HOLLAND PARK S

A place of scholarship; determinedly academic with examination results in the top 2% of state schools and outstanding A level and GCSE results.

A place of ambition, endeavour, drive and creativity, with outstanding success in placing students in top flight universities.

A place of self-effacing confidence.

A place to find oneself and hear the still small voice.

A place where the potency of academic prowess embraces the human beating heart.

A place which believes that lives and futures can be altered and that chance can be marginalised.

Thriving in a brand new state of the art building, Holland Park is an outstandingly successful and oversubscribed school with a vast range of accolades and a commitment to avoid the complacency that can be attendant on such heady success.

HEAD: Colin Hall | ASSOCIATE HEAD: David Chappell

AIRLIE GARDENS, CAMPDEN HILL ROAD, LONDON W8 7AF

www.hollandparkschool.co.uk | admissions@hollandparkschool.co.uk

THE GOOD SCHOOLS GUIDE

London North

www.goodschoolsguide.co.uk

First Edition published 2014 by Lucas Publishing Ltd
Address Good Schools Guide, 10 Greycoat Place, London SW1P 1SB
Website www.goodschoolsguide.co.uk
ISBN 978-1-909963-01-6
Copyright (c) 2014, Lucas Publications Ltd
Printed by Berforts Information Press Ltd

Acknowledgments

Writers

Amanda Lyath	Grace Moody-Stuart	Melanie Sanderson
Beth Noakes	Jackie Lixenburg	Nicky Adams
Charlotte Phillips	Janette Wallis	Ralph Lucas
Denise Roberts	Judith French	Sandra Hutchinson
Emma Jones	Lisa Freedman	Sophie Irwin
Emma Lee-Potter	Mary-Anne Smillie	Susan Bailes
Emma Vickers	Mary Langford	Susan Hamlyn

Design: David Preston, Harriet Plyler

Typesetting: Theresa Hare, Optima Information Design

Editorial review by Beth Noakes and team: Janita Clamp, Emma Lee-Potter, Kathryn Berger, Amanda Perkins

Advertising sales: Charlotte Hollingshead and Jo Dodds, Publishing Matters

Web manager: Anthony Back

Project management: Katja Lips

Keeping us updated: Martin Husbands

Editorial coordination: Shari Lord

Junior League of London for excerpts from *Living in London: A Practical Guide*

Photography: Thanks to all the schools who responded to our requests for photographs. Additional photography by Hannah Palmer and Laura Radford

Thanks to these schools for their cover photos:
The American School in London
Notting Hill and Ealing High Junior School
Ilford County High School
Queen's Gate Junior School
Mill Hill School
Latymer Prep School
Kensington Prep School

BROMLEY HIGH SCHOOL

Exceptional Education Since 1883

For Girls 4-18 years

Fees assistance & Scholarships available in the Senior School

Find out more about life at
Bromley High School

Tel: 020 8781 7000

admissions@bro.gdst.net **www.bromleyhigh.gdst.net**

gdst Girls' Day
School Trust

Contents

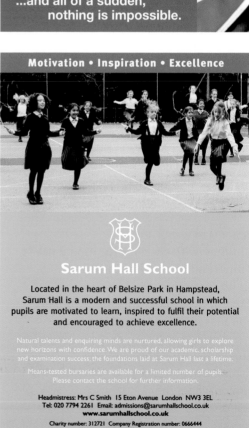

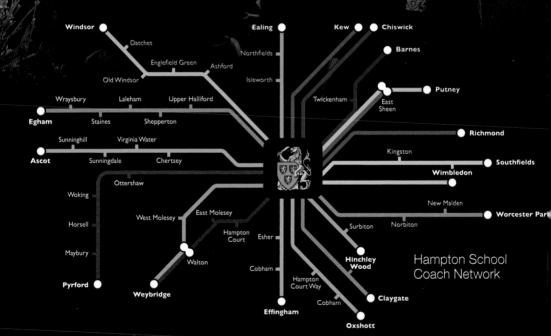

How to use this book

The age range of a school is indicated by the colour assigned to the title bar.

Junior School

Senior School

The circular symbols found within the title bars indicate the following school characterics:

 Girls' school

 Boys' school

 Co-ed school

 Boarding available

 State school

 Independent school

 School for children with special educational needs

London North map

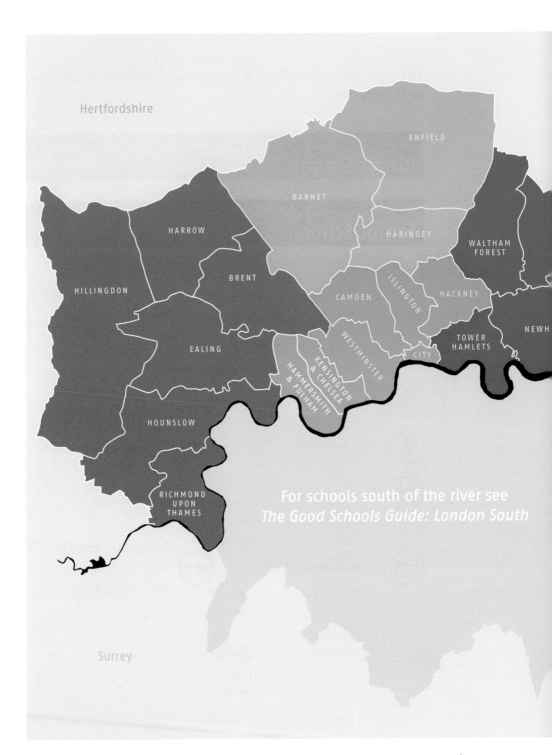

Hertfordshire

ENFIELD

BARNET

HARROW

HARINGEY

WALTHAM FOREST

HILLINGDON

BRENT

ISLINGTON

HACKNEY

CAMDEN

NEWH

TOWER HAMLETS

EALING

WESTMINSTER

CITY

KENSINGTON & CHELSEA

HAMMERSMITH & FULHAM

HOUNSLOW

RICHMOND UPON THAMES

For schools south of the river see
The Good Schools Guide: London South

Surrey

CENTRAL — 51

Camden
City of London
Hackney
Islington
Westminster

CENTRAL WEST — 217

Hammersmith & Fulham
Kensington & Chelsea

WEST — 359

Brent
Ealing
Harrow
Hillingdon
Hounslow
Richmond-Upon-Thames

NORTH — 479

Barnet
Enfield
Harringey

EAST — 571

Barking & Dagenham
Havering
Redbridge
Tower Hamlets
Waltham Forest

Introduction

Welcome to the first Good Schools Guide to London North. We offer you our knowledge, inside information, experience and opinions on what parents tell us are the capital's best schools north of the Thames.

Along with many of the highest performing independent schools, London has some of the best state schools in the country. It also has one of the fastest growing populations, seemingly with consequences predictable to everyone except government planners. We don't think that more temporary classrooms eating up playground space is the answer and we suspect you don't either.

In Barking and Dagenham for example, almost all primaries, faith schools excepted, are now multi-form entry. Christchurch Primary, down the road in Redbridge, has five forms in a year, and, over in Richmond, Stanley Primary has over 700 pupils. Few primaries built to house 350 children can comfortably accommodate 600. While some primaries in comfortable areas seem able to raise funds and rebuild – look at the excellent Montpelier in Ealing, for instance - for others there is little space and less money. Parents are, understandably, underwhelmed and increasingly concerned that their shy or quiet child is simply not getting his fair share of attention and support.

Free primary schools, touted by some as the white knights of education, have turned out to be rather more selective about where they mount their rescue missions. Many have opted to open in leafier areas, by-passing the grittier bits, or cherry-picking middle class pupils via faith selection criteria.

Not, of course, that this situation applies solely to London. Many conurbations with rapidly expanding populations have comparable problems. But London, particularly with its influx of rich overseas immigrants, has unique challenges. Londoners who might, in previous decades, have bought family houses in eg Hammersmith, Shepherd's Bush,

Islington, Maida Vale are now priced out of this market and have moved to Acton, Kilburn, Dalston or Ilford. This also increases pupil numbers in local schools.

Overseas money coming into central London puts pressure on independent schools which, despite the recession, are seeing unprecedented numbers of applications. The North London Consortium schools, the City of London schools and the few academic co-educational schools are, amongst others, ever more popular and over-subscribed. And it doesn't stop inside the North Circular. The Barnet and Enfield grammar schools, too, are seeing ever-longer queues at their gates.

To some extent, all this is deserving of celebration. It is not by accident that so many of our schools – state and independent – are so popular and astonishingly over-subscribed. London schools are leading the way in all kinds of excellence. Fewer schools are now failing their pupils, despite the strains of such high numbers who, for example, speak a language other than English at home. It is a challenge and London schools are rising to it. Our astoundingly diverse school populations work, learn and play harmoniously together – a model for the wider world and one we applaud. We have a raft of excellent head teachers in both sectors, we have innovation and imagination and teachers of extraordinary dedication. London children are achieving highly and bringing credit to the capital.

This guide celebrates this resurgence. Here you can read about local areas, the best schools in each borough and learn what they are really like – from the inside. We invite you to contribute to making London schools the best they can be. Let us know about your own experience and join us in keeping up the pressure on all sectors of education in London to continue raising standards for the future of our children and for us all.

GSG Charter

No school can pay to be included in (or choose to be excluded from) The Good Schools Guide, and we do not charge schools for reviews.

In recent years we have helped to defray our costs by selling advertising space and licensing schools to reprint their own reviews for a fee. We make these offers only to schools that are already in the Guide on merit. Whether or not they choose to advertise has no bearing on their inclusion in the Guide nor on the content of their review. Schools we have not chosen for inclusion in the Guide are not allowed to advertise.

The Good Schools Guide Advice Service is a fee paying, personal consultancy service for parents. The Guide and our website also offer other advice on a vast range of education matters, free to subscribers. We receive no commission nor any other payment from any school for these services. We provide information on tutor companies on our website, and may charge these companies for carrying out a review, but they are only included after careful vetting.

We take our independence very seriously and the separation of commercial and editorial content is absolute. If you have any questions or concerns about our commercial policy, please write in the first instance to editor@ goodschoolsguide.co.uk.

More and more children are coming to Lancing from London

· We don't pre-test ·
· We love learning for its own sake ·
· We encourage and support but we don't pressurise ·
· We believe Art, Music, Culture and Sport enrich lives ·
· We are a community and family, not just a school that pursues results ·
· Our children love to board and can go home at weekends ·
· Our stunning campus is only an hour from London ·

Come and see us and discover the difference

Lancing College
Senior School & Sixth Form

www.lancingcollege.co.uk
Tel 01273 465805 | West Sussex BN15 0RW

Registered Charity Number 1076483

The British education system

State schools

Many families head for London hoping for a place in a good local state school. There are huge advantages: at primary level in particular, your child's friends will almost all be local, you will soon feel part of the local community and you won't spend hours in a car trying to navigate London traffic or have to squeeze onto a rush hour tube or bus. Many London schools are used to young children arriving without fluent English and have systems in place to help. And of course they are free. At primary level you don't get the specialist teachers that many private preps employ, nor probably the level of facilities, but the quality of teaching at a good state school shouldn't be inferior (see Prep or primary, page 29). With a good comprehensive down the road, you are home and dry. However, state primaries don't prepare children for 11+ entrance exams, so if you are aiming at a selective secondary school you will probably have to rope in a tutor in year 5 or so (see Tutors and tutoring, page 631).

Admissions

The tricky bit. Many families moving to London want to find a school before they commit to renting or buying a house. However, you won't be offered a state school place without proof of a local address.

Normal primary school admissions are at 3+ into the nursery or 4+ into the reception class (beware: getting a nursery place doesn't usually guarantee a reception class place, you will probably have to reapply). Some are divided into infant and junior schools, the latter starting at 7 years. Most secondary schools start at 11. For a normal application, you will need to apply – with a local address – by around mid-January for primary schools and the end of October of the year before entry for secondary schools, with some leeway for change of address up till mid-December. Apply later,

Secondary schools use various forms of selection, including ability, location or both.

and you become a late applicant, probably joining the queue behind all those who applied on time (see Getting into a good state school, page 37). NB selective grammar schools now set entrance tests in September, often with a closing date for applications in July.

Most state schools, primary and secondary, give preference to looked after children, those with specific medical or social needs, then siblings. While no state primary school selects by ability or aptitude (except the London Oratory Junior House, which tests all applicants for general academic ability and musical aptitude), faith schools mostly give preference to regular church-goers. Secular primary schools give most of their places to those who live closest (which can, in many areas, mean more-or-less spitting distance).

Secondary schools use various forms of selection, including ability, location or both. Secular comprehensives give most of their places to those who live closest. Academically selective grammar schools (NB not all have 'grammar' in their name) range from those that offer places to the highest scorers in their entrance tests, regardless of where they live, to those that offer places only to local children. Some schools award a proportion of their places by 'aptitude'; some by church attendance; some use 'fair banding' to get a spread of ability. St Marylebone uses a combination of all three: 60 per cent of places are given to church-goers; it divides applicants into four ability bands, with equal offers to each band; and there are 12 'performing arts' places. For most, distance is the tie-breaker. The local authority will usually tell you how far the cut-off was for the previous year.

Independent schools

Many areas of London are well-equipped with prep schools. These are likely to have small classes, specialist teachers and a relatively biddable intake – if not the sports facilities you find in a country school. They also prepare your child for entrance exams to secondary schools, and advise on which are likely to be most suitable. Don't assume the teaching will be better than at a state school – both sectors include those who would be better off in a different profession. A prep school is judged at least partly by its leavers' destinations, so it will do its best to ensure your child moves on to a decent secondary school, even if it has to dampen down your expectations.

Don't assume the teaching will be better than at a state school – both sectors include those who would be better off in a different profession.

A stand-alone pre-prep, that usually goes from age 3 to 7 years, may be a good bet if you are arriving in London at short notice. Some of the children who join at 3 may move on at 4 or 5, so places do come up. The disadvantage is that they are, inevitably, obliged to spend a significant part of the upper years preparing children for 7+ entrance exams.

Independent secondaries range from ferociously selective power-houses such as Westminster and St Paul's to those that provide a gentle haven from hothousing or social integration – with admissions policies to match. A glance at the league tables will give a clue as to the degree of selection they operate.

Admissions

Prep schools generally don't care where you live, as long as you can pay the fees. Many London preps give the illusion, at least, that if you don't sign your child up at birth you are too late. Some selective schools do close their waiting lists early, or have specific dates for registering; others operate on a first-come-first-served basis and do fill up – on paper at least. However, it is always worth a phone call. London is a very mobile area and last-minute places come up at the most sought-after schools.

The thought of putting your 3 or 4-year-old through a selection session or two may seem round the bend. Indeed, all-through schools (those with a senior school attached) that select this young rarely guarantee that a place at 4 will see you through into the senior school. Even those selected at 7 or 8 are sometimes weeded out at 11 or 13.

Nevertheless, your child may have to go through it. At 3, they may be asked to draw a picture, listen to a story and answer questions, cut out a circle, do a jigsaw, build a tower, match dominoes. Many schools send them out to play together, no doubt with an eye out to see who bites whom.

London is a very mobile area and last-minute places come up at the most sought-after schools.

Selection at this age is not an exact science, and certainly does not mean your child is doomed to failure because he didn't get a place at 3.

At 7, 8 and 11, most schools set maths and English exams, perhaps combined with reasoning tests. Many have previous papers on their websites. They will generally interview likely candidates and ask their previous school for a report, and may include some sort of group activity. Entry at 13 is getting more complicated, with increasing numbers of London schools setting pre-tests (generally maths, English and reasoning) in year 6 or 7. Those selected usually need to confirm their places by doing well in the Common Entrance exam (in a range of subjects) in year 8. This system is tricky to navigate if you are arriving with a child already in year 7 or 8, and you may need to track down one of the (dwindling number of) schools that don't use the pre-test system.

Many pupils change schools in the sixth form – whether

Does your child possess a strong scientific gene, or shine out for a whole body of reasons?

The aim of Fulham Prep is that all students should not only reach their potential, but exceed it, giving them the confidence to set their sights high. This may be achieved through academic channels or through sport, art, music, drama or whatever inspires the particular individual.

Find out how your child can reach their full potential by calling **020 7371 9911** (reception to year 2) or **020 7386 2444** (years 3 to 8). Visit www.fulhamprep.co.uk

PRE-PREP OPEN DAY 20 NOVEMBER 2014

FULHAM PREP SCHOOL

Ofsted Outstanding School 2013|2014

FULHAM PREP SCHOOL

from single sex to co-ed, boarding to day, state to private or vice versa. Some single sex schools admit pupils of the opposite gender into the sixth form. Both state and private schools almost always have some sort of entrance requirements at this point, generally involving GCSE grades, interviews and perhaps entrance exams.

E L T H A M COLLEGE

GLORIA FILIORUM PATRES

LARGE ENOUGH TO EXCEL SMALL ENOUGH TO CARE

All That Jazz performed by a sporting trio.

At Eltham College everyone is someone else. A Sixth Form Mathematician organises art workshops for visiting primary school children, the Captain of the 3rd XV is the lead actor in West Side Story and the General Secretary of the Model United Nations helps out at the local care home. In a challenging yet caring environment, we nurture each student's skills and talents. All of them.

We develop well-rounded individuals.

Eltham College, Grove Park Road, Mottingham, London, SE9 4QF
Telephone 020 8857 1455
www.eltham-college.org.uk

Is this your daughter's diary...

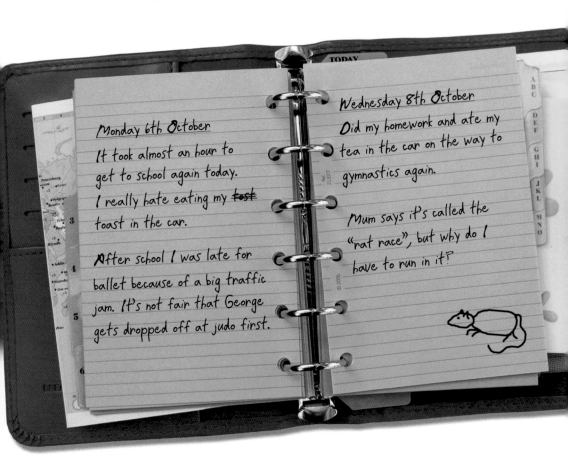

Monday 6th October

It took almost an hour to get to school again today. I really hate eating my ~~tost~~ toast in the car.

After school I was late for ballet because of a big traffic jam. It's not fair that George gets dropped off at judo first.

Wednesday 8th October

Did my homework and ate my tea in the car on the way to gymnastics again.

Mum says it's called the "rat race", but why do I have to run in it?

Then take a look at weekly boarding at Godstowe Schoo

Godstowe is an independent day and boarding school just minutes from the M40 in High Wycombe, Buckinghamshire. Girls board in our special junior house from the age of seven and enjoy school, clubs and supervised homework all under one roof.

If it sounds too good to be true why not come and see for yourself? Contact the Registrar at registrar@godstowe.org or 01494 429006 to arrange an appointmen For more information, visit our website a www.godstowe.org.

Godstowe Preparatory School for girls aged 3-13.
Shrubbery Road, High Wycombe, Bucks, HP13 6PR. Tel: 01494 529273. Email: schooloffice@godstowe.o

Prep or primary?

One of the questions most frequently asked of the Good Schools Guide Advice Service is, 'Should I send my child to a prep school or send him to the local primary and save the money for an independent senior school?'

This question is particular knotty for Londoners. While the standard of state schools in London is improving, the problems facing these schools are becoming more complex. Among them are shrinking budgets, growing pupil numbers and the fact that, increasingly, schools have to fund eg the needs of children with learning difficulties out of their existing budgets.

A primary school should be one to which all the children can walk so that your child's friends will be local.

Primary

There are many excellent reasons for sending your child to the local primary – assuming, that it really is local. A primary school should be one to which all the children can walk so that your child's friends will be local – people to whose homes he can run round after school when he is old enough. You may find, if your children go to such a school, that your own circle of friends, well into later life, is still largely made up of those parents you met there. If your local school is well-run, the children are happy and the learning that goes on there is evident and interesting, then you are lucky and it would be hard to see why you would consider anything else.

However, not all state primaries offer such a start in life. Many are dilapidated, with transient populations of both pupils and staff. Discipline is lax, often because the parents do not back up the school, aspirations are low and energy levels – amongst the staff, the governors and the parent body – are insufficient to lift the school out of mediocrity. If that is your local school, you may, understandably, be looking for alternatives.

Prep

London prep schools are generally on the small side – though some have as many as 550 children. They always have smaller classes than city primaries and this is a particular draw for many families. They are exactly what they say they are, ie preparatory schools. Their reason for existing is to prepare children for senior schools – in most cases, for academically selective senior schools – and they stand or fall in a highly competitive market by their success in doing just that. A prep school which does not send its leavers in year 6 or year 8 to good selective schools will rapidly lose applicants.

Many people worry that if they don't get their child into a good prep at 4 or 7, they forfeit his chances of getting to a good academically selective – independent or state – senior school at 11 or 13. This is not the case.

The means by which senior schools assess children at 10, 11 or 13 have become very sophisticated. They are increasingly designed to identify children with natural innate ability. The modern computerised reasoning tests cannot be tutored for or even prepared for in any genuinely helpful way. Tutoring a child in English and maths is usually a good idea on educational grounds – all children improve if they have one-to-one time with good teacher – but even this, though it can help, cannot guarantee that a child of average ability will get through stringent entrance tests. Nor should it. Likewise, sending your child to a prep school from the age of 4, while he may have a lovely time in his small, orderly classes with good teaching and lots of sports, cannot guarantee that he will make it to a top London independent school.

Most London independent senior schools will take 50 per cent or more of their year 7 intake from the state sector.

Most London independent senior schools will take 50 per cent or more of their year 7 intake from the state sector. These academically selective schools are exactly what they say they are and it is the performance of your child in their subtly constructed tests which will, in the end, determine whether or not he gains a place.

Of course, tutoring or a prep school will help, but only in marginal cases will it tip the balance. And a child is done no favours by putting him into a fast-paced intellectual environment in which he will struggle from his first year and onwards – if he manages to stay. The schools are good at selecting those who will thrive in the academic atmosphere they offer, but we do get the occasional demoralised 13 or 14 year old who is struggling in a school where, through no fault of his own, he was always going to slip further and further behind. This can be demoralising and damaging for years to come.

Of course, tutoring or a prep school will help, but only in marginal cases will it tip the balance.

State primary to independent senior

If your child is at a state primary he will not be prepared for entry to independent schools. That is not the job of state primaries – much though many parents wish it were. Consequently, it may well be that your child gets to year 5 or even 6 without ever having done a comprehension exercise to a time limit. To that extent, any state school child is at a disadvantage compared to a prep school child who will have been drilled and tested daily in order to give him the familiarity and practice he needs to tackle entrance tests.

This is when a tutor will help. A state primary child needs that little bit of extra help in doing maths and English tests to a time limit and having the support of an experienced and expert teacher will help to plug gaps, demystify problems and build confidence (see Tutors and tutoring on page 631).

In general, a bright child from a state primary and with supportive parents like you (you must be or you wouldn't be reading this) has as much chance of gaining a place at an academically selective senior school – state or independent – as any child from a prep school and, quite possibly, more. Prep schools may vaunt the 'special relationships' they have as 'feeder' schools to the seniors, but no decent senior school would turn down the bright and naturally sparky veteran of a good state primary.

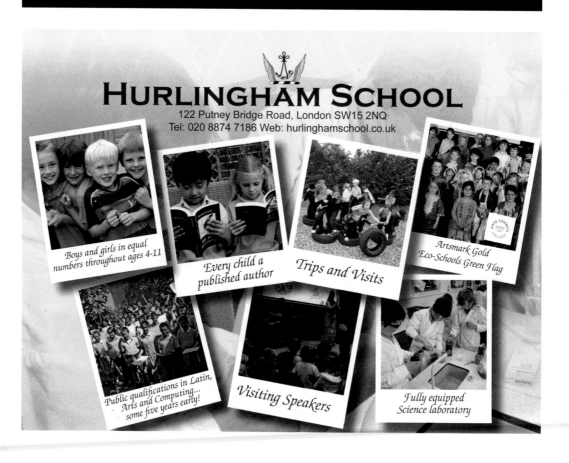

FINE ARTS
COLLEGE

WE OFFER A WIDE RANGE OF SUBJECTS AT A LEVEL AND GCSE

GRADED
OUTSTANDING
BY OFSTED

ISA INDEPENDENT SCHOOLS ASSOCIATION
Accredited Member

020 7586 0312

www.hampsteadfinearts.com

Getting into a good state school

You may have flawless local state schools which effortlessly accommodate all the local kids. If not, here are some tactics to consider:

Get moving
Consider moving to a part of London with long-established state school excellence. Generally, but not always, suburbs trump inner city locations when it comes to good-for-ever schools. See our run throughs of the best state schools in each London borough. If you need to know which street to buy or rent in, the Good Schools Guide website features invaluable catchment area maps.

Get God
Failing that, get religion early so your child can be baptised (by 6 months for many Catholic schools) and the family engaged in weekly services and church activities. This will improve your chances of access to an excellent Catholic or Anglican faith school, something that enabled Tony Blair's children to complete their education in one part of London while living in another.

Get stuck in
Your local schools may be going through a purple patch or you may be within range of the scattering of selective secondary state schools around London. They're so over-subscribed that getting in is a lottery, but your (bright) child has as much of a chance as anyone else's if you find a good tutor (see Tutors and tutoring on page 631).

Some secondary schools also admit a small proportion of out-of-catchment pupils based on aptitude – language at Grey Coat Hospital, in Westminster, for instance, or music at Camden School for Girls – while an increasing number use ballots to prevent parents gaming the system.

Get real

It may come down to helping your child do their best in a less than ideal school environment. This takes time and dedication and is a reason why thousands turn to home education.

Get the information

Research all the schools within your patch. Check to see which are reviewed in the Good Schools Guide. None will be perfect, so look at them from a range of viewpoints, and avoid being over-influenced by reputation and rumour (both can be substantially outdated).

Are the Ofsted reports confidence-inspiring? Are they reasonably up to date? Don't take them as gospel, though: a school may have got its outstanding rating by ticking the right boxes rather than by providing the sort of educational environment that will suit your child. Equally, it may have been rated 'requires improvement' for a failing that does not greatly concern you (and is anyway being dealt with). Do the able get stellar exam results? Do ordinary children do well, too? Do websites suggest a broad and fascinating as well as a successful education? Roughly what does their catchment area look like?

Even if secondary education is a long way off, research secondary schools in the area too. If they are poor, you could face more disruption when your child reaches 11. If good, do they give preference to children in named primaries and are your preferred choices amongst them?

Having arrived at a long list of potential schools, research the admissions process. Though increasingly complex, with every academy and free school entitled to set its own entry criteria, and faith schools providing various numbers of hoops to jump through, your local authority website should round up the lot.

Work your way through the admissions rules. The higher up, the more powerful they are. Find the one that best describes your child. Scrutinise cut-off criteria – often related to distance from the school but calculated in idiosyncratic ways. Note the preference given to siblings, which can benefit families whose younger children are admitted as a matter of right wherever they live, but scupper newcomers' chances in a year with a bumper crop of reception age brothers and sisters.

Don't take it as gospel though: a school may have got its outstanding rating by ticking the right boxes.

Get practical

Once you know which good schools you like, might conceivably get into and are in areas you can afford to live in, go and check them out.

Schools are individual places with their own styles and cultures. Though a comfortingly large number in London have come good over the last few years, reputation or results alone won't tell you whether they would suit your child. You need to find pupils who match your child in character and ability, and parents who share your outlook on education, and see the school through their eyes.

A visit is essential; being shown round by children during an ordinary school day is best, an open day less so, though it will give you a better chance to chat to teachers, and see everything that school is doing.

Talk to locals, ask what the schools are like or – as a long term measure – consider volunteering to get a unique, in-depth insight.

Get going

At the end of all this work, you should know which schools you would like your children to attend and what you have to do to be sure of getting them there.

Nine times out of ten, at least in London, living in the catchment area is a non-negotiable. Move, live there for at least two years and don't cheat. The penalties if you do can range from cold-shouldering from other parents to the loss of a school place. Some boroughs may even disqualify you if you still own the home you lived in previously. What you do after serving your time is up to you – but check that siblings get priority over distance if you have younger children.

Move, live there for at least two years and don't cheat.

If you need to change school later on, the rules may be different. Once the main process of entry is finished, some schools are individually responsible for filling any 'in year' spaces that may arise through pupils moving elsewhere (and, in London, people are always moving).

Although, nominally, the same entry rules apply, in practice things are much less clear. Schools, or the local authority, keep a waiting list, but the allocation of places can be hard to track. Sound out your favourite school: you are looking at a house nearby, might they have room for your children, if not immediately then over the next year or so? If you get a helpful response, visit them and make good friends. Persistence – and charm – can pay off.

Passion for
learning
Inspiration
for life

www.thameschristiancollege.org.uk

Refreshingly
independent

Not only do our pupils
achieve top grades, they
also leave with the depth
of character and values
that set them apart.

A brief London North tour

From nursery to sixth form, in the state and private sector, those living north of the Thames and south of Watford are unbelievably spoilt for choice. What's more, the range of outstanding schools will suit almost any parent's outlook or pocket and any child's aptitude and interest.

This range and variety, however, will not necessarily make choosing a school any easier, nor, for those who have targeted examples in mind, will it allow a laissez-faire approach to the admissions process.

If you're thinking of paying fees from the word go, you will often need to register your child's name as soon after birth as possible. Popular pre-preps, like The Children's House in Islington or The Phoenix in Hampstead, are accustomed to parents ringing straight from the delivery room (if not before).

At these schools, experienced staff are required to make Solomon-like judgements on the Oxbridge potential of those just out of nappies.

Even the promptest application, however, is only of moderate benefit if you are applying to selective prep schools like The Hall (for boys) or St Christopher's (for girls), or hoping to get in on the ground-floor to leading secondaries like North London Collegiate, South Hampstead High School or Highgate. At these schools, experienced staff are required to make Solomon-like judgements on the Oxbridge potential of those just out of nappies. They freely admit they don't always get it right and sensible parents take the outcome philosophically – as well as having a strong back-up in place.

If a state primary is your preferred route, there is more flexibility in terms of timing (the application process only begins the year before entry), but it still makes sense to study the admissions policy well in advance, particularly if your intended means of entry is living nearby. Popular non-denominational schools, such as Rhodes Avenue, Tetherdown or Coldfall (all in Muswell Hill) will require a ruler when buying or renting in the relevant catchment. Though not a definitive solution, a call to the local authority will at least establish how far away successful applicants have lived in previous years.

Many of north London's most successful primaries – as elsewhere in the UK – are affiliated to a specific religious faith, giving priority to those who follow it. The degree of commitment, however, will vary considerably and, here again, it pays to familiarise yourself with the entrance criteria. Catholic schools tend to be the highest sticklers, expecting early baptism and consistent church attendance thereafter. Other faiths can be more forgiving, but Anglican foundations, like Marylebone's Hampden Gurney or St Michael's Church of England Primary in Highgate, will also expect plenty of evidence your faith is sincere.

At secondary level, north London and its surrounding suburbs boast such an abundance of outstanding schools that parents' main difficulty can be choosing between them.

At secondary level, north London and its surrounding suburbs boast such an abundance of outstanding schools that parents' main difficulty can be choosing between them. Those facing the leap from junior to senior will often spend sleepless nights wavering between single sex and co-ed, selective and non, state and independent.

The area is justly celebrated for its high-flying selective schools in both the state and private sector and, if you're looking for the best on offer and want it for free, you will be putting your hope in schools like Henrietta Barnett, The Latymer School, Edmonton, Queen Elizabeth's School, Barnet and St Michael's Catholic Grammar. Unsurprisingly, they are also amongst the hardest schools in the country to get into, often with more than 10 applicants for every place.

Those unwilling to confront the cut-throat competition can still enjoy an excellent education as some of the

country's leading comprehensives, such as Mill Hill County, Fortismere, Alexandra Park, Ashmole and Camden School for Girls. To guarantee a place at one of these successful institutions, however, you will undoubtedly have to live within a brief stroll.

North London's independent sector is equally renowned for academic excellence with schools such as North London Collegiate, South Hampstead High School and University College School consistently delivering top-20 results. Those who favour co-education can find it at Highgate, or, for those who value creativity and holistic education over competition, King's Alfred's School in Golders Green.

North London parents are not, perhaps, the biggest consumers of boarding education, but here, too, those looking for weekly or full boarding for boys or girls will find a range of strong options. Mill Hill, Westminster and, indeed, Harrow (not perhaps everyone's notion of a north London school, but easily reachable by tube and enjoying spectacular views of Wembley

The Good Schools Guide Advice Service

The Good Schools Guide Advice Service (GSGAS) is a personal service for individual families covering every aspect of schools and education. The advisors are our most experienced and knowledgeable writers and most of them live and work in or near London. They have visited countless schools, quizzed innumerable parents, children, teachers and heads. This vast experience, coupled with the data, inside information and expertise of the entire team, is available to any parents who need assistance with their child's education.

How can we help?

Because The Good Schools Guide Advice Service is a personal service, run on a one-to-one basis, we can help you in whatever way you need us to. You tell us what you require and we tell you how we can help, whether it's advice about places in London schools or something entirely different. Our website: www.gsgexpertschoolsconsultants.co.uk shows you all the services we offer. You can also see details about our advisors and how they can help you.

If you're not sure what academic level your child is at, we can undertake academic assessments; we also have a superb team of experts in SEN. Our advisors have professional links with leading experts in fields such as educational psychology and tutoring. Two other unique components of our consultancy are the Scholarships and Bursaries Service and State School Service, the only such resources in the UK. Just tell us what you need and we will find an expert schools and education advisor to work with you.

Perhaps most importantly, our advisors understand how challenging it can be to be a parent. We are sympathetic and will help in whatever way we can to set you and your child on the right track.

What should I do?

Phone us on +44 (0)203 286 6824 or send us a brief email to advice@goodschoolsguide.co.uk outlining what you need. Tell us the age of your child and where you live plus your contact details. We will contact you within 48 hours of your initial phone call or email and make sure that we match you with the right advisor. Consultations can be conducted over the phone or email but our advisors are happy to meet you face to face if you prefer. Urgent enquiries are dealt with urgently. We can find an advisor to speak with you within the hour if necessary.

How much?

We provide one of the most competitively priced tailor-made advice services in the UK. Check our website for current fees.

The Good Schools Guide promise

All information is treated in the strictest confidence. We will refund your fee if you are not entirely satisfied with the results.

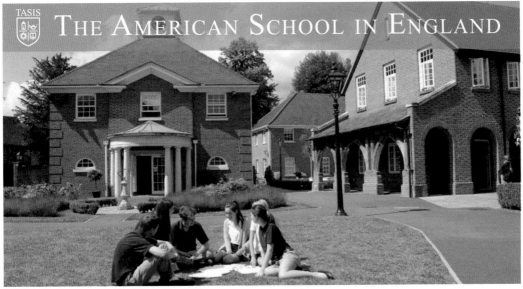

"MOST FORWARD-THINKING SCHOOL IN THE UK"

THE WEEK
Magazine

"BEST PUBLIC SCHOOL"

TATLER
Tatler Schools Guide 2014

- "*Excellent academic standards are matched by exceptional levels of achievement in the co-curriculum, including sports and the creative performing arts*" - ISI Report 2014

- Located less than 40 miles from London

WELLINGTON
COLLEGE

Crowthorne, Berkshire RG45 7PU | www.wellingtoncollege.org.uk

Central North

Crouch End
ross
Hampstead Heath
Stoke Newington
Upper C
8
11 12
29
39
36
20 21
27
1
16
Holloway Road
37
Hackne
28
3 4
7
18
22 23 19
10
London Fie
24
13
6 9
5
2
Highbury & Islington
Kilburn
25
17
26
Camden Town
40 41
St John's Wood
14 15
Islington
35
Shoreditch
42
Regents Park
Kings Cross
38
31 32
Maida Vale
49
56
54
Bloomsbury
33
Liverpool Street
59
Holborn
34
hite ity
52
51
53
55
Soho
30
Notting Hill
43
64
44
Covent Garden
erd's h
Kensington Gardens
Hyde Park
Kensington
St James's Park
60
63 Waterloo
Southwark
Bermondsey
57
Westminster
45
58
61
50
Lambeth
47 48
62
46
Fulham

CENTRAL

CAMDEN

An introduction to Central London and its state schools

Today London's state schools are amongst the best in England. This may come as a surprise to those who can remember back to the bad old days of the 1980s and '90s, when many parents were choosing to send children to independent secondary schools or to move out of London altogether to avoid the perils of the local comp.

This turnaround was largely due to the highly effective London Challenge, which operated between 2003 and 2011. This scheme saw strong heads mentoring those in weak schools, zero tolerance of low expectations and the smart use of data to track pupil progress. At its core was a commitment to breaking the link between deprivation and low attainment. The injection of energetic, new graduates from top universities in the Teach First scheme contributed, as did the success of some of the early sponsored academies.

We can review only a small proportion of London's state schools, but here is a brief tour of the boroughs, their characteristics and a selection of notable state primary and secondary schools.

Camden

Camden stretches from the mansion blocks of Holborn and Bloomsbury to Hampstead Heath, with its wooded walks and swimming ponds, and from the council estates of Somerstown to the mansions of Hampstead – which, with its winding, hilly streets, exclusive boutiques and streetside cafes, has the ambience of an affluent village.

Camden has long been known to have a good local authority education department – and, most likely in consequence, none of its schools have converted into academies. The only academy in the borough at time of writing is the new and very popular UCL Academy at Swiss Cottage, which was shocked to receive a tepid judgement from Ofsted in its first report.

The most famous and popular secondary school is Camden School for Girls qv (which takes boys in the sixth form). It uses banding to select pupils of a range of abilities, and such is its popularity that it will only assess those who live within a mile, whilst offers are generally confined to those living within half that distance (apart from a few music aptitude places). Girls are also well served by School qv and La Sainte Union qv, the latter with a strictly Catholic intake. These two are part of a sixth form consortium, LaSwap qv, with William Ellis boys' school qv (on the up after some rocky years) and co-ed Acland Burghley (still reeling after an Ofsted hit squad visit in the first week of the 2013 new school year). Hampstead School qv on the western edge of the borough is popular too. WAC Arts College is a new free school in Belsize Park, offering a creative curriculum to disengaged 14 – 19 year olds.

A good range of primary schools, though very much weighted on the faith side – Christ Church C of E, Hampstead Parochial, St Paul's C of E, Emmanuel, Holy Trinity and St Silas qv and The Rosary are amongst the most popular, alongside the free school St Luke's in Hampstead. A secular free school, Abacus Belsize primary, opened in 2013 after much lobbying by parents who wanted to redress the balance. It hopes to move into a permanent home in the vacated police station on Rosslyn Hill in 2016. Non-church-goers may also want to consider Eleanor Palmer (in the news because of some families briefly renting properties close by in order to gain a place), New End, Torriano, Fleet, Brookfield, Kingsgate or Christopher Hatton further south.

City of London

City of London, the original Roman settlement that still makes up the square mile of so of one of the world's financial centres, includes the Barbican, some of the Inns of Temple and many financial institutions. Its relatively few inhabitants live amongst medieval street plans, Wren churches and 21st century skyscrapers, and it throngs with suited and high heeled City workers thronging outside the packed pubs on Friday afternoons, and no place for coffee or a crust of bread on weekends. It also has several independent schools, senior and junior, but no state secondary schools – though the corporation does sponsor city academies in Islington, Hackney and Southwark. Its only state primary school, Sir John Cass qv, is an excellent, multi-ethnic school C of E school, giving priority to regular church-goers.

Hackney

Just north of the City of London and east of Islington, Hackney is an inner city borough that includes trendy Shoreditch and Hoxton as well as the Hackney Marshes and Lea Valley (home of the 2012 Olympic canoeing and kayaking competitions). Its educational landscape is characterised by a high proportion of state and independent schools for the orthodox Jewish community in Stanford Hill. It also has a Muslim free school, the Olive.

Its best known – and very sought-after – secondary school is Mossborne Community Academy qv, whose founding principal was Sir Michael Wilshaw, now chief inspector of schools. It has complicated admissions criteria involving fair banding and inner and outer zones. Clapton Girls' Academy (places allocated by fair banding and distance) is also successful. Popular primary schools include Lauriston, London Fields, Grazebrook, William Patten, Northwold, Queensbridge, Orchard and Jubilee.

Islington

Islington is uncompromisingly urban, with little green space but Georgian squares, trendy converted warehouses, Arsenal football club, canal side walks and street markets, thick on the ground with City workers escaping for lunch or window shopping the antique shops of Camden Passage.

It used to have the reputation of being a black hole for good state schools, with parents commuting en masse to Hampstead, but times are a-changing. Highbury Fields is an up-and-coming comprehensive, and St Mary Magdalen a good all-through school that does IB in the sixth form. City and Islington Sixth Form College qv has links with some of the top universities and often transforms the prospects of students who arrived with uninspiring GCSE results.

Primary schools to move house for include William Tyndale, Yerbury, Grafton qv and Gillespie, with St John's Highbury Vale C of E, St Joseph's RC and St Peter and St Paul RC attracting parental bums onto pews.

Westminster

Westminster includes Buckingham Palace and the Houses of Parliament, Mayfair and Belgravia (with its streets of garden squares and creamy white stucco terraced houses, painted in the Cadogan colour code of magnolia). It includes Little Venice, the area of large stucco houses round the Grand Union Canal; Soho, famous for its sex industry venues but rapidly undergoing gentrification; the massively redeveloped Paddington Waterside area; parts of Knightsbridge, some of whose streets are lined with distinctive and imposing six story red-brick Queen Anne-style townhouses with Dutch and Glemish gables, between high sided canyons of commercial exuberance. It also includes shabby social housing estates and some very ethnically mixed communities.

It has two of the most popular girls' comprehensives in London, both faith schools with various associated admissions hoops: St Marylebone qv and Grey Coat Hospital qv. St Marylebone has some performing arts places (a linked school, Marylebone Boys, opened in September 2014, and a linked special school in September 2013) and Grey Coat Hospital gives some places to girls with a talent for languages. All these use 'fair banding' to offer places to children from a full range of abilities. Several academies are doing well: Westminster Academy, King Solomon Academy (an all-through school) and Pimlico Academy are all rated as outstanding. A controversial new sixth form college, Harris Westminster, a collaboration between Westminster School and Harris Federation, opened in 2014 at a cost of £45 million, much to the chagrin of other state sixth forms that have suffered massive budget cuts.

The church schools tend to be the most sought-after primaries: Hampden Gurney qv, St Peter's Eaton Square qv, St Saviour's C of E, St Joseph's RC and St Vincent's RC. Non-church Millbank (beloved of MPs' families), George Eliot, Gateway and Barrow Hill are also well thought of.

The Academy School

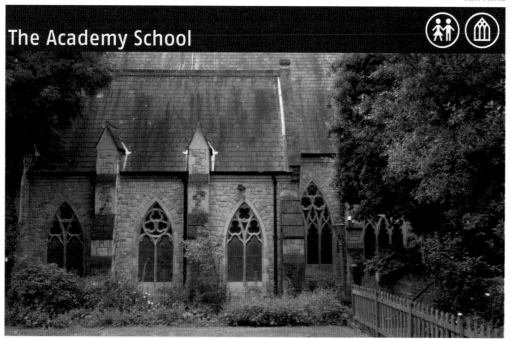

3 Pilgrims Place, Rosslyn Hill, London, NW3 1NG

Independent · Pupils: 90 · Ages: 6–13 · Fees (per term):£5,605

Tel: 020 7435 6621
Fax: 020 7435 7457
Email: office@academyhampstead.com
Website: www.academyschoolhampstead.com

Joint principals: Mr Garth Evans (50s), and Ms Chloe Sandars (40s), are joint principals of this small Hampstead school, which they founded in 1997. Chloe studied at the Royal Academy of Music, followed by postgraduate work at Trinity College of Music, then played in a trio while teaching music part-time. Garth, whose great-grandfather accompanied Captain Scott to the Antarctic, was educated at Falkner House, Westminster School and Queen Mary College, London, where he read English. He started tutoring privately at the age of 16 ('to fund my beer money') and went on to work at Trevor-Roberts, where he met Chloe. As private tutors, Garth and Chloe developed quite a following and parents encouraged them to start their own school. 'They liked the way we taught,' says Garth. 'Their children were inspired and given confidence.' The pair are an excellent foil to each other, she calm and organised, he a passionate and reassuring instructor. Chloe has two teenage daughters, both of whom attended the Academy, Garth a teenage son and daughter. Garth's wife, Bea (who teaches geography and acts as the school nurse) and Chloe's husband, Andrew (ex-City, who runs the finances and also teaches history and maths) are very much part of the four-person leadership team.

Entrance: Though they have occasionally taken a younger sibling, this is essentially a school which begins at 6, once children have learnt to read. 'We start with specialist subject teaching from the word go,' says Chloe. Pupils join at every stage thereafter, including mid year, if a place is available and the

> *'We're happy to work with the very strong and the very weak. The questions we ask are: Do we think we could do a good job? Do we like the family?'*

school feels it can meet the child's (and the parents') needs. Maximum of 90 pupils, however, and the school tends to be fullest in the summer. Pupils are assessed rather than tested, taking part in a class to see how they fit in. 'We're happy to work with the very strong and the very weak,' says Chloe. 'The questions we ask are: Do we think we can do a good job? Do we like the family?' Occasional year 7 places for boys after the 11-plus exodus of girls.

Exit: To a wide range of schools but most get their first choice. St Paul's Girls, North London Collegiate, City of London, Westminster, UCS, Highgate, Mill Hill, South Hampstead, Francis Holland, The Latymer and St Christopher, with several scholarships. 'Sometimes we have to work with parents to adjust their expectations, particularly if they've set their heart on a specific school from an early age, but most parents trust our judgement,' says Garth. Others are just grateful for the help given in pointing them in the right direction. 'My daughter is not at all academic,' said one mother, 'but they did everything to find a school that worked for her and she is now immensely happy.'

Remarks: The Academy is by no means a traditional school and its approach is perhaps defined by the backgrounds of its heads, who spent their early careers mopping up the fall-out from a traditional education elsewhere. The basis of their philosophy is that all learning stems from a happy child. 'It really is true,' says Chloe. 'If children are happy, everything follows from that.' Year groups here are soft-edged ('We're very flexible about birth dates') and so are classes. 'The whole school is planned round the individual and how best to work with their ability. If there's a problem we solve it.' Class sizes of about 14, but pupils are moved up a set in the middle of a term or taken out of a class to be given additional support. A significant part of the

'I looked at every church in the area. Then one snowy evening I knocked on the door here and the vicar said, "Step this way."'

process is instilling the essentials. Teaching, particularly in the core subjects, is rock solid and maths and English are thoroughly engrained. Though most pupils can read fluently on arrival, they continue to read aloud two or three times a week. Older children read for 15 minutes at the end of every lunch hour and all have a reading list and a carefully monitored reading record. Maths is unusually strong. 'Children like being good at maths,' says Garth, who believes that any subject, no matter how complex, can be taught well if communication is clear. As proof, on the day the Guide visited, his class of 11-year-olds had clearly grasped logarithms, a topic normally reserved for sixth formers. The effect lingers into secondary school. 'My daughter has stayed in the top maths set at a competitive school,' said one parent, 'I feel that's down to the teaching at The Academy.'

The Academy started out with just seven children in the premises of a Unitarian Chapel in Hampstead village. 'I looked at every church in the area,' said Chloe. 'Then one snowy evening I knocked on the door here and the vicar said, "Step this way".' The lower years are now housed in two dainty white Georgian cottages, with room sizes that reflect the era, older pupils are taught in the chapel. Facilities are relatively restricted with only a small library and science taught on the move, but pupils are engaged and enthusiastic. 'They give us quite a lot of freedom,' said one, 'but work us very hard.'

The school day starts bright and early with the first lesson at 8. 'We always felt the best part of the day was lost if you started with assembly at 8.30,' says Chloe. There are no 'class' teachers (though the youngest do have one specifically devoted to their needs). The school believes that 'every child is special', but this is not a place that specialises in those with serious learning difficulties. It copes well, however, with those on the margins and a special-needs expert visits weekly. Whatever the child's ability, most parents agree every ounce of potential is fully exploited.

Games are certainly not the raison d'être here and if you had a madly sporty child, whose primary motivation was to be captain of this or that, The Academy would not be an obvious choice. PE is taught on site by a sports teacher and swimming

The Academy is inspiration for all, but particularly so for those who've lost their way or lost confidence elsewhere

at the nearby Royal Free Leisure Centre, but there's little in the way of team sports. This is more a place where the question is who would like to be in the team – if the answer's yes, you're in. There is, however, a recently established netball squad and matches have been played against other schools in cricket and football, as well as handball, badminton and netball. Music and art are more of a priority. Double art every week, with woodwork on offer and a separate pottery room with its own kiln. Music, too, is taken seriously. 'We do a lot of singing, since it's very inclusive,' says Chloe and the school has a violin teacher and a 19-piece orchestra. 'It's a pretty odd orchestra, with one person on brass and 11 violins, but it's fun and they learn what it's like playing together. Occasionally, an exceptional player will raise the bar for everyone.' The annual school musical, which involves the entire school, is the highlight of the summer term. School food is packed lunch.

Pastoral care is what this school is all about. 'Children are nurtured and encouraged and set very simple objectives,' says Garth. 'We then build it up little by little and make them believe in themselves.' The Academy is inspiration for all, but particularly so for those who've lost their way or lost confidence elsewhere. 'We're good at turning them round,' says Garth, and parents couldn't agree more. 'It's a bit of a cliché,' said one who'd sent two children from two different schools, 'but they do care passionately about the children. In the case of both my children, they were completely transformed both academically and emotionally.' The school has its own visiting counsellor, who teaches PSHE and is available for any pupil who wants to talk. 'They feel it's OK to cross a line with me,' she says. Boundaries here, however, are firm, just further back than might be the case elsewhere. 'We deal furiously with unkindness or making capital at someone else's expense,' says Garth. There is no expulsion. 'We never send them away, we just remove them from society from 8-3.30 unless they behave.' The school has a uniform – a navy sweat top with the school's logo – but it's not strictly imposed. 'We don't really mind as long as they're neat,' said Chloe.

Families are mainly Hampstead locals and the relationship with parents is fundamental. Garth gives out his mobile number and parents can ring whenever they feel the need, a privilege he say they don't abuse. The parents themselves are immensely grateful. 'This is the school we all wish we could have gone to,' said one.

The American School in London Lower School

Linked school: The American School in London, 63

1 Waverley Place, London, NW8 0NP

Independent · Pupils: 425 · Ages: 4–10 · Fees (per term): £7,316

Tel: 020 7449 1200
Fax: 020 7449 1350
Email: admissions@asl.org
Website: www.asl.org

40

Head of School: Since 2007 Coreen Hester. This energetic Californian was ASL's high school principal from 1995-1997, and returned in 2007 to inherit a well-oiled machine in a newly-renovated campus. Highly visible, 'larger than life', with 'lots of presence', Mrs Hester is praised by parents who describe her as 'smart, insightful and approachable. She's a great communicator, and she's had a huge impact on the school. She has really upped the game for the teachers.'

She's looking at everything from top down and bottom up, aligning the programmes so that what is taught to 5 year olds makes sense when they are 15. Development of the already highly-qualified teaching staff is another priority.

Entrance: Apply as soon as possible after 1 July of the year before entry. School asks for copies of report cards and a teacher recommendation.

Exit: Kids rarely leave the primary at ASL unless the family is transferred away from London and nearly all go through to the middle and senior

'She's a great communicator and she's had a huge impact on the school. She has really upped the game for the teachers.'

school. Some families re-negotiate contracts just to stay on. Many want to see their children through to graduation.

Remarks: The lower school's project-approach aims to develop attitudes and habits that set up these youngsters for life-long learning, with critical thinking skills and solid foundations. During our stroll through the lower school we saw a full range of teaching contexts – children working one-to-one with teachers and assistants, working in pairs, small groups working collaboratively on projects, whole class groups seated in a big circle on the floor playing a language game, or engaged in teacher-led instruction using an interactive whiteboard. Spanish is introduced from the start, and lower school classes occasionally spend the day at the school's learning centre in Cannon's Park for outdoor and environmental studies. In-house specialists support children with mild learning problems, providing individual support to help them develop coping skills and strategies. Spaces are limited and there's an additional fee for the programme. Up to grade 4, an EAL programme helps non-English speakers come up to speed.

The school uses every inch of its limited space. The outdoor spaces have been adapted for different age groups. The lower school has a pod centre for each grade level; classrooms radiate from a central information space housing computers, reading corners and other teaching resources. Pupil work is displayed everywhere. The primary library is well stocked and always busy; parents either volunteer or browse the shelves for books to borrow. Children can bring their own lunch or buy it in the cafeteria.

Although there are 50 nationalities at ASL, the character of the school is definitely American, albeit 'global American'. As one parent described it, 'If you are an American coming from another international school, it feels American, but if you are from the suburbs of Chicago or Westchester County, it feels international.' Preponderance of parents from corporate world, particularly financial.

The school is very security conscious: security fending surrounds the perimeters and security men keep watch on all comings and goings (no entry without a school pass or photo id).

In her opening letter to the parents, the head spoke about 'striving for the best in American education'. Well, this school isn't far from that. The resources and facilities are excellent, attitudes are positive and results are good. Bright, curious, motivated kids do well here and middle of the road ones end up surprising their parents.

The American School in London

Linked school: The American School in London Lower School, 61

1 Waverley Place, London, NW8 0NP

Independent • Pupils: 1,350 • Ages: K to Grade 12 • Non-demon • Fees (per term): £7,316 – £8,550

Tel: 020 7449 1220
Fax: 020 7449 1350
Email: admissions@asl.org
Website: www.asl.org

41

Head of School: Since 2007, Coreen R Hester (degrees in English Literature and Education, Stanford University), previously head of Hamlin School in San Francisco. Was ASL's high school principal from 1995-1997, when her children were both pupils there. Early in her career, Mrs Hester taught English at University Liggott in Michigan; she then spent 10 years at the Branson School as teacher, dean, college counsellor, assistant head and interim head of school. Was also previously director of the Western Region Educational Services.

This energetic Californian inherited a well-oiled machine in a newly-renovated campus. She aims to strengthen the already high-qualified teaching staff, is looking at the role of support staff and reviewing the curriculum so that what is taught to 5 year olds makes sense when they are 15. Highly visible, 'larger than life', with 'lots of presence', she gets lots of praise from parents who describe her as 'so smart and insightful', and couldn't be more approachable. 'She's a great communicator'. 'The impact she has had on the school is huge. She has really upped the game for the teachers. We think the world of her!'

Academic matters: ASL's reputation is tops and an expectation of excellence must be pumped in through the air ducts; parents say that ASL aligns itself with the top US independent and public schools. Classes are no larger than 20 (15 the average in high school) and children are encouraged to take risks and view mistakes as natural learning. To quote a high schooler, 'Being smart is admired here. It's not about showing off, it's about showing what you can do.'

The middle school programme is designed to develop independence and organisation. While some parents initially worry that middle school begins at grade 5, a tad younger than the norm in many US and international schools, the structure is well designed so that grades 5 and 6 share one floor, and grades 7 and 8 another, facilitating the transition from primary to secondary education. 'Think of it as lower middle and upper middle school,' parents say. 'It works.'

High school is preparation for higher education with plenty of options in several subject areas, including over 20 AP subjects, making ASL one of the most prolific AP schools outside the US. In 2014, 240 students sat 631 AP exams in 32 subject areas, 81 per cent scored grade 3 or higher (out of a possible 5). The average SAT 1 scores were 666 in critical read-

Two libraries, very inviting and always busy, parents there either volunteering or browsing the shelves themselves

ing, 666 in math and 675 in writing (out of a possible 800 in each). Recent appointment of an all-school curriculum coordinator, who is reviewing the entire academic programme from soup to nuts, should iron out any kinks and has the approval of parents.

Older students say that this is a school where you need to be motivated and work hard. It's more of an unspoken expectation throughout, but all confirm there is good support in place and teachers willing to put in the extra hours to help. However, it comes a bit easier if you are proactive about seeking that help out. One parent said, 'If a child is highly sensitive, it is not always the kindest and gentlest place to be. But if they can access the education, it is a great experience'. All the departments are strong, improvements to language provision previously noted, although we have spoken to some dual-language families and kids who say they no longer consider themselves to be truly bilingual, having not maintained the other language.

ASL keeps up with US pedagogy, forging strong relations with leading US educationalists, such as Project Zero at Harvard, and not only sends teachers there to learn as part of the school's generous professional development programme but also hosts ASL learning institutes so other educators in the UK and abroad benefit.

Two libraries, very inviting and always busy, parents there either volunteering or browsing the shelves themselves. Computer terminals all over and all students have computer classes. Grades 7 and 8 are given laptops which they are expected to master. High school students can bring their own or use the many on site.

ASL can handle students with mild learning problems; specialists provide individual support; spaces are limited and there's an additional fee for the programme. One parent we spoke to wanted to dispel the myth that ASL does not deal well with learning problems. Her child's problem, overlooked by previous schools, was diagnosed right away and the SEN team have been 'fabulous'. The English as an Additional Language (EAL) programme helps non-English speakers up to grade 4 come up to

speed for better integration in the mainstream. Intermediate and advanced English speakers are integrated up to grade 10. After that, total fluency is required to handle the rigorous academics.

Faculty of 175, average tenure is nine years which is good for international schools. Not only do 75 per cent of the teachers have higher degrees, so do many of the teaching assistants. Despite this longevity of service, a new high school principal, and a new lower school principal and assistant principal joined the staff in 2013. It's early days but parents seem happy with the new arrivals.

Games, options, the arts: Academics are important but so are the arts, sports and other activities, with a growing emphasis on community service. Framed paintings, drawings and photos by former students line the walls, forming part of the school's permanent collection and setting the bar for the arts. Everyone learns an instrument in the band or orchestra and sings in the choir through middle school. These enthusiastic musicians then take up seats in the bands and orchestras at the high school level. Opportunities available to travel in Europe with the choir and orchestras, or with the drama programme. Photo labs and art studios busy throughout the day. The new auditorium looks like a not-so-mini version of the Barbican, and it's always in use either for concerts and plays or hosting speakers.

Sports are part of the DNA at ASL but, unlike some stateside schools, sports at ASL complement the academics rather than competing with them. At least 85 per cent of high school students play on at least one school team. There are two gyms, 21

If word gets back to the high school dean about a party, he'll phone the host's parents just to make sure they are aware

acres of playing fields a tube ride away (students are bussed there, though distance means that this is restricted to after-school activities) and a display case filled with trophies leaves no doubt about the school's athletic standing in the international school world.

Special interest clubs too many to mention – all the usual ones and lots of unusual ones, in school and off campus. The PCA funds up to £1,000 for a well-thought-out one-time project put forward by faculty, students or staff. The head also has a fund to support new projects: for example, the school's robotics program began this way.

High school students accompanied by faculty members participate in annual spring Alternatives programme, choosing between recreational, academic or cultural activities done over four days. Community service with new emphasis on local interaction has 270 kids volunteering in charities and projects based within a few miles radius. They're also building bridges with the nearby comprehensive school thanks to a student-led joint-school Lego robotics club initiative. The kids themselves form lots of service-related clubs that do their own independent fundraising for good causes they want to support. Students encouraged to assume leadership roles, challenge themselves and take advantage of London. Field trips, not just in London but all over Europe and Africa, organised to broaden perspectives.

Background and atmosphere: Founded in 1951 as an alternative to the British schools for London's burgeoning American diplomatic, military and corporate community, this London city school uses every inch of its space; through innovative planning and successful fundraising initiatives they continues to embellish that. Compact brick buildings set on a city block encase the 1,350 student body, which is at capacity. Security fencing surrounds the perimeters and smart security men keep a watchful eye on all comings and goings (no entry without a school pass or photo id). Outdoor spaces adapted to different age groups.

ASL has a strong and proactive board of trustees in the style of US independent schools. They are active and hard-working and take their role very seriously. The last the big development project added an extra floor, a gym, new labs and a theatre. The lower school has a pod centre for each grade level; classrooms radiate from a central information space housing computers, reading corners and other teaching resources. The middle school students move around between classes more, and the high school is what you would expect: animated kids rushing around halls, definitely happy to be there. Pupil work is everywhere, for example an impressive student-designed notice board about the US elections conveyed both the US-essence of the school and the calibre of creativity and critical thinking these kids possess.

Middle and high school classes run for 80 minutes with an hour for lunch. Students bring their lunch or buy it in the cafeteria, which is very good, though many in grades 9-12 opt for the off-campus privilege. We hear some grumbles about pressure on lunch facilities; one parent said she was not particularly happy with the early timing of her lower school daughter's lunch sitting. Lower school students eat a packed lunch (from home or purchased from ASL) in their classroom.

Pastoral care and discipline: It seems that students at ASL work hard and play hard. The kids are motivated to try hard to do their best, to try lots of new activities or get better at the ones they excel at. While allowing for individual initiative and responsibility, the organisation and structure is in place to ensure plenty of support so that no one drifts off course.

Parents report few serious disciplinary problems, saying the school plays it 'close to the vest', and that if there are, they're dealt with quietly and confidentially. School rules not onerous but expectation is that they will be followed and the school will take transgressions seriously. When news circulated about a recent (and rare) cheating incident, the head responded swiftly and firmly. Parents say, however, that teachers and principals are not always consistent doling out the consequences and sanctions which result from misbehaviour.

The school recommends that families abide by US drinking rules – no alcohol for under 21s – which are stricter than those found in Britain, but this is difficult to enforce. If word gets back to the high school dean about a party, he phones the host's parents just to make sure they are aware. At times this makes him more popular with parents than the kids! No dress code, but jeans seem to be the uniform of choice. If you do see the odd shirt and tie, it means a team is off to an away game.

Students arrive at this urban school with different levels of 'street wisdom' and 'stranger danger' awareness. Parents appreciate the way ASL takes pains to speak frankly to parents and kids about the potential problems and equip students with the right skills to protect themselves. A noteworthy issue is that middle schoolers are sometimes targets for muggings in the streets of affluent St John's Wood. Perpetrators are usually other kids

looking for the portable technology now standard kit for many students. Nobody ever gets hurt, but it happens a few times a year. Door-to-door bus service available in the morning and after school and also at the end of the after-school programme, covers central, north and west London.

ASL high schoolers do not have an advisory or home room teacher, a concern for some parents; instead, a dean of year looks after the year group, working in partnership with principals and subject teachers. In grade 11 deans hand over to the university counsellors, each of whom has a light case load so they can give plenty of attention to each of their charges. Daily bulletins and notices are sent by email to all.

Pupils and parents: The school may be in London but the tone is definitely American – let's call it 'global American'. Eighty per cent of the 1,350 students hold US passports, and half of those are multi-passport holders from dual-national families. There are 50 nationalities in the school and the group of great kids who turned up during break to meet the GSG visitor didn't contain a single American! As a rule, ASL students are bright, curious and confident, and willing to express their views about anything you ask them. But, as one middle school pupil observed, 'international passports do not make a place international; the school is pretty American'. The popular award-winning student newspaper The Standard debates this question from time to time. Non-Americans at this school are largely attracted by the academic, social and college counselling preparation for entry into US universities. Lots of 'third culture kids' (professional parents raising children in a country not their own), and expats from the finance world, though the transiency is diminishing as more families stay longer.

As one parent said, 'If you are an American coming from another international school, it feels American, but if you are from the suburbs of Chicago or Westchester County, it feels international'.

The school has revised its mission statement to incorporate the 'global perspective', and 'bursting the bubble' is one of Hester's goals for the school, which she describes as 'somewhere in the mid-Atlantic'. After 9/11 the school heightened its security and understandably drew inward but now, Hester explains, 'it's time to bring ASL into London, and London into ASL', with more intentional planning for programming, including emphasis on community service activities.

There is a perception on the part of some parents that it's economic diversity that is lacking, with concerns that 'too many kids are fretting about the right trainers or Prada handbags, and the presence of a few kids so wealthy that their security guards come to school with them, which is a bit weird.' This is something the school hopes will change through its diversity statement – and a target to grow the financial aid pot to a level equivalent of 8.5 per cent of the tuition income.

It is worth noting that lots of ASL families are there for the second time. Families sometimes choose London as a posting in part because of ASL; it is regarded by many as one of the key attractions of moving here.

Entrance: Admission is based on school records, teacher recommendations and standardised test results (ERB/ SSATs). Turnover is diminishing, with waiting lists at all grades, which means there may not be space for all family members. Unlike other international schools, ASL will only accept applications a year before admission; the first round of offers is made on 1 February. After that, it's rolling admissions.

Huge praise for the school's support for new arrivals – both parents and kids – including seminars, social events and newsletters. 'It's tremendous how much they reach out to pull you in, because they know you are lost.'

Exit: Most students leaving before graduation do so because of family transfers. For those planning to finish the course, university preparation work begins in grade 11 for students and parents. One parent told us that the rumour that everyone has to go to a 'top 10' is untrue. ASL's US Advanced Placements (APs) are welcomed by British universities, and although more ASL students are getting offers from top UK universities, most still opt for the USA. Graduates go on to all the big and little Ivy Leagues, as well as the major state universities in the US (Harvard, Yale, Princeton, Stanford, University of Pennsylvania), the major players in Canada (McGill,

Toronto) and British Russell Group unis (Cambridge, Bristol, Queen Mary London). A recent graduate entered University of Virginia as a prestigious Jefferson Scholar with full university funding.

Money matters: Tuition covers textbooks, laboratory fees and all required activities except for the Music Tour for band, orchestra and choir members. There are occasional additional expenses – usually travel – associated with some middle and high school classes. Tuition does not include expenses for trips related to extracurricular activities such as athletics, Model UN or service learning. Needs-based financial aid is available for tuition and also for school-related trips and activities.

Parents say there is a definite expectation that everyone (including staff) will participate in the school's fundraising initiatives; this presents a challenging adjustment for some, particularly families who are less familiar with a US independent school tradition. Besides annual funds, there is a major auction every other year ('Think Sotheby's,' one parent says.) Another parent says that the level of importance attributed to the expectation of significant donations is a lingering legacy of previous heads, and the days when a family's status at school was, albeit subtly, linked to the size of a financial benefaction, are long gone.

Remarks: In her opening letter to the parents the head spoke about 'striving for the best in American education'. Well, this school isn't far from that. The resources and facilities are excellent, attitudes are positive and results are good. Bright, curious, motivated kids do well here and those who are in the middle of the road end up surprising their parents.

Arnold House School

1 Loudoun Road, London, NW8 0LH

Independent • Pupils: 260 • Ages: 5–13 • C of E • Fees (per term): £5,650

Tel: 020 7266 4840
Fax: 020 7266 6994
Email: registrar@arnoldhouse.co.uk
Website: www.arnoldhouse.co.uk

42

Headmaster: Since 2006, Vivien Thomas (50s). A user-friendly, down-to-earth chap with an easy warmth and an unscholarly taste in garish ties (red flowers and giant yellow fish on the day we visited). Makes a point of being accessible on school gate duty at least twice a week and is generally popular with parents. 'Relaxed, confident, intelligent, and understands how parents feel about their children,' says one. Educated at University College School, Hampstead, followed by St Luke's College, Exeter, where he studied PE and history. Had a trial for QPR aged 17 and dreamt of becoming a professional sportsman but, after failing to make the grade (at football, tennis and rugby), he turned his talents to education. Taught PE and maths at UCS, followed by a spell at an international school in Venezuela. He returned to London to become deputy head at Arnold House, then head of Keble Prep, Winchmore Hill, until 2006. Married to Rowena, he is a man of varied interests, who 'struggles with golf', enjoys travelling and takes guitar lessons with 'a madman in Dollis Hill who used to play with Ginger Baker of Cream'.

Entrance: Application form (plus the usual £100 fee) due before child's second birthday, followed by an open evening held in April/May approximately two and a half years before the intended entry date. Interested parents (roughly 170 families for 38 places) are then invited to meet the head for a 20 minute chat. As always, it is the parents who are being assessed as much as the child. Don't say, 'I need you to get my son into Westminster'. Do say, 'I'd like my child to be happy and enjoy an all-round

---

He is a man of varied interests, who 'struggles with golf', enjoys travelling and takes guitar lessons with 'a madman in Dollis Hill who used to play with Ginger Baker of Cream.'

---

education'. Prospective pupils then invited for an informal one-to-one assessment and places offered 15 months before entry date. 'I hate the idea that it'll be down to the little boy, that he might be "not good enough",' says the head. 'What I want to know is, will he be a nice little boy to teach? When you open a book, is he able to be engaged? Or is he climbing the walls, unruly and impolite? I don't want it to be a skills-based test, and I find it astonishing that there are tutoring agencies for 3 and 4 year olds.'

Main entry-point is into year 1, with occasional ad-hoc places in other years. Younger siblings and sons of Old Boys looked on favourably. Partial and full means-tested bursaries are available in years 5, 6 and 7.

Exit: Strongly 13-plus focussed school. A wide intake means a broad exit, but high fliers get into all the top schools, often with scholarships to boot. Two-thirds go on to London day schools, with the

remainder heading off to boarding school. Strong links with Westminster, St Paul's, City of London Boys, Highgate, UCS and Mill Hill. Boarders go to Eton, Harrow, Rugby, Marlborough, Winchester and Bradfield, amongst others. Over-ambitious parents are discouraged from entering their son for exams all over the place. 'After 12 years of headship I know the system inside out. I am very honest with parents. What may look like an opportunity to them is in reality a rejection letter on the mat. Granny's all keyed up, everyone is rooting for him, but I know it's just not going to happen. I'll say, "your son is moving along quite happily, do you really want him to get that knock back?"'

Roughly 25 out of 30 boys get their first choice school, the remaining five or six take a bit longer. 'When boys are on the waiting list it's my job to turn that into an offer. We have excellent relations with schools, and that's when the prep school head really earns his corn.'

The school offers excellent results with less of the stressful, hothouse hysteria that so often accompanies the 13-plus experience. 'I offer places to parents who understand the Arnold House ethos,' says the head. 'They should want their son to join knitting club, cooking club, play music and sport, and not be getting anxious if he doesn't get three hours homework a night. We are here for bigger things than getting into a top academic senior school.'

Remarks: While some sniff that it is old fashioned, for others the traditional values of Arnold House are its strongest selling point. 'It's just like the perfect country prep school, but in London,' sighs one happy parent.

In the stressful, results-oriented atmosphere of the London prep school system, Arnold House is an artfully constructed oasis where boys can still be boys. Pupils are even encouraged to have snowball fights and inter-house conker competitions (safely supervised, of course). Admission is non-selective and the school frowns on hothousing, yet year after year leavers gain entry to the holy trinity of Eton, St Paul's and Westminster.

'These boys don't need to be pushed,' claims the head (rather airily). 'It's a question of 'nudging' and bringing a boy nicely, like a fine wine, to the point where he is ready.'

Arnold House was founded in 1905 with nine pupils by a Miss Hanson, who was keen to prove boys could be prepared for public school entrance by a woman. She was successful, and the school has now expanded to fill three adjoining houses in a quiet St John's Wood side-street. The buildings lack any particular architectural pizzazz, but inside it feels spacious and well laid out, and is probably one of the cleanest schools we've visited. Even the boys' loos were sparkling, and instead of the usual dank, unloved urinals we found modern boutique-style plumbing with glossy lime green and red cubicles.

Entrance is into year 1, with 38 places split into two classes, though classes are smaller at the top of the school due to natural shrinkage. They are mixed up every couple of years to ensure academic parity and 'social refreshment'. Setting begins in year 3 for maths and English, with subjects taught by specialists from year 5. French from year 1, Latin from year 5, and ancient Greek is an option in year 7. No separate scholarship class, but boys with scholarship potential are identified at the end of year 7 and invited to join specialist lessons.

Lots of examples of creative, value-added education. The Compass Course in years 5 and 6 aims to foster independent thinking, public speaking and IT skills. Pupils work collaboratively to design an EU leaflet, make an animated film, write a play and create a charity PowerPoint presentation. Instead of the bog-standard year 8 battlefields trip, pupils spend time researching Arnold House Old Boys killed in WW1 before visiting France and finding their graves in the war cemeteries to pay their respects. An inspired way to bring history off the page. There is an embarrassment of before-school, after-school and break-time activities ranging from an 8am Quiz Club to Mad Scientist Club, Bug Club, darts, French Fun and Games plus all the usual sport, music and art activities.

Like many London schools has a shortage of outside space. There is an adequate playground, but boys must travel to the school's seven acre sports ground in Canons Park (35 minutes away) for games. The younger boys travel by coach, years 7 and 8 by public transport. ('You'd expect, with the fees we pay, that the boys wouldn't have to get there by tube', mutters one disgruntled parent.) Here there are classrooms, a theatre, tennis courts and pitches for football, cricket, hockey and rugby. Older boys play team games twice a week, younger boys once a week, and there are additional PE and sports sessions at local leisure centres. A busy fixtures list for A, right down to G teams, means that even the most athletically-challenged pupil has an opportunity to represent the school.

The music department is outstanding and has many scholarships under its belt. Some 85 per cent of pupils study at least one instrument and many learn two. Twenty different ensembles on offer, from flute group to jazz and African drums, with lots of opportunity to perform in concerts. Years 7 and 8 can use the whizzy i-music suite for production, recording and pod-casting.

Art is taught to a high standard and doesn't get quietly side-lined as exams loom for older pupils. No need to feign enthusiasm when pupils arrive home clutching yet another art project. We saw wonderful Cubist self-portraits from year 3 and some very accomplished papier-mâché shells that any parent would be proud to put on display.

SEN support is excellent and, with a year of free one-to-one sessions before charges kick in, is more generous than at many comparable schools. One permanent SEN qualified staff member is supported by three visiting specialists for dyspraxia, speech and language and occupational therapy. Pupils who need extra help are identified in years 1 and 2 and either given classroom support by the six teaching assistants, or allotted one-to-one sessions as necessary. Dyslexia screening for every pupil in year 4 as a 'final trawl' to identify those with SEN needs, which can often mean brighter pupils in which dyslexic tendencies are masked.

So what type of child does Arnold House suit? 'My son has been blissfully happy, but there is a certain rough and tumble that goes with a boys' school, and I think if they are very fragile they might find it easier at a co-ed. They don't have to be uber-sporty though, there's drama, singing, art, something for everybody.'

'We take the boys as they are,' says the head. 'We have boys with IQs below 100 all the way up to 140. Once we take a boy on we're looking to be together as a team for eight years.' He admitted that, occasionally, if a boy looks like he is struggling by year 4 or 5, he will have a meeting with parents to decide 'whether or not this is looking like a good plan'.

Behaviour at the school is generally accepted to be good. 'We expect the boys to rise to a certain level of behaviour. I don't know if you can teach kindness, but you can certainly teach consideration,' says the head. There's the usual system of sanctions and rewards with Good Citizenship badges for 'being a good egg' and Industry badges for trying hard. Senior boys get ties for art, music, games and responsibility. 'I'm always pleased to hear how strict the school is,' says one parent. 'My son is well-behaved, but I occasionally hear of other boys being told off, and they are properly told off.'

Bullying is rare but, as in all schools, it happens. Usually nipped in the bud early by class teachers, but suspension has been used when necessary. 'In 7 years I've had only four situations where I've had to step in,' says the head. 'There isn't a parent I've met who thinks their son could actually be the bully, so it always has to be thoroughly investigated.' The head is very hot on cyber bullying. 'If a boy is being talked about in a derogatory way on Facebook on Sunday night, then it's going to cause problems at school on Monday morning. Even if it happens outside school, I will deal with it.' Only one parent we spoke to was unhappy, feeling that a situation had been dealt with 'too late'.

Parents are a mix of multi-national successful professionals, with 50 per cent close enough to walk to school (should they ever choose to leave the 4x4 behind) and others coming from further afield (Notting Hill, Islington, Highgate). Reputed to be a friendly, sociable parent body, though the higher-than-average fees mean there's a lot of wealth sloshing around. 'There are a few amazingly flash cars, but also plenty of beat-up cars like ours. It's an easy, mixed group and I've seen no snobbishness whatsoever.' This is not the place for wags, trophy wives or school gate show-offs. 'It's definitely not a "women who lunch" school,' said one mother. 'All the mothers have, or have had, interesting careers. At my son's nursery I was the only working mum and had nothing in common with anyone, so I find the professional ethos here a relief.'

School lunches would definitely win a triple gold star from Jamie Oliver. A very jolly cook was making roast beef, Yorkshire pud, parsnips and broccoli on the day we visited, and the gravy was even made with a dash of wine.

The Camden School for Girls

Sandall Road, London, NW5 2DB

State • Pupils: 970 • Ages: 11–19 • Non-denom

Tel: 020 7485 3414
Fax: 020 7284 3361
Email: csg@camdengirls.camden.sch.uk
Website: www.camdengirls.camden.sch.uk

Headteacher: Since 2010, Elizabeth Kitcatt BA MA (Institute of Education). Ms Kitcatt has been at the school for many years, joining from Parliament Hill School, where she was head of English. At Camden, under the previous regime, as well as teaching English, she was deputy head, responsible for 'teachers' professional development' and 'school improvement planning'. Looks a bit like Delia Smith and has the same reassuring, measured presence. Clearly strong on detail, but generally considered rather more cautious and less charismatic than her predecessor. 'She's a bit bland,' said one long-term parent. 'She's quite a lot stricter, but otherwise seems to have made little impact.' Determined to maintain the school's high standards and inclusive approach. Enjoys singing in her spare time.

Academic matters: Camden is one of the country's most successful comprehensives. Latest Ofsted rated it 'outstanding' in every respect (except attendance) and commented that 'it rightly deserves the outstanding reputation it has among parents and in the community'. In 2014, 77 per cent of pupils got 5+ A*-C grades at GCSE, including English and maths, and 43 per cent of grades were A*/A. But the sixth form is the jewel in the crown and A level results are stellar, with 83 per cent A*-B and 58 per cent A*/A grades. 'Top class curriculum,' says Ofsted, and that includes a hard-going compulsory core at GCSE of English, maths, science, philosophy and theology, physical education, French or Spanish and PSHE. Mixed-ability classes of about 28 pre-GCSE, 20 in the sixth form, and work carefully monitored with individual targets set at the beginning of each year. Homework, too, taken seriously, with detentions for slackers.

Drama too – with the already professional among the sixth form – is strong, with an annual Broadway show and sixth-formers mounting their own production

The sixth form decidedly less mixed-ability than the lower school, as only those who make the grades make the transfer. The curriculum here is traditional and academic with classical civilisation, history of art, ancient Greek, economics and philosophy supplementing the mainstream subjects. ('Softer' options such as media studies and DT are only taught to AS level). Extended Project Qualification (EPQ) also popular. Intellectual stretching taken even further for Oxbridge aspirants with after-school masterclasses covering everything from the Economic Downturn to The Wasteland. Much inspired instruction, particularly in the sixth form. 'It's like an old-fashioned grammar school,' says one parent. 'The teaching is really rigorous.' Lower down, there are those who struggle with more challenging pupils. ('Some teachers just can't control the class,' said one year 9 parent. 'There are subjects where my daughter has completely given up.') Though sciences are well taught with strong results, this is a noticeably arty school – possibly not the ideal place if medicine is your ultimate goal. Special needs well catered for, with sensitive individual support in class or by withdrawal in small groups. After-school homework club for dyslexia and spelling. Middle-class parents, too, tend to pick up the slack when students flag.

Games, options, the arts: 'Art and music are fantastic here,' said one mother with two daughters, one artistic, the other musical. Most parents (many in the media) agree. The school has specialist music status with dedicated music places at both 11 and 16, and this pool of talent forms the core of two orchestras (including a 70-piece symphony orchestra), various chamber music ensembles, three choirs, a wind band, a jazz group, a jazz choir and a recorder group. Both music and music technology offered at A Level. Energetic and dedicated head of music. Art, too, is incredibly strong ('Art is really big in this school,' said one student fan) with powerful work on display throughout the halls and a glorious traditional art studio (formerly the gym), with a suitably bohemian skylight, as well as a pottery studio. Textiles equally vibrant. Art is the fourth most popular A level choice (after English, maths and history) with a good number of A*s. The keen also use the EPQ to extend their range (a short film made by a student was recently shown on the South Bank) and about 20 per cent of leavers go on to art-related degrees. Drama too – with the already professional among the sixth form – is strong, with an annual Broadway show and sixth-formers mounting their own production. (Stage management is offered as an enrichment activity and last year one pupil left to take up a recording contract.)

Sport, on the other hand, is probably not the school's forte. An on-site gym, outdoor netball court and attractive dance studio are supplemented by excellent facilities at Cantelowes Park, a few feet from the gates, but play-up, play-up and play the game is not really the ethos here. Plenty of clubs from art, technology and modern languages to specialist make-up and knitting, and sixth formers devote Wednesday afternoons to 'enrichment studies', ranging from creative writing to personal finance and tag rugby. All the more traditional ornaments, too, including a sixth-form newspaper and a debating society. Though there's plenty going on, you do have to be self-motivated to make the most of it. 'My son was supposed to do football as an enrichment activity,' said one mother, 'but no one monitors it. He just has Wednesday afternoons off.' School trips (Austrian tour for musicians, ski trip) and work experience abroad organised annually.

Background and atmosphere: Camden, founded in 1871 by Frances Mary Buss, is an iconic school in the history of education. Buss – and her limerickly-linked counterpart, Dorothea Beale, who founded Cheltenham Ladies' College – were responsible for establishing three of the great landmarks in women's education. Buss founded North London Collegiate in 1850, and then, specifically for girls

of more modest means, Camden, which opened in 1879 and until 1920 (when it established its own sixth form) regularly sent scholarship girls on to North London for sixth form. The school went comprehensive in 1977.

Relatively restricted site with a motley collection of buildings, from the high-ceilinged, large-windowed Victorian through 60s concrete to red-brick modern. Good facilities with new science labs, a well-stocked library, modern computer rooms and classrooms and a building which houses

Camden is a cool school, an obvious haven for the daughters of the north London, left-leaning media classes

design technology, English and music. Socially, the atmosphere is relaxed but purposeful. 'I was at quite a strict girls' independent school before I came to Camden in year 10,' said one sixth former, 'and I much prefer it here. You're treated like an adult.' Good food – pasta and garlic bread, curry – at reasonable cost.

Pastoral care and discipline: Deliberately few rules, but Ms Kitcatt is generally noted for having tightened up on the detail, clamping down on latecomers and absentees. 'Camden Compass' spells out the behaviour code, but generally a strong sense of trust and girls are 'let out into the unknown' from year 9. That doesn't mean, however, their activities remain unobserved. 'The one time my daughter was absent without leave, you knew immediately,' said one parent. 'They really have the girls sussed,' said another, with a daughter who'd encountered considerable difficulties. 'I really feel they listened to my worries.'

Highly praised induction programme eases new pupils into the sixth from, where the approach is definitely 'young adult', with signing in rather than register and no requirement to be on site during study periods. 'We see it as transition between school sixth form and college,' says the head. Loose-rein it may be, but a strong team of tutors oversee 18 students each and offer advice on everything from study skills to gap years. Elected prefects organise the leavers' ball and help out younger girls. Parents in general think the outcome is all that could be desired. 'It's a terrific environment and produces really feisty girls, who are encouraged to think for themselves and question.'

Pupils and parents: 'Camden girls have a sense of their place within the world that is immediately recognisable,' says one former head girl, and who could dispute her standpoint? 'Girls are confident beyond belief,' said one parent with a more ambivalent view. Camden is a cool school, an obvious haven for the daughters of the north London, left-leaning media classes. Current and former parents include the sculpture Antony Gormley, Random House chief Gail Rebuck, and Tate Modern director Sir Nicholas Serota, and old girls in the same style number Sarah Brown (wife of Gordon), Professor of Networking Julia Hobsbawm and actress Emma Thompson. The mainstream here is street-smart and sociable and frequently blessed by names like Hermione, Indiana and Genevieve. But while all participate in the uniform non-uniform of skinny jeans and stylish footwear, this is not a socially homogeneous institution. The school serves a catchment where the proportion of those eligible for free school meals is well above average, and it educates a plentiful sprinkling of refugees and asylum seekers, from Kosovo to Kurdistan. 'It's multi-dimensional and multi-ethnic,' said one mother. 'It's an urban experience, but excellent.' In the sixth form, there's a significant influx – boys and girls – from the independent sector.

Entrance: At 11 – unless you have an SEN statement, are in local authority care, have a sibling still at the school or are a talented musician – you will have to live no further away than 0.982 miles of the school entrance 'in a straight line as the crow flies' in order to sit a 'banding' test (40 minutes of verbal and non-verbal reasoning), set to ensure all classes are of mixed ability. Once the four bands are established, 28 places are offered in each band according to the general criteria. Camden is definitely one of those London schools which people move house for (and sometimes only pretend to move house – a naughtiness the school clamps down on firmly). If that's your plan, living within a few feet of the gates is your only sensible course of action. At 11, there are eight music places awarded independently of all other criteria. Music candidates take a multiple-choice aptitude test to whittle down the numbers, then the top 60 are invited back for a five-minute audition. In the sixth form, Camden goes co-ed, admitting a further 150-170 new pupils (from about 1000 applicants), no more than half of whom can be boys. Once again siblings are given precedence (but only if the sibling is still at the school on the date the applicant starts). Other places are dependent on distance from the gates, academic references and GCSE grades, predicted and actual (documentary proof required for all three). Grade Bs essential in at least five subjects, including maths and English language. At this point, a further 15 music places on offer to those who play 'an orchestral instrument to a high standard.'

Exit: Quite a number leave at 16, either because they don't make the grade or because they prefer a sixth-form college, apprenticeship or employment. Vast majority of leavers at 18 to further or higher education, including generaly 15 or so to Oxbridge and occasional one to Harvard. Art foundation and music schools also very popular.

Money matters: Camden is a voluntary aided school and, as such, has to contribute 10 per cent to its buildings costs. Parents give generously and there is an annual fundraising appeal, with monthly donations from £10. Plenty of further fundraising activities, too, where celebrity watching is the order of the day.

Remarks: One of London's best and coolest schools. Suits the self-motivated, self-assured, creative individualist, particularly those who might find the atmosphere elsewhere pettifogging and unimaginative.

The Children's House School

King Henry's Walk, Islington, London N1 4PB

Independent • Pupils: 60 • Ages: 2–8 • Fees (per term): £2,505 – £4,340

Tel: 020 7249 6273
Fax: 020 7923 4336
Email: info@childrenshouse-upperschool.co.uk
Website: www.childrenshouseschool.co.uk

37

Head: Jill Rothwell BA PGCE (50s). Mrs Rothwell (Jill to all) took her first degree in English and drama (at Manchester), then a PGCE at the Institute of Education, followed by two years teaching in the state sector. She became a parent at the Children's House in 1985 and a member of the parent's committee, but it was only when she came to register her third child in 1995 that she was invited in to teach. 'When I rang up, they said, "We'd like to offer you a place"; that's when I discovered my vocation.' She took over as head of the nursery in 2003, then, in 2005, oversaw the launch of the pre-prep. Retired temporarily in 2011 but, after a brief interlude, was back. Parents confirm both her commitment to the school and her devotion to the children. ('She's the most child-centred person; whatever else is going on, she never loses that perspective.')

Entrance: Register for nursery as soon as possible after birth and (crucially) register separately for nursery and pre-prep (deposits of £1500 and £2000 respectively). Places offered by date of registration and sibling priority. Most places in the pre-prep are filled from the nursery, but 'one or two' spaces available in reception, again based on date of registration.

Exit: Some leave at the formal entry points to other schools at 4 and 5. 'Parents ask if we mind,' says the head, 'but our advice is always to do what's best for the child.' Twenty-eight start out in two reception classes, but numbers generally reduce to a manageable 20 by year 2. Boys at all stages to the main north London preps (The Hall, St Anthony's, Hereward House, etc) and, at 7 plus, to the junior schools of major senior schools (Highgate, UCS). Girls to South Hampstead and nearby City of London School for Girls. Significant numbers, too, to St Paul's Cathedral School, Forest and The Cavendish.

Remarks: Founded as a nursery in someone's front room in 1973, when 'there was little in the way of Early Years provision and nothing in the way of policies and procedures', the nursery is now a fully-formed school, housed independently in a converted chapel in central Islington and headed

by Emma Berou. Here children from 2 enjoy a rich and dynamic offering (including conversational French, dance and sport) taught by fully qualified teachers. 'It's a lovely, friendly place,' said one parent. 'They really care about each child.'

The pre-prep came into being when a former parent spotted a school to let in the local newspaper. 'Our nursery parents always felt it was a pity children had to move on at 4 and 5.' Now they can remain in the fold, housed in a petite and picturesque Victorian schoolhouse nestled in the shelter of its big brother church. 'It's idyllic, like Enid Blyton,' says one parent.

Mornings are devoted to the three Rs, with much of the work 'topic based'. 'We take an overarching theme and help children make links across the curriculum,' says Jill. (Typical subject matter, for example, is Ourselves, in which children might explore the senses in science, study old toys in history, make a toy in design technology, and visit the Bethnal Green Museum of Childhood.) Often chil-

---

Working the nearby community garden provides further time out of doors and educational avenues

---

dren work in groups. 'We like them to work collaboratively, one child supporting another.' A very creative school; arts and crafts is central to learning. Children, for example, make shoebox interiors as a part of a home topic, create tetrahedron mobiles in maths, and paint and embroider textiles to study printmaking. Homework introduced gently in reception and year 1, with a more significant push towards 7 plus.

Specialist teachers extend the core. French and ICT, with a dedicated teacher and a full-class supply of laptops, throughout. Singing and rhythm taught by a music teacher, plus a weekly half-hour violin lesson from a professional violinist. 'I want the children to be at the end of passionate teaching,' says Jill. Dance, too, taught by an external expert.

The school prides itself on being 'very inclusive' and a hard-working SENCo addresses both minor and significant difficulties. Good support, too, for those with English as an additional language, addressing the requirements of an increasing number of bilingual children.

Not the school for those looking for an early introduction to competitive team games, but a specialist teaches PE and balls skills (relay races, running, pitching) in one of the two large adjoining church halls. Well-equipped playground provides further scope for fresh air, exercise and, most importantly, play. 'We have a lot of play resources and use them to extend their learning with carefully planned activities,' says the head. Working the nearby community garden provides further time out of doors and educational avenues.

Plenty of 'enrichment'. 'The school is fantastic at making lovely things happen for the children,' says one parent. Two visits a term, a least one in the form of 'entertainment', plus numerous themed days (dressing-up day, book day, etc). All stay for after-school clubs (sewing, fencing, cookery, drama, football, arts and crafts and yoga).

School uniform minimal and practical (navy and white sweatshirt with logo). No hot food; children bring in lunch boxes, supplemented by a snack and fruit in the morning.

Traditional values of courtesy and consideration central to the ethos. 'Being kind is paramount,' says a mother. Monitors chosen weekly, with top-of-the school Year 2, given increased responsibility. 'They're so helpful and dependable,' says the head. 'If you ask them to do something, they'll get it done.'

One of the things parents like most about the The Children's House is its home-away-from-home atmosphere. In break, for example, children wander in and out of the school office. ('We're doing plaits,' confided one pair, 'can you help us?') 'There's no such thing as a closed door,' said one happy parent.

Founded by parents, The Children's House remains a parent-driven operation, with active participation from its Parent Committee. 'No one owns it,' says the head. 'It's a collective.' All vote for the Council of Management, which administers the school. Unsurprisingly, families (Hackney and Islington media, City, lawyers and artisans) form a tight bond both with each other and the school, regularly arriving to read, organising the summer fair, quiz night, etc. 'I couldn't do it without the parents,' says the head. 'They're amazing.' 'We're always made to feel welcome,' says one.

About 10 per cent of children are on means-tested bursary places, covering up to 100 per cent of fees.

City and Islington College

283 – 309 Goswell Road, London, EC1V 7LA

State • Pupils: 1,350 • Ages: 16–19 • Non-denom

Tel: 020 7700 9333
Fax: 020 7520 0602
Email: courseinfo@candi.ac.uk
Website: www.candi.ac.uk

38

Director: Since 2001, Ms Keren Abse BA MA PGCE (50s). First degree in English, second in history, both from Sussex. Started teaching English in 1978 at Reynolds High School, Ealing, then to Quintin Kynaston in Westminster. She joined the college in 1984 and says, 'it's changed dramatically.' There were just 120 students back then. 'By the time we got to 700 I had been a senior teacher, head of English and then deputy head,' she says. When she became head in 2001 the college had 1,000 students.

With a robust structure of tutors, lead tutors and teachers in place, her vision is more growth, but '1600 is our limit.' She enjoys working with this age group because it marks the 'transition from children to adults' – the period when 'they are enquiring about the world and are enthusiastic.'

Also likes the fact that 'they are only with us for two years – so you get quick feedback.' Her days in the classroom are a distant memory now as she no longer teaches.

Due to its size and the layout of the building the college does not come together as a whole. 'When we were smaller we used to have a termly assembly but we can't do that,' she says. 'We have student council meetings and I meet reps once a term but it is more distant in some ways than I would like because of the size of building.' A parent whose child recently left said she never saw the head during the two years her daughter was there – probably a good thing, since the head says she only sees a student and their parents if the student is experiencing problems.

Strong management team in place with expertise in education, business and local community. Head says high quality student outcome is the primary purpose and managers who do not share the college's values are 'managed out'.

Academic matters: Takes students from a wide ability range but most come here with reasonably high grades. 'We would let someone do three A levels with five A* to Cs; to do four subjects they have to have four Bs at GCSE.' Requirement is lower than Woodhouse College or Camden School for Girls, but the college also attracts 'some with all A grades.' Many come from abroad with EAL needs and do very well – 'although not all are capable of maintaining the high grades expected here, the majority do'.

Results have been pretty consistent since 2010. A level results for 2014 show 40 per cent A*-B grades. Strongest subjects include further maths, French, geography, film studies, Italian, media studies, Spanish and Turkish.

Teacher/pupil ratio of 10:1. Teachers are A level specialists, many of them examiners or IVs (internationally recognised certificate that allows teachers to evaluate other teachers). Others come with vocational or industry experience and do in-service training with other teachers. 'We are one of the biggest providers of A levels, if not the biggest in the country, so we have expertise about teaching A levels, what kids need to do to progress and the ability to tailor everything to that,' says the head. The wide range of subjects attracts many. 'I wanted to go to George Moneaux but they didn't

Political awareness also drives the agenda for a wide number of talks and debates, on subjects like the London riots, conflict in Serbia, responsibility and justice

have the courses – I came here for the range,' said one student. The college also offers the IB, which head is keen to grow.

While the past has been about helping those who have under-achieved to reach their full potential, head says the present is about 'finding a way to stretch the ablest,' without neglecting the mission to enable past under-achievers to progress to higher education, if not necessarily to a Russell Group university. College is noted for its strong support for students with learning difficulties and disabilities. The school's self-assessment report notes that success rates for those with learning difficulties have been increasing, especially those with Asperger's and hearing and mobility impairments. Learning support team provides literacy, numeracy, dyslexia, ESOL, examination and disability support to learners at all levels. Support is provided in class, in one-to-one sessions, workshops and in small groups.

Games, options, the arts: Sport is not huge here although there is a football team and a basketball court. Plenty of enrichment activities though,

and visits to theatres and galleries. Joint projects between different years and partner schools are common. 'We did an art exhibition with year 11s from a partner school and primary schools have been coming to use it for inspiration for work,' said one pupil. Performing arts centre, comprising studio and theatre space, teaches drama, dance and music and benefits from partnerships with Sadler's Wells, Almeida, Welsh National Opera and Islington Community Theatre. Productions often have a political, cultural or campaigning focus – for example, World Mental Health Day and a Dance 4 Life production to promote sexual health. Political awareness also drives the agenda for a wide number of talks and debates, on subjects like the London riots, conflict in Serbia, responsibility and justice and 'the nature of female rebellion.'

Enrichment activities are tailored to helping students develop employability skills and are backed up by a very good careers department. 'I don't think (other places) have as much as we do in terms of help with employment,' a student told us.

Students are introduced to the careers service from the start and can visit at any time to talk about future plans or concerns about subject choices or to get help with writing a CV or university applications. Well-equipped careers centre (interview rooms, library resource areas, dedicated staff team and plenty of information) organises talks by different universities and employers, including UCL and Cambridge. 'We put an enormous amount of effort into building links with universities and employers and stretching kids,' explained the student careers advisor.

Ready, Steady, Job is a programme comprising self-directed study, tutor-led activities and careers talks, for those seeking employment rather than university. Moodle site provides detailed information and advice on jobs and employment and training fair takes place in the autumn. Law support group arranges visits to the Old Bailey, magistrates' courts, supreme court and law firms.

Students attend masterclasses, taster courses, open days and summer schools. The Lloyd's scheme is run at the bank's HQ near St Paul's and provides an employment gateway for 40 students 'who want to work somewhere in finance or law and want to apply for a degree maths or economics,' says the head. Similar partnership with Barclay's Capital. The head is upfront about the aim behind these partnerships: 'We are lucky as we're just down the road from many of these centres. We are such a big provider so teachers can use that to create relationships with outsiders.'

Background and atmosphere: The college is located in Islington – the 14th most deprived borough in England. It is housed in a modern, four-storey

building with subject departments on the upper levels, and careers centre, student support office, cafeteria and resource study centre on the ground floor. Students say, 'whenever a book isn't in the library they order it from another library. All you have to do is to ask.' Glass building has a bright, corporate feel against its city landscape – it is walking distance from Holborn, St Paul's and Kings Cross.

Walls are decorated with pictures of influential thinkers as well as student council members, anti-bullying stance ('It's not big to make others feel small'), learning agreement in full and tips on completing AS level portfolios. Students' fine art, painting and photography work on show in the general administration office. Accolades like outstanding Ofsted in all categories, Queen's Anniversary Prize for Education (second time), Silver Investor in People Award, STEM Assured status (reflecting excellence in science, technology, engineering and maths) and reaccreditation by MATRIX all help create a sense of achievement and pride here.

The site was purpose built as a sixth form college for 1,100 students, so there are works to extend toilets, administration blocks and meeting areas. Head describes it as an 'exciting place to work,' where 'teachers end up staying a long time.' Students say 'everyone in the college is nice, so you settle into your work straight away,' although one or two commented on the 'cliques that gather around in groups in the cafeteria' and said, 'you have to walk through to go to lessons and it can feel intimidating.'

Pastoral care and discipline: In this college environment students are expected to develop independence in their approach to study. However, there is a very strong tutorial/pastoral system in place to help them make the transition from school. Tutors are supported by more experienced lead tutors who operate like heads of year and manage any 'at risk' students referred to them. 'We try to move them from dependency on teacher and home as a lot will go to university so will have to become independent in more ways,' says the head. 'There are rules and structures in place to "frighten" the student into arriving promptly. You have to be in your lessons and do all your work otherwise you don't need to be here. You cannot come here and just do nothing.'

Each student has an individual learning plan, used to set 'challenging but realistic long and short term academic and personal goals.' These are monitored through regular one-to-one tutorials and course team reviews and can be tracked online via the college intranet – 'so we can see where we are

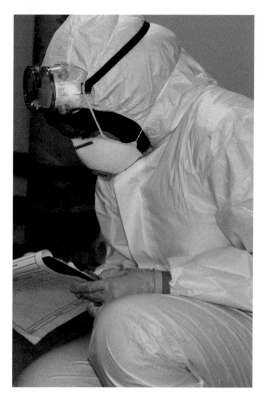

any time,' say pupils. Lots of support for students who are struggling, like A2 buddies, mentoring, one-to-one support and drop-in workshops.

Punctuality is good on the whole and bullying rarely happens. 'Not that we're well behaved,' a student told us. 'We're just too busy and there's so much work you don't have time to do anything else.' Parents say: 'It's not like school, where if your child misses a day they give you a call.' Some felt there could be more contact, adding that 'here it's a bit like just turn up and get on with it.'

Pupils and parents: Students from ethnic minorities predominate, with many from abroad. Twenty-eight different languages spoken here. Students come from 200 schools across London. Head says: 'All aspire high. We have the inner London characteristic of lots of kids from immigrant communities. Parents want them to do well, so you can find higher aspirations here than you would have in many suburbs.' Parents are largely a mix of first and second-generation immigrants, professionals and semi-skilled workers.

Despite lamentations from parents about 'not much contact with the college,' they are kept updated by a newsletter, emails, annual report and parents' evenings. There are also HE information for parents of A2 students, giving information about university application process and finance. Annual bus trip to Cambridge for parents – to educate them about what is on offer. 'We have a large number of students whose parents have never been to university or to university in this country,' says the head. 'We try to demystify that.'

Past pupils include actress Zawe Ashton, presenter Reggie Yates and singer Paloma Faith.

Entrance: Open day in November. Applications must be received before end of January, with interviews held in March. Enrolment dependent on GCSE grades meeting entry requirements and on places being available. A local school partnership with five Islington schools (Elizabeth Garrett Anderson, Holloway, Islington Arts and Media and Mount Carmel) means pupils from these school get priority.

Exit: Eighty per cent of students go to university, including four to Oxbridge and seven to UCL in 2014. Many students also take advantage of the other courses on offer at other centres at the college, choosing apprenticeships, BTec courses, and/or employment rather than university and a degree.

Remarks: Careers advice is exceptional, with a good range of choice and information given to students on university, training, employment, gap years and other post-sixth form options. Clearly offers a good range of opportunity to develop political and social awareness through the wide cultural mix and unusual blend of enrichment activities. To get the most out of all that this college has to offer students need to be pretty outgoing, independent and open-minded, or they may find the environment too much of a harsh contrast to school sixth form. That said, it does very well by most of its pupils.

City of London School

Queen Victoria Street, London, EC4V 3AL

Independent · Pupils: 930 · Ages: 10–18 · Non–denom · Fees (per term): £4,771

Tel: 020 7489 0291
Fax: 020 7329 6887
Email: admissions@clsb.org.uk
Website: www.clsb.org.uk

30

Head: Since April 2014, Sarah Fletcher MA PGCE (late 40s), previously head of Kingston Grammar School. An Oxford historian, she has also been deputy head at Rugby and taught at Wycombe Abbey, St George's Montreux, Habs Girls' in Elstree and Lawrence Sheriff Grammar in Rugby – an admirably varied career with child protection, housemistressing and Pre-U experience along the way. We described her at Kingston as 'softly spoken, sparkly, diplomatic and clever.' She has two grown up sons. She told the London Evening Standard that she applied to City because of its good bursary scheme; her grandfather's life was transformed by a man who helped financially with his education.

Academic matters: An academic school of high expectations rather than high pressure. 'You work as hard as you need to work,' said a sixth former. 'You know who is good at what – and you accept

that.' 'They welcome your strengths, whatever they are,' said a parent. Talented linguists can take French or Latin GCSE in year 10, whilst also studying Russian or Greek. Musicians, too, can take their subject a year early and some boys do additional maths alongside maths GCSE. In 2014, 88 per cent of I/GCSEs were A* or A; at A level, 72 per cent A*/A.

'Most departments have at least one amazing teacher,' said a sixth former. A good mix of long-serving and newer staff. Strong emphasis on science in the sixth form – several boys coming in from linked state schools with science scholarships; history also extremely popular, with numbers taking it to A level second only to maths.

Excellent support for those with mild dyslexia/dyspraxia – 'It needs to be mild or they wouldn't cope' – with 100 or so boys receiving extra help in small groups. 'It's wonderful and very low key,' said a parent. The building is accessible for wheelchairs, but so far only boys with a broken leg have made use of this.

Games, options, the arts: In Tardis-like fashion, the compact-looking school building encompasses a sports hall, gym and swimming pool as well as squash courts and fencing salle. Seventeen acres of playing fields a half-hour coach ride away and a couple of concrete playgrounds on site. 'When I looked out before school this morning there were four cricket matches, a football game and some basketball going on,' said a sixth former.

Teams have reached London cup finals at cricket, football and water polo, and the school fields teams in 12 competitive sports, including golf and sailing – 'Sailing suits our boys because you need a mixture of intellectual and physical aggression and you don't have to train too hard'. Pupils have represented their country in fencing and table-tennis in recent years, with recent successes in football and athletics. School's sporting profile increasing, with more teams in the lower years playing matches against feeder prep schools.

But it is fair to say that the average City boy is not a fanatical sportsman. He is likely to be equally interested in debating, singing in the choir, playing Warhammer. 'We push debating and public speaking because it makes the boys more thoughtful and considered. It counters any yob culture.' Zillions

of clubs before, during and after school: Model UN (with annual conference); railway society (with its own model railway room); Jewish society (generally involving food); Square Mile club (with eminent speakers such as Jeremy Paxman, John Bercow and Nick Robinson) et al. 'We're very keen on being an out-looking school. The boys will have to make their way in a global setting.'

Pupils in year 9 get to know their city well on eight visits to, eg, the Museum of Surgery and the Globe. Over 140 other school trips ranging from a Chinese exchange to geography field trips to India, Iceland and Cuba. European work experience in year 12. Extremely popular CCF, with hundreds of

---

'Sailing suits our boys because you need a mixture of intellectual and physical aggression and you don't have to train too hard.'

---

pupils learning to fly, going camping at home and abroad, skiing, canoeing, driving powerboats – 'It was one of the best things I've done at school,' said an ex-pupil. Community service is an alternative and charity fundraising is high profile – over £58,000 raised for READ International.

The school theatre was revamped and drama is strong, with frequent theatre visits and many productions in conjunction with City of London Girls' School. Joint orchestras and choirs, too, bolstered by the choristers who join at the age of 10. The music is 'fantastic', said a parent, and a sixth former agreed, 'If you're good you become sucked into the music department and your life revolves around it'. Two terms' free instrumental tuition for everyone in the younger classes.

Background and atmosphere: Has its origins in a 1442 bequest of land to support the education of poor men's sons. This endowment became so valuable by 1834 that it enabled the Corporation of London to found City of London School in Milk Street, near Cheapside. Unusually for the time, it was a day school that did not discriminate against non-Anglicans and offered a practical and progressive education which included science and English (as opposed to classical) literature. It moved to Blackfriars in 1879 and to its present red-brick purpose-built facilities in 1986.

Wonderful site with many balconies and windows looking out across the Thames to Tate Modern, adjacent to the (alas, no longer) Wobbly Bridge, with St Paul's right behind. Very urban, very buzzy. Keen on outreach – staff seconded to help East London state schools with maths, sports, drama etc. Boys not cosseted, expected to be independent, used to getting about London on their own from the age of 10 upwards. A teacher recounts approvingly how she overheard a group of 11 year olds, who had finished exams early, organising their own trip to a pizza restaurant across the river to celebrate. 'The boys are immensely proud of being part of the City of London,' said a parent.

Some boys who joined at 13 found it took time to integrate; they also mention an atmosphere far less pressured than their prep schools, with time to coast for a while.

Pastoral care and discipline: Strong anti-bullying culture. Pupils report some scapegoating in the younger classes, but no physical abuse, 'And people soon grow out of it'. 'They work very hard to deal with it,' said a parent. 'It's a very welcoming place. There's space for all sorts of diversity – black and white, rich and poor.' By general consent a complete lack of racial tension. Clear expectations, rules strictly enforced. 'It's relaxed but firm,' said a pupil.

Pupils and parents: Extremely cosmopolitan. Few local families so nearly all travel in by tube, train or bus, from all points but particularly north and west. The huge catchment area and generous bursaries encourage a rich ethnic and social mix emanating from St Albans to Mile End. 'It makes teaching RE very interesting. In a class of 20 there will be 100 different opinions, and they educate one another

about their own religions.' OBs include Daniel Radcliffe, Peter Ware Higgs, Julian Barnes, Lord Levine, Kingsley Amis and Herbert Asquith.

Entrance: Takes around 40 boys at 10, some of these Temple Church or Chapel Royal choristers on scholarships. The main intake – about 60 boys – is at 11. Around 60 per cent of these come from state primaries. Another 45 come in at 13, almost entirely from prep schools. Now examines and offers places to 13+ candidates in year 6, so no chance of a retake for those who don't make an 11+ place.

Around 15–20 join the sixth form, often with science scholarships, and mostly from state schools, including linked schools Stepney Green and St Thomas the Apostle.

Exit: Around 12–15 leave after GCSEs, almost invariably for state sixth forms. Nearly always gets 20+ Oxbridge places (24 in 2014, plus 13 medics), with the vast majority of the rest going to Russell Group universities, many to read science or engineering.

Money matters: A good place to try for a scholarship or bursary – total of 106 full fee, means-tested bursaries throughout the school, plus 30 academic, sports and music scholarships a year.

Remarks: Very urban, very happening, very cosmopolitan school that achieves high standards without undue pressure and produces independent, outward-looking boys. 'We're happy as Larry,' said a father. 'We'd recommend it to anyone.'

City of London School for Girls (Prep School)

Linked school: City of London School for Girls, 84

St Giles' Terrace, Barbican, London, EC2Y 8BB

Independent • Pupils: 100 • Ages: 7–11 • Fees (per term): £4,803

Tel: 020 7847 5500
Fax: 020 7638 3212
Email: admissions@clsg.org.uk
Website: www.clsg.org.uk

31

Headmistress: Since 2010, Miss Jane Rogers MPhil BA (London). Worked for 10 years in the state sector before moving to the Institute of Education as a science lecturer and educational researcher. Moved back into education when she took a post of senior teacher at the Lyceum School, after which she came to the Prep, because 'I'm interested in academic excellence'. Educated at Chelmsford County High

School for Girls, University College London (geography) and Institute of Education. Has two teenage children.

Entrance: Twenty-four hotly contested places at 7+, sitting nationally standardised tests in English, maths and verbal reasoning plus some spelling and writing tests of the Prep's own authorship. Register your daughter early to be sure of her being seen: the school assesses a maximum of 150 girls, and is always over-subscribed. Of those 150, the top 50 are called back for a further day's appraisal, during which they're examined in English, maths, science and DT – this last because it allows the girls to be observed in practical activities and working as a team. The 24 places are then offered to those 'with academic ability and the potential to become independent, happy learners.' Girls are seen in the November of the year preceding entry; closing date for accepting or declining offers is mid-February.

Exit: Parents take note: entry to the senior school is not automatic. By Easter of Y5, reserved places (ie places that are guaranteed) are offered only to those girls 'who continue to develop'. Any child who joined the school later than Y3 doesn't get one at all, and must sit for a place along with the external candidates. Head insists that 'the vast majority go through.' Some parents' perceptions are different; see below. Destinations of those who do go elsewhere include St Paul's Girls, North London Collegiate, Francis Holland, Channing and Queen's College London. 'We've been hugely successful in placing girls at other schools,' says head. 'Schools like City Prep girls, and they don't get them that often.'

Remarks: Broad curriculum, with specialist teachers from the senior school coming in to teach music, art, DT, PE, Latin (Ys 5 and 6) and modern languages. The girls learn a different language each year: Spanish in Y3, French in Y4, German in Y5 and Mandarin in Y6. The idea is that the girls acquire

> *'If you're prepared to buy into the idea of City and have a daughter capable of swimming in its often competitive seas, it will be a worthwhile experience.'*

an enthusiasm for languages which then helps them to choose the right ones when they go on to senior school, which is certainly commendable. It struck us as odd, however, that they only studied each language for a year before having to drop it and move onto the next one; a Y5 girl we spoke to admitted that she'd now forgotten the Spanish she'd learned in Y3.

As well as benefiting from the senior school teaching expertise, the excellent senior school facilities – swimming pool, sports hall, library, Astroturf, tennis courts – are all available to the Prep school, which doubtless explains why there's no difference in fees between the two (though prep fees do include lunch). Sports and gymnastics are strong, and music likewise, with the Y6s doing a Prep Opera every year. Impressive LAMDA results in 2014, with virtually everyone getting distinction. There are also lots of residential trips which are perennially popular. Wide variety of clubs, and after-school care provides an opportunity for girls to do their homework as well as have fun. ('They have a register to make sure you don't wander off,'

said one of our tour guides, earnestly.) Sixth formers from the senior school run clubs for the Prep girls, which, says head, creates 'a big sister culture. They're great role models for the younger girls.'

Other than some worrying reports which we outline below, it took a long while for parental feedback to reach us about this school. Our first invitation was met with complete silence, and even a second appeal didn't yield very much. (This was in contrast to the parents of girls in the senior school, who were quick to tell us how happy they were.) Those who did eventually contact us agreed that the girls are worked hard but achieve highly. A couple remarked on the school's competitive nature: 'The girls are incredibly competitive, but also very supportive of each other, and have a strong sense of loyalty to their school,' said one. Another observed, 'If you're prepared to buy into the idea of City and have a daughter capable of swimming in its often competitive seas, it will be a worthwhile experience for her and for your family.' These parents emphasized that their daughters were enjoying their time at the Prep, had made friends and embraced the opportunities on offer there.

However, some of these same parents expressed disquiet about the entry process to the senior school. 'The goal posts seem to have been moved,' said one couple, 'The message about not everyone getting reserved places is stronger now than it was when our daughter got in.' The same worried mother continued, 'Choosing to put a child through an entrance exam when they're 6 is not an easy decision; in our case we hoped to avoid the stress at 11 plus, which we now find we may not do. I suspect the feeling of rejection and the dent to self-confidence is higher if you don't get a reserved place from the Prep and can stay with your friends, than if you apply and fail as an external candidate.' Miss Rogers told us that an average of four girls leave City Prep's Y6 every year: two out of choice, and two who were 'advised to go elsewhere.' School figures show an average of three girls a year recently have not been given reserved places. This figure seems high to us, given both the stringent nature of the admissions process and the acknowledged high workload put upon the girls during their time here; and we did ask the head to comment on it. 'Not all girls develop the same,' was her comment. 'Some go upwards and some go downwards,' adding, 'sometimes things happen in families to disturb girls.'

Parents and former parents are divided in their feelings about the school. On one side of the argument, accounts have been passed to us of recent City Prep girls whose confidence, and even health, had been so undermined by the school's approach that their parents voted with their feet and took them out. These parents write with angry eloquence about the school's 'complete lack of nurture and care' and claim that it 'values malleability

and obedience over originality and sparky intellect.' They allege that there is poor support for special needs such as dyslexia, and that some of the teaching is sub-standard ('After we moved her, we discovered that she had been so poorly taught that she needed to relearn a year's worth of maths,' said one mother, and another mother reported an identical experience.)

The head insists that the school works closely with parents, and that the girls' happiness is paramount to her. 'We love quirky individuals. We've got lots and lots of those. Girls are allowed to be themselves here.' And indeed, other parents told us that their daughters loved coming to school. One, whose child had excelled there academically, spoke of the school's 'really good pastoral side.' 'The Prep is a nurturing and non-threatening environment,' said one mother whose child was now at CLSG senior, 'and I would have no hesitation in recommending it.'

Picking our way through such contradictory accounts was difficult. We can only conclude by suggesting that, since entry to CLSG senior school isn't guaranteed, parents should think closely about whether City Prep is the right choice for their daughter; or whether a prep school not linked to any senior school, but with a proven record of getting its leavers into the destination of their choice, might suit their family better.

City of London School for Girls

Linked school: City of London School for Girls (Prep School), 81

St Giles' Terrace, London, EC2Y 8BB

Independent • Pupils: 615 • Ages: 7–18 • Non-denom
• Fees (per term): £4,803

Tel: 020 7847 5500
Fax: 020 7638 3212
Email: admissions@clsg.org.uk
Website: www.clsg.org.uk

Headmistress: Since April 2014, Mrs Ena Harrop. Was previously director of studies here and before that was head of modern languages at RGS Guildford. English is her third language (after her native Spanish and French). Has a first class degree in classics from Salamanca University, an MA from Munich University and an MPhil in classics from Cambridge. She also has a PGCE from the Institute of Education and recently concluded her MA in education management at King's College London. She is married with three young daughters.

Academic matters: Up there with the top selective schools – 78 per cent A*/A grades at A level in 2014, with maths, history and English the most popular subjects. Praised for imaginative teaching methods. Everyone does two modern languages from year 7, choosing between French, Spanish, German and Mandarin, and studies at least one to GCSE. Some take Spanish a year early – most get A*s – then start the AS course. In 2014, 96 per cent A*/A grades at GCSE and nearly 74 per cent A*. Top set mathematicians do additional maths alongside GCSE maths,

and everyone studies three single sciences. Teaches thinking skills to year 10 and 11 pupils, who can take the AS exam alongside GCSEs: 'It's good for university assessment tests and interviews and we like to give them the opportunity to be stretched.'

Part of the East London Schools' Consortium, exchanging good practice with other girls' independent and state schools, and hosting the Urban Scholars Intervention Programme Saturday school – some 60 gifted and talented state school girls from surrounding boroughs follow a varied programme encouraging them raise their aspirations and attainments.

Games, options, the arts: Music particularly vibrant, with numerous orchestras, ensembles, groups and choirs, many run jointly with City Boys. 'It's very inclusive,' said a parent. 'Anyone can go along to the orchestra and they all get a good experience of performing.' Most peripatetic teachers come from the nearby Guildhall School of Music. High quality art and DT – the innovative coffee tables in the reception hall were designed and built by a student.

Often produces Arkwright engineering scholars. Plenty of drama – 'lively and good,' said a parent – again, often in conjunction with the boys' school.

'It's not the place for someone who wants to chase a ball around playing fields,' said a pupil, 'but they do pack things in.' It particularly suits those who shine in the compact arenas of swimming pool, netball court and gym, with successful swimming, fencing, gymnastics and netball teams. Diving, canoeing, climbing, running and water polo are other sporting options, alongside cricket, hockey and football on the new five-a-side Astroturf pitch. City girls always make up a large proportion of the City of London team for the London Youth Games and pupils have represented England at karate and fencing.

Makes good use of its central London location, with numerous outings to museums, art galleries, concerts and theatres, as well as strong connections with City banks and businesses. Sixth formers set up and run lunchtime clubs ranging from Asian society to cheerleading, with plenty to choose from. Residential trip destinations range from Bideford to Beijing.

Background and atmosphere: Founded in 1894 with a bequest from coal merchant William Ward as a school for girls that 'would correspond, as near as may be, to the City of London School... making all proper allowance for the difference of the sexes.' It moved to its purpose-built, five-storey, Barbican home in 1969. Uncompromisingly urban, surrounded by multi-tiered flats and office blocks, it shoe-horns in everything from a food technology room to a multi-gym and sixth form centre with pool table, beanbags and computer suite, looking out over a khaki-coloured lake. Corridors are lined with noticeboards crammed with information.

Buzzy, busy atmosphere. Girls are encouraged to be independent; nearly everyone arrives by public transport. 'Our girls are pretty savvy. We give them support and advice on dealing with potential

---

It particularly suits those who shine in the compact arenas of swimming pool, netball court and gym

---

problems and they're streetwise in the nicest possible way.' Plenty of emphasis on ambition and women in leadership, with City mentors, visits to City institutions and talks by scientists and journalists, bankers and army officers.

Joint activities with City Boys include concerts and plays, lectures, careers conventions and mock Oxbridge interviews, plus social events organised by parents for the junior classes – 'by year 9 they prefer to organise their own social life.'

Pastoral care and discipline: No easy ride academically – but the pressure to succeed comes from students as much as staff. 'There's a focus on academic success,' said a pupil, 'but everyone wants to do well. And staff are aware of other things going on in your life apart from work, so you feel supported.'

Four houses give a strong sense of identity and belonging, as well as opportunities to get involved in drama and sports competitions. Strong pastoral support – 'they do look out for them,' said a parent. Parents can even log on to keep tabs on what their daughter ate for lunch and what she has to do for homework.

Pupils and parents: Girls travel from Chelmsford and Croydon, Bromley and Buckinghamshire, though the majority are the children of 'North London intellectuals and City bankers,' said a parent. A fair social and ethnic mix – 'It's a melting pot of girls. They learn to respect each other and value other people's opinions.' Girls tend to be independent, opinionated and ambitious, inspired by the location of their school.

Entrance: Part of the North London Consortium, which sets joint maths and English exams each January. Applicants to City also sit GETINTU – a computer-based cognitive test – in November. From some 500 applicants, 280 are interviewed, to choose an intake of around 70, who join the 20 or so coming up from the prep school. A few girls join the sixth form.

Exit: A fair outward trickle after GCSEs (a fifth in 2014), mostly to co-ed state or private sixth forms. All sixth form leavers go on to university, art or music school – 14 to Oxbridge in 2014; Bristol, KCL, UCL and Durham popular; history, politics, philosophy and languages amongst the most common degree subjects.

Money matters: Scholarships and bursaries help support 23 per cent of pupils. Academic, drama, art and music scholarships, generally worth £1,500 a year, available at 11 and 16, plus means-tested bursaries – 'we have a strong means-tested programme, so we have the flexibility to give bursaries to those who need it.'

Remarks: Vibrant, ambitious, high-achieving school in the centre of London, producing confident and articulate girls.

College Francais Bilingue de Londres – Junior Section

Linked school: College Francais Bilingue De Londres, 87

87 Holmes Road, Kentish Town, London, NW5 3AX

Independent • Pupils: 340 • Ages: 5–11 • Non–denom
• Fees (per term): £2,421 – £2,680

Tel: 020 7993 7400
Fax: 020 7267 2325
Email: info@cfbl.org.uk
Website: www.cfbl.org.uk

3

Headteacher: Since 2011, François-Xavier Gabet (50s). He has degrees in teaching French and French as a second language from University of Lille. Has taught in French schools in France, Saudi Arabia, USA and Australia and was a French language adviser to the US state of Louisiana. Set up the first bilingual French/English school in Melbourne (while also teaching at Monash University).

Head of primary is David Gassian, and Cerian Maraviglia is the deputy head of primary.

Entrance: This school is highly over-subscribed, with some 800 applications for 140 places. We have heard that a maximum of 30 per cent of places are allocated to children whose parents work for the consortium of French companies that helped to secure the school building. The school says that the list of partner companies is available for inspection if required. As with the other French homologue schools, entry is not easy and some families start out at other schools. Getting one sibling in helps boost the chances of the others. The priorities are: siblings (both primary and secondary), children

from another official French school (locally or abroad), including students following the CNED (the French distance-learning programme), then any miscellany of Francophones fortunate to get in. It seems there are some last minute surprises. The nearby La Petite Ecole is a popular feeder and others opt for local British independent schools while they wait for the coveted place at CFBL.

Exit: The good news is that upon completion of their primary education at CFBL, children continue to secondary at CFBL. At this point some move to British independent or state schools but the vast majority stay on. No testing, no interviews, no worries.

Remarks: The French primary model has two divisions – maternelle (reception and year 1) and primaire (years 2 to 6). At the junior section of the CFBL 50 per cent of children have French and English language instruction and 50 per cent follow the French national curriculum. Half the staff are UK qualified and half are French. The teachers are timetabled in

such a way that when classes are being taught by French teachers, the English-speaking staff are freed up to support students whose English language skills need bolstering and to ensure that English literacy standards are of a high level.

There are two forms of 25 students each for the youngest classes, 30 per class from the age of 7+. Classes are of mixed ability but the combination of French and English teachers means that they are able to differentiate the curriculum. English and French as a foreign language taught up to four times per week. Other specialists include teachers of PE, music and ICT (interactive whiteboards in all classrooms), while the bilingual French librarian works closely with the teachers in developing the literacy scheme and creating class libraries. No specialist SEN support but class teachers are able to provide some support and there is a part-time educational psychologist too. Parents pay for diagnostic testing. A speech therapist is available.

Though 'curricular extras' do not traditionally loom large on the French educational landscape, they do make an effort at CFBL. We heard lots of talk about a Camden-based project called the English Pocket Opera Company, where 700 children participated in a production of Orphée. Judging from the parents we spoke to, this involved the whole community. The school is working on developing a choir and activities for instrumental music and there are hopes that the school's new sports facility will mean some new sporting activities.

The CFBL was established with a mission to offer a French curriculum in a bilingual context to 700 students. The school was at one time known as L'Ile aux Enfants and was located in a nearby building that now houses Le Petite Ecole, a French primary school that also feeds the CFBL. Now housed in a Victorian school building in Kentish Town, the school backs on to attractive residential streets but its front sits on a street that is less so. Step inside, however, and it's another story. The refurbishment is brilliant, with high ceilings, large windows drawing in masses of light and parquet wooden floors, plus modern touches like internal stairways with lots of glass. Cosy primary library in its own little building on the playground – most of the resources are French, although they are developing the English language collection.

A small portion of the central playground has been forfeited for the sake of a new cafeteria. Bright and airy, it provides an attractive place to serve equally attractive lunch menus for the youngsters. (Lunches are compulsory, with meat and fish served daily, or vegetarian options available for those observing kosher or halal diets).

Parents are happy with the level of attention given to their children, particularly when they first arrive at the school. There were no disciplinary concerns expressed by parents, who say the children are very accepting and welcoming. Deputy head of primary appears to have the confidence of the parents who speak highly of him and were happy when they heard he had been appointed in this role after several years as a teacher.

A real mix of families at CFBL, including expat corporates on international assignment in London, entrepreneurs, local business owners and French nationals whose marriages have created bicultural families. CFBL families suggest that the socio-economic atmosphere at CFBL is 'less rarified' than the more salubrious environs of the Lycée Charles de Gaulle in South Ken. Some end up at CFBL by default (no room at the Lycée) while others genuinely prefer this school. The size is another factor – it is much smaller than the Lycée and this is something that parents of primary pupils particularly like.

College Francais Bilingue De Londres

Linked school: College Francais Bilingue de Londres – Junior Section, 86

87 Holmes road, London, NW5 3AX

Independent · Pupils: 460 · Ages: 11–15 · Non–denom · Fees (per term): £2,421

Tel: 020 7993 7400
Fax: 020 7267 2325
Email: info@cfbl.org.uk
Website: www.cfbl.org.uk/en

Headteacher: Since 2011, François-Xavier Gabet (50s). He has degrees from University of Lille – in teaching French and French as a second language. Has taught in French schools in France, Saudi Arabia, USA and Australia and was a French language adviser to the US state of Louisiana. Set up the first bilingual French/English school in Melbourne (while also teaching at Monash University).

He was the ideal founding head for this newish London school and arrived a year before it opened – to plan every facet. Despite his traditional website photo, when we met him he was fashionably turned out in jeans, turtleneck jumper and blazer – looking more like a high-tech dot-com CEO on London's Silicon Roundabout than what one might expect for the head of a prestigious French school.

Steeped in the high standards associated with French educational tradition, he is refreshingly internationally-minded and aims to help his multilingual students recognise the advantages of being part of a global network of schools. While well aware of the rigorous demands of the French system, he asks teachers to be flexible, creative

---

He was fashionably turned out in jeans, turtleneck jumper and blazer – looking more like a high-tech dot-com CEO on London's Silicon Roundabout

and generous in their approach. He cares about the school's relations with the local Kentish Town community (he does not want CFBL to be a 'French bubble') and works closely with the board (whom he describes as 'capable, professionally-accomplished and yet humble') to find ways to improve this full-to-capacity school.

Fit, energetic and quite the coolest head this Good Schools Guide editor has met, he is married with a daughter at university in Belgium and a son at CFBL. His 'tour of duty' is up in 2015 and he will leave a big pair of shoes to fill.

Academic matters: The French secondary model has two divisions – College (years 7 to 10) and Lycée (years 11 to 13). CFBL offers college, following on from the school's primary section.

As of 2015, students (already working in French and English) will have the option to join the Anglais Renforcé section, where 45 per cent of the curriculum is delivered in English, preparing them nicely for the new international diploma (DNBI) section at the Lycée Charles de Gaulle. Others will be able to opt for the Plurilingue stream, where they begin a third language (German or Spanish). Music, sport, IT and art are taught in English. Parents have mixed views – some feel the bilingual programme gives their (French-speaking) children lots of good exposure and immersion in English while others say the level of English is not as challenging as they'd like and that it's essentially French with a few English classes. Bilingual school models are never straightforward, with different perceptions about what exactly it means. IT is taught weekly – some parents would like to see a bit more, but concede that with the extra time already devoted to languages, this would be challenging.

The pupils work long hours – the additional English language means more hours than usual – so parents should be clear on this before they enrol their children. This is in addition to the homework load. The French educational system is regarded as one of the best in the world and academic standards are not an issue here. It's deciding if you want to do this with the added challenge of a bilingual or trilingual programme.

Games, options, the arts: Though extracurricular activities don't traditionally loom large on the French educational landscape, they do make an effort at CFBL. We've heard lots of buzz about the

English Pocket Opera Company, when 700 youngsters participated in a production of Orphée which seems to have involved the whole community. More sports on tap here than is the norm for French schools – the football team practises locally and took part in a tournament in Paris. Netball js popular with girls. The school is working on launching a choir and developing interest in instrumental music activities. Sixième students (first year secondary) go on a residential trip with outdoor pursuits activities aimed at integrating new students and team building.

CFBL has an exchange programme with schools in Uruguay and Berlin for students studying Spanish or German and strong links with a school in Spain. Mandarin club recently introduced. The head hopes that these experiences will help students and parents value the importance of learning languages and about other cultures.

Background and atmosphere: The College Français Bilingue de Londres was born out of the recent French ambassador's call for increased capacity to meet the growing demand for French education in London. With funding from the French government and from French companies (we're guessing banks and perhaps Eurostar, whose London base is conveniently nearby), who formed a charity to acquire the school property, the school's mission is to offer a French curriculum in a bilingual context to 700 students. The school was at one time known as L'Ile aux Enfants and located in a nearby building that now houses Le Petite Ecole, a feeder primary school.

Housed in a Victorian school building in Kentish Town. The head is aware of the impact that the mass arrival of a French community in the heart of this traditionally working-class area of north London has had and is working to win over the hearts and minds of locals. Most families living in the area were attracted to the Victorian terraced properties and the 'gentrification' of the area is thought to be partly thanks to the school (as well, of course, as the long-standing local Camden School for Girls). Part of the neighbourhood charm offensive was the introduction of French language classes for the local community.

The school backs on to some picturesque residential streets, though it fronts onto a street that is less so, and a bit of planting and tidying of the outside pavements and garden patches would improve the first impression. Step inside, however, and it's another story. The refurbishment is brilliant, taking full advantage of the Victorian features, with high ceilings, large windows drawing in masses of light, brick and glazed tile walls and parquet wooden floors, while incorporating modern touches. The upper school library – with

We've heard lots of buzz about the English Pocket Opera Company, when 700 youngsters participated in a production of Orphée

high ceilings and huge windows – is fully equipped with impressive French and English collections, loads of computers and armchairs.

A small portion of the central playground has been forfeited to create a bright and airy cafeteria. Lunches compulsory, with meat and fish served daily and vegetarian options available for those observing kosher or halal diets.

The school has recently acquired an outdoor space a five-minute walk away. This will feature a massive inflatable structure for sports and other activities and will be available to the local community too.

Part of the AEFE (Agency for Teaching of French Education Abroad), CFBL is one of an international network of schools directed by the French ministry of education. The school is managed by a 12-member board – six representing the companies that helped fund the acquisition of the building and six elected by the parents. Its goals are to provide continuity of education to the French expat community in London, but also to prepare students to go to the best French universities. In fact 80 per cent of students who graduate from the Lycée Charles de Gaulle head to British or US universities. The head feels that the internationally-minded, multi-lingual emphasis of the school serves to provide good preparation for these options later on.

Pastoral care and discipline: Parents are very pleased with the school, many jumping through hoops to secure places. A parent of a child with SEN described it as particularly caring and attentive to her child. Classes are smaller than most French schools – a maximum of 30 in a class, with a two or three form intake. Discipline is not a worry for parents – one parent speculated that the presence of more UK-trained teachers (there to deliver the bilingual programme) strengthens the pastoral care perspective of the teaching faculty (not always as high on the French teachers' radar). The school runs careers counselling through a jobs forum that parents help to organise.

Pupils and parents: The community is a blend of expat corporate types on international assignments and more permanent French families who have found themselves in London for other reasons, including entrepreneurs, local business owners,

French nationals whose marriages have created bi-cultural families. Parents suggest that the socio-economic atmosphere at CFBL is less 'rarified' than one finds in the more salubrious environs of the Lycée Charles de Gaulle in South Ken. While some end up at CFBL by default (no room at the Lycée), others prefer this school. The size is another factor – even with its capacity of 700, it is much smaller than the Lycée. French families who find the Eurostar terminal at St Pancras convenient are increasingly moving into neighbourhoods that are handy for the train journey through the tunnel to France and for the school.

The community is about two-thirds French. Some parents feel the school is less international than they would like, while others who come from France find it very international by comparison. There is obviously an underlying French cultural and educational foundation, but it seems that with a school community consisting of many dual national families, they seek to honour all cultures and traditions. Parents are happy that the children integrate easily, although some say teachers don't make as much of this diversity as they might. A parents' association provides lots of volunteer opportunities for those who want to get involved.

Entrance: Highly over-subscribed with some 800 applications for 140 places. We hear that a maximum of 30 per cent of the places are allocated to children whose parents work for the consortium of French companies that helped to secure the school building. The list of partner companies is available for inspection if required.

As with the other over-subscribed French homologue schools, some children start out at other schools. Getting one sibling in helps boost the chances of the others. Admissions priorities are: siblings (both primary and secondary), children from another official French school (local or abroad), including students following the CNED (the French distance-learning programme), then any miscellany of Francophones fortunate enough to get in. It seems there are some last minute surprises. The nearby La Petite Ecole is a popular feeder, while others opt for local British independent schools while they wait for the coveted place at CFBL.

Exit: Some expat families move abroad and continue their education in the French system. Others, finding the fees an issue (though remarkably good value when compared to most London independent schools), enter local state schools. Students who are less confident about their French language skills may leave after quatrième to do GCSEs in the local British sector, although the English section at the Lycée Charles de Gaulle is an option for them. The vast majority head to the Lycée Charles de Gaulle to enter their Baccalauréat programme. As of 2015, a new lycée in Wembley will become an alternative option and parents anxiously wait to hear how the selection/allocation process will work.

Money matters: The fees at CFBL are reasonable by London independent school standards (although CFBL fees are marginally higher than the Lycée Charles de Gaulle). As a charity, school engages in some fundraising activity – such as its annual gala event.

Remarks: An interesting school that embodies all of the academic rigour associated with the French tradition, but with a strong emphasis on languages and English. A sparkling little gem in the heart of Kentish Town, it is a bilingual environment with a truly international mindset.

Connaught House School

47 Connaught Square, London, W2 2HL

Independent • Pupils: 85 • Ages: 4–11 (boys leave at 8) • Non-denom • Fees (per term): £4,650 – £5,583

Tel: 020 7262 8830
Email: office@connaughthouseschool.co.uk
Website: www.connaughthouseschool.co.uk

43

Joint principals: Since 1991, Mrs Jacqueline Hampton (early 60s) and her husband, Mr Frederick Hampton MA RCA; both studied at art school. Mrs Hampton, aged 19, came here to lend a hand to her mother, Mrs Nancy Keane, who founded the school in 1952 with just six pupils, and never left.

An intimate, cosy, family-run school, refreshing in this age of private equity backed independent schools. Mr and Mrs Hampton are very hands on and complement each other in their skills and strengths. She is form teacher for year 5 and he teaches English and art. Mrs Hampton describes

herself as a 'big picture' person. She wants to see the children having fun while they learn and is determined to withstand the pressure, that faces all London schools, to turn into an exam sausage factory. However, she recognises that there has to be a balance and there needs to be some push to enable them to move on to good schools. The couple have two grown-up sons (both of whom were here).

One of their daughters-in-law, Mrs Victoria Hampton (late 30s), who runs the early years part of the school and has taught here for more than six years, is being groomed to take on the reins of headship. Not that she needs much training. She comes with a wealth of experience of young children, having started and run her own nursery in Oxfordshire, been deputy head of a nursery in Clapham, as well as having a host of qualifications for teaching young children – Montessori diploma, Early Years foundation degree, Hornsby diploma (dyslexia). She has two young boys of her own who will come here and loves being part of the fabric of the school. Gentle, pretty, with a mellifluous voice and perfect diction (which we suspect matches her handwriting), the children clearly love her as do the staff. She knows them all, is actively involved in observing and participating in lessons throughout the school and has already initiated and implemented changes and improvements. One of these was to bring the reception class (known at Junior One) up from the ground floor so that they can have plenty of space, free flowing between two large, high ceilinged rooms.

Although this is an independent, privately owned school, it has none of the trappings of a profit-motivated business. 'We are a school first that happens to have to run as a business,' say Mr and Mrs Hampton in unison. Phew – such schools do still exist. The Hamptons are wonderfully down to earth and direct. No kow-towing to demanding high net worth parents goes on here. The children are their focus. They know the children, enjoy the children, and put their interests above all else. They are proper educationalists, in the more traditional mould, and despite the competitive pressures common to all London day schools, are ensuring that music, art and drama are as central as the academics. They are firm believers in the theory that a happy child will be a successful child.

Entrance: At age 4 into reception (here called Junior One). Sixteen places for girls and boys. 'Very gentle assessments' take place when the child is 3 to ensure that they will get as much out of the school as possible. Children are assessed by two teachers and also have some one-to-one time. Absolutely no preparation is necessary. Priority is given to siblings and second and third generations. After that, proximity to school. 'The local community ethos is something we value very highly and would not like to lose,' says Victoria Hampton. Applications can also be made for entry into the upper end of the school. Academic and music bursaries are available to those applying at 7 or 8. Many come from local nurseries, including Great Beginnings and Paint Pots, and there is some liaison with nurseries after places have been offered.

Exit: All boys leave at 7 or 8 and tend to go to local prep schools such as Westminster Under School, Sussex House or Wetherby, the odd one going north to UCS junior school. The girls stay until 11 and generally opt for London day schools – Francis Holland, Clarence Gate, is currently the most popular, but also many also to Godolphin and Latymer, City of London, More House, Latymer Upper, Queens Gate and South Hampstead High. Those wishing to board generally choose Wycombe Abbey or St Mary's, Ascot. Despite leaving a very small school to go on to these much larger establishments, none of the pupils seems to be fazed – the confidence they acquire at CHS gives them the ability to cope in a broader environment.

Remarks: There is no danger of the slightly old-fashioned, wonderfully personal and child-centred ethos of this tiny school changing. The school has not expanded at all since it was first founded. It still occupies the same building, and is very small; you will know quite quickly if you love it or not, but if you don't, be careful not to write it off too soon. This is a rare little boutique in the increasingly branded, competitive world of London day schools and it offers a uniquely personal touch that many similar schools are in danger of losing. Despite its small size, good use is made of the environs. Hyde Park is only a short walk away, and children enjoy

---

We were shown wonderful wooden red buses and fire engines, built by the children, and split-pin dolls clothed in fabulous petite Victorian dresses and hats

---

lots of outdoor activities there all the year round, including parachute games, obstacle races, rounders and football. Fencing, dance, and martial arts all take place at Little Venice Sports Centre. Tennis, football, hockey, basketball and the annual sports day happen at Paddington Recreation Ground. Swimming is at Queen Mother's Sports Centre in Victoria. There is sport every day of one kind or another. Although we heard some whispering from former parents of boys here – that the boys didn't get to run around enough and there were insufficient sporting opportunities – we could see no evidence of this. The Hamptons clearly understand boys well, with two sons and at least two small grandsons of their own.

Art and music are the main extracurricular strengths of the school. Plenty of music assemblies

and lots of performances. Everyone takes part, and the large, high-ceilinged room in the middle of the building is a comfortable and intimate place to perform. We were treated to a mini concert, which included violin and recorder players as well as piano and singing – impromptu concerts of this kind are not unusual, we were told, and you can see how much confidence is imbued into these tiny performers as a result. The art room is a relatively dark, pokey room in the basement, but the quality of art that is produced defies the facilities. Perhaps to be expected, since both heads are trained artists. We saw small children beavering away at covering balloons in newspaper to create hot air balloons. We were shown wonderful wooden red buses and fire engines, built by the children, and split-pin dolls clothed in fabulous petite Victorian dresses and hats. Colourful displays adorn the walls – work obviously done by the children rather than touched up by the teachers (what a relief), and bright Chinese lanterns and colourful fish were bobbing from almost every ceiling.

Plenty of drama; each junior form does its own play once a year (these have included the Gruffalo's Christmas and Charlie Cook's Favourite Book), and years 4, 5 and 6 have performed Sleeping Beauty. Drama productions and concerts take place at the Carisbrooke Hall down the road or the Steiner Theatre close to Baker Street. Although this is very much a mixed community school with no particular religious bias, there is an annual carol concert in St John's Church, Hyde Park Crescent, which everyone is expected to attend. 'We would rather it were inclusive,' says Mrs Hampton.

Clubs are varied and numerous. The Hamptons make a huge effort to ensure that everyone from years 2 – 6 try everything. There is lots to try, from embroidery, pottery, board games and mini beasts to any kind of dance from country to zumba as well as chess and music. Full advantage is made of the school's cosmopolitan location – recent trips have included to the Globe Theatre, the Courtauld and the Tate Modern, the Celtic Harmony Camp, London Zoo, and to the obvious museums – Science, Horniman, and Transport.

You need not worry about little Freddie not getting enough attention either. There are only 16 pupils in a class – they try to keep an equal number of girls and boys in the early years. Junior One (reception) has two teachers and a qualified teaching assistant. Forms 1, 2 and 3 have both a form teacher and qualified teaching assistant in each class. All children use personal Fizz books (little laptops, as far as we could tell), there are MacBooks in every classroom and the Hamptons pride themselves on recruiting excellent teachers with 'diverse interests'. There is a competitive fives player on the staff at the moment. With such a small school, and class sizes, it is relatively easy to pick up any learning difficulties, we were told. They have a few cases of children with glue ear who may need speech and language therapy. Specialist therapists, for, eg, dyslexia are brought in at extra expense for parents but Victoria Hampton herself is a dyslexia therapist, and they prefer to keep as much support in school as possible. We were told that there is usually only one child in each year group who needs any kind of help at all. There are a high number of children with English as a second language, and although they need a reasonably good grasp of English at assessment, because of the high level of teacher support (and a recently introduced EAL club) they usually progress very quickly.

All in all, a very special little school which is loved by parents and pupils alike, where the children feel challenged every day and their parents are constantly amazed by what they know. 'The closest you can get to home schooling,' declares one. If that sounds appealing, take a little trip to Marble Arch now.

DLD College

100 Marylebone Lane, London, W1U 2QB

Independent • Pupils: 340 • Ages: 14–21 • Non–denom • Fees (per term): £6,000

Tel: 020 7935 8411
Fax: 020 7935 0755
Email: dld@dld.org
Website: www.dldcollege.co.uk

44

Principal: Since September 2013, Rachel Borland, previously principal of Abbey College in Birmingham. She is principal of both DLD and Abbey College in London, as they increasingly integrate before moving to a single, purpose-built site with student accommodation on Westminster Bridge Road in September 2015. She has previously been principal of an international boarding school in Nigeria, assistant director of studies at the British Council in both Hong Kong and Jordan, and worked at Bath University.

Academic matters: A small minority of pupils are there to do one-year GCSE courses, the rest one- or two-year A level courses. College offers a two-year GCSE programme geared for SEN students, also retake courses of varying length, up to one year. Maximum class size 10. Commendable results from a mixed ability intake. Most GCSE students take seven subjects, from a limited list that includes the basics plus French, religious studies, art, graphics and drama. Russian, Chinese, Spanish, Italian and German are available via individual tuition. In 2014, 23 per cent A*/A grades.

'They're unfussy about clothes and about students in clinches on the stairs,' said an insider. 'But academically they're pretty tough.'

A level students get a choice of 35 subjects, including music technology, photography, film and media studies, sociology, psychology and languages, in more or less any combination. Art, economics, religious studies and philosophy are consistently popular, alongside English and maths; 61 per cent A*-B grades and 32 per cent A*/A in 2014.

Some students are disaffected when they arrive – 'But it is unusual for them to be anti-education after a few weeks. It's important to fit the right course to the right student. Because of the small class sizes they get lots of individual feedback and huge amounts of encouragement, and most start making progress very quickly'.

The college can cope with a wide range of special needs, generally picking up several previously undiagnosed cases each year. Most students need group support with study and essay writing skills; individual help is also available at extra cost. 'Our SEN students get more or less the same level of results as the others – due to getting the subjects right and plenty of support. Apart from English for academic purposes, students can also have individual sessions with our SENCo.' Accredited by CReSTeD, whose most recent report speaks of it as a unique school.

No quarter is given academically – 'We will not accept scrappy work. We believe in raising standards and in helping students believe they can move up to the next level'. Many staff are from Oxbridge and some come from non-teaching backgrounds – the theatre, the City, the BBC. 'They work unbelievably hard,' said an insider. 'They put in a lot of effort for the students.' The most recent ISI report reports that students like being at the college and are very happy with the personal support that they receive.

Games, options, the arts: A surprisingly arty college – A level art and photography are two of the most popular and successful subjects and several students are refugees from high-powered academic institutions where the creative side is less valued.

The main aim of most students is to pass their exams – extracurricular activities are not high on the agenda, except for those in plays and sports teams. A level students, in particular, often work long days. However, all GCSE students play curricular sport at local centres on Friday afternoons, including football, basketball, tennis, netball, dance, rock-climbing and aerobics – sports clubs and matches after school. The DLD youth theatre puts on two performances a year; the house band – organised by the drummer of Van der Graaf Generator, who is also the music technology teacher – plays well-attended gigs; film, Duke of Edinburgh Award, EPQ, debating and art clubs.

Background and atmosphere: Now one of 17 schools owned by the Alpha Plus Group, founded in 1931 to provide tutoring for Oxbridge and Colonial Service entrance exams. After World War II it began to specialise in A and O level teaching. In 2004 it moved from Notting Hill to light, airy, refurbished premises in Marylebone, with an 80-seater theatre, recording studio, three art studios, science labs and photography studio. Will be on the move again in 2015, as it amalgamates with Abbey College at a new, purpose built site on Westminster Bridge Road.

Informal atmosphere, closer to a college than a school, with staff and students on a first name basis. 'They're unfussy about clothes and about students in clinches on the stairs,' said an insider. 'But academically they're pretty tough. Students don't get away with things.'

Pastoral care and discipline: Strong pastoral system. 'Many students have had a shifting lifestyle and it's a real haven for them,' said an insider. 'There is a lot of respect because students know we care about them.' A register is taken in every lesson and parents are texted or emailed. Each student has a weekly meeting with their personal tutor to talk about progress and future plans; five directors of studies work closely with the personal tutors. Tough sanctions for misusing drink and drugs – those under suspicion are sent for drugs tests, to general parental approval. 'There are a few troubled and troublesome students,' said a parent, 'but most buckle down eventually.'

'Occasionally there are students we don't manage to turn round. Then we'll often suggest to parents a gap year in the middle of the sixth form, preferably working in Waitrose. It concentrates their minds on the consequences of failing to work and the difference in maturity when they come back is often amazing.'

Sanctions include supervised study; also a system of verbal and written warnings based on employment law. Bullying is taken very seriously – 'They don't care about superficial things,' said an insider, 'but on work, drink, drugs and bullying they clamp down very quickly'.

Pupils and parents: Most students have come from private schools. Some have had enough of boarding; some have been ill; some have found their previous school too rigid or too stressful. Others come from peripatetic diplomatic families. Some lack confidence and need to learn good working habits. Most thrive in the informal but structured atmosphere.

Entrance: Those going into the sixth form need a minimum of five grade Cs at GCSE; if they haven't passed maths or English they will need to retake these. Everyone is interviewed and previous schools are asked for references. The college will not consider students who have been disruptive elsewhere.

Exit: A few GCSE students move on elsewhere – perhaps to state sixth form colleges – but most go through to the sixth form. Those aiming at Oxbridge are given an intensive course including lectures,

seminars, mock interviews and individual tuition – three Oxbridge places in 2014. Extra help also for potential vets, doctors and dentists, via a bespoke medical programme. Wide range of degree courses, with business, management and finance being the most popular, also art foundation, mechanical engineering, sports and exercise science.

Money matters: Several scholarships available, worth 10-100 per cent of fees, plus bursaries.

Remarks: Good at stimulating the very bright as well as re-motivating the disaffected. Informal atmosphere with strong staff/student relationships underly a structured regime where everyone is kept up to scratch.

Eaton House Belgravia

Linked schools: Eaton House The Vale, 246; Eaton House the Manor Girls' School; Eaton House the Manor Preparatory and Pre-Preparatory Schools, see *The Good Schools Guide: London South*

3-5 Eaton Gate, Eaton Square, London, SW1W 9BA

Independent • Pupils: 230 • Ages: 4-8 • Non-denom • Fees (per term): £4,710

Tel: 020 7730 9343
Fax: 020 7730 1798
Email: admin@eatonhouseschools.com
Website: www.eatonhouseschools.com

45

Headmistress: Since 1998, Miss Lucy Watts (40s) Dip Montessori. Previously taught at a co-ed Montessori prep school before joining Eaton House in 1990. She started her career as a class teacher, moving on to become head of science and deputy head and, eight years later, headmistress. A calm and efficient leader, full of energy and good humour, say parents. Over the years many strong friendships have formed and Miss Lucy has several godchildren amongst the siblings of her earlier pupils. She maintains excellent relations between staff, parents and pupils and emphasises that the Eaton House group of schools is like an extended family with all looking out for each other, working hard and respecting each other's individual roles. Still very much a hands-on head, teaching handwriting to younger children, maths to the top years and also acts as a supply teacher to cover sick leave. Her door is always open to parents and the weekly newsletter keeps everybody up to date with all the Eaton House group happenings.

Entrance: At 4+ non-selective – places are allocated on a first come first served basis with priority given to siblings, children of staff, ex-staff and old boys. Put your son's name down early – £50 for a confirmed place and £30 for a waiting list place. Deposit of a term's fees, two terms before the child starts, which is credited against your final term's fees.

Exit: At 7+ and 8+ mainly to London day schools – Westminster Under, Westminster Cathedral Choir School, Colet Court, Sussex House, St Philip's, Eaton House The Manor Prep and Wetherby. A few head off to board at Summer Fields, The Dragon, Ludgrove and the like.

Remarks: Traditional 3Rs curriculum with lots of added extras, particularly in the arts and science – the school boasts its own lab, boys enjoy potion and crystal making amongst their many experiments and discoveries. Pupils are divided into small classes, no streaming but informal sets for maths to ensure that everybody is meeting their potential and able to go at their own pace. As in the past, the school's aim is to give boys a good grounding and a full understanding in all maths and English topics, rather than rushing ahead.

No outdoor space so school days are very structured – boys are bussed to Hyde or Battersea Park every day to let off steam and play sports. Swimming takes place at the Queen Mother's sports centre. Good choice of after-school and optional weekend sports clubs encourage boys to choose and try out different activities. Chess lessons for years 2 and 3. An actor visits the school to help train the boys for junior debating club. Lots of spirited music and drama, which is reflected in the many assemblies, plays and themed days, which often see teachers dressing up too. Excellent choir for ones so young, performs at a local charity events and is thought to be adorable by parents and anyone lucky enough to catch one of their performances. Five small practice rooms in the basement for young instrumentalists – boys can learn piano, flute, violin, recorder and guitar.

Well-organised SEN supports children with specific learning differences; Move Fit group is run by physiotherapists for anyone who needs to improve coordination, and touch typing tuition for year 2 upwards.

Mainly local clientele with many parents working in the City as bankers and lawyers, although much more international than in the past. Staff and parents have high expectations for the boys as the majority move onto academically selective prep schools. Boys are set numerous challenges, both physical and intellectual, and well trained so they become familiar with class exams in preparation for the formal 7+ and 8+ entry examinations. Miss Lucy and her staff are always on hand to advise parents about suitable choice of prep schools.

Bustling kitchen runs two lunch sittings a day; where possible the food is fresh and cooked on-site. Birthdays are special days, with boys bringing cakes or biscuits to share with friends and staff. Boys present as cheerful little chaps. School remains a popular and successful recipe for pre-preppers as ever.

Fairley House School

30 Causton Street, London, SW1P 4AU

Independent • Pupils: 180 • Ages: 5–14 • Non-denom
• Fees (per term): £9,797

Tel: 020 7976 5456
Fax: 020 7976 5905
Email: office@fairleyhouse.org.uk
Website: www.fairleyhouse.org.uk

46

Headmaster: Since September 2013, Mr Michael Taylor BA PGCE FRGS (40-ish). A geographer, he came here from four years as deputy head at More House near Farnham, another good specialist school. Too early to tell how he will turn out, but first reports are

very encouraging – he clearly gets on well with both parents and children. Parents say 'boyish', 'deals with problems well', 'has a laugh with the pupils but keeps their respect', 'hands shaken, greeted by name, knows if they have been away.'

All the classrooms, including the science lab, are buzzing with activities, visual reminders and clues, anything that is memorable

Previous principal, Jackie Murray, is now school's principal educational psychologist. Still a force in the land.

Academic matters: Regularly inspected and accredited by CReSTeD, the register for specialist schools with provision for dyslexia and SpLDs. Pupils are split into a junior department – 5 to 9 years – and a senior department – 10 to 14 years, class size usually 8-12 pupils. The main emphasis being on numeracy and literacy, everyone is put into a small group to match their ability and skills for maths and English and rejoins their class for other subjects. Children are taught to understand their own learning styles and shown strategies to overcome barriers to learning to achieve their targets. The aim is to return children to mainstream schools as soon as they are able, which has great success in doing. Test results such as Sats are very respectable, especially from children who can have quite pronounced difficulties.

Every child has an IEP which is regularly reviewed by the trans-disciplinary team to monitor progress and ensure that individual needs are being catered for. Mornings start with exercises; depending on the individual, this could be physical, orthoptic or attention focused. All the classrooms, including the science lab, are buzzing with activities, visual reminders and clues, anything that is memorable: models made by the children, word banks for a current history topic or colour-coded parts of speech. Every teacher has specialist qualifications which ensure that all classes are fully accessible and multisensory. 'Having teachers who are nice to you and understand has changed my life,' said a 10-year-old. The learning support is an integral part of the whole school approach to teaching. The transdisciplinary approach is used across the curriculum, helpfully allowing therapy delivery to be linked to specific subjects and development. Homework is colour-coded to help with the organisation, and deadlines must be met to prepare the children for returning to mainstream school. Help and advice is on hand for those who get stuck.

Depending on the individual needs of the pupil, speech therapy and occupational therapy are incorporated into classroom learning, art, drama and sports. Younger children will be making 'ch' out of chocolate buttons whilst older ones are baking round pies to help understand and remember the mathematical sign pi. Children are taught to touch-type once they have achieved a reading age of approximately 8 years. In-house speech and occupational therapists run their own sensory integration programmes and motor coordination classes. The therapy staff organising the motor coordination classes have been specially trained in America and continue to attend training in the USA to keep up to date.

'It was like letting a different child into my house. Cool and collected where he had been crying and angry.'

Parents thrilled to have found the place. A typical story: 'His previous school [a well-known London prep] had given up on him: "He will never learn his times tables". He had shut down completely. On his first day here he learned his nine times table. He has made huge progress, so much more confident, maths is no longer an issue.' Or: 'It was like letting a different child into my house. Cool and collected where he had been crying and angry.'

Games, options, the arts: Wonderfully imaginative art displays line the corridors and even the ceilings are decorated in many areas of the building. Pupils make their own ceramic tiles depicting various scenes from history and also design and execute murals. The most recent addition is the newly-built art studio and kiln room. The children enjoy a great variety of artistic activities including textiles, fashion, design and technology, sewing and puppet-making.

A range of sports – all the traditional ones, alongside canoeing, fencing and yoga. Although doesn't have its own playing fields, they make good use of local facilities at Battersea Park and the Queen Mother sports centre. Music and drama are taught as separate subjects and integrated into other curriculum areas to help children develop good communication skills. Everyone is encouraged to learn a musical instrument and the school runs its own acting awards and music medals scheme. Parents pack into the termly dramatic and musical productions.

Extracurricular activities include museum and theatre trips along with a wide choice of lunchtime and after-school clubs. Club options change regularly depending on the clientèle and demand.

Background and atmosphere: Founded in 1975 by a speech therapist, Daphne Hamilton Fairley, as a charitable trust in memory of her oncologist husband, killed by an IRA bomb. The upper school site, originally a church, has been cleverly converted into a four-storey building. The junior school pupils are housed in a Victorian infants' school in the shadows of Lambeth Palace, backing on to Archbishop's Park, complete with sports facilities and an adventure playground for the children's use. Both buildings are well decorated, with a lot of space dedicated to the children's achievements, visual timetables and fantastic works of art. The atmosphere is purposeful, peaceful and well organised, encouraging pupils to be themselves. Lots of smiling and cheerful faces – nobody should feel the odd one out here.

Pastoral care and discipline: Structured mentoring system involving 18 members of staff to whom children can refer themselves. Aim is to work in a strong partnership with parents to help ensure things do not go wrong for pupils due to simple misunderstandings. Seems to be working, as parents feel pastoral care has improved over the last few years. 'Not too strict. Jokey,' said a parent, but at the end of the day kids waiting for the bus are orderly, and board quietly.

Pupils and parents: Scattered all over London, and a few from the edges of the home counties – requires an effort to get to know other families. Everybody and anybody affected by neuro-diversity. By all accounts, lots of very supportive and enthusiastic parents who are keen to get involved with school activities. Most recently the parent group has fundraised to update and restock the school library. Weekly newsletters, back-up information on the website and parents can use a communication book or email teachers. Comprehensive, well-designed website, but not 'read friendly' as yet.

Entrance: Children are invited to spend two days here, where they will have a transdisciplinary all-round assessment to ensure that the school will be able to meet their needs. After the assessment, parents are provided with reports from an educational psychologist, speech therapist and occupational therapist and then invited for a conference to discuss how the school can help and support their

child. Assessments cost £290–£890. In the event of the school not being able to offer a place they will suggest other options to parents.

Most pupils have a diagnosis of specific learning differences, usually dyslexia and/or dyspraxia and the related conditions ADD, ADHD and Asperger's. Also able to accommodate some pupils who have non-conventional learning styles and find mainstream schools inaccessible.

Exit: The average stay for pupils at Fairley House is approximately two/three years. Depending on when a child arrives at the school, there is a tendency for the Fairley programme to end at odd ages (from an entrance point of view) like 12 or 14, which some potential next schools get stuffy about. Some parents clearly feel that the school could have been more helpful in the search for where to go to next. Top destinations are Bedales (senior and junior), DLD College, Hall School (Wimbledon), Kingham Hill, Millfield (senior and junior), Milton Abbey, Portland Place, Bedes (senior and junior), St Christopher and Windlesham House – but there are a wide range of others who welcome Fairley pupils.

Money matters: A few bursaries are available for trainee teachers. As yet, unable to offer bursaries to pupils, but will assist parents with tribunals and the statementing procedure. Approximately 26 per cent of pupils have a statement of special educational needs and are funded by their local authorities.

Remarks: Certainly good value for money, but the fees are terrifying and beyond the reach of many without local authority funding. A remarkable school for its holistic, multi-sensory and transdisciplinary approach. A beacon for children with learning and processing differences and parents who have been tearing their hair out trying to cope in other situations.

Fine Arts College Hampstead

Centre Studios 41–43 Englands Lane, London, NW3 4YD

Independent • Pupils: 150 • Ages: 14–19 • Non-denom • Fees (per term): £6,110

Tel: 020 7586 0312
Fax: 020 7483 0355
Email: mail@hampsteadfinearts.com
Website: www.hampsteadfinearts.com

5

Joint principals: Nicholas Cochrane and Candida Cave (50s). Both studied at the Ruskin School of Drawing and Fine Art, Oxford. Cochrane then went on to work for the Old Masters Department at Christies. The pair started teaching at a tutorial college and found 'we were quite good at inspiring people'. The decision to set up a college of their own was something that just 'came about', but clearly had a market, and has grown steadily ever since. Nicholas Cochrane teaches fine art, while continuing to exhibit with The Royal Society of Portrait Painters. (Has won the Prince of Wales's Award for Portrait Drawing.) Candida Cave, too, remains a practising painter and playwright, while teaching art history. Parents and pupils are great fans of their warm and relaxed approach. 'Candida Cave is what all parents dream of in a teacher, but think they'll never meet,' said one. 'She's imaginative and nurturing, but not a push over. My daughter just fell in love with her.'

Academic matters: A very broad, almost exclusively, arts-based curriculum (no science in the sixth form, though a few mathematicians). The visual arts remain, as one might expect, exceptionally popular. Photography is the number one subject choice (80 students this year) but also large numbers for fine art and art history, English literature, textiles, graphic design, film studies and media studies. The fine arts approach provides a strong traditional grounding (from classical busts and life models), which leaves many students with strong enough technical skills to bypass foundation courses. (The college also runs a two-term post A level portfolio course, to ensure preparation for art degrees and art college is tip-top). An extensive curriculum (29 subjects in all) of liberal arts, social sciences, modern languages (French, Spanish and Italian), and classical studies (Latin, Greek, ancient history and classical civilisation), can be taken in virtually any combination. Strong results overall (25 per cent A*/A and 70 per cent A*/B in 2014), with English and fine art particularly stellar. Exceptionally high 'valued added' between GCSE and A Level (fourth highest in the country) produced by caring teaching in small groups (classes never exceed nine).

'My daughter had failed spectacularly at two fee-paying schools,' says one appreciative mother of

The fine arts approach provides a strong traditional grounding (from classical busts and life models)

a daughter now at a Russell Group university. 'She thought she was a dunce until they took her under their wing. They produced an incredible turn around and she went from Cs to As.' Also offers GCSEs, with two year groups of about 20 in all. 'We find there's a real need in year 10,' says Candida Cave, 'particularly when schools start saying, you should drop this or that.' GCSE subjects include biology and some physics but probably not the place for nascent medics. In 2014, 27 per cent A*/A grades. Staff long-serving and enthusiastic (including three ex-students and Candida Cave's daughter), with a fair proportion who also have alternative lives as professional artists, film makers, etc. Teaching style relaxed but enthusiastic; student style, co-operative competition. 'It's very much teaching in discussion, they want to impress each other in a nice way,' says Candida Cave. Good information given to parents and pupils about progress, with fortnightly reports and two parents' evenings. Rated outstanding by Ofsted in latest report.

Games, options, the arts: Plenty of opportunity to display talent, with an annual art exhibition, music and drama recital, and short films shown at the local Everyman Cinema. (One girl was recently runner-up for the Young Film Critic Award at Bafta). Loads of outside speakers and cultural outings, with annual study trips to Florence, Paris and Venice. Not at all a hierarchical place, and students organise their own entertainment – 'a certain number tend to take the lead each year' – including charitable fundraising (for Breast Cancer awareness, the Red Cross, a local hospice) and other social events. Certainly not the ideal environment for the sporty (and few here care) but GCSE students have fencing lessons plus PE at a local sports centre and the College's long-standing football team plays against other sixth-form colleges. Popular table tennis, too, on site.

Background and atmosphere: Started in 1978 in the YMCA in Tottenham Court Road, teaching art and art history. 'We started because there wasn't anyone else specialising in the arts,' says Candida Cave. Moved to Belsize Park in 1982, started offering GCSEs in 1994, and then, in 2002, added a converted Victorian dairy, which now forms the hub of the school, providing rambling lateral space around a cobbled courtyard. A good mix of classrooms (some more spacious than others) and excellent studio space, for art, drama, photography (with its own darkroom for traditional-style printing) and media studies. The atmosphere is intentionally informal and teachers are called by their first names. 'The college was very much founded as a bridge between school and university. Many students come here because they're looking for something more flexible.' Students congregate in the common room, where free coffee is on offer, but no food supplied on site. Some bring sandwiches, the majority visit the multitude of local eateries. Dress code vaguely artistic and bohemian (the odd fur gilet and extreme make up, the majority in UGGs and tracksuits), but kept well within limits. 'If it offends, we tell them to dress properly. It's just common sense.'

Pastoral care and discipline: 'What we liked about the college,' said one parent, 'is the industrious informality. They take the job seriously, but don't wear it too formally.' Pupils' work and well-being is immaculately monitored. Everyone has a personal tutor, whom they see for an hour and a half each week. The tutor goes through reports, helps with essay-writing and advises on university applications. All GCSE pupils sign in at 9am and again at 1.30pm. If pupils are not in class an email is sent to parents within half an hour. 'Pupils turn up because they want to,' said one parent. 'But, equally, they know that if they can't be bothered to turn up, the attitude will be, don't bother to come back.' Most have no problems with this. 'I've never been to a school before where all the other pupils want to learn,' said one boy. Students sign a contract of behaviour, so know exactly what is expected, and misbehaviour, social or academic, is followed by an oral warning, a written warning, and then a parental meeting. 'We've not excluded anyone for eight to nine years, and not even suspended anyone for a long time,' says Candida Cave. 'We're run here on mutual respect and they do seem to rise to that.' Most see the college as a place where they can be confident concerns will be dealt with quickly and in confidence. Definitely a haven for those for whom more boisterous or insensitive environments have just not worked. 'The college made my daughter believe in herself. I feel I owe them,' said one parent.

Pupils and parents: A mix of mostly local professional/artistic families, who tend to be profoundly relieved that their children have found such a civilised and creative niche. Some of those who come to do GCSEs have previously been educated abroad. Others have had enough of boarding school, or failed to fit into more conventional schools. Alumni include Orlando Bloom and Helena Bonham-Carter.

Entrance: All applicants are interviewed with their parents and the college makes offers based on two criteria: candidates 'really want to be here' and 'they intend to go on to higher education'. Minimum five GCSEs with C or above, but this liberal benchmark is generally well exceeded, not a few arriving garlanded with a multitude of A*s. Most from local independents and leading boarding schools, a few from the state sector and schools further afield.

Exit: Around 30 per cent leave after GCSEs. For the rest, a generous sprinkling into every permutation of arts and media – from film studies and fine art to fashion retailing and creative writing – but also to history, psychology and sociology. Sussex, Falmouth, Nottingham Trent and Leeds currently popular.

Money matters: One scholarship of 100 per cent (based on academic merit, a statement of why they deserve a scholarship, and an interview). Two of 25 per cent may be given for outstanding exam performance at GCSE ('We wanted to show we appreciated their intelligence.') A limited number of bursaries awarded to students who have previously been educated in the state system who would not otherwise be able to afford private education.

Remarks: A low-key, calm and friendly place, with strong teaching and results, particularly in the arts. Ideal for the 'arty, urban misfit' who has wilted in a more conventional environment.

Francis Holland Junior School, Sloane Square

Linked school: Francis Holland School, Sloane Square, 103

Graham Terrace, London, SW1W 8JF

Independent • Pupils: 165 • Ages: 4–11 • C of E • Fees (per term): £5,095 – £5,790

Tel: 020 7730 2971
Fax: 020 7823 4066
Email: education@fhs–sw1.org.uk
Website: www.fhs–sw1.org.uk

47

Headmistress: Since 2010, Miss Sarah Styles BA, QTS in theology and MA in philosophy of education. Previously director of studies at Wheathampstead House. Was a member of the royal navy and now a member of the royal naval reserve at weekends and in school holidays. Seen by parents as being 'approachable', 'sweet' and 'fair,' with a strong team around her. This celebrated junior school is

Highly anticipated Princess Margaret ballet competition every summer term – her daughter is an old girl

in a very safe pair of hands. Teaches English to year 6. Likes cycling, walking and being on the go.

Moving on in January 2015 to head St Hilda's Prep in Bushey.

Entrance: Assessments at 3. Some 150 girls tested in January for 24 places. School assesses 'girls' potential and readiness to learn.' Head was horrified when a parent asked about tutoring for their 3 year old. She advises, 'Parents need to read to their children, take them to the park and talk to them. That's the best preparation for these tests.' Places occasionally available further up the school and prospective pupils are then assessed in the classroom setting. Barely a spare seat in the house.

Exit: Fairly evenly split: one third to the senior school, two-thirds to other London day schools or boarding. One parent remarked that she thought it would be 'a hard jump to go from Francis Holland Junior School to a large co-ed. Girls are protected here and can be quite gentle. I'm not sure they are always ready for the hurly burly of senior school.' Popular day destinations are St Paul's, Godolphin and Latymer and City of London Girls. Current boarding favourites are Wycombe Abbey, Downe House and St Mary's Ascot.

Remarks: A small, academic school, tucked away behind Sloane Square. One form per year of 24 maximum. Shares a site with senior school. 'Low pressure in the early years,' says head. Reception children have naps after lunch in first term when sleepy. From year 4 it hots up, with summer exams in maths, English and science from then on. No setting but plenty of differentiation. The consensus among parents we spoke to was 'You need to be academically robust to cope here. There are so many projects and tests, and parents are expected to be able to support their offspring massively. It feels almost relentless at times.' More academic than senior school: 'The girls here are clever and motivated,' said one parent. 'Strong foundations are laid but the girls work hard for it,' according to another. The standard of work on display was astonishingly high. The girls themselves feel that they are well prepared for the 11+, but 'we don't feel too much pressure.' Year 6 pupils kept working to proper timetables once 11+ exams are over;

no coasting here. Teaching is superb and staff considered by the parents to be high quality. Teachers come over from senior school to teach PE, science, French (from 8) and some art. Well motivated staff. 'We're a strong team,' says head.

Bright classrooms, inventive displays, beanbags and colour everywhere. Wonderful library, shared with senior school, and huge numbers of books at every turn.

Girls have beautiful manners and stand up with military discipline when adults enter the room. Highly articulate and fluent. Very keen to show their projects to us when we visited and tell us what they had learnt. Highly engaged in lessons, from early years upwards. Pretty tartan uniform. One girl in top year thought it would be worth staying at the school just so she could get to wear the new kit.

Plenty of time for fun, with highly-anticipated trips to Cornwall in year 6 and Canterbury in year 5. Sport is a real strength. Ballet taken seriously: compulsory in the first years, fabulous ballet studio. Highly anticipated Princess Margaret ballet competition every summer term – her daughter is an old girl. Lots of music and drama, including impressive end of year 6 musical. Girls take the initiative by providing the costumes, designing the posters and rehearsing on their own at break times. Great emphasis placed on creativity throughout

Girls have beautiful manners and stand up with military discipline when adults enter the room

the school. Junior choir from year 3 and a very select chamber choir for the most talented singers. Significant numbers learn Instruments from year 1 onwards. Head feels, 'girls need time to be bored. They should not have every moment of their lives timetabled.' Wants them to discover what interests them for themselves. Plenty of clubs on offer including chess, speech and drama, pottery, art and French.

A very caring school in which older girls are expected to, and do, look after the younger ones. Year 6 pupils write and illustrate books for year 1 pupils. Lots of raising money for charity. All year 6 girls are prefects, though badges confiscated for poor behaviour.

Families are 'more and more international', says head. 'A bewildering number of languages spoken in the playground at pick up time,' according to one mother. Children come from nearby Westminster, Chelsea, Knightsbridge and Pimlico.

'A happy school,' is the general consensus amongst parents. Bullying very rare. Head feels girls are 'traditional and polite'. One pupil acknowledges, 'It will be the saddest day of my life when I leave Francis Holland to go to my next school.' Head believes her school is 'vibrant', and it was certainly buzzing on the day we visited. A real energy about the place. Francis Holland girls have a wonderfully stimulating start to life here, with devoted care and attention from outstanding teachers and a capable head. No wonder there's a queue to come here.

Francis Holland School, Sloane Square

Linked school: Francis Holland Junior School, Sloane Square, 101

39 Graham Terrace, London, SW1W 8JF

Independent • Pupils: 335 • Ages: 11–18 • C of E • Fees (per term): £5,790

Tel: 020 7730 2971
Fax: 020 7823 4066
Email: registrar@fhs–sw1.org.uk
Website: www.fhs–sw1.org.uk

48

Headmistress: Since September 2012, Mrs Lucy Elphinstone MA PGCE MEd FRSA (50s). Educated at Barnstaple Grammar School, Devon, and Newnham College, Cambridge (English). Very varied career, including stints in publishing, bookselling, catering, property and ghost-writing. Wide teaching experience from 3 to 18 years, and countless leadership roles including head of a pre-school, head of English at King's Taunton, director of studies in two prep schools, director of drama and resident tutor at Fettes College. Came here from Downe House where she was head of sixth form, senior leader and Oxbridge co-ordinator. Four highly successful adult children. Living in London for the first time since her 20s and loving the culture. Hobbies include ski-ing, watercolour painting, Scottish reeling and Victorian children's literature. Acknowledges she is very different from her long-serving predecessor, who was 'a mathematician with very different strengths from mine.'

Keen to build up girls' resilience to help them deal with the challenges ahead, including multiple changes of career. Wants pupils to be confident risk-takers. In her assembly on the day we visited, she encouraged girls to take on board Christopher Robin's advice to Winnie the Pooh: 'You are braver than you believe, stronger than you seem, and smarter than you think.' One parent described her as 'ambitious for the school and highly visionary'. Another claimed, 'She's shaken the school up. It was good before but she has lifted our spirits.' Girls consider her to

She encouraged girls to take on board Christopher Robin's advice to Winnie the Pooh: 'You are braver than you believe, stronger than you seem, and smarter than you think.'

be 'a great role model.' Dynamic, vivacious and engaging.

Academic matters: In 2014, a disappointing 35 per cent A*/A at A level; 66 per cent A*-B. History of art and English currently popular, with ever-increasing numbers taking maths and science. Compulsory extended project qualification in sixth form, introduced by head to develop girls' research skills and to prepare them for the next stage. Photography, business studies and music technology recently introduced at A level. Seventy-seven per cent A*/A at GCSE. Spanish, chemistry and history results impressive. Setting in English, science and maths by year 9. 'Not onerous amounts of homework in first couple of years,' said one parent.

Excellent reports about provision now on offer to pupils with special needs: 'no longer just lip service,' said one parent. All pupils screened for dyslexia on arrival. A handful of pupils have EAL requirements and are seen on a one-to-one basis by specialist staff. Extra support continues to sixth form.

Some teaching described as 'fantastic', but one parent we spoke to felt there were 'still some members of staff who need weeding out. They aren't inspiring the girls and aren't getting the results.' Approximately a third of staff has been there at least 10 years. Recent appointments, particularly of younger members of staff, seen as very positive. Staff feel 'empowered' by newish head.

Academic success is recognised with flamboyant prize giving at nearby Cadogan Hall, with performances by talented dancers and musicians. The girls were hugely excited to see staff wearing their graduation gowns and 'felt proud' to be part of Francis Holland. A great success, recently introduced by head, who is clearly keen to celebrate success in all fields.

Two parallel classes throughout senior school. Classes start at 16 on average and rarely go above 20 in lower years, diminishing to six to eight in sixth form. Would split sixth form classes if they exceeded 10 pupils. From year 11, all girls have an academic mentor, so everyone is fully supported and no one is left floundering. Girls genuinely feel that staff are keeping a close eye on them and

that they are guided through university entrance 'incredibly well'.

Games, options, the arts: Sport now taken very seriously, at all levels, and is compulsory for all. Head believes, 'Sport is important as it teaches you that you can't always win, but you can pick yourself up and carry on'. Newly appointed head of sport who everyone is raving about. Well-equipped gym and netball / tennis court on site. Outdoor sports in Battersea Park, including tennis, hockey, athletics and rounders. Top years can try pilates, yoga, squash and boxercise as well as more traditional team sports. Most parents are delighted that fixtures are now arranged on Saturday mornings and the school wins the majority of matches.

Music is flourishing. Nearly 60 per cent learn an instrument. Choirs, orchestras, chamber groups and jazz groups galore. Two choir tours to Europe each year. Head wants creative and enterprising pupils and girls recently set up own theatre company. Highly successful theatrical collaborations with boys from nearby Cardinal Vaughan School, with minimal adult input. Parents consider drama to be a real strength. Speech and drama very popular with many reaching top grades in exams.

Impressive selection of clubs including debating and philosophy, as well as animal club for younger girls. School has a renowned menagerie of

animals, from gerbils and snakes to chinchillas, and younger girls get to take home animals for the weekend. Girls encouraged to become proficient in public speaking: debating club from year 10, and mock elections and English Speaking Union events arranged. Broad horizons and an informed awareness of current affairs expected.

Background and atmosphere: Set up by the Rev Francis Holland, Canon of Canterbury, in 1881 as a C of E foundation but all faiths welcome. Sister school to Francis Holland Regent's Park: the schools share a governing body, staff training days and have the same ethos. Same site as junior school, in a Tardis-like building behind Sloane Square. Head aware that being in the same place from 4-18 years has its disadvantages and is keeping her eye out for property nearby. Beautiful interior decorating: stunning new entrance hall lifts morale on arrival and upper sixth common room seriously plush.

Pastoral care and discipline: Described by parents as being 'nurturing'. Lower sixth girls are paired with year 7 girls in 'Big Sister' programme, to make sure they settle on arrival at the school. Head concerned that 'high performing parents have high expectations of their children.' Aware that girls can feel pressurized to perform and a well-being programme has been set up to help girls to cope, when it all becomes too much. Head is a trained counsellor and pastoral care is high on the agenda.

Strong ethos of service fostered, whether fundraising for school in Uganda or organising tea parties for elderly in Battersea. Girls are expected to give something back.

Head would expel a girl for drug taking; those caught smoking pay money to a cancer charity, phone their parents from head's office and do community service within the school grounds. Won't tolerate unkindness or rudeness and girls we met were fantastically polite. Sixth formers allowed out for lunch but 'school food is delicious so we prefer to stay at school for lunch and just go out for a coffee,' said one.

Pupils and parents: Happy, confident and charming girls who seem ready to take on the world. Well-heeled and polished with ready smiles. Couldn't wait to tell us how lucky they felt to be here. High octane, international families: mainly French, Spanish, Italian, Russian and American. Most live within a three mile radius of school. Communication with parents now greatly improved with regular newsletters and reports. 'We are delighted that we finally know what is going on,' said one.

Notable former pupils include Vanessa Mae, Sienna Miller, Cara Delevingne and Rose Tremain.

Entrance: At 11+, exams in English and maths, as well as half a day spent at school consisting of interview and taster lesson. Part of the North London Consortium Group One. Some 500 girls sit for 50 places. Bar raised each year. At 13+, exams in English, maths, science and French. For sixth form, by entrance or scholarship exams in proposed A level subjects

Exit: A trickle leave after GCSE. Most sixth formers to university. Generally one or two Oxbridge places. As one girl put it, 'I have applied to Oxford, but it's just one of my choices. It's not made into a big deal here. My other choices are great too.' Art foundation courses also popular. Medicine, economics, history and psychology are favoured courses; Leeds, Bristol and Nottingham regular destinations. Increasing numbers to US universities, especially for liberal arts degrees, and not only those with a direct American link; others to Spain, France and Canada. Head of careers is a very

---

School has a renowned menagerie of animals, from gerbils and snakes to chinchillas, and younger girls get to take home animals for the weekend

successful recent appointment; she asks girls at beginning of sixth form, 'What is your dream?', and then helps them to chase it. Higher education fair organised by school. Girls well supported once they leave, throughout university and beyond if needed. Relations with alumnae now actively fostered.

Money matters: At 11, four academic scholarships, as well as music, art and drama scholarships. Bursaries at 11+, 14+ and four in sixth form. Daughters of clergy offered remission on a third of fees.

Remarks: This school is undergoing a transformation and the excitement is palpable. Expectations are high and challenges are being set, but the girls and staff know they have a strong leader and are following her willingly. 'An excellent appointment,' said one parent. 'We feel seriously lucky to have our girls here on Mrs Elphinstone's watch,' said another. Though small, this school is now punching above its weight. An exciting and exhilarating place to be.

Francis Holland School, Regent's Park

Clarence Gate, Ivor Place, London, NW1 6XR

Independent · Pupils: 465 · Ages: 11–18 · C of E · Fees (per term): £5,560

Tel: 020 7723 0176
Fax: 020 7706 1522
Email: admin@fhs-nw1.org.uk
Website: www.fhs-nw1.org.uk

49

Headmistress: Since 2004, Mrs Vivienne Durham MA (50s). Prior to her arrival at Francis Holland, much-loved deputy head at South Hampstead High and had taught at Guildford High and Haberdashers' Girls, where she headed the English department. Deservedly one of the most popular heads in the business, loquacious, enthusiastic, fervent in her belief in 'education' rather than in specifically 'girls' education', highly articulate and jolly good fun. She is a people person writ large, but also a clever strategist and manager of resources. You want to give her your daughters and we spoke to no-one who regretted having done so. 'Mrs Durham is very caring, very switched-on and really nice to deal with,' vouchsafed one grateful mother, who spoke for many. The staff clearly love her too and the girls plainly see her as a role model. We could quote much of what she says but will settle for: 'I've never seen an online facility which could replace a good human being in the classroom'. She is infuriatingly svelte and chic and married to the ex-head of University College School.

Academic matters: Small classes – especially at A level – are an almost USP here. No class is bigger than 25 and, in the sixth, 14 max – many are far smaller. For a relatively small sixth form offers a creditable range of subjects including economics, history of art and psychology. Most popular subjects tend to be art, biology, English, history and maths; the best results in RS, politics, geography, history of art and art. Economics less strong. Theatre studies offered at A level though not at GCSE. Outstanding results in many subjects – 57 per cent A*/A in 2013. Extended project (worth half an A level) can be taken in addition to A levels and challenges the most able.

GCSEs and, increasingly, IGCSEs (79 per cent A*/A) also include a good number of options – most popular are history, art and geography. Wisely, allows girls to take either three separate sciences or double science – we approve.

SEN support is generally by withdrawal or out-of-lesson individual support. Most of those who receive help are mildly dyslexic/dyspraxic but additional support also for those perceived as G and T. Three-strong 'learning enhancement' team. 'We give girls extra support the entire time – it's simply part of what we offer,' says head, and parents concur, 'The girls can refer themselves for support and there's excellent liaison between the subject staff and the team'.

But the academic input here is far more than just good teaching. Weekly lectures by outside speakers open to all from year 9 up. Lots of trips hither and yon and good use made of privileged location and the proximity of the odd museum, House of Parliament, Bank of England or three.

Games, options, the arts: Minutes from Regent's Park, where most sports take place. Onsite is a tiny Astro playground – good for netball shooting practice but no more – but a good sized gym, fitness suite and, surprisingly, basement swimming pool, opened 1996 by, somewhat improbably, Old Girl Joan Collins – swimming one of the more competitive sports. Sport compulsory for all, but lots of choice by the time you're in the sixth and Zumba is a recent, popular addition – along with yoga and the use of the fitness suite.

Art is exceptional here – lots of it lines the corridors and we felt inclined to snaffle some of the best pieces to hang at home: really attractive, skilful, imaginative work. Top floor now houses the two studios, plus kiln, dark room, and printing press; views over the grey slate, Georgian rooftops and grey, steel satellite dishes must inspire artistic freedom, as it clearly burns bright.

Music also housed up here, though you'd not imagine the few small rooms result in the level of skill and performance managed by the girls here. Seventy per cent learn at least one instrument. Orchestras, choirs – large and chamber – and other ensembles thrive and surprise. Annual concert with the boys of Harrow School is a highlight. Music and drama combine to produce major annual show, plus drama competition – these draw in most, one way or another, though more drama – especially in the upper years – would be appreciated by many. Young Enterprise and Duke of Edinburgh Award scheme both thrive, along with more than 70 clubs and activities.

Background and atmosphere: Founded by Canon Francis Holland in 1878 at the instigation of his wife, Mary Sibylla, an interesting woman, mother of six, who pushed for the education of 'girls from the middle and upper classes' and later converted to Roman Catholicism. The second school with Canon Holland's name was founded shortly after just off Sloane Square; the two schools still occupy their original sites and are run by the same foundation. Sibylla's letters were published by her children and make for touching reading.

Minutes from Baker Street and Regent's Park, the main building is a classic 1900s red-brick school – smallish classrooms, corridors, lots of floors and a wonderful hexagonal hall with three galleries and lots of polished wood. But the Tardis cliché really applies here. From the unassuming outside, you can't imagine how the school could accommodate more than a few dozen girls, but inside it goes on and on and has some surprisingly spacious areas. The library is also a decent size and has acquired

---

Basement swimming pool, opened 1996, somewhat improbably, by Old Girl Joan Collins – swimming one of the more competitive sports

a new area for computers in addition to the trad bookshelves and table space. Sofas and armchairs – we approve of that too. The stock is good, but some updating might inspire more to use books along with Google.

The hall – used for all major events – is not an ideal performance space but has extendable staging and clearly works. The acquisition of the adjacent Gloucester Arms pub and its consequent reopening as the Gloucester Wing was a major advance – Mrs Durham is on the lookout for a further property to enable further expansion, not in numbers but in facilities. Now possesses two good art studios, seminar rooms and a splendid, well-used lecture theatre. The old saloon bar is a useful space for drama work, charity activities and talks. School is an admirable mix of traditional and up to the minute – computer system recently renewed and everyone now wired in and up, as you'd expect.

Right at the top is the sixth form area and it's super – lots of space, though it can get crowded at breaks – with a roof top garden, a workroom, silent study area and common room with cooking area, sofas and lockers. Staff allowed in to pop marked

work etc into sensible pigeon holes. School is accessible – lift enables wheelchair-users to get almost everywhere, though some corridors and steps make odd corners impossible.

The food is 'the best in London' – certainly the salads were lusciously inviting, as were the plates of fruit – pomegranates, passion fruit and melon slices: drool! Kitchen staff clearly popular with sixth formers – 'They are so kind – they bring us up hot chocolate and muffins,' we were told, and that really is kind, as four flights of stairs are involved.

Pastoral care and discipline: Universal praise for the pastoral care – 'the school could not be more supportive'; 'The staff are incredibly sensitive and caring. They are firm when it's needed, but you are always supported,' parents told us again and again. 'The staff are inspiring – they are more than just academic: they look after the whole child,' is another theme'. Heads of year have overall responsibility and a counsellor visits weekly. Home and social difficulties – as anywhere – but few discipline problems; Mrs Durham the ultimate arbiter.

Backup for practical as well as emotional needs: 'The UCAS support here is amazingly impressive,' an Oxbridge hopeful told us. 'The school has been so on top of everything – you get at least three teachers helping, loads of sessions; our head of sixth is amazing and she makes us feel completely secure in how we approach our applications.'

'I want them to be confident and self-possessed but not trumpet about it,' asserts the head. 'We are absolutely about nurture. We are kind and academic. Kind is central.'

Pupils and parents: Interesting mix. Professional families from all over – hence the higher than usual incidence of relocating ins and outs that

> *'They are so kind – they bring us up hot chocolate and muffins,' and that really is kind, as four flights of stairs are involved*

results in places appearing at odd stages: academics, medics, thesps and financiers, as you'd expect. The very rich – 'There are a few "princesses" in the sixth form,' muttered one or two parents – along with those who struggle to find the fees.

Notable Old Girls include Theresa Villiers, Joan and Jackie Collins, Tamara and Petra Ecclestone, Emilia Fox and Holly Branson.

Entrance: From over 170 preps and primaries. Majority from Pembridge House, Bute House, Sarum Hall, St Mary's, Hampstead, St Christopher's, Hampstead, St Christina's. Applications via the North London Consortium – exams in English and maths plus interviews. Oversubscribed of course, but as for many parents whose daughters also apply to the other powerhouses in the area the school, for all its virtues, is not always the first choice, a good chance of a place at 11+ if your daughter is able and would fit in. Location in central London means that relocating families come and go more than elsewhere and places often occur in other years – it is always worth a call.

At 16+ very few are taken – Mrs Durham has a sizeable sixth form and is not straining nerves to cram in more. Perhaps two to three places awarded to, perhaps, 20-30 applicants. A/Bs needed at GCSE.

Exit: Around 10 leave after GCSE and head for mixed sixth forms, notably Highgate – some come back. Mrs Durham is not the head to throw you out if you have problems or your GCSEs disappoint – 'We take them in at 11: we'll stick with them till 18'; also several families whose daughters have found refuge here from unhappiness elsewhere.

No identikit FH leaver – fledglings go everywhere including New York University, Durham, Warwick and Imperial College. One of Oxford in 2014 and two medics.

Money matters: A few bursaries and scholarships and worth enquiring, but, like most girls' day schools, not munificently endowed.

Remarks: Your clever daughter will be well taught and will do as well here as anywhere. Your shy and gentle soul will be loved and encouraged. Definitely no hothouse but a school that warms and nurtures. A gem in the heart of the metropolis.

Grafton Primary School

Eburne Road, Holloway, London, N7 6AR

State • Pupils: 462 • Ages: 3–11

Tel: 020 7272 3284
Fax: 020 7272 5709
Email: graftonschool@grafton.islington.sch.uk
Website: www.graftonschool.co.uk

39

Head: Since 1993, Mrs Nitsa Sergides OBE (awarded in 2012 for services to education), (60s). Qualified as a teacher in 1973, followed by 19 years of teaching at a local school. Became deputy head of Grafton Primary in 1991, and head two years later.

Cypriot born Nitsa (as everyone calls her), is the embodiment of Mediterranean warmth. Her pupils adore her, 'lovely to all of us, talks to us like family.' Her teachers are loyal (incredibly low turnover of staff) and parents marvel at her dedication: 'She's quite amazing, her enthusiasm never wanes and she genuinely wants the best for everybody.' Another parent told us, 'She is truly exceptional. Apart from her incredibly nurturing side, she has a gift of being able to get hold of every resource going for the school.'

Nitsa came to the UK at the age of 13 with teaching firmly on her radar, 'I think I was seven when I realised that's what I wanted to be.' Now in her 23rd year at Grafton School, she still wants to make a difference. 'I believe that children must be given every chance to succeed regardless of background or ethnicity. We try to create opportunities some pupils may not otherwise have.' This could be a yearly trip to the coast (which for some pupils is their first experience of the sea), or the chance to learn a musical instrument.

One of Nitsa's proudest achievements is that she hasn't had to exclude a child for 11 years, 'I always believe more in preventative measures rather than reactive measures.' She also believes that, given the correct guidance, inner-city schools can be as good as any: 'My three children are all products of Islington comprehensives. My son is now a neurosurgeon and both my daughters are barristers.' Married for 40 years to an engineer 'my bouncing board', she loves visiting art galleries and museums and spending time with her grandchildren. Such is her infectious enthusiasm that we left her office grinning.

Entrance: Standard local authority criteria of siblings, proximity to school and children in care etc. Competition for places is fierce – most recently 354 applicants for 60 places. As word spreads about this school there is concern about wealthier parents buying property in now trendy Holloway to get their kids a place, with predictable consequences for Grafton's rich diversity.

Exit: Mixed bag on offer for secondary schools in the Islington area. Most go on to Acland Burghley (if they live close enough), Highbury Fields, Highbury Grove, Mount Carmel school for girls, St Mary Magdalene and others including Islington Arts school or Central Foundation Boys' School. A few try for grammars like Latymer or Dame Alice Owen and independents such as City of London

Remarks: A tricky one to find, Grafton Primary runs adjacent to the Holloway Road, off Seven Sisters Road, accessible by car via a tiny slip road. Most pupils walk to school thereby avoiding the perils of Holloway's one-way system.

We were expecting great things and we weren't disappointed. Rated outstanding by Ofsted for the past 10 years and awarded the title of Beacon School, Grafton defies its demographics. A staggering 55-60 per cent of its pupils would qualify for free school meals (although in Islington, these are fully funded for all pupils), 25 per cent of children have SEN, 12 per cent with statements. Grafton is genuinely inclusive – big on equal opps for pupils with disabilities and a vast ethnic mix. One pupil told us, 'I have friends from so many different cultures and we are like a big family.' We heard the word 'family' used frequently and there is definitely a sense of unity and loyalty as well as pride in this school.

Grafton has recently become a teaching school, meaning that they now train teachers and support staff from other primaries. It is also one of only a few pioneering schools to have been chosen to introduce the CAME maths programme (Cognitive Acceleration through Mathematics Education), which promises to have a significant impact on both pupil and teacher development. Maths is

already a very strong subject at Grafton. In 2013, nearly 18 per cent of year 6, achieved a level 6 in maths SATs.

On entering one is immediately struck by the spectacularly colourful lobby. Rarely have we seen so much artwork, sculpture, ceiling displays (including a wonderful tree of life installation which ran the length of the lobby and through the school's

---

'If they're not hopping on a bus to St Paul's Cathedral, visiting the zoo or going to art galleries and museums, they are doing a walking tour around London.'

---

office). Grafton has partnerships with art professionals, a specialist art and design teacher and an artist in residence, believing that time given to creative subjects helps children achieve in other areas.

The interior of the school is charming, if a little cramped (could be because every inch of space is covered with student displays). The Victorian building is DDA compliant and has a lift for wheelchair users. A 3.5m refurb means all classrooms are now up to spec and there's as a new sports hall and reception play area. Library is still a work in progress but promises to be a great space.

Outside is an oasis of calm – amazing considering proximity to the very urban and not very pretty Seven Sisters Road. Grounds are fairly large for an inner-city school and in addition to the playground there is a quiet formal garden with benches for students to have lunch and read (undergoing a refurb during our visit) and a wildlife garden. This mini eco system with pond and bug hotel feels a million miles from the city. 'Many parents volunteer their time in the garden and elsewhere', we are told. At the end of the wildlife garden is a glass building that we thought was a greenhouse, it's actually the art room, a quirky space crammed with creative materials.

In the assembly hall we were treated to a music assembly in Swahili, just one of the 34 languages spoken here. On site translators assist parents from the three main non-English speaking groups – Somalian, Turkish and Bangladeshi and the school told us, 'We do what we can to make parents from all sectors of society feel included.'

The students we met were a highly articulate bunch – happy, confident and engaging. They loved their school and the opportunities it offered. One told us, 'Julia Donaldson has visited the school and some paralympians came to talk to us, which was amazing and inspiring.' Another said he loved the cricket and football 'and we've won many

tournaments.' A few negative comments about the lunches (free of charge for all pupils) and we thought that some of the food did look pretty unappetising. It seems almost churlish to mention this when for some pupils it may be the only cooked meal they get in a day.

Parents and pupils generally seemed extremely happy with their school. One parent did mention that she would like more sporting activities within the school day as opposed to just afternoon clubs, although she added that the Grafton school day is such a busy one, she's not sure where they would fit it in. Another told us, 'The school is amazing at being pro-active, especially with day trips. If they're not hopping on the bus to St Paul's Cathedral, visiting the zoo or going to art galleries and museums, they're doing a walking tour around London. That's the benefit of being so inner city with free bus travel.' The quality of teaching came in for particular praise. One mother told us, 'My older children go to private schools and I know that the teaching my youngest is getting here is better than they received at her age.' She also said that there is

a very high ratio of staff to pupils – 1:6 in the first two years – again, as good, as if not better than at some independent schools.

The Grey Coat Hospital

Greycoat Place, London, SW1P 2DY

State • Pupils: 1,010, 40 boys in the sixth form • Ages: 11–18 • C of E

Tel: 020 7969 1998
Fax: 020 7828 2697
Email: info@gch.org.uk
Website: www.gch.org.uk

50

Headteacher: Since 2011, Ms Siân Maddrell BA (40s). Educated at Surbiton High, followed by a degree in French at Durham. After gaining her PGCE at Oxford, she began her teaching career at Grey Coat in 1992, soon becoming head of modern languages and one of the first advanced skills teachers in the country. Left Grey Coat in 2000 and later became the first vice principal of Pimlico Academy. Friendly, thoughtful, efficient and clearly devoted to her school. Takes great pride in her pupils and their achievements. Not above picking up stray litter in the playground.

'We want to enable girls to take charge of their learning, make decisions based on Christian values, live in the world as independent women and meet the challenges of the 21st century,' she told us. 'We just try to focus on our pupils. It's a very ambitious school and the students will tell you that the expectations and aspirations are really high for everybody. It's about empowering the pupils to do their best. We want girls to be confident enough to be able to seize every opportunity.'

Enjoys sport, theatre and travel – 'I'm very interested in other countries and cultures.' Married with two sons, so 'most of my free time is spent with my family.'

Academic matters: School is regularly rated outstanding by Ofsted. Recently received congratulatory letter from local MP and schools minister praising pupils and staff for position in the performance tables and saying 'it is clear that your school has equipped its pupils to be successful hereafter, both in terms of their readiness for further study and in terms of their readiness to enter the world of work in due course.'

Excellent exam results again in 2014. Eighty-five per cent of students gained five or more A*-C GCSEs including English and maths. Girls take between nine and 13 GCSEs. At A level, more than 71 per cent A*/B. For the past two years, Grey Coat has been in the top 100 non-selective schools in the country in terms of GCSE results and progress. Good range of subjects on offer to GCSE, including Latin,

business studies and computing. Pre-U offered in Latin, Greek and art history, all of which are taught at neighbouring Westminster School. 'The pupils love their lessons at Westminster,' the head told us. A level subjects include film studies and sociology as well as more traditional fare. Biology, English, history, maths, psychology and religious studies currently very popular. EPQ is becoming increasingly fashionable.

Grey Coat is a specialist language college that emphasises the learning of languages and has an outward looking, global focus. 'We encourage an international outlook as well as strong grades,' says the head. 'It is important for our students to gain an understanding of other countries and cultures and to have an open and inclusive approach, as well as to develop their linguistic skills.' All students

---

External inspirational speakers come in regularly to motivate and encourage the girls

study Spanish and a second modern language (French or German). Most continue with two foreign languages to GCSE. Opportunities to study Mandarin, Japanese and ancient Greek out of school hours. Japanese exchange offered to girls in year 10; other exchange trips to France and Germany, as well as opportunities for work experience in Germany.

International May Fair for younger pupils is an annual highlight. Students are encouraged to represent a country – through fashion, food, dance, ecology and culture. The competition is judged by staff and the prize, awarded to the most impressive tutor group, is a trip to Paris. School is excellent at offering incentives to pupils; girls are encouraged to be competitive. Pupils regularly win local and national science and maths competitions.

Grey Coat prides itself on being an inclusive school. SEN pupils make good progress academically and are fully involved in school life. All year 7 girls are screened for learning difficulties on entry to school. Small support groups for literacy, numeracy and social skills run at lunchtime for younger girls. Five per cent have a statement of special educational needs. Gifted and talented extension programmes in place for more able.

Average class size is 26, with a maximum of 30. No setting in year 7. Year 8 pupils setted for English, maths, science and languages.

Games, options, the arts: Good level of participation in wide variety of sport. 'We are the Westminster sports champions in practically everything and we provide a rich variety of sports,' says the head. Opportunities for fencing, squash, ice-skating and athletics as well as team sports. Currently Westminster netball champions. 'We've struggled a bit with athletics as we have to bus the pupils over to Battersea Park,' admits bursar. Massive sports hall at Regency Street site. Annual gym and dance display.

Creative subjects taken seriously. Excellent facilities in art and design; these remain very popular subjects and the quality of art displays is very high. 'The standard of art work is mind-blowing,' according to one parent. Music and drama both strong. Instrumental and singing lessons are subsidised by school's foundation. Good range of choirs, bands, string and jazz groups and orchestra. Several concerts every year. Successful gospel choir recently reached semi-finals of BBC's School Choir of the Year competition.

Roughly 15 pupils a year achieve D of E gold award. Good spread of clubs, including maths challenge, debating, football, trampolining and creative writing. External inspirational speakers come in regularly to motivate and encourage the girls.

Talent show at the end of the Easter term is eagerly anticipated while staff pantomime is apparently 'the best day' of the school year

Workshops led by outsiders a regular feature of the education offered here. School takes part in BBC News School Report, enabling pupils to make their own news reports for a live audience. Students develop their journalistic skills and have a ball.

Lots of time for fun here too. Talent show at the end of the Easter term is eagerly anticipated while staff pantomime is apparently 'the best day' of the school year. 'It's absolutely hilarious watching the teachers,' said one pupil. Post-GCSE celebration for year 11s includes a fashion show of their textiles work.

Background and atmosphere: Originally founded for boys – by eight merchants of Westminster on St Andrew's day in 1698. In 1706 Queen Anne granted the Grey Coat Hospital Foundation a royal charter and her portrait hangs in pride of place in the Great Hall. Original wooden boards detailing the names and donations of 18th century benefactors line the stairs. In 1874 Grey Coat Hospital became a girls' school, under church management. Whole school was evacuated during the war and its buildings suffered significant bomb damage.

A C of E school – head says 'Christian values play a key part in what we aim to do here.' Church services held each term either in Westminster Abbey or St Margaret's, including a service on Ash Wednesday and a July celebration to which new pupils (and their parents) are invited. 'It's a lovely event – beautifully done,' said a parent. Confirmation services take place at Westminster Abbey and school has its own chaplain.

School occupies two fabulous buildings in the heart of Westminster. Huge quantity of traffic and people encircling it on the streets outside.

Strikingly beautiful building in Greycoat Place, freshly painted and well polished. Statuettes of Grey Coat boy and girl adorn the front façade of the school. Wonderful entrance hall, glistening with trophies and artwork. School celebrates the achievements of the girls at every opportunity. In 1998 the school celebrated its 300th anniversary by opening a new upper school building on Regency Street, having sold another site on Sloane Square.

Original building at Greycoat Place is used by the younger pupils (years 7 to 9) but lots of coming and going of pupils from one site to another. Fantastic new arts block, includes swish drama studios where recent productions have included Shakespearean plays and The Madness of George III. 'Drama is one of those things that is taken very seriously at Grey Coat and the performances are very professional,' we were told. Facilities hired out to National Youth Theatre in holidays.

Welcoming staff. Healthy female/male ratio and mix of long-servers and newly qualified teachers. 'A positive balance,' says the head. Turnover of staff can be high, with up to 20 per cent a year leaving, but 'there's no clear pattern.'

Symbiotic relationship with Westminster School. Grey Coats go there for lectures, some lessons and Oxbridge preparation, while graduate trainee teachers from Westminster come here to

gain experience of teaching in a state school. 'It's wonderful for our students that they have these opportunities,' says the head.

Pastoral care and discipline: Pastoral care is a major strength of the school. 'Each girl is part of a tutor group family and a year group family, so each feels looked after here,' says the head. Strict code of conduct, but relatively few behavioural issues here. Older girls are given plenty of responsibility, with 40 prefects in final year. Girls can become ambassadors for their year group, having successfully explained at interview why they should be chosen. 'There is a strong sense of community here,' says the head. 'We have counsellors, student counsellors, and older students working with younger pupils. It's about creating a sense that we're all in this together.' It certainly seems to be working well. A learning mentor is on hand to help girls organise themselves if needed, as well as a drop-in school nurse.

Girls start off in smaller, lower school – helps them cope better with the progression to upper school. 'It's rare to hear of anyone being miserable here,' a parent told us. 'The school keeps a close eye on its pupils and intervenes quickly if things are going awry.'

Food thought to be 'very good, with lots of choice' according to one pupil. Vast quantities of pizzas being eaten at break on the day we visited

Food thought to be 'very good, with lots of choice' according to one pupil. Vast quantities of pizzas being eaten at break on the day we visited. Oyster card system in place so girls don't need to carry money and the canteen is open from breakfast onwards. School is confident that 'we'd know if a girl wasn't eating.'

Head is justifiably proud of the excellent attendance record of 98 per cent throughout the year – rating it the third highest in the UK. 'All our pupils came in when the recent tube strike was on,' says the head. Pupils with 100 per cent attendance and punctuality for a year get a trip to the theatre.

Pupils and parents: 'A real mix,' the head told us. Twenty-eight per cent of pupils eligible for Pupil Premium. Two-thirds from minority ethnic groups. A quarter whose first language is not English – more than 50 languages spoken at home, including Yoruba, Swahili, Spanish, French and Dutch.

Big inner-city blend of families, including daughters of politicians and education professionals. School recently hit the headlines with the news that former education secretary Michael Gove is sending his daughter here. Old Greys include TV presenter Sarah Greene and Tamsin Dunwoody MP. Recent leaver is Ebony-Jewel Rainford-Brent, the first female black cricketer to play for the England team (she presented awards at last prizegiving). Many old girls remain loyal to the school and return to the annual school celebration service in Westminster Abbey each year.

Entrance: Huge catchment area from the dioceses of London and Southwark. Pupils travel from as far away as Essex and Kent and are rarely local. Total of 151 places offered in year 7. Fifteen language places (following an aptitude test which 450 sit); 88 C of E places; 28 other church places; 20 open places.

Priority given to looked-after children, then siblings, church attendance for church places and a distance tie-breaker. The comprehensive intake is placed into bands following an assessment test – 25 per cent places to band 1, 50 per cent places to band 2 and 25 per cent to band 3. Offers sent out in March.

Open events for year 6 pupils in September and early October each year. Sixth form open events in November. Relatively little movement of pupils.

'We are a very stable population,' says the bursar. Once pupils are here, they tend to stay put, even if it means travelling long distances. In-year admissions are dealt with by the local authority. Forty boys in sixth form, all 'charming,' according to one member of staff.

Exit: Around a quarter leave after GCSEs, usually for schools closer to home or offering subjects not available here. Their places are taken by a fresh intake – the head says 'it's a fresh start for all.' Around 90 per cent go on to higher education. School encourages pupils to aim for top universities and some 40 per cent go to Russell Group universities. In 2014 destinations included Oxford, Cambridge, Exeter, St Andrews, Leeds, Durham, Nottingham, Bristol and Manchester. Popular subjects include medicine, sciences, maths, English, religious studies and classics.

Money matters: Parents' Guild raises money each year for both the school and charity. Recently paid for a beautiful stained glass window by Michael Coles. Parents are asked to contribute a small amount of money on a monthly or annual basis.

Remarks: A sensational mix of high academic standards strongly supported by caring and devoted staff. No wonder they are prepared to travel for hours each day to be part of this buzzing school. The girls we met were charming, articulate, interesting and purposeful. Their pride in the school was striking. Not only are they ambitious and successful but they're also happy. On the day we visited, groups of girls were sitting cross-legged on the tarmac playground at break time, chatting and laughing as though they didn't have a care in the world.

The Hall School

23 Crossfield Road, London, NW3 4NU

Independent • Pupils: 460 • Ages: 4–13 • C of E • Fees (per term): 4,820 – £5,480

Tel: 020 7722 1700
Fax: 020 7483 0181
Email: office@hallschool.co.uk
Website: www.hallschool.co.uk

6

Head: Since September 2013, Christopher Godwin, previously head of Bedford Prep. Read geography at Loughborough, then masters in Middle Eastern studies at Durham. Joined Bedford in 1993 as second master and director of studies before taking over the headship four years later. Gentle and unassuming; keen and active sportsman, particularly rugby – now as coach rather than player.

Entrance: Competition for entrance is keen and applications restricted to those registering before their first birthday – even so, the school is three times over-subscribed. At 3, parents discuss with the head whether a child will enter at 4 or 5 (32 places at 4, 22 at 5). All applicants are tested in the same year – 4+ entrants in January for September, 5+ entrants in late April/May for the following September (school tests close together to ensure the comparison is as fair as possible.) Boys are assessed in groups of six and the school is looking for 'happy, well-adjusted little chaps who want to have a go,' says junior school head, Kirsty Anderson. 'We want

---

A hard core of clever boys is stretched in every direction, producing confident and ever more articulate pupils

---

them to be responsive, able to concentrate and integrate with others. We're not looking for them to be intellectually precocious, just natural and spontaneous.' Even so, mistakes have been known, and though every effort is made to support the strugglers, a child may occasionally be guided elsewhere. Until now, the school has relied solely on its own testing, but is contemplating contacting feeder nurseries for more background. Looks 'fondly' on siblings, but no guarantees – 'It has to be the right school for the individual child'. Occasional places arise at other times, so always worth contacting the school.

Exit: Seventy per cent to top London day schools, particularly Westminster and St Paul's, but also largish contingents to UCS, City of London, Highgate, Merchant Taylors' and Mill Hill. Sizeable minority to traditional single-sex boarding schools – Eton, Harrow, Winchester, Tonbridge; school trying to spread the word about co-ed boarding but singles only to St Edward's Oxford, Aldenham and Uppingham. Boys carefully guided in their secondary school choice. 'We start talking to parents when boys are in the middle school, suggesting what type of boy would fit what school; we don't like to leave it with a year to go.' The match is made by annual assessment of verbal and non-verbal reasoning – 'We track them over the years on a graph' – as well as day-to-day performance. Scholarship form in year 8 for those contemplating the demanding exams of Westminster and Eton, but not all scholarships derive from this form.

Remarks: Remains confidently the top north London prep school for those looking towards the country's top academic secondary schools. A hard core of clever boys is stretched in every direction, producing confident and ever more articulate pupils. 'They're already talking when they come in at 3 and never stop,' said one teacher.

Long-serving, experienced and enthusiastic staff who clearly love their jobs and the school have won the respect of parents. 'The teaching here is wonderful,' said one parent, whose son arrived in year 5. 'My son just blossomed.' Primarily female teachers in the lower years, predominantly male from year 5, and younger staff encouraged to stay by the clever recent addition of an on-site crèche.

Specialist French, science, music, sport and ICT more or less from the word go. Latin added in year 5, Greek in year 7 for scholarship candidates. Setting in core subjects from year 5 and Latin from year 6. Three sciences, one taught each term. Very well-stocked library with library sessions once a week. ICT provision already notable but the head is looking to spend over £300,000 to create a single network for the entire school. Homework starts gently but builds up to a considerable volume in the upper forms, averaging two preps of 45 minutes for years 7 and 8. No Sats but exams taken seriously with all subjects examined twice yearly in the upper forms.

Housed in three airy and orderly buildings with the junior school (reception to year 3), middle (years 4 and 5) and senior school (years 6-8) on separate sites all within a short walk. Two classes of 16 in reception, re-shuffled to three of 18 in year 1. By year 8, four classes of 12 to 14, with a scholarship form, fast common entrance form and two further parallel classes.

Strong special needs support provided gratis with a full-time learning support co-ordinator and four part-time specialist staff. Most difficulties – mainly problems with literacy – are picked up at the earliest point in the junior school.

On the games front, like most London preps, not overly endowed with outside space, though the junior school benefits from a colourful and imaginatively refurbished playground. Rather tired playground for older boys is on the brink of a re-think. Nonetheless, sport taken seriously with the boys dispatched by coach to East Finchley two afternoons a week and rugby, hockey, cross-country, gymnastics, fencing and five-a-side all on offer. All boys get the chance to represent the school at some time in a team game (nine football teams). County and national representatives at chess, fencing and tennis. Cricket tour of Sri Lanka, football tour of Holland.

Music outstanding at all levels, both in the classroom (two specialist music lesson a week) and outside, with a host of peripatetic teachers. More than three-quarters of the boys play at least one instrument and are encouraged to perform in the large orchestra, string quartets, jazz group and choir, leading to an abundance of music awards. Excellent drama with a highlight annual drama production in summer term which includes every boy in the final year. Boys throughout the school are encouraged to perform in plays, concerts, and in public speaking. Lovely, bright roof-top art room, with a potter's wheel and annual exhibition.

Senior school boys enjoy an enviable common room, known as the Pit, with a focal snooker table and daily newspapers. Vast range of clubs, including cookery, Mandarin, model making, computer maths games etc.

Far more traditionally religious than many nominally Christian schools. Recently built chapel for quiet contemplation, which includes a corner for Jewish worshippers. Grace said before meals, morning assembly, with hymn practice. House system encourages boys to raise money for charity.

Parents mainly from high-powered, high-income backgrounds in the professions, banking and business, who can be – some would say frequently are – fairly demanding. Most are local but a percentage are happy to make the trek from Notting Hill, Holland Park and Islington.

Undoubtedly a super school for the brightest boys, who take away the best grounding possible and a real intellectual curiosity. 'It's often described as a hothouse, but I don't feel it's like that. They're not boffins, just normal, cheerful boys, who are particularly enthusiastic about a concert, a play, football or a piece of pottery.' Most parents concur. 'My son suffers from quite serious dyslexia but he still received the most marvellous education,' said one. 'His general knowledge is really astonishing.' For the right boy there can be few better schools, but some have been known to feel a bit left out in the drive to achieve.

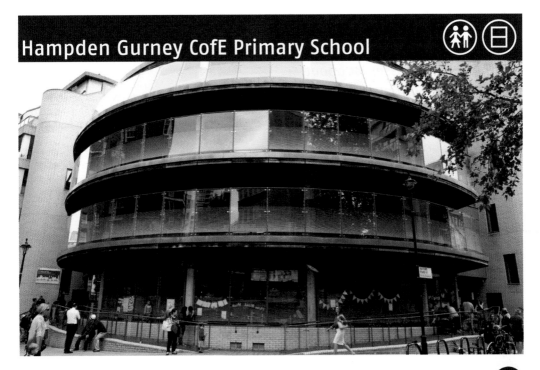

Hampden Gurney CofE Primary School

13 Nutford Place, London, W1H 5HA

State • Pupils: 240 • Ages: 3–11 • Cof E

Tel: 020 7641 4195
Email: office@hampdengurney.co.uk
Website: www.hampdengurneyschool.org.uk

51

Headteacher: Mrs Evelyn Chua (40s). A firm and fashionably-dressed visionary, originates from Malaysia and has worked immensely hard to transform this inner-city C of E primary to a school with beacon status, recently ranked third in the country. A formidable figure, the children certainly respect her, the punishment of last resort for the naughty, but those who've experienced her teaching also find her an inspiration. No British embarrassment about supporting the gifted and talented, but equally determined that every child in this exceptional school will come out a winner.

Entrance: School is affiliated to the High Anglican Church of the Annunciation in Bryanston Street near Marble Arch, and gives priority to church-going applicants, so if sung mass and ample evidence of the Virgin are not part of your belief system, not the school for you. Don't relax your church attendance either once your eldest has secured a place – sibling priority only as a tie-break. Heavily oversubscribed, with 55 applicants for nursery and 160 for 30 reception places in 2014. No automatic transfer from nursery to reception.

Exit: Results to make many a prep school head weep. Last year, 16 academic, four music and three art scholarships, as well as two bursaries. 'We don't give specific preparation, but we just teach them very well,' says the head, and clearly 'very well' is

---

No British embarrassment about supporting the gifted and talented

very well indeed. Recent awards have taken pupils to Latymer Upper, City of London Boys and Girls, Notting Hill and Ealing, St Benedict's, Westminster Under, St Paul's Girls, Cardinal Vaughan and Colet Court, with others to eg Highgate, Queen's College, St Marylebone, Holland Park and Chelsea Academy.

Remarks: Long-serving head is clearly able to stretch and enthuse young minds and the busy, well-organised classrooms and dedicated staff (three male teachers) are testament to her management skills. Clearly no area of the curriculum here where good is good enough. Half the pupils come in speaking little English; the rest are prosperous middle class, many from international backgrounds, but nearly all those moving on to secondary school attain top marks in maths, English and science. Specialist teaching in PE, art, DT and music, with a rotation system of teachers two afternoons a week.

Particularly noted for its gifted and talented programme – this is definitely a school where it is cool to be clever. Mrs Chua has high standards and many students reach or exceed them – 'In year 6, some of the children are doing GCSE maths,' said one mother. But also strong (individual and group) out-of-class support for every child who needs it.

A fairly hefty homework diary, particularly for a state primary: 30-45 minutes a night in years 3-5, one hour in year 6, with English, maths and science set nightly and other subjects once a week. Optional holiday homework as well. Well-equipped ICT suite with digital cameras and laptops. Interactive whiteboards in every classroom. ICT taught creatively with an annual ICT week, where even the youngest gets a chance to demonstrate their Spielberg potential. Light and well-equipped rooftop science 'pod'.

Despite its restricted playground space, the school performs sporting miracles with daily sport clubs and specialists provided by the local authority to teach PE, netball, cricket, tennis, tag rugby. Young footballers play for Westminster and regular football competitions with other local schools. Swimming at nearby Seymour Leisure Centre.

Several years ago the school decided to rebuild its worn-out classrooms to match its league-table-topping position and, working with architects Building Design Partnership, sold off part of its land to fund a new building. Now The Beehive, a six-storey dome of steel and glass, has become both a local landmark and an inspiring place to learn, with nursery pupils starting out on the ground floor and progressing to the tent-covered roof as they rise through the curriculum.

Neat and practical red and grey uniform. Strong house system with houses named after eminent Brits and points for everything. Ample extracurricular activity, ranging from sewing and gardening to writing and publishing the school newspaper. Strong emphasis, too, on charitable fundraising. Residential trips to the countryside.

Heavy emphasis on attendance and punctuality (head firmly warns prospective parents against sinful thoughts of mid-term breaks). Escalating punishment system (warning, missing play time, time out, Mrs Chua) but minimum behavioural problems. Indeed classrooms are a model of well-ordered enthusiasm.

Founded in 1863 by Reverend Hampden Gurney, Rector of St Mary's Bryanston Square, the school's ethos is still strongly High Anglican, with compulsory attendance at weekly sung Eucharist and RE teaching firmly rooted in the Church of England.

Mrs Chua has collected more awards than a Brown Owl, everything from the National Association for Able Children Award to Service Excellence Award. Not unnaturally, most parents are immensely positive: 'You couldn't find a better education in the state system,' said one mother, who'd taken her children out of the private sector. And the articulate, confident and happy pupils are the school's best advertisement. One boy, asked about what he liked about the school, replied, 'Everything.'

Hampstead School

Westbere Road, London, NW2 3RT

State • Pupils: 1,245 • Ages: 11–19 • Non–denom

Tel: 020 7794 8133
Fax: 020 7435 8260
Email: enquiries@hampsteadschool.org.uk
Website: www.hampsteadschool.org.uk

Headteacher: Since 2006, Mr Jacques Szemalikowski MA BSc PGCE NPQH CPhys MinstP (early 50s). This head needs no Red Bull! Positively explodes with energy, a dynamo. Five minutes in his company and you are left exhausted. With four young children of his own, this guy is driven. He is here to make a difference, and in his tenure as headmaster of Hampstead School, he has.

A graduate in astrophysics, and a teacher for 25 years before his first headship at The Warwick School, Redhill, Mr Szemalikowski is somewhat old school in his principles and discipline. A misbehaving student can find themselves holed away for the day in the exclusion zone, 'our naughty step' – a small building situated at the back of the playing fields. He makes no apologies for his rigorous approach to education, both for his students and staff members alike. His mantra is 'Every child can achieve, every child will achieve, whatever it takes' – and he does what he can to ensure this is not just hot air. He organises trips to Oxford so that his students can be aspirational: 'I want them to know this can be for them too. I want them to be the movers and shakers of the modern world.'

His staff are not allowed to rest on their laurels either. He doesn't do 'good' – he wants outstanding from his staff and they are expected to attend weekly regular after-school workshops in order to achieve this (the latest Ofsted report commented that there 'wasn't yet enough outstanding teaching.') A recent high turnover of staff, he says, was testimony to their 'tremendous training' which secured them promotional posts in other schools. Like him, don't like him, 'I'm not here to be popular, I'm here to get the job done.'

Hit the headlines recently for reporting the student author of a blog critical of the school to the police and to the universities where he hoped to study.

Academic matters: 2014 saw 55 per cent of pupils achieve 5+ A*-C grades at GCSE including English and maths. A disappointing fall from the year before, after five consecutive years of rising results, but consider that nearly half the pupils are bilingual (63 different nationalities), five per cent are statemented and nearly 40 per cent are on free school meals. Fifteen per cent of grades were A*/A.

A level results 39 per cent A*/B and 19 per cent A*/A. In the top 20 UK state schools for continuing into science A levels after GCSE. Big emphasis on science, and there is the option of triple rather than double science for students who attain at least a level 6 at the end of key stage 3. Maths, too, is

---

A melting pot of culture and diversity, and a whole host of activities to keep even the most apathetic child interested

strong and the school is very involved in maths challenges with students achieving above national average numbers of gold, silver and bronze certificates. The school also offers free Saturday school maths masterclasses for gifted mathematicians from years 5 and 6 of local primary schools.

English and media are popular subjects, and students also have the option of learning Arabic and Italian (as well as French and Spanish). Bilingual homework support is offered. Pupils have six BTecs to choose from including catering and hospitality, and a wide variety of A levels including three new ones in philosophy, creative writing and culture and communication. No subject is offered at GCSE level which can't be carried through to A level. 'We don't stream, we set, so there is movement', the head points out. Maths, English and science setted from year 7. Every faculty in the school has a remunerated teacher responsible for gifted and talented children. There is a clear focus on standards and students are tracked from the moment they arrive. They have individual charts and are monitored six times a year. As soon as a student starts to slip, staff want to know why. An appreciative parent commented that the school is 'quick to congratulate children if they've done well – very good at praising.' Strong curriculum support and SEN help, notably those who arrive with little English, and catch up is rapid: 'assessors couldn't tell the difference between SEN students and non-SEN students', we were told.

Archaic-looking but well-equipped classrooms, most notably the music department, where a large cash injection has meant up-to-date technology. Through their status as a technology college they have been able to implement a £0.5 million upgrade to the library, creating an independent learning centre combining traditional library resources with new technologies. (That said, the library is actually quite scant on books itself.) Masses of extracurricular activity perhaps also reflects the academic ethos of the school: the school's debating society has had spectacular success in Model United Nations – with ongoing victories both as a delegation and individuals. Involved in Jack Petchey Speak out Challenge and has a Youth Parliament.

Games, options, the arts: Fizzes with activity – plenty to do. Music is popular and heavy investment in this department has meant that each of the school's 1,300 students is offered the opportunity to learn a musical instrument. Pupils can choose to join a wide variety of musical activities, including senior or junior orchestra, guitar orchestra, jazz band, junior choir and many more.

Enthusiastic drama – great on site replica fringe theatre, partnerships with the Hampstead Theatre Club, Royal Court and Tricycle all help to inspire; a few students had extras parts in the Dustin Hoffman movie Quartet.

Strong sport, particularly football, basketball and table tennis. The football team recently won the Bliss Inner London Cup, becoming the first Camden school to win the trophy; the girls' basketball team won the Under 15 Championships in 2013. A team of students and staff also recently completed the 56-mile London to Brighton bike ride. Limited playing fields, but somewhat redeemed by its other on site facilities including a basketball/netball court, a dance studio, a fitness suite, a multi-use Astroturf and an on-site pool (that could do with some love).

The plethora of extracurricular activities includes gardening (they have an allotment which grows produce for the catering department), poetry, rugby, dance and aikido clubs, plus several music ensembles. For the more dedicated student, those who lack quiet space at home and those who need extra help, there are after-school homework sessions.

Background and atmosphere: Hampstead Schmampstead – this school is no more in Hampstead than Arsenal (FC) is in Arsenal! Situated in between colourful but definitely not posh Cricklewood, Kilburn and semi-posh West Hampstead, you can see the flag before you see the school. Red and emblazoned with the school logo, the flag waves proudly high above this impressive large red-brick building. The main building, formerly the old Haberdashers' Boys' school, was built in 1908, and indeed on first appearance promises great things.

One is immediately struck by the amount of banners displayed on the building's facade: 'Best ever GCSE results', 'Read more, earn more, learn more', 'Leaders of tomorrow' and so on. Mr Szemalikowski, who has been on three trips to the USA (Chicago, Boston and DC), says it's very much an American thing to do: 'It reinforces key aspirations at all times.' Tear your eyes away, walk up the ramped approach, through a plate glass entrance into a fairly modern foyer and see more slogans – this time on a wall-mounted flat screen TV, and from the wisdom of Galileo: 'Measure what is measurable,' the theme of the week.

Mosey on through the foyer to a vast concrete, central open air atrium faced by a modern teaching block and broken only by a dark and reedy pond – 'there are fish in there.' Mr Szemalikowski smiles brightly on our tour. The school was due for a substantial rebuild in 2011, but sadly the national school redevelopment scheme was axed by the coalition government. Refurbishment started and ended on new loos – £125,000 spent on giving them a spruce up as 'the test of any state school is its loos', says the head. (Although why the staff room is right next to them – the mind boggles).

A well-equipped ICT and catering block (with industrial spec kitchens) looks in stark contrast to the rest of the school. Good sixth form centre with huge common room overlooking the central atrium. Lucky sixth formers can feast their eyes on yet more banners – this time displayed on the walls around the central atrium – (did we mention Big Brother?) Wheelchair access throughout – the school is completely DDA compliant. There is a disability resource which can cater for up to seven students with complex needs. These students are fully integrated into mainstream lessons.

This is a big, sprawling campus, and easy to lose your bearings, especially for new pupils coming from little primaries. Lest you forget where you are, fear not, everything is logoed – from school water bottles to the dustbins, another of the head's ideas of constant reinforcement of group identity. Pupils are a mixed and diverse bunch, but all seem to share a common loyalty towards the school and enjoy being there. One 13-year-old pupil told us: 'I love the responsibility they give us. I was on a panel to help elect the last deputy head of the school.' Badges are awarded to students who meet standards and display good behaviour – bronze through to platinum. Get platinum, you can have lunch with the head! Students' pride in their school is evident in the total lack of graffiti, vandalism and litter.

Commendable efforts to involve the outside world and lots of whole school charity work. An appreciation of the diversity of the school is prevalent – Black History Month, Gay/Transgender Month, a recent trip to Auschwitz, to name but a few. The school culture involves loads of celebration and reward of achievement and improvement.

Pastoral care and discipline: If punctuality and attendance ain't your bag, this ain't your school. Mr Szemalikowski and the entire senior management team are at the gates to greet pupils from 8.40am, after which sluggards have to report individually.

(Early risers' club offered from 7.30am onwards for an extra cost of 50p). Attendance has improved dramatically since Mr Szemalikowski came on board. He is completely intolerant of any absence during term time (other than illness) and allows pupils two days a year for religious holidays. 'Every day counts', is one of the school's many slogans.

He is the head that reintroduced uniform to the school, and according to an ex-student, it has made a huge change – 'now everyone is on a level playing field.' Different ties denote whether or not a student has been trained in peer mentoring, and any student feeling vulnerable can approach those who have. Automatic exclusion for fighting, drugs, alcohol or carrying a weapon (as was recently the case with a student found to be carrying a knife). The head walks around daily to keep in touch, and lo and behold, if a student is wandering aimlessly in the grounds, they are stopped and questioned – and only when Mr Szemalikowski is entirely satisfied with their response are they sent on their way. Good level of security – brings to bear the stark reality that you are in an inner-city school.

However, despite Mr Szemalikowski's robust attitude to discipline, one parent says, 'it doesn't go far enough'. She feels that students are given too many chances, although she does acknowledge that the exclusion zone is a good deterrent – 'my daughter was in there once, and has said she won't be going there again.' (It is a small outhouse building, which can hold up to six students at any one time, with no contact with their peers for the

whole day). Classes seemed to be well behaved for the most part – with the exception of the odd class joker – and a good level of concentration in what they were doing. PE, however, was on the very raucous side.

Non-teaching heads of year are one of Mr Szemalikowski's brainchilds. The idea is that the heads of year are there solely for the pupils' welfare needs and not to be distracted with marking homework. It works brilliantly, one parent enthused. 'It means that if I have any concerns about my child I know I can contact the head of year, and they are always available to speak to, no matter what time of day.' Year common rooms are 'exclusive to Hampstead School' – the idea being that year groups can eat together at lunchtimes and the heads of year have their offices in there and are always available at lunchtime too.

Buddying, mentoring and restorative justice schemes all bolster pupils' sense of security, and bullying is rigorously kept in check. 'The House', situated a stone's throw from the Exclusion Zone, is a cuboid block on the perimeter where you go if you are troubled – or troubling – and is well staffed with welfare workers, counsellors and other supportive types.

Recent school awards include: British Council International Award at Outstanding level; The Prince's Teaching Institute English kite mark; UNICEF Rights Respecting School (Level 1) Award; Pupils' and Parents' Achievement for All Quality Mark (first school to achieve this and now a national roll-out school); International School Award; School Games (Silver) Award; Gold TfL Sustainable Travel award; Safe School Award.

Pupils and parents: From moneyed West Hampstead, to recent refugees in temporary housing, the demographic is diverse – all the more admirable when one considers how far the school has come. One pupil told us, 'I love the fact that one of my best friends is black, the other wears a hijab'. A real feature of the school, we were told, is that no ethnic groups predominate. Nineteen per cent is white British – the largest group.

Former pupils include Sadie Frost, Rachel Yankey, ex-MP Julia Drown, Alec Bogdanovic, Jake Lensen, Tobias Hill, Zadie Smith.

Entrance: From up to 71 primary schools (no named feeders; totally non-selective), and covering three boroughs – Camden, Brent and Barnet (admissions managed by Camden) – the school is now oversubscribed in every year. One parent, a born and bred Cricklewood local, remarked how the school used to have a 'terrible reputation', and no right-thinking parent, given the choice, would have sent their kids there – but she said, 'that's changed since Mr

Szemalikowski came on board'. Oversubscribed sixth form both from internal and external candidates. Twenty year 12 places are available to external applicants that meet the entry requirements – which vary according to the level of course they want to pursue.

Exit: About 70 per cent stay for the sixth form, the remainder go to other colleges and sixth forms. Some 70 per cent of sixth formers move on to an impressive range of higher education – from chemistry at King's College, law at Bristol and maths at Leeds to a paid apprenticeship in aerospace engineering with Air Bus, at University of Surrey (which was big news because the student beat a large number of applicants for the prestigious placement). One former student has become an international DJ and producer as a result of studying A level music at the school.

Remarks: The head's energy and vision has already worked wonders on this school. A melting pot of culture and diversity, and a whole host of activities to keep even the most apathetic child interested. However, this school ain't for the faint hearted – large and imposing, and big on discipline and punctuality. In need of a massive cosmetic makeover (Mr Gove!)

Heathside Preparatory School

16 New End, London, NW3 1JA

Independent • Pupils: 250 • Ages: 2–11 • Non–denom • Fees (per term): £3,200 – £4,250

Tel: 020 7794 5857
Fax: 020 7435 6434
Email: info@heathside.net
Website: www.heathside.net

Headmistress: Since the school's foundation in 1993, Ms Melissa Remus Elliot MA PG Dip (40s), who is also joint owner. She grew up all over the US, following her father's work, and attended Duke University and The American University, Washington. She worked as a Washington intern and on several Broadway shows before moving to the UK and training as a teacher. During three years' teaching she formulated an idea of her ideal school and set up Heathside with her business partner and co-head (now retired), Jill White, becoming the youngest head teacher in the country in her 20s. She also got an MA in counselling aspects of education. She is married with four children, all at Heathside, 'which gives me a good insight into what actually goes on in the classrooms'. Overflowing praise from parents: 'a very open-minded and dynamic person, relentlessly striving to find ways to make the school better'; 'open and honest in a very refreshing way'; 'both pragmatic and inspirational'; 'extraordinary ability to retain a thorough portrait of each child'; 'unbelievably energetic and gung-ho'.

Entrance: Takes 10 2 and 3-year-olds into the nursery class. Most places go to siblings and those who sign up very early, though it's worth trying for an afternoon place if you have been less well organised. More join to form two reception classes of 15. Children visit for a day to ensure they and the school are a good match. 'If there is any question mark we may ask them to come in for several days. We try to be careful to make sure that the school suits the child. We don't take children with behavioural difficulties or serious special needs, and if we have any concerns about academic ability, we would speak in detail with the parents and teachers about whether we could create a special programme to support the child.'

Exit: Most move on at 11, the vast majority to the local independents: Highgate, Haberdashers, UCS, South Hampstead, Francis Holland and Channing. Some to City Boys' or Girls', some very bright children to Westminster, St Paul's or North London Collegiate, and some who prefer a less intense environment to Aldenham. A few to local state schools, eg Camden School for Girls and St Marylebone. Generally a good haul of scholarships. Parents

Everyone from year 1 upwards goes to Hampstead Heath for an hour at lunchtime most days to climb trees, run around, build dens, play in the snow

comment on 'Melissa's dogged commitment to find places for all her pupils....she reads children exceptionally well'.

Remarks: Started in 1993 on the site – and with much of the equipment and quite a few of the staff and pupils – of a former prep school that had come to a rocky end. Occupies two buildings a couple of hundred metres apart in the middle of Hampstead, and uses every inch of the limited space. Aims to let every child follow their strengths and interests, with plenty of extracurricular activities and fun, practical lessons.

The lower school is housed in a converted and extended church hall, which includes a music practice room, a hall used for gym, yoga, music and drama as well as assemblies, a nursery room with comfortable sofas, and art and science rooms. 'Science teaching brilliant – really hands-on and fun,' said a parent. 'And my daughter is very excited to be allowed to chop wood and use a glue gun in DT.' 'Can't imagine my kids being more stimulated or jolly,' said another.

Since the school is non-selective it includes a fair ability range, but classes are small and the lower school has plenty of teaching assistants. 'Learning is really celebrated,' said a parent. Several ability groups for maths from year 1 upwards. 'Children have different ways of learning, and we group them accordingly. Some need lots of reinforcement, but we never assume that a child is no good at maths. We work in a way that helps them to understand, and once the building blocks are firm, they can fly.' When we visited, a group of children who found times tables challenging were learning them through pictures and stories, whilst another group (of year 4 pupils) were working on secondary level problems.

Several literacy groups – 'They are all good readers, but some have difficulty with writing'. These get intensive tuition in years 3 and 4, ready for the lead-up to year 6 exams. 'Because we don't have to prepare them for 7+ exams, it doesn't matter if they take longer to come through.'

French is taught throughout the school, with plenty of songs and games, by a teacher who talks entirely in French from the start. 'They think she only speaks French, and they learn amazingly quickly.' Latin is a 'massive hit,' said a parent; also a Mandarin club.

Inevitably the pressure rises as the 11+ approaches, but parents praise the imaginative approach. 'They're pushed in their ability to write essays and do comprehensions, but it's not a brutal régime,' said one. 'In a typical Heathside move, an ex-parent who is a literature professor comes in twice a week and encourages them to read and enjoy sophisticated texts. They're worked incredibly hard, but it's very exciting.'

The full-time identified needs coordinator is renowned for helping with dyslexia and dyspraxia. One-to-one help costs extra, but most learn in compatible groups. The school would not suit an autistic child – 'We're too busy and active' – and would hesitate to take one with other behavioural difficulties – 'We have to think about the rest of the class.' However, a girl who came into year 4 with limited experience of maths 'blossomed, and got into all the secondary schools she tried'.

Small groups work at their own pace in various nooks and crannies. 'You may find your child having a lesson in what looks like a broom cupboard – but they are learning,' said a parent. Prose and poetry competitions, with everyone writing poems and learning a piece to recite, and plenty of drama from Macbeth to Pirates of Penzance. 'We do really challenging stuff, but in a fun way.'

The full-time music director is 'amazingly inspirational' – everyone learns the ocarina and recorder and many play the piano and other instruments too. Several instrumental groups and choirs, and termly formal and informal concerts 'spur them on'.

Chess is a big deal here – teams go off for weekend tournaments, and Heathside has been the English Primary Schools Chess Association National Small Schools champion for eight years. 'It's a big social scene,' said a parent, 'and they're very good at encouraging girls to play.' A 'huge variety' of other clubs including gym, art and science. Parents talk of 'amazing trips', including ice skating at the Tower of London and 'going to France for the day to meet pen-pals'.

The school's only outside space is a small playground with climbing frame alongside the lower school. However, nearly everyone from year 1 upwards goes to Hampstead Heath for an hour at lunchtime most days – the younger ones go three times a week – to climb trees, run around, build dens, play in the snow. The children also play sport every day, at UCS and Swiss Cottage; on Friday morning they have a swimming and multisports programme – ranging from rock climbing to judo – at Swiss Cottage leisure centre, culminating in a Dim T lunch. Specialist coaches include an ex-international Sri Lankan cricketer and an ex-professional footballer, and the football, swimming and cricket teams are rarely beaten. Many teams are co-ed – 'Our best footballer is a girl' – and girls' sport was boosted by the arrival of a coach specialising in rounders, field hockey and netball. Sports day includes 'proper races' at Parliament Hill Fields running track.

Parents praise the family atmosphere, with friendships across the year groups. 'There's a real relationship between teachers and children,' said a parent. 'They are strict about talking and noise, because they have to be in a building that size, but then you see a child hurtling downstairs with no shoes on to do some photocopying for their teacher. It's an adventurous, common-sense and human approach.' Another parent commented that she is delighted with the 'close and intimate, nurturing

atmosphere which generates a real appetite to learn. It's very warm, very flexible'.

Huge mix of families including some wealthy, famous parents and quite a few international families. But it tends to attract those who are not happy with the more traditional private sector ethos; quite a few have moved their children (often reluctantly) from state primaries. Parents tend to become closely involved: one dad runs a gifted maths club, another comes in to talk about astronomy, many parents help with festivals such as Chinese New Year and Halloween, others help run the library or become class reps. 'We're an interesting mix,' said a mother. 'Most people are very friendly and very engaged with the school.' 'We absolutely love it here,' said a father, 'and so does every other parent we've met.'

Hereward House School

14 Strathray Gardens, London, NW3 4NY

Independent • Pupils: 180 • Ages: 4–13 • Non–denom • Fees (per term): £4,480 – £4,965

Tel: 020 7794 4820
Fax: 020 7794 2024
Email: headmaster@herewardhouse.co.uk
Website: www.herewardhouse.co.uk

Headmaster: Since 2011, Tom Burden MA (40-ish), formerly deputy head. Mr Burden grew up on the Isle of Wight, where he was educated at local schools before proceeding to Oxford (with a scholarship) to study theology. After graduating, he started

teaching as a bit of fresh air before settling down to something earnest, but was soon gripped. Five years at Alleyn Court School, Southend, then a further five at boarding prep Lockers Park, Hertfordshire, where he headed the English department and ran the scholarship set, while still managing plenty of sports coaching. 'I loved every minute and took away the idea that boys should be boyish, enjoy their childhood and be trusted to have responsibilities.' A similar combination in a London day school is rare, but Hereward House was a 'good match', and his headship has been more about evolution than revolution. Continues to teach English, plus some sports coaching. 'I love teaching and you really get to know the boys.'

Prides himself on 'not being a distant chap', and boys clearly warm to him. Hands go up faster than lightning in the classroom or on the stairs and text messages are sent mid cricket match to update him on progress. Still dedicated to getting the best out of each boy at CE, he gives up holidays and weekends for extra tuition.

Parents are appreciative of his approach and approachability: 'He's on the doorstep every morning to greet each boy – to congratulate him on a brilliant prep or great cricket innings – or simply to suggest he may wish to straighten his tie.' Keen on improving communication with parents, he's recently introduced a newsletter and weekly email. 'He's contactable round the clock and responds promptly to text, emails and phone messages,' said one mother. A sports fan and regular at Lords, Mr Burden relaxes by playing football, bowls and

cricket. His Boy's Own enthusiasms include: Bletchley Park, the Underground, the Gothic Revival and the London sewer system. He's also 'hugely interested' in politics, philosophy and religion.

Moving on in January 2015 to head The Pilgrims' School in Winchester. His successor will be Pascal Evans, currently director of studies at Westminster Under School; he was previously head of French there. A keen runner, he is married to Akiyo.

Entrance: Register by the time your son is a year old at the latest. Head sees all parents and boys, when boys are 3. 'I make a significant commitment to finding the right boy,' he says. Siblings guaranteed a place, the rest chosen on 'suitability' rather than ability. 'We could test to find the most academic, but we're not going down that route,' says the head firmly. 'What we're really looking for is a good chap to have in the place, a player rather than spectator.' Offers – conditional on staying till the age of 13 – are made one year before entry at rising five. Occasional places thereafter due to relocation, but those on the waiting list get first dibs. Occasional places at end of year 6.

Exit: The school won't prepare for entrance tests at 7 or 8. 'Our record at 13 is so strong, there's no need to exit early,' says the head.

Historically, Highgate the most popular choice at 13, followed by City and UCS, but good numbers to all the other London day schools, with regular scholarships. 'Our scholarship record is broadly comparable per head to the best schools in the area,' says the head. Scholarships in 2014 included one to St Paul's, one to Highgate, two boys to Westminster via the Challenge (Westminster scholarship exam) and one to Eton with a starred place. Regular places at Eton, Harrow, Rugby and Winchester.

Careful guidance given in the run up to CE. 'Parents here will typically ask: "What is the right school for my son?" rather than saying "which school can you get him into?" They really do want the best fit.'

Remarks: The school was founded in 1951 in its current red-brick Hampstead house. In essence it's still a family business, though now governed by a trust made up of members of the Sampson family.

Though not a school in which selection is made on academic grounds, almost every boy here is above average, with 'the top third as bright as anywhere'. Generally no setting until year 8 (occasionally from year 7), then only in English, maths and Latin. Specialist teaching, in part from year 4, entirely from year 5. French from the start, Latin from year 5, Greek from year 8 (potentially from year 7). Teachers know boys well and respond quickly to their needs. ('Teachers are often outside

Rules kept to a minimum. Beyond the basics, the main principle is that boys should treat one another well and make the most of what's on offer

during pick-up time,' said one parent, 'and will seek you out to talk about your child.') Learning support also fine-tuned, with two specialists to help the struggling ('in the majority of cases, boys come out the other end without a problem,' says the head.) A former barrister provides the stretch needed for the most demanding scholarship papers. Parents feel the school works well for all abilities. 'Our older son is very academic and remains challenged with lots of extra work,' said one, 'while our younger son is smart, but playful, and the school uses a very different approach to stimulate him.' Homework at manageable levels. 'It should be do-able in an hour if working at a steady pace,' says the head.

Sport is 'central to the school life'. Two afternoons of games a week, one on Hampstead Heath, the other in Brondesbury. Cricket and soccer particularly strong and every boy gets to play, with a first, second and third team. 'This is simply too small a school for a boy to be sitting on the sidelines handing out oranges. They love to represent the school.' Punches above its weight – the Colts remain unbeaten for nearly two years – but can struggle against the largest schools. Cross-country also taken seriously, with weekly lessons in the spring term. Fencing, tennis and hockey on offer as clubs, plus timetabled swimming at Swiss Cottage baths just down the road. Smallish playground with an intricate system of who uses what bit when – seems to work like a well-rehearsed ballet.

Almost every boy plays an instrument, half play two or more (the orchestra has nearly 60 members). Form concerts every term. Art, too, highly valued. One of the head's first acts on taking over was to hang boys' work around the school ('I wanted to take art out of the art room') and a cricket-themed display now ornaments his study. Pottery and DT also popular (though a cleverly crafted crossbow did have to be confiscated). Drama taught until the final two years, when academic works takes precedence. Major drama production every other year, with every boy involved.

Loads of clubs, including photography, fencing, tennis, typing, art, music theory, chess, Spanish and science. 'If boys want something else we make it happen,' says the head. Handy prep club, too, nightly from 4pm to 5pm (with flexibility to stay till 6pm). Popular annual ski trip, accompanied by head and parents, where card playing is often a focus of evening activity. 'I believe in cards,' says the head. 'I don't see why they shouldn't learn to play whist and basic bridge.' First school disco held this year, so boys can 'learn how to treat a lady.'

Bright, high-ceilinged classrooms, originally the living quarters of an affluent turn-of-the-century family, complemented by relatively flimsy science and music space, which are top of the head's agenda for a make-over.

This small school revels in its size. The head wants a family atmosphere and does his utmost to make this happen. 'Academic performance is based on the foundation that the school is happy.' All boys are known by name and all are given a position of 'meaningful' responsibility at the top of the school, with eight prefects, four house captains, and further captains for music, drama and games. 'Every boy must have his moment in the sun,' says the head. Parents definitely approve: 'Senior boys thrive on the responsibility and have the confidence to display a fair amount of individuality in how they fill their role.' Two senior boys, for example, are at the door each morning to greet each boy by name. Head has also introduced merit prizes, with bronze, silver and gold awards, form prizes for effort and contribution to the community and school colours for non-academic achievements. Elected school council has considerable sway, 'They wanted more pasta and sweet and sour chicken and that was delivered.'

Rules kept to a minimum. Beyond the basics, the main principle is that boys should treat one another well and make the most of what's on offer. 'Hopefully boys have a sense they are part of the system, not ruled by it. We're looking for good chaps, gentlemen with a general sense of decency.' Parents remark on how considerate boys are to each other – even out of school. Disciplinary problems only of the extremely minor variety like tipping chairs and talking in line. 'I'm very close to the operation,' says the head. 'I walk the school and go out in break to see what's happening.' Staff eat lunch with boys every day to engage boys in friendly conversation. 'It's a great time to find out how things are going.' The head also meets with prefects weekly to discuss concerns they may have about younger boys. 'Everyone knows everyone else; older boys look out for younger ones; the more confident encourage the less so.'

Parents are typical north London professionals, with a cosmopolitan range of nationalities, generally reasonably local. Newly founded PTA, very much part of the head's drive for a sense of community. 'Everyone is very welcoming to newcomers,' says one recent arrival. 'My two boys, who joined higher up the school, have had plenty of invitations.'

Holy Trinity and Saint Silas CofE Primary School

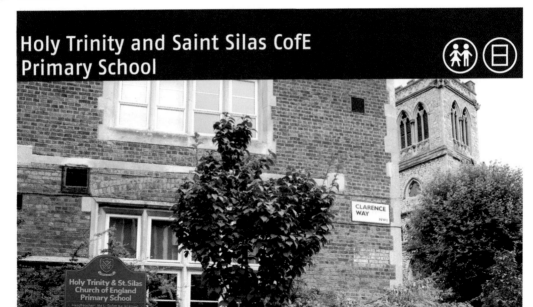

Hartland Road, London, NW1 8DE

State · Pupils: 210 · Ages: 4–11 · Church of England ·

Tel: 020 7267 0771
Fax: 020 7916 5881
Email: admin@holytrinitynw1.camden.sch.uk
Website: camden.schooljotter.com/holytrinitynw1

10

Head: Since 2013, Lorraine Dolan, who was appointed after the tragic death of inspirational head Annie Williams in December 2012. She was previously deputy head of St Paul's Catholic Primary School in Wood Green.

Entrance: After the customary priority for looked-after children, the primary admissions criterion is church attendance, either at The Most Holy Trinity Church across the road or at St Silas the Martyr in Kentish Town. About a third come via this route. When Ms Williams became head, school was very much bottom of the parental-choice agenda, but the intake has altered and now gets more professional parents (including some high-profile political ones). Not too many, school hopes – 'we have a good social mix and want to keep it that way'. At the moment, remains a class and ethnic melting pot, with the largest minority being Bangladeshi and Somali families.

Exit: Mainly to the local comprehensives – Haverstock, William Ellis, Parliament Hill, St Marylebone and Camden School for Girls – but

school has also developed a relationship with The Hall, one of north London's leading prep schools and some year 6 boys have gone there with bursaries before proceeding to leading London independent day schools.

Remarks: This, in the words of Ofsted, is 'an exceptional school' and, without a doubt, its exceptional quality stems from the passion and focus of its 'talented and hardworking' previous head. Ms Williams was a woman who had edited the word 'compromise' from her vocabulary. She built up a team of energetic, often newly-qualified teachers ('we grow our own') – 'I'm very snobbish about teachers – they have to have been to a good university and to have travelled. It gives them a cultural understanding'. The teaching staff is unusually well qualified, with three MAs, two law degrees and three teachers who speak fluent French (so French is taught convincingly from reception), as well as a number of graduate teaching assistants. Ms William's management philosophy included encouraging staff to take a year-long sabbatical every three years to do voluntary work mentoring and coaching.

Housed in a typical Victorian schoolhouse, a meander from tourist-packed Camden Lock. Inside its pristine, soothing interior, however, you'd never guess where you were – fresh flowers, polished parquet and a big red school bell are all from another era.

Despite the fact that the majority of pupils arrive at Holy Trinity with well below average attainment, the school is at the pinnacle of the league tables, with results in English in the top one per cent nationally. Literacy is taught for two hours a day, primarily through poetry and prose. School is strong on story-telling. On the day we visited, a group of eight-year-olds listened spellbound as a young male teacher first played the flute, then, in true Jackanory style, announced: 'And now I'm going to tell you a story'.

All the arts are fundamental to the curriculum. Drama 'has a very big focus' – every year school mounts a whole-school Shakespeare play including every pupil and member of staff and has now helped found a borough-wide Shakespeare festival with five neighbouring primaries. Hardly surprising then that, according to Ofsted: 'Pupils' empathy with the works of Shakespeare is quite remarkable'.

Despite limited square footage, has its own art department and pupils' work is hung boldly throughout the building. Painting even spills out into the large urban playground, where one inner-city wall has been reborn as a rural, summer scene (with a 3D vegetable plot to extend the experience). Music is equally central and Ms Williams insisted all staff learn a musical instrument to perform alongside pupils. Trips are very much part of the education. Visits – free of charge – to the theatre, opera, ballet and museums are planned on a regular basis

Though about 75 per cent of pupils are not Anglicans, the Christian message is strong, with a thoroughly involved parish priest, regular church attendance and class mass held half termly. Grace is said before lunch. Lunch itself is entirely healthy ('We had the smoothie debate. And one person's smoothie is another's fizzy pop') and mealtimes, too, are considered a development opportunity. Music is played and, on Fridays, tablecloths laid. A firm emphasis on good manners. The 'golden rules' dictate: don't talk with your mouth full; learn to use your knife and fork correctly'.

Rules elsewhere are equally clear cut. Attentive good behaviour is the norm, but for those who stray, the first offence means displacement to another class; further disruption means an encounter with the head. Badly behaved parents can also find themselves hauled in front of the head.

Standards may be firmly upheld, but the school is also compassionate and warm. Ms Williams kept an ever-open door. On the day of our visit, one child came in to recount the details of her special day out, quickly followed by an entire class offering cakes they'd just baked. With mums and dads, the same policy applies: 'You can never let anything fester, otherwise it just goes round the playground'.

Takes a pro-active approach to its parents, offering jewellery classes as an incentive to engage with catch-up maths, and parents respond with energetic fund-raising. 'We are very grateful for the wonderful education our children receive,' said one. Ms Williams herself was no ingénue when it came to fund-raising and had won considerable support from charities like John Lyons and the Mercer's Company, who have underwritten school trips and paid for 30 laptops.

Superb is Ofsted's summary of the Holy Trinity and St Silas experience and parents agree: 'Children want to come to school. They think it's fun'.

La Sainte Union Catholic Secondary School

Linked school: LaSwap Sixth Form Consortium, 135

Highgate Road, London, NW5 1RP

State · Pupils: 1,220 · Ages: 11–18 · RC ·

Tel: 020 7428 4600
Fax: 020 7267 7647
Email: general@lsu.camden.sch.uk
Website: www.lasainteunion.org.uk

Headteacher: Since 2008, Mrs Maureen Williams (40s). Educated at a convent school in Hampshire, read English and medieval literature at Exeter University before taking her PGCE at Digby Stuart College, Roehampton. Taught English at St Joseph's College, Croydon and La Retraite Roman Catholic Girls' School in Lambeth, before taking over from long-serving head Sister Teresa and becoming the school's first lay principal, charged with a mission to gently modernise while maintaining the

The gardens to the rear are elegantly laid out with a small orchard and an ample stock of summer roses (sensibly, girls are required to keep to the path)

traditions of La Sainte Union. A calm and competent presence; no doubt the school's illustrious tradition remains in safe hands. Married to a senior probation officer, she enjoys running, walking and good food in her spare time.

Academic matters: One of Camden's top-performing comprehensive schools. In 2014, 81 per cent of pupils achieved 5+ A*-C grades at GCSE including English and maths, with 36 per cent A*/A grades – a significant achievement for a school with no academic selection, and not reached by any fudging of the exam system. Pupils here take a demanding curriculum, with nine and half subjects kept going until GCSE, including a compulsory modern language, ICT and RE. Has specialist status in science and maths and 25 girls a year take all three sciences. Everyone, however, benefits from the science enrichment programme, with a multitude of speakers from UCL and Imperial College (both of which offer work placements). 'Many of the girls come from backgrounds where there is limited experience of higher education,' says the head. 'The programme raises their aspirations.' Science

results have improved significantly, though A level physicists are still a relative rarity. Setting in maths from year 7, broad banding in science, English and languages (French and Spanish) from year 8. The gifted and talented are led along at a brisk pace, taking some subjects early and adding to the basic diet with astronomy, geography, Italian and statistics. 'The school has some really clever girls,' said one mother, 'and they really nurture them.'

All abilities and interests, however, are well catered for, with young apprenticeships and diplomas increasingly popular. 'Not everyone has to be brilliant, but everyone has to achieve what they can,' commented a parent. 'They say, this is your goal, go for it – but not everyone's goal is the same.' About 70 per cent proceed to the sixth form, which forms part of the popular local consortium of four comprehensives, La Swap. A commendable 41 per cent A*/B grades and 11 per cent A*/A at A level in 2014, though results post-16 are not quite as starry as at GCSE. 'We could raise the entry requirements,' says the head, 'and attract a higher ability cohort, but we know we can achieve these results without doing so.' Some 20 pupils have statements of special needs, including one with Down's; has wheelchair access by means of lifts. 'They try to help everyone,' commented one parent.

Games, options, the arts: Music is a particular strength ('super,' says Ofsted) and is based here for the entire consortium sixth form. The standard of singing is unusually high with a 'talented' voice coach in residence. Whole school enthusiasm manifested in a 130-strong gospel choir (a Tour Choice,

which performed recently in Barcelona Cathedral), a year 11 jazz band and a strong chamber choir. About a third of pupils take individual instrumental or voice tuition.

Definitely not a 9am-4pm place – 50 clubs operating, before, during and after lessons, everything from rowing and trampolining to keep fit and cookery. For hard-pressed working parents, the homework club, with supervised study before and after school, is a real boon – as it often is for girls. Thriving art department. The spacious walled grounds include a decent range of pitches, made full use of for two hours' compulsory weekly sports, including rounders, netball, athletics, basketball, trampolining, football and aerobics. 'There's no sitting on the side here,' says the head.

Background and atmosphere: One of a number of schools founded by the Sisters of La Sainte Union de Sacre Coeur, a teaching order founded in the early 19th century. The Camden school has now been in the borough for the past 150 years. Housed in a gracious Victorian building (with later additions), maintains the stately and soothing presence of the former convent boarding school it once was. The classrooms in the main block are light and high-ceilinged, the floors polished to a mirror sheen, the gardens to the rear are elegantly laid out with a small orchard and an ample stock of summer roses (sensibly, girls are required to keep to the path and admire from a distance).

Though now very much a modern comprehensive, with a broad intake of practising Catholics from across the capital, still has the purposeful air of calm you might expect from its history. The last teaching sister departed in 2010, but the tradition of the founding order and those of the Catholic faith are well maintained. 'We see our mission as promoting the values of the gospel and spirituality, preparing children for a life centred on Christ, celebrating the sacrament and providing links with other parishes and the international LSU community,' says the head. Has its own pretty chapel and pupils attend mass once a weekly rota. Founder's Day is marked with mass –and ice cream.

Pupils wear the distinctive uniform of tartan kilts and white stockings with pride and recently voted to retain this particular tradition. Strong sense of community, both local and international, including its sister school in Tanzania. Vocal school council (with elections for president and vice president) has its say on bullying and school food as well as uniform.

Pastoral care and discipline: Despite its affluent north London location on the lower slopes of Highgate, intake is anything but indulged – 65 per cent of pupils from low income families, 10 per cent

on free school meals. The student population reflects the Catholic population of London – a third speak English as an additional language; a sizeable percentage are first and second generation immigrants from Nigeria, Ghana, the Congo, Poland, South America and southern Europe. Parents are active in their own churches and in the school. 'There is a real sense of community,' said one. No linked parish but many families attend nearby St Joseph's, Highgate and St Dominic's in Kentish Town.

Pupils and parents: 'This is an inner-city comp,' insists the head, though anyone dropping in from outside might be excused for thinking the term doesn't match the orderly space within. Behaviour is generally exemplary but, for those who stray, bad marks and detentions, as well as fixed-term exclusions. Girls with difficulties are certainly not left to fend for themselves. 'Some girls are from families with real problems and they would rather be at school on weekends and holidays than at home,' says one mother. 'This is a safe place to be.' Offers both parental support and additional help with behaviour management and conflict resolution. Teaches about the temptations of drugs and alcohol but drugs are not a significant issue, at least on-site. Problems mainly concern friendship disputes that change social boundaries. Good induction day in year 7 brings pupils from disparate locations and homes together. 'My daughter has really blossomed here,' says one happy parent.

Entrance: 180 girls admitted to the heavily over-subscribed year 7, mainly from Catholic primary schools. No selection on ability but must be prac-tising Catholics baptised in the first year, then able to demonstrate regular church attendance for at least three years. Pupils arrive from seven boroughs (from Walthamstow to Barnet) as distance is meas-ured by public transport rather than metres from the gates. Eighteen places offered on musical apti-tude, with an aurel test and a small audition. Entry to La Swap sixth form requires mostly Bs for A level. All girls who enter between 11 and 16 base them-selves at the school for the sixth form.

Exit: About a fifth to Russell Group universities, with UCL a favourite option. Popular subjects include English, history, business studies and art foundation. Medics get specialist coaching for BMAT tests. One or two to Oxbridge each year, including medicine.

Money matters: Despite the fact that two-thirds of parents here are on a joint family income of £30,000 or less, most manage the £100 a year volun-tary contribution. 'Parents are very generous' and very active, constantly raising funds with second-hand uniform sales etc. 'This is not a rich school,' said one, 'but the school and parents make every effort to give the girls the opportunities that others might take as a given.'

Remarks: A calm and orderly universe, demand-ing (and getting) high standards of achievement from girls who might not always be expected to reach this high.

Lansdowne College

40–44 Bark Place, London, W2 4AT

Independent • Pupils: 210 • Ages: 14–19 • Non-denom
• Fees (per term): up to £6,480

Tel: 020 7616 4400
Fax: 020 7616 4401
Email: info@lansdownecollege.com
Website: www.lansdownecollege.com

52

Principal: Since September 2014, Mark Love BEd PGCLME (50-ish). Educated at Bristol Polytechnic and Sheffield Hallam University. Twenty-three years' experience of working in post-16 education sector, the majority with independent sector organ-isations. Taught A level economics, business and accounting and spent seven years as principal of Abbey College before becoming principal of CATS College London.

A former GCSE and A level examiner, he lists his main interests as team building and leadership, general management, curriculum development and pastoral care. His wife is an interior designer and they have two daughters. In his spare time he is interested in politics, rugby, football, film, read-ing, current affairs and travelling.

Academic matters: There is a small GCSE cohort of some 40 pupils, but this is essentially a sixth form college offering one and two year A level courses, plus short retake courses. With the demise of January retakes, it now offers February to June courses. 'They can come to us in September to sort out UCAS, then go off for a gap few months before getting down to work. We hope they'll come back with renewed vigour.'

Colleges like this stand or fall by the value they add, and Lansdowne claims an average one to two grade increase at A level on its short courses. 'We're expert at getting people with Cs up to A/Bs. And at getting Cs for people who were predicted to fail.' However, they are coy about their latest results. Classes are tiny: six is average, with one or two not unusual, especially for more esoteric sub-jects such as Russian, Japanese or geology. Around half are retake students and half do their entire A level course here. Maths is the most popular sub-ject, with large cohorts also for biology, chemistry, English, psychology and economics. Courses range from accounting to graphics to philosophy.

The college starts in year 10, teaching core GCSE subjects plus a carousel of options, but the GCSE course runs over one year and most join in year 11.

Passing exams is the raison d'être here – stu-dents are 'very focused on achieving examination success', said Ofsted, mentioning 'interesting and challenging lessons' – and tutors make sure the foundations are in place. 'They went back to basics, and kept repeating them, but they did make her enjoy her subject again,' said a parent. Teaching focuses on exam technique. 'Because time is so

Abilities range from those who have failed first time round to those who need top results for competitive courses

short, we have to concentrate on ensuring they know how to get the best results – to understand what examiners want,' says the principal. 'They have to know how to tick the boxes.' Students have weekly exam practices in the hall where they will sit the real thing. 'If they do it once a week they don't panic when the time comes.' GCSE and lower sixth students have at least three hours a week of supervised study periods. No exam study leave or June half term: 'We run our own revision programme. We teach right up to the last exam in the last subject.'

Abilities range from those who have failed first time round to those who need top results for competitive courses. 'But in a small class this range doesn't matter. Stronger students tend to pull up the weaker ones. If you put all the C grade students together they tend to stay at that grade. However, if we find we have a particularly weak group we may add on extra lessons.'

The college rarely accepts students with statements – 'we don't have the facilities or staff' – but has improving learning support, with a third of students on the register. 'We've just bought 25 new laptops for those who need them.'

Very flexible timetabling – organised by the principal – means the college can offer any combination of its 47 A level and 27 GCSE subjects. It also enables sports stars or those with medical problems to fit in lessons round other commitments. 'Every single timetable is written for an individual. And they are organised for the convenience of the students, not the teachers.'

Many of the teachers have higher degrees. 'This sector attracts highly qualified staff, because every class is an exam class.' Ofsted rated the college outstanding, commenting on the 'very wide and flexible range of courses' and the teachers' 'excellent knowledge of their subjects'.

Runs a medics' programme for those aiming at medicine, dentistry, pharmacy or veterinary degrees, and Easter revision courses, with plenty of individual careers advice and help with UCAS applications.

Games, options, the arts: Plenty of creativity going on, with GCSE drama students rehearsing their devised piece during our visit, photography and artwork adorning the corridor walls, a bright north-facing art studio, graphics room and 'fantastic' photography department with its own dark room.

GCSE students have one PE lesson a week, the football team plays in a league, and there are ad hoc rugby and netball teams. There's an annual ski trip, a chance to do the Duke of Edinburgh Award, and a post-exam activities week that includes paintballing and a trip to Thorpe Park, 'to say thanks for working so hard'. In the autumn term, GCSE and AS students

spend Friday afternoons visiting museums, galleries and other London sites or listening to outside speakers. They go ice skating, bowling and to the cinema together. There's a Christmas party and a summer ball, organised by the student council. However, it is fair to say that these students' main focus is on their studies, and no-one joins the college for its extracurricular offerings. As a parent said, 'you're not going to go there for the night life.'

Background and atmosphere: In a quiet back street between Notting Hill and Queensway, the 60s building could be an anonymous block of flats. Inside is a maze of classrooms, science and language labs, art and photography rooms. Noticeably, whilst there is a study centre with plenty of computers, magazines, reference material and past exam papers, there is no library. It is bright, but one parent commented, 'You have to fight the look. There's not a frill to be had.'

Originally a primary school and community centre for the neighbouring synagogue, it became a college in the late '70s. Once individually owned, it is now part of Astrum Education, which also includes Duff Miller and Chelsea Independent Colleges, and is owned by private equity firm Sovereign Capital. Happily, the firm is prepared to invest in the infrastructure, and building work to create more classroom space and freshen up the

fabric is planned for the short summer break. No common room but students socialise in the canteen and on the small outdoor patio area.

Pastoral care and discipline: Relaxed atmosphere – 'having no uniform breaks down a lot of barriers' – but a stringent approach to punctuality and attendance, with a register taken at the beginning of each lesson. The college has a full time attendance officer who will phone or text any missing student, then their parents. Each student has a personal tutor who keeps an eye on their well-being and progression. 'Because our groups are so small we can keep tabs on things and deal with any problems quickly.'

The college will expel for smoking drugs repeatedly. 'If they're caught once they're suspended; if they're caught again they're expelled. I can't pretend it doesn't happen – we are in central London. It's the worst day of my life, but I do have that ultimate sanction, and there's no shying away from it.'

Pupils and parents: A mix of backgrounds, including around 13 per cent international students from countries ranging from Kazakhstan to Libya, a percentage liable to increase over the next few years. Some pupils come from state schools in year 11 for intensive small-group GCSE tuition, others are recent arrivals in London. Some have been ill or been asked to leave their previous school. Most join the sixth form to improve on previous grades.

Entrance: All applicants are given a tour and interviewed by the principal or vice principal. 'We ask about their background and how we can help them.' The college is not selective, but will look at previous exam results.

'It was the tutors convinced us when we looked round,' said a parent. 'They told us it would be hard work for our daughter, and could be lonely, but they thought they could get her through. And they did.'

Exit: Of the GCSE students, around 50 – 60 per cent stay on for A levels. A level students nearly all to university: occasional one or two to Oxbridge; around half to top universities ranging from Durham to Sussex to SOAS, for subjects ranging from medicine to anthropology and aeronautical engineering.

Money matters: Several means-tested bursaries and academic scholarships up to 40 per cent of fees awarded each year, the latter via the autumn scholarship exam.

Remarks: Extremely good at its job, which is concentrated and detailed preparation for passing exams. Few frills or frivolities. 'It's a sleeves rolled up place,' said a satisfied parent.

LaSwap Sixth Form Consortium

Linked schools: La Sainte Union Catholic Secondary School, 129; Parliament Hill School, 147; William Ellis School, 212

William Ellis School, Highgate Road, London, NW5 1RN

State · Pupils: 1,300 · Ages: 16–19 · Non-denom

Tel: 020 7692 4157
Fax: 020 7284 1021
Email: laswap@williamellis.camden.sch.uk
Website: www.laswap.camden.sch.uk

12

Joint Heads: LaSwap is a sixth-form consortium composed of four neighbouring comprehensives – Parliament Hill, La Sainte Union, Acland Burghley and William Ellis, and the heads of the four schools share the headship. They meet monthly to plan a strategic overview.

Academic matters: These four comprehensives, geographically within a few hundred yards of each other, created an amalgamated sixth form to provide the widest possible subject variety and range of qualifications. Lucky sixth formers here have a choice of a remarkable 39 A levels, as well as BTecs, NVQs, a certificate in childcare and GCSEs (for those who need further preparation before going on to A levels). About 80 per cent of students follow a purely

> *Despite the consortium's leafy surroundings on the eastern edge of Hampstead Heath, all four schools are inner-city comprehensives with a socio-economic intake reflective of the term*

academic course, the rest sit vocational exams, but those who want to can mix and match. In 2014, 40 per cent A*/B grades at A level. The consortium's strengths lie in vocational subjects, the visual arts (with consistently outstanding results) and arts subjects, like RE, media studies and English. Still possibly not the ideal location for scientists.

Teaching (with over 300 teachers) is enthusiastic, knowledgeable and well prepared. 'We've generally found the teaching to be very good,' said one parent, 'though, as always, you'll get the odd dud.' Some criticism for not always taking into account the wide range of ability in this relatively unselective sixth form, but not all would agree – 'In my classes, some people have 10 A*s and others mainly Cs, but I haven't found that a problem,' said

one boy. All students are allocated a base school but most study on a number of sites. Some subjects are taught on all the sites, the more rarefied – philosophy, textiles and dance, for example – on only one.

Each pupil is given target grades on entry based on GCSE results and is carefully tracked thereafter, with good exam preparation and help with study skills, as well as twice yearly reports. 'The communication with home is excellent,' says one parent. 'If my son has done something well they email me. Equally, if he's not doing his homework, they'll let me know.' The academic side is clearly complex, but well organised. 'I wanted to change one of my subjects early on,' said a pupil. 'I went to see the head of year and it was sorted by the end of lunch hour.'

Games, options, the arts: The extracurricular here is a significant part of what LaSwap has to offer, being as varied and extensive as the academic range. The generous enrichment programme, which largely takes place on Wednesday and Thursday afternoons, provides 35 options, from ballet and debating to theatrical make-up, DJ-ing and maths masterclasses. Off-site sports include sailing and climbing. The programme is not compulsory, but everyone is encouraged to have a go, regardless of previous knowledge or expertise.

Background and atmosphere: The four schools (La Sainte Union, an all-girls' Catholic school, William Ellis, an all-boys' former grammar school, Acland Burghley, a co-ed comprehensive, and Parliament Hill, an all-girls' comprehensive) decided to unite their sixth form offering 25 years ago. Each school retains its distinctive ethos and pupils generally enjoy the change of pace. 'I really like the different atmosphere in each school,' said one. All four schools retain the pupils they take in at 11 and each has its own director of sixth form and heads of year.

One great plus of the model is the halfway house it offers between school and sixth-form college. 'My daughter originally wanted to leave and go to college,' said one mother, 'but once she'd started at LaSwap, she found the teachers treated her with more respect and she was given much more responsibility for her assignments.' The advantage for students who opt for continuity is that they remain in familiar surroundings while meeting new people and conquering new horizons. 'In the earlier years, my daughter's friends were all local,' said one parent. 'In the sixth form, she suddenly had a whole new set of friends from all over London.' New students, however, don't feel excluded – 'I felt everybody was in the same position as I was,' said one. 'People had friends from their original school, but they didn't know anyone from the other schools.'

LaSwap is careful about taking both existing students and recent arrivals to a more independent level of study, with a well-planned induction programme, including a thorough briefing on the outline of each course and relevant dates and department procedures. Students like the friendly, laid-back but organised approach and strong sense of community.

Pastoral care and discipline: All students register at their base school, where they take most of their lessons. Here they have a head of year and a tutor who monitors their work and well-being, with regular interviews to discuss problems and set appropriate targets. Also a confidential professional counselling service and regular PSHE, with outside speakers, group work and discussions.

Pupils and parents: Students, from a huge range of ethnic and social backgrounds, apply from a vast swathe of north London. Despite the consortium's leafy surroundings on the eastern edge of Hampstead Heath, all four schools are inner-city comprehensives with a socio-economic intake reflective of the term. Generally, pupils are confident and mature and get on well.

Entrance: LaSwap has about 1,300 places on offer. Eight hundred of these generally go to existing students; a further 300 are available for students from schools outside the consortium. The entrance procedure is intricate and careful attention must be paid to every step and date. First step is to register interest online by the end of the autumn term. Then, armed with a ticket and a parent, prospective candidates attend the open evening in January. Applications must be submitted by post or by hand in early February – those who miss the deadline are immediately put on the waiting list. All applicants who meet the deadline are offered an interview at the school in February or March to discuss subject choice and given conditional offers based on GCSE grades. Those with offers must attend the one-day induction course held before the start of the summer holidays, when summer assignments are set. Post GCSE results, further interviews and places are confirmed. Now asks for mostly B grades at GCSE (rather than C grades, as previously) to study A levels.

Exit: About 400 students go on to 60 universities to study 50 different subjects, from medicine and accountancy to drama and international relations. About 20 per cent to Russell Group universities. A large contingent to leading art colleges, mostly to the University of the Arts, London (Central St Martin's, Chelsea, Camberwell and London College of Fashion etc). Three to Cambridge in 2014.

Remarks: A good compromise between school and a sixth form college, with an extraordinary range of subjects on offer. Tends to suit the motivated and the self starter, but not ideal for those who will be distracted by studying on a number of sites or who require the disciplined parameters of a school sixth form to function at their peak.

The Lyceum

Kayam House, 6 Paul Street, London, EC2A 4JH

Tel: 020 7247 1588
Email: admin@lyceumschool.co.uk
Website: www.lyceumschool.co.uk

35

Independent • Pupils: 105 • Ages: 3–11 • Non-denom
• Fees (per term): £4,600

Head: Since September 2014, Edwin Brown, previously head of Quainton Hall prep in Harrow. He has also been head of St Columba's College Prep in St Albans and a Hillingdon primary school. He has a CertEd and BEd from Lancaster and an MA from London. Particularly interested in teaching environmental sciences, thinking skills and creative arts; keen supporter of Newcastle United and Saracens. He is married to Lesley, also a prep school teacher, and they have four grown up children.

Entrance: Places at 3 and 4 are offered on a first-come first-served basis with priority to siblings. A few places for 7 year olds and the odd vacancy later on, awarded after assessment. The school does not set out to cater for special needs and one parent with older children at the Lyceum told us she chose not to send her youngest child because she required more specialist support. Nevertheless, in recent years, the school has employed a SENCo and part-time speech and language therapist, which has helped as the needs of individual children have become apparent. Before parents accept a place, they are invited to meet the head to ensure they fully understand what the school is about before making a commitment. Many families use public transport from Hackney or Islington but the demographics have altered in recent years, as more mothers are working or living close by in the City

Exit: The majority stay until 11, with a few leaving earlier for schools like City Girls' Prep. The school does not prepare pupils for 7+ examinations; however, the top year is skilfully prepared with plenty of 11+ examination technique and care. Definitely not a hothouse, the Lyceum offers an alternative to hothouses on the one hand and very laid-back schools on the other. One parent said, 'I chose The Lyceum deliberately because I didn't want my child stressed out going to school'. Another remarked, 'The school doesn't come across as overly academic, however, it should promote its achievement in getting children into good quality schools.' Destinations have widened over the years to include City of London, Highgate, Channing, North Bridge House, Dulwich College, Queen's Gate, Forest School, South Hampstead, Frances Holland Clarence Gate and Portland Place, as well as a few boarding schools like Headington and Cheltenham Ladies, with several academic, art and music scholarships. The variety of destinations reflects the mixed ability of the pupils.

Remarks: A short walk from Liverpool Street and Moorgate, the building which houses the school was originally a distribution warehouse for the Radio Times. Parents find the packed lunches a chore but accept the location of the school and lack of space cannot be helped. Throughout the building there are massive silver pipes for filtering air, not air conditioning. The school is sure they have 'less asthma as a result' but it is utilitarian.

Apart from the nursery, the classrooms are open plan and grouped together chronologically with a shared library in the centre. The bright strip lights in the hall are functional, whilst central pink chandeliers in the open plan classroom area are quirky and fun. We saw teachers working and sharing, encouraged to support one another, with plenty of resources but no smartboards. 'The relationship with the teachers is very important,' commented one parent of three, 'as the pupils see them as allies, friendly, someone to help them, rather than adversarial'. Another praised the fact that 'the children come out very comfortable with themselves, not brash', and another added, 'They develop interpersonal skills, are comfortable talking to adults' – as we experienced in our con-

Each day begins gently with music playing as a signal for parents to depart

versations with a group during our visit. There is a good balance of staff age with some long-serving teachers and energetic young ones. Some of the teaching assistants we met are old pupils, who loved the school so much they wanted to return. Each day begins gently with music playing as a signal for parents to depart. Specialists teach French (from reception), and music; afternoons are devoted to creativity and sports.

Year groups are paired for trips and non-academic lessons, or to make up the numbers for games. This results in the children knowing each other and looking after one another, taking responsibility without the need for houses or prefects. We saw small classes, 16 on average, each with a teaching assistant (including one man), thoroughly enjoying their learning. In small classes friendships can become an issue, but parents are remark: 'The school deals well with this and talks through any situation quickly and effectively. There is zero tolerance of bad behaviour.'

Despite the urban location, the children all have plenty of physical activity and play on a daily basis. There is a reasonably large, indoor courtyard, which works well for breaks and small sports, as well as a gallery/hall for drama, dance, music and gym, plays and assemblies. For half the year they use the local Broadgate Centre ice rink for skating and parents really appreciate the use of local facilities such as the vast Artillery Ground, Bunhill Fields and Golden Lane Sports Centre for tennis, swimming and netball. One parent commented on the disadvantage that the children are taught the basic sports skills but do not have much experience of team fixtures and matches, but they quickly learn when they move on to secondary school. Another parent appreciated the fact that 'the children are learning to love the City and all there is on offer'. They come and go in their navy and white uniform, with smart caps for boys and felt hats/boaters for girls. All the pupils we spoke to said they like the uniform and feel comfortable in it.

We saw a good mix of artwork in lively topic displays and a developmental whole school (nursery to year 6) set of colourful paintings of poinsettias in the hall. The school is keen to stress the many opportunities to perform, with regular plays, assemblies and concerts. The majority learn instruments and take examinations, and they reach a high standard of performance. We watched an impressive big band rehearsal and a chamber choir practice. As one boy proudly stated, 'It's great fun. For a small school, we can play loads of instruments'. Charlotte Barbour-Condini, an ex-pupil, was runner up in the BBC Young Musician of the Year playing the recorder.

Recently-introduced Mandarin clubs, plus an IT consultant, who has been working alongside the staff. The school is keen for children to be 'producers of content, not just consumers', and we saw children producing sophisticated animations, websites, mobile apps and even their own ebook. Hooray! Much of this work is related to the Living History topics and annual year 5 and 6 residential trips for years 5 and 6 to eg Edinburgh, Paris and Amsterdam. Parents praised these as being 'vivid and memorable', though one emphasised the need for careful budgeting, as they are in addition to the annual fees.

The emphasis is not on cramming and there are no end of year examinations, but parents feel that pupils are successfully prepared for secondary schools. Working parents can drop off their children, pop back for an assembly or attend sports day in the knowledge a nanny or grandparent would be equally welcome. 'The Lyceum produces well rounded children who are happy,' say parents, and 'It manages to strike a good balance between creativity and very good results,' no mean feat.

New owner, equity-backed Minerva Education, has agreed to maintain the school's ethos: parents will be anxious to ensure this is a reality.

Mossbourne Community Academy

100 Downs Park Road, London, E5 8JY

State • Pupils: 1,350 • Ages: 11–18 • Non–denom

Tel: 020 8525 5200
Fax: 020 8528 5222
Email: enquiries@mossbourne.hackney.sch.uk
Website: www.mossbourne.hackney.sch.uk/

36

Principal: Since 2012, Mr Peter Hughes (30s), who took over when founding principal Sir Michael Wilshaw left to lead Ofsted. An Australian, he came to Mossbourne as part of the Future Leaders programme, which identifies, supports and trains potential head teachers. He has taught at Pimlico and Highgate Wood, and was an advanced skills teacher. He can be seen out running at 6am with rowers (the school has a liaison with London Youth Rowers and is close to the River Lee.

Academic matters: Truly outstanding results: in 2014, 88 per cent of pupils got 5+ A*-C grades at GCSE including maths and English. More than 36 per cent A*/A grades. At A level, 63 per cent of grades were A*/B and 8 per cent A*. Not only are these some of the best state school results in the capital, they are also all the more extraordinary given the fact that a significant proportion of the pupils arrive in year 7 hardly able to read.

The country's highest ranking school for 'value added' – how is it done? Well, a formula that bears no relationship to wishy-washy liberalism – a tough-love approach with a strict uniform policy, ferocious discipline, meticulous monitoring with weekly target setting and a 'can-do' culture. Young and enthusiastic teaching staff (who receive performance-related bonuses) have no official office hours and parents universally praise their dedication. 'My kids never complain about their teachers,' said one mother. 'They seem to be in school at seven every morning. They recognise that not everyone is going to be a rocket scientist, but still manage to make every child feel relevant, included and loved.'

The banded intake is set on entry in all the main curriculum subjects (English, maths, science, humanities, ICT and modern languages), though considerable movement between sets. Music, drama, dance, PE, art and design technology are not setted. Three languages on offer at GCSE – French, German, Spanish – as part of the core curriculum, but students also have the opportunity to take public exams in Turkish, Latin, Bengali, Swedish and Italian. Both vocational and academic exams on offer post-GCSE (though considerably more academic than vocational), with a BTEC in business studies and level 3 ICT. Homework is set in abundance. Two specialities: ICT and RATL (raising achievement, transforming learning). ICT facilities are therefore state of the art, with interactive whiteboards in all classrooms and all students offered access to the internet and laptops. What really makes the school excel academically, however, is the minutely monitored assessment – the 'personalised learning agenda' is certainly not just government jargon at this school.

The SEN provision is particularly remarkable, with its own well-resourced teaching centre and well-qualified specialists who cope with the full range of difficulties from autistic spectrum to dyslexia. All pupils with academic, social, emotional or behavioural difficulties have a learning mentor and those who require learning support work with a teaching assistant (in class or outside), receive specialist teaching and the support of external specialists if required. Handwriting club and homework club. Additional English classes, too, for non-native speakers on Saturday mornings. Strategies to suit all, including the brightest. The head quickly followed up on one parent's suggestion that Latin might be a desirable addition and equally quickly found himself with 30 students, who went on to take GCSE.

Games, options, the arts: Extracurricular here is part of the curriculum, with an additional, compulsory, off-piste period every afternoon from 3.10 to 4.10pm. This time is used to help strugglers, and also to broaden horizons, with more than 70 activities on offer. All pupils required to take a minimum of two extension classes, which include everything from journalism to marathon running. Saturday morning school provides a safe place to have fun and weekend activities include the City explorers club, to discover the joys of London. Sports include football, netball, basketball, cricket and even rowing, and 'best in Hackney' for athletics. Wonderful head of sport, reports one mother – 'my son had no problem getting up at 6am three mornings a week to be at cricket practice at 7'. Clearly

A tough-love approach with a strict uniform policy, ferocious discipline, meticulous monitoring with weekly target setting and a 'can-do' culture

buzzing on all fronts – annual junior concert, dance and drama production; trips to Edinburgh, Belgium, the Isle of Wight, language trips to Spain and German; Spanish play, poetry competition, debating, links with London College of Fashion.

Background and atmosphere: Founded on the site of Hackney Downs School, once a successful local grammar school, whose alumnae include Sir Michael Caine and Harold Pinter. By the 1990s, however, it had become notorious as 'the worst in Britain' and was eventually demolished. Mossbourne was rebuilt on the same site, a tricky triangle bounded on two sides by railway lines. Founding principal Sir Michael Wilshaw worked alongside architects, Richard Rogers and Partners, to design a school (costing £325 million) which met his requirements. Now one of the largest wooden structures in England, it was created in a V shape, which holds in its arms a triangular social area. Wilshaw believed that pupils need to be kept under

constant observation, so the head's office and the classrooms all overlook the grounds. No corridors – hotspots for bullying – and no staffroom, since Wilshaw felt teachers need to be involved at break times and after school, when most trouble occurs. Indoors, the triple-height space is light and airy and learning takes place in 'learning areas'. Sixth form centre added in 2009.

Pupils' aspirations always focused upwards. Rather than the Lord's Prayer, students recite the Mossbourne reflection: 'Throughout this lesson I aspire to maintain an inquiring mind, a calm disposition and an attentive ear, so that in this class and in all classes I can fulfil my true potential'. Parents without hesitation describe the school as 'absolutely amazing' – 'the kids are plainly very well cared for, polite, helpful and considerate. You feel that they are looked after and they are looking out for each other'. An incredible loyalty between kids from completely different ethnic and social backgrounds. Perhaps the greatest compliment any parent can pay is: 'You walk into the school during the day and there is an air of studiousness and control. I don't think about it any more – I know the teachers are in charge'.

Pastoral care and discipline: As celebrated for its discipline as for its academic success – little opportunity to slip up here. Particularly in the early years, pupils are drilled in army-like expectations. Detentions commonplace, for lost homework, left-at-home games kit, being more than 10 seconds late when the morning whistles goes at 8.40am, and students stand when a teacher enters the room. Wherever the potential for rule breaking, staff are on hand – stairwells manned between lessons and students monitored after school. Pre-GCSE pupils wear smart grey and red school blazers and neatly knotted ties, sixth formers graduate to business-like

suits and skirts (at or below the knee). No piercings allowed, except for ears, hair must be kept to an acceptable norm (those indulging in the shaven look work in isolation until locks re-grow). Mobiles banned and students not allowed to enter shops on their way home or loiter outside the gates in groups. 'Structure sets a child free,' says the head. And it certainly seems to – a 96 per cent attendance rate.

Pastoral care is as strong as the discipline. Few personal problems go unnoticed, whether bullying or self-harm. At the first sign, parents are invited to come and speak to the staff. One grateful mother has nothing but praise for their intervention. 'They made it very easy for my children speak to a counsellor. Mossbourne is a place where you can talk and get support when you can't always get that at home'. Food healthy and delicious.

Pupils and parents: A large percentage of the intake comes from the adjacent Pembury estate, an urban sprawl which tends to hit the headlines for its shootings and drugs rather than its high educational aspirations. Four-fifths of pupils are from minority ethnic groups (many Turkish Kurds), two-fifths speak English as a second language, fifty per cent are on free school meals. But also a fair number of clued-up, middle-class parents – the kind who used to go private or bus their children out of the borough – who fight from a great distance to get their children the superb education the school offers.

Entrance: Total of 200 places –- now one of the country's most over-subscribed schools. The head is looking for a balanced intake: 'We want a comprehensive – we don't want a secondary modern'. Applicants sit reasoning tests to divide into four equal ability bands. 60 per cent of places in each band are given to whose who live within the inner zone (now less than 500 metres from the gates); 40 per cent of places go to those outside the zone. For those inside the zone, priority is given to those in public care and statemented children, then siblings, then distance from the gates. For those outside the zone, the order is the same, though the final criteria is not distance from the gates but distance from the home address to a co-ed, non-selective comprehensive. Those who live furthest from that type of school are given priority at Mossbourne. Introducing a lottery system from 2014.

The lower sixth form has only 125 places and priority is given to those who have come up through the school. Most places are filled automatically, though pupils looking for academic courses need to meet the demanding criteria of seven A*-C GCSEs, including English and maths; those wanting vocational courses need four A*-C.

A few candidates come in at this stage from other Hackney comprehensives.

Exit: Most proceed to the sixth form. Three to Oxbridge in 2014. Many others to Russell Group and other top unis, including the US.

Money matters: Money is not a problem at this well-resourced school – everything from the buildings

to the technology is of the highest standard and whatever the head wants to get done he has the means to achieve.

Remarks: Proof that with sufficient resources and the right direction, the kids who life intended to fail can succeed. Parents rightly fight to get into its safe, inspiring and eco-friendly classrooms.

North Bridge House Junior School

Linked schools: North Bridge House Preparatory School, 142; North Bridge House Senior School, 144

8 Netherhall Gardens, London, NW3 5RR

Independent • Pupils: 410 • Ages: 2+ – 7 • Non-denom • Fees (per term): £4,705 – £4,900

Tel: 020 7435 2884
Fax: 020 7794 1337
Email: junior@northbridgehouse.com
Website: www.northbridgehouse.com

13

Headteacher: Since January 2014, Joanna Hockley, previously deputy head of Clifton Lodge school in Ealing, another Cognita school.

Entrance: Life begins at playgroup level and children are mostly siblings of current pupils. Then the nursery takes around 30 children out of the 120 applicants. Reception, the following year, takes the same number out of a similar number of applicants. Occasional places thereafter, but around 10 children out of 40-odd are taken into year 3.

Criteria are refreshing – first come siblings, then children of former pupils, then families who live closest and finally, those who fit the age bracket the school wants to fill. Makes a point of covering the entire chronological year in any class year group.

That doesn't mean no assessment. All applicants visit and parent and child are interviewed. So the emphasis is more on whether the child – and family – fit the school's ethos rather than on academic potential. The result is a spread of ability, ethnicity and just about everything other than location – most live within three miles of the school, many near enough to walk. Equal split of boys/girls. Runs a good coach service to obvious areas.

Exit: Virtually all move on from the junior school to the prep school in year 3, despite the different location. Those who leave at this stage mostly do so for single sex education.

Remarks: Highly confusing for outsiders. The nursery and junior school are housed in two buildings moments from each other in Hampstead. The preparatory school lives off Regent's Park, whilst North Bridge House Senior School amalgamated with the Royal School in Hampstead in 2012 resulting in NBH Senior School moving to the Royal's central Hampstead site. Another NBH senior school, covering years 9 – 13, opened in Canonbury in September 2014.

Life begins in the nursery building – a splendid Victorian house on Fitzjohn's Avenue, used as a nursery school for decades but only acquired by North Bridge in 1989. Classrooms are full of happily absorbed children. We saw year 1s engaged in water play and modelling while the parallel class had a friendly 'show and tell session'. Art was fun – we enjoyed Mondrian-inspired collages on the walls and appreciated the principle that 'everyone's work goes up – not just the best'. It's well-equipped – a music room doubles as an eating room, a good gym/ hall for concerts and shows – and does not feel as crowded as some similar schools, though we found some of the rooms uncomfortably hot. Everyone learns French from reception and PE is four days a week. Outside space, again, compares well with comparable schools – some safe surfaces, a lovely wooden play train and caterpillar, with some covered nooks for secret conversations and conspiracies.

The Fitzjohn's site houses the playgroup, nursery and reception. The building on Netherhall Gardens is the main site for the junior school and has the year 1 and 2 classes. This is a quieter corner – a cul de sac overlooking the Finchley Road; the house is a five-storey red-brickery, interestingly sited between the British College of Osteopathic Medicine and the former home of Sidney and Beatrice Webb. It's a corner favoured by independent schools – South Hampstead Junior School is opposite and nearby, Southbank International (also owned by Cognita, the owners of North Bridge) is up the road, and others not more than a rubber's throw away. Efforts are made to stagger drop-offs and pick-ups. From the top of the main building splendid views – over to Harrow-on-the-Hill one way and to the North Downs the other.

As in the nursery building, every inch is covered in displayed work – much to intrigue and delight the eye. Classrooms are occupied by quiet and relaxed children, clearly engaged and interested. Music, French and PE are said to be the school's specialties – everyone learns music and a third or more learn piano, guitar or violin in school; choirs and bands. Outside space is less impressive, though. A marked out chess board and a climbing frame on the tarmac. Sports mostly at the Talacre Centre in Kentish Town. More could be done to make this a livelier area.

A full-time learning support teacher sees around 25 pupils regularly – up to three times a week – for varying types of support. Despite the manner of entry, nothing more than mild dyslexia/ dyspraxia surfaces here. All children are monitored twice-yearly to check progress.

Junior and nursery school parents praise the friendliness and welcome they find here and feel what is offered at this level hardly differs from what the overtly academic neighbours do.

North Bridge House Preparatory School

Linked schools: North Bridge House Junior School, 141; North Bridge House Senior School, 144

1 Gloucester Avenue, London, NW1 7AB

Independent • Pupils: 295 • Ages: 7–13 • Fees (per term): £4,995

Tel: 020 7267 6266
Fax: 020 7284 2508
Email: prep@northbridgehouse.com
Website: www.northbridgehouse.com

14

Headteacher: Since 2005, Mr Brodie Bibby BA PGCE MEd (40s). Took his first degree in archaeology and ancient history at Exeter, followed by a PGCE at Roehampton, then taught in state and independent schools, including time at The Banda School, Kenya and as deputy head of Westminster Under School. Still teaches history, drama and games.

Energetic and efficient, he's a man who gets things done, but wants what's done to combine high achievement for all with happy kids protected

as much as possible from the early pressure of the modern exam system. Parents rate him highly. 'He's really involved in all areas,' said one, 'and knows and welcomes every parent. You feel he's really proud of the school.' Has recently run the senior school during the previous head's maternity leave, but is now happily back on his own stomping ground, with more room to move around and year 3 now under his wing. His own son and daughter attended the school, always a recommendation.

Entrance: Non-selective in nursery, so names down at birth or as soon as possible thereafter. Parents are invited to tour the school in the November prior to entry. For entry in year 3 (when up to 20 places become available), assessment in January in English, maths and reasoning. Open mornings held throughout the year.

Exit: Plenty of guidance about appropriate secondary school starting in year 5. 'It's important to be honest with parents and make sure the school is the right fit,' says the head.

Excellent results at 11 for girls. Good chunk each year to Channing and South Hampstead, but to a wide range of state and private, including impressive numbers to Henrietta Barnett. Boys, too, go everywhere, with impressive results at 13+ and Common Entrance. A solid handful to Westminster and St Paul's and significant numbers to City, as well as all the usual north London suspects. Those who wish to continue to North Bridge House Senior School in Hampstead are now more or less guaranteed a smooth passage, though occasionally someone may be asked to look elsewhere.

Remarks: North Bridge, one of the largest stand-alone prep schools in London, opened in 1939 in St John's Wood and is now part of the growing stable of schools run by the Cognita group. It is a school that has undoubtedly benefited from the recent relocation of its senior school to a new home. Now years 3 to 8 are grouped together on the same site, with considerably more elbow room.

Formerly a convent chapel, then a Japanese school, the site has gradually been updated to provide a spacious welcoming reception and good playground space. Still a bit of a rabbit warren (younger children are carefully guided round), but some impressive features, such as the lofty pillared and gilded assembly hall, two newly equipped science labs and music rooms.

Teaching – by friendly, well-qualified staff in classes of about 20 – is lively and fun, with the national curriculum followed in the early years, then stretched well beyond later on. 'My son is looked after really well,' said one mother. 'His teachers completely understand his strengths and weaknesses and seem to catch his imagination.' Pupils' progress is meticulously tracked on a database. Specialist subject teaching in ICT, French, music and games. French, taught by native speakers, from reception; Spanish added in years 3, 4 and 5; Latin and Greek from year 6. Plenty of 'professional development,' too, so teachers are kept on their toes. Classroom style is relaxed but orderly.

Children with special needs are given excellent additional support, with group work in class plus one-to-one attention outside if necessary. In years 3, 4 and 5, teachers are supported by assistants who help out with reading and group activities.

Girl-boy balance kept as even as possible in the younger years then in year 6 boys are hived off into a separate all-boys prep on the top floor to prepare for Common Entrance. The school prides itself on its support for those taking 11+and 13+ entrance tests. 'The exams can be quite ruthless and it's important pupils feel good about themselves,' says the head.

Strong emphasis on art, music, drama and sport. The art room (home to art club and regular exhibitions) has now been freed up for use by all pupils. Music – with an orchestra, a number of choirs and plenty of informal concerts – is vibrant. Annual school play (most recently The Pied Piper) attracts enthusiastic auditioning. Sport, played twice a week, offers a good choice for both boys and girls (kayaking, rock climbing, basketball, dance and table tennis in addition to the standard fare) and regular matches against other local schools. Two well-equipped playgrounds and afternoon break in the open spaces of Regent's Park, just across the road. The school is non-denominational, but pupils receive education on all major faiths.

Exciting range of out-of-class activities (at lunch and after-school) includes flamenco, yoga and cookery, as well as arts, sport and drama. Chess particularly popular, with a coach training potential grandmasters for national competition. Reorganisation has allowed space for a purpose-built library, with bean bags, newspapers and library lessons. Plenty of trips, including abroad (Rouen, Vienna). Energetic charitable involvement (recent fundraisers include a Readathon and cross-country run). Lunch, featuring traditional favourites like fish and chips and jelly with ice cream, is served in the assembly hall and eaten alongside the teachers.

Excellent communication with parents, with an informative handbook distributed at annual info evening and email access to teachers. 'They send you an email if they have any concerns and you can email them with anything that worries you.' Pastoral care, too, comes in for high praise. 'Problems are picked up immediately and dealt with sensibly and sensitively,' said one parent, whose daughter had experienced some low-level bullying.

Families live fairly locally (mainly Hampstead, Islington and Queen's Park), but are metropolitan and cosmopolitan (Russian, American, Chinese, Japanese, African), often in the arts and media. The approach certainly appeals to those who might find other local schools too formal. 'I like it because it because it's unpretentious,' said one father of three. 'It doesn't take itself too seriously.'

A successful school (which received 'outstanding' in every category in its last Ofsted report), but also a happy and friendly place which seems to find room for everyone to thrive. 'We get very good results, but we don't want to pressure someone into getting into a school. We let children be children,' says the head. A philosophy which clearly works. 'I really like coming to school in the morning,' said one girl in her final year.

North Bridge House Senior School

Linked schools: North Bridge House Junior School, 141; North Bridge House Preparatory School, 142

65 Rosslyn Hill, London, NW3 5UD

Independent · Pupils: 290 · Ages: 11–16 · Non–denom
· Fees (per term): £4,995

Tel: 020 7267 6266
Fax: 020 7284 2508
Email: seniorschool@northbridgehouse.com
Website: www.nbhseniorschool.co.uk

15

Head: Georgina Masefield BA MA PGCE (40s). Australian by birth, Mrs Masefield grew up in north London, where she attended Channing School. Then to UCL to do a BA in English literature and linguistics, followed by an MA in medieval literature. She also holds a PGCE and is currently completing a masters of education from Buckingham University (where she has worked as a mentor and tutor). Started at North Bridge in 1998 as a supply teacher, moving quickly up the ranks from form teacher and head of art to head of English in the senior school. 'She's a fantastic teacher,' says one former pupil. 'Everyone she taught used to get A*.' In 2010, she left (temporarily) to become an adviser and then education officer for the school's owners, Cognita, helping to develop curriculum and standards across the group. ('I loved it, but in the end, I felt I wanted to shape and drive my own school.')

Remains passionate about teaching. 'I still observe lessons, sitting where the children sit and doing the activities.' Glamorous and ebullient, she's also clearly effective, and the rate of change since she took over has been rapid and decisive. Married to an archaeologist, she has one son at university.

Academic matters: North Bridge has never been (and has no desire to become) a hothouse, but there's definitely a sense that academic outcome has now been put higher up the agenda (with a considerable exodus of old staff and influx of new). In 2014 92 per cent of pupils achieved five A*-C grades at GCSE, with 37 per cent A*/A. Don't be surprised, however, if these statistics improve in the coming years. 'We're very keen to retain diversity,' says the head, 'but we also want pupils to leave with the best possible grades.' (Some parents feel the shift is entirely positive, 'She's really pushing the school in the right direction'; others are less convinced, 'I preferred it when it was a bit quirkier.')

Since taking over, Mrs Masefield's made a number of significant alterations, introducing specialist subject teaching in year 7 and increasing the academic content. All pupils take nine GCSEs, including English lang and lit, maths, double or triple science (about half do triple) a social science (history or geography) and a modern foreign language (those with dyslexia can be absolved). French from year 7, German and Spanish in year 8. Latin now compulsory in year 7 ('It's not only helpful for understanding English linguistics, but useful in terms of developing modern language skills,' says the head). A rich GCSE offering beyond the core includes textiles, photography, media studies, food technology, art, music, classical civilisation and (newly added) computer programming to complement the existing offering of IT.

North Bridge has always done well by those with mild learning difficulties, and about 10 per cent of pupils here need some sort of support (usually able dyslexics and dyspraxics). Lovely, large, bright dedicated room (with its own sofa), overseen by a full-time SENCo and a medley of part-timers (all with specialist dyslexia qualifications). 'There's no stigma attached to special needs here,' says the head of learning support. 'Children want to come.' Regular assessment for all and informal support with study skills, revision techniques and exam strategies available at break and after school on a drop-in basis. The school also has a lift, and can provide additional support for those with English as a second language.

Games, options, the arts: Always a creative place, particularly in the visual arts and drama, the new building has extended the range, with well-designed, dedicated space for textiles, ceramics and DT, as well as a new media suite (fully equipped with Macs), dark room and de-luxe food technology department.

Music teaching now provided entirely in-house, with more music in the curriculum and a carousel of additional opportunities. Compulsory choir in year 7, music theatre in year 8 and plenty of performance, including Battle of the Bands and clubs for close harmony singing, grade V theory and jazz.

For a small school, a very decent amount of sport, with a multitude of teams and access for everyone. Pupils already participate regularly in out-of-school competitions and sports trips and the soon-to-be completed sports hall and newly landscaped grounds (with market garden and netball court) will undoubtedly improve on-site possibilities.

Perhaps the most popular recent innovation is the enrichment programme, a weekly 50-minute slot embedding in the timetable activities generally considered add-ons. 'If extracurricular activities just take place in clubs,' says the head, 'they tend to fall off the radar.' Now the whole school mingles in a choice of 26 varieties (changed termly), encompassing a broad and imaginative sweep, from archaeology and cheerobics to origami and animation.

Background and atmosphere: First established as a junior school in 1939, the senior school was set up in 1987. In 2004, the entire outfit (junior school, prep, and senior school) was bought by Cognita. The group runs 64 schools across three continents, but encourages each to retain its founding ethos. 'Here, it's to celebrate the individual in a caring way, to offer a wide breath of experience, to aim high and push pupils a little bit further so they exceed their potential,' says Mrs Masefield. North Bridge is Cognita's flagship and the association comes with undoubted benefits – centralised services and long-term planning – but some feel it's also accompanied by just a whiff of the corporate.

In 2012, the senior school separated physically from the prep school, moving out of the cramped site in Camden Town to take over the premises (and pupils) of the Royal School in Hampstead. The 60s building has now been entirely refurbished, combining all the positives of the era (acres of windows, light and spacious classrooms, outstanding views) with all mod cons. Comfortable, well-stocked

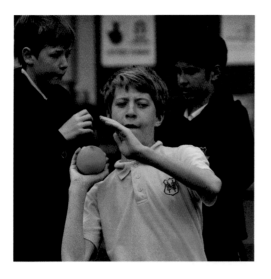

library, with enthusiastic librarian who arranges tantalising displays of 'banned books' and interesting guest speakers. Delicious food (freshly baked bread, minted pea and quinoa soup, vegetarian option) provided by outside caterers. Free inter-school shuttle bus aids parents needing to pick up from the prep or pre-prep, plus a reasonably priced school coach taking in a broad sweep of north London.

Pastoral care and discipline: School prides itself on its family atmosphere and this, all agree, is one of its chief strengths. 'Kids really look out for one another,' said one happy parent. 'What I love about the school,' says another, 'is that way that everyone from the oldest to the youngest gets on. There's a real sense of camaraderie'. Others are upbeat about the individual, confidence-boosting attention. 'My son came home from a residential trip declaring, "Now, I'm not afraid of anything any more." He's really flourished at the school.'

Transition to secondary carefully managed, with the entire year contained on one floor and newcomers linked with year 11 'buddies'. Twice daily form periods make sure no pastoral (or disciplinary) issue is overlooked and head holds weekly open house ('Masefield Mondays') when pupils can come and 'tell me anything'.

An unpretentious and civilised place, where good behaviour and good manners are paramount. 'This is a nurturing school, but we have clear expectations and firm boundaries,' says the head. (The latter are now being made more explicit, with detention for uniform lapses, for example). Usual disciplinary ladder, starting out with discussion in form time. Good behaviour and achievement acknowledged by 'head's tea' and activities like ice skating and bowling.

New World of Work initiative, targeted at year 10, has upped the careers offering. Older pupils now do a week of work experience and gain a wider understanding of a range of professions (from local government officials to astronauts) through weekly speakers interviewed by the head or groups of students.

Three houses compete throughout the year (in maths, poetry and cake baking, amongst other activities), with winners rewarded with a trip. All of year 10 invited to apply for positions of leadership and responsibility. Prefects, house captains and head boy and girl appointed in year 11. Student voice throughout loud and clear. 'We want children to run things.'

Pupils and parents: Families generally local, many within walking distance, then trickling out to Highgate, Muswell Hill, Finchley. A few from further afield. Quite a cosmopolitan bunch, often less intensely exam focused than parents elsewhere in north London. 'They want a happy, stimulating, wide-ranging education for their children that won't turn them into nervous wrecks,' says the head. Pupils are often those who flourish in a more intimate, less pressured environment. 'When we looked at some of the bigger secondary-school options, my son just hated the idea of them,' says one parent.

Entrance: Entrance is selective, but not unduly so. ('Pupils are admitted who are performing at or above the national average'.) At 11+, considerable numbers from the state sector. Apply one year prior to entry, with a (flexible) closing date in December of year 6. A number of assessment days held in the spring, with applicants invited in in groups of about 20 for a two-hour assessment in English, maths and an informal interview with the head or deputy. 'It's quite relaxed. We want to find out how much they know and whether they'll fit in here and do well.' Those with 'scholarship potential' invited back to sit further papers or demonstrate skills in sport, music, art or drama. School does its best to balance the girl-boy mix, but still tilted 60:40 in favour of boys. Pupils at North Bridge House prep guaranteed entry at 11, but not at 13 (though they still get priority). Siblings, too, are favoured.

Exit: All leave at GCSE with plenty of advice and preparation (including interview practice) from year 10. Significant numbers to Camden School for Girls, Highgate, UCS, City, as well as to a range of sixth form (Woodhouse) and tutorial colleges. Can now transfer to the new North Bridge senior school in Islington.

Money matters: Range of scholarships, academic, creative (art, music, performing arts) and sport. Limited number of bursaries, but schools does its best to support existing parents.

Remarks: An inclusive, nurturing school, which gets the best out of many children who would struggle in a larger pond. New head making energetic waves in a positive direction.

Parliament Hill School

Linked school: LaSwap Sixth Form Consortium, 135

Highgate Road, London, NW5 1RL

State • Pupils: 1,100 • Ages: 11–19 • Non-denom

Tel: 020 7485 7077
Fax: 020 7485 9524
Email: headteacher@parliamenthill.camden.sch.uk
Website: www.parliamenthill.camden.sch.uk

16

Headteacher: Since 2005, Ms Susan Higgins MA (Cantab) MA (Ed) (50s), previously head of Brentford School for Girls for five years. She studied English at New Hall (now Murray Edwards) College, Cambridge, after a peripatetic school career, as her family moved around the country. The first Oxbridge student from her Bradford comprehensive, she was enthused by 'an inspirational English teacher'. She was head of English at Walthamstow School for Girls for much of her career, taking time out to become deputy head at Skinners' Company's School for Girls in Hackney and spending time as a school-based PGCE tutor for the Institute of Education before returning to Walthamstow as deputy head. She has two children.

A strong and capable leader with a good back-up team, who is currently also in overall charge of Acland Burghley School whilst it seeks a new head.

Parents say: 'I'm very impressed by her.... She's personable and engaging, with great people skills. She has a firm grasp of what needs to be done....The girls love hearing about her experience of going to Cambridge as a working class girl...She's a great role model for them.'

Academic matters: A huge ability range here, with lots of bright girls and also plenty in need of extra support, whether educational or emotional. Accordingly, the school offers a range of options. Everyone studies for a core of GCSE subjects which includes maths, English, core science, RE, and short courses in PE and citizenship. They can add on more GCSE subjects, or choose a vocational BTec from a range that includes business, art and design, ICT and health and social care, or go for a young apprenticeship. Most of the latter two options are taught elsewhere in Camden. Everyone is allocated to either French or Spanish classes for the first three years, and can start the other language in year 9; about a third take a modern language GCSE. Other popular options at KS4 include additional AS maths and triple science; ICT AS and photography GCSE are taught after school as twilight classes.

In 2014, 68 per cent of girls got 5+ A*-C grades including English and maths at GCSE. English has been very strong, maths and science historically rather weaker. However, maths now taught in ability sets from the second term in year 7, and the curriculum has been redesigned substantially. Girls arrive at the school with, on average, much higher verbal than non-verbal aptitude scores – 'but as a technology college we focus on building up their

Harmonious atmosphere. Despite the huge range of pupils, both ethnically and socially, girls tend to get on well together, with few reports of bullying

confidence and aptitude in maths and science'. The science department has appointed some very highly qualified teachers over the last few years. Triple science courses very popular, with excellent results. 'They're very good at assessing strengths and weaknesses,' said a parent, 'and throwing lots of energy at weaknesses.'

The head is reviewing all the schemes of work in key stage 3, including building in greater differentiation for ranges of ability –'in a comprehensive you have to keep revisiting this and doing it better'. Homework and marking – aspects raised by parents as sometimes inconsistent – are other key priorities. 'Every department has produced its own guidelines with clear expectations. Parents need to know these'. The latest Ofsted report, under the new, harsher regime, downgraded the school from outstanding to good, citing the gap in achievement between poorer students and the rest. However, parents generally feel it still deserves an outstanding rating.

SEN provision has been 'transformed', with an assistant head leading the way on SEN and inclusion. Consultants brought in recently to review the

provision were 'very positive'. Few state schools feel that they have sufficient funds to provide all the help every child needs, but 'we feel we've made substantial progress'. The Extra Mile project targets under-achieving year 10 girls, who are mostly from white low-income families.

Gifted and talented provision focuses on what goes on in lessons. 'In a comprehensive you've got to make sure you're providing stretch in the classroom. We get professionals in to make sure we're getting it right'. Also masterclasses and mentoring, and year 7 girls recently visited Murray Edwards College, Cambridge, to meet undergraduates and visit the zoology department. 'Many of our girls wouldn't naturally consider applying to a university like this. It's essential they have their aspirations raised'.

Joint sixth form with next-door William Ellis School, with co-ed tutor groups. It is also part of LaSwap, which includes La Sainte Union and Acland Burghley schools too. Each school teaches the core sixth form subjects, but students visit other schools in the group for more minority subjects eg film studies and further maths. The ability range encompasses those aspiring to read medicine at Cambridge and those working for an introductory BTec diploma in health and social care, with appropriate entry requirements. A scheme in conjunction with La Sainte Union targets very able scientists, who study together and take part in organised work experience and masterclasses. English is the most popular A level subject at Parliament Hill, with psychology second. In 2014, LaSwap achieved more than 40 per cent A*/B grades at A level.

Games, options, the arts: Everyone takes DT GCSE, with a choice of four options – year 7s were busy cooking muffins during our visit. The single storey DT block was built to an environmentally-friendly design with a green roof, and forms the fourth side of a grassy courtyard, twisting up to meet the original Edwardian building. On another corner of the building is the performing arts block, clad in green glass, which provides music rooms and dance and drama studios. The top floor corridors are lined with expressive GCSE and A level photography and artwork, and textile designs hang in the stairwells.

Music probably not the highest profile subject here, but many girls have instrumental lessons and play in the orchestra or in the jazz, string or brass ensembles, or sing in the choir. Those on free school meals get free music lessons. Two hours' timetabled PE a week for everyone. Two tennis/netball courts at the front of the school and a grassy area at the back where the football teams practise, plus a rather ageing hall for gym and badminton with a fitness suite. On the wish-list is a new sports hall. All year 7s learn to swim at Swiss Cottage baths and the head hopes in future to make more

use of the Lido, which is more or less next door. Sports teams play successful matches against other Camden schools.

A breakfast club every morning at 8am and plenty more activities ranging from Italian and chess clubs to basketball and rounders. Girls perform in musicals such as the 'excellent and ambitious' production of The Wiz, run round Parliament Hill in fancy dress to raise funds for Sports Relief, visit China and go on physics trips to Switzerland.

Background and atmosphere: Opened in 1906, has an idyllic site on the edge of Hampstead Heath. Plenty of grassy space, including a sculpture park and kick-around area. Buildings range from solid Edwardiana to the 21st century award-winning DT and performing arts blocks. Is at last – hooray – in receipt of £19.2 million to rebuild the well-past-its-sell-by-date Heath Building ('we're all going to lean against it until it falls over,' promised head when we visited) which houses maths, English, science, canteen and library.

Harmonious atmosphere. Despite the huge range of pupils, both ethnically and socially, girls tend to get on well together, with few reports of bullying. Recently one of six in the country to win a Diamond quality mark for cultural diversity. 'They manage the mix very well,' said a parent.

Pastoral care and discipline: Many vulnerable pupils here, including refugees and those with learning difficulties, who get 'excellent' support, says Ofsted. Liaises with its feeder primary school to identify girls likely to be in need of extra help with making the transition to senior school. It works with outside agencies that provide therapy or counselling to those in need. It also runs many programmes to motivate disaffected pupils, stretch the aspirations of bright girls and ensure everyone gets a chance to broaden their horizons. Assertive classroom management keeps most lessons running without disruptions.

Older girls are allowed to go out onto Hampstead Heath at lunchtimes, together with pupils from nearby schools, William Ellis and La Sainte Union, and locals have complained about litter problems. 'We're very concerned. The girls regard the Heath as very special to them, and we're doing work on social responsibility to educate them that it's for everyone in the community'.

Pastoral care is very good, report parents. 'I've always felt they know my daughter very well,' said one. 'They've contacted me whenever they've had concerns, and they've dealt with any problems quickly and well.'

Pupils and parents: 'Amazingly diverse' student population speaks some 50 different languages at home, though few are at early stages of learning English. Over 200 refugees. Nearly half of the girls are on free school meals, but also good support from some local middle-class families. OGs include actress Katrin Cartlidge, BBC journalist Laura Trevelyan and Lola Young, Baroness Young of Hornsey.

Entrance: Takes 180 girls into year 7, with admissions organised by the LA. Priority for particular SEN, siblings, children in care and those with exceptional social needs. Then by distance – generally within a mile and a half. Those joining LaSwap sixth form to do A levels must have at least eight GCSE passes including three C and two B grades; various vocational courses available for those with lower grades.

Exit: Between two-thirds and three-quarters of pupils join LaSwap sixth form. Some move on to other sixth forms, eg Camden School for Girls or Woodhouse College, others to colleges such as City and Islington or Westminster Kingsway to do vocational courses.

One or two a year to Oxbridge; three to Cambridge in 2014. Many others reading sciences eg biomedical science, pharmacy and physics. London universities popular – King's College, UCL and Queen Mary recently. Sussex, Nottingham and Leeds popular for a range of subjects – languages, history, English, architecture and psychology. Quite a few to art foundation courses.

Remarks: Popular girls' comprehensive in idyllic situation on the borders of Hampstead Heath, with a diverse but harmonious student population. Strong, popular head who is a driving force in building on strengths and tackling weaknesses. 'My daughter has been so happy there that she has become an ambassador for her school,' said a parent.

Phoenix School

Linked schools: University College School Junior School, 195 and University College School, 196

36 College Crescent, London, NW3 5LF

Independent • Pupils: 130 • Ages: 3–7 • Non-denom • Fees (per term): £4,645

Tel: 020 7722 4433
Fax: 020 7722 4601
Email: thephoenix@ucs.org.uk
Website: www.ucs.org.uk/the-phoenix.html

17

Headmistress: Since 2011, Miss Caroline Froud, previously head of lower school, Belmont (Mill Hill Prep School) for five years. Taught abroad for six years before returning to the UK to teach in both primary and further education establishments.

Moving on in December 2014; deputy head Miss Watt will take over the reins until a new head is appointed.

Entrance: Two main entries, each taking a balance of boys and girls. The afternoon nursery class takes children whose 3rd birthday falls between September and December. Approximately 20 places are offered for the morning nursery classes of 16 each, attending for five mornings and two afternoon sessions. Register in January 18 months before admission. Most places go to siblings or to those with University College School (UCS) connections. Occasional vacancies at 4+, 5+ or 6+; prospective pupils are invited for a half-day assessment.

Exit: Most boys go to UCS Junior School at 7, subject to passing the entrance exam. Girls are also expected to stay till they are 7 and most move on to South Hampstead High's or Highgate's junior departments. A few pupils to eg Westminster Under

School, North London Collegiate, North Bridge House, Academy School.

Remarks: Was purchased by the UCS foundation in 2002 as its pre-prep and benefits from sharing the funding and facilities. Compact site up above the Finchley Road near Swiss Cottage, which nevertheless includes a hall, art room, music room, library and playgrounds with sandpits, climbing frame and wendy house, as well as classrooms. Children also use the UCS junior branch ICT suite

and the senior school swimming pool and theatre, and spend an afternoon a week at the UCS playing fields in West Hampstead.

Specialist music, art and PE teachers. Before and after-school clubs include ballet, yoga, Taekwondo, Mandarin and art. Plenty of visitors and trips to eg museums and art galleries.

Can cope with mild special needs, eg dyslexia. Though not a hothouse – 'we don't do never-ending practice exam papers' – it has a strong academic focus and prepares well for the next stage.

Portland Place School

56–58 Portland Place, London, W1B 1NJ

Independent • Pupils: 430 • Ages: 9–18 • Non denom
• Fees (per term): £6,035

Tel: 020 7307 8700
Fax: 020 7436 2676
Email: admin@portland-place.co.uk
Website: www.portland-place.co.uk

53

Headmaster: Since 2011, Timothy Cook BA (50s). Educated at Chislehurst and Sidcup Grammar School in Kent and Leeds University (first in modern languages). Previously head of middle school and head of upper school at Dulwich College, London (where he spent 14 years), then deputy head at St Dunstan's College, London.

Wife Karin – senior post in financial services industry; son at Dulwich College, daughter at Nottingham University. Parents describe him as 'very professional and an excellent communicator.'

With two teenage children of his own, he understands the challenges of these years and brings a human touch to the job as well as aeons of professional experience. So hands on that he is known to respond immediately to emails sent at the crack of dawn in the morning (he cycles in, rain or shine, from south east London and is at his desk by 7am). He may well be the one to answer the phone in the middle of the afternoon and will be in a position to reassure an anxious mother by personally confirming the exact whereabouts of her child. The door to his study is always open and he sees most children at some point during the day. This is a man who when he says he enjoys knowing every pupil, means it. 'It's the joy of running a relatively small school,' he says with a humility, which, one suspects, is typical of him.

While learning to adapt to a more informal approach than he has been used to, he embraces the founder and former head's legacy of a small, nurturing environment that can genuinely meet the needs of every individual and bring out the best in them – in terms of their wider interests, academic and social. 'Boys and girls at Portland Place gain a sense of self-worth from being valued for who they are and what they can contribute. This in turn instils a sense of self-belief, which is the platform for both academic achievement and success in later life.'

Thorough, earnest, completely without affectation and as straight as a rod, he is a head you feel you can trust but 'not the type that wants to be your best friend.' remarked one parent with relief.

Academic matters: A broader band of ability than in most of the fiercely competitive London day schools – something the school takes pride in and, together with its small class sizes, sees as a 'unique selling point.' Only 12 in a class in years 5 and 6, an average of 15 in years 7 to 11 (we saw several smaller ones) and smaller still in the sixth form means that attention can be given to each child – you can be sure that there will be both stretching and confidence building. A godsend for the discerning parent who can see through the merry-go-round nature of 11+ and wants to ensure their child is educated rather than exam-processed. Hence the increasing

demand for places lower down the school; there is now one class in year 5 as well as two in year 6. Piles on the value added – 'We're always near the top of the value added tables' is the boast.

No Latin or Greek at GCSE ('there isn't the demand from our parents,' we were told). Economics,

---

A godsend for the discerning parent who can see through the merry-go-round nature of 11+ and wants to ensure their child is educated rather than exam-processed

---

computing, sport studies and media are offered, along with the traditional subjects. All pupils take at least one of French, Italian or Spanish, not much enthusiasm for taking up a second modern language. If your daughter speaks Italian at home, she is encouraged to do Spanish as her GCSE option. If you want your child to take a GCSE in, for example, Arabic, the school will facilitate it within the timetable, but the onus of paying and finding the teacher is on you.

At GCSE, 75 per cent achieved five or more A*-C including English and maths, 32 per cent of grades A*/A in 2014. The value added shows at A level, where the results are more impressive, most being in the B-D bracket, with a decent sprinkling of As (18 per cent A*/A grades and 48 per cent A*/B in 2014). We saw small tutor groups of as few as five – notably these were in science subjects. Clever ones, with

offers from Oxbridge as well other Russell Group universities. Arts subjects tend to be busier (up to 15 in a group). Library manned by full-time librarian and a nice place to sit and read. Lots of fiction, used for competitions, book club and quiet study. As an academic resource it is risible (school prefers 'needs developing' and reminds us that the individual heads of departments keep library resources in their offices). Good IT suites and resources for the popular media and film options.

Setting in maths, science and English from year 7. Plenty of movement between sets, we were assured. Sizeable number of mild dyslexics but no additional support in lessons apart from general support from class teacher. Staunch policy of no withdrawals from classes (except once weekly for children who have EAL). School employs four specialist learning support teachers who will arrange to see children outside lesson time in groups of two or three to devise strategies to help them access the mainstream curriculum. No screening on admission. However SENCo oversees general provision and monitoring – 80 to 90 children perceived as having some kind of mild learning disability or difficulty and some have IEPs. Most with more than the mildest difficulties seek support outside school. Inside school, the attitude is healthy – 'I'm not treated as if dyslexia is a crime, unlike at my last school,' we were told. Two of the three buildings have lifts but school will be helpful if someone breaks a leg and move lessons to the ground floor.

Games, options, the arts: Well known for sporting prowess despite there being virtually no facilities on site. Pupils are bussed or walk everywhere – mostly to Regent's Park, with pitches and courts of all kinds, Seymour Place for swimming – and the results and achievements, given the conditions, are impressive. Years 7 to 9 have sport timetabled four times a week (one of the advantages of no canteen and shorter lunch breaks: time can be reallocated to sport). Football and netball tours of Barbados, swimming teams win competitions (Westminster champions five years in a row), masses of medals in cross-country and local honours in athletics and team sports. Pervasive pride in school sports, helped, no doubt, by classy Olympians on staff. However most really keen sportsmen and women do their serious sport outside school – girls' football a particular highpoint. Sport now compulsory to year 12 – one afternoon a week minimum of netball or football.

Music and drama similarly 'massive.' Music mostly means pop and jazz (we saw lots of ukulele enthusiasts). There are also a few violinists and woodwinders amongst the jazz pianists, guitarists, drummers and bassists who predominate, but eclectic range of music taken seriously. We were shown

round by a budding actor in year 10 who enthused about the opportunities he has been given to develop his talent. Wholehearted, whole school productions annually – West Side Story, Singing in the Rain, The Producers and Annie are recent offerings; not on-site as no suitable space but venues include The RADA Studios in WC1. Upper school recently performed a resoundingly successful Richard III – which was then a sell-out at the Edinburgh Fringe. Lower school (up to year 9) most recently performed Skellig as their annual production. Good-sized on-site drama studio can accommodate smaller productions (we were impressed with the assortment of costumes and props).

Art in the lower school is lively and inventive. We saw ink portraits in the style of Peter Howson, as well as Pop Art-style Creme Eggs. Fewer than 10 do art A level – facilities limited, though there is a textiles room and school excels in photography. DT similarly energetic – resistant materials, pewter casting, CAD and CAM, though all in rather small and poky rooms in basement. Lots of extracurricular stuff – when we visited a stress management workshop was being delivered to all GCSE students. Trips galore – we have seldom seen such a full programme. Much use made of London's galleries, museums and exhibitions, plus the nearby wider world and the opportunities it offers for field, sporting and other educational exercises, both here and abroad.

Background and atmosphere: This is a young school, founded only 20 or so years ago by the visionary head of science at St Paul's Girls, Richard Walker (Tim Cook's predecessor). His aim was to create a smaller independent co-ed senior school that wasn't super selective. Part of the Alpha Plus group, it forms one of their 19 UK schools and colleges, bringing the advantages of the economies of scale. Portland Place – the road – is a broad, straight thoroughfare in the heart of regency London, two minutes from Oxford Circus to the south, two minutes to Regent's Park to the north. It is lined by august embassies (China, Kenya, Poland, Portugal) and the HQs of royal and learned institutions (architects, physicists, radiologists, anaesthetists). The main school building – Portland Place – identifies itself with a modest brass plate and is elegantly splendid. It is rare for us to compliment a school on its decor but a pleasure to do so here. Eye-catching blue carpet up and down the stairs (not just on the ground floor for show as elsewhere), magnificent ceilings, cornices, columns, capitals and fireplaces: nowhere more so than in the old ballroom, rescued from its carapace of false ceiling and fluorescent tubes and very much in use. All in tip-top nick. This building houses the lower years, the hall (used for gym and dance) and the top floors (formerly the servants' quarters) accommodate music and languages.

A second building in Great Portland Street, five minutes away, houses the upper years and has a breathtaking eyeball-to-eyeball view of the BT Tower, seemingly within grabbing distance. Harford House, also in Great Portland Street and with a facade resembling that of a corporate HQ, is home to art, drama and science. It's a logistical nightmare – five or seven storeys to be up and down all day, three buildings and it all has to be timetabled, supervised and navigated. We suppose everyone to be very fit – a real bonus for children who need lots of movement and exercise if they are to perform well mentally.

No school kitchen. Pupils bring packed lunches or order in from local cafés (which deliver dozens of paninis etc in little brown carriers). Years 10 and 11 and the sixth hang out in the many cafés in or around Great Portland Street and just love the privilege of this kind of freedom.

Pastoral care and discipline: Definitely an informal feel to the place. Although not quite on first name terms with teachers, one can sense an equality in the relationships not seen in more traditional establishments. Good use of sixth form mentors for years 7 and 8 – really fosters inter-age group understanding and friendships, especially helpful in so small a school. Solidly structured pastoral care hierarchy picks up and deals with problems. but there's a pervasive sense of everyone looking out for everyone else. People seem to know each other's little brothers and sisters here. Parents praise the home-school communications and especially the termly parents' evenings. 'The teachers are mostly young and energetic,' enthused a parent, 'and you really get to know them.'

Pupils and parents: More boys than girls (about 60:40 in lower years) – simply because there are so many more girls' and co-ed schools in London. Mixed, as befits its location – trad, moneyed independent education veterans alongside newbies and newcomers from here, there and everywhere, blended with those who couldn't get into the 'academic' schools and for whom PP has been a jolly lucky find. From the whole urban sprawl – no longer just the north and west but around 30 per cent from east and south too. Mostly UK born and based but also from pretty much the rest of the globe, solar system and beyond, in a great undivided family. Brains? Yes, though common denominator more palpably pleasure, pride and enthusiasm for the place.

Entrance: There are now 9+ and 10+ intakes – partly to steal a march on the competition and partly to meet the needs of those who dread the 11+ circus and will do anything to avoid it (wise move). 'Informal tests' in English and maths with deputy/head of year. Year 7 has tests in English and maths and a chat with a teacher. For places at 12+, 13+ and 14+ – same format plus additional test in science. School keen to dispel image that it's the go-to place for a child on the dys-strata. Child has to be able to cope and pupils who can't will be turned down. A few join at year 12, on flexible terms. They come, at 11, from a large number of schools – state and independent.

Exit: About a quarter leave after GCSE. Wide range of post-A level destinations and courses, including sports and exercise science, mechanical engineering and forensic investigations at the newer universities. The odd one to study music and to art college, as well as maths, philosophy and English at Sussex and Italian at Bristol. About 30 per cent leaving after GCSE (mostly to non-fee paying sixth form colleges).

Money matters: Five scholarships for academic, music, drama, sports and art. All worth 25 per cent of fees. No bursaries.

Remarks: Small, nurturing and refreshingly relaxed. A haven of creativity in the pushy academically competitive world of London day schools. A place for engaged, lively, normal kids – privileged, yes, but Sloanes, no. Becoming ever more popular as more and more people discover it. The challenge will be to maintain its ethos of 'broader academic intake' in the face of increasing demand.

Queen's College Prep School

Linked school: Queen's College London, 158

61 Portland Place, London, W1B 1QP

Independent · Pupils: 200 · Ages: 4–11 · C of E · Fees (per term): £4,985

Tel: 020 7291 0660
Fax: 020 7291 0669
Email: info@qcps.org.uk
Website: www.qcps.org.uk

54

Headmistress: Since 2008, Mrs Annie Dempsey BA Cert Ed. A history graduate and specialist English teacher, she has wide experience in preparatory and secondary education. Previously head of St Dunstan's College Junior School, a co-ed independent which she took from 'good' to 'outstanding.' Her own two daughters have been through the London day school system and now work in the City. Parents describe her as 'efficient, very clear and empathetic' and are full of praise for her achievements, 'Under her guidance the school has gone from strength to strength,' we were told.

Smart and engaging, with a gentle manner, head is well established and fully committed

to her role. She is proud of the school and cares deeply that her charges become 'well-grounded, well-mannered, with the ability to make relationships.' She is keen that whilst pupils are at school they learn 'how to think and what not to think.' Has created a very strong management team, including male deputy head (academic), and male assistant head (pastoral care and administration). 'Head greets every child daily by name,' said an appreciative parent, valuing how well she knows each girl. Parents feel pupils are thoroughly prepared for the entrance examination procedure. 'We have received excellent guidance – spot on,' said another. 'We had regular meetings and if we

needed more detail there has been flexibility and an open door.' Head said: 'It's about finding where her soul's going to sing.'

Something of an Aladdin's cave when you climb up past the big, bright science room to art studio on the top floor. Large windows, with great views of nearby rooftops, fill the room with light

Entrance: Most children join in the September after their 4th birthday. No formal assessment but entry to reception involves a parental interview with the headmistress. Two forms in every year, with an average of 16 in a class. Entry to all other year groups (if places become available) involves an assessment of the child's academic achievement and potential, an evaluation of social skills and school reports, plus a parental interview. Two open mornings, by appointment only, are held each term and parents who have registered are invited to attend.

There is no one main feeder as pupils come from a wide range of nurseries in north London. They include Broadhurst, the Liberal Jewish Synagogue Nursery School, Hope Montessori, Marylebone Village Nursery, Great Beginnings and the Windmill Montessori Nursery School. The catchment area includes Marylebone, Regent's Park, St John's Wood, Maida Vale, Mayfair, Fitzrovia, Little Venice, Hampstead and Islington. Pupils are international, multi-cultural, multi-faith, with majority living locally and with English as their first language. 'We love a family,' says the head.

Exit: 'We prepare for choice,' says the head – and the results show a variety of destinations, with around 40 per cent choosing the senior school (all by competitive entrance examination so the Queen's College Prep candidates on a level playing with outsiders). Girls regularly win academic, art and music scholarships. London girls' day schools are popular choices, including both Francis Hollands, Channing, City of London School for Girls, South Hampstead High, Godolphin and Latymer and St Paul's Girls' School. A few head for boarding at Cheltenham Ladies' College and Downe House.

Remarks: This small, traditional girls' day school is well situated, very close to Regent's Park. 'Surroundings really matter,' the head told us and her study with its soothing, grey and cream décor provides a calm setting for dealing with parents and daily concerns. School is housed in two tall Adam buildings – ornate ceilings and ground floor classrooms with columns and fireplaces. All attractively light and bright.

The imaginative use of space and excellent modern resources work well, from the ICT suite to the transformed first floor drawing room (with sprung floor for dance, drama and fencing). Basement has a well-lit music room, dining room and gym. It was good to see girls enjoying reading in the well-stocked library (with part-time librarian). Older pupils can bring Kindles in for leisure reading. Something of an Aladdin's cave when you climb up past the big, bright science room to art studio on the top floor. Large windows, with great views of nearby roof-tops, fill the room with light. Good to see younger pupils creating colourful Elmer-inspired elephants – freely drawn rather than using templates. No kiln, but girls produce batiks in the senior school. Senior school theatre used for top year productions and All Souls Church at Langham Place for harvest and carol services.

School offers a broad curriculum. Each day begins and ends with form teachers – to help pupils organise themselves and their homework. Mornings are dedicated to English and maths and the timetable has been constructed to build in time for travel to various sports facilities nearby. Older pupils have longer days on Tuesdays, Wednesdays and Thursdays. Specialists from reception up for music, French, PE, ballet and musical theatre. Specialist art from year 1, Latin from year 5 and study skills in year 6.

Rather than girls going out of class for individual learning support lessons, the emphasis is placed on differentiation in small classes. Recently appointed male SENCo manages the department, reporting to the deputy head, and there is a clear policy with procedures in place to identify girls with SEN as early as possible. Outside specialists for speech therapy, occupational therapy and dyslexia – by arrangement with parents. Head informs parents on entry that girls must be able to access the curriculum on offer and told us: 'This is the right school as long as we can meet their needs.'

Parents are full of praise for the high standard of teaching and care taken to cater for individuals. The small class sizes help, along with the use of teaching assistants (unusually up to year 4). Underpinning it all, however, is an effective, carefully honed monitoring system for pupils' progress – implemented by the management team and used to share information at regular meetings. Parents told us: 'The girls are happy as they are treated as individuals and there is an excellent balance between academic and life experiences.'

Vibrant displays, and imaginative artwork act as a stimulus for learning and celebrate the pupils' achievements. We loved the walk-in mermaid's cave' for an 'under the sea' topic in year 1, complete with relevant books on display. 'The teachers really take trouble,' a parent said, adding that teachers dressed up as astronauts during a recent project about space.

The pupils we spoke to felt very well supported and encouraged by the reward system (includes head's commendations and house points). Setting in maths and, where appropriate, English from year 3. This works well. We saw enthusiastic teaching, with girls focused, challenged and thoroughly enjoying their learning.

School takes full advantage of cultural opportunities and there are two class trips every half term. A parent told us: 'For me this makes up for other areas as like other inner London prep schools, there are limitations to sports provision.' Having said that, the girls get a very wide and varied diet of sports, including tag rugby and football. They also use nearby Regent's Park and other sports venues across London (some form of physical activity timetabled each day for the older children). Younger pupils enjoy a lovely private garden across the way. Tennis is not in the curriculum. Enthusiastic PE staff run sessions at weekends and are willing to try out new ventures (trampolining when we visited).

Head wants the girls to work hard and play hard. Music and dance are very popular, with vast numbers seizing opportunities to learn instruments, sing and attend the dance academy that operates after school and in the holidays.

At morning break older girls socialise in the dining room, and at lunch times there are organised activities to enable them to relax, have fun and mix. We watched a lunchtime marimba ensemble rehearsal. Girls concentrated hard and produced delightful syncopated African rhythms alongside their enthusiastic teacher. The energetic dance teacher runs a variety of classes from ballet and jazz to street dancing and tap and the girls love it. The performing arts are a real strength of this school.

Confidence is a key word and is nurtured and developed throughout girls' time here. All the pupils we spoke to during our visit were polite, well mannered and happy. In lessons they readily explained what they were doing and were eager to throw themselves into activities, finding mathematics fun as they devised and budgeted for their own theme park or discussed performance poetry and how to communicate with an audience. They understand the importance of being kind, showing mutual respect to their teachers and each other. They are mindful of the code of conduct (present in every classroom and emphasised in assemblies taken by the head).

Active parents' circle for fundraising and social events. Parents are encouraged to be involved, with two form representatives for each year. Communication with parents is excellent. Alongside the usual there's a general weekly newsletter. The school has also introduced specific year group newsletters with valuable curriculum information, key dates, details of pupils' achievements and splendid photographs.

Parents complimentary about the weekly menu. Food is prepared in the senior school and the parent of a daughter with allergies felt very supported by the school Smart uniform. Only niggle expressed by parents was that they'd like winter hats to be reintroduced (girls love their summer boaters).

Parents told us that this is a school 'that raises the bar.' They praised 'the quality of education, staff retention, creativity and happy children' and said that above all it's a place 'that takes genuine pride in its charges and allows each individual to flourish.'

Queen's College London

Linked school: Queen's College Prep School, 155

43–49 Harley Street, London, W1G 8BT

Independent • Pupils: 350 • Ages: 11–18 • C of E • Fees (per term): £5,410

Tel: 020 7291 7000
Fax: 020 7291 7090
Email: admissions@qcl.org.uk
Website: www.qcl.org.uk

55

Principal: Since 2009, Dr Frances Ramsey MA DPhil (Oxon) (40s). Completed doctorate in medieval history before starting teaching. Taught at Westminster School, where she was head of history and director of studies. Discovered the importance of the pastoral side when she became Master of the Queen's Scholars. Cerebral and professional, she is determined to lead the school onwards and upwards. Says it has the same feel and ethos as Westminster and parents and staff feel familiar. All the latter have full lives beyond day-to-day teaching, which she thinks is important. Very much likes the all girl set up – 'no distraction in the classroom'.

'The school has a certain quirkiness and it is important that this is not ironed out,' say parents. They are impressed with 'the buzz of the school and the direction it is going in'. There were mixed reactions from parents to the introduction of uniform for years 7 to 9, mainly because they didn't want general informality of the school to change. But, as Dr Ramsey is a firm believer in 'evolution not revolution', we don't feel they need to worry and the change was enthusiastically welcomed by prospective parents. She misses having the time to teach but makes sure that she is as visible as possible, taking assembly twice a week, having coffee/tea meetings with the senior girls and congratulating younger ones who bring her their 'show

Founded in 1848 and given a royal charter in 1853, a pioneer in education for women, this was the first institution in Great Britain to give academic qualifications to girls

principal' reward cards. Is also seen at all school performances. She interviews all the parents of new applicants and the school maintains a continuous open door policy (parents tell us that they can go in and go anywhere any time they like), so she is not inaccessible.

Married to an Oxford academic, with two children in central London schools. We think that Queen's College is lucky to have her.

Academic matters: Excellent results across the board, with a curriculum that covers a broad range of subjects and is as strong on the creative side as the academic. Parents say: 'Well structured, but girls don't feel it is rigid and therefore thrive on it. Art is taken as seriously as maths.' Dr Ramsey has upped the academic ante, increasing the number of subjects taken as IGCSE and bringing in triple science for the top set. She says that despite the

---

'Well structured, but girls don't feel it is rigid and therefore thrive on it. Art is taken as seriously as maths.'

---

school not being super selective, the girls are all able and ambitious. In 2014, 58 per cent of GCSE grades were A*/A. Parents say the school 'embraces a girl's whole brain'; is 'sympathetic, understanding and supportive'. All agree that the school is not a hothouse, the atmosphere is relaxed, yet it manages to bring out the potential in all girls, academic or artistic.

Teachers praised for their dedication and support. The director of studies, one of the good proportion of males on the staff, is bright and approachable and was appointed to oversee academic developments. Appears to cater well for different types of children guiding them towards opportunities. No EFL tuition but will give support for EAL if necessary. Small classes in the sixth form (average eight) are, a parent said, 'the jewel in the crown'. A huge range of subjects available to be studied, including several languages. Maths, English literature, history and biology seem the most popular. In 2014, 46 per cent A*/A grades at A level.

Popular, fully trained and experienced SENCo four days a week. Can cope with the milder end of the spectrum. All children assessed in year 7 and extra tuition given where necessary. Deputy head says head of English superb at finding any problems – in fact, all teachers good at spotting and communicating concerns: 'Nobody gets through the net'. Classroom assistants not needed as class sizes small (15-20 in years 7-11) and varied. Parents kept fully in the picture – communication lines are good.

Games, options, the arts: As in many town schools, physical activity an ongoing problem, but one they do seem to have cracked here. Head of PE has

completely reorganised the system and all girls have at least one sport-type session four days a week. Could be gymnastics, in a beautifully refurbished, fully-equipped hall, ballet, seasonal games in Regent's Park, swimming or anything else that demands physical activity. In fact, when we were discussing the school uniform issue, one parent suggested that they didn't really need to bother as 'my daughter seems to wear her sports kit most days!' Lots of matches played against other schools and the Duke of Edinburgh award is a popular option. Senior girls can go to the University of Westminster gym for exercise or pilates and yoga type classes. Very grown-up.

Wonderful pictures on display everywhere. Well-equipped art room up in the eaves (north lit, of course), showing coverage of all aspects of the subject. We were fascinated by a huge sculpture made of wire coat hangers. Talented head of art develops ability and encourages imagination, as is evidenced by their results. Music from beginner to grade 8. About 50 per cent learn an individual instrument or have voice tuition. Several concerts, formal and informal, and musical ensembles each year, as well as musical theatre productions and opera. Enthusiastic head of drama finds many different ways to stimulate and stretch her students such as The Crucible being performed in the round

– an exciting first. This school is not scared of experiment or innovation.

Clubs abound and take place in the middle of the day as well as at the end. Each day is jam-packed with activity. Lots of girls stay late on Tuesdays to attend the thriving running club. No excuse for any girl ever to sit twiddling her thumbs. Plenty of outings making use of all London has to offer. Regular trips home and abroad, both educational and social. Lots of charitable involvement and fund-raising activities.

Background and atmosphere: Founded in 1848 and given a royal charter in 1853, a pioneer in education for women, this was the first institution in Great Britain to give academic qualifications to girls. Still on its original site in four elegant, well-proportioned Georgian houses, internally it has often been altered through the years in order to provide the best modern education possible. Wouldn't those early Victorian students be amazed to see the state-of-the-art glass computer room, 'the goldfish bowl', so cleverly integrated, science and language laboratories beyond their imaginations, the wonderful libraries and the great hall, where modern lighting and sound equipment helps to enhance perhaps almost recognizable costume dramas? They would certainly enjoy the more relaxed atmosphere and the idea of learning through discovery rather than rote. Teachers who really care and want to help their pupils to learn and discover in an informal way. A happy atmosphere in the school today that gives girls confidence and helps them find their own way to go forward.

Two of the earliest students, Miss Buss and Miss Beale, went on to found the North London Collegiate School and Camden School for Girls, and St Hilda's College Oxford, respectively. Katherine Mansfield and Jacqueline du Pré also stand amongst

> *Wouldn't those early Victorian students be amazed to see the state-of-the-art glass computer room, 'the goldfish bowl'*

the long list of distinguished old girls as well as, more recently, writers Daisy Goodwin and Imogen Lloyd Webber. A distinguished tradition and history in the making.

Pastoral care and discipline: Dr Ramsey has added a layer of pastoral staff giving, she believes, better co-ordination and consistency. Girls have a year tutor as well as a form tutor, so should always

> *Lots of girls stay late on Tuesdays to attend the thriving running club. No excuse for any girl ever to sit twiddling her thumbs*

have someone to talk to if necessary and should not slip through the net if difficulties arise. Has also introduced mid-term mini reports in every subject, 'a quick reality check', as she calls them, which should help highlight potential academic problems. Apparently the girls have responded well to this idea. Strong anti-bullying policy – would not hesitate to exclude an offender.

Pupils and parents: The usual cosmopolitan London mix of nationalities and backgrounds. About 10 per cent don't speak English at home.

Entrance: Mainly at 11+ via the North London consortium exam. Must also have reference from previous school and be interviewed by the principal or a senior member of staff. A good percentage from Queen's College Prep, about 25 per cent from local state primaries, the rest from other private preps. Another intake at 16+ subject to GCSE results and letters of recommendation from their previous schools. All prospective entrants at this level interviewed by the head of sixth form.

Exit: Around 30 per cent leave after GCSEs, mostly for co-ed sixth forms. A levels leavers to top universities eg Edinburgh, Leeds, Manchester, Nottingham, UCL, York, to study everything from art and design to science subjects.

Money matters: Several means-tested bursaries available at 11+ and 16+, funded by the Old Queen's bursary trust fund. Academic, music and art scholarships, for up to 25 per cent of fees, for both internal and external candidates. Would hope always to be able to find a way of keeping a pupil in need.

Remarks: A happy, rounded school where girls are encouraged to be individuals in an informal, unstressful environment; where nurturing teachers bring out the best in them and help them to find their own paths; where they develop confidence and a desire to succeed. Where being yourself is respected and really matters.

St Anthony's Preparatory School

90 Fitzjohn's Avenue, London, NW3 6NP

Independent · Pupils: 295 · Ages: 4–13 · RC · Fees (per term): £5,320 – £5,430

Tel: 020 7431 1066
Fax: 020 7435 9223
Email: gill.hooper@stanthonysprep.co.uk
Website: www.stanthonysprep.org.uk

18

Headmaster: Since 2010, Paul Keyte MA. Educated at Bloxham and Oriel College, Oxford, where he read philosophy and theology, graduating with a first. Fell into teaching during his postgraduate research (on Wittgenstein and Kierkegaard). 'I thought I'd teach for a couple of years before going back,' he says, but, instead, became hooked. Started out at Dulwich, where he taught philosophy and RE, before becoming head of liberal studies. Then to King's College School Wimbledon, where he set up the philosophy and RE department and was under master (pastoral). 'You have to understand the shadow side, the theft and the bullying.' Then, senior master academic at Winchester and director of studies, deputy head at Highgate and at South Hampstead.

St Anthony's is his first prep school. ('I was attracted to the job because it was big enough to be interesting yet small enough for me to be a father.') An undoubted enthusiast, he remains passionate about teaching ('I feel anchored in the classroom'), and continues to teach RS to year 8 and 'learning enrichment' to all. Knows virtually all his pupils by name. A convert to Catholicism and married to a Catholic (who teaches at South Hampstead), he has one son (now at the school). Outside (and often imported) interests include singing, Schubert ('I learnt German to understand it better'), musicals and Leeds United (much to his pupils' amusement). Energetic, enthusiastic and intellectual, yet accessible, parents feel fortunate to have him. 'He's incredibly supportive and gracious,' said one parent. 'He's the reason we chose the school,' said another.

Entrance: St Anthony's has changed its entrance from a two-stage process with entry points in year 1 and year 3 to a single admission of two classes in reception. 'We feel it provides a year of consolidation,' says the head, 'and a greater run up to secondary school pre-testing.' Tour, then register, as early as possible. All boys are interviewed. 'I'm looking for teach-ability and sociability,' says Mr Keyte. 'They have to be able to cope with the pace and adapt to our style of teaching. We're not competitive, but we're famous for creating independent learners.' Boys from about 25 feeder nurseries, but Catholics have often attended nearby St Mary's and St Christina's in St John's Wood.

Exit: In large numbers to UCS, City and Mill Hill, then everywhere with chunks to Highgate, Haberdashers' and Merchant Taylors', a solid sprinkling to Westminster and St Paul's, as well as to leading boarding schools (Eton, Oundle and Ampleforth). Plenty of scholarships, including for sport and music. No one is ever asked to leave. 'That's our duty, once they're here,' says the head. Occasionally, some may decide that the academic pace is not for them and are 'gently helped' to find somewhere else.

Remarks: The head's heavyweight presence sets the tone and is a good match with the school's highly qualified staff (many with Oxbridge degrees and interesting first careers).The school is split into two sites across the road from each other, each with its own spacious Victorian building. In the junior school (reception to year 3), you'll find a sweeping staircase, turn-of-the-century tiling, large light classrooms and a good-sized dining room (which doubles as an assembly and concert hall). Class size is kept to a maximum of 16-20. Specialist subject teaching in French and music from reception. Mandarin from year 1. 'We aim to send them from the junior school happy and well adjusted, able to cope with the demands of exams,' says the head. 'We're building the personality rather than drilling.' But skills are thoroughly inculcated. 'In the junior years,' said one mother of two, 'the teaching is very precise. They really get the handwriting and spelling under control, which reaps benefits as they get older.'

In year 4, a move to the senior school (years 4-8) is accompanied by greater subject specialisation, more male teachers and recently renovated premises. Some setting in maths, flexible setting elsewhere. No scholarship set, but plenty of

'learning enrichment.' 'Exams require sophisticated skills and we introduce enrichment early on,' says the head. Philosophy, Latin, Greek and Arabic all on offer. The head also runs lunch-hour discus-

---

'St Anthony's boys are never the same. There's no stamp.'

sion groups which any boy can attend. Parents feel he has got a firm grip on the rapidly changing exam landscape. 'The school used to be not quite as rigorous,' said one mother, 'but now the head is really on top of it.'

Good support for SEN with two specialists, one with expertise in dyscalculia. Sophisticated early screening identifies those who may require additional support. Discreet withdrawal to two small bright dedicated classrooms for those who struggle as well as those who need stretch.

The arts, now as always, remain core to what this school is about. The head has tripled the number of music lessons and managed to acquire a baby grand as well as introduce a state-of-the-art music studio. 'My head of music says, "No boy leaves here who couldn't do grade 5 theory",' he says happily. A fair number are gifted musicians, one carrying off a recent Eton music scholarship, another singing with the ENO. Outside school hours, boys are given plenty of encouragement with the school providing the weekend venue for Trinity Laban's by-audition-only classes. Other art forms not neglected, with a big annual Shakespeare production and two weeks of film-making post common entrance. A wide range of hobbies and clubs – logic and puzzle, general knowledge, chess, dance, touch typing – cover a range of enthusiasms (the lunch-time chess players packed out one classroom on our visit).

Not traditionally known as a 'sporty school', but the head is keen to give sport an increasingly important role. 'This is one area I'm working on developing. I'm passionate about what sport brings to children.' Traditional carousel of rugby, football, hockey, cricket, played twice weekly at Brondesbury, a 10-minute coach ride a way. On site, the school has its own pool and two good-sized playgrounds. At St Anthony's, however, sport is as much about taking part as winning, with as many boys as possible participating. 'I'd rather the boys lost nobly and honourably than win for the sake of it. But, there's nothing wrong with really nice sportsmen who get gold medals.'

As a family-owned prep school founded in the 19th century, St Anthony's was run in its own highly individual way, with a famously alternative 'vibe', creative and quirky, underpinned by a strong Catholic ethos. Parents felt concern when the school was taken over by the efficient operator Alpha Plus, but have found that a professional distance has been kept, while judicious investment has brought the infrastructure into tip-top shape.

The only all-boys Catholic prep school in north London (with an 'outstanding' Diocesan report), this remains very much a Catholic school (about 80 per cent of families are practising Catholics). 'Faith is part of the heartbeat of the school,' says the head. Prayers said morning and afternoon, as well as grace at lunch, and you'll find a crucifix in every classroom as well as the Catholic RE syllabus at common entrance. The head, however, feels the function of religion is not to exclude. 'We have a mission to provide for the Catholic community, but inclusivity is important.' And most feel included. 'Families with other beliefs get incredible respect,' said one Jewish parent.

Despite its slightly bohemian reputation, good manners and ethics remain key. Discipline here is done with the lightest of hands, but the boundaries are clearly in place. All teachers known by their first name and learning very much a cooperative enterprise. There's a golden toffee for those who've done something special (such as sing a song in the style of Johnny Cash), but those who break the Code of Conduct are entered into a 'green book' and parents are brought in to discuss anyone who's managed to rack up a third offence. Higher up the school, boys discuss what they've done wrong and what they've learned from it. 'I've only given one detention since I got here,' says the head. 'It never gets to that point. I try to give them a dignified exit.' Strong anti-bullying policies. 'The teachers are exceptionally kind and nurturing,' said one parent. 'They'll always do their best to help, whether it's finding a lost rugby kit or providing interview preparation for senior school tests.'

Parents usual north London lawyers, bankers and advertisers, but Catholic purpose means plenty of Italians, Germans and Spanish. Media parents often come with useful benefits. 'One allowed us to preview films, another offered tickets to the Wigmore Hall.' Boys are not necessarily the neatest, but are undoubtedly enthusiastic and individual. 'St Anthony's boys are never the same. There's no stamp.'

St Christopher's School

32 Belsize Lane, London, NW3 5AE

Independent • Pupils: 240 • Ages: 4–11 • Non-denom • Fees (per term): £4,325

Tel: 020 7435 1521
Fax: 020 7431 6694
Email: admissions@st-christophers.hampstead.sch.uk
Website: www.st-christophers.hampstead.sch.uk

19

Head: Since 2003, Mrs Susan (Susie) West (60s), BA PGCE MA Educational Management. Educated at Howells, University of Newcastle, Oxford (PGCE) and the OU. Then taught extensively in the private sector in England and abroad, at Oakham, at St Bede's, Eastbourne (where she was head of the pre-prep school), at Sherborne (where she was a housemistress), in Kuala Lumpur (where she was head of English), and at Sussex House, before becoming deputy head of Kensington Prep. An energetic figure who cycles to Hampstead every day from Pimlico, Mrs West is divorced with a grown-up son and daughter. She continues to teach some English to years 4 and 5, feeling that not only is this the best way to get to know the children but also the ideal means to understand the issues faced by her staff. Down to earth, positive and straight talking, with a clear passion for educating and a genuine empathy with her pupils.

Entrance: St Christopher's is one of London's highest-achieving academic prep schools, with results at 11 the envy of many of its neighbours. This, however, is a school which selects primarily on ability. Part of the selection procedure is standardised tests, so summer birthdays don't lose out. 'It is not an academic assessment,' says the head. 'We observe how they play together and how they interact with other children.' The school operates a split entry and successful candidates are allocated a place either for reception or for year 1, depending primarily on 'school readiness'. Tests dates and results are co-ordinated with other leading selective north London prep schools. Early registration is essential (as near birth as possible) for those already resident in London. Entry lists are closed at about 300 to be assessed for 38 available places. The head, however, is always willing to be flexible for those who've just arrived. Siblings are given an automatic offer, unless it is considered 'they will not flourish'. Not flourishing, however, is fairly loosely interpreted. 'If you have two clever daughters and the third is not as bright,' says the head, 'some parents think she'll upset the exit poll, but that's not the way we work.' Parents confirm that year groups cover a (relatively) wide spread of ability. Occasional vacancies after entry. One 100 per cent means-tested scholarship available per annum and other support available as necessary.

Exit: 'We're fortunate in London that there are so many great schools,' says the head, 'and we are proud of the achievement of all our girls. There's no scholarship board here. We don't want to make some pupils feel instantly diminished.' That said, this is generally a school of bright sparks and ambitious parents and the majority proceed to the highest performing London day schools. City of London, North London Collegiate and South Hampstead top the list, with St Paul's Girls and Highgate close behind. Quite a number of scholarships amongst them. A handful to board and a few to Henrietta Barnett.

Remarks: St Christopher's was founded in 1883 by two local literary lesbians, but established in its current form in 1950 by the writer Rosemary Manning. It became a charitable trust in the 1970s. Housed in a large Victorian family house (with modern additions) in fashionable Belsize Park, this is a top-flight prep school for top-flight north London parents and the ethos and atmosphere are reflective of that. The education the pupils receive here is thoughtful and

The message that banking is as worthwhile a career for girls as nursing is instilled with visits to the Bank of England and a mock Dragon's Den

exciting. It concentrates on the fundamentals, but only after the fundamentals have been carefully considered. 'We have to ask the question what are we educating children for,' says the head. 'It's a world we know nothing about, a world very different from our own.' The school has carefully analysed the impact of technology. 'The girls think technologically and it can be much more difficult to get them to listen to a story and concentrate.' The issue is addressed by concentrated focus on the task of reading and understanding and girls read aloud every day from reception to year 3 and regularly thereafter. 'If you can't read, you can't do maths,' says the head. No concessions are made when it comes to literature ('We don't use abridged texts') and Dickens and Lewis Carroll are digested in the original. An excellent library underlines the school's priorities.

Much of the timetable follows the national curriculum ('It would be foolish not to, there are some very interesting things, but we cut away the trivia. We don't reject it, we tweak it.') and the approach is based on 'child-initiated learning' with pupils

taught to question and take responsibility for what they learn. Work is then tailored to the needs of each pupil, with maths books, for example, customised to the age and stage. (Though those in need of learning support are in the minority – mainly younger siblings – parents consider this tailoring, too, to be strong.) Spanish ('one of the most widely spoken languages in the world') is taught throughout, Latin from year 5 and French as a club from year 3. Specialist subject teaching from year 4, with drama added to the curricular mix, joined by history of art in year 5. Flexibility of mind is encouraged by the inclusion of chess. ('It's a brilliant thinking exercise.')

Hard-working, well-qualified staff, particularly in the final two years. 'I cannot imagine better teachers than the maths and English teachers in years 5 and 6,' said one parent. 'They are really transformative.'

Despite the school's outstanding scholarship record, there is no scholarship class and no setting, except in maths in the final two years. Nor is this a school that crams for exams; preparation lasts just one term, when practice papers are given weekly. 'They're not missing core subjects from year 5, they still have time for all the extracurricular, they're not pressured and processed,' says the head. The approach here is enriching and the head believes there is as much value in creativity as in the core subjects.

Music is generally considered strong and enthusiastic, with two music classes plus a singing class each week. What's learnt here is put into practice with a junior orchestra, a wind group, a string group, piano club, junior and senior choirs and a chamber choir. This is media land, too, and there is also a thriving film club, where girls learn to make their own. Cultural outings are very much part of the offering, with regular visits to theatres and museums and a young writers' workshop.

Sport is perhaps less important than it might be elsewhere (some parents complain that unless you're in a team, this can be a rather neglected area). Netball court and gym on site and regular matches against other schools in netball and rounders. Short tennis is also taught in the summer term and senior girls play lacrosse. Swimming lessons only in year 3 at nearby Swiss Cottage baths, sports day held at Hampstead Cricket Club. Though the outdoor space here is not unduly extensive, it is used very effectively, with an outdoor classroom, an Alice Garden and a science-themed garden. 'Children today have a very boring existence, chauffeured here and there,' says the head, 'and we wanted to create an environment where they were allowed to be imaginative.' Indeed, the thread that runs throughout St Christopher's is that a good education is stimulating, interesting and exciting.

The extracurricular is therefore addressed as energetically, with everything from public speaking to self-defence and Indian dance and, while there may be a Florence Nightingale workshop, the message that banking is as worthwhile a career for girls as nursing is instilled with visits to the Bank of England and a mock Dragon's Den. All staff are required to run two clubs a year and the offering is extensive.

Four houses, Bronte, Nightingale, North and Pankhurst, provide the basis for inter-house competition. The school has a strong family feel, sheltered and relaxed. There are no school rules ('We just ask for respect in the classroom and for them to be polite to teachers.') Good behaviour is instilled by discussion. ('Why did you do that? How do you imagine that would look?') Occasionally parents feel that emotional difficulties are not picked up as quickly as they might be. ('If you mention a problem, they take it seriously, but it's not always spotted,' said one.) Assembly every Friday is non-denominational. School meals exclude pork, shellfish, ham and nuts in order to cater for all. The facilities here have been brought thoroughly up to date, too, with a smart extension providing additional classrooms and state-of-the art IT. The green and blue uniform of Aertex shirts and blue trousers is practical and durable.

Over a third of pupils live within walking distance and the rest travel from affluent nearby postcodes like St Johns Wood, Maida Vale, Islington and Highgate. Parents are often intellectual, professional, international and Jewish – and occasionally celebrities. 'They are interesting and incredibly well-informed,' says the head. 'They are very involved and desperately keen to support their children's education. ('Sometimes too keenly involved,' remarked one father. 'There are a lot of non-working mothers who once had high-powered careers and are now directing their energies on their children.') Occasionally expectations have to be gently adjusted.

A high-octane education producing confident, well-informed and articulate girls. 'The nice thing about St Christopher's is that it provides an excellent education without trying to breed a master race,' says one happy customer.

St Margaret's Junior School (London)

Linked school: St Margaret's School (London), 167

18 Kidderpore Gardens, London, NW3 7SR

Independent • Pupils: 80 • Ages: 4–11 • Fees (per term): £3,470 – £3,930

Tel: 020 7435 2439
Fax: 020 7431 1308
Email: enquiry@st-margarets.co.uk
Website: www.st-margarets.co.uk

20

Principal: Mr Mark Webster. (see senior school review opposite).

Entrance: From reception to year 2 assessment involves girls coming in for the morning and working with the class teacher. From year 3 upwards they take a standard set of English and maths assessments.

Exit: About 80 per cent of girls stay on to the senior school, though a small number move to more selective senior schools such as North London Collegiate or City of London School for GIrls.

Remarks: Junior and senior schools both occupy the same building and have the same head, with different uniforms but little separation between them. The school has three houses, where pupils of all ages work together to raise funds for charities of their own choice and compete at sports. Very much a family school in every sense – 45 per cent of pupils are sisters or relatives of current or ex-pupils.

'There are, in fact, 158 options, so they do have some choice.'

In the juniors, all pupils follow the national curriculum (with the addition of French) from reception. An unusual addition is the head's own invention, '125' – a tribute to the school's 125th anniversary – which provides pupils with a list of activities to attempt at some point in their schooldays. 'There are, in fact, 158 options, so they do have some choice.' The range includes the practical, the cultural and the altruistic ('Do a nice thing for something who can do nothing in return').

Swimming throughout; teams for eg netball and rounders play inter-house and inter-school matches from year 4 upwards, variety of sports clubs. School has largish garden and there is a sports area a couple of minutes' walk away.

Gentle and nurturing with a strong family atmosphere.

St Margaret's School (London)

Linked school: St Margaret's Junior School (London), 166

18 Kidderpore Gardens, London, NW3 7SR

Independent • Pupils: 155 • Ages: 11–16 • C of E • Fees (per term): £3,470 – £4,020

Tel: 020 7435 2439
Fax: 020 7431 1308
Email: enquiry@st-margarets.co.uk
Website: www.st-margarets.co.uk

21

Principal: Since 2008, Mr Mark Webster BSc (mid-40s). Educated at Highgate School and University College London (where he read psychology), PGCE at Cambridge. Spent 15 years at the Royal School, Hampstead (first in primary, then IT, psychology and maths, before becoming deputy and acting head). Never planned to become a teacher – 'If you'd asked me early on what job I wanted to do, I'd have said teaching was 999th out of 1000'. A chance encounter changed his mind. 'I was working in publishing, when I met someone who said their job in teaching was fantastic. I'd never met anyone who felt that way about work.' Now equally enthusiastic about his chosen profession, Mr Webster continues to be hands on in his approach, teaching mathematics and '125' (see below). Particularly positive about working in a small school – 'I like the proximity and enjoy seeing the children grow up. You feel you can make a significant difference'. Operates an open-door policy and is constantly updating and improving what's on offer. Fundamental to his approach is the view that education is about instilling a sense of curiosity – 'Qualifications are a passport to the next stage, but if you remain curious you will never be bored'. He himself retains a

---

Drama is taken seriously. Performance is compulsory – 'We don't do Hamlet and let some people end up as third tree on the left.'

---

passionate interest in art, history and reading. Also plays football for Highgate Old Boys. A tactful, sympathetic enthusiast, Webster is a good fit for this family-like school. 'It's unusual to have a man,' said one mother, 'but I think he really cares.' Married to a teacher with two young sons.

Academic matters: GCSE options include Spanish, French, psychology, drama and music. An unusual addition is the head's own invention, '125' – a tribute to the school's 125th anniversary – which provides pupils with a list of activities to attempt at some point in their schooldays. 'There are, in fact, 158 options, so they do have some choice.' The range includes the practical, the cultural and the altruistic ('Do a nice thing for something who can do nothing in return'). In years 7, 8 and 9, 125 is a designated lesson.

In 2014, 42 per cent of GCSEs graded A*/A and 76 per cent A*-B. The majority take additional science (taught in a compact, but efficient, lab), enabling them to go on to science A levels, which many do. A modern language is compulsory (enthusiastic chatter about letters from French pen pals on the day we visited). The school is relatively non-selective and the ability range always includes the very able and those with more modest aspirations: in mathematics in year 11 there will be at least one girl taking the Foundation paper, whilst another achieves A* at A level. The plus side of a small school is class size (between 11-15 in the junior school, 11-19 thereafter) and personal attention – 'You don't get excellent results without teachers having spare time to help'. Setting introduced when necessary but, with limited space, teaching is usually differentiated rather than physically separated.

Outsiders have been known to view the school as a haven for the struggling, but it is only the right school for those with up to moderate special needs. 'We don't have the depth of resources for learning support that a larger school would have,' says the head. SENCo, plus a couple of teachers trained in dyslexia and dyscalculia, but the main support comes from classroom teachers. All abilities equally well catered for – 'We aren't results-driven and we exhaust every avenue'.

Games, options, the arts: The head's view is that education is a 'can-do', 'must try' matter and, inspired by the celebrated art historian Sir Ernst Gombrich's attitude – 'You don't have to like it, but it's important to understand why other people do..We compel them to try lots of things. They may moan, but we make them give it a go'. Drama is taken seriously. Performance is compulsory – 'We don't do Hamlet and let some people end up as third tree on the left. We make them write their own script and perform on a series of nights'. Music, too, is important – 'We have a super-motivated music teacher' – with a variety of traditional and less traditional extra-lesson options ('Handbells are very popular'). A number of choirs, plus a junior school orchestra. Some 80 per cent of girls have private instrument lessons at the school. Art immensely popular, with excellent results at GCSE: two studios, one reasonably spacious, the other definitely petite.

Outside space, too, is relatively restricted, with a largish garden transformed into an Astroturf playground. A local hall is used for gym and the school now has a sports area for netball, tennis and

other sports two minutes' walk away. Minibus takes girls to Hampstead Heath for rounders or running, to Hendon Leisure Centre for aerobics, rock climbing and badminton and the Welsh Harp for rowing. In David and Goliath mode the school is unafraid to compete with much larger north London schools like Highgate and Channing – 'We often lose' – but succeed when more evenly matched. Plenty of clubs (fencing, theatre, cookery, bicycle maintenance, knitting, philosophy, book club, tennis) and trips, local and international, from walks on Hampstead Heath to Spain and Iceland.

Background and atmosphere: Founded in 1884, it moved to its present site in a quiet, suburban Hampstead road in 1943. Senior and junior schools both occupy the same building and have the same head, with different uniforms but little separation between them. The school has three houses, where pupils of all ages work together to raise funds for charities of their own choice and compete at sports. It is small, cosy and friendly; a parent commented: 'It allows the girls to achieve whatever they can – but in a safe, non-confrontational environment'. Red and white uniform in the junior school, black and white in the senior. 'The head has changed the uniform and it's much more flattering,' said one mother. 'These things matter to teenage girls.'

Pastoral care and discipline: Discipline not a significant issue. Though head insists this is not the garden of Eden, disciplinary issues tend to be confined to infringements of uniform – 'We can live with earrings if there's no drink or drugs'. Bullying – 'We get a case every year' – is dealt with promptly. 'Parents tend to be very supportive. They come to this school for its caring environment and they're

---

Though head insists this is not the Garden of Eden, disciplinary issues tend to be confined to infringements of uniform – 'We can live with earrings if there's no drink or drugs.'

---

quick to back us up.' Parents couldn't agree more – 'You get ups and downs with some of the girls, but if you ever get a problem it's dealt with straight away,' said one. Most parents feel one of the school's greatest strengths is its pastoral side, allowing girls to fulfil their potential and know exactly who they are. 'It's too small a school not to be a community. Girls, for example, will discuss a problem on

Facebook and say, let's resolve this.' The school has its own head of pastoral care but also relies on a school counsellor when needed and pro-actively encourages 'bonding' with a variety of trips. 'The girls mix across the years and are often close to girls in the year above and below,' said a parent.

Pupils and parents: Nice, well-behaved, confident girls from a cosmopolitan range of backgrounds reflecting the school's north London location. A sizeable chunk come from within walking distance, then in an arc stretching from Wembley to Islington (school minibus on offer for those who require it). Very much a family school in every sense – 45 per cent of pupils are sisters or relatives of current or ex-pupils. 'A lot of people like the sense of support and nurturing.' Most newcomers hear about the school by word of mouth, though the internet (and recent accolades in The Sunday Times) have slightly altered the traditional intake. Those relocating can find it a particularly valuable resource. 'I like it because there is more of a mix than usual in north London,' said one mother.

Entrance: Guaranteed transition from within at 11. 'Once we've made the commitment, unless there are particular special needs we can't support, we stick to it.' External candidates take English, maths and verbal reasoning exams.

Exit: School has no intention of opening a sixth form despite parental requests. 'By then it really is time to move on.' Notably successful with applications at 16. Most popular choices at that point are local co-ed sixth forms like Highgate and UCS, and similar atmosphere girls' schools like Channing. A reasonable number to the state sector (St Marylebone particularly popular). Good guidance on offer at both 11 and 16 – 'It's really important to make an informed choice. Not every school will suit every girl and they are used to being supported here'. School also works with them on interview practice and personal statements. Girls generally get their first-choice sixth form – 'My daughter got in everywhere she applied,' said one parent.

Money matters: Not an expensive school by any means, but not much scope for additional funding. One 50 per cent scholarship at 11, about five per cent get some sort of bursary.

Remarks: A gentle, nurturing school with a strong and secure family atmosphere providing a stimulating, tailor-made education. 'A little gem,' to quote one parent, though possibly not the ideal venue for the child that needs plenty of space to run around or one who requires the challenge of a big stage.

St Mary's School, Hampstead

47 Fitzjohn's Avenue, London, NW3 6PG

Independent · Pupils: 280 · Ages: 2+ – 11 · Fees (per term): 2,235 – £4,020

Tel: 020 7435 1868
Fax: 020 7794 7922
Email: enquiries@stmh.co.uk
Website: www.stmh.co.uk

22

Headmistress: Since 2003, Miss Angela Rawlinson BA MA (fifties). A New Zealander, she did a degree in education and psychology at Auckland University, then trained as a teacher at Auckland Teachers' College. Taught in NZ for seven years, before arriving in the UK in 1989 to 'stay for a year'. After research at Cambridge (on drama in the curriculum), she worked in the state sector (as deputy head at the Servite RC Primary in Fulham and head at the Marlborough School, Kensington), before taking over at St Mary's.

Immensely professional, enthusiastic and energetic, she loves her work: 'In what other job would you find 300 people coming in and saying "I love you" every day?' Weekends are spent on the south coast reading, playing tennis and golf. 'She's amazing,' said one mother. 'You'll come in in the morning and find her skipping with the children. My daughter always rushes in to give her a big cuddle'.

Entrance: Names down at birth, but even delivery-room efficiency will not guarantee a place. These go first to siblings, then to Catholics, then to non-Catholics. Parents generally tour the school nine months before entry, sign the acceptance form and pay a deposit. Nursery arrangements are particularly parent friendly. Children are admitted from 2 years and 9 months and can stay to lunch or all afternoon with minimum notice. Boys make up a third of nursery entrants. A few further places for girls often become available in year 3.

Exit: About 85 per cent to leading academic secondary schools – South Hampstead, City of London, North London Collegiate, Highgate, Haberdashers' etc – quite a number with scholarships. Also to selective state schools (St Michael's Catholic Grammar, Henrietta Barnett). Secondary school advice is a strength, starting with individual parent meetings in year 5. 'Most trust us and listen to what we recommend', says the head. Boys leave by the age of 6, many to neighbouring Catholic prep St Anthony's.

Remarks: Founded in 1871, by the Congregation of Jesus, the school moved from Belsize Park in 1926 to its present building, a turn-of-the-century mansion with polished mosaic floors and vast country-like gardens. Against this gracious period backdrop,

facilities are thoroughly up to date, with a super, Mac-filled IT suite, large, new assembly hall and well-stocked library located in the panelled former billiards room. In 1992, when there were too few teaching nuns to manage the school, a charitable trust was formed to continue the good work under lay management.

A non-selective school, it still manages to pull off high-flying results at 11. Teaching (as described in the recent ISI report) is 'excellent' – sharp, lively and very pupil focused. 'The teacher worked out my

---

Most pupils adore the school ('my daughter can't wait to get back after the holidays') and parents are equally appreciative

---

daughter in three minutes', said one parent. Praise is appropriate and immediate. 'My daughter had been struggling to write a longer essay. On the day she did so, the head immediately called her in and gave her two merit points. It encouraged her so much'.

The brightest are stretched through a curriculum enriched with plenty of arts-related activities and sport. 'We wanted to make it more relevant', says the head, 'and incorporate risk taking and thinking independently'. Interesting extra work for those who need stretch (lunch-time puzzle club, for example, is a big hit).

Fluid ability grouping throughout, then setting in maths and English in year 6 in the run up to 11 plus. Excellent support for strugglers, too, with three special needs teachers providing help in class and out of it (in lovely, bright teaching space). 'The learning support is fantastic', said one mother with a daughter finding maths a mountain. 'Very few independent schools are non-selective, but St Mary's does very well by all'. Another told us: 'You really feel they care about every single girl. If someone is not up to scratch, the response is "what can we do to help them shine?"' External specialists are invited in to keep absence to a minimum.

Strong sport, with a double court for netball and a well-equipped gym. All the usual team games (rounders, netball, hockey, football), plus swimming at Swiss Cottage baths (for years 3 to 6) and athletics in Regent's Park. Gymnastics particularly popular, with pupils competing at regional and national level. High achievement too, in music and excellent dance and drama (including an all-encompassing production in year 6). Heaps of clubs (Latin, Spanish, needlework, craft, lingua franca) and plenty of trips (year 5 to an adventure camp in Devon, year 6 on a five-day break in France to meet pen pals and make croissants, little ones to a farm and the seaside).

Boys are well integrated and given appropriate scope in the Big Boys Club, in which football is played and steam let off on imaginary motor bikes. 'It lets them be boys in this all-girls environment', said one mother.

Very much a Catholic school, with about 70 per cent Catholic parents. 'I think one of the most wonderful things about it is that the Catholic ethos permeates every aspect of the children's life', said one. Those who wish can be prepared for First Holy Communion by much-loved Father Chris on his twice-weekly visits to the school chapel. Pupils participate in Mass and study Catholic Christianity. 'Many of our parents have had a Catholic education themselves and want that for their children', says the head – but even those who haven't feel included. 'As a non-Catholic', said one parent, 'I was quite concerned at the outset, but Father Chris is so lovely and give such interesting talks. They really teach the children how to be a good and loving member of a community'.

Pupils are beaming and notably well-behaved (not a peep was heard when our guide was chatting to one teacher as children queued to leave the room). 'We really work hard at being positive. We want to catch children doing the right thing', says the head. Plenty of rewards for those who are caught doing things 'the St Mary's Way'; those who

---

'In what other job would you find 300 people coming in and saying "I love you" every day?'

---

slip up are gently reminded of 'expectations'. 'We want pupils to do their best to be their best,' says the head. Most pupils adore the school ('my daughter can't wait to get back after the holidays') and parents are equally appreciative. 'You're never made to feel unwelcome, you never feel you shouldn't be there', we were told.

Mostly professional families from Hampstead and the surrounding areas, with a wide range of backgrounds (from Europe, the US, Asia and the Far East). About half speak at least one other language at home (with good in-school support for newcomers on the foothills of English). Mums 'really involved' (with reading, bazaars, the library, uniform sale). Despite its Hampstead location, this is a fairly understated place and, unusually for a prep school, offers a number of full bursaries.

The St Marylebone C of E School

64 Marylebone High Street, London, W1U 5BA

State • Pupils: 800 • Ages: 11–18 • C of E

Tel: 020 7935 4704
Fax: 020 7935 4005
Email: info@stmaryleboneschool.com
Website: www.stmaryleboneschool.com

56

Headteacher: Since January 2014, Kathryn Pugh, previously assistant head. A Cambridge graduate with first class honours in English, she joined St Marylebone in 2005 as English teacher and learning co-ordinator, and became assistant head in 2008. She has experience in business and the developing world as well as teaching.

Academic matters: St Marylebone's offers a lot of subject options – 'an amazing variety,' enthused one parent. Dance, health and social care, Latin and business studies canter alongside the front runners at GCSE and all are in the ribbons. Seventy-nine per cent 5+ A*-C grades in 2014 including maths and English with some outstanding performances (48 per cent A*/A). RS results are knockout and the curriculum is praised for its earnest inclusiveness. The Englishes are good, so are the single sciences though most take the double award. Maths more than respectable. Good to see German holding its own but no other lang apart than French, which does pretty well too. Art and history strong and popular. School has policy of taking some subjects – langs, ICT, RS – early to excellent effect. RS and German especially successful.

At A level, 74 per cent A*-B with 35 per cent A*/A in 2014. English by far the most popular. Psychology, sociology and economics among the options – the first much the favourite with a spread of results. Low take up for German and French – more support for modern langs seems needed here. Some parents wonder how the results are achieved with so little homework. Relatively good teacher:pupil ratio and school spends money on retaining good staff.

Gifted and talented programme. School caters for a range of SENs, has a SENCo, a full time SEN teacher, learning support assistants and specialist centres for students with learning difficulties. It is a centre of excellence for severe emotional and behavioural difficulties and can provide for ASD, ADD and Down's – if not severe. Can provide for moderate physical difficulties too.

Games, options, the arts: By all accounts it's the arts that flourish here and sports come a very poor second. 'Sports are useless,' said a parent, 'they just don't bother apart from the regulation double period.' 'You can do it if you feel like it,' said a pupil. 'We get our fitness from dance and drama. There are after-school clubs for people who are good' – open to all, says school. And there are – netball, football, trampolining, rugby and tennis as well as before school sessions in fitness, running etc. Underground sports hall – more than many

so urban a school could muster. Nonetheless, St M's is a performing arts college and this is evident whomever you speak to. Dance and music are outstanding and production values are high. 'The girls take huge pride in their performances,' we were told, 'even if not everyone can take part. It is inspirational.' The inspiration is further fuelled by the long-awaited £6m performing arts centre. This makes a huge difference – not least to the amount of space it frees for other curricular activities. In all respects the arts reign here. You can make everything from jewellery to ceramics and print your own photos. Debating, dance and musical performance of all kinds thrive.

To an extent these options are only available for the brightest and best. Parents who rave about the musical standards – 'The concerts just blow you away – it's like going to a serious musical event' – acknowledge that only the best will get in on the act. Opportunities like GCSE photography work in the highly professional Metro Studios only available to the three or four girls whose applications to take the course are considered sufficiently impressive. This is the reality of a state-funded school but it must be trying for the also-rans and would-bes.

Background and atmosphere: Unique city setting – off Marylebone High Street with Regent's Park over the (horribly busy) road. Victoriana with some attractive features – high ceilings, gothic windows and plenty of light. Radical building plans now completed. Cramped and crammed – though the performing arts building makes a big difference, as does

Much appreciated are the proper, old–fashioned termly reports which don't just parrot at you what the class has done but actually talk about your own daughter

the newish sixth form centre on Blandford Street; every nook has something educational squashed into it. No space for lockers so girls are adept at carting their lives around with them and being organised about what they need for each lesson. Lunch is eaten in form rooms, though year 10 examinees and upwards are mercifully allowed out to settle in the numerous cafés round about at lunchtime.

The admissions policy (see below) dictates that active membership of the C of E is the main criterion for entry and this also influences the ethos. Parents are, in general, impressed. 'I trust it,' said one, 'to give my daughter a good education.' 'It's highly organised,' said another. 'Very efficient,

there's plenty of notice about everything. They're very attentive to detail.' Far better equipped and resourced than most such schools largely due to incessant and skilful fundraising and the band of supportive parents.

In September 2013 opened The St Marylebone Bridge School, a co-educational free special school for children with statements for speech, language and communication, which shares some governors and teachers with the main school.

Pastoral care and discipline: Discipline reportedly 'fearsome' and 'slightly on the petty side' but generally felt to be effective and well understood by pupils. Not a whisper of drugs or even smoking being 'issues'. Links with home are excellent, say parents – and not only when there are problems. 'They write and tell us if our daughter has improved at something or just made a big effort,' nodded a parent. Much appreciated are the proper, old-fashioned termly reports which don't just parrot at you what the class has done but actually talk about your own daughter. Good, realistic and collaborative target-setting also works. House system. Pastoral care and support seen as very good overall on both academic and personal matters and many teachers seen as good and dedicated – but a few glaring exceptions and some just felt to be uninspiring.

Pupils and parents: About 65 per cent from ethnic minority backgrounds and from 90 different countries. Over 50 per cent of pupils are bilingual. More than 60 languages spoken at home. Sixty per cent C of E members; the largest second religious group is Muslim. Some feeling among parents that little is done to encourage friendships between the different ethnic and religious groups. Others reported that 'the school is big enough for girls to make real choices about friendships and there's a very open environment.' School clearly tries hard – has an annual World Culture Day among many other initiatives – and attracts fierce loyalty. Active parents' group works hard though has problems involving all but the usual – mostly white, middle class – suspects

Entrance: Absurdly and maddeningly oversubscribed – something like 1,000 applicants for 150 places. School no longer allowed to interview applicants – 'they hate that,' said a sympathetic parent. Admissions criteria are primarily that you have to be C of E – 60 per cent are – though looked after children and those with statements have priority. Thirty per cent of places are 'open', with distance the only criteria. Twelve places annually given to those with outstanding aptitude in an aspect of performing arts (music, choral, dance or drama). Applicants divided into four ability bands with equal numbers accepted from each band. Tie breaker of how near to the school you live. In the sixth, 275 – priority to existing students, though they have to fulfil requirements (minimum of five A*-C GCSEs). Boys are taken into the sixth and, again, more apply than there are places for. School receives five applications a week for occasional places.

Exit: One-quarter leave after GCSE and go to sixth form colleges, the independents, eg Latymer Upper, or other state schools, eg Camden, largely for a greater range of A level objects or for boys. Most stay, though entrance to the school's own sixth form is not a given, even for their own. Sixth form leavers to good universities and a range of courses; four to Cambridge in 2014.

Money matters: National funding programmes such as Excellence in Cities ended many years ago so bidding for extra money from various sources takes up a lot of time. The result, however, is a school that is well-staffed and well-equipped, if not to lavish private school standards.

Remarks: Exceptional, successful inner-city school serving a diverse community with a strong middle class core. Combines best traditional values with best modern practice. New head will undoubtedly take some time to make the school her own after her predecessor's 20 year reign.

St Paul's Cathedral School

2 New Change, London, EC4M 9AD

Independent • Pupils: 255 • Ages: 4–13 • C of E • Fees (per term): Day £4,167 – £4,487; boarding +£2,595; choristers £2,595

Tel: 020 7248 5156
Fax: 020 7329 6568
Email: admissions@spcs.london.sch.uk
Website: www.spcslondon.com

33

Headmaster: Since 2009, Mr Neil Chippington MA (Cantab) FRCO (40s). Music scholar at Cranleigh, organ scholar at Cambridge, Fellow of the Royal College of Organists, music is certainly in his blood. Came from Winchester College where he was a housemaster for eight years and, having himself been a quirister (chorister) at Winchester Cathedral, seems to be the ideal person to have taken the responsibility of 30 boarding choristers and a school bursting with music. Says he wants to make sure that all children reach their academic potential and are stretched to the limit of their abilities without the school becoming a hothouse. Feels it is crucial to get the balance right so that both choristers and day children get a wide breadth of educational experience and benefit from each other's talents.

Currently reviewing the curriculum, looking at different ways of approaching CE. Open minded and not afraid of change. Says 'the bottom line is to instil a love of learning'. Has introduced a more significant staff appraisal system. Communication apparently an issue when he arrived but believes he has opened up the lines. Responds quickly to emails and maintains an open door policy. Parents acknowledge this improvement. Married with two small sons, the elder of whom is at the school.

In amongst the hustle and bustle of the City of London, an oasis of orderliness and calm. Boy choristers have been around since 1123

Entrance: Seventy on list for 20 available places at 4+, so best to put children down early. Informal assessment in November before year of entry. More places at 7+ when boarding choristers also start. January assessment and short test for day children (also taken by those in pre-prep); informal audition with director of music for choristers, followed by formal audition and same academic test as day children. More places for choristers at 8+ and occasionally 9+. Choristers' fees paid by Dean and Chapter of St Paul's Cathedral with parents paying boarding fee. This will carry on even if a boy's voice breaks early. If in need, bursaries available for day children also. Head is keen to build up a fund and expand this.

Exit: At 11+ and 13+ to a mixture of London day schools and top boarding schools. Majority of girls at 11+ though head eager to keep girls and maintain balance. Choristers mostly to boarding schools at 13+. An impressive number of music and the occasional academic scholarships. Westminster appears high among day schools, with City of London (girls and boys), Highgate, Forest School and JAGS also featuring. King's Canterbury popular amongst a wide selection of good boarding schools. Recently, Eton, Stowe, Uppingham and Oundle have all offered academic and music scholarships. Famous ex pupils include Alastair Cooke (England cricket captain) and Simon Russell Beale (actor).

Remarks: A small school, nestling in the precincts of St Paul's Cathedral, providing an excellent all round education in a traditional setting with a formal, spiritual context to everything it does. In amongst the hustle and bustle of the City of London, an oasis of orderliness and calm. Boy choristers have been around since 1123, originally linked to a grammar school which became St Paul's School, London, about 400 years later. Only tenuous links remain. In 1989, the Dean and Chapter decided to expand the tiny choristers' only school to include day boys as well. Girls arrived in 1998 and the school grew to the size it is today.

Two low concrete towers house the classrooms and are linked by the school hall, the gym, the library and various other communal activity areas. We seemed to wander up and down and across as enthusiastic pupils showed us their school but 'once you know the two towers it's easy,' they assured us. Three lovely bright classrooms for the pre-prep years, two each for years 3 and 4, then subject-based doubling up as home rooms from year 5 onwards.

Broad-based curriculum with all subjects well taught. Parents praise 'inspirational teachers' who are 'passionate about everything they do'. Average age 39 seems about right. Our guides also spoke enthusiastically about their teachers, singling out

science and Latin/Greek as exceptional. Certainly pupils did look happy and absorbed in the excellent science lab, however the French class we looked in on appeared chaotic. Mixed ability classes throughout with some discreet setting, particularly in years 7 and 8. Previously some complaints about lack of preparation for 11+ entrance exams but head is driving this forward and has made important changes, revamping part of the curriculum and timetabling non-verbal reasoning, study skills etc into earlier years. Parents very happy about this. Creative writing, apparently, a great strength. Latin compulsory from year 5. Modern languages not the strongest point, though French taught from the beginning and Spanish available as an extra. Head's wife a linguist, so change could be in the air. Interactive white boards in classrooms and new IT suite. All special needs problems dealt with by head of learning support. Teachers flag up concerns and he is immediately involved. Any necessary help is provided, mostly free of charge. Additional staff available for one-to-one and in-class support when necessary. Parents kept fully in the picture and involved from the beginning.

Reasonable art. Studio also contains a printing press (given by the Stationers' Company) and a kiln for firing imaginative clay models. Location excellent for visiting Tate Modern as part of extended art lesson. Drama strongish and everyone gets a chance to take part in a production. As one of our guides said, 'if you're not particularly musical, you can still do drama and have fun'. LAMDA exam course available.

Inevitably the greatest strength is music, huge both instrumentally and vocally. Virtually every child in the school learns an instrument of his or her choice (no bagpipes!). Choristers learn two, piano being compulsory. Over 300 music lessons

Virtually every child in the school learns an instrument of his or her choice (no bagpipes!). Choristers learn two, piano being compulsory

given each week, beginners all the way to grade 8. At least six different choirs plus 15 orchestras and ensembles from classic to rock band. Something for everyone you might say. For musical, creative children it is a great place to be. Opportunities abound. Choristers are in the minority but it is their talent that is the backbone of the school. Head feels that one of the most crucial things he needs to do is clarify the way they are perceived. The day school exists because of them and they are getting a wider breadth of education because of the day school. Thus both sides are gaining a huge amount and it is important to maintain the balance. Choristers are acquiring an excellent academic education and day pupils are seeing, hearing and being involved in music of an exceptionally high standard. All of them are equally at home in the cathedral, which they treat as an extension of the school. Assemblies and occasional special services held and the majority get the chance to sing there. A parent told us, 'the Christmas service was something to behold.. about six or seven different choirs were fielded, including a combined one which seemed to involve most of the school'.

Choristers have a pretty heavy schedule with singing practice before school every morning, evensong on Tuesdays, Wednesdays, Fridays and Saturdays plus Saturday morning rehearsals and Sunday services. Alongside a multitude of other occasions when they have to perform. One of the first things the head did for them was to negotiate Monday evenings off as well as Thursdays. Seems only fair after an action-packed weekend. He also stresses the importance of watching the development of their voices and becoming more aware of change – necessary with the earlier physical growth that now occurs. Thirteen-year-old trebles are rarer. Both the cathedral's director of music and organist are also committed to their personal development and nurture.

A father said, 'Sport at the school is active, fun and inclusive'. Despite its inner city site, it is well catered for. Pupils are bused to Coram's Fields and Regent's Park for seasonal activities. Matches fielded against other schools in hockey, football, cricket, rounders, fencing and netball. Have been runners up in U12 London Schools' Cricket Association Cup, winners of the Girls' Football South London

Tournament and pupils have been selected for the U10 National Fencing Squad and the U11 Surrey County Cricket squad. Also swim at local baths recreationally and competitively. Rubber surfaced playground, marked up for ball games, for the prep where teachers also arrange impromptu games and sports practice. Brand new, larger, grass and wood-chip playground with climbing equipment for the pre-prep. Older children allowed to play quiet games here but not allowed to climb.

A variety of after-school clubs, mainly on Thursdays to enable choristers to join in, but on other days too. Range from cookery to dance to computer etc. Bound to be something for everyone. Also children may stay to do supervised prep at school, charged as an extra but useful for working parents. Plenty of outings and expeditions, academic, cultural and sporty. Home and occasionally abroad. A lot to see within walking distance as well.

Parents stress the happy atmosphere – 'it has been the making of our little boy' – (of a chorister) and 'our unsettled, troublemaker has been transformed' – (of a day boy). 'Very good discipline, they don't tolerate bad behaviour'. General feeling that children are treated as individuals, academically stretched and made to work to their own levels; that the school is 'well managed and well ordered'. Much of this appears to lie in the vertical tutor system. Pupils are assigned to a tutor from day one and, in normal circumstances, remain with him/her until they leave the school. Thus tutor groups mixed in both ability and age and there is easy

rapport between all children across the school. The older ones love helping the younger ones.

According to parents excellent pastoral care, particularly for the boarders. 'They get well cared for, individual treatment and feel they are part of a family'. Several raved about the deputy head (pastoral) who, they say, really carried the school through recent difficult times. Definitely feel there's a good team in place now.

Effective and active PTA. General feeling is that head is in tune with all pupils and ideal person to be running the boarding section as well. Watch this spot for further developments.

St Peter's Eaton Square CofE Primary School

Lower Belgrave Street, London, SW1W 0NL

State • Pupils: 340 • Ages: 3–11 • C of E

Tel: 020 7641 4230
Fax: 020 7641 4235
Email: office@stpeaton.org.uk
Website: www.stpeaton.org.uk

57

Head: Since 2010, Ms Nicola Cottier BEd Cantab (40s). Previously head of St Matthew's, Westminster, since 1996. Educated at Sutton High, her first job was at Moira House, an independent girls' school in Sussex. She has worked in the Bahamas, United States, Canada and Wales, but most recently in London schools with church links. She is married with two children, and lives in Kew. She revolutionised the music provision at St Matthew's, where she was described as an 'inspirational headteacher' who

'created the most wonderful spirit in the school'. She is hugely enthusiastic, rhapsodising about the 'fantastic' ethos and supportive community at St Peter's.

Entrance: Ten part-time nursery places. No automatic transfer to reception – must re-apply and meet criteria. Nearly all of the nursery places go to baptised children whose families worship regularly at St Peter's Church Eaton Square; preference after that to siblings, then to baptised children who attend other churches without their own church school. Families come from a wide area and a huge range of backgrounds – 'duchesses to dustmen'. Apply through the local authority, with supplementary school form, during autumn term a year before entry. Takes 50 children into reception, again according to criteria.

Exit: Girls to Grey Coat Hospital, St Marylebone, Lady Margaret's; boys to London Nautical, Pimlico Academy etc. Over half to independent schools: Westminster Under School, JAGS, City of London, St Paul's, Godolphin and Latymer, Emanuel, Streatham & Clapham High etc. Children not encouraged to move on to independents at 7 or 8: 'We won't go out of our way to support it. It is disruptive, and our children do very well getting the places they want at 11.' A parent commented: 'Why would you want to move earlier when they all do so well here?'

Remarks: Very popular and over-subscribed central London primary school, tucked away in a side street just round the corner from Victoria Station. Consistently excellent, lively teaching, with each child's progress closely tracked. The majority of pupils reach level 5 in year 6: a huge achievement. Languages strong: Latin from year 3 upwards. Dedicated IT suite with 30 computers. Inclusion Manager has responsibility for EAL and G&T as well as those with SEN. Teaching assistants deployed to support children as needed. Parents also pitch in as eg volunteer readers. Good at spotting problems with vulnerable children and liaising with outside agencies where necessary. 'We always cater for a wide

range of needs.' Two reception classes of 25; higher up, the children in each of years 1/2, 3/4 and 4/5 are divided by age into three classes over two year groups.

'We are blessed that we have really fabulous music.' No orchestra, but peripatetic teachers for recorder, violin, drums, guitar, piano and brass, as well as class music lessons, trips to concerts at the Barbican etc, singing at the Royal Albert Hall and at Friday's Sung Eucharist service. Very little space for sport on site – the hall is used for gym and PE and the small, soft-surface playground has a climbing wall

Girls from Grey Coat Hospital do work experience at St Peter's, and pupils visit Westminster City School for their science week

along one side. However, they swim at the Queen Mother Sports Centre (notable successes in galas), play sports in Battersea Park and Hyde Park (year 1 were off for a multi-skills session when we visited) and borrow Westminster School's Vincent Square sports site. Professional sports coaches run twice-weekly sessions, and football, cricket and tennis teams play in inter-school matches. 'It's such a cramped site that we try to get them out as much as possible.'

Enrichment is a buzz word here and there are plenty of outings – 'It's a fabulous situation: everything is on our doorstep' – to eg the V&A, National

Gallery, London Zoo. Year 6 visits Sayers Croft field centre in Surrey. Girls from Grey Coat Hospital do work experience at St Peter's, and pupils visit Westminster City School for their science week. Strong tradition of raising funds for charity.

St Peter's was first mentioned in an 1860s survey as an infants' school in Ecclestone Square. Moved to its present site, donated by the Marquess of Westminster, in 1872; became an infant and junior school in 1949. Building and site compact, but even the basement nursery classrooms are light, bright and cheerful; youngest classes have their own indoor/outdoor partly-covered play area. The upper floor classrooms, carved from the top half of a hall, have beautiful large, round windows. Airy feel but very cramped for space: every nook and cranny has at least three different uses. A major building project in 2012 remodelled the school to create sufficient classrooms to introduce two forms incrementally into each year group.

School follows Anglo-Catholic tradition and there are services at school and in Westminster Abbey as well as in the strongly-linked namesake church: clergy pop in and out and are available for counselling. The church interior, redesigned after an anti-Catholic arson attack 20 years ago, is a beautiful, simple, open space which 'lends itself to our nativity plays' and is also the setting for year 6 productions, concerts and speech days as well as services.

A tightly-run ship: children are neat and tidy, with tucked-in shirts and tied-back hair. They are orderly in class and move quietly around the building. The atmosphere is welcoming, friendly and purposeful. Parents appreciate the combination of excellent behaviour, kind ethos and inspiring teaching. 'It is a warm and safe place,' said one.

Active PTA which organises social events such as Burns Night and helps with eg Easter Fair. This is not a local school – families come from a wide area – but there is a strong community of parents, many of whom also meet at church events, including those who attended the school themselves. Children who have moved on to secondary school come back to do work experience and spread their news. 'We know they do well wherever they go.'

St Vincent de Paul RC Primary School

Morpeth Terrace, London, SW1P 1EP

State • Pupils: 250 • Ages: 3–11 • RC

Tel: 020 7641 5990
Fax: 020 7641 5901
Email: office@svpschool.co.uk
Website: www.svpschool-primary.org.uk

58

Head: Since 2002, Jack O'Neill STB MA (50s). Studied theology at university. His teaching career started in Hammersmith and Fulham, arriving at St Vincent de Paul as deputy head, then promoted to head.

He shares his passion for Roman history with pupils, accompanying the children on visits to local sites and teaching the Minimus Mouse Latin course to year 4 and year 5. Parents say head's dynamic and considered approach shines through in a number of areas – particularly music, pastoral care and efficient management of the school's budget. He is supported by a dedicated team of assistants, teachers and committed parents.

Entrance: Always oversubscribed. Nursery children are not guaranteed entry into the main school at 4+. Priority given to practising Roman Catholics, with distance from the school used as a tiebreaker. First priority goes to looked after Catholic children, then baptised, practising siblings, then baptised Catholics. A waiting list is kept for occasional places.

Exit: Most pupils get their first choice secondary school. Popular choices include Sacred Heart, London Oratory, Cardinal Vaughan and St Thomas More as well as others further afield including Westminster Cathedral Choir School.

Remarks: School was founded in 1859 by the Sisters of Charity of St Vincent de Paul to enable them to work with the poor of Westminster. Moved to current premises in the shadows of Westminster Cathedral, conveniently next door to St Paul's bookshop, in 1974.

Pupils come from a wide variety of backgrounds. Around three-quarters speak English as an additional language. Fairly compact site – outdoor space has been redeveloped to create three separate play areas for nursery children, infants and juniors. Cleverly designed, with lots of greenery and modern play equipment. Pupils also use the playgrounds and local sports facilities for team sports and have a dedicated sports coach for all PE lessons. Inside, school is light, modern and well

School is part of the Westminster Cathedral Choir School outreach programme and the choir performs at Westminster Cathedral

designed. Peaceful chapel is very much at the heart of this friendly and well-disciplined school.

While this is a Catholic school, pupils are taught to understand other faiths and cultures. Good behaviour, thinking of others and cooperation goes without saying. Pupils are monitored regularly to assess their progress and there are plenty of parent evenings, giving everyone the opportunity to discuss their children. Written reports at the end of each year.

Alongside the national curriculum, the arts and sports, pupils benefit from being taught Spanish from the age of 7. Latin is introduced in year 4. Academic results are exceptional. Staff have high expectations and have created a good learning ethos. The SENCo coordinates additional needs and runs a Units of Sound action programme. There is also a school counsellor.

Multi-coloured and multimedia displays of artwork adorn classrooms and corridors. Large, multi-purpose hall where children practise for termly concerts and plays and musical performances. School is part of the Westminster Cathedral Choir School outreach programme and the choir performs at Westminster Cathedral as well as regularly singing at family Mass. Well-stocked music room with an impressive selection of instruments – from glockenspiels to bongo drums. All have singing and music lessons, provided by a dedicated music teacher. Pupils talk excitedly about how they are encouraged to create their own music. Small charge is made for individual lessons on a wide range of instruments.

Sixth formers from neighbouring Westminster School work as volunteers, acting as classroom assistants and helping to run school clubs. ICT room doubles up as a cinema for film club.

Not a place for those who wish to sit on their laurels. Energetic PTA meets regularly to discuss the organisation of numerous fundraising events for the school. Each family is asked to make a small annual contribution towards the maintenance and building fund – for the benefit of the present community and to ensure continuation for future generations. Pupils are active fundraisers and run regular charity events. The school also works with Mission Together, a charity that encourages children to care about mission through prayer, learning and fundraising.

A lively and impressive school that produces caring and thoughtful individuals. Recently downgraded by Ofsted to 'requires improvement', largely due to lack of challenge at KS1. However, parents praise it to the rafters and pupils say they look forward to going to school.

Sarum Hall School

15 Eton Avenue, London, NW3 3EL

Independent · Pupils: 175 girls · Ages: 3–11 · C of E · Fees (per term): £3,860 – £4,180

Tel: 020 7794 2261
Fax: 020 7431 7501
Email: admissions@sarumhallschool.co.uk
Website: www.sarumhallschool.co.uk

23

Headmistress: Since 2008, Mrs Christine Smith BA Cert Ed RSA (SpLD) (50s). Mrs Smith spent the previous 17 years at Lochinver Prep in Potter's Bar. Began her career teaching home economics and textiles at Edmonton County School before having her two daughters. Lured back to teaching to work with deaf children, eventually becoming director of studies at Lochinver and setting up their learning support unit. When her children left home, she felt ready for a new challenge. 'I walked into Sarum Hall and knew immediately I could see myself here'. Describes herself as 'a calm person', and is widely seen as a sensible, soothing presence.

Parents find her very approachable – 'Mrs Smith is so nice. She smiles all the time'. Married to an actuary. Interests include tai chi, cooking, the theatre and martial arts (she spent time in Beijing learning about swords).

Entrance: Main intake in September after 3rd birthday. Register as soon after birth as possible with a non-refundable deposit of £100. Parents are invited two years before entry to visit the school on a working day and then write to confirm their continued interest in a place. The school is non-selective, but priority is given to siblings and to the children and

grandchildren of former pupils. The remainder of the 22-24 nursery places are based on the head's decision – 'I meet all the parents and discuss what kind of school they hope for for their daughter. This is very much a community school'. Most pupils are local, ideally within walking distance. Occasional vacancies arise after nursery. From year 1, applicants are tested in English and maths.

Exit: Practically all to their first-choice school at 11: Channing, City Girls, Francis Holland, Godolphin & Latymer, Highgate, Immanuel, North London Collegiate, South Hampstead, St Helen's and St Paul's. Also, unusually for a north London prep, a reasonable contingent to board at eg Wycombe Abbey, Queenswood, St George's Ascot.

Remarks: If a school can have the 'wow factor', then Sarum Hall definitely does. Housed in a superb, RIBA-lauded contemporary building, which provides plenty of well-planned light and airy space to work, move about and play. 'Even on the most dismal day,' says the head, 'the school is flooded with natural light.' High design standards are complemented with attractive displays of fresh flowers and a rooftop extension provides a quiet room for music exams and practice.

The head has a clear vision of a continuing tradition – 'Sarum Hall is an academic school whose girls go on to further education and develop a lifelong love of learning. But the school places as strong an emphasis on the cultural and social as the academic. Music, art and drama have a central role'.

Good, solid, traditional teaching using the national curriculum but not the dreaded Sats. 'The school really prepares pupils superbly for 11 plus,' says one mother with two daughters who've successfully surmounted that hurdle. Specialist subject teaching in PE, music, IT and French from nursery, science from year 3, English, maths and humanities in years 5 and 6. Inspired science teaching ('very practical and relevant,' said one parent), taught in a well-furnished lab to the accompaniment of classical music. Some setting in maths, but 'we don't make too much of that'. However signifi-

> *Imaginative cross-curricular teaching. 'One girl found a flattened toad in Africa and it was incorporated into the study of Macbeth,' says the head*

cant differentiation to meet individual needs, with additional work, for example, for those sitting boarding school entrance exams and plenty of classroom assistance throughout. Imaginative cross-curricular teaching. 'One girl found a flattened toad in Africa and it was incorporated into the study of Macbeth,' says the head. Long serving ('people come to stay'), highly-regarded staff. 'Some of the teachers have a real passion for their subject,' says one mother.

Learning support unit (with one dedicated member of staff) copes with dyslexia, dyspraxia and the 'gifted and talented', at no additional cost. (Girls are taken out of lessons for individual or group support, though this is 'not a huge part of the school'.) Homework introduced gently in year 2, rising to a maximum of one hour a night in year 6. All pupils expected to read daily. Bright and breezily decorated library open to all in lunch and break, plus library lessons as part of the curriculum.

Music, art and drama all lively and strong. Majority of girls study one or more instruments after year 2 and get plenty of opportunity to show off in class assemblies, frequent concerts and house drama. Also sit the English Speaking Board exams to build up communication skills. Stunning studio art room with north-facing light is made full use of – pupils study sculpture, print, textiles and woodwork. Also frequent exposure to the real thing, with outings to exhibitions as well as in-house visits from professional artists.

Though outdoor space is not extensive, the outside is as well planned as the interior and daily sport or PE takes place on three Astroturf courts (used for netball, hockey, rounders, soccer, cricket and tennis) or in the assembly hall, which triples as a gym (for dance as well as gymnastics) and theatre. Swimming once more part of the curriculum, at nearby Swiss Cottage Baths. Annual athletics meet on Hampstead Heath.

Plenty of nourishing after-school clubs (yoga, sewing, knitting, Mandarin) and enriching outings to theatres etc – 'We take full advantage of what's on our doorstep'. Year 6 summer programme to manage post 11-plus drag offering first aid, cookery, Mandarin and other handy skills. Residential trips to Flatford Mill and a château in France.

Very much a family-based school. 'We care about the whole family and want to nurture the natural talents of every girl,' says the head, and parents feel it lives up to its aims. 'I've had three daughters here and enjoyed it all the way; it's a wonderful school,' says one. Traditional good manners (from year 2 girls leap to their feet when head enters and chorus, 'Good morning, Mrs Smith'). 'We don't have any behavioural problems,' says head. Positive rewards for good behaviour, constant emphasis on Golden Rules – 'we are gentle, kind and helpful. We listen and are honest and work hard. We look after property. We don't hurt anybody's feelings' etc. Three houses, with house points for good work and good behaviour, lots of praise and positive reinforcements. Food prepared daily on site with vegetarian option and faithful stalwarts like syrup sponge and custard. No packed lunch. Staff eat with girls. No mobile phones, no email, supervised internet use only. Affiliated to the Church of England and the large number of Jewish girls and other faiths join in daily assembly with the Lord's Prayer and hymns.

Enthusiastic charitable fundraising. 'These girls are very privileged and we try and get them to see that,' says the head. Parents and pupils are predominantly affluent, white, middle-class professionals – accountants, lawyers, city, etc, not too many media – with a strong international contingent, mainly European, Indian and Chinese. Many girls have brothers at The Hall and Arnold House (and head does her best to ensure coordinated term dates). No scholarships or bursaries, though will support parents if they fall on hard times.

A very well-run, small, intimate, traditional girls' prep in a wonderful modern setting that gets the very best out of a broad range of ability without too much pressure and provides a rich education in every sense. Possibly not the ideal school for the maverick child (or parent) or one who doesn't deal happily with authority.

Sir John Cass's Foundation Primary School

St James's Passage, 27 Duke's Place, London, EC3A 5DE

State · Pupils: 270 · Ages: 3m–11 · C of E

Tel: 020 7283 1147
Fax: 020 7626 5071
Email: sirjohncassprimary@cityoflondon.gov.uk
Website: www.sirjohncassprimary.org

34

Executive Headteacher: Since January 1993, Mr Gerry Loughran (early 50s), a bright eyed-Geordie who steadfastly refuses to be tempted away into inspecting or the like – 'I don't want to leave the chalkface!' He's taught and co-ordinated and led at four other primaries in central London before Sir John Cass and still works alongside teachers.

Efficient and enthusiastic, he moves easily between talking to pupils ('why are you in the classroom at lunch? I'm listening, you listen to me'), parents (about updating their work skills and what they need to look for in a secondary school) and bigwigs such as the mayor. Very proud of success stories, eg a young mother just finished qualifying in Cambridge and keen to return to her old school to teach.

Entrance: At 3+, oversubscribed (75 applications for 30 places) and priority given to families/children in need in the City of London, then those who attend St Botolph's or neighbouring churches and live in the area, then siblings. Worth ringing, since places do open up when families move out of the area. If your child gets a place in the nursery, the school will do its utmost to keep them throughout the school.

Exit: To full range of secondary schools – church, community, independent and residential eg City of London Girls, City of London Boys, Christ's Hospital, City Academy in Southwark. Since performing arts and music are so strong here parents are advised to look for opportunities for their children to continue.

Remarks: Founded in 1710, the only voluntary aided school in the City of London (so not short of resources); this Georgian mass is open 50 weeks a year and is so much more than just a school. An oasis in the traffic that is Aldgate (the pollution monitor in the playground registers remarkably low readings), pedestrians can peer down at the little ones in the courtyard of the Cass Child and Family Centre – 90 reading and language partners from surrounding offices volunteer at lunchtime. The main entrance is opposite a café, and visitors walk directly into the playground. The day we did, there was a line of helmeted children ready, with their trusty steeds, for their cycle safety test.

Between them pupils and parents speak 36 languages, and backgrounds range from two families sharing a flat to one with a Barbican pad and a house in the country. A teacher and a nursery officer work alongside class teachers to support those with English as a second language (50 per cent of the kids are Bangladeshi). A SENCo liaises with children, four LSAs and nine TAs for reading development, and school is also in touch with CAMHs. Snoezelen room in the nursery section is fully equipped with sensory equipment to calm children (and staff!). The school is totally inclusive of those with relevant support – at present three with statements and one with Downs Syndrome.

A key worker is assigned to four or five families and they are visited before children's entrance. The centre also offers an extended school service to the community with health and social visitors, Jobcentre Plus and lots of advice and support sessions for parents in a family learning room and Sp@

ce: computer lessons, volunteering at your school, child development classes, first aid, ESL and getting back to work training. Many social functions for parent and community group (eg summer market, international food night) and art projects have led to work exhibited in the V&A and the Bethnal Green Museum of Childhood.

The teaching team is stable and ranges from the newly qualified to those with 30 years of experience. RE is popular, with two terms on Christianity, the other on another world faith and, as with sex education, parents can withdraw their children from these lessons but none do. The curriculum is made real in all manner of ways: artist and poet residencies, a roof garden with class planters and

Between them pupils and parents speak 36 languages, and backgrounds range from two families sharing a flat to one with a Barbican pad and a house in the country

greenhouse overlooked by the Foster's Gherkin, maths linked to musical notation and vice versa, the home beat police officer in class to talk about peer pressure and avoidance of gangs, after-school clubs (including knitting with senior citizens who provide tales of the war years to those kids with no extended family). Key stage 2 get to go on two school journeys for a week to experience life with their friends outside London.

A musicianship teacher begins strings project with the little ones (nursery to year 3) and by years 4, 5 and 6 all play a violin, cello etc of their own – groups have performed for the Lord Mayor, Prince Phillip, Bill Clinton and Tony Blair. The choir has sung on the Queen's Christmas broadcast and at the Royal Albert Hall (three-part harmony!).

The school coach runs relays to St George's Pool on the Highway or a crocodile of children snakes to the one in Golden Lane. The annual sports day takes place at Mile End stadium, the school competes as the City's team for the London Heathrow Games and occasionally plays rugby against other schools but, since it is the only one in the borough, there is not much competition. There's a traditionally equipped sports hall (huge windows and high ceilings throughout the school) on the second floor, in addition to the lines of different courts painted in the playground.

The basement (a secure area in case of bomb threat) houses the computer suite with 15 workstations networked to a couple in each class and an interactive whiteboard. This technology doesn't come without an awareness of the environment: the school received an award for work on recycling paper, printer cartridges, composting and installing timers on light switches.

Food is cooked on the premises and served in what is now called The Restaurant on the top floor; there are themed days with the menu scribed up on a whiteboard (tropical fruit, bread), and a comments book for the children. Some 35 per cent get free school meals. Manners are incredibly important here (one child says a prayer before everyone

tucks in) and everyone learns to behave politely according to their surroundings, whether it is lunch at Mansion House or breakfast club.

The Behaviour for Learning Policy is applied positively; however, a series of sanction slips is given out for ignoring the school code of conduct (respect, cooperation, truth and honesty, trying your best etc) – four of these mean the child will be excluded and this hardly ever happens. Fire drills and bomb alerts are necessarily slick with the head's bleeper linked directly to the City of London police.

South Hampstead High School Junior Department

Linked school: South Hampstead High School, 186

5 Netherhall Gardens, London, NW3 5RN

Independent • Pupils: 260 • Ages: 4–11 • Non-denom
• Fees (per term): £4,023

Tel: 020 7794 7198
Fax: 020 7431 2750
Email: junior@shhs.gdst.net
Website: www.shhs.gdst.net/junior-school

24

Headmistress: Since September 2013, Mrs Gabrielle Solti BA PGCE, previously head of Notting Hill and Ealing Junior School, who has returned to her roots – she used to teach at nearby Trevor Roberts and was then deputy head of Primrose Hill Primary. Always wanted to be a teacher, but was told while reading

history at Oxford that she would be head by the time she was 30 and couldn't see the point. 'What then?' she asked. So she headed for the European Commission in Brussels – where she met her husband, then working in the marketing department at Nestlé in Paris and London and now a lawyer

'It's not just girls holding clipboards. They all get their turn and love being scientists.'

– before she could no longer resist the lure of teaching and went to train at The Institute ('A gold standard – stands out on the cv; I always appoint graduates from there if I can'). We described her at her previous post as 'destined for great things', and she is clearly on her way.

Entrance: North London parents tend to be somewhat obsessive about getting their daughters into a top school from the word go, and South Hampstead is vastly oversubscribed at 4, with about 240 applying for 24 places. School, however, is not looking for prodigies. 'I tell parents not to coach. There's no need at all for reading or writing. We're looking for focus, concentration, stamina and – hopefully – a spark.' In the first round of assessment, girls are observed at play, in the second, in groups of five with short activities. A rejection at 4 is certainly not a no for ever. Many reapply at 7+, when there are a further 24 places. At this stage, skills come into play, along with non-verbal reasoning, but school tries to 'peel back layers of coaching'. Priority is given to siblings, but 'only if they're the right fit.' Feeder schools include Hampstead Hill, Devonshire House, The Phoenix, North Bridge House, St Mary's, The Children's House and Brooklands.

Register at least two years in advance for 4+ entry. Assesses the first 250 applicants to deliver their applications on 1 October – queues form early outside the school. Registration for 7+ opens 18 months in advance and assesses the first 140 applicants.

Exit: Nearly all to the senior school. A few, who it is felt might need something 'gentler', are guided elsewhere. This is flagged up early on and help is given to find an appropriate school. 'We never ask anyone to leave. These are our girls until year 6.' Some, however, exit in year 5 to avoid 11 plus.

Remarks: Two bright, Victorian buildings across the road from each other in a quiet road five minutes walk from the senior school. One building houses reception to year 4, the other years 5 and 6. Though the school is madly competitive on entry, once inside the atmosphere is enthusiastic but relaxed. School feels this is due to the fact that girls here won't generally need to sit 11 plus. 'We're not teaching them to jump through hoops, we're here to open doors.' And, though the basics are rock solid, the academic offering is less about drilling and more about a spirit of inquiry. 'The sheer fun and enthusiasm for teaching are extraordinary,' said one father. Mandarin taught from year 1 as a second language ('I wanted them to experience something really different'), French added in year 4. Philosophy for all. 'Girls can sometimes be too compliant; this pushes them a little bit further.' Science has improved radically since space rearranged to create new labs. 'I think that's one of the great advantages of a single-sex education. It's not just girls holding clipboards. They all get their turn and love being scientists.'

The senior and junior schools overlap in their teaching style with a lot of independent inquiry, including two themed homeworks set annually across the school (a recent topic was black and white). 'It liberates them to do research.' An approach that clearly works. 'My daughter wasn't particularly interested in reading,' said one parent, 'but then they did a project on the Romans and you couldn't stop her. She read everything there was on the subject. She just became passionate.' Two libraries, one in each building, with all taking library lessons.

Special needs provision is strong. 'We try raise to raise any potential problems and get parents involved without panicking them. We don't want them immediately going off to get their child tested. Occasionally we recommend an educational psychologist or good outside tutoring.' Some 70 pupils speak a second language at home and, in year 5, the school peps up the reading and comprehension to ensure they aren't disadvantaged.

Music a key part of the curriculum. 'I want them to learn about sound. We do a lot of singing.' All girls, too, take the Royal Academy Young Strings project in year 1, with violin and cello taught using the Kodaly method. Large orchestra of 50-60, plus a quartet, quintet, wind band and jazz band. Art and DT taught in small groups in separate classrooms. Reasonable London playground plus use of

'We're not teaching them to jump through hoops, we're here to open doors.'

the senior school's playing fields a five-minute coach ride away. Two double periods of PE each week, plus gymnastics, netball, hockey and athletics clubs. 'It's important to instil an enjoyment and love of sport.' Excellent range of general clubs, including lateral thinking, chess, fashion illustration and languages (French, Spanish and Latin) and these energetic girls tend to be actively involved on numerous fronts.

Pastoral care is undoubtedly a strength. Parents, generally local and professional, feel they can always have a chat. 'Every child is recognised and appreciated, whether they're extrovert or quite shy,' said one. School cook is 'a bit of a legend', providing delicious freshly-cooked food with vegetarian options. Girls dine in batches and queue politely. They also open doors. 'It's not a backs-against-the-wall place, but we expect consideration.' Supportive parents are significant fundraisers (for playground equipment and extra laptops).

A school which produces articulate, well-educated, confident – and very happy – girls. 'It's a fabulous school,' said one happy parent. 'It lets every child be an individual.'

South Hampstead High School

Linked school: South Hampstead High School Junior Department, 184

3 Maresfield Gardens, London, NW3 5SS

Independent • Pupils: 640 • Ages: 11–18 • Non-denom
• Fees (per term): £5,077

Tel: 020 7435 2899
Fax: 020 7431 8022
Email: senior@shhs.gdst.net
Website: www.shhs.gdst.net

25

Headmistress: Since September 2013, Miss Helen Pike MA (Oxon) (early 40s), previously director of studies at the Royal Grammar School, Guildford. An Oxford history graduate, she studied for a Master's in modern history in the States, has an MA in fiction from Birkbeck and a PGCE from the OU. Miss Pike, who is working on her second novel, had hitherto taught entirely at top boys' schools – Westminster, City of London and St Paul's as well as RGS. Her partner is an Oxford don, she has an adult step-daughter and two school-age step-sons – and she is, judging from first impressions, exactly what this flagship school has needed for some time.

Very striking, tall, with evident sparkle and style, she has the personality, wit and flair to give this school the blast of energy and confidence it deserves. She oversaw the extraordinary rebuild which will, in many ways, be a new school. Hampstead and its clever, creative girls will doubtless rise to meet the challenges set by their new clever, and creative head. Another good GDST appointment.

Academic matters: A superstar in the exam league tables. In 2014, nearly 90 per cent of GCSEs were A*/A and more than two-thirds of A levels were

A*/A. Particularly impressive, however, is the percentage of A*s at A level, with 22 per cent of exams taken last year receiving the top grade (national average eight per cent). Though one of the previous head's ambitions was to make the school 'fly' academically, teaching to the tests is not part of the school's agenda. Girls here are provided with significantly more substantial nourishment than mark schemes to feed their intellects. 'They're very creative and individual, they need a challenging environment.' All years do a beyond-the-curriculum themed project (year 8, for example, focused on murder mystery, year 10 created a language), and sixth formers undertake the school's own (unexamined) extended essay. 'They have the old public school ideal of the whole person,' said one parent. 'You feel they're confident about getting the results, so can afford to be less obsessed by exams than elsewhere.'

A good balance between arts and science. Six compulsory subjects at GCSE, plus 10 options (including Latin and Greek). Over 20 subjects, including art history, philosophy and economics, in the sixth form, with maths, economics, chemistry and English amongst the most popular. Very strong emphasis on teaching and learning and

Girls here are provided with significantly more substantial nourishment than mark schemes to feed their intellects

plenty of lunchtime clubs to clear up difficulties. Form tutors provide one-to-one chats every half term and girls rate teacher support highly: 'They really want to help you rather than just seeing you as someone who will produce good results,' said one A level student.

Special needs here primarily mild dyslexia and dyspraxia, though some experience, too, of autism. About 10 per cent get help. 'We give them the support they need, whether that's improving study skills or using a word processor in every lesson.'

Games, options, the arts: Music exceptional (with generous scholarships at 11 and 16). Fourteen instruments taught, numerous ensembles, bands and orchestras, as well as two junior and four senior choirs. High rate of finalists at national music competitions; and a school radio station to rival Radio 3. The visual arts equally vibrant, with healthy numbers going on to art school and plenty of enthusiastic part-timers, who pursue it alongside more traditional academic disciplines.

(One recent leaver studied art foundation before reading politics at Cambridge.) Sport, compulsory throughout, is taken seriously by the school, with four acres of playing fields a five-minute coach drive away and a games staff ornamented by high-flying internationals. That said, for the majority, traditional team games are perhaps not top of eve-

She has the personality, wit and flair to give this school the blast of energy and confidence it deserves

ryone's to-do list. 'It varies from year to year,' said one keen athlete. 'It's there if you want it.' Fifty-plus clubs, from Mandarin to trampolining, and plenty of trips abroad (classics to Sicily, geography to Iceland, World Challenge to Peru). Regular guest speakers and active participation in out-of-school activities, from Young Inventors to the Arvon writing course. 'The extracurricular is very good and the girls really participate,' said a parent of two.

Background and atmosphere: Set up in the 1870s on enlightened principles, South Hampstead was one of the founding members – and is now one the flagships of – the Girls' Day School Trust, typical of its approach in prioritising fine teaching rather than frills. Until the previous head's arrival the school buildings were perhaps a bit too unfrilly. 'They were no longer fit for purpose,' she said decidedly. 'The girls deserve a beautiful environment.' Persistent lobbying has finally resulted in a state-of-the-art schoolhouse designed by world-renowned firm Hopkins Architects (designers of the Olympic

Girls are enthusiastic, hardworking (very) and sensible (this is not a school where being 'cool' is considered 'cool').

velodrome), open in October 2014. The sleek glass-and-steel tour de force will include ultra-modern facilities for art, DT and music, as well as a first class library, classrooms and sports courts. The 20th century science block and elegantly refurbished Arts and Crafts Oakwood House remain. In the meantime, pupils are based for four days a week in temporary classrooms at the sports ground in West Hampstead.

Our recent tour – in hard hat, builder's boots, fluorescent jacket and goggles – of the nascent new school was very exciting. There will be nothing quite like it anywhere in north London. The building plus its very modern, enthusiastic and inspirational head will make this school very hard to beat.

Pastoral care and discipline: Girls are taught meditation, 'mindfulness' and 'keeping it real' by two designated members of staff. 'Clever girls will always think, if, but, what... We want to keep them grounded in the now.' Nurture week encourages thinking, too, about others. The previous head reintroduced the house system which allows girls to get to know each other across the year groups, with annual competitions in dance, drama and music. Plenty of leadership opportunities too, with both house captains and elected school prefects. Navy and yellow uniform in the lower school; sixth formers wear their own clothes – mainly tidy jeans.

Pupils and parents: About 60 per cent of girls live locally, the rest come from as far afield as Notting Hill and Brixton. Parents are cosmopolitan, often professional, with a high proportion of foreign nationals. Financially the range extends from bus drivers to hedge-fund managers and, though some parents see the latter in the ascendant, South Hampstead is generally considered considerably less flashy than some of its local counterparts. 'There are all types of parents,' said one. 'It's like a breath of fresh air.' Girls are enthusiastic, hardworking (very), and sensible (this is not a school where being 'cool' is considered 'cool'). 'It's more real, more honest than some other schools,' said one girl, 'and it's not as cliquey'. Parents care about achieving the best possible education for their bright daughters. 'All the girls here are motivated and have very high standards. I tell them, "You're

diamonds, go out and sparkle".' Old girls include Helena Bonham-Carter, Rabbi Julia Neuberger, Fay Weldon.

Entrance: About 40 come up from the junior school, the rest sit the North London Girls' Schools' Consortium joint 11+ exam. Competition is fierce, with as many as six applicants per place. Occasional vacancies are filled from the waiting list. Sixth-form entrance tests include data analysis and an essay and, if relevant, subject tests. Offers are made on the basis of results and interviews. At all levels the school is looking for the intellectually engaged. 'They've got to be up to it academically,' says the school. 'We won't take someone who won't thrive here intellectually.'

Exit: Used to be a reasonable exodus post GCSE to co-ed independents, particularly Westminster, but the flood has slowed to a trickle. No doubt the introduction of a stunning sixth-form centre – which looks like a boutique hotel – is part of the magic potion. One or two to state schools at 16 (Camden,

'Clever girls will always think if, but, what...We want to keep them grounded in the now.'

LaSwap). At 18, about 10 per cent to Oxbridge, a handful to medical school, three or four to art school or music colleges, the rest to Russell Group universities, with Durham, Warwick, Bristol, Birmingham and Nottingham the most popular.

Money matters: Fees, in keeping with the Girls' Day School Trust philosophy of a value-for-money education, are generally competitive. Five per cent of annual income is spent on scholarships and means-tested bursaries (with increasing emphasis given to the latter) at 11 and 16. New applicants are automatically entered for scholarships; those moving up the school need to sit the entrance exam to qualify. Excellent music scholarships (up to 50 per cent off the fees), with grade VI generally required for auditions at 11.

Remarks: A school once considered all work and no play. Now better results than ever achieved with a broader education and vastly improved pastoral care. Will shine even more brightly under sparky new head.

Sylvia Young Theatre School

1 Nutford Place, London, W1H 5YZ

Independent · Pupils: 230 · Ages: 10–16 · Fees (per term): £3,100 – £4,250

Tel: 020 7258 2330
Fax: 020 7723 1040
Email: info@sylviayoungtheatreschool.co.uk
Website: www.syts.co.uk

Principal: Since 1981, Sylvia Young OBE (70s). The founding principal, she is something of a legend in London's theatreland and has been supplying junior talent to the West End stage for over 30 years. With some early training, she decided 'performance was not for me', but soon realised she had a knack for spotting and inspiring talent in others. She started on a small scale, working with local children at a youth club in east London, then launched a full-time school at the suggestion of one of the parents. The school is her passion and she now lives on the site with her husband. Two grown-up daughters have both entered the profession, one (Frances Ruffelle) as a Tony-winning actress and singer, the other (Alison) as a theatrical agent. Her granddaughter is the pop singer Eliza Doolittle. Sylvia Young is a sympathetic soul, whose persistence and drive has developed the school from a walk-on role to full stardom. 'It's the Oxbridge of theatre schools', said one parent. She was appointed OBE in 2005 for services to the arts.

Since 2005, Ms Frances Chave BSc PGCE (40s) has been the academic and pastoral head. Ms Chave read maths at Exeter University, followed by a PGCE at Southampton, then taught at two large comprehensives (Cranford Community College and Feltham Community College), before helping to set up a third, Overton Grange School in Sutton, where she was deputy head. 'When I decided to move on, I wanted something completely different', she says. Sylvia Young is about as different as it gets and Ms Chave has steadily improved the academic offering, particularly on the science side. A strong and sensible presence, she enjoys theatre, 'but only as a spectator', and in her spare time plays golf and other sports.

Academic matters: The school has long been known for the high standard of tuition in the performing arts, and has put increasing emphasis on the more academic side of the curriculum. 'We decided early on we didn't want our pupils to lose out by coming to a theatre school', says the founder. The school is unusual in that it hives off academic lessons into three hard-working days on Mondays, Tuesdays and Wednesdays, leaving Thursdays and Fridays free for professional studies. The subdivision is reasonably demanding. 'Both staff and students have to be very focused,' says Ms Chave. Unsurprisingly, the academic curriculum is more compact than you'd

189

find in a mainstream school – so no PE (no need with all that dancing), geography or DT – and the emphasis is definitely on the arts. All pupils study English lang and lit, maths, science (core and additional), expressive arts and drama to GCSE, when other options include music, art, media studies, history and Spanish. English, drama and theatre studies are the most successful GCSEs, but the head has worked hard to bring up attainment in science and maths (both of which are set).

Results are respectable, though 2014 saw a steep decline in the percentage of pupils getting five or more GCSEs at A*-C including English and maths, from 70 to 52, with the percentage of A*/A grades falling from 33 to 25. 'Most of our pupils do better than expected', says Ms Chave. 'If you're somewhere you really want to be, it does have a knock-on effect'. Parents agree: 'My daughter was at a mainstream academic school before. Here she's achieved because she wants to, not because she's being pushed'.

The school, which is non-selective academically, tests all pupils for learning difficulties on entry and copes well with moderate problems, from dyslexia to Asperger's. 'We have two children here on the autistic spectrum, one's a great dancer, the other a great actor'. Well-qualified SENCo oversees help in class and out, with teachers kept well

in the loop. Inevitably, lessons here are interrupted by professional work, but no one is allowed to lag behind. 'We have very good systems in place to catch up,' says Ms Chave. 'Every week staff write out what has been covered in class and what has been

---

When a professional engagement is protracted, staff liaise directly with on-set tutors

---

set for homework and everyone gets a copy'. Students are expected to make up what they've missed in their own time. 'They're amazingly adaptable, they just fit straight back in'. When a professional engagement is protracted, staff liaise directly with on-set tutors.

Games, options, the arts: The performing arts are of course the raison d'être of this all-singing, all-dancing institution and Thursdays and Fridays are devoted to the training needs of aspiring stars. Many of the performing arts staff are themselves working professionals and don't spare their students from the profession's harder knocks. (At one lesson the Guide attended, the class was asked to vote on the best singer.) Students are set by ability across the age range in all the performing disciplines – so, for example, a talented year 7 may be in the same ballet class as a less nimble year 11. Everyone studies all aspects of drama, music and dance, with classes ranging from voice production to recording technique, and all take annual LAMDA exams in speech and drama. All pupils, too, are represented by the in-house Sylvia Young Agency and put forward for professional work, ranging from West End musicals (the school regularly supplies cast members for Matilda and Billy Elliot) to advertising voice-overs and language tapes. 'You have to understand what a real performance is like', says Sylvia Young, 'and you have to learn that you may not get picked because you're not right for the part, no matter how talented you are. It's part of the training'. The school takes care, however, to ensure work doesn't interfere with academic priorities. 'My daughter has GCSEs coming up and they don't allow her to go off every five minutes', said one parent. 'School work comes first'.

Background and atmosphere: The school started out by running part-time classes in the 1970s, then opened full-time in Drury Lane in 1981. In 1983 it moved to Marylebone and in 2010 transferred into spacious premises in a converted Christian Science church just behind Marble Arch. The newly

refurbished building provides excellent facilities for both the vocational and academic, with 10 purpose-built studios, two computer rooms, two science labs, two bright art rooms and a small library (mainly used for catching up with homework). Priorities, now as always, remain the family atmosphere and care and attention of children, whether they're constantly in work or destined for a civilian career ('we do sometimes have to tell parents a child doesn't have what it takes for performance'). Regardless of the eventual outcome, all are equipped with valuable 'transferable skills' – confidence and the ability to communicate well and work with adults: 'The aim is to ensure they're secure in themselves', says Sylvia Young. Parents say pupils take on board the virtue of industry. 'They know the world they're contemplating is fiercely competitive', said one mother, 'and it's not going to be an easy ride. They learn a very strong work ethic'. Though clearly those who've gotta dance or act or sing (or all three) are ideally served here, the school works equally well for those who might want to enter the profession in more self-effacing roles. 'They teach you about every aspect from choreography to TV'. Twenty or so pupils board with London host families (generally present or past parents), often in groups of two or three. 'The woman my son boards with is marvellous', says one mother. 'She picks him up from the theatre at night, makes sure he does his homework, and arranges fun evenings of singing or games'.

Pastoral care and discipline: This is a school which is essentially about self-discipline, and disciplinary problems of the mainstream sort are rare. 'We don't have bullying', says Sylvia Young firmly, 'just children being silly sometimes'. The school monitors each child carefully, with an individual log kept on each. 'The children know they can come to us and we'll listen'. Parents feel confident their children are happy. 'My son feels so lucky. He is doing what he wants to do every day and there aren't many adults who can say that'. The school has a strong disciplinary structure. 'We're very firm about the basics,' says Ms Young. Rules are clearly spelled out – no make-up, no micro skirts, no uploading of photographs onto the internet (a serious danger in a school where celebrity is a daily fact of life) – and consistently enforced. 'Other schools have these rules, but at Sylvia Young they really impose them', said one parent. 'It's quite old fashioned'. Two uniforms, one for academic work (white shirts, blazers, jumpers and ties), another for vocational days (tracksuits and unitards). Both are neatly worn.

Pupils and parents: Parents cover the full range. 'They're not pushy stage-school parents at all', says Ms Young. 'They're a very normal group, from all backgrounds'. Though certainly some are affluent, many really struggle to send their children here and travel considerable distances to do so. The children, of course, are as diverse as the parents, but significantly more talented than the average. They're all here because they really want to be. One parent told us: 'My son, who'd been at a local primary school, said when he first saw Sylvia Young, "Mum, it's amazing. I just fit in there".' Others who fitted in equally well include Billie Piper, Denise van Outen, former Spice Girl Emma Bunton, Jade Ewen from The Sugababes, Nathan Sykes of The Wanted and the late Amy Winehouse, whose father has recently set up a scholarship in her memory.

Entrance: The first entry point is year 6. 'Year 6 is a good time to come', says Sylvia Young, 'because either pupils can continue into year 7 or they have time to go elsewhere. A few decide it's not what they want'. Most enter at year 7, with the occasional place at other times. At all ages, the audition is the most important part of the process. The school offers a preliminary audition, with low-key workshops. Those with most potential are invited back to perform two drama pieces (one from Shakespeare and a modern work), a song and a dance. Candidates also sit academic tests in English and maths. 'But we're not a grammar school. We just need to feel happy they'll cope with the pace and be able to get done in three days what most do in five'. That said, the stronger an applicant is on the professional side, the more leeway is given academically. Motivation, too, is carefully examined. 'There's a lot of discussion about what the child wants and what the parents are looking for'. The school sees up to 500 applicants for 40 places at 11.

Exit: Pupils are assessed at the end of years 8 and 9, which provides an opportunity for families to reassess their child's career path. Currently all move on at 16 (though the school is contemplating a sixth form). About half (mainly dancers) go on to specialist colleges, the rest to traditional academic sixth forms to do A levels and then frequently to study drama at university. Close links with all the central London tutorial colleges (Lansdowne, Ashbourne, Duff Miller, DLD etc) and quite a number of pupils proceed to these with scholarships.

Money matters: Three official scholarships (one full and two half), and many more get some sort of help. Quite a number put their theatrical earnings towards the fees.

Remarks: A school which combines a sound academic background with outstanding vocational training and professional opportunity. Hard work, but hard work undertaken with purposeful pleasure.

Trevor-Roberts School

55–57 Eton Avenue, London, NW3 3ET

Independent • Pupils: 100 • Ages: 5–13 • C of E • Fees (per term): £4,090 – £4,690.

Tel: 020 7586 1444
Fax: 020 7722 0114
Email: trjuniorweb@trevor-robertsschool.co.uk
Website: trevor-robertsschool.co.uk

26

Senior Head: Since 1999, Simon Trevor-Roberts BA, 50s. Son of the founder, Trevor-Roberts studied at Westminster School before reading English at Aberystwyth. In 1983, he joined his father Christopher in the family firm, where he learnt his trade by example. (He has since been joined by his sister Amanda, who heads up the Junior School). Mild mannered and reflective, he has a very clear sense of what the school is about: 'We try to get children to enjoy the process of learning.' Continues to teach maths to the 13 plus candidates, because he's found he, too, now has the knack of putting things across clearly. 'I shadowed my father for a long time and learnt how to do it by osmosis.' Parents find him immensely approachable and engaged. 'You always have complete access to the head and he knows all the kids incredibly well.' Married with two grown children, both of whom attended the school.

Entrance: Register as soon after birth as possible. About 80 sets of parents are contacted when their child is 1 and offered a tour. Those who then wish to proceed confirm this in writing, and the school assesses the first 50 children on their list in the September prior to the calendar year in which they turn 5. 'We're not expecting any preparation, but

---

'I shadowed my father for a long time and learned how to do it by osmosis.'

---

we want to make sure it will be a happy transition,' says the registrar. 'We're looking for inquisitive children who want to learn. Getting that is more a dark art than a science.' The school generally tries to give priority to siblings, 'but only if it's the right school'. Often takes in one or two more in year 4, when the year group divides into two classes.

Exit: Girls mainly – though not exclusively – at 11, generally to Francis Holland, South Hampstead and other north London favourites. Most boys (and some girls) at 13, to a wide range of day and boarding schools, including regular placements at City of London, Eton, Harrow, Highgate, Latymer Upper, Merchant Taylors', UCS and Westminster. 'The head is very good at managing parental expectations,' says one former parent.

Remarks: This is a family-run school with a very distinctive ethos, deriving in large part from its origins. Founded by the current heads' father in the 1950s with just 14 boys, it was originally seen as a refuge for the 'unteachable'. 'My father had a reputation for taking those whom other schools had given up on and getting them through entrance exams to leading public schools,' says Simon Trevor-Roberts.

Today, the school can takes its pick of north London's brightest, but continues to select a mixed-ability (now co-educational) intake and provide a tailor-made education for all. 'They want every child to work to his or her potential and really do treat every child as an individual,' said one parent.

Children start in year 1 in a class grouped according to the calendar year of their birth. In year 4, this is re-arranged to allow everyone to be in place for secondary school entrance. One class of 16-18 in the early years, two classes in year 4 and year 6, then a single form again for the final two

years. 'We like to move children around so they're not in the same group for eight years,' says the head. 'It give us the flexibility to allow those who require it a bit more time and accelerate those who need it.' Parents confirm this is skilfully managed. 'They're constantly re-adjusting their approach for different levels of learning, but not in a way that disturbs the children.'

Specialist subject teaching from the word go, with a classroom teacher for the core subjects, but music, history, geography, science and art all taught in their own space. 'It keeps the week fresh.'

Plenty of imaginative teaching by intelligent (including many Oxbridge), though not always qualified, staff. French from year 1, Latin from year 5, some Greek in year 8, Mandarin taught as a club. Special needs addressed by weekly sessions with the learning support coordinator and outside specialists.

Everyone staying for the final two years sits common entrance. 'We take it very seriously,' says the head. 'Eleven plus is about flexible problem solving; by 13, it's more structure on the page.' Senior schools praise the 'structure on the page' received.

Very good at ensuring the basics are in place. 'Sometimes you have to be a bit tough,' says the head. 'We insist that children use a pen rather than touch type. If you have to write an essay under exam conditions, you have to be able to discipline your thoughts.' No truck with overly formalised exam training. 'Non-verbal reasoning is not a subject,' he says crisply.

Formal homework from year 3, starting out with 20 minutes in English or maths ('It shows them how to work by themselves and for themselves'), up to two hours a night for the top forms. 'They do work very hard, but the atmosphere still manages to be reasonably relaxed,' says one mother.

Good relationships with staff are fundamental ('The teacher is not someone they're trying to hoodwink,' says the head), as is the view that effort should be lauded over achievement. 'Children are perfectly aware there's competition elsewhere,

---

No truck with overly formalised exam training. 'Non-verbal reasoning is not a subject,' head says crisply

---

they don't need it reinforced. We want them to be in competition with themselves.' Good work is rewarded with a 'digniora', with recipients queuing in the lunch hour to have their accolade verified and registered. Three merits win a £4 token

'My son almost died of nerves the first time he had to read out a poem, but now he loves drama and performing.'

(designed to reflect the season) to be spent at independent local shops.

Breadth well beyond the exam curriculum is given enormous emphasis. Outstanding music – 'We love music' – with a dynamic head. Taught in the classroom from years 1 to 6, outside throughout, with numerous ensembles (brass, jazz, string, woodwind, chamber choir, rock band) and much external participation (at the Royal Festival Hall, St John's Smith Square, etc.) Twice weekly art lessons (one in year 7) in a bright art department at the top of school, with its own kiln. Extra art and DT on offer for enthusiasts on Wednesday afternoons.

Cultural values that have largely been submerged elsewhere – 'Everyone is encouraged to have a novel on the go' – with half an hour of silent reading daily after lunch. Poetry and drama matter and prove great confidence builders. 'My son almost died of nerves the first time he had to read out a poem,' said one mother, 'but now he loves

drama and performing.' 'The plays are unbelievable,' said another.

Plenty of fresh air and exercise, with a good-sized, well-equipped playground, including popular table tennis, miniature railway and chicken coop ('the chickens are a great comfort to quieter shyer children.'). Primrose Hill, a few hundred yards from the door, enables twice weekly games. Definitely not a school, however, where 'go-fight-win' is on the agenda. 'Children love sport, but I don't want a First Eleven ethos, with the captain of games strutting around,' says the head. 'We do play matches against other schools, but everyone has a go.'

The senior school building, a fine example of the Arts and Crafts, was the founder's own home and still offers delightful domestic interiors with William Morris wallpaper in the front hall and mid-century classic tables used instead of desks in the top forms. The juniors are housed in their own building with a separate dining room and science lab.

The atmosphere is civilised but structured ('It's a nice mix of the very strict and the nurturing and kind – teachers are always willing to talk things through.'). Pupils sit down to eat their biscuits at break before rushing off to the playground. Everyone has a hot lunch, served through an open hatch, 'so they can see where it is made.' Staff share the dining hall with pupils. 'Eating is socialising.' Food is freshly prepared on site using local produce.

Manners and uniform are both reasonably relaxed (no backs against the wall here). Light blue polo shirt for younger children, dark blue for older ones. Trousers and skirts, 'something reasonable'. 'Jeans are fine, jeans hanging off the hips are not.'

Often the school of choice for the liberal, media intelligentsia (including some famous names), the type of parent who genuinely believes in the well-rounded education, not the rush to the top of the league tables. (Competition here, though it undoubtedly exists, tends to be on the level of how

Popular table tennis, miniature railway and chicken coop ('the chickens are a great comfort to quieter, shyer children.')

many operas your child has seen rather than where the family went skiing.) Mainly local, some from Notting Hill, Queen's Park, Islington. The head feels 'there's no typical child, but I've heard people say our children are very kind.'

University College School Junior School

Linked schools: Phoenix School, 150; University College School, 196

---

11 Holly Hill, London, NW3 6QN

Independent • Pupils: 250 • Ages: 7–11 • Non-denom
• Fees (per term): £5,495

Tel: 020 7435 3068
Fax: 020 7435 7332
Email: juniorbranch@ucs.org.uk
Website: www.ucs.org.uk

27

Headmaster of Junior: Since July 2014, Lewis Hayward, previously deputy principal of Highgate School. He has an MA in classics from Oxford and one in educational leadership and management from the Open University. He started his teaching career in Nairobi, moving to Saudi Arabia as an EFL teacher at the Saudi Aramco Oil Company and being promoted to editor and analyst. Has since taught classics at Holmewood House and Highfield Prep, joining Highgate in 2009. He is married with two children.

Entrance: Some 170 applicants for 60 places at 7. At the initial assessment, in the autumn term, staff hear boys read – 'we're looking for two years above chronological age' – then read them a story and ask them questions in groups. Meanwhile, the head takes parents on a tour of the school, 'to make sure they want us'. Confident readers are asked back for English, maths and non-verbal reasoning tests in the spring term, with attention also paid to how they interact in groups.

The main feeder pre-preps tend to be The Phoenix, Mulberry House, Golders Hill School and Hampstead Hill School. Although The Phoenix is the UCS pre-prep, applicants take the same entrance test as everyone else. 'All things being equal they'll get a place. But they must be able to cope.'

Exit: Virtually all to the senior school, without taking the entrance exam. 'If a boy is really struggling we'll talk to his parents – but that has only happened once whilst I've been here.'

Remarks: Compact site tucked away at the top of Hampstead behind the Everyman cinema with views across London from every classroom. Nice boy-friendly science lab with tarantulas and poisonous frogs, which doubles as recording studios where boys can come in to write and record songs at lunchtime (an apprenticeship, no doubt, for the rock band culture of the senior school).

Art, woodwork and cookery rooms, all well-used: plenty of time here for creative activities. Some impressive photography displayed: came third in the Prep School Photographer of the Year competition. Smallish rubber surface playground/football pitch; boys play rugby, football, cricket and hockey at the senior school grounds in West

Giant chess set in the playground; the under 11 team recently won the National Schools gold award

Hampstead. Also use the senior school swimming pool and theatre and have concerts in the great hall. Giant chess set in the playground; the under 11 team recently won the National Schools gold award.

Does not have to prepare boys for common entrance, so no huge academic pressure – can spend less time on maths and English and more on other activities. Relaxed pace. Undoubtedly some parents feel that their children are not stretched academically and some complain of lack of homework, though the latest Independent Schools Inspectorate report (following a bad inspection previously) praised standards. 'I think we've turned it round'.

Happy to accept able boys with physical disabilities. 'If they're bright and can cope we'll take anyone.' 'They've been amazing helping with all his needs,' said the parent of one disabled boy. Full-time school nurse who 'knows all the boys and is involved in their personal development'. Two part-time SEN teachers.

Warm, friendly atmosphere. 'It's a very happy school,' said a parent.

University College School

Linked schools: Phoenix School, 150; University College School Junior School, 195

Frognal, London, NW3 6XH

Independent • Pupils: 790 (co-ed in sixth form) • Ages: 11–18 • Non-denom • Fees (per term): £5,945

Tel: 020 7435 2215
Fax: 020 7433 2111
Email: ssadmissions@ucs.org.uk
Website: www.ucs.org.uk

28

Headmaster: Since September 2013, Mr Mark Beard (40s). Formerly deputy head of Brighton College. Studied chemistry at Oxford and has a master's in education management from King's College London. Taught at King Edward's Birmingham and St Paul's before joining Brighton College. He is married with two young children, lives in North London and enjoys squash, reading and ancient history.

Is apparently tightening up on school's previously relaxed attitude to untucked shirts and late homework. 'Liberal scholarship is not the same as liberal attitudes,' he told the local paper. Has also introduced a GCSE points system for internal and external sixth form applicants.

Academic matters: Says it does not measure success by exam league tables – can afford not to, with an impressive 88 per cent of GCSEs and 70 per cent of A levels graded A*/A in 2014. An unusually wide GCSE choice – two English, maths, a science and a modern language (Mandarin available from year 9) are compulsory but boys have a free choice of their other five subjects. 'The kids do the subjects

they enjoy and we achieve good results in every subject.' There is guidance to ensure that, for example, someone with an inclination toward medicine does not end up doing only one science.

But the numerical bias is undoubtedly towards the social sciences – economics, government and politics and history are particularly popular A levels and around a third of leavers go on to do social sciences at university. 'This says more about the families; the boys are encouraged to talk and discuss and think a lot from a young age, so they tend towards the discursive, argumentative subjects.' Having said that, plenty take maths A level and the sciences have a good minority showing.

Everyone is assessed when they enter the school and those in need can get extra help outside the classroom and can eg use laptops. 'But they must be bright enough to cope with the classroom work.' At this liberal school the emphasis is on self-motivation, and some north London parents find it insufficiently pushy. It is stricter, say pupils, in the early years. 'As the workload increases you develop an instinct for getting on and doing it.' Undoubtedly, some develop more of an instinct than others, but there are safety nets. 'We have huge rafts of processes in place to help them develop their own motivation. But we want to get them off those systems as soon as possible and get them self-supporting.'

Teaching styles vary from the military to the liberal but tend toward the latter. 'The relationship between teachers and pupils here is very individual,' said a sixth former. 'You can disagree and question their views. But it is disciplined in the classroom because we respect the teachers. If someone you respect is talking you'll listen to them.'

Games, options, the arts: The swish Sir Roger Bannister sports complex includes a swimming pool, sports hall, multi-gym and dance studio – and a Costa Coffee bar. Small Astroturf pitch on site and sports fields a couple of miles away in West Hampstead. Most people play twice a week and sports include hockey and basketball as well as rugby, soccer and cricket. The teams win reasonably often but it is fair to say that macho ultra-competitiveness is not a UCS characteristic, and the captain of rugby is equally at home giving a camp starring performance in the school play. 'We're not triumphalist. We like to do things for the hell of it.'

A range of orchestras, choirs and ensembles, including a joint symphony orchestra with South Hampstead High School. Plenty of concerts including a lunchtime classical series in the great hall and jazz evenings in the Lund Theatre. But UCS is best known locally for its rock groups, such as Bombay Bicycle Club, formed to play in assembly and now touring worldwide. The annual Battle of the Bands showcases talents like this to a boisterous audience of north London teenagers. Revamped lecture theatre can now be used as a flexible rehearsal and performance space for music and drama departments.

Excellent art, DT and modern language facilities are housed in the Jeremy Bentham Building, providing fully-equipped studios, workshops, classroom and two language laboratories. Drama strong

---

At this liberal school the emphasis is on self-motivation, and some north London parents find it insufficiently pushy

---

too, with a large variety of plays from West Side Story to Macbeth, including some joint performances with South Hampstead High School. Plenty of opportunities for those with a technical bent to get involved backstage.

Numerous extracurricular activities: Ten Tors challenge, skiing in Colorado, cricket in Florida, language trip to Hamburg. Raises £20,000–£30,000 a year for charities, some of which goes to linked schools overseas – one in Uganda, run by an OG (Old Gower), schools in India and Sri Lanka and an orphanage in Romania. Pupils go out to work there during holidays and gap years and many find it a life-changing experience.

Background and atmosphere: Founded in 1830 by the University of London as the 'Godless College' of Gower Street, it was one of the first schools to teach modern languages and sciences, and one of the first to abolish corporal punishment. It moved to Hampstead in 1907 and maintained its liberal and secular outlook. The main building – including the panelled great hall with organ – is a notable example of Edwardian architecture. There are no school bells, no religious observance and technically no religious education – though a few boys each year, nonetheless, do take RS at GCSE. 'It develops free-thinking, self-assured and entrepreneurial boys,' said a parent. 'It fosters independent thinking and makes the boys feel that they are very clever.'

The Independent Schools Inspectorate commented on a 'lack of clarity about the required standards of dress and appearance', and there used to be a feeling that uniform was a somewhat voluntary matter, though by all accounts the new head has different ideas.

Pastoral care and discipline: Renowned for its friendly atmosphere and caring attitude. The lower school, years 7 and 8, is organised largely apart from the rest of the school, with its own building and pastoral staff. In year 9 boys join one of five Demes – roughly like houses – and are looked after by Deme wardens and form tutors.

Boys report that bullying is virtually non-existent. The tolerant and open-minded atmosphere reaps good relationships between pupils and between staff and pupils. 'There's no set code of

Macho ultra–competitiveness is not a UCS characteristic, and the captain of rugby is equally at home giving a camp starring performance in the school play

conduct except that you behave responsibly,' said a sixth-former. Boys feel that it is very hard to get punished: 'The gardener is the only one who's strict when it comes to discipline. You don't mess with his flower beds.'

'Boys do get punished,' says the school, 'but we don't have a tariff of offences. We try to treat each offence and each pupil as an individual. So some kids spend a lot of time talking to teachers about what's going wrong. Most north London boys like talking about themselves, so they don't see it as a big deal.'

Pupils and parents: Mostly wealthy families from a relatively small area. The school does not record the ethnic or religious background of its pupils but they mirror fairly accurately the inhabitants of the Hampstead/Garden Suburb/Hendon/Finchley catchment area, with around half Jewish and a good sprinkling from various ethnic minorities.

Pupils tend to be confident and self-opinionated. 'They go through an arrogant phase,' said a parent, though the school feels that most teenagers do so, and prefers to say, 'we at UCS are quite good at developing assurance rather than arrogance.' Another parent commented, 'You need to be the life and soul – to throw yourself into things. It's probably not ideal for a quiet, bookish boy. They like you to get involved.' Students say, 'You have to be open-minded and accept other people and their views. And it helps if you have an in-built inclination to do well. There's space for all here – but the UCS type does tend to be out-going.'

OGs include Sir Chris Bonington, Sir Roger Bannister, Sir Dirk Bogarde, Alex Garland and – yes! – the Hampstead-liberal-hating Daily Mail editor, Paul Dacre.

Entrance: About two-thirds of 11-year-olds come from the junior school in Holly Hill. They move up without needing to take an entrance exam. Another 30 or so come from outside – mostly local state primaries. About 200 applicants take maths,

English and non-verbal reasoning tests, and about half are called back for group activities and interview. Another 30 come in at 13, mostly from local preps. They are assessed during the summer term of year 7 in maths, English and non-verbal reasoning, with half invited back for interviews, with offers conditional on common entrance.

A few boys and some 30 girls join the sixth form. The school sets its own assessment test, which is not subject-specific but measures thinking skills, problem-solving, interpretation of data. Head has introduced new guidelines for sixth form entry: current pupils and new entrants must get at least 14 points at GCSE (with three given for an A* and one for a B).

Exit: Nearly all end up at university, around half after a gap year. Bristol, UCL, Manchester, Imperial and Durham popular, with 20 to Oxbridge in 2014.

Social sciences, as mentioned, particularly popular, alongside humanities and languages.

Money matters: The school has successfully met its target to double the amount of means-tested fee assistance available and provides over 50 bursaries per year. There are also various scholarships, though the school regards these as 'basically pat-on-the-back awards', feeling that they should be means-tested rather than handed out to those who can well afford the fees.

Remarks: Achieves impressive exam results with a relaxed atmosphere. An ex-pupil insists that we describe it as 'the top liberal public school' and says, 'I look on my time at UCS as a golden age.' Certainly parents and pupils are uniformly happy – 'My son is having a fantastic time. If you're enthusiastic, there's so much scope to do what you want to do.'

Westminster Abbey Choir School (♟) (⌂) (🛏)

Dean's Yard, London, SW1P 3NY

Independent · Pupils: 35 boys · Ages: 8–13 · C of E · Fees (per term): £2,346

Tel: 020 7222 6151
Fax: 020 7222 1548
Email: headmaster@westminster-abbey.org
Website: www.westminster-abbey.org/choir-school

60

Headmaster: Since 2002, Mr Jonathan Milton BEd (50s), married, formerly head of The Abbey School in Tewkesbury. Bred, if not born, into the choir school tradition – he was a choral scholar at York. Music was his degree subject, though he now teaches geography. A gentle man, whose quiet, friendly manner betrays a profound love of his unique school, the tradition it enshrines and the community of boys and staff which gives it ever-fresh life. Clearly, an inspired appointment. Mr Milton is, at once, a traditionalist and a moderniser – exactly the right balance for the place. 'When I came, there were no carpets or curtains and it felt tense – that's now completely gone. It was dark too. We've tried to make it gentler.' He showed us the little IT room next to the dormitories, 'it's a marvellous way for boys to stay in touch – much simpler than writing a letter. And the staff communicate with parents every week electronically.' Gentler the school may well be but he has also tightened the academics, keeping step with the outside world in which senior school places are no longer assigned in little chats between heads of 'big' schools and trusted prep heads. Mr Milton's openness, thoughtfulness and warmth are mirrored in his boys. Those we talked

to were similarly relaxed, candid and friendly. Head and boys share their view of life here, 'it's tough, you get very tired but.. it's fabulous.'

Entrance: No formal entrance test day or the like. Over the year, school will see around 25 boys for voice trials – usually in ones and twos – and usually in year 3. The Master of the Choristers will hear them and the head will chat to the boy and parents

'They have to enjoy being part of a close-knit team and they must have personality and character,' says Mr Milton

and, if the lad looks promising he will be invited back to spend a day in the school. This will include a more formal voice trial, a chance to play their instruments and testing in maths and English. What is looked for is not grade 8 in six instruments but musical aptitude and the kind of attitude to

199

music, community and learning that make for a happy and successful Westminster Abbey chorister. 'They have to enjoy being part of a close-knit team and they must have personality and character,' says Mr Milton. Academic brilliance is less important though, clearly, the boy must enjoy learning. Of the 25 they see, places may be offered to between four and six, on average, though one or two may be invited to come back some months later.

These days, more than half come from state primaries and can be caught up and supported where necessary. 'With year groups of six or seven, we can tailor-make classes,' says head. School fees are subsidised by the Abbey and no-one, however impecunious, should be put off applying if their boy is a natural chorister. Funds will be found. 'Some pay nothing at all,' says Mr Milton. Boys now come from further afield – Yorkshire and even overseas. Quite tough for an 8-year-old, you might think. 'And,' says Mr Milton, 'few of our parents would have chosen a boarding school – when they see it, they realise it's a way of life.' Yes. This represents the most amazing opportunity for the right child and a peerless preparation for life.

Exit: An astonishing list of leavers' destinations over the last three years. Everyone wins a music scholarship to a prestigious school and many win academic and/or art schols too. Most popular senior schools are King's Canterbury, Eton and Winchester with the rest hither and yon, and doing very well wherever they end up.

Remarks: This is the only choir school in the country which is only a choir school – no day pupils, no girls, no non-choristers. Average class size six, maximum is nine – in a way that says it all. The place hums with quiet activity – mental, physical and musical. It all happens in a tall, unobtrusive building in Dean's Yard – right under Big Ben, the Houses of Parliament and Westminster Abbey. Dean's Yard is a grassy square lined by augustly solid houses. Opposite is the modest arch which leads to Westminster School – no connection with the choir school except that the large pupils and the little choristers see each other passing all day which makes the business of scholarship and growing up in this – the heart of the great centre of London – seem quite the normal thing.

Five floors accommodate all learning, admin and living space. All is freshly-painted and feels light, comfortable and well-cared for. There's a super ground floor 'music room' used for assemblies and the like – a splendid stained glass window commemorating Purcell and the other Masters of the Choristers who between them make up a history of English choral music – Gibbons, Blow, Simon Preston et al. Classrooms are small with conventional desks, whiteboards and it all looks a bit dolls house in scale – enhanced, when we visited (during exam week) by the very cuddly teddies (for good luck) sitting reassuringly on desks. More teddies in the dorms which – it is a boys' school – are, if not Spartan, certainly not prettified. Bunk beds with integral cupboards in airy rooms. Good shower rooms, good ICT provision and a very nice sitting room with sofas, piano, TV, books and games and feeling really snug.

Everyone does standard prep school curriculum but flexibility can be built into the system with such small classes and so small a school. Individual help is the norm. No boys with SENs, we are told, though the odd mild dyslexic may creep in. A boy with dyslexia would find chorister-life tough, says Mr Milton – what with having to read music and a foreign language at speed and so on. 'It wouldn't

be fair.' Yes. Sports take place via buses to Battersea Park, The Queen Mother Sports centre in Victoria and water sports in Docklands – Mr Milton is a keen sailor. They kayak, rock climb and sail and Mr Milton sees this – and the opportunity to get away from the closed chorister world – as essential for good relations.

Evidence of boy-life and wit abounds. 'WACS Lyrical' – the boys' own noticeboard – details competitions, initiatives, jokes and notices – full of fun and ideas. The art room, open in the evenings, similarly lively – we were terrified by the huge multi-tusked cardboard, paper and paint beast which 'would be tamed by listening to Palestrina'. Boys enjoy textile work, DT – they make fan-powered vehicles for racing – and knitting: 'very popular', we were told. Obviously, music is central to life. Singing practice in the song school happens each morning and each afternoon before evensong – except on Weds and alternate Mons. Instrumental practice is timetabled and very much a normal part of everyday life. Musical guests and ensembles visit, there is a composer in residence – a real privilege for such boys

– and school takes full advantage of the concert halls and galleries roundabout. Likewise, the school goes into local primaries – boys take their instruments – to inspire others, 'just to give music a boost'.

What do the boys say – and their parents? 'You have to be very independent and organised,' a seasoned 12-year-old told us. 'You can't rely on your parents to pack your bag and find your pencil case – you have to do it all yourself. You have to manage your own revision and music practice.' (Sounds like a course in choristership might be handy all round!) 'It is very tiring – I'd like to have more of a rest after concerts.' On the other hand – 'singing all the special services we do is brilliant. We did a special service for the spies! (100 years of MI5.) They just looked normal. They don't wear T-shirts saying "I'm a spy".' And 'We're on TV, we go on tours and make CDs.' 'It can be exhausting,' said a parent, 'but they bounce back. It's unbelievably rewarding.' And they clearly enjoy the abbey community with whom they share Christmas and Easter meals and so on. A choristership here is a treasure. A huge commitment for boys and family while it lasts, but a gift for life.

Westminster Cathedral Choir School

Ambrosden Avenue, London, SW1P 1QH

Tel: 020 7798 9081

61

Independent • Pupils: 170 • Ages: 7–13 • RC • Fees (per term): Day £5,350; chorister boarders £2,861

Email: office@choirschool.com
Website: www.choirschool.com

Headmaster: Since 2007, Mr Neil McLaughlan (40s). Married with a young son and daughter, and a man who radiates humour, decency and charm in equal measure. Read philosophy and politics at Durham and spent a few years with Andersen Consulting in London before embarking on a teaching career in 1997. After spells at Stonyhurst and Worth, he took up a post as head of English and director of development at Downside School, before joining WCCS as headmaster. He hopes to be there 'for the duration.' Parents hope so too. 'Lovely guy!' said one. 'So easy to approach!' said another. 'An extremely dedicated head and a great promoter of the school,' said a third. Typically modest, he hopes to do 'lots and lots of small things right.' We think he's doing lots of big things right too. Under his visionary yet kindly leadership, this has become an inspiring school that is going from strength to strength.

Entrance: Main entry points for day boys are at 7+, where 14-15 places are available, and 8+ (a further eight or so places). Applicants sit tests in English,

maths and non-verbal reasoning in January of the year before entry. Occasional places in other year groups, notably at 11+. The school is always oversubscribed, and, once boys have met the required academic standard, will give preference where possible to practising Roman Catholics and to boys with a brother at the school.

Choristers, who must be Catholic and must be boarders, join at 8+. Would-be probationers have to pass informal and formal tests with the cathedral's master of music, as well as succeeding at the academic assessment; and if they manage all that, they spend two nights at the school to see whether chorister life will suit them. Only then will they be offered one of the six available places. As the school's popularity grows, so inevitably does the competition; there are now half a dozen serious candidates for each choristership, and for the first time in over a decade, the school has not had to go recruiting for them.

Up to full fees assistance for choristers; none for day pupils, whose families just have to fork out. As a result, there is more cultural than social diversity here. Boys come from a wide range of nationalities, among them France, Spain, Italy, Russia, Ghana and Korea, making this a truly international school. With some 80 per cent of the boys now from Catholic families, the school is less religiously diverse than it was, but remains open to day boys of all faiths provided their families are happy to support the school's Catholic ethos.

Exit: The head has worked tirelessly to raise the school's profile, and WCCS's exit record is superb. Boys regularly leave for boarding schools like Eton, Harrow, Winchester, Uppingham, Stonyhurst and Ampleforth, and for a raft of top London schools, including Westminster, St Paul's, City of London, KCS Wimbledon, Latymer Upper and Dulwich College. Others to Cardinal Vaughan and the London Oratory. 'The school is much more linked into the senior schools than it was a few years ago,' reported one satisfied parent. 'Oh yes, the head's always going on about schools,' confirmed one of the boys, equably.

Remarks: The school was endearingly shabby once, but not any more. A five-year programme of refurbishment has just finished, and everything is now bang up to date. Visitors are welcomed in the beautiful glass-fronted foyer, where handwritten Music for Mass schedules from 1905 are hung beside huge photos of current pupils radiating health and cheeriness. Throughout the building, ceilings, floors and lighting are all new, and all the classrooms are gleaming and well resourced, with interactive whiteboards in each one. Large and much-loved playground, where boys play 'crazy games' on the climbing apparatus, just covered with Astroturf. 'That was a real selling point for

'The key thing,' says head, 'is to have good, kind people around the boys, good accommodation, and excellent food. An army marches on its stomach.'

me,' said one parent. 'The boys have a chance to be boys.' 'The way to the heart of little boys is good food and football at playtime, and WCCS excels in both,' confirmed another. We didn't try the football, but we can confirm that the food is splendid, a delicious combination of tasty and healthy. Boarding facilities have also been upgraded. We can't comment on the refurbished boarders' common room, because a curmudgeonly old trumpet teacher therein told us we were interrupting his lesson and to get out, but we did manage to see the sleeping accommodation, which was cheerful, light and airy. The rigours of chorister life notwithstanding, feedback on the boarding experience from both parents and boys was uniformly positive. 'The key thing,' says head, 'is to have good, kind people around the boys, good accommodation and excellent food. An army marches on its stomach.'

Years ago, parents had disquiets about aspects of WCCS. Nowadays, they cannot find enough superlatives with which to express their delight. 'We have been thrilled by both the teaching and pastoral care provided by the school.' 'The staff generate a wonderfully positive energy.' 'It's an amazing school, the teachers are so kind!' 'You couldn't choose a better school, I recommend it to everyone.' 'A wonderful warmth and care is present everywhere.'

A father of a new chorister told us, 'My son absolutely loves it. He's thrilled to pieces. The first weekend they were eligible to go home, he didn't want to come.' (Poor mum!) And a mother of two day pupils wrote, 'Happiness is guaranteed at this school; it is such a nurturing, caring and stimulating environment. I can honestly say that the only problem I have ever had is to find a way to drag my boys out of the playground and back home at the end of the day.' What's behind this remarkable success? 'The one ingredient a Catholic school should have is joy,' said the head when we asked him, simply and without any side.

There is joy in the teaching here, that's for sure. A quiet revolution is taking place in the WCCS curriculum that made this reviewer go all excited and wobbly at the knees. Schemes of work have been painstakingly redesigned, with scholarship and a genuine love of learning at their heart. 'The idea is to present knowledge as a unified whole,' explained the head, 'so for instance, whilst they're studying Adam and Eve in RS, they'll be doing C S Lewis's The Magician's Nephew in English. Likewise, we use geometry and graph-plotting in maths to support map skills in geography, and they'll draw antique maps in art at the same time. If the boys are doing the human body in science, they'll look at what the Greeks and Romans discovered about it in history.' The boys we spoke to praised the lessons as 'really good fun,' adding, 'The work's challenging, but in a good way'.

Much emphasis on poetry, with poems studied every week, as well as learnt by heart and declaimed. 'We want them to know the great poets of the English language,' said the deputy head, and to further this, the school has produced its own wonderful anthologies, where the selection is 'unashamedly classic.' In addition to regular English lessons, boys receive two lessons a week on formal grammar and punctuation, and Latin is compulsory from the off – 'Latin is crucial for grammar, it's not an academic luxury,' insisted the deputy head. 'As an international school, the story of the world's great civilisations interests us. But children of this age also need connections, and they need the basics.' All those who have wrung their hands at the disjointed, shallow content of so many modern lessons, lift up your hearts and hope.

This is clearly a scholarly yet joyful environment, and the quality of student work we saw reflected that. We read, misty-eyed, a set of poems by the year 7s about Westminster Bridge (inspired by Wordsworth's sonnet) that were outstandingly creative and well-written; likewise, a history essay on Thomas Becket was not only mature and insightful, but skilful and lucid in its use of language. But mightn't this approach favour only the brightest? WCCS's SENCo emphatically denied it, asserting

We read, misty-eyed, a set of poems by the year 7s about Westminster Bridge (inspired by Wordsworth's sonnet)

that boys at the school with SEN benefited from understanding how language works. We were impressed with the support the school gives to those with dyslexia and dyspraxia, as well as to ESL students, such as the two grave and courteous Russian boys we saw having extra English tutorials. And all the staff we met were purposeful, well-bred (curmudgeon excepted), cultivated, devoted to what they do, and, according to parents, 'incredibly dedicated.'

As you'd expect, the standard of music here is outstanding. The choristers are completely immersed in music-making at the highest level (listen to the downloads on the website, and marvel), and the day boys, swimming in the same element, also achieve great things. We saw year 8 boys composing their entries for the school's Christmas carol competition, and heard much excellent instrumental playing as we went round the school. 'The music programme is amazing,' enthused one parent, 'My son's piano playing has come on by leaps and bounds in just a few weeks.' Many pupils achieve grades 7 or 8 in their chosen instrument(s) by the time they leave.

Football, rugby and cricket are the main sports here, played at local pitches, and swimming and PE are held at the nearby Queen Mother Sports Centre. Lots of extracurricular activities, including debating, philosophy, chess, scrabble, code-breaking, the Airfix model club, current affairs, and cross country running. 'But where do you run?' we asked, glancing with some surprise at the surrounding streets. 'Oh!' said our tour guide, 'Green Park, Hyde Park, St James's..'

Lucky lads, you might think. And they are, of course. But what struck us most about this lovely little school was how considerate, well-mannered and sanguine about life its pupils seemed to be. They are achieving great things, while remaining likeable and happy boys. As one mother wrote, 'My son is neither Catholic nor musical, but has been recognised for other things he has to contribute to the school. They're grounded children with good values. It's a perfect place for my son to grow into a confident young man.' We agree with her. For boys fortunate enough to come here, this is as near perfect as it gets.

Westminster Under School

Linked school: Westminster School, 206

Adrian House, 27 Vincent Square, London, SW1P 2NN

Independent • Pupils: 265 • Ages: 7–13 • C of E • Fees (per term): £5,460

Tel: 020 7821 5788
Fax: 020 7821 0458
Email: under.school@westminster.org.uk
Website: www.westminsterunder.org.uk

 62

Master: Since 2010, Mrs Elizabeth Hill MA Cert Ed Dip Ed (50s). The daughter of two head teachers, Mrs Hill grew up in Leeds, where she attended Leeds Girls' High School. Then onto Homerton College, Cambridge (where she studied biology and physical education) and the Institute of Education, achieving an MA in education and psychology. Wide-ranging teaching experience in the state and private sector (St Ivo School, Cambridgeshire; Raines Foundation School, Tower Hamlets; Camden School for Girls; Alleyn's Junior School), including 15 years as deputy head of Dulwich Prep London. She also serves as an ISI inspector. The Under School is her first headship, but one she was prepared to wait for. Capable, enthusiastic and sympathetic, she continues to teach, aims to know every child (and every parent) by name. Keen to maintain tradition – despite being the school's first female head, she's retained the title of 'Master' – but equally keen to be forward-looking and develop the school. Married to Humphrey, a former lawyer, she spends her out-of-school hours with her extensive family (three boys, two girls, all now in their 20s), and enjoys bridge, sport, music and travelling.

Entrance: Academically selective (very) at 7, 8 and 11. Some successful applicants are merely 'well above the national average', about a third 'far above'. All candidates need to read fluently well beyond their chronological age and approach the unexpected logically and imaginatively. No obvious feeders, though all the usual central London pre-preps represented. At 11+, a reasonable chunk from state primaries, most of the rest from schools which end at year 6. (The master encourages entrants from 'those leaving at a natural point.') Twenty-two places at 7 (175 applying), a further 22 at 8 (175 applying), then 28 places at 11 (250 applying). About 40 invited at each stage for interview and further testing. 'We want to understand each child and decide if this is the right school for them.' What makes the fit? 'The school is about passion, enthusiasm, determination and

a hunger for achievement. We're looking for boys who are independent, intellectual and individual. Everybody here loves learning.'

Exit: About 80 per cent go on to the senior school (including all those who come in at 11), with a good number of scholarships (seven in 2014), but the school is equally happy to prepare for entrance and scholarships elsewhere. About a dozen each year to Eton (often those with family connections), quite a few with major scholarships (three King's Scholars, two Oppidans in 2014). Generally a couple to Winchester, and a sprinkling to City, Dulwich, Alleyn's, etc.

Remarks: Academically top of the tree. Well-qualified staff (a number with PhDs) provides teaching that is strong, lively and challenging. 'We're looking for boys who will think and problem solve,' says the master. 'We want them to work things out, not be spoonfed.' Most boys seem to relish the offering. 'I really like all my lessons,' said one. 'The teachers are very enthusiastic and if you have a problem they just want to help,' said another.

Specialist teaching in all subjects from year 5. In English, boys are encouraged to 'develop their own voice'. Books are seminal, with even the smallest scouring the library shelves in their lunch hour. Reading lists updated termly and topped up with an in-house bookshop and regular swapshop. Weekly maths competitions hone skills both for lessons and the Intermediate and Senior Maths Challenge, where plenty achieve gold and beyond. Programming from year 3. French throughout, taught by native speakers. Classical studies combined with Latin from year 5, stand-alone Latin from year 6, Greek in year 8. Annual Latin play competition. 'There's a real sense of intellectual endeavour,' says one parent.

Thorough monitoring, with internal exams November and June, plus mocks in the Lent term of year 8, as well as regular subject testing. Lots of rewards for achievement with cups and shields for virtually everything. Homework load significant

---

'We don't require parental support and you absolutely don't need a tutor. If you need a tutor, you shouldn't be at Westminster.'

---

at all levels. An hour a night in years 3-5, an hour and a half in years 7 and 8. Some parents have voiced the view that supportive homes are essential. The master says this shouldn't be necessary: 'We don't require parental support and you

absolutely don't need a tutor. If you need a tutor, you shouldn't be at Westminster.' We do, however, hear rumours of unhappiness in both staffroom and parental circles.

New arrivals at 11 – two forms of 12-14 boys – are given Saturday morning lessons from the moment they're accepted, then segregated for lessons (but not other activities) in year 7. 'We give them lots of attention, before dividing up the whole year group into scholarship and CE forms in year 8,' says the master. Those from state primaries can find the transition taxing. 'Catching up to common entrance in two years was difficult,' says one parent. 'There was an enormous amount of work and my son found it stressful.'

Few struggle in the conventional sense, but an experienced SENCo provides support with study skills, exam technique and organisation, arranging clinics where help from peer mentors is particularly productive. Plenty of 'enhancement', too, through debating, history of art etc.

Music of an exceptionally high standard (many boys with grade 8 and beyond and plenty of music scholarships to senior schools). Head of music (also musical director of National Youth Music Theatre) oversees over 500 lessons a week, an outstanding choir and biannual music trips.

Not everyone's idea of a sporty school, but the athletic ante has been raised recently with the addition of a number of well-qualified coaches. ('One boy attends the Chelsea football academy one day a week, but still manages his academic work,' says the master). For a central London prep, notably well-endowed with playing fields, and the expansive garden square opposite the front gates provides an ample supply of pitches and courts as well as an adventure playground. Games twice a week, with regular inter-house and inter-school tournaments in football, hockey, cricket, tennis and basketball. Newly-acquired sports hall just down the road (also able to accommodate mass gatherings of parents) offers further scope for indoor games, including judo, fencing, karate, wall climbing and nets.

Exciting theatrical tradition maintained by an 'inspirational' head of drama, with three productions annually (recent highlights include Lord of the Flies, School for Scandal) and a large, new drama studio with a separate 'Green Room' in the pipeline. Art now housed in it its own light and lovely double studio, with a self-contained art history library. Clubs every night (history, Mandarin, debating, etc). Chess (taught by a Grand Master) particularly popular, with 90 members and England players. Competitions galore, including hotly contested Scrabble tournament. (Some find the atmosphere slightly too competitive. 'They don't just have a Scrabble club or a chess club, they have a Scrabble competition or a chess competition.')

Plenty of external speakers and trips in London and further afield. (Recent adventures include classics to Sorrento, cricket to South Africa, geography to the Grand Canyon.) Philanthropy a core value. 'They learn to enjoy giving and love raising money for disadvantaged children,' says the master. (Parents and boys raised £45,000 last year, £18,000 in the popular Readathon.)

Founded in 1943 as a class of 17 boys located in the senior school, then decanted to Ecclestone Square, the school took up residence in its current spacious premises in Adrian House – a red-brick Victorian former hospital – in 1981. The Under School continues to share both governors and outlook with the senior school, allowing the same careful planning over future development. A large new building, directly opposite the existing school, opened in 2013, providing a loft dining hall and indulgent stretches of well-equipped teaching space.

Discipline not an issue. 'You don't have to shout at Westminster; we encourage good behaviour through positive behaviour management and high expectations,' says the master. Certainly, one boy unbidden held open a door, all answered questions readily and politely. Immaculate uniform, perhaps, not a priority. ('Shirts look better in than out,' the master gently chides.) She teaches PSHE: 'They have to learn about emotional intelligence and empathy for others. We talk about life.' She hopes that all feel confident to 'tell'. 'We want them to be able to talk with us about anything and it will be OK.'

At 7 and 8, parents primarily prime-central-London (often City) high achievers. At 11+, more diverse, with pupils coming from as far afield as Dagenham and Guildford. Plenty of bilingual, multicultural homes. Parents tend to be proud (and occasionally pushy). Boys are extremely articulate (one 8 year old, asked how he'd cope with a broken arm, responded, 'I will just have to become ambidextrous') and can undoubtedly be boffiny ('Thus, you can see,' explained one 11 year old).

No scholarships, but a few means-tested bursaries of up to 100 per cent at 11 (which take the recipient through the senior school). 'Our philosophy is that the children who can come here should not be prevented from doing so for financial reasons,' says the master.

An exciting, demanding education for the intellectual, industrious child.

Westminster School

Linked school: Westminster Under School, 204

17 Dean's Yard, London, SW1P 3PB

Independent • Pupils: 740 • Ages: 11–18 • C of E • Fees (per term): Day £7,800 – £8,546; boarding £10,930; Queen's Scholars £5,632

Tel: 020 7963 1003
Fax: 020 7963 1002
Email: registrar@westminster.org.uk
Website: www.westminster.org.uk

63

Head Master: Since July 2014, Patrick Derham MA (late 40s), previously head of Rugby School. At 11 was sent to live and study on the naval training ship, Arethusa, run by the children's charity, Shaftesbury Homes, to prepare young men for the navy. His potential was spotted and he was

transferred to Pangbourne College, where he eventually became head of school. Read history at Pembroke College, Cambridge (first class degree), and began his teaching career at Cheam School. Moved to Radley, where he was head of history and a housemaster, and joined Solihull as headmaster in 1996. Dynamic, level-headed and caring. Very popular with parents. Married to Alison, a teacher, with two grown up children.

Academic matters: Second to none. Always in the top five of any league table, but that is a by-product of what goes on here. Syllabuses can be almost incidental, to the extent that a check needs to be made near exam time to ensure that the actual requirements of the course have been attended to, as so much else has. Teachers teach from immense depth and breadth of knowledge of their subjects and far beyond. Many are acknowledged experts in their fields. This enthusiasm is met by that of their pupils who may not all be boffins but who have lively, questioning minds, turned on by the general buzz of the intellectual life on offer.

If you want convincing, in 2014, at GCSE, 87 per cent of subjects taken got A*, 97 per cent A*/A grades. All GCSE subjects, and some others, can be taken to A level or Cambridge Pre-U and these results are equally impressive. In 2014, 51 per cent of subjects taken achieved A* or the Pre-U equivalent (grades D1 and D2), and 84 per cent A*/A (nearly all take four A levels or Pre-Us, and many five). Most popular are maths (massive), history (nearly so), sciences, English and economics. There are equal numbers of Latin and French takers and languages are always strong. German, so sadly moribund elsewhere, taught in

part via poetry and song. Theatre studies, electronics, music and RE are taken by minorities as exam subjects but all have lively profiles on the extracurricular side of life. Pupils sit the Pre-U in all classical and modern languages, English, art history and art. In all other subjects they sit A levels

Everyone does DT and electronics in year 9 and school owns an electron microscope in its up-to-the-minute labs. Computerised projection system in all classrooms, whiteboards for mathematicians. Each dept has a supply of laptops available on demand. The library – in a stunning set of rooms – is open until 9.00pm and has its own much-

Most pupils come from moneyed and clever families resident in London but originating everywhere, so many languages spoken at home

praised website. Overall teacher:pupil ratio of one to eight. Recent injection of young teachers appreciated by Westminsters who also revere their sages. Some teachers seen as 'wacky and inspirational' rather than efficient but, of most, we are told, 'nothing is too much trouble'.

School bemused at the thought that anyone with the right kind of intellectual capacity might be denied a place because of an SEN eg mild or moderate dyspraxia – 'there's no problem'. Study skills coordinator sees all who need support, whether the super-bright but chaotic or those with a dys. All pupils provided for on a case by case basis. 'I believe that as you go through the academic life you move from one level of learning to another. Our study skills co-coordinator helps everyone think about the skills needed to empower their learning at different stages.'

Games, options, the arts: The Westminster extra-curricular programme, extraordinary by universal consent, is impossible to encapsulate here and is much enhanced by the contribution of the academic staff who offer activities founded on their private enthusiasms. It is further embellished by a unique list of outside speakers. Recent visitors include Rowan Williams, Simon Singh, Martin Rees, Christopher Ricks, Colin Thubron, Tony Benn, David Ramsbottom, Margaret Hodge, Oliver Letwin, George Galloway, Robert Fisk, Jon Snow. There are evening concerts given by the like of Ian Bostridge, Imogen Cooper, Felicity Lott. If Westminster parents sometimes niggle that their children do not go out into London sufficiently that is because London comes to them. There are esoteric trips everywhere – to Iceland for plate tectonics, to New York for art, to the Crimea for rock climbing, Venice to row in the regatta and to Chios for classicists and on and on.

The arts are privileged and more so since the acquisition of the Millicent Fawcett Hall, now an excellent flexible studio theatre and the opening

of the Manoukian Music Centre – an ex-army drill hall with recital room, teaching and practice rooms and recording studios. Outstanding music and drama and school mounts productions of eg Mozart and Weill operas to professional standards. Drama taught throughout school. Art, too, is breathtakingly good – four studio areas, a tradi-

The history of Westminster reads like the history of England and its list of Old Westminsters is a list of main players in that story

tional printing press and much emphasis on the traditional skills – people can draw and paint here. Other options, reflecting the staff's eclecticism, include bookbinding, Warhammer, languages, board games, D of E, jazz, philosophy, carpentry, comic films etc. Debating is famously strong. PHAB, like other community service projects, gets enthusiastic participation.

Games (known as 'station') played vigorously and joyously and with stunning success in, particularly, rowing, cricket and cross-country. There have also been successes in football, fencing, netball and fives. Sporting opportunities are multifarious but no-one would claim world class sportiness for Westminster overall. Games mostly played on the surprisingly large playing fields in nearby Vincent Square and school acquired a large sports centre adjacent to these playing fields which used to be one of the Royal Horticultural Halls.

Background and atmosphere: The history of Westminster reads like the history of England and its list of Old Westminsters is a list of main players in that story. The thousands of tourists who tramp the precincts of Westminster Abbey must be startled to see knots of vaguely uniformed teenagers comfortably chatting round about Dean's Yard – the adjacent grassy square. They would need to peer through the inconspicuous archway that leads into Little Dean's Yard – the school's central quad – to find the hotch-potch of houses that form the nucleus of the school.

Westminster began in 1179 and has been in continuous existence since the fourteenth century. Elizabeth I bestowed royal patronage upon it in 1560 and is celebrated as the school's official foundress. The abbey is its chapel – an astonishing privilege in itself. Many meals are eaten in College Hall – a medieval room with coats of arms, portraits of former heads and wonderful painted corbels under a beamed ceiling – in which the abbots and monks gathered to eat in the early years of the abbey. It is an integral part of the deanery and adjacent to the Jerusalem Chamber. School has, of course, its own argot and it can be mystifying. Also its own traditions – ask about 'The Greaze'.

The school buildings have been built, acquired and developed over the centuries, most of them abutting Little Dean's Yard, the houses named after revered and redoubtable former housemasters and Old Boys. They include a series of rooms in the beautiful Ashburnam House which make up the library – a national monument in itself. The quiet streets round about provide outposts, all only minutes away. These include the girls' boarding house, in the Georgian silence of Barton Street (opposite T E Lawrence's former house), the Robert Hooke Science building on the far side of Smith Square, the theatre and music centres and the Weston Building on Dean's Yard which provides airy, spacious new teaching rooms in a very Westminster mix of modern technology, cornicing, panelling and parquetry. The latest acquisition is a former monastery building in Tufton Street (next to the main site in Dean's Yard) which is now a house called Purcell's for boarding girls and day boys.

Girls arrived in the sixth form in 1973 and are much valued though there are no plans to include them lower down the school. School appreciates how a Westminster sixth form works for both sexes – 'The girls' results are the highest nationally, they thrive on our debating style of teaching and the boys pick up on their work ethic'. The Westminster sixth form life is relaxed and collaborative. A pupil told us, 'People make their own relationship with the school which the teachers respect.. problems are worked out through a kind of bantering interaction with the teachers'.

Boarding recently upgraded. All rooms are now comfortable and most are well-appointed. Many are surprisingly spacious and, of course, have views over the abbey, school or college buildings and gardens. Younger boys in rooms of between two and eight and all pupils have their own rooms in the last three years. Thumb print recognition or key pad entry systems. Good kitchens, common rooms, games rooms and sensible, relaxed discipline maintained by resident housemasters (male or female are called this), many of whom have young families on site. All boarders in the lower school (up to the age of 16) go home every weekend. Some sixth form boarders stay at school at weekends but the school is very quiet on Saturday nights.

Overseas numbers remain small though school sees Westminster in a global context in interesting ways. 'We're not dragging in pupils from abroad but we need to see ourselves as a world-wide school competing with the best pupils from everywhere. We're interested in links with the top academic schools worldwide and in learning what they do educationally. That's where our future competition for university places will increasingly come from – rather than from UK schools.'

Pastoral care and discipline: Famously relaxed and liberal as has been felt appropriate in a school which thrives on the individuality of its members. Despite an undertaking to smarten up, to our seasoned eye Westminster pupils look much as they have ever done and shirts seem to not to stay tucked in for long. Girls have a dress code – plain colours, no denim, jackets rather than jumpers since '08, etc.

No serious drugs-related disciplinary incidents recently. 'We're probably more concerned with alcohol than drugs but believe in taking a firm line.' The approach is very much to educate and to involve parents, establishing a collaborative and supportive home/school relationship. 'We have a disciplined system which, if it is to be fair, has to be consistent.. you've got to keep talking to your young but, whereas we would look at infringements on a case by case basis, we can't be individualistic at the expense of the school community'.

Maybe not individualistic but individuals really count here and great efforts are made to support and nurture those taken into the school fold – sometimes at unconventional times in their careers. Pastoral care, not always the school's strength, now impressive and it's hard to fall through the net. Some parents feel that, for girls, the pastoral side 'has a bit of a hole in it'. One said, 'I don't think they really take on board that girls have certain issues', and some take longer to settle in than others, though the boarders have a cosy nest in their homely house. The tutor system, at its best, is supportive and comradely though 'some tutors are not really involved and are pretty useless,' we were told. 'People who are thought likely to get into trouble are allocated to really good tutors.'

Pupils and parents: 'We are more metropolitan and cosmopolitan than most public schools.' Most pupils come from moneyed and clever families resident in London but originating everywhere, so many languages spoken at home. Only a quarter boards and most of those are Londoners with busy-busy families. Very few from really far away – Russia, China etc. Pupils are quirky, sparky, irreverent, natural sceptics, though seldom 'cynical' as reported in the rhapsodic recent ISI inspection report. They are articulate, endlessly intellectually curious, creative, individual, challenging in the best sense. Their parents, many of whom are active in supporting the school, know exactly what it is they are paying for and love it – 'it's fantastic'.

Former pupils (Old Westminsters) include some rotters, for example most of the officers in command during 'the disaster in the Crimea' such as Lord Lucan. Also Kim Philby. But then there are also Ben Jonson, George Herbert, John Dryden, John Locke, Christopher Wren, Robert Hooke, Henry Purcell, Charles Wesley, Earl Howe, Warren Hastings, Edward Gibbon, Jeremy Bentham, GA Henty, AA Milne (who vastly endowed the school), Adrian Boult, John Gielgud, Angus Wilson, Norman Parkinson, Andrew Huxley, Peter Ustinov, Flanders and Swann, Tony Benn, Corin Redgrave, and, still with us, Peter Brook, Nigel Lawson, Roger Norrington, Andrew Lloyd Webber, Stephen Poliakoff, Helena Bonham-Carter, Ruth Kelly, Imogen Stubbs, Louis Theroux, Dido and Mika etc etc.

Entrance: Register your son by the end of year 5 for 13+ entry. He will be screened in the autumn of year 6 – ISEB computer tests in maths, English and VR and interview – places conditional on CE performance offered thereafter. At least 70 per cent expected. Further interview at 13 – 'we like it as it opens the teacher/pupil dialogue'. Alternative method of entry is the Challenge – a competitive exam for scholarship places. Those who don't win scholarships may be offered places with other financial help if they do well enough. Around 400 are seen at 11 when conditional offers for the 120 places are made. Boys and girls applying for 16+ places must register by the October before entry. Offers based on interview, tests and meeting GCSE requirements.

Exit: In 2014, 97 Oxbridge places and 16 to leading American unis, though pupils stress, 'they make a big deal about not going to Oxbridge if it's not for you – they try to educate the parents that it's OK if we want to go somewhere else.' Most of the rest to Bristol, UCL, Imperial, LSE, Edinburgh, Warwick, Durham. Principal degree subjects history, economics, PPE, management, maths, languages, medicine. But they go everywhere and study everything to distinguished levels.

Money matters: Eight Queen's scholarships annually worth 50 per cent of the boarding fee and scholars must board. Music scholarship worth 25 per cent of the day or boarding fee at 13+. Means-tested bursaries of up to 100 per cent of fees. Expensive trips highly subsidised by school when appropriate.

Remarks: For the right boy or girl, simply the best.

Wetherby Preparatory School

Linked school: Wetherby School, 356

48 Bryanston Square, London, W1H 2EA

Independent • Pupils: 305 • Ages: 7–13 • Non denom • Fees (per term): £6,135

Tel: 020 7535 3520
Fax: 020 7535 3523
Email: admin@wetherbyprep.co.uk
Website: www.wetherbyprep.co.uk

64

Head: Since 2008, Mr Nick Baker BA PGCE (30s). After reading geography at UCL, acquired teaching qualifications at Newcastle. Taught in state secondary and middle schools and then Chesham Prep in rural Buckinghamshire. Joined Wetherby Prep at its inception in 2004. Initially senior master, then deputy head, before taking over the reins in January 2008. Quiet, does not have a huge ego and doesn't push himself forward but parents are full of praise for him, say he is honest and open and 'a very strong leader for boys'. 'Totally transparent, what you see is what you get'. 'An inspiration for boys and staff alike'. Feel he has definitely put his own mark on the school and they like it. Has a completely open door policy as wants to have a community, family school. Feels it is important to

be a high profile head and stands outside to greet all the boys as they come off the buses in the morning. Teaches geography to common entrance classes and helps out elsewhere when he can. Watches, listens, thinks and really does seem to know each boy. Married to an ex-teacher with two small sons who he adores. Parents say 'when he is making decisions he thinks like a father.' Has high expectations of his pupils and runs 'a tight ship with no shady corners. If one appears he deals with it.' Boys like and respect him. A head who is constantly striving to improve his school and looking for ways to make it the best in London.

Entrance: At 7 and 8, tests in English, maths and reasoning during an assessment day at the school, when will also take part in group activities. Places further up the school will be treated individually. Open evening in autumn term but otherwise no open days. However, parents are invited to visit the school and meet the head at any stage, doors are never closed. Unless circumstances are exceptional, automatic transfer from the pre-prep.

Exit: Early days yet but so far results impressive. Harrow, Westminster, St Paul's, King's Wimbledon, Eton and Latymer Upper currently most popular. The future looks rosy.

Remarks: A well-structured, well-balanced, caring school offering a slightly less pressurised alternative to the top London preparatory schools. One parent feels that, at the moment, it is her 'little secret'. We doubt it will stay that way much longer.

Opened in 2004 in Notting Hill Gate, has now moved to larger premises in tall, elegant listed Georgian house in central London. Parents and boys alike are delighted. 'Fabulous,' said one, 'and the busing system is brilliant'. The additional space means that classrooms can now be subject-based with each floor having its own identity. Two staircases, one, stylish and unadorned, for up in the old part of the house, one for down, winding round the lift shaft, in the newer, non-listed back addition. Rules say no running anywhere in the school. Huge hall right across the front on first floor, so far lacking in much wall decoration as conservation limits what can be done. Used for various activities and three times a week assemblies. Rooms aplenty, all bright and airy, staff can even escape to their own suite for R and R.

Broad curriculum and good teaching prepare the boys well for CE. Young staff (average age mid-30s), half male, half female and smallish classes, max 20, at the moment more like 14/15. Standard high and boys are expected to perform well. Setted from year 4 in English, maths and French but classes are names not numbers – on English floor, Dickens, Conan Doyle and Woolf – so no superiority and boys do not know which set they are in. Interactive white boards and a computer in every classroom. IT embedded in curriculum with 60 laptops (in IT suite) available to be collected and used by the boys whenever and wherever necessary.

Good music. About a third learn individual instruments, some to grade 8. Choir (audition necessary) and string ensemble. Two concerts a year, all perform in the first one. Art and design room at top of the extension, so no problem putting stuff on the walls there. Humanities at the back on the ground floor and two decent sized science labs in basement, with more advanced equipment for the seniors. These boys have everything. Lots of outings and visits, within London, the UK and overseas.

No outdoor exercise area on site but much use is made of Seymour Leisure Centre just a few minutes' walk away and parents say 'loads of sport'. All the usuals plus rowing to competitive levels. Awards for all. We met some older boys in the basement lining up to go in for a delicious looking lunch, wonderful quirky menus sent home for parents to see each week. We asked what the symbols on their ties meant: 'I've got my football half colours' and 'I've got my full ones'. This is a traditional prep school with modern innovations. A particularly effective one has been to cancel all Friday afternoon lessons and have compulsory clubs instead. Range from the cerebral, like European culture or maths, to the creative, like model making, to the sporty such as badminton and horse riding. Several others as well. So Friday afternoons are fun and both boys and parents think this is a brilliant idea.

Excellent pastoral care and help for SEN children. They are aware of how boys are learning and quick to pick up on any problems. Teachers plan weekly and make sure that those who need extra help are given it. Specialist teachers are available out of lesson time for more severe cases and if they feel all is still not going right they bring in other agencies. Their sister school, Abingdon House in South Kensington, is always there to help and the Dyslexia Centre round the corner provides occasional teachers. Policies for everything. PSHE for all every week. Head of PSHE and boys' fitness 'a real father figure who the boys find easy to talk to.' Parents very impressed with communications. Any email sent to a staff member is replied to within 24 hours and feedback is equal for all children, academic or non-academic. Parents say that learning difficulties are well dealt with and the individuality of each child is properly catered for. 'If a boy is picked on the head is on to it in milliseconds and deals with it.'

Not a cosy, laid back school but one where every pupil is expected to perform and participate. Where parents are constantly kept up to date with their child's progress and tutors have been known to ring them even over half term. Not all expected to be A students but are expected to try and all boys are rewarded in some way or other. Parents say, 'very inclusive. Lots of leeway for each boy to be rewarded in front of the school.' 'You can trust the school to keep you in touch.' 'Very traditional, very strong values. Manners, decency and social responsibilities count. So does respect for peers.'

William Ellis School

Linked school: LaSwap Sixth Form Consortium, 135

Highgate Road, London, NW5 1RN

State · Pupils: 870 · Ages: 11–18 · Non-denom

Tel: 020 7267 9346
Fax: 020 7284 1274
Email: info@williamellis.camden.sch.uk
Website: www.williamellis.camden.sch.uk

29

Head: Since 2011, Mr Sam White, chemistry graduate and previously deputy head of the London Oratory. Good news, say parents: 'He has an exceptionally good manner with boys and parents.' 'The boys like and respect him.' 'Whenever I go in I see him chatting with a boy, and he seems to be genuinely interested in them.' A pupil concurred: 'He has been really keen to get to know us all. He is a good influence on us.'

He was appointed during the interim headship of Jill Hislop, who took over after the school had suffered a budget deficit, got through two heads in quick succession and been slated by Ofsted. Ms Hislop, who still has strong links with the school as its 'professional partner', started the upward trajectory that Sam White has continued. Ofsted returned in 2012 and pronounced the school 'good', quoting a teacher's remark that 'The headteacher is leading and pulling everyone here along.'

He felt that he was taking on 'a challenge, but manageable...it was a school that desperately wanted to improve'. His first job was tackling behaviour – 'we needed to re-establish clear boundaries' – and his first two years saw a high rate of temporary exclusions, which has now dropped significantly. He has also continued the work on improving the quality of teaching and, despite some initial staff turnover, maintained teacher morale and encouraged staff to work collaboratively to produce good schemes of work.

Camden is one of the few areas of the country where no schools have converted to academies, and the local schools (which collaborate as a joint sixth form, LaSwap) work closely together. 'I get lots of support from Sue next door [at Parliament Hill], Maureen across the road [at La Sainte Union]...'

Academic matters: Huge ability range, with year 7 reading ages ranging from 8 to 17. The upward trend in GCSE results, with a blip in 2013 due to English, has continued: in 2014, 64 per cent of pupils got 5+ A*-C grades including English and maths, with 20 per cent A*/A grades. Parents report that English, once a weak point, has been turned round by the 'very impressive' new HoD. The school now teaches the IGCSE English language, and those who took the exam early achieved 'brilliant results'.

The school has a language specialism, and everyone starts French in year 7, with around half studying it to GCSE. School has links with the nearby Collège Français Bilingue de Londres. Most take up either Spanish or German in year 8 (offered in alternate years), but this is no longer compulsory, and some spend extra time on English fluency instead. Latin and Mandarin are taught in clubs, and fundraising has enabled a sixth form Mandarin and geography trip to China in 2014 – the first for three years.

Around a quarter of boys take single sciences to GCSE. Those with a more vocational bent can take OCR science, and choose from various other courses with a large coursework element such as business studies, travel and tourism, and ICT. Some spend a day a week in years 10 and 11 at Westminster Kingsway College studying eg catering, construction or motor mechanics.

Fluid grouping rather than setting across the curriculum from year 8 (school hopes to group maths and science from year 7 in future) at the discretion of each faculty head. 'If a set of boys has a particular weakness in a subject we may put them

---

Some parents would prefer more rigorous setting, but praise the willingness of staff to go the extra mile for boys at all levels

---

together for a term, but there's plenty of movement.' Some parents would prefer more rigorous setting, but praise the willingness of staff to go the extra mile for boys at all levels. 'They will take time and a lot of patience with those who are bright but

not pulling their finger out. I don't feel they are just settling for the easiest way of getting them through exams.'

Parents are mostly optimistic, though one complained about a lack of homework. 'We've found the teaching really good so far,' said another. 'My son is very happy here and seems to be doing well.'

School uses Future First, set up by old Elysians, to help it keep in touch with alumni and get them involved in giving careers advice, work experience and mentoring

---

'My son, who is very academic, is being well supported,' said another. 'I had severe reservations about some of the teaching during my son's early years here,' said a long-standing parent, 'but I don't now. I've never felt I had to get a tutor in.'

Teaching assistants are increasingly being trained to help with particular subjects, or with behavioural or language difficulties, rather than being velcroed to a particular child. The school uses some of its pupil premium funding (alongside sponsorship) on its City Year team of volunteers, who act as mentors, support teachers in class, run breakfast and homework clubs and supervise in the playground. The funding also helps with small group and one-to-one teaching, particularly in English, as well as counselling and interventions to improve attendance.

Joint sixth form with Parliament Hill School, which is part of the LaSwap consortium that also includes La Sainte Union and Acland Burghley. This enables a wide range of courses for a wide range of abilities, from a BTec in health and social care to further maths A level. In 2014, 13 per cent A*/A grades and 41 per cent A*-B. Students stay in their base school (which for William Ellis boys will be their own school or Parliament Hill) for the majority of lessons, but may go elsewhere for minority subjects.

As well as working with Camden to provide one-to-one careers advice, school uses Future First, set up by old Elysians, to help it keep in touch with alumni and get them involved in giving careers advice, work experience and mentoring. It organises career sessions here and brings back old boys to talk about their work.

Games, options, the arts: A large trophy on the head's table when we visited is the new house cup. Houses, reintroduced in 2012 and run by 'young, enthusiastic staff', are named after local historic buildings (Lauderdale, Burgh, Willow, Keats and

Fenton). Pupils gain house points by competing at sports and taking part in talent shows, spelling bees, chess, model building, cake sales et al.

Year 7 and year 9 have a week camping at the school's field centre, The Mill, in Surrey. Boys also go on ski trips, language exchanges and field trips. 'The extracurricular activities have improved markedly over the past few years,' said a parent, citing her son's sessions at the Royal College of Music, playwriting with professionals, theatre and concert trips, Model UN.

Football and basketball are the most popular team sports, but rugby is up and coming – the RFU provides coaching and talented players are encouraged to join local clubs. The eight table tennis tables get enthusiastic use. Takes part in the annual Camden Shield boys' competition, which sees teams from six Camden secondary schools compete in football, table tennis, basketball, badminton, athletics and cricket. Pupils report that team sports peter out in the higher years: 'The teachers do try, but we tend to get a bit lazy in years 10 and 11.' The school has a newish sports hall, with facilities for

---

'Whenever I've emailed to ask questions, I've had an immediate and pleased reply. They are extremely responsive to an interested/meddling parent.'

PE and basketball and a multi-gym, and the playground doubles up as five-a-side football pitches. Sadly, the school cannot afford to hire the field next door, groomed for cricket when we visited, but it does play games on other parts of Parliament Hill Fields and use the athletics track there. Clubs include cricket, running and trampoline.

Light top floor art rooms display impressive work; a sixth former was recently a finalist in the Camden Art Competition, and students have exhibited their work at the local Lauderdale House. Some parents find the music provision underwhelming, but there are choirs, ensembles and a range of concerts for all, from beginners to advanced musicians, often in conjunction with Parliament Hill School and La Sainte Union, which form a joint orchestra with WE. There are also workshops and masterclasses run by professional musicians. The head of music 'has been very supportive of my son writing and performing his own music,' said a parent, and a school group recently reached the finals of the Roundhouse Band Slam competition. School subsidises instrumental lessons for boys on free school meals.

Not a school that goes in for full-scale musicals, but there are many smaller drama performances, such as the recent drama club interpretations of the Ancient Mariner and Christmas Eve in the Trenches at the Winter Concert. Pupils work with outside organisations such as the Donmar Warehouse, and take part in the Shakespeare Schools Festival. 'They do it thoroughly and well,' said a parent.

Background and atmosphere: William Ellis was a public-spirited businessman who founded several schools in the mid-nineteenth century, believing children should be taught 'useful' subjects such as science and to develop their reasoning faculties, rather than rote-learning religious tracts and ancient languages. William Ellis School, the only one of his schools that still exists, was founded in Gospel Oak in 1862 and recognised as a boy's secondary school in 1889. It moved to its present site, on the edge of Parliament Hill Fields, in 1937. Originally a grammar school, it turned comprehensive in 1978; the red-brick vine-clad buildings still have a grammar school feel.

'My son has had a very happy time here,' said a parent. 'He has a sense of belonging and pride in his school. It fosters a nice attitude and spirit in the boys – confident but not arrogant.'

Pastoral care and discipline: As mentioned, one of the head's first actions was to tighten up on discipline, with plenty of fixed term exclusions in his first couple of years. He also appointed a new and effective head of pastoral care. This has helped to cut down on the low level disruption that once marred many lessons, and has made boys feel safer inside and out. 'They are much stricter on uniform than they used to be, and you no longer have to hack your way through a posse of boys smoking round the gate,' said a parent. Year 7 has its own quad, with table tennis and picnic tables. The year 7 head has links with most of the feeder primary schools, and boys are invited to summer school before they start.

One parent commented: 'The pastoral care is very good. A few years ago I went through a difficult divorce and they were brilliant at supporting my son.' Another said, 'Whenever I've emailed to ask questions, I've had an immediate and pleased reply. They are extremely responsive to an interested/meddling parent.'

Increasing emphasis on carrots rather than sticks, with boys earning house praise points for good work and good attitudes, from persistence to creativity. 'Relationships can be much more relaxed once ground rules are established,' says the head. Deep Learning Days, part of the PHSE curriculum, see timetables dropped for a day in favour of discussions on relationships, including peer pressure and bullying, careers and the world of work, with plenty of outside speakers. 'We try to make it circular – get the boys to present back to their peers what they have learned. Recently 25 year 9 boys did a play for the rest of the school.' One parent commented on her despondence at a lack of creativity in the PHSE teaching, but another said, 'They are very good at raising the boys' social and political awareness. They don't shy away from issues that can be sensitive, such as homophobia and religion.'

Pupils and parents: Huge ethnic mix, with fewer than a third of pupils from white British background, and others ranging from Irish to Turkish to Somalian. Huge social mix too, from the large social housing estates of Gospel Oak to the multi-million pound houses of Dartmouth Park. 'There were cliques lower down the school, but in years 10 and 11 everyone hangs out together and we all get on,' said a pupil. 'The fact that the boys come from a huge range of backgrounds doesn't seem to matter one bit, which is a very impressive trick for a school to pull off,' said a parent.

Old Elysians include Toby Young, Robert Elms, Sean French, Andrew Sachs and Len Deighton.

Entrance: Usual admissions criteria for 125 year 7 places: looked after children, medical and social need, siblings, up to 12 musical aptitude places, then by distance (usually up to about two miles). Generally around 300 outside places for LaSwap sixth form consortium, with an intricate admissions system and a range of entry requirements for different levels of courses.

Exit: Around 70 per cent move on to LaSwap sixth form. Some go off to eg Camden School for Girls, Woodhouse College, St Marylebone, Fortismere or FE colleges. Around 20 per cent of LaSwap leavers to Russell Group universities, including several a year to Oxbridge (four in 2014).

Money matters: Voluntary aided by the William Ellis and Birkbeck Schools Trust, but otherwise is as hard up as most other state schools.

Remarks: Small boys' comprehensive in idyllic situation on the borders of Hampstead Heath, now emerging rapidly from the doldrums under strong, popular and enthusiastic head. 'It can only get better and better,' said a satisfied parent.

Central West

Hammersmith & Fulham
Kensington & Chelsea

CENTRAL WEST

An introduction to Central West London and its state schools

Hammersmith & Fulham

A long borough that travels from north to south, albeit with numerous bus routes linking the two ends. Just west of Chelsea, this is a hard borough to pin down, with Fulham's pockets of large mansion flats near the river and Victorian terraced houses within sound of gentle thwonk of tennis balls at the Queens Club – cheek by jowl with council housing and some fairly mean streets. But some of the harder areas are on an upward trend, particularly near the recently gentrified Fulham Broadway and in Hammersmith with bustling King Street, ever improving pubs and new development spreading out from the huge Westfield shopping centre.

A high percentage of children used to attend secondary schools outside the borough, but the arrival in 2011 of two very different schools has changed the face of secondary school provision here. The Hammersmith Academy had a wobbly start in the face of the sudden and fierce competition from the much publicised and surprisingly popular West London Free School. The latter, with its public-school-like stipulation that Latin be learnt by all and that boys play hockey and rugby, not football, was a London middle class magnet. However, as the years roll on and its pupils are still nowhere near being housed in the premises they were promised (the elegant and spacious Palingswick House on King Street), and reeling from losing two heads in three years, the West London Free School is starting to lose some ground to its more established, well-resourced rival. The Hammersmith Academy is modelled on the highly successful Thomas Telford Academy in the Midlands. It has three hour lessons conducted in the splendid circular premises between the Goldhawk and Uxbridge Roads, and the Mercers (the Guild that is behind St Paul's boys and girls, among others) as sponsors.

Burlington Danes Academy – towards North Kensington – is one of the ARK academies, with the associated financial and expert support. The school has become a serious contender – results are good and becoming better, and Ofsted judges it to be outstanding across the board. Phoenix Canberra, in Shepherds Bush, benefitted enormously from the tight control and charismatic headship of Sir William Atkinson. While he has gone now, academic performance remains reasonably steady with some improvement. A good choice of vocational subjects as well as academic, but probably not the place to sit A levels.

Sacred Heart High qv in Hammersmith is a reason for parents of girls to convert to Catholicism and choose a local Catholic primary school (siblings are quite low on the priority list).

In the south of the borough, Fulham Cross Boys' School (once called Henry Compton) and Fulham College Girls' School (both 11 – 16 years) are now in a federation with the new Fulham Enterprise Studio. This is a vocational 'studio school' for 14 – 19 year olds, specialising in construction and performing arts (production). Free schoolers are at work here too, setting up The Fulham Boys' School (C of E but welcoming all faiths and none) in West Kensington. Controversially, the local authority agreed to close down popular and successful Sulivan Primary, moving its pupils to New King's Primary School, and freeing its site for Fulham Boys' (at time of writing, with Labour now in control of the borough, this decision is under review).

Lady Margaret qv in Parsons Green, an all-girls, Church of England school with over 50 per cent church-goer places, feels more like Wycombe Abbey than a London comprehensive. This end of the borough is also home to the highly prestigious London Oratory qv – the holy grail for Catholic parents with sons. Boys are accepted from across

London, the admission requirements stringent, but the lucky parents who have succeeded in jumping through those precarious hoops (including Blairs and Cleggs) are satisfied customers.

Popular primary schools include John Betts qv, traditional and small, lots of parents opining that it reminds them of their own primary school, Brackenbury, and Greenside (the latter despite a string of highly disappointing Ofsted reports). The West London Free School primary school has made a promising start, say parents cautiously, with automatic entry into the senior school. The Ark Conway Primary School in the far north of the borough, part of the ARK group of academies, is in a relatively deprived area but is well managed and in a splendidly characterful building (the old library).

There is a plethora of good church schools, most notably the outstanding St Stephen's on the Uxbridge Road, which sends large numbers to Twyford C of E high school in Acton as well as the West London Free School (its founder's children go there), and the ever-popular St Peter's in the leafy Hammersmith square of that name off King Street. For the Catholics, Larmenier & Sacred Heart in Brook Green and The Good Shepherd off Askew Road feed boys to Cardinal Vaughan and the London Oratory, girls to the ever-outstanding Sacred Heart.

Kensington & Chelsea

The Royal Borough of Kensington and Chelsea is one of London's smallest boroughs geographically and yet one of the most densely populated areas in Europe. It includes Holland Park, the area named for the eponymous park, which features leafy streets and some of the largest detached and semi-detached houses in London. Notting Hill of Hugh Grant fame is home to the Portobello Market and hosts the largest annual street party and carnival in Europe, held over the August bank holiday weekend.

The borough houses some of London's wealthiest as well as its poorest. Half the residents educate their children privately, half of the state school pupils receive free school meals, and half of the borough's children go to secondary school in another borough. It is also, on DfE statistics, the best performing area in England for GCSE results.

There are only five mainstream secondaries and of these only one, Holland Park qv, is a community school. It is rated outstanding and is hideously oversubscribed, but gives up to 10 per cent of places to students who show an 'aptitude in art and design.'

The rest have a religious requirement as part of the admissions process. Three are Catholic (St Thomas More – co-ed – in SW3, Sion-Manning – girls – in North Kensington and Cardinal Vaughan qv – boys – in Holland Park) and one, co-ed Chelsea Academy (Fulham), is C of E (50 per cent faith and 50 per cent open places, with some preference for children from K&C primary schools). Cardinal Vaughan, with its tight entrance rules and tight discipline, is the number one choice of school for the children of a number of prominent political figures.

Fox qv, with its tiny catchment tightly focused primarily on and around Kensington Church Street and south of Notting Hill Gate, is a very vibrant and a reliable primary school choice. Half of the 27 primary schools are either Catholic or C of E, St Barnabas and St Philips and St Mary Abbots – the latter attracting leading lights in the parliament – perhaps the most coveted. Further south towards Chelsea, the Oratory is a popular choice for Catholics and Christ Church for the Anglicans. If you're not religious and live close to a salubrious area that incorporates, inter alia, The Boltons, then Bousfield qv is likely to be your number one choice. Other less well known schools that have a good reputation in the (slightly) darker corners of the borough include Barlby and Thomas Jones.

Ashbourne Independent School

17 Old Court Place, London W8 4PL

Independent • Pupils: 240 • Ages: 16–19 • Non-denom
• Fees (per term): £7,000 – £8,333

Tel: 020 7937 3858
Fax: 020 7937 2207
Email: admin@ashbournecollege.co.uk
Website: www.ashbournecollege.co.uk

20

Principal: Since 1981, Michael (Mike) Kirby BApSc MSC (60s), who founded the college. Mr Kirby read aerospace engineering in Toronto (he retains a soft Canadian burr) and Birkbeck where he did a masters in statistics. Very tall, laconic and seemingly inscrutable, but a warmth and a smile escape him occasionally and the man is momentarily revealed. After 32 years, unsurprisingly, he and his school mirror each other. Focused and clear-sighted, he has made a place where little distracts from work but where the work ethic is underpinned by the sense of support felt by the students. His involvement with the students is integral to the day-to-day running but the touch is light. 'I know a lot of them personally – they can be a bit wide-eyed and innocent but they're just nice kids and they're great fun.' He still teaches maths revision classes – as ever, we applaud – and, unlike many in his position, sees the students very much in their own home context. 'We positively encourage parents to get involved.'

Prominent member of CIFE (the Conference for Independent Further Education) and the British Council Education Counselling Service, he is the owner and proprietor of Ashbourne. This and the length of his tenure make him unique. He is keen that Ashbourne be recognised as a 'bona fide part of

the independent school system', hence his resolve not to be the first resort for resit students – though they do come in penny numbers. He launched and continues to steer a pretty effective school.

Academic matters: Most students come for the two-year A level course, although one year and 18 month A level programmes also on offer – these popular with, mostly, overseas students. Separate classes for those AS students who want to improve their grades – a growing trend. However, AS students who significantly 'underperform' – having been warned that they are in danger of doing so – are shown the door. No embarrassment at this – 'We filter,' says Mr Kirby. 'That's how we get the results'. A small middle school offers two year (years 10 and 11) and one year (year 11) GCSE programmes – currently 30 students.

At A level, 37 subjects on offer and all taught in small classes – seven is average, 10 is max and even ones and twos for some subjects. In 2014, 76 per cent A*-B and 54 per cent A*/A grades. Maths much the most popular subject and with the most impressive results – almost all A*-B. Similarly with further maths. The sciences also taken by many – again with a decent crop of results. We witnessed one Eng Lit class – all girls. Languages holding up well and business here, as everywhere, gaining a more mixed bunch of results. Unsurprisingly, no Latin, no Greek. All language teachers are native speakers. Lunchtime critical theory seminar much-praised and very popular: 'It's way beyond the A level syllabus so you learn about Marx and Freud and feminism and then apply the theories to film and literature. I learned so much from doing it that way,' an A2 student enthused. All lessons are two hours long. Teachers much praised for their enthusiasm and care. Many are long-serving.

Few SEN students with anything other than mild dyslexia/dycalculia/ADHD and neither building any good for those with mobility difficulties. No SENCo though SEN overseen by affable head of middle school. Mr Kirby says: 'The school is happy to accept those with SEN but makes no special provision beyond arrangements for exams.' A few here have extra exam time, a laptop in exams or a scribe.

Games, options, the arts: Some variance between the college which claims to offer 'a very wide extra-curricular programme' and the students, some of whom seem to know little about it – mostly, apparently, the Brits who don't live locally. However, much enthusiasm from those who do partake and especially from those who have gone on overseas subject-related trips with the college. We are told

that the college has now appointed an officer who is specifically responsible for student activities and for ensuring that everyone knows about them.

Art is legendary here and the art room – where we were glad to see some mess – was full of concentrating artists and makers of textiles when we visited. Lots of colour and art seemingly derived from diverse influences. College runs a choir but no orchestra/ensembles. Lots of societies – held in lunchtime and after college; good college newspaper written by students. No sport to speak of and some join gyms etc (there's one next door) but, as everyone agreed, it's the price you pay. Very popular Christmas Revue in which virtually all take part – local fringe theatres are hired for these and other performance events.

Background and atmosphere: In two buildings, separated by Ken High Street. 'Old Building' (in Old Court Place) is tucked down a side road – helpfully guarded by two policemen holding rifles (actually outside the Israeli Consulate) – and so discreet, it's very easily missed. Most sixth form classes take place here. 'Young Street Building' in – you couldn't make it up – Young Street opposite houses the middle school and the rest of the sixth form classes including a huge art room – by far the biggest of the school's rooms. Internally, both buildings are pristine – white walls relieved by stylish and undistracting prints and some larger artwork made on site. Plain carpet, bare wood stairs. Sofas only in one common room and the two staff rooms which are as severely workful as the rest of the establishment. There's nowhere to doss, nowhere to hide. You come here, you work. If you want to mess about, you go out. And they do. Ken High Street, the park, cafés and shops – it's all on the doorstep and, if the inside of the school is cramped, up close London is huge, spacious and full of things to do. Students would welcome kitchen space – somewhere to warm up lunch brought from home (daily eating out is expensive) – but every inch counts here and the common rooms are small. Lockers only for GCSE, art and photography students.

Can accommodate up to 250 students. Teaching rooms are definitely small. Interactive whiteboards in use everywhere and Mac PCs everywhere too. The 'library' is all Macs and the shelves have text books and uni guides. There is no library. Good music room – again, all tech, as far as we could see though there is, apparently, a piano and a guitar. Good film/media room and photography studio has dark room. A pervasive air of relaxed purposefulness. And a fantastic location.

Pastoral care and discipline: The parents we spoke to paid tribute to the excellence of home-school communications and this is true equally of local or UK-based families and the overseas ones. Few such colleges offer the community feel and nurturing to be found here – strengthened by everyone being on first name terms and easy exchanges of emails between parents and staff. Staff room doors are glazed and usually open – little sense of 'them and us'. Everyone has a personal tutor – the same throughout their time – c20 tutees to a tutor. This is not the place if all you want is processing to achieve results. The staff gain much praise for being on top of their game educationally but also for 'really caring' and being very approachable. Drug use would lead to immediate expulsion but this sanction very rarely used. Probably not your first shot if you've been ejected elsewhere.

Pupils and parents: Students come from state and independent schools in the UK, as well as from private schools abroad. Around half the students from around 40 different countries – the rest from the UK. Fewer Chinese than hitherto – more now from Vietnam and Malaysia but college recruits from Russia, Botswana, Ukraine and Kazakhstan and elsewhere. All students have to speak good English and must speak English during the school day – even when with compatriots. About 40 per cent of the students have dedicated English-language classes (no extra cost) – up to six per week – however, best not to choose Ashbourne if you need substantial EAL reinforcement. Of the UK students, around third to a half from the state sector. No boarding though college has halls shared with other educational bodies close by and in Hampstead. Some international students' families find their own more local accommodation. Slightly more girls than boys overall and girls vastly outnumber boys in the humanities. Students here don't look like rebels, dropouts or rejects but wholesome and focused – much as at any academic, independent school's sixth form. All relish the social mix and the internationalism. Students on bursaries complement the loaded with no discernible difference. 'It's a bit cliquey,' we were told, 'especially if you're not into smoking and drinking,' but that's what they do at this age – it's part of being a teenager and drugs seem not to feature here, unlike elsewhere. The principal notes that Ashbourne appeals particularly to 'pupils from good local girls' independents who want something different at A level'.

Entrance: January and September intakes makes for flexibility and a great help to those who need time to re-group after, perhaps, mind-numbing GCSE results. Entry via interview – telephone or face-to-face with either principal or director of studies plus a subject-related entrance test. Auditions for drama/music applicants and portfolio for those who wish to pursue fine art – in which the college

has a distinguished tradition. Also, most recent school report/grades/predictions and a personal statement. Bs expected for entry to A level courses – though some flexibility. International students must have minimum 5.5 IELTS or equivalent.

Exit: To a diverse list of colleges and university – no processed clones leave here. Oxbridge places and unis abroad not uncommon (one off to Cambridge to study maths in 2014). Perhaps predictably, London universities figure prominently, along with eg Edinburgh University. Courses taken mostly point to solid professions and vocations. Many ultimately into law and finance but this is no mere spawning ground for the suited professions. Creatives include artist and photographer Marion Sosa, fashion designer Chau Nguyen, actors Calum Witney and Vicky Pasion, and the writer Dane Weatherman (founder of the literary periodical Black and Blue).

Money matters: Some bursarial help for students of exceptional ability, especially in drama and music, which offer a very few full scholarships.

Remarks: Solid, reliable and effective place to study. Not for socialites, smack-heads or slackers.

Bousfield Primary School

South Bolton Gardens, Old Brompton Road, London
SW5 0DJ

State • Pupils: 430 • Ages: 3–11 • Non–denom

Tel: 020 7373 6544
Fax: 020 7373 8894
Email: info@bousfield.rbkc.sch.uk
Website: www.bousfieldprimaryschool.rbkc.sch.uk

21

Headteacher: Since September 2014, Helen Swain BEd MA, deputy head for last eight years. Has been in teaching for 26 years and joined Bousfield as a year 6 teacher 16 years ago.

Entrance: Due to cuts in funding there are now 60 part-time places in the nursery on offer, rather than the previous 30 full-time places. Two parallel classes from reception to year 6, each with 30 pupils. Applications for the nursery are done through the school; applications to the main school are done via Royal Borough of Kensington and Chelsea.

No automatic transfer from the nursery to the main school – parents must reapply. Children who are in care or have an SEN statement are considered first, followed by siblings and then proximity to school (currently approximately 0.5 of a mile and shrinking). Distance measured as the crow flies. Places do become available further up the school, due to high mobility rates of pupils, so worth persevering. Hugely over-subscribed. As one current parent puts it: 'If you get offered a place here, you'd be mad to turn it down.'

Exit: Most popular secondary schools are Holland Park, Chelsea Academy and Lady Margaret's. Over a third go on to independent senior schools, including Latymer, City of London, The Harrodian, Putney High and Francis Holland. No special preparation given for those doing 11+ exams. School knows a large amount of tutoring probably goes on, but says pupils get plenty of exam practice anyway. Much parental advice and support given when it comes to choosing next school.

Remarks: Strikingly international, with 41 different first languages currently spoken at home. Sixty per cent have English as an additional language. After English, the most prominent languages are French and Arabic. School sees this cosmopolitan element as a real strength and the high level of harmony being something to celebrate. A significant number arrive with very limited English. It is 'sink or swim, but usually swim.' Much language teaching on offer, including Italian classes laid on by the Italian Consulate and French to all KS2 pupils. Bilingual pupils tend to outperform monolingual ones. Much coming and going due to large expat intake. Lots of French families have departed recently due to job losses in the City. Only about half the class in year 6 have been there from reception.

Superb academic results, particularly given the huge EAL contingent, though school always looking to 'up the ante.' English, maths and science Sats results well above national average. There are plans

---

'After the ceremony, I go away feeling that at this point in their lives perhaps they really have all won.'

---

afoot introduce some setting for maths and reading in year 6, though lack of space means separating children into groups is a challenge. Pupils' progress is tracked carefully.

When we visited, children were beautifully behaved and all engaged. A sense of calm pervaded the school. Manners and presentation clearly high on the agenda. No uniform. Packed lunch or school lunch. Fruit given to the younger years, funded by School Fruit and Vegetable Scheme.

One full-time teacher and one teaching assistant in each class, as well as extra support staff for pupils with statements and EAL pupils in the early stages of learning English. A great team of dedicated staff, who 'put the hours in.' Many loyal, long-serving teachers (20 members of staff have been there more than 10 years), as well as newer ones. A strong team – 'no prima donnas.'

Bright, vivid displays throughout the school. Some classrooms smallish; every iota of space used. School is a 1950s listed building which makes expansion and development problematic.

Arts are very strong in the school, though not at the expense of academics. Lots of music, dance and drama going on. School believes performance helps to build children's self-esteem. Pupils are offered a rich curriculum, full of workshops, plays and concerts. More than 90 learn a musical instrument. Guitar and strings ensembles, two choirs but no orchestra. Parents attend practice workshops so they know what a good music practice at home should involve.

Plenty of sport – gym and games as well as after-school clubs offering tennis, football, cricket and even cheerleading. Swimming for years 3 and 4. Pupils take part in borough events (including athletics) in the summer term.

Quantity of homework has been reduced – parents were completing too much of the pupils' project work ('you can always spot the hand of a parent,' we were told) and copious amounts were

being downloaded unthinkingly from the internet. Homework now more focused on the basics, with reading, spelling and maths given from early on.

Some children with SEN statements. More on the SEN register, receiving support of some kind. No specially trained teachers but school feels they have strategies and experience to help those in need. Has experience of pupils with Asperger syndrome, autism, ADHD, emotional/behavioural difficulties and moderate/severe learning difficulties, as well as dyslexia, dyspraxia and hearing and visual impairment. School is not a centre of excellence for all of these – very occasionally pupils move to special schools, either when Bousfield can no longer adequately support them or when they move to secondary school. Staff say Bousfield is 'an inclusive school' that does its best to accommodate those with difficulties.

Strong parental involvement, with school questionnaires showing overwhelming parental support and high levels of satisfaction. Numerous opportunities for parents to attend curriculum workshops and 'book looks' (when they visit to look at children's books). Parents welcomed in at the beginning of the day.

Some wrap-around care available, albeit not all on-site. Breakfast club on offer and pupils can be escorted to a neighbouring school (with more provision) at the end of the day if required.

Bousfield has close connections with artist Quentin Blake, who attends prize-givings and pops in regularly. All leavers receive a prize at the final

---

School sees this cosmopolitan element as a real strength and the high level of harmony being something to celebrate

---

assembly and Blake says his spirits are raised as each leaver is celebrated. 'After the ceremony, I go away feeling that at this point in their lives perhaps they really have all won,' he adds.

A great sense of purpose permeates this thriving school, with pupils bright-eyed and focused, offered a lively, dynamic and interesting education. As one satisfied parent lamented: 'I just wish it could go on into secondary school.'

Bute House Preparatory School for Girls

Luxemburg Gardens, London W6 7EA

Independent · Pupils: 310 · Ages: 4–11 · Non-denom
· Fees (per term): £4,439

Tel: 020 7603 7381
Fax: 020 7371 3446
Email: mail@butehouse.co.uk
Website: butehouse.org

Head: Since September 2012, Mrs Helen Lowe (early 50s) BA Oxford Brookes, LGSM Guildhall School of Music and Drama. Married to Phil, whom she met at drama school. They have two grown up children. Having 'got acting out of my system' she started her teaching career in big Essex comprehensives where she taught drama. She is verging on the evangelical about the profoundly positive benefits a background in drama can have – 'everyone should go to drama school because it's all about people and understanding other people's point of view'. She then went on to teach at primary schools in Richmond and became the literacy consultant for the whole of the borough. Her experience in the independent sector includes being a drama teacher at St Paul's Girls' in the 1990s, curriculum coordinator at Lady Eleanor Holles junior department and head of juniors at King's House in Richmond, where she taught for three years. Bute House is her first 'stand alone' headship, ending the 20 year tenure of the formidable Sallie Salvidant.

Bright and bubbly, Mrs Lowe likes to make an impact. Never one to be seen without her pink lipstick, snazzy glasses and white blonde hair well coiffed. Her confident manner ('I'm very bossy,' she

admits with a twinkle) could be overbearing were it not delivered with such warmth and humour. Parents remark on her enthusiasm and ability to make changes without a fuss. Good changes, that few had even noticed were needed – a whole school Christmas celebration at a local church for example. 'I am a great communicator,' she says. Parents agree. She holds open house individual appointment sessions where parents can discuss any of their concerns about the school. She can not only put her point across impressively but listens too – and, what's more, the parents listen to her – even when it might be news they don't enjoy hearing – that their daughter won't suit a school they have set their hearts on, for example.

She knows the girls properly, and by the time the 11+ process kicks in, she is well equipped to write their reports for senior schools and advise the parents on the best school for each one, having taught all girls in their second half of year 5 and first half of year 6. 'I have the best interests of the child at heart,' she avers. This may not always coincide with pleasing the parents but it doesn't faze her. When it comes to decisions about boarding school, however, she is sensitive to the fact that this is a decision that affects the whole family, not just the girl. A refreshingly modern and human touch from a prep school that sends a fair few to the top girls' boarding schools.

Entrance: There are two entrance points: reception – a one form entry where 22 places are allotted by ballot (after taking into account siblings, which could mean that the number is easily halved), and year 3, when girls are selected after sitting the 7+ exam (in the January of year 2). About 400 girls are entered into the ballot, two years before entrance, which is then scrupulously and rigorously drawn – by the chair of governors, with the head, the bursar, the school secretary and a lawyer in attendance. No question of rigging, and absolutely no point in ensuring that little Emily can recite her 10 times table.

For year 3, about 200 register for 38 places. Assessments in English, maths and non-verbal reasoning are carried out in a relaxed way along with various activities which focus on team work and social interaction. The girls are carefully observed by a number of teachers and Mrs Lowe said, 'hand on heart', they weren't just looking for the most academically able and – don't choke on your skinny flat white – they have turned down girls despite their marks being among the highest. They are looking for girls who respond well to learning, with a positive and enthusiastic attitude. This is a school determined to maintain their mixed ability, academically non-competitive ethos (this and the ballot were the two non-negotiables in her interview, Mrs Lowe tells us).

No sibling preference at 7+ assessment, but school 'looks very carefully at sisters'. Occasional places thereafter are competed for by test, and the school has a waiting list for each year. Girls come from the local boroughs and as far as Barnes, Ealing, Kew, Putney, Wimbledon and north London. Vast diversity of backgrounds, the US and Asian contingent is fairly significant and a number are bilingual in combinations of French/Mandarin/Italian/German, to name but a few.

Exit: Over half each year go either to St Paul's or Godolphin & Latymer. Even if they don't go there, these are the two schools that most parents aspire to. The rest either board – Wycombe Abbey, Downe House, Cheltenham Ladies' the current favourites – or go to other all girls' day schools eg Putney High, Lady Eleanor Holles, the Francis Hollands. Recently greater interest among parents in co-ed – Latymer Upper is becoming increasingly popular. Interestingly, around the same proportion of those who enter at 4+ as those who come at 7+ go on to the most academic schools. Bute girls trail scholarships: in 2014, the leavers were offered, between

them, 33 scholarships (including 15 academic, and not just brainbox awards either, 13 music too).

Remarks: One can be forgiven for thinking that this is the prep school for St Paul's Girls' School; it used to be years ago, but hasn't been since the 1950s, and it's a dangerous mistake to make. Although Bute is lucky enough to share the St Paul's swimming pool and some games pitches, and is only a stone's throw away, it is an entirely separate and distinct institution. You may have won the jackpot to get your daughter in here in that she will have a fabulous education during her early years, but you haven't been granted a stepping stone into the hallowed halls of St Paul's Girls. There are no friendly ears to be bent. Iris will have as great a chance of getting in there from any of the good London preps as she does from Bute House.

An outstanding prep school, Bute House manages to combine solid substance with flair and panache. There is lots going on: the academics are excellent despite – or probably because of – its non-competitive ethos, but this is one of the most passionately competitive about sports of any of the girls' day schools we have seen. In the classroom, however, there is no setting, streaming or ranking, and marking is all done by comment: 'That's what contributes to the girls being so good and kind to

Her confident manner ('I'm very bossy,' she admits with a twinkle) could be overbearing were it not delivered with such warmth and humour

each other – and makes it such an amazingly warm, happy and friendly place,' comments Mrs Lowe.

Learning support is known as 'learning enrichment' here – SEN and G&T girls occasionally removed from their lesson in order that their learning be 'enriched'. The head of the learning enrichment department is an SEN specialist, as are the other members of staff who both support those girls needing extra help or extend the more able girls. Teachers from the LED work in class alongside class teachers as well as sometimes taking groups of girls out of the classroom. The teaching is clearly, for the most part, inspired, and this is true of the learning enrichment programme too. Fifty-two girls are on the LE register, many needing only minimal support. This support is free. Those who don't speak English at home have one weekly support session. Some see the SENCo on a one-to-one basis and some in small groups. Ninety on the G&T register. School says that any difficulties are diagnosed early and dealt with as soon as possible.

We detected some sensitivity around the issue of special needs. The school says that it 'makes it clear in its parents' contract that girls with specific learning difficulties who need a great deal of additional support may be encouraged to look for another school that can meet their needs better'. A few parents, albeit under the old regime, felt that their daughters with learning difficulties were not getting sufficient attention compared with those who were 'gifted'. School is keen to point out that this is changing. A dynamic SEN teacher coupled with a change in priority and ethos from the top means that everyone here gets the attention they need. However, there does appear to be some tension between the non-competitive academic ethos and the fact that ultimately this is an academic school with parents who have academic aspirations. Mrs Lowe asserts that early identification of any issues should enable all the girls to achieve highly, and she is especially keen to ensure that every girl achieves to the best of her ability. She says she also looks carefully at the transition from year 2 to 3, since this can cause anxiety for parents who perceive that the new intake may well be more academically able, and the flood of new girls will result in their daughter becoming 'lost'. The strong non-competitive academic ethos comes as a shock to a lot of parents who are attracted to the idea of Bute House as a top prep school with a history of a relationship with St Paul's – often in competitive professions themselves, they find themselves feeling frustrated not knowing whether Molly is top of the class or not.

Any competitive instincts can find an outlet in the sports programme, however. Bute girls are known in the prep school world to be formidable netball players and there is a D team as well as an A so everyone should get a chance to play. Some mutterings among mothers that this is not the case – but we suspect that the kudos of playing in the A team is such that both daughter and parents aspire for that. Gymnastics is also very popular and of a high standard. Although gym squad, run by external coaches, is only for the most talented, school says that those not in the squad have plenty of opportunity to be involved in gymnastics. Excellent sports facilities, especially considering its inner urban site, with use of St Paul's pool next door, and swimming is strong – plenty of squads and galas so that everyone gets a chance. Mrs Lowe attributes the excellent team spirit among the girls to the lack of competition in the classroom.

Very young, innovative head of drama (complete with red glasses and severe fringe) injecting some exploratory imaginative work into the drama curriculum; the class we saw were all lying on the floor with their feet in their air waving their arms. Head of music also young and energetic – a benign 'Jack Black school of rock' type, he arranges lots of different groups, bands and orchestras ('smiley strings', 'string fever', 'jammmy jazzers' to name a few). Girls have class music twice a week from reception through to year 6 and most learn at least one instrument, from the double bass through to the bassoon.

Rich curriculum – everyone does French from reception, Spanish from year 5 but no Latin at all. Specialist teaching from reception in drama, music, sport and art (and DT) as well as French. Specialist science teaching from year 4 and proper DT facilities – saws, work benches, as well as a well-equipped art room – first class and unusual in a London prep school. Huge superbly-equipped science lab and lots of outside space – netball courts as well as playgrounds, comfortable sitting areas and plenty of greenery. Every floor has stairwell storage for laptops, which are available for the girls to use when needed. Excellent library, well-stocked, well-organised (there are two librarians) and most importantly well-used. Lots of music rooms for lessons and practice. All the girls do one drama performance once a year. The show at the end of year 6 is a highlight, with the most recent being Annie.

The Bute building itself is a surprise – a somewhat futuristic 1950s neo-greenhouse farrago with add-ons in pine, pink render, louvred glass and warm-toned brickwork in a quiet Victorian terraced street just off fashionable Brook Green, five minutes from the Hammersmith jungle. It has a splendid atrium with the reception and offices and big screens with the news of the day, timetable changes etc; even the day's birthdays – rather nice. One eye catching and charming tradition is the corridor outside the hall, the walls of which are covered by little ceramic tiles, each one made by a Bute pupil as a record of their time at the school. The school, thereafter, in the head's words, 'is a bit of a Tardis' and one is not prepared by the hotch-potch exterior for the spaciousness – of each classroom, the immense hall and outside space as well as of the airiness and uncluttered feel of the whole.

The classrooms are a feast. Reception is big and there is plenty of space for everyone at the little tables and around the many activities. Everything is beautifully laid out – pencils in pots, a discovery table with 'new life in spring' exhibits – most remarkable – a canopied and cushioned book corner and lots of lovely dressing-up stuff including some pretty cool shoes. All the children use the garden, complete with lots of climbing things and a real – not a bouncy – castle and sandpit. Reception children have their own times when they also use large wheely toys. This is perhaps the most colourful school we know – everywhere are displays, pictures and models – all bursting with vitality, wit and fun. Many rooms, including the hall, are flexible, and divisible into two. All classrooms have smartboards and, oh joy! – all are air-conditioned. The girls eat in one half of the hall and drool over the food. 'It's just the best'..'it's cooked to perfection!' Free cucumber and carrot wedges are served at break and there are water-fountains inside and outside school.

If your daughter is lucky enough to get a place here she will have stimulating and exciting time, making good friends and building excellent foundations for her future. Your aspirations and ambitions need to be tempered, however; the school she ends up going to next will be right for her, but it may not necessarily be the one you had in mind when you set out on this odyssey.

Cameron House School

4 The Vale, London SW3 6AH

Independent • Pupils: 120 • Ages: 4–11 • Non–denom • Fees (per term): £5,550

Tel: 020 7352 4040
Fax: 020 7352 2349
Email: info@cameronhouseschool.org
Website: www.cameronhouseschool.org

22

Headmistress: Since 2007, Mrs Lucie Moore BEd. School founded in 1980 by Josie Cameron Ashcroft, who is the proprietor and, as Mrs Moore puts it, 'is her one and only governor'. A member of the IAPS, Ms Ashcroft taught at Thomas's and coached children privately before setting up her own school in St Luke's Church, Sydney Street. She remains principal and still keeps a close eye on the ongoing vision and image of the school and knows all the parents as well as the staff.

Mrs Moore, as headmistress, is in charge of the day-to-day running of the school. She started her teaching career in a state primary in Winchester, then in international schools in Italy and Bangkok, before settling into the hurly burly of London day schools. She spent seven years at the Hampshire School, where her career took a meteoric rise under the paternal guidance of Arthur Bray: 'He was like a mentor to me'. He soon identified her talents and she swiftly became head of prep and vice principal of the Hampshire Schools before he encouraged her to apply for the post here.

Her husband, the finance director at City Airport, is always by her side at school events. A young headmistress (she was 36 when she started), Lucie (as she is known to everyone, pupils, staff and parents) is attractive and bubbly. She has a huge sense of fun and clearly adores the children. Each sentence is peppered with 'Aren't they just so sweet?' She's got a point – children here are very cute: girls clad in fresh blue and white striped summer dresses with cherry jumpers and cardis, boys bumbling, adorable in blue cord shorts.

Parents enthuse about her smiling enthusiasm, warmth, excellent communication and understanding of each child. We heard reports of her firm but sensitive approach to the big issues that arise in a child's life, whether it's an instance of unkindness – difficult to conceive of a child being actually bullied here – or problems at home. She also has enormous reserves of energy and is very driven. As well as teaching every class in the school once a week ('It's important that I keep my feet on the ground for the sake of the children and the staff'), coordinating the SEN, and working on the weekly newsletter, she is at the front door every afternoon and morning greeting each child.

If any parent expresses an interest in a senior school she doesn't know, she will make sure she spends plenty of time there – not only to establish important links with the head but also to make sure in her own mind that the school would suit that child. Highly efficient ('I'm a Virgo,' she says. 'I need to be organised and to plan ahead') and not at all concerned about getting her hands dirty, she describes the job as 'fitting like a glove'.

Entrance: All children are assessed at 3, so no need to rush to get your baby onto a list; register up till a year before entry. A popular school – over 200 applicants for 20 places and Mrs Moore acknowledges how difficult it is to choose – 'It's heartbreaking to reject anyone,' she says. Ultimately they look to create a class with a balance of the confident and the shy and some happily in between. They work closely with nurseries and rely on their reports (children come from a wide range including Pippa Poppins, Paint Pots, and Miss Daisy's). Putting school down as a genuine first choice always helps.

Exit: A few boys at 7+ or 8+ to, eg, boarding or Catholic schools (Ludgrove, St Philip's), but head actively discourages year 3 leavers so fewer and fewer now. Mrs Moore has fine tuned the 'stepping stones' options for boys who want to do 13+

Bubbles the maths clown visited, the hall was filled with balloons and children came to school dressed as shapes

common entrance and sends them for two years at 11 to, eg, Newton Prep, Fulham Prep, Sussex House, Wetherby or the GEMS Hampshire School. Lots of advice given to parents from year 5 onwards.

At 11 girls and boys go to a broad range of schools each year – current favourites are Latymer Upper, St Paul's Girls, City of London Girls' and Boys', Dulwich, Alleyn's, Emanuel, Godolphin & Latymer, Queen's Gate and Francis Holland. They nearly always get their first choice school, we're told (due in large part to Mrs Moore's determination that parents choose the school that suits their child, whatever they themselves might prefer). 'And they interview beautifully because they're so confident,' she gloats. One or two girls every year board at, eg, Wycombe Abbey or Downe House.

Remarks: A tiny (one class per year of about 20), cosy, pretty school, but don't be misled into thinking it's just chocolate boxy – Cameron House is a serious player in getting children into sought-after London schools. Wide range of ability, but what all children have in common is that they are confident and very, very smiley.

They are given a lot of preparation in the final year. In year 6, class sizes shrink so everyone gets more attention, compulsory homework club gives all children an extra hour at school and removes the pressure from the parents. 'We shoulder the worry,' says Mrs Moore, 'and the last thing I want is to see 10 year olds being counselled for stress.' A lot of staff channelled into year 6, when they do group work, prepare for scholarships, have mock interviews and confidence-building workshops. The formula clearly works – they get results, but no-one could describe this as a hothouse.

Approximately 15 children are helped with mild to moderate SEN – dyspraxia, dyscalculia, dysgraphia etc. The school takes a holistic approach. Learning support is timetabled and structured with clear IEPs drawn up – parents pay extra. Programme for the gifted and talented run within the class. In addition a select few are invited to join the Discovery Club and Explorers Club. Mrs Moore explains the cautious approach to the gifted and talented programme. Children are identified towards the end of year 1 – 'We wouldn't want to have to say, "You weren't gifted after all!"' she says.

A town house with not a great deal of space, but the soft plush tartan carpet throughout the stairwell, lavatories with pretty wallpaper, water filters, attractive blue furnishings and every teacher referred to by their first names – without even a Miss or Mister attached – give the school a homely, uninstitutional feel.

Children have fun here, whether it's enjoying music, drama or sport, watching caterpillars transmorph into butterflies or playing giant magnetic chess in the playground (a good excuse to see the lovely Lucie, to get the chess pieces). Even maths can be made to be an excuse to dress up and laugh – Bubbles the maths clown visited, the hall was filled with balloons and children came to school dressed as shapes. In Book Week everyone dresses up, even Mrs Moore, who is not at all fazed when she greets prospective parents dressed as Captain Hook. 'If they don't like to see their future headmistress being able to laugh at herself, then we're clearly not the right school for them nor them for us,' she says.

Nearly everyone plays an instrument or has singing lessons – the lessons happen in a little Wendy house type hut in the playground. Major dramatic productions – The Lion King, A Midsummer Night's Dream among them – take place in a closely guarded secret venue – 'Let's just say a theatre off Kensington High Street,' is as far as Mrs Moore will be drawn. 'We aim high,' she says proudly, as she lists the impressive artistic accomplishments for such a small school, which include getting to the final for young choir of the year at the Royal Festival Hall. They have an orchestra, string quartet and three choirs.

One of Mrs Moore's challenges has been to stop the boys leaving at 7+ or 8+ – signs of success. Although previous year 6 classes have had few boys, some none at all, when we visited there were an equal number of both sexes. 'Parents are starting to realise that they can get their boys into Westminster Under, Colet Court or Latymer at 11,' she says, 'and there are plenty of stepping stone options between 11 and 13.' Children are kept a lot more active here than at many similar schools. Games takes place three times a week – children can do cricket, football, hockey and netball as well as martial arts in the huge loft space at the Boudokwai centre. Lots of matches (most of which they lose, comments one parent) but the advantage of being a small school is everyone gets to have a go – it's not just the sporty types who do everything.

A lot of expat families, mainly from the US, Canada and Australia, reflecting the cosmopolitan area. We saw masses of glamorous long-haired mothers off to the gym after drop off. Lots of city types, but also more than the usual number of creatives – artists and actors, as well as doctors and art dealers. All parents are very involved and enjoy the open door policy of the school.

A charming school that will discover your child's strengths, nurture and support them.

The Cardinal Vaughan Memorial RC School

89 Addison Road, London W14 8BZ

State • Pupils: 950 (co-ed in sixth form) • Ages: 11–18 • RC

Tel: 020 7603 8478
Fax: 020 7602 3124
Email: mail@cvms.co.uk
Website: www.cvms.co.uk

23

Headmaster: Since 2011, Mr Paul Stubbings, previously deputy head, appointed after a row over admissions criteria between the school governors and the Westminster diocese – the diocese objected to the parental involvement criteria as discriminatory against poorer parents – which resulted in a purging of the governing body, injunctions and a stalemate resolved by a governors' U turn and Mr Stubbings' appointment (very popular with parents).

Academic matters: Consistently impressive results and school makes no bones about aiming for academic excellence in its comprehensive intake. School has specialist status in mathematics and IT and computing is BIG here – though some would like to see computer science on the curriculum in addition to IT. A level results 87 per cent A*-B grades in 2014 and 53 per cent A*/A. Range of subjects offered not immense but includes economics, music tech, philosophy and sociology. It has to be said that the 'newer' subjects do not attract vast numbers. School also offers applied A

level in business – Bs for most. Most popular – and successful – A level subjects are maths and Eng lit – both astonishingly good. GCSEs: again not a huge range of options – French and Spanish now the only modern langs though Latin thrives and Greek is up-and-coming. Most popular subjects are engineering – a double qualification – French and ICT. Everyone takes RS. In 2014, 57 per cent A*/A grades overall – and remember this is a comprehensive school.

This degree of success is not achieved by having independent school sized classes. In the lower school class sizes are 28-30 though music, DT, art and IT groups have 20 pupils. At KS4, class sizes vary but core subjects are taught in groups of 25-30. Most sixth form classes are under 20. Girls and boys seem to achieve similarly though there are some mutterings about AS candidates being 'encouraged' to drop subjects rather than continuing to A2 if it is felt they are unlikely to do well. Accolades abound – the Vaughan is in the top 20 of just about every league table – often near the top. It is regularly named 'top Catholic comp in the country' by those who have such plaudits to give away. Parents and pupils, for the most part, add to the encomia. No-one could eulogise the school's shiny new facilities – apart from all the IT stuff – or accommodation. The level of achievement here is down to the quality of the teaching and the staff and pupils' pride in the place. We heard of 'lovely teachers', the good monitoring of progress and much high praise, especially, of the music dept. Bright pupils speak warmly of their 'inspiring' teachers – 'they are amazing – best in the business' – and they mean it.

All applicants are tested – to ensure that school takes across the ability range and to better enable banding once they arrive. School takes 'more than our fair share of statemented children' and it is a beacon of hope for those parents of children with significant difficulties, seeming, as it does, to offer real education in a compassionate community. Majority with SEN, though, are mild dyslexics and dyspraxics. Who goes where is decided, of course, by the LA but school is concerned about the sheer additional physical space taken by extra LSAs who accompany some of the children with more severe SEN. And this is understandable. Many rooms are small and rather poky and corridors are not spacious. Busy SENCo and others give in-class support but parents give mixed reports. One parent felt that her dyspraxic son's problems were picked up very late and that the support he was subsequently offered was barely adequate. Similar reports from others. School, however, tells us that such comments are 'vastly outweighed by parents delighted with our SEN arrangements'. School unashamed of its high octane essence. 'Here we have traditional, hothouse academic teaching. It can be a bit of a shock for those who come in from outside.' G and T pupils offered Greek – where else in the state system is this a growth area?

Games, options, the arts: Very little space on school premises. This is hardly uncommon in London, but it cannot help the potential for the school's sporting excellence to parallel its academic prowess that, for the most part, games depend on a coach trip 30 minutes away to Twickenham – a major part of any school day, however inspiring the location when they get there. Games, nonetheless, played with immense energy and enthusiasm and, especially on the rugby pitch, are done well. Cross-country also popular and successful – especially for the girls; rock climbing and indoor rowing equally so – four rowers offered schols to train for 2012. Football and basketball also played with vigour and rigour. Complaints of too little sport in the recent past now being remedied.

Over 30 per cent of pupils receive individual music tuition and music is a glory of the school – now enhanced by superb new space and facilities

on the top floor – big rehearsal/recital rooms, lots of practice rooms and music tech facilities which must induce composing even in the tone deaf. All under a busy and smiley head of dept. Lots of ensembles include the popular Big Band. Schola Cantorum – the celebrated choir – tours and gives concerts all over the place. In London, this includes Westminster Cathedral, Westminster Abbey, St John's Smith Square, The Royal Opera House – they recently provided the boys in Turandot – The Barbican and the Queen Elizabeth Hall. Outside the UK, this includes Italy – all the grandest places in Rome – plus Spain, Greece, Holland, Germany, the USA and France. In 2007, they sang High Mass at Notre Dame. The Schola now has its own

---

Schola Cantorum – the celebrated choir – tours and gives concerts all over the place. In London this includes Westminster Cathedral, Westminster Abbey, St John's Smith Square, The Royal Opera House

---

Songschool – just like in a regular cathedral choir school – in which the choir rehearses – a real boon. Drama, never a strength here and not an academic subject is, however, enthusiastically pursued and results in popular productions of, mostly, musicals. School's original main building began life as a theatre and we wondered why so little use is made of it in this way – the stage and gallery are intact, if a little dog-eared. Good art – we liked what we saw of the ceramics, sculpture, mobiles, printing et al – lively creative stuff – and equally good DT – wood, metal and plastic work. Lots of imaginative and rewarding extra-curricular trips and visits – especially for the musicians – parents glow.

Background and atmosphere: The Vaughan is located in posh Holland Park – wide, quiet streets lined by well-appointed Victorian villas and mansion blocks. Shepherd's Bush, on the other side of the monster roundabout round the corner, is a world away, whereas Kensington High Street – about 15 minutes walk the other way – seems a natural neighbour. Founded in 1914, the school is a memorial to the third Archbishop of Westminster, Herbert, Cardinal Vaughan. It began life as an independent school with 29 pupils but became a grammar school in 1944 and a comprehensive in 1977. Girls were first admitted to the sixth form in 1980 and their presence – 'an adornment to the school', according to previous head – is established.

No chance of going co-ed throughout – simply no room. The original building – Addison Hall – was a musical theatre, but its exterior – possibly what attracted its purchasers – is more reminiscent of a Rinascimento palazzo in pink stone. It now boasts an entrance with highly-wrought grillwork in which the school's motto, Amare et Servire, and crest are displayed. 'The Old Building' as it is known, houses years 11-13. The 'New Building' was built in the 1960s and much added to since then. It has an attractive exterior with a pretty little garden and an impressive reception area which abuts the main hall – full of pupils on supervised private study when we visited – no 'free' periods here. DT and IT are housed in the Pellegrini Building, named after a former head. Some roomy places inside but the overall impression is of a rather cramped school with little space – especially outside – and many rather bleak areas. Most rooms have air-conditioning but we almost passed out in the heat of some of them. Few rooms or corridors have displays or much colour and the ambiance is not so much monastic as a little neglected.

Situated in these leafy, pricey avenues, you'd expect an upmarket local school population. But it isn't so. School takes from all over and the only common denominator is a commitment to the Roman Catholic faith. Previous head was wearily, but pugnaciously, defensive of the charge of being

The original building – Addison Hall – was a musical theatre, but its exterior – possibly what attracted its purchasers – is more reminiscent of a Rinascimento palazzo in pink stone

socially or academically elitist. He wrote, 'people ask why our pupils' performance goes so far beyond national averages. After all, our top results at A level and at GCSE, over the last five years, have improved six times more than national results. Is it because, as some would like to believe, we "cherry pick" pupils from privileged backgrounds? I don't think so. More than 18 per cent – almost a fifth – of those boys who achieved such staggering results at GCSE last year were on free school meals. The national average of pupils on free school meals is 14 per cent. So much for the slander that the Vaughan is socially selective.' Maybe the slander persists because the staff wear academic gowns – must be anathema to Dave Spart, head of St Jargon's, and those who pump out new brainless 'initiatives' every morning.

The life of the school is imbued with its Roman Catholic inspiration. Everywhere are photographs of pontiffs, cathedrals and the school's own choir singing in various glorious cathedrals. Year groups go on retreats at Tyburn Convent and at Farm Street and the school day and week are punctuated by regular Mass, confession, Benedictus, angelus and so on – all lessons begin and end with the Sign of the Cross and some teachers have prayers in each of their lessons – to a degree rare even in RC schools. But there is also a spirit of enquiry. Vaughan pupils address seriously 'the Dawkins Delusion', 'the problem of Free Will' and 'the Just War theory'. Philosophy pupils attend Heythrop College for talks on philosophy of religion, epistemology and ethics and theology pupils explore the history of Israel. The ethos is embraced and warmly defended by pupils when appropriate. They are aware of the privilege of being here and of the secular – and other – pressures that might have it otherwise. While most parents express great satisfaction with the school in general, we heard a few murmurs from those who are less than ecstatic. 'It's fine as long as all goes well'.. 'they're not brilliant at dealing with problems'.. 'they're not great at getting back to you' – (school says, 'we pride ourselves on excellent communications with parents and prompt responses to their queries') – and 'it's best for the really bright'. School warmly disputes this too. And most are truly grateful for what they receive.

Pastoral care and discipline: Discipline is tight but, by now, so well-established that it works and few transgress. Sixth formers have more latitude though their common-room is open only at break-times. Occasional bullying is 'firmly and speedily dealt with'. Zero tolerance of drink or drugs is seldom tested. The occasional idiot caught smoking in the streets – sixth form pupils are allowed out of school in breaks – is punished. We saw lots of Vaughan pupils out and about and they definitely do not frighten the horses. 'Old-fashioned good manners' expected and, in general, displayed. The atmosphere is orderly and we saw only quiet classes. Catholic ethos underpins everything and is palpable. Sex ed taught 'by the RS dept for the moral side and the science dept for the biological details'. Four houses – Campion, Fisher, Mayne and More. Real sense of camaraderie between pupils.

Pupils and parents: Pupils come from a wide area covering most of London, some from as far away as Hertfordshire and Surrey. Around half are from ethnic minority groups. Some 30 per cent speak English as an additional language. Here the offspring of a few of well-heeled 'old' RC families from Kensington learn alongside those of their Filipino, Portuguese or Spanish live-in domestic staff and the children of Irish immigrants from Wembley, in a context hard to find elsewhere. Parents very appreciative of parents' evenings when teachers come to find them rather than the usual ghastly queuing for a two minute slot with a glazed-eyed teacher. Notable former pupils include actors Richard Greene – Robin Hood in earlier days – and Roger Delgado, footballers Bernard Joy of Arsenal and Fulham and the last amateur to represent the England national football team, Paul Parker and Eddie Newton, novelist Helen Oyeyemi and comedian Dominic Holland. Also WWII flying aces Donald Garland VC and Paddy Finucane DSO and recent Olympic rowing gold medallists Martin Pross and Gary Herbert. Many seem, however, to have worthy careers in the City.

Entrance: Pupils come from over 50 schools. Around 725 apply for the 120 places at 11+. At sixth form, around four apply for every place. Most of the sixth form entrants will be girls – lots from Sacred Heart – and the entrance requirements at that stage are academic, rather than devotional – As and Bs in the subjects they will study in the sixth. School has long been (in)famous for the rigour of its admissions' criteria and stories abound of devoted little church-goers being rejected on account of imperfect catechism or knowledge of parables. 'Nonsense!' bellows school. Early baptism, weekly attendance at mass, Holy Communion – all are taken for granted in applicants; no mention now of the 'family involvement' that was so contentious. Applicants split into three ability bands, 12 music places.

Exit: A regular mighty handful to Oxbridge (10 in 2014), all doing solid subjects at real colleges. Most of the rest to heavyweight universities to do heavyweight subjects – law at King's, maths at Imperial etc and a sensible fistful to eg sports psychology at Bournemouth. A notable number to architecture and engineering. Some 10 per cent leave after GCSEs – most to join other schools, a few to employment, another few to other RC colleges.

Money matters: Voluntary aided. School asks for a voluntary contribution of £300 pa for the Governors' Fund and the vast majority stumps up – some more, some less but no-one comes after you if you don't. A few instrumental bursaries for sixth form entrants who must have reached at least grade 6 on an orchestral instrument.

Remarks: A unique opportunity, not to be missed if you can meet the requirements and stay the course. The kind of school parents everywhere cry out for and few, very few, ever find.

Chepstow House School

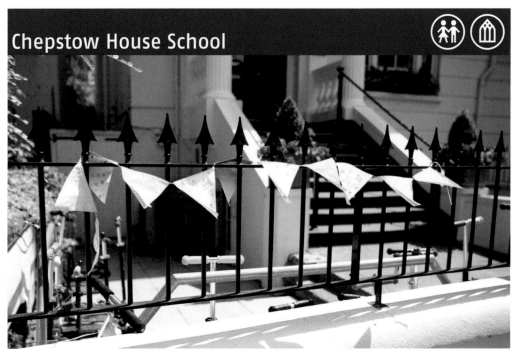

108a Lancaster Road, London W11 1QS

Independent • Pupils: 140 • Ages: 2–13 • Fees (per term): £5,435

Tel: 020 7243 0243
Email: info@chepstowhouseschool.co.uk
Website: www.chepstowhouseschool.co.uk

24

Headteacher: Since 2010, Mrs Angela Barr BA Ed (40s). Has been head since school started. Previously head of the lower school at Pembridge Hall, another Alpha Plus school. Studied geography and education at Christchurch College, Kent University and then taught in a state school in Essex before taking off and travelling around Africa for a year, where she met her husband, Simon. 'I loved school and always wanted to be a teacher,' she says with passion.

Blonde, youthful, warm and attractive, head is a spirited, independent character who lives for the moment and is all about the 'doing now.' Asked where she sees herself in five years time she looks dismayed and then, grinning, says: 'on a beach with a gin and tonic.' She is very hands on and personally supports youngest pupils with their reading. 'I am a big believer in getting children reading,' she says. Also works hard to make sure her staff are teaching with all the different learning styles in mind – 'essential in a co-educational school.' Plenty of internal training – for assistants as well as for teachers. She says her biggest challenge is maintaining a sense of community among her 17 staff. When we visited a strong team spirit was evident. Head is very much a 'primus inter pares,' in the old style of monarchy.

Entrance: Non-selective, so it's a case of registration at or as soon as possible after birth (current cost £150 – non refundable if you don't get a place). School allots five definite places a month, and tries to stagger them among children born at the beginning, middle and end of the month, so no advantage in booking your Caesarean for the first of September. Attempts are made to keep an even number of boys and girls and those who drop out are replaced like with like, as far as possible from the waiting list. That way they don't get a surfeit of, say, boys born in August. Priority given to siblings. Has just opened a nursery class, additional reception class and a year 3 class and moved to new premises is expanding gradually to year 6 and possibly year 8.

Exit: Pupils can now stay on to year 6 and perhaps beyond. Up to now, large number of boys, as you would expect, to Wetherby, and girls to Pembridge Hall (via a test, but most have got a place). Bute House a popular choice for girls but not many jump through that hoop. A small number get to Colet Court and Westminster. Latymer Prep a popular choice as more and more parents opt for co-ed. The odd one to Thomas's, St Philip's or outside London.

Remarks: Born into the now well-established stable of Alpha Plus Group schools, the young colt that is Chepstow House barely wobbled on its hind legs before it was up and running. No doubt thanks in part to the huge demand there is for good schools in this leafy, sophisticated area of Notting Hill.

Asked where she sees herself in five years time she looks dismayed and then, grinning, says: 'on a beach with a gin and tonic.'

However, the school has risen to meet that demand with style as well as results. Children look enchanting in their quaint red berets and jackets, girls in tartan pinafores, boys in red tank tops and grey shorts (some parents worry about their sons getting cold knees in the winter).

Classes named after birds – the further up the school, the bigger and more fierce the bird. Two classes of 20 in reception and year 1. Pupils start in Robins and Sparrows and then move into Woodpeckers and Kingfishers. For year 2, with exams looming in January, they divide into three groups of 12, with classes named after three types of owl – Barn, Snowy and Tawny.

With a teacher and teaching assistant in each class the children get lots of support and attention. French and music start from reception. Three sets for maths in year 2 and lots of differentiation in the lower years. Each child has the use of an iPad – technology skills are learned on the job rather than in a separate lesson devoted to IT. We saw 5-year-olds using their iPads in a geography lesson, as well as other imaginative methods of teaching, including reception children learning how to tell the time in the playground through movement and action. Good-sized playground is frequently used for learning, both academic and physical.

Any learning difficulties are identified quickly, says head. High standards are set for reading and writing and development and progress are tracked in-house with a reading test as well as SEN assessment. Guided reading from reception helps with comprehension. Head told us: 'If a child has not taken off in reception we know that they will need support in year 1 and someone will work with that child every day – either me, or one of my assistant heads.'

The sense of purpose is palpable. When we visited children were working on 'big write,' a weekly activity for years 1 and 2 where pupils learn to develop their vocabulary and style of writing.

Music is vibrant. The only male teacher here is the music teacher and he introduces pupils to a number of different genres – Portuguese singer/songwriter Caetano Veloso when we visited. A number of pupils have violin, guitar and piano lessons taught by peripatetic teachers. Colourful and expressive art adorns the walls. Evidence of physical activity everywhere; much-loved Little Foxes franchise gets them learning ball skills. Fencing and martial arts clubs in the morning. Swimming up the road at Porchester Baths, otherwise all sport happens on site. The children are get fresh air and exercise come rain or shine. Delicious food cooked on site and there is a remarkably civilised atmosphere as the children enjoy their lunch.

Ofsted (who visited just two terms after the school launched) concluded it was good across the board. All credit to the way the head and her team hit the ground running We suspect the esteemed government inspectors will be even more impressed when they return.

Parents from all over the globe – plenty of Americans, Australians and Canadians, a fair few from Scandinavia, Eastern Europe and Russia, as well as French and Italians. Attracts the less traditional English who prefer co-ed at this stage. Parents are in media, finance, law as well as in the arts. Head makes good use of the parents' experience. One parent arranged for someone from Sky News to give a talk in assembly while another

hosted expeditions to private art galleries hosted by another parent. Plenty of trips, including the favourite Bushcraft as well as to churches and Science Museum.

Lots of smiling faces, both parents and children, when they arrive first thing. Head welcomes everyone and is proud of school's open door policy. 'We are not hiding anything,' she says. Nor does she have to. These children are very lucky indeed to have such a focused and privileged start to their education.

Parents are generally very supportive and enthusiastic. 'It's a tight ship – with high energy,' we were told. All good, but there was some regret from a few quarters that the pressure of the 7+ perhaps took the joy out of learning for the child who finds it hard to sit still and concentrate on reading and writing. All this has now changed, with the whole school move to considerably larger premises in Lancaster Road (bang opposite rivals Notting Hill Prep). This not only makes for a larger school at the bottom, with a new nursery class, but will also enable expansion to the age of 13. There is no longer the pressure to enter and pass an exam at the age of 6 and there should be scope for much more drama and a structured sport department, two things the school has lacked so far.

Definitely one to watch if you live in or near this very oversubscribed area of London.

Christ Church C of E Primary School

1 Robinson Street, London SW3 4AA

State · Pupils: 210 · Ages: 4–11 · C of E

Tel: 020 7352 5708
Email: info@chchchelsea.rbkc.sch.uk
Website: www.chchchelsea.rbkc.sch.uk

25

Head: Since September 2009, Mrs Avis Hawkins, who was previously joint acting head.

Entrance: Application by late January for the following September for reception class. All other ages on an ad hoc basis. Priority given to (i) children with siblings in the school; (ii) children of families who are regular worshippers in St Luke's or Christ Church, Chelsea; (iii) children living in the parish; (iv) children of families who are regular worshippers in a neighbouring parish church etc. Complete the school's supplementary admissions form as well as applying through the LA.

Exit: Chelsea Academy, Burntwood, Lady Margaret School, The Grey Coat Hospital, Holland Park etc. Around a quarter to private London day schools – Alleyn's, Emanuel, Dulwich, More House, Godolphin & Latymer, Whitgift etc – many on scholarships.

Remarks: Excellent primary school in super location tucked away in a quiet corner of Chelsea, with – by London standards – lots of space, including good-sized playground and extra area of garden/pond etc. Judged outstanding by Ofsted in every category. Founded 1840, affiliated to local churches. Cherry-coloured uniform. Newly-refurbished prize-winning buildings. Approximately 50 per cent of pupils from Chelsea, the rest from Wandsworth, Westminster and beyond – very mixed intake.

Good core and cross-curricular and SEN provision; all children have experience with computers. Maths and English very good. French and Spanish on offer after school; swimming for year 2 and above. PE in much-used all-purpose school hall as well as local green space. Keen games and music. Even here parents sending children on to private schools usually opt for a year or two of coaching. Continuing good and happy reports from parents, though some would like to see an 11+ class. Oversubscribed for all year groups.

Collingham Independent GCSE and Sixth Form College

23 Collingham Gardens, London SW5 0HL

Independent · Pupils: 220 · Ages: 14–20 · Fees (per term): £5,865 – £6,250

Tel: 020 7244 7414
Fax: 020 7370 7312
Email: london@collingham.co.uk
Website: www.collingham.co.uk

26

Principal: Since 2012, Dr Sally Powell BA MA PGCE (early 40s), a London and Oxford English specialist, lively, welcoming, delightful. Has notched up a not inconsiderable 10 years here (in fact many staff are of long standing and committed to the place).

Mr James Allder BA, a geographer (40ish), is deputy principal and director of studies; an enthusiastic skier and snowboarder.

Ms Emma Clay MSc oversees the GCSE department in Queen's Gate.

Academic matters: You go to Collingham for two things – the academics and the sense of being independent while, in reality, being nurtured and carefully monitored. The place, though, stands or falls on its teaching – 'We integrate modern methods with traditional teaching – the emphasis is always on the teaching; the rest is back-up.' So don't come here if you want wall-to-wall technology – not that it isn't where it's needed: interactive whiteboards in, eg, geography rooms and students port their laptops hither and yon. Facilities for both digital and trad photography indicate an imaginative approach and a small IT room right at the top of the school for the actual teaching of it. Twenty-nine GCSE subjects and an extraordinary 36 A level subjects offered. In 2014, 30 per cent A*/A and 62 per cent A*-B grades at A level; 74 per cent of pupils got 5+ A* – C grades at I/GCSE including English and maths, and 32 per cent of grades were A*/A.

All A level subjects taught in designated subject rooms, which are functional, not over-crowded with displays or other distractions and well-maintained. At GCSE, the average class size is five and never more than nine; at A level much the same, though, depending on what subjects you choose, you can be taught one-to-one – great for the students, and the teachers like it, too, of course. GCSE students usually in college 9.15am – 6.00pm; AS students get 20 hours of teaching weekly, A level students get 18. 'GCSEs are brilliantly taught,' one recent alumnus told us. 'I was rescued.' A few more popular classes – no room is huge – are rather cramped, but no-one minds much.

Learning support tutor sees those with SEN difficulties (charged extra) and subject teachers also do one-to-one as needed. Probably not for those with more than mild dyslexia or similar. Up to eight hours' weekly EAL support.

Games, options, the arts: Art produces an impressive range of work in many media, given the fact that college has only one small studio, with intense and dedicated ('fantastic' and 'amazing', students told us) practising artist, whose domain it is. 'I'm interested in teaching them to be artists – to express themselves in art,' he imparted, and students love it here. Corridors and stairwell round about display varied work in many disciplines – we liked especially the horse mobile made from cleverly coloured twisted paper. Twelve GCSE and 20 A level art students at the time of our visit – testament to the small is beautiful as successful ethos.

Sport is limited. GCSE students have a supervised two hours sports slot on Friday, where activities range for football and tennis to swimming. A level students can take part in weekly football training and are in a small inter-college league playing at the Westway sports centre. Clubs run if someone wants to run one, so debates happen one year and not the next. Drama is enthusiastic and curricular – classes take place in the Study Room, a small studio theatre is borrowed for exams and exam prep. Theatre studies trips to London shows. Citizenship course involves a good range of mind-broadening trips. Skiing and walking trips plus an annual concert. But you won't come here if the extracurricular life is what feeds your roots – this is a plus for most here: 'There's nothing to distract you from work'.

Background and atmosphere: Modest and understated six-storey house in Collingham Gardens – an equidistant five minutes' walk from Gloucester Road and Earl's Court tube stations in an unshowy bit of west Kensington; has been a school of a sort for much of its 130 years, having previously accommodated Gibbs' Prep School until the mid-1970s. So it is quite remarkable that the building retains many attractive features and is maintained in such a way as to preserve that sense of its being a house, not an institution – friezes, cornices, attractive mirrors and chandeliers about the place and a minimum of ghastly fluorescent tubes, sludge-coloured paintwork and other municipally-inspired excrescences. In the black and white tiled hallway are little tables with students playing chess – no, they weren't put there to impress us: it is student-inspired and a

A fabulous opportunity to regroup and get on track if things have gone awry – and a good place for friendships too

student-pursued activity. The splendid first floor drawing room – now the Study Room – is library/exam/private study area, where, when not in use for exams, students go between taught periods to do homework etc. The individual subject rooms have small specialised book collections.

No outside space to speak of – a small patio at the back – but students are encouraged to use Kensington Gardens or Holland Park in the summer, not more than 15 minutes' walk away. Earl's Court is not devoid of bars and cafes and students know where they are. Tiny cafeteria in the basement, rather like the art room, produces range and quality of food in inverse proportion to its size: aroma of frying mushrooms nearly did for us – until we opened the door to the chemistry lab further down the basement corridor (very labby labs here).

The GCSE building in Queen's Gate Place – all white Regency elegance – accommodates most of the needs of the smallish contingent of students at this level. Supervision and monitoring very important here for students as young as these; the school secretary has an important pastoral role – this is a significant commitment to the other site and its, on occasions, perhaps more vulnerable denizens. Several full-time academic staff – the place

succeeds largely on account of the inevitably close and trusting staff:pupil relationship which develops: 'We combine a homely, personal feeling with cutting edge teaching'. Interestingly, the families of the two founders still own the college – this contrasts, perhaps significantly in terms of ethos, with the much larger concerns which own most other tutorial colleges in central London.

Most students live locally, though some from further off stay with family – 'We love grandmothers'; a few overseas students board with host families. 'If we get it right, we can restore the spark they may have lost at their big schools' – many come having failed to thrive at their public schools, through sickness, bullying, perhaps some gentle eccentricity or simply just not being happy. 'Some who may have loved prep school boarding can just outgrow it..We hope to be a village school in the middle of Kensington.' It doesn't feel quite like that – too much general sophistication in the air – but in terms of the smallness and closeness of the community, it is spot on. Seen by many as providing a dry run for university without the sense of being cast adrift that some experience there.

Pastoral care and discipline: Punctuality is important – you are signed in for each class, not at the start of the day, and parents are called within 15 minutes in the case of no-shows. But you don't need to come in early if you don't have a class – think what that means to a 16 year old! A few smoking Collinghamers lurk on the pavement and college is pragmatic – 'We don't allow it on site and we don't like it, but we'd rather they do it where we can see them. Everywhere they are, we are'. Clear

Tiny café in the basement produces range and quality of food in inverse proportion to its size : aroma of frying mushrooms nearly did for us

sanctions for those who don't work and occasional expulsions if they just won't. Not an option for druggies or bullies from elsewhere, 'We're too small to be a second chance saloon'. But, 'We are very happy to take anyone who's been ill or in a muddle, sensitive souls who need individual attention, perhaps if they've had an eating disorder – we will look after them'. Expulsion for drinking or drugging or bullying here virtually unheard of.

Parents have open access to their child's tutor – easy communication. 'They rescued my son,' one mother told us. 'I can't speak highly enough of their care.' 'The teachers are incredibly friendly,' an A level student told us. 'I was welcomed with open arms.'

Pupils and parents: You have to be able to raise the cash – and some pull out all the stops to do so – but it's cheaper than boarding. So everyone from global bankers to school secretaries, and the students mix, seemingly seamlessly. No scope for ostracising oddballs here – everyone accepts and is accepting. Considerable range of ability too. Very few join from the state sector. Roughly 55:45 boy:girl split. Notable leavers include Minnie Driver and, more, recently Georgia May Jagger.

Entrance: Interviews, references from current/previous school and, if necessary, an exam – 'They've got to want to work with us'. Can take people at any time, so great for relocaters and those who've just gotta get out – flexible.

Exit: Around half move on elsewhere after GCSEs. Practically all to university. In 2014, one to Oxbridge; around a third to London universities.

Money matters: Given the small classes and the individual care and attention, it's not as much as you might think. Additional one-to-one tuition is charged extra by the hour, exams and materials for practical subjects likewise extra, so do check what you sign up for. Some bursaries in case of need.

Remarks: 'I am so happy here,' one bright A level spark told us. 'I'm with a lot of clever people; we're brilliantly taught. Everyone is perfectly normal – they just didn't like the regimentation of school life.' A fabulous opportunity to regroup and get on track if things have gone awry – and a good place for friendships too. Some come back years after to see staff. A gem.

Eaton House The Vale

THE VALE SCHOOL

Linked schools: Eaton House Belgravia, 95; Eaton House the Manor Girls' School, Eaton House the Manor Preparatory and Pre–Preparatory School, see *The Good Schools Guide: London South*

2 Elvaston Place, London SW7 5QH

Independent • Pupils: 80 • Ages: 3–11 • Non–denom
• Fees (per term): £4,710

Tel: 020 7584 9515
Fax: 020 7584 8368
Email: admin@eatonhouseschools.com
Website: www.eatonhouseschools.com

27

Headmaster: Since 2008, Mr Robin Greenwood FTCL ARCM, BSc (40s) a scientist and musician. He was educated in South Africa, then London University, where he studied biological sciences. An accomplished pianist, he also studied music at Trinity College, London. Mr Greenwood taught at the Eaton House Schools before becoming headmaster of Wetherby Prep and has now returned to the fold to become headmaster of The Vale. Parents say the school is like one big family and Mr Greenwood is always on hand to discuss their child's progress.

Entrance: At 4+ non-selective entry on a first-come first-served basis. Children attending the nursery enter in the term leading up to the third birthday.

Exit: At 8+ boys to Colet Court, Eaton House The Manor Prep, Fulham Prep, Westminster Under or Westminster Cathedral Choir School; occasional one to boarding school. Girls at 8+ to eg Bassett House, Norland Place, Knightsbridge School; at 11+

eg Francis Holland, Godolphin & Latymer, St Mary's Calne, Downe House, Tudor Hall.

Remarks: The Vale is currently a co-ed nursery and prep school catering for boys from 3 – 8 and girls from 3 – 11. Traditional 3Rs curriculum with a focus on developing every child's abilities, both academic and non-academic. No streaming and class sizes are kept small to ensure lots of individual attention.

The school occupies a large six-storey Georgian house just off Gloucester Road, complete with kitchens and a dining area. Facilities are excellent for a small school, although slightly tight. Well-stocked library, ICT room, multi-purpose hall and their own science lab. No outdoor space – pupils go for short walk during morning break and midday playtimes are held in Kensington Gardens. Two afternoons a week children go to Battersea Park with the games master for PE lessons. Pupils are introduced to around 10 different sports, including tennis, cricket and athletics, with matches, competitions and summer sports days being popular events. Exciting whole class drama and music; with around a third of the children learning an instrument, everyone performs in the regular plays and musicals.

For those with SEN, a part-time adviser organises additional support as needed by pupils. The school welcomes visiting specialists including speech and occupational therapists to support pupils with individual needs. Home/school communication is considered paramount – reading and message books are exchanged every day and

five simple rules for everyone to follow to encourage thoughtfulness and sensible behaviour.

The children also benefit from being taken out to visit a variety of London sites and museums. After-school clubs include French, cookery, chess, healthy kids and lifestyles. Mr Greenwood has an open door policy for parents which helps create the nurturing and friendly atmosphere and, most importantly, yummy lunches, say the young ones.

Ecole Francaise Jacques Prevert

59 Brook Green, London W6 7BE

Independent · Pupils: 260 · Ages: 3–11 · Non–denom
· Fees (per term): £1,500 – £1,730

Tel: 020 7602 6871
Fax: 020 7602 3162
Email: info@ecoleprevert.org.uk
Website: www.ecoleprevert.org.uk

Director: Since 2011, Patrice Possenti BA History (University of Lyon), Diplome Professeur des Ecoles (French national certification), early 40s, previously director of a primary school near Lyon for six years, and simultaneously at University of Lyon training new teachers and specialising in IT training for teachers. Special interests are languages and how children develop as multilinguals. He is also keen on the use of IT to improve learning. At Jacques Prevert he is always considering means of expanding the premises, but this is an on-going challenge in urban London.

The school is under the auspices of the AEFE (French Agency for the French Education Abroad, run by the French Ministry of Foreign Affairs), which oversees a network of French curriculum

Youngsters of all ages call out to greet him and clamour for his attention to share news or show him their work

schools around the world, and appoints the directors of all its schools. The northern European ones meet regularly, and they are are generally rotated every five years.

Parents speak highly of Mr Possenti and the respect and affection with which he is held is tangible when walking through the school: youngsters of all ages call out to greet him and clamour for his attention to share news or show him their work.

Acknowledging them by name, he makes each one feel important, even whilst escorting us through the school. He comes across as completely dedicated to his work, though he admits to a passion for figure-skating, which he now teaches as a school activity.

Entrance: Most children start in September, although as the community is an international one there is occasional movement during the school year. The cut-off date for birthdays is December, so those accustomed to September birthday deadlines may be surprised to find there are some younger peers in the class.

The admission criteria are aligned with those of all AEFE schools. Priority is given to siblings, pupils coming from other AEFE schools abroad or in the UK (typically La Petite Ecole Française in Notting Hill and L'Ecole du Hérisson (Hammersmith); academic ability isn't a factor. Siblings get preference. The school is normally over-subscribed with one or two forms in a year. Twenty-eight pupils admitted at age 4 and 16 new pupils at age 6. Parents recommend getting on the waiting list at the earliest possible opportunity and hanging on even if you don't get an offer for the first year, as vacancies can arise in later years. They also advise that if you aren't on the waiting list, and are not transferring in from a French school, 'you can forget it'.

Exit: Most pupils go to the London French Lycée Charles de Gaulle, where the director is able to track his pupils' progress, as the Lycée regularly sends progress reports back to Jacques Prevert. However from 2015, in addition to the French Lycée Charles de Gaulle in South Kensington and the College Français Bilingue de Londres in Kentish Town, parents will also have the option of applying to the new Lycée opening in Wembley. Some parents (Anglophones) opt to move their children into the English system at the end of the primary years. The school does not advise parents on specific schools, but the parents' association organises information sessions about the English system and the French Lycée organises a meeting in March about the French secondary system.

Remarks: French curriculum, with the addition of English classes taught by native speakers. Main language of instruction is French, in keeping with school's mission to promote bilingual education, which begins in kindergarten. As the children get older (8 upwards), some the subjects such as history, geography and eventually science are partially taught by English teachers working in parallel with the French colleagues.

Parents are pleased with the early childhood programme that integrates arts, crafts, singing and pre-reading skills such as learning letters. They move to the primary section at age 6, and are usually reading by the end of the first term. The school is exempt from following the EYFS.

Those in the primary section follow the prescribed French curriculum, which includes seven

The Maternelle Grande children were making elaborate models of castles in anticipation of a visit to the Tower of London

'pillars': mastery of the French language, speaking a modern foreign language (English), acquiring basic knowledge in mathematics and science, developing a humanist culture, mastering common ICT, acquiring social and civic skills, and developing autonomy and initiative.

The first two-year cycle (roughly equivalent to British KS1) includes PE and sport, visual art, music and a modern foreign language (in this case, English, taught by native speakers). This is followed by a three-year 'consolidation cycle' (ages 8-11) roughly equivalent to English KS2. This is where the French imperative to teach grammar shines and the rigorous French history syllabus covers pre-history to the Middle Ages, the Enlightenment to the French Revolution, the 20th Century and the European Union. Geography is similarly Franco-centric.

Teachers are encouraged to integrate IT into the curriculum from 4-year-olds upwards. A cheerful library holds an impressive French collection; the English classroom holds the English language materials. There are no national exams for French primary school students; progress is internally assessed and there are detailed termly online reports.

Because pupils are not necessarily fluent English speakers, juggling the English language levels is an continuous challenge; English classes are streamed by ability groups from 7 years, and the school provides some support to help new arrivals in the English-medium classes. The curriculum includes English grammar and comprehension.

Though the school is crowded, it is orderly. Some special classes give teachers the opportunity to work with smaller groups. On our visit we saw lots of variety in teaching approaches and learning activity, including PE, music and artists at work, all the students looking engaged and happy. The Maternelle Grande children were making elaborate models of castles in anticipation of a visit to the Tower of London.

Typical of many French schools, there is no specialist SEN support, but teachers use their free lessons to provide one-to-one teaching to pupils who are lagging behind. More flexible than most UK schools, it is not unheard of for a particularly strong or bright child to move up a year, or a struggling pupil to stay down.

PE includes ice skating, rock climbing, acrosport and badminton. Music is taught by a specialist, art mostly by class teachers. Parents point out that while extracurricular activities are not a big feature of traditional French schools, here a super-involved parent body organises clubs for eg tennis, judo, karate, chess, arts and crafts and singing at nominal extra cost. Morning club from 8am.

Founded in 1974 as a smaller, more family-friendly French primary school alternative to the larger Lycée Charles de Gaulle in South Kensington, the school is in a large converted house. There is a small outdoor playground, and children sometimes have free time on spacious Brook Green.

Discipline is quite strict. Pupils have the same teacher for most subjects so they know each other well. Lunches (included in the school fees) are well balanced and freshly prepared. On Wednesdays, which are half days, those staying on for afternoon activities bring a packed lunch.

The community is an international one with many dual-national bilingual families: more than half are French or French/British, about 15 per cent are British and the remainder come from a variety of countries, with speakers of Spanish, German, Arabic, Chinese all represented. It's not unusual for students to speak three or four languages. However, parents tell us that the lingua franca is English.

Most families are local, but there is a school bus service organised by parents. Active parents' association, kept up to date by a snazzy online newsletter with video links. In this small community where everyone knows everyone else, parents feel obliged to play their part in committees, fund raising or generally helping out.

Subsidies from the French Government keep the fees down. French nationals are eligible to apply for scholarships.

For London families who want their children to have the advantage of developing or keeping up French language fluency in a small and friendly school environment, parents advise: 'Get on the waiting list'.

Eridge House School

1 Fulham Park Road, Fulham, London SW6 4LJ

Independent · Pupils: 200 · Ages: 3–11 · Fees (per term): £4,850 – £5,240

Tel: 020 7371 9009
Fax: 020 7371 9229
Email: admissions@eridgehouse.co.uk
Website: www.eridgehouse.co.uk

Headteacher: Since September 2013, Ms Pippa Hogg-Andrews (50s), previously head of lower school at the Royal Ballet School for 10 years. BEd from Cambridge; three teenage children; likes 'beach hut life' and walking her border terrier.

Entrance: Non-selective, ie first come, first served. Number of registrations increasing as word spreads – now you need to put your child's name down at birth if you want to be sure of a place at 3 or 4. Nursery children given priority for entry at 4. Occasional places do crop up further up the school.

Exit: In 2014 to a range including Godolphin and Latymer, King's College School, City of London Boys', The Hall Wimbledon, Ibstock, Lady Margaret's, Emmanuel and The Hall Wimbledon. Round hole policy rather than preparing all children for the swankiest or most academic schools – Ms Hogg-Andrews will make sure they progress to the school that best suits them; she knows the children well enough and has built up networks with a mix of London day schools and boarding schools. She says, 'Our parents are likely to want a school with a similar ethos to ours and won't want to go too far for it, but it will depend in the individual child, of course.' Parents given everything they need to inform their choice.

Remarks: The aim of founder Mrs Waring was to create 'a village school in the middle of Fulham'. Impossible? You'd have thought so, and she waited till she had found the right property to try out the idea. School housed in handsome former lodge to Fulham Palace, a generously-proportioned Victorian house, comfortably on a corner in leafy, residential Fulham. A modern extension makes it feel like the Tardis. Excellent multi-purpose hall where they do drama, dance, music, gym and eat freshly cooked food at lunchtime. No cramming into tiny rooms – space to move, play, feel relaxed. And that's not just inside – the former lodge must have had large and leafy gardens, as school has an extraordinary amount of space around it. An Astroturf pitch (carefully cut round mature trees) and several outdoor adventure playgrounds, thoughtfully designed to develop little arm muscles ('good for handwriting') as well as to allow

their imagination to fly. Matches happen here, but they also walk two streets to Hurlingham Park with tennis, netball and athletics facilities. Few preps in this part of London could compare.

Emphasis is on providing an all-round education. The school cherry picks the best of three education systems – the Montessori (for nursery and transition), the national curriculum and the French programme. Attracts a wide international mix of pupils, particularly French. A small – but significant – number is taught a carefully planned version of the CNED by school's resident French native speaker and highly experienced teacher, which is co-ordinated into the main curriculum.

The former lodge must have had large and leafy gardens, as school has an extraordinary amount of space around it

All children have French twice weekly. Syllabus varied with much specialist teaching, including music, sports and dance. Lowest class has 'lots of structured play' but can run in and out of the garden at any time – plenty of fresh air had by all. Parents are not shooed off the premises at drop off as in many schools. Quite the contrary – if you watch your child's assembly you can stay for coffee, croissants and a chat afterwards. Useful after-school clubs until 4.30pm, from fencing and Mandarin to cooking and board-games.

School's prospectus states it welcomes children with SEN. Head reiterates that they would always see what they can do to accommodate special needs and would never automatically say no. All good stuff, but no evidence of much experience yet. The year 2 teacher doubles up as SENCo and has a few people on her books needing help with handwriting and organisation. Otherwise only one dyslexic pupil. Gifted and talented pupils are catered for in the whole class. Very mixed ability classes, but 'classes are small enough to be able to cater for each individual's needs,' assures school.

Children encouraged to take responsibility for each other as well as themselves. When we visited, a French boy was helping a fellow French speaker who was struggling with his English. House system fosters good relations among children in different years. On the eagerly anticipated 'House day' each term, normal lessons are off; instead everyone works together on activities – whether it be building something out of newspaper in total silence or designing a house flag. The reward: highly-coveted house points. They are big on certificates and rewards here – each week in assembly prizes are awarded for a range of achievements, eg we saw a desperately shy girl win the headteacher's award for being chatty. Everyone gets a chance to shine. One parent explained why she chose Eridge House, despite the school not being on the dinner party gossip list – 'I needed a school where my daughter would be noticed, and she is'. Sports teams are circulated so everyone gets a chance. 'Although they want to win, it's not the only important thing. We also keep a watchful eye on each of the houses to prevent one from becoming too strong in every area.'

Laughter and happiness are key – if that means allowing your daughter to wear her fairy dress over her uniform, so be it: 'The important thing is to get them running through the door in the morning'.

This is not a place where you'll see ordered children filing through the school – 'We like our corridors to be filled with chatter,' says head. The focus is as much, if not more, on how they learn rather than what they learn. Absolutely no Sats, 'But we do inform parents regularly of where their child is according to the national curriculum'. If parents want to see written evidence of how their child is doing, they are shown ongoing assessment and self-assessment forms filled in by the children, with targets set by themselves as well as by their teachers. 'Some of our parents need educating,' admits school. Be prepared to be given a lump of playdough at a parents' evening and come up with bright ideas on what you might learn from it.

Many heads – and parents – claim to be against pressure early on. This is the real thing. 'We are not the soft option – there are some very academic children at the school,' asserts the head. However those who aren't will not be pushed; otherwise they risk ending up somewhere where they can't cope. All pupils come from minutes away. Many can – not all do – walk to school, so the place has a real local feel. It's a bit of a gem. Can it preserve its ethos while continuing to expand? Tough one, but if you live in Fulham and are not paranoid about league tables, it could well be for you.

Falkner House

19 Brechin Place, London SW7 4QB

Independent • Pupils: 150 • Ages: 3–11 • Non-denom • Fees (per term): £2,675 – £5,350

Tel: 020 7373 4501
Fax: 020 7835 0073
Email: office@falknerhouse.co.uk
Website: www.falknerhouse.co.uk

28

Headteacher: Since 1999, Mrs Anita Griggs BA PGCE (early 60s). Educated at Queen's College, Harley Street, then studied history and economics at York University. Spent her early career at the Bank of England, before heading the economics department at St Paul's Girls' School.

Her mother, Flavia Nunes, was Falkner House's founding head and her father ran a successful boys' prep so she has the central London education system embedded in her DNA. Today she unites the best of British tradition with the decisively innovative. 'As soon as someone has a good idea, I would like it to happen,' she says. 'I'm an impatient person.'

Very much a hands-on head, she's at the gates every morning, constantly available to parents (her home number is on the school's website), pupils ('I don't teach, but I know the children from the back of their heads') and teachers. Forthright, purposeful and positive ('never think you can't do something'), she's also bracingly down to earth. 'While I want girls to be happy and successful at 11, I also want them to be happy and successful at 31 and 41.'

Her mother, Flavia Nunes, was Falkner House's founding head and her father ran a successful boys' prep so she has the central London education system embedded in her DNA

She has no immediate intention of passing the baton to one of her four adult daughters (two of whom work in the school). 'There are other things I could do with my life. I do it because I love it.' Parents definitely appreciate this. 'She's immensely charming,' said one, 'and really fights for the girls.' 'She's given my children the most wonderful education,' said another.

Married to a city lawyer, she lives across the road from the school and in her off-duty hours is an 'obsessive reader' and enthusiastic traveller.

Entrance: Register as soon as possible after birth. Some enter at nursery (including boys), but a nursery spot does not guarantee passage to the main school. In the January before entry, about 130 girls compete for 22 reception places in an assessment that looks for 'focus, working memory and enthusiasm,' as well as more elusive qualities such as 'grit' and good manners.

'A child cannot be prepared and we don't assess whether or not they can read,' says the head. Many will inevitably be disappointed, but parents are let down as gently as possible. 'No selection system is perfect. We don't get false positives, but we sometimes get false negatives.' Occasional places (an average of one a year) are again filled by assessment. 'I'd rather leave a space than have the wrong fit,' adds the head.

Exit: The 'next step' is considered thoughtfully, with parents invited in for a planning meeting in year 5. 'We take endless care to ensure girls not only get into the best schools but the schools that are best for them.' The majority, now as always, to London's leading academic girls' schools (St Paul's, City of London, Godolphin & Latymer etc) but co-ed Latymer Upper is also attracting increasing attention. Reasonable numbers to board, with Wycombe Abbey and St Mary's Ascot featuring strongly. Girls frequently leave garnered with scholarships, academic, music and sporting.

Remarks: Flavia Nunes set up Falkner House in 1954 with the intention of providing girls with the same standard of academic excellence enjoyed by their brothers – by no means a given in those days – and the school continues to provide a broad and challenging education taught by a dedicated, energetic and innovative staff. 'They're the real stars,' says the head.

Reading is central to the offering. All younger girls are expected to read nightly at home and a love of words and books is encouraged by regular attendance at two libraries, well-considered reading lists, a weekly library lesson from year 3 and freedom to bring in Kindles from year 4. Poetry is learned by heart and recited in class and competitions. Girls become articulate and confident, both on the page and in conversation.

Beyond the three Rs, a rainbow of opportunity. French throughout (with a fortnightly French assembly), classics from year 3, Latin from year 5. The arts, too, taken seriously. Music strong (seven music scholarships in 2014) and varied with plenty in the way of performance (wind band, string group, choir, chamber music ensemble). Art room buzzing and history of art taught from reception, with regular outings to museums and galleries. Dance and drama included in the core curriculum and a popular after-school ballet club allows those who wish to take external exams.

Technology here is not just for display on the timetable, but blazing a trail – a hardworking teacher has reinvented the year 5 and 6 curriculum

to be delivered on iPads. In 2014 Apple named Falkner House one of six groundbreaking schools worldwide for its innovative approach.

Homework and exams introduced early (the former in reception, the latter twice yearly from year 3). 'It's important for girls to learn to take both the test and the results in their stride; to learn their best is good enough,' says the head.

This is a selective school and few have serious special educational needs. Mild difficulties, however, are addressed successfully by experienced staff and high fliers given regular extension work.

Despite a handkerchief playground, sport played competitively to a high level. Coaches ferry girls to Battersea, Kensington Gardens, Latchmere Leisure Centre and Chelsea and from year 3 the school fields A, B, and often C squads in netball, athletics, swimming, rounders and cross country. 'It's a culture of "play the game within the spirit of the game",' says the head. 'We do not kill to win.' Win they do, however, producing recent champions at the London Schools Swimming Association and the British Schools Team Fencing Championship. Numerous extracurricular activities include clubs, trips (abroad and to the head's house in West Sussex) and treats (on Founder's Day an English National Ballet soloist came in to teach choreography).

Fresh food cooked daily – and described as 'amazing' by our guides, with staff monitoring manners and a balanced diet. 'We've taken out all mention of healthy eating,' says the head. 'All children here eat healthy food, so why create more anxiety?'

The school is still located in the two spacious, multi-storeyed Victorian houses where it was founded and retains the echo of a post-war family home, with carpeted corridors and the head's office elegantly kitted out with antiques. Tradition, too, maintained with daily 'prayers' (Christian hymns

Parents kept at well-informed arms' length. 'I'd prefer them not to come in and hang up the children's coats – children come to school to learn independence,' says the head

and the Lord's Prayer) held in the delightful, parqueted assembly hall. All faiths welcome. Remembrance Day, carol service and the Queen's Jubilee accorded due dignity. 'The girls should understand the culture. That's not deprivation; it's enrichment.'

Other traditional strands include both a house and prefect system. Head girl, deputy and prefects appointed for half term stints, so most get a go, while other routes to glory include sports person or artist of the week, eco monitor and badge girl (responsible for helping the teacher).

Head's mission is to endow pupils with self confidence, independence of mind, kindness and good manners, and girls clearly enjoy the process. 'It's fun,' said one. Though the inevitable friendship groups form, all seem to get on. 'No one is not friends,' said another. Top year girls are paired with those coming into reception, and this union of

Retains the echo of a post-war family home, with carpeted corridors and the head's office elegantly kitted out with antiques

'grandes' and 'petites' means new arrivals are never left stranded. 'We play with them and introduce our petite to our friends' petites.' Precocity definitely discouraged (no nail varnish, no jewellery and only 'sensible' shoes).

Parents kept at well-informed arms' length. 'I'd prefer them not to come in and hang up the children's coats – children come to school to learn independence,' says the head, who is also firmly anti-PTA. 'I'm very proud of that. I don't want some alpha mummy in charge. I'd prefer her to come in and give me her bright ideas.'

The home-school link, however, is strong, with parental involvement expected with homework and music practice. Parents regularly invited to attend events, from ballet recitals to Father's Day breakfasts. The school website, updated weekly, keeps all in the loop, while the flexible early birds and late birds system allows drop off and pick up from early morning till late afternoon. 'If you're stuck in traffic you can just telephone,' said one parent. 'It's fantastic for working mothers.'

Families mainly within walking distance, then spreading out to Hammersmith, Chiswick, Fulham and Battersea. Predominantly British, highly qualified, working in financial services, but also numerous global citizens. Unsurprisingly, some can be a tad competitive, something the head keeps firmly in check. 'If someone rings up to demand why their daughter's not in the netball team, you just have to say, "I'm sorry you're cross, but let's try and be reasonable. There are other people better at netball".'

Given the location, families tend to be affluent. The website includes requests for housekeepers and year 6 parents are politely asked to plan family holidays 'to avoid jet lag'). No formal bursaries or scholarships, but the school has always helped out existing pupils in financial difficulties.

Fox Primary School

Kensington Place, London W8 7PP

State • Pupils: 330 • Ages: 4–11 • Non-denom

Tel: 020 7727 7637
Fax: 020 7229 4628
Email: info@fox.rbkc.sch.uk
Website: www.fox.rbkc.sch.uk

29

Headteacher: Since 2006, Paul Cotter BA PGCE (40s). Previously deputy head at Avondale Primary in North Kensington, bringing much of what he learnt there with him, including his young, extremely bright and capable deputy, Emma Madden – they make a formidable team. Swiftly injected energy and fresh blood into this ever-popular local school. Savvy – knows how to access funding and use it to the max.

Entrance: Heavily oversubscribed – over 200 applicants for 45 places. Priority (rather than catchment) area is mainly to the south towards Kensington rather than the north to Notting Hill, where greater density of state school provision. Lots of mobility, however, so places do crop up, and further up the school they have admitted children beyond this area. Siblings have priority but no one else. Entrance procedure is administered by the borough and the head can exercise no preference. Children come from over 40 different nurseries, but parents we spoke to mentioned Strawberry Fields, Rolfes, St Peters and Kids Unlimited.

Exit: About half each year to Holland Park, a handful to the new-ish Chelsea Academy. More than a third to independent schools – a wide range including Latymer Upper, Godolphin and Latymer, City of London Boys' and Girls', St Paul's Boys' and Girls', some board at, eg, Christ's Hospital and Cheltenham Ladies' College, some win scholarships to, eg, Charterhouse. 'They can go wherever they want,' said one parent. Mr Cotter meets all secondary heads – 'they generally like Fox children,' he says proudly. Parents notice that he sees this as an integral part of his job – makes no judgement about the choice other than finding what's best for each individual.

Remarks: A buzzing local primary with a liberal, funky feel to it. A sea of colour greets you as you enter the well secured gates – brightly clad children (no uniform) playing noisily (as you would hope) in the imaginatively and tastefully decorated playground. As well as the main area for football and netball, a quieter arbour with wooden tables, canopies and lavender, the gentle rushing of water running around the perimeter. A popular place to trade Match Attacks and Go Gos on a Friday and for parents to discuss their next fundraising project after drop off. A giant chess board and climbing wall in the far corner while, behind the school, in the younger years' playground, allotments (where the children tend radishes and chillis as well as lychees) and a woodland trail. Dedicated play area with sand and water for reception children with beautiful mosaics on the walls.

The school is housed in a large 1930s building and has all the hallmarks of being purpose built, with wide corridors and staircases. Large windows into bright, spacious, airy classrooms. Every inch of space is used to benefit learning – the deputy head's office also has an interactive white board and desks. Music rooms, dedicated learning rooms for smaller groups, an IT room with 30 flat screen computers, a large hall with a huge white screen. IT is used to liven things up at every occasion, particularly the assemblies (which happen at 3pm, when 'everyone has had enough rather than first thing, which is prime learning time,' says head sensibly). We saw the house (named after four different species of fox) spellathon conducted like a prime time quiz show. Everyone had fun and everyone learnt something. This is clearly key to the ethos here.

A strong, dynamic teaching staff, average age less than 30. Larger number of women than men. They bring fun and lots of motivation to the daily curriculum. Parents enthuse about the cohesive staff – by all accounts Mr Cotter has built a team of excellent teachers. Energy saving schemes (they are aiming for green flag system and have an 'eco team' of pupils to help them do it) and clever organisation have resulted in his being able to employ more staff and ensure the school is extremely well equipped. One of his cleverest achievements has to be the class sizes – reduced at every opportunity. Currently only 22 in two classes in reception, year 1, and years 4 to 6, with an ingenious scheme to allow for differentiation according to age and stage in years 2 and 3. Rightly proud of this innovation – 'Standards have shot up as a result,' he observes – Fox now rates as one of the top primary schools in the country.

Everyone achieves here – the bright ones as well as those with special needs. High ratio of staff to children in each class, and the SENCo teaches smaller groups of up to 10 who have learning difficulties (PTA funded laptops for this). About 15 per cent of children are currently on the SEN register, some with statements. One or two reports that it took a bit of prodding before school diagnosed, eg, dyslexia (school denies this, 'We have rigorous monitoring systems,' they say) but by all accounts, once any problems are discovered, school gives tremendous support. English is the second language for about one third of children – they catch up quickly. School accepts child as s/he is and works enthusiastically with what they've got, say parents – they don't try to iron out the problems and pretend they're not there.

Music and dance are central to the school day. Years 2 and 3 all learn the recorder in key stage 1, with over half the school going on to learn an instrument in key stage 2. An orchestra with regular concerts, jazz and dance throughout the year. Science week happens in the autumn term, arts week in the winter term and sports week (where they canoe and climb, do archery and judo as well as the sports you might normally expect) in the summer. Some 40 clubs are offered either before or after school – children can choose almost anything from Chinese to table tennis, sculpture to archery.

Delicious lunches cooked by their own chef (no imported catering service here) allow for every penny to be put back into the menu. Staff eat with pupils in the school hall. They don't need persuading to eat fresh Greek salad – after all, 'They are as fussy as the children,' acknowledges head.

Very supportive and active PTA raises significant sums of money each year, helping to fund, eg, the stunning areas of the playground. One parent described the parent body as having 'a can do attitude that you find in some private schools'. A number of parents were at Fox themselves – always

School thrives on multiculturalism and diverse influences but 'doesn't see that as an excuse for poor performance,' emphasises one parent

a positive indicator. High number of professionals – barristers, journalists, diplomats, authors as well as artists and musicians, and 17 per cent of pupils are on free school meals. One parent spoke of the relief she felt that her daughter wouldn't grow up thinking everyone had a second home in Barbados.

A school with a strong, very positive identity (witness the 'mighty Fox' anthem, sung by the whole school at every successful achievement). One parent described it as mini UN – can be up to 15 nationalities in one class. School thrives on multiculturalism and diverse influences but 'doesn't see that as an excuse for poor performance,' emphasises one parent. School quick to point out that bilingual pupils outperform their monolingual peers. Bright eyed, confident, articulate and above all happy children who enjoy coming to school. A rare and precious jewel showing real life at its best – not to be overlooked in this super-affluent patch of London.

Fulham Prep and Pre-prep School

200 Greyhound Road, London W14 9SD

Independent • Pupils: 595 • Ages: 4–13 • Non-denom
• Fees (per term): £4,800 – £5,325

Tel: 020 7386 2444
Fax: 020 7386 2449
Email: prepadmin@fulhamprep.co.uk
Website: www.fulhamprep.co.uk

4

Principal: Mrs Jane Emmett is back in charge after the short-lived tenure (less than a year) of Richie Howells. She founded the school in 1996 along with other members of her family (it is a family company with some external shareholders).

Head of the pre-prep is Ms Di Steven BEd, educated at Glasgow University with PGCY Ed from Dundee and an NPQH. She has been with the school for a decade, has one son in the pre-prep, a second younger son in a nearby nursery. Clearly in touch with the concerns of the modern parent, juggling work pressure with teaching her son to ride a bicycle. She is thorough and thoughtful with a pleasant manner and high standards. Her IT expertise ensures that the pre-prep is very well equipped.

Entrance: The pre-prep is non-selective in reception, with 90 places offered on a first come first served basis. Priority and a discount given to siblings. Entry after reception involves spending a morning at the school. Automatic transfer to the prep. The prep holds examinations and interviews at 7+ 8+ and 11+.

Exit: Majority of pre-prep pupils move on to the prep. Has a reputation for getting each prep school child into the right next school. Results are impressive with regular scholarships and places at a variety of boarding and day schools. School is keen to encourage more girls to stay until 13 but this very much depends on the choice of destination as many girls' schools want them at 11+. Girls move on to boarding schools including Benenden, Downe House, Tudor Hall, Wycombe Abbey, or to day schools such as Francis Holland, Godolphin & Latymer, Putney High, St Paul's Girls', Wimbledon High. Boys leave at 13 except those destined for Latymer or Westminster Under at 11. Their destinations include: King's College School, Dulwich, Eton, Harrow, Hampton, Marlborough, St Paul's, Wellington, Westminster and Winchester.

Remarks: The school is on two sites: there are transport arrangements between prep (on Greyhound Road) and pre-prep (on Fulham High Street) to assist busy parents, and January exam candidates are given the opportunity to visit in November for a treasure hunt so that they feel more at home when they come in for the dreaded tests.

The curriculum is not straitjacketed, and parents appreciate its variety and breadth. Although one class is given an accelerated pace (selected according to pupils' school destinations) this

would 'not be fair on the others who do not need it,' remarks the principal. That said, there is an expectation that every child will be able to keep up with a dynamic academic programme. All are being prepared for competitive entrance examinations and although some allowance is made for pupils from abroad there is limited EAL support in school. Experienced and extremely caring SENCo supports those with mild learning difficulties. Parents confirm that if serious difficulties were to develop, a school move would be suggested. Pre-prep has its own SENCo, a 'godsend,' remarks Ms Steven and we noted some very good examples of provision for different abilities.

Until year 4 pupils are classroom based, then they move round specialist facilities. Latin from year 5 and philosophy for years 4 to 6. Greek available in years 7 and 8. 'The teachers make lessons interesting, often involving games in them', pupils remarked to us. They also appreciate the way staff

---

Very much a local school, as evidenced by the numbers of bikes and scooters parked inside the gates

---

'offer advice and support'. We saw a number of young, enthusiastic staff, with more males in evidence than is often the case. The principal is keen to stress the role models provided by the female head of science (who is also a great skier), and the male head of art. Class sizes between 14 and 20.

A listed Victorian school building accommodates the pre-prep reception classes, library, activity room and ICT suite. Adjoining is a modern three-storey block for years 1 and 2 as well as the spacious gym/hall, dark music room and light art studio. Large, well-equipped play areas including fabulous Astroturf and garden with shallow pond. We saw plenty of imaginative play equipment that can be re-arranged with different themes.

Do not expect soft furnishings, carpets and tasteful flower arrangements, or a palatial office for the principal. The prep school was originally a Victorian board school and the building still shows this, although it is light with high ceilings, classrooms leading off the wide corridors on several floors, and an impressive meeting room with raked seating. Welcoming library with enthusiastic librarian. Classrooms contain attractive displays and are well equipped with the usual interactive boards. Some access to laptops, but though good use is made of the intranet to support learning (a recent development), we felt that the ICT in the

prep is not cutting edge (schools says, 'we have been very proactive in implementing a great deal of computer science, coding and digital literacy within our current programme.').

More boys than girls in the school, especially noticeable in years 7 and 8 when many of the girls have left for London day schools. Those girls that do remain can be assured of being given responsibility and participating in many sports. Pupils look happy and move about purposefully; they are polite and responsive but not precocious, though it takes a certain robustness to flourish here. Parents like the fact that 'there are all walks of life' and the school is not 'glitzy'.

Heaps for all to do here. 'There are lots of opportunities for children to try new activities, with loads of clubs from jewellery to street dancing,' commented a parent. 'There's also plenty of music, from award winning chamber choir to African drumming, orchestra and jazz group.' Music is a strength of the school with four choirs including school choir apprentices and chamber choir, a boys' choir, plus a parents' choir which sings at the carol service. All classes have two music lessons with three-quarters of the pupils taking individual instrumental or singing lessons in spacious accommodation. Pre-prep pupils learn the recorder and percussion.

The school has its own Astroturf, netball court and cricket nets, and there is one afternoon a week at Barn Elms. In years 3 and 4 every child is given the chance to play in a team. The second half of Friday afternoon is for sport, as are some Saturdays (though both of these may be avoided). The deputy head is especially pleased with the up-and-coming rugby players, and cricket is very popular. Girls play netball. The pre-prep makes frequent use of

Clearly in touch with the concerns of the modern parent, juggling work pressure with teaching her son to ride a bicycle

Hurlingham Park for games, swimming takes place at Fulham Pools and there's summer tennis coaching for years 1 and 2 in Bishops' Park.

'Pupils show tremendous loyalty to the four houses,' remarks Mr Howells. The house names fit the locality: Bishops, Crabtree, Hurlingham and Peterborough. Older pupils take their responsibilities seriously and look out for younger pupils. Even in the pre-prep pupils start to take responsibilities eg as house captains. All the houses raise funds for charities, and the school supports, for example, a local state primary for severely disabled children.

Discipline system understood by all and parents believe any bullying is quickly acted upon. Pupils we spoke to were clear that the head sees anyone who seriously misbehaves, and cited swearing as a major offence. Matters are dealt with promptly. Strong communication between home and school, including an open door policy and regular daily contact, means potential problems are nipped in the bud.

Sibling discount; some bursaries for families in difficulties. Scholarships available for years 7 and 8.

Very much a local school, as evidenced by the numbers of bikes and scooters parked inside the gates. The pupils are polite and express themselves confidently; one parent commented that some parents choose Fulham Prep because they have been impressed by the behaviour of the children outside school and asked where they were educated. A 'really vibrant, caring school where pupils are nurtured and understood' is the parental consensus. No wonder it has grown so fast.

Garden House School

Turks Row, London SW3 4TW

Independent · Pupils: 495 · Ages: 3–11 · Non–denom
· Fees (per term): £4,240 – £6,800

Tel: 020 7730 1652
Fax: 020 7730 0470
Email: info@gardenhouseschool.co.uk
Website: www.gardenhouseschool.co.uk

30

Principal: Since 1973, Mrs Jill Oddy BA. She also runs three pre-prep schools in New York. As a long-serving member of the administrative department – who appreciated the school's move in recent years to Turks Row just behind Sloane Square – proudly remarks: 'She has tremendous vision.'

Head of girls' school since September 2014, Mrs Charlotte Crofton BA (modern history, Newcastle) and PGCE (London), who has been a year 5 teacher here for eight years. She works alongside established, popular head of the girls' lower school – Mrs Wendy Challen Cert Ed Froebel.

Head of the boys' school since 2006, Mr Christian Warland, with BA from Exeter, mid-40s, left his work in the City as a lawyer and seems here to stay. He has found the change very satisfying: 'We spent considerable time analysing what went wrong in the City whereas here we are constantly forward-looking and this is very positive.' An old Garden House boy himself (and son of the principal), his three sons have been, or are being, educated at Garden House.

All three heads value taking time to get to know the children, from shaking hands with

them and making eye contact first thing in the morning to teaching. Head of boys teaches ICT to year 2 and current affairs to the rest. Mrs Challen teaches throughout lower school whenever possible, as well as being available for small groups for shared reading.

Entrance: As part of the school's desire to involve parents from the start, the family is seen as a unit. Usually girls are interviewed by head of lower school in January for the following September and boys by headmaster in October/November. Regular tours are organised for prospective parents, Tuesdays for the boys' school and Wednesdays for the girls', and there is no entrance examination, thankfully, so it really is important to secure a place on the lengthy waiting list with £120 as soon as possible. The school states that GH children live in Kensington, Chelsea, Fulham, Battersea and Westminster and that English is spoken at home by at least one parent, so very much a day school serving its local, smart area. The school does not offer scholarships in the lower school but scholarships and generous bursaries are available to children – mostly boys – entering at the age of 8. Once a place is offered, a registration fee of £2,000 is payable. There is a 10 per cent discount for all siblings. Around 50 boys and 45 girls join reception. Entrants at 8+ (by exam and interview) are nearly all boys, to replace the 30 – 40 who leave at this stage. There is a small amount of coming and going as families relocate so it is definitely worth checking.

Exit: Boys leave at 8+ (30-40) and 11+ (12-15) for top London day schools, including Sussex House, Westminster Under, Northcote Lodge, Wetherby Prep; one or two to boarding prep schools such as Ludgrove and Cothill House. Nearly all girls leave at 11; just under half go on to boarding schools including Downe House, St Mary's Ascot, Wycombe Abbey, with a consistent number to Queen's Gate, Godolphin and Latymer, St Paul's Girls', both Francis Hollands etc. Some go on with academic, art or sporting scholarships and awards.

Remarks: The exterior of the school, originally a British army barracks, is well maintained, but what awaits inside is quite magical. We were struck by the attention to detail and aesthetics; the entrance hall is beautifully arranged with rocking-horse, pupils' models and high quality art works by professionals, including an appealing watercolour of the school by a parent, Martin Millard, whose wife helps in the library. Classical music plays and flower arrangements and lighting produce a calming, civilising effect after the noise and bustle outside. Every corridor and every room shows a

care for the surroundings, whether it be the recital room, art room, well-equipped ICT suite or classrooms with vibrant displays, and this contributes to the attention paid to individual pupils. As a cur-

Classical music plays and flower arrangements and lighting produce a calming, civilising effect after the noise and bustle outside

rent parent remarked: 'This is above all a nurturing school, where boys and girls receive a wonderful education. It is so nurturing both for parents and children.'

Heads are proud of broad curriculum and use of cross-curriculum planning. Every class has a teacher and classroom assistant, with specialist teachers for music, drama, games, French, IT, ballet, Latin, fencing, art from year 2 upwards and RE in the upper school. Boys and girls are taught separately after kindergarten but come together for playtime and musical and drama performances, as well as some trips. Average class size is 15 for girls and 14 for boys, with mixed ability teaching for all and some streaming only in mathematics. There is a learning zone on the website and plenty of Inter Activ boards and laptops for research. There is a well-qualified learning support team with a range of expertise, including speech therapy, so pupils can be assessed in-house; some classroom assistants

The FebFest programme, involving the whole school from year 2 upwards, is linked to a fictional character travelling the world and hearing music from many cultures and heritages

are trained in dyslexia. Alongside the learning support, there is also a gifted and talented coordinator, and year 6 get help with creative writing and mathematics ready for 11+ exams. The boys and girls share the same broad curriculum, but many boys sit 8+ exams, so there is a different emphasis at this stage even for those staying till 11. Practice papers and internal assessments throughout the year help pupils to cope with different styles of questioning. Plenty of advice and guidance available to parents but tutoring is discouraged as unnecessary pressure.

The attractively-equipped kindergarten accommodates tiny tots in a separate building attached to Holy Trinity Church. There are morning sessions for 24 children and afternoon sessions for 12, and they share a play area with the C of E primary school over the road.

The behaviour policy, using traffic lights, is well thought out. A parent commented on how seriously the children take it and said that the red light is very rarely used – 'it is brilliant, a clear not emotional system.' The head was also reassuringly definite that she would have no hesitation in using the red light and contacting a parent if the need arose: if, for example, a child were bullied.

All three heads are keen for school to be fun and stimulating, as the enormous array of activities and events demonstrate. During our visit boys were producing leaves in IT and art enthusiastically for FebFest, and the older girls spoke of the delights of preparing music and performing at Cadogan Hall in the spring term to a packed audience. The FebFest programme, involving the whole school from year 2 upwards, is linked to a fictional character travelling the world and hearing music from many cultures and heritages. The school is handy for galleries, exhibitions, museums and concerts. Music is popular with pupils as the teacher makes 'music enjoyable using actions' and 'is not too serious but friendly.' We heard the boys singing with gusto, and the percussion teacher clearly had year 1 boys enthralled. Every year the chamber choir goes on tour to Normandy and sings in the chapel of Emmanuel College, Cambridge. The musical calendar is packed. Four productions a year at the Royal Court and the Christmas concert is held in the Holy Trinity Church. Numerous events and competitions include Varsity Challenge, House Shout and Garden House has Talent.

Sport is taken seriously with football, rugby, cricket, rounders, hockey, lacrosse, tennis, netball at nearby Burton Court and Ranelagh Gardens as well as swimming at the Queen Mother's Pool. As a parent remarked, 'It all happens seamlessly despite the school not having its own extensive grounds, as so much is in easy walking distance.' Pupils were keen to explain how inclusive the school is, with team places and encouragement even for the less talented.

Active and supportive PTA with a predominantly Anglo-American parent body. The pupils feel they are respected by the teachers; as one parent remarked, 'There is always a seasoned staff member who has expertise and experience alongside another with energy, who comes across as positive and not world-weary. The school is amazing'.

Fridays are half days, though older children can do supervised homework until 2.30pm. Popular with parents who feel younger children are ready for the shorter day by Friday, and with those who want to leave early for the country.

Not a cheap school, although the Harrods uniform is also available secondhand and there is a complimentary bus service at 4.00pm to Fulham.

Sparky teachers, male and female, give a sense of energy in a school community in which care, respect and kindness for all is very much the ethos.

GEMS Hampshire School

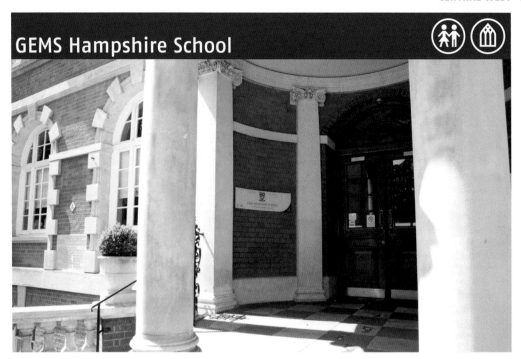

15 Manresa Road, London SW3 6NB

Independent • Pupils: 265 • Ages: 3–13 • Non–denom
• Fees (per term): £3,755 – £5,320

Tel: 020 7352 7077
Fax: 020 7351 3960
Email: info@ghs.gemsedu.co.uk
Website: www.ths.westminster.sch.uk

31

Headmaster: Since January 2014, Donal Brennan BEd (Dublin), previously under master and director of studies at Hill House International.

Entrance: From 3, an informal interview; older children attend an assessment day – nothing too daunting. School is currently expanding, so plenty of places at various different levels in both the prep and the pre-prep. As school fills up, likely to be entrance points at rising 3, 4 and 5 (kindergarten and reception based at Wetherby Place) only, with the occasional place further up the school.

Exit: Handful of boys leave at 8, majority at 13, most girls at 11, very few to boarding schools, most to a (very) wide range of London day schools. Favourites with the girls are More House, Francis Holland and Godolphin & Latymer; for boys Latymer Upper, Westminster, Dulwich, Emanuel, Colet Court and City of London.

Remarks: Founded as a dance school in 1928 by June Hampshire; on moving to London in the early 1930s became mainstream. Her daughter, Jane Box Grainger, took over as head in the 1960s;

another daughter is the well known actress Susan Hampshire. Now part of the GEMS group. Pupils in year 1 to year 8 accommodated in impressive premises on Manresa Road (marbled Corinthian columns, no less). Formerly a King's College library and, prior to that, the public library built by Earl Cadogan in 1891; the building is listed – after extensive negotiations with various bodies, including English Heritage, the staff have created their dream building for the school.

State of the art technology throughout – whiteboards that are not only interactive but also move up and down walls (wonderful for children in the early years, who still sit on the carpet) and even move around the room (an ingenious way of getting round English Heritage's intransigence about having a whiteboard installed in the grand library). Individual computer desks in many of the classrooms already and more are planned – soon all children from year 6 to year 8 will have their own computer, carefully hidden away inside the smart wooden desks, at which they can also write. ICT a great strength – children become highly competent with technology and are given the opportunity to learn touch-typing.

Lifts throughout the building – children with physical disabilities can now be accommodated – as well as individual staircases and entrances for different sections of the school to keep the homely atmosphere and ensure that the younger children feel secure. A large kitchen, which can prepare banquets for 160. Children arrive in the morning to the smell of fresh bread, baked daily, and eat lunch with the staff at round tables in the impressive June Hampshire Hall, complete with moveable stage and soundproofed screens. Gym also takes place in here; plenty of space to tuck things away, so you would never know it serves so many different purposes. Space is the overwhelming impression you get as you are shown round – no cramped stairways and classrooms in this central London school (what a welcome change from the norm); good sized walled garden, where all children can get some fresh air during break times.

Games take place at Battersea Park, swimming at Chelsea swimming baths (younger ones still swim at Fulham pools). Wonderfully atmospheric library which smells of studiousness. Domed window in the ceiling – balcony bursting with bookshelves but treacherous balustrade, too dangerous to use so just for show. The downstairs, however, teems with genuine learning – old and new: the hallmark computer desks again, a long wide mahogany table around which a whole class can work, mobile interactive whiteboard, as well as doughnut cushions for the younger ones in an intimate space carved out for them between two marble pillars.

Family-based, community-spirited atmosphere; pupils are friendly and encouraged to look after each other. They work hard and are much praised. A wide curriculum, including four languages. During a week in May each year the prep school section closes down and relocates to a château in France where they rock climb and canoe etc, as well as continue with academic subjects.

Careful assessments of the children at every stage through a combination of PIPs, NFER, national curriculum levels and CATs testing. Maximum 20 to a class, a watchful eye is kept and special needs are quickly identified. A dedicated SENCo (highly praised by one parent for her direct approach and ability to make her sessions fun) is employed full time, and works one-to-one with children diagnosed with, eg, dyslexia and dyspraxia. The gifted and talented, after a lengthy and careful assessment, are given a programme of accelerated learning. Visiting speech therapists, and EFL is catered for in-house. A lot of demand for this, as school is made up of a significant number of foreign pupils whose parents are on temporary postings.

Good inclusive arts programme: everyone is in an annual drama production, often a musical. Busy choir and orchestra (more than half the school play an instrument). Children entertain each other over lunch with informal piano recitals. Enthusiastic noises from parents, who are pleased with the breadth of education their children are getting at this stage. A relaxed and secure environment for the normal child who wants to have a go at everything.

Glendower Prep School

87 Queen's Gate, London SW7 5JX

Independent • Pupils: 220 • Ages: 4–11 • Non-denom
• Fees (per term): £5,500

Tel: 020 7370 1927
Fax: 020 7244 8308
Email: office@glendower.kensington.sch.uk
Website: www.glendowerprep.org

32

Headmistress: Since September 2012, Mrs Sarah Knollys (rhymes with tolls) BA PGCE (mid 40s), educated at Wycombe Abbey and St Paul's Girls', Exeter (a degree in French and Italian) and Roehampton Universities. Started teaching career as SEN assistant at Finton House School, London; rose from form teacher to maths co-ordinator, SCITT mentor, key stage 2 manager, senior management team and school governor at Allfarthing School, London, a busy state school in Wandsworth, (1993-2000); founding head, Maple Walk School, London (2005-2012). Married to Christopher; they have two teenage sons.

Bright and bubbly, Mrs Knollys exudes warmth and is highly accessible. She is the kind of person who rolls up her sleeves and gets on with it, whether it be teaching netball, transforming school lunches or wearing her slipper socks round the school on Red Nose day and dressing up in something crazy on Fun Friday. She is a woman who gets things done – as can be seen from her previous job at Maple Walk, the pioneer New Model school which started 'out of a trunk' as she puts it, with two pupils, and increased exponentially to 150 pupils by the time she left.

This is her first experience of a single sex school. 'I thought I'd miss the boys,' she remarks, 'but I don't miss the scraps in the playground – and our girls are very feisty.' She loves the girls, she says, because of their enthusiasm for everything, their lack of shame about excelling in science and maths and the more stable class dynamic – which can often be distorted by a predominance of one gender, she explains. She makes herself available to the parents, emails are responded to promptly, and she is there every morning to greet families. She is particularly on top of the 11 plus process, which starts with private meetings with her as early as year 4.

She is a good listener and we were told by one girl that 'she took on board our suggestions so we have much better lunches now, we no longer have to serve the younger children their lunch, and the loos and sinks are much nicer.' Her visible presence around the school includes teaching year 6 Latin, supporting maths in year 5 and English comprehension in year 4. That way she can properly understand each child and write detailed reports for the senior schools as well as giving fully informed advice to parents. She has one-to-one meetings with everyone from the kitchen staff through to the teaching staff and the parents. No one gets special treatment but everyone gets proper attention. This is a woman who throws herself into every aspect of the job and has been seen wiping her tears away during a music assembly. 'These are my girls,' she says unapologetically.

Entrance: Selective at 4 years. Far too many applicants for the 36 places. The girls are assessed on an informal basis – essentially to see if they interact well and can do the basics competently. Any parent who thinks coaching at this age is a good idea – forget it now. Sensible sibling policy means that often there are a fewer than 36 places open to newcomers. The tinies are assessed for 40 minutes in small groups. Older children applying for an occasional place will be assessed for longer – a morning or perhaps a full day, careful note being taken on whether they can cope and how they interact with their peers. No particular feeder nurseries. Occasional places occur but school unlikely to fill them after year 5 – the cohesion of the year being seen as paramount. It's worth a call, though. Some bursaries available for needy local girls or those already in the school who fall on hard times. Unsuccessful applicants for 4+ entry and later applicants to the school will be placed on a waiting list for consideration should an occasional place arise.

Exit: Recently, quite a number to top boarding schools – among them, Benenden, Downe House, St Mary's Calne, Wycombe Abbey. A wide range of offers from London day schools – including the odd co-ed one – but girls tend to go to St Paul's, Godolphin & Latymer, Francis Holland SW1, St James's and even as far afield as South Hampstead and Putney High. Always a handful of scholarships each year – art and music as well as academic.

Remarks: Think purple. Think elegant. Think Glendower. Natty purple berets, charming purple checked and striped uniform, purple website, purple chairs and folders in the class rooms, purple benches and tables in the playground as well as the purple scooters that the girls arrive on. Plush carpets and sweeping staircase in a building that feels much more like a comfortable home than a school. The 1830s white building – Thomas Cundy III? – on Queen's Gate occupies a large corner plot facing Stanhope Gardens. Part of the adjacent building integrated with the school through a major development and refurbishment programme. The resulting six storey building is remarkably spacious. An airy, panelled and white-painted entrance hall, complete with wonderful large Quentin Blake originals, greets the visitor and is also used, with the doors opened to the adjacent library, as an assembly space. Library attractive and well-stocked. Excellent displays of work everywhere, lots of up-to-the-minute equipment in all rooms, which are remarkably orderly with inviting and interesting-looking work and resources.

From the moment you enter Mrs Knollys' study with its oak panelled walls, large Victorian partners' desks and oil portraits on the walls, you know this is a school with history. Founded by two spinsters in 1895, one of whose eyes (Edith Lloyd's) follow you around the room from above the fireplace, Glendower is a charitable trust, and has always been run as a not-for-profit organisation. A nostalgic relief as spanking new profit-making companies pop up throughout the city, establishing expensive schools to meet demand.

Girls get lots of attention here. One teacher/assistant to 11 girls, class sizes of between 16 and 18. Not a school for those with serious SENs but school will pick up and support those with mild difficulties and make individual learning plans for those who need them. Between five and 10 per cent of girls are on the SEN register, more are being monitored. No stigma, just lots of support. There's a handwriting club during lunch break, some who have been

diagnosed dyscalculic get support from outside – Emerson House for example; a learning support assistant will go into the classroom to give support with organisational/processing skills etc. No extra charge for this. Some five per cent come needing a little extra help with English and EFL is given in small groups or one-to-one as needed. Parents a real mix, US, Chinese, European – lots of bilingual, trilingual, English as a fourth language – but they are here for the duration – not much to-ing and

---

She is the kind of person who rolls up her sleeves and gets on with it, whether it be teaching netball or wearing her slipper socks round the school on Red Nose Day

---

fro-ing. Specialist teaching right from the start – French, music, drama and PE, and by year 4 almost all teaching is specialist. The academic programme includes DT and ICT, and Mrs Knollys is no Luddite – plans afoot to introduce tablets in the classrooms. Science is well equipped and busy. The girls enthused about identifying cells under a microscope using iodine.

The post 11 plus programme is excellent and includes touch typing, Latin and lots of public speaking – balloon debating competitions against other schools is a popular one. Poetry competitions all through the school, poems recited by heart, girls vote for the winners and finals judged by eg famous actresses and poets. Lots of music – and the twice weekly music assemblies can feature anything from Bollywood dancing to a harp recital. Most girls play at least one instrument and many take musical theatre exams. 'Music is as natural as breathing here,' glows Mrs Knollys. 'No-one is concerned about performing and there are no divas.' This school is no slouch when it comes to sport either, despite having no grounds to speak of. They are fiendish at netball and compete at national level as well as against other local schools and among themselves in inter-house matches. We saw several girls snatch some precious moments during break to practise their shooting skills. Theatrical productions and swimming take place at Imperial College, athletics in Chiswick. The girls also play tennis and rounders. Lunch: 'we are no longer vegetarian!' – another change introduced by the attentive Mrs Knollys. Fish on Fridays. Only vegetarian options on Mondays but the rest of the week meat galore. Food cooked fresh on the premises and they eat in their own dining room – no packed lunches here – hurrah!

The Godolphin and Latymer School

Iffley Road, London W6 0PG

Independent · Pupils: 780 · Ages: 11–18 · Non-denom
· Fees (per term): £5,760

Tel: 020 8741 1936
Fax: 020 8735 9520
Email: registrar@godolphinandlatymer.com
Website: www.godolphinandlatymer.com

Head Mistress: Since 2009, Mrs Ruth Mercer BA (50s), read history at London University and is passionate about the subject – 'One of the reasons I chose to teach', she says, 'is so that I could continue to learn history'. Previously head of Northwood College, where, after a bumpy beginning, she was a considerable success. She grew up in Preston – her northern accent is just discernible after years of teaching in independent London girls' day schools; head of history and politics at Notting Hill and Ealing for 12 years, deputy head here at Godolphin from 1998 until 2002 and thence to Northwood College, which she ran for seven years.

Married to the deputy head of Greenford High Comprehensive in Ealing; they have two teenage children, both at single sex schools. 'I practise what I preach,' she says. Wholeheartedly committed to single sex education: 'We fail both boys and girls if we educate them together because we can't meet their very different needs,' she says. One staff member said, 'We were thrilled with her appointment – she is so hands on'.

Thoughtful, honest (prefers careful accuracy to hard sell) and tactful, Mrs Mercer is serious but clearly enjoys humour and is not afraid to join in and make a fool of herself, whether it be in the chorus of Mamma Mia directed by the girls or in a fitness contest, organised by the students, clad in blue wig and hood. Teaches history to year 7 – 'I need to know what the girls are like as learners as well as individuals'. This is a head who rolls up her sleeves and gets on with it at the coal face. During her first two terms she shadowed several classes, sitting with the girls, doing all the set tasks – 'quite a challenge when you are in a GCSE chemistry lesson and you haven't done chemistry for aeons'. It was an invaluable exercise, one of the results of which was the appointment of a thinking and learning coordinator (a refreshing departure from the usual 'teaching and learning'). She identified that teaching here needs to move away from the didactic – 'predictable hoop-jumping isn't training them for the real world'.

Popular with the girls, who appreciate her warmth and friendliness. None of the parents we spoke to had much, or indeed any, contact with her. They don't seem concerned. As one parent put it, 'She may tweak a few things but she isn't going to screw it up'.

Academic matters: Examination results are impressive – 74 per cent of A level results at A*/A in 2014 and those doing the IB achieved well too – average point score of 41 out of a possible 45. English literature, history, maths and biology particularly popular, with chemistry and history of art close behind. A level choices include philosophy, government and politics, music technology, Russian, classical civilisation.

IB take-up varies but Mrs Mercer is a great fan because it makes girls think ('exam technique has dumbed down A levels') and is right up the street of your typical self-reliant and busy Dolphin (that's what girls here are known as – past and present). All A level students can now do an extended project so they can be as stretched (nearly) as much as the IB candidates. In 2014, 96 per cent of GCSE grades were A or A*.

Over 50 per cent of staff have been here for over 10 years, 25 per cent of staff are men (not bad for a girls' school). Some parents comment on how results driven the school is – As are expected the whole time and 77 per cent is a poor mark. One mentioned her horror when parents were told in the November of their daughter's first year – two months in – whether their daughter was meeting her expected targets.

Positive noises from the girls. Teachers are supportive and always available to help, they say. No tutor system, however, and, as one parent pointed out, there is no one person who knows your child really well academically and has done all the way through so you can have a productive discussion with them about, say, their choice of A levels.

Full-time individual learning needs coordinator (Mrs Mercer doesn't like using the pejorative sounding 'special needs'). Needs mainly on the mild to moderate dys-strata and organisational skills, though have had statemented children in the past.

Girls take responsibility for a number of shows throughout the year – producing, directing and acting in them

Each case will be judged individually but girls here need to be able to stand the pace. 'All our girls are Gifted and Talented,' says head and the aim is to constantly stretch and stimulate them with the quality of the lessons. No extra charge for extra help.

Games, options, the arts: If your daughter is passionate about sport but gawky on the pitch, probably not the school for her. Although the teams – hockey and netball in particular – are strong, if your daughter isn't picked she is likely to get sidelined – a common complaint among parents. Astroturf (floodlit) hockey pitch, courts for netball and tennis – all on site and girls here are competitive and keen. Involvement rapidly declines for the not so sporty and as they move further up the school – one girl told us there is very little sport beyond year 10. Fencing, yoga and pilates as well as rowing (they share a boat house with Kings, Wimbledon). Not much swimming though they do have use of Latymer's pool.

Drama and music are a different story – very inclusive, ambitious and hugely popular. Girls take responsibility for a number of shows throughout the year – producing, directing and acting in them. Splendid new facilities housed in the Bishop Centre (nothing ecclesiastical meant by the nomenclature – it is in fact named after Dame Joyce Bishop, headmistress until 1963, but building is made up of St John's Church together with the vicarage, which school acquired in 2008). Concerts and theatrical performances take place here with state-of-the-art lighting and seating facilities (though one parent controversially complained that the acoustics were terrible and you couldn't see a thing – 'that's now been fixed,' school assures us). The Rudland Music School is connected to the Bishop Centre by a bright glass corridor. First class facilities for music playing and music making – you can burn discs in high tech studios, store your instrument in a discreet but secure locker and practise in comfortable soundproofed music rooms. A joint orchestra with Latymer Upper School as well as various choirs, ensembles and bands including a jazz band. 'You can get involved even if you have no musical talent whatsoever,' said one pupil, approvingly.

Art is strong. One girl commented that it was best thing about the school. Pottery a little disappointing. They still have a kiln but no longer have any wheels.

Huge range and number of trips – domestic and global – whether it be classics trips to the British Museum, Bath or Athens, skiing in the US or trekking in the Sinai desert. Swimming is not the only contact girls have with Latymer Upper. They go on French and German exchanges together and sixth formers do joint work experience in Versailles and Berlin.

Impressive amount of work in local community, especially with the elderly. One old Dolphin fondly remembers that her first experience of the indignities of old age was while she was at school here helping old ladies onto the loo. A 'social services' team led by about seven girls in the sixth form coordinates whole school charitable efforts – every week they choose a different charity. They raise money by any means possible – cake sales or charging fellow pupils to watch all the staff perform Mamma Mia during lunch break.

Background and atmosphere: Built as a boarding school for boys in 1861, became an independent day school for girls in 1905 and evolved, through different state-aided statuses, before turning independent again in 1977 rather than becoming a comprehensive school or being closed down altogether. Situated at the end of Iffley Road in W6, it's encased by hectic Hammersmith on one side and leafy Brackenbury on the other. There is a definite churchy feel to the architecture.

What was formerly St John's Church is now the Bishop Centre. The original buildings are yellow brick Victorian, with some distinctly church-like windows and a formal panelled assembly hall. Recent yellow-brick additions blend in fairly harmoniously and have provided science labs and art studios, a pottery room, computer studies rooms and language labs. 'I like the way different buildings have different feels,' said a pupil. The ecology garden is used in biology lessons, there's a quad with pond (plus dolphin statue) and a courtyard where girls can eat lunch in warm weather. The spacious top floor sixth form centre resembles an airport lounge with roof terrace and tuck shop. 'We feel privileged to come up our own staircase to our own room,' said a sixth former.

Although almost every girl we spoke to said they loved the friendly and supportive atmosphere, a number of parents complained of poor communication and an 'us and them' attitude from the senior staff – 'they prefer to support the teachers rather than sympathise with the concerns of parents,' said one. That said, it is universally acknowledged that school responds swiftly when something can be done.

This is a close knit community where there is mutual trust between staff and pupils. Girls here are real joiner-inners – for many of them the school day runs from 7 in the morning until 8 at night. They are given a lot of responsibility and there is healthy contact between younger and older girls. One parent described the atmosphere as buzzing. We would have to agree.

Pastoral care and discipline: Head says behaviour is good, and better than when she was here as deputy. No instances of drugs found in school: if they were, each case would be dealt with individually, but likely to result in expulsion. Regular surveys about bullying – school council (chaired by head girl – with one member of staff – the rest are girls) produced its own anti-bullying strategy, recently revised to incorporate Facebook cyber-style bullying.

Sixth form can go out to Hammersmith at lunchtime – a privilege that can be withdrawn for bad behaviour.

Mutterings among parents about poor communication – 'it's hard to get hold of teachers' – and one said that her daughter's form-mistress hardly knew her: 'They only have 10 minutes with the girls in the morning'. A parent of a younger girl said she was still working with the reputation of the school as being a good one rather than what she has experienced – 'I wish I knew what she was doing in the day,' she said.

Pupils and parents: Parents are professional – city types and lawyers, a few in media and publishing. Ambitious with high expectations. Not as much diversity as there used to be in the days of Assisted Places, though school tries hard with a bursary fund to maintain some socio-economic spread. Lots of Gucci and Fendi handbags at the school gates as well as the odd chauffeur dropping off a daughter of a Russian magnate. Quite a high number of children from the States and France who live in SWs 1 and 3. A few from Ealing, Kew and Richmond and a small number from north London, otherwise it's largely local.

Girls are feisty, confident, independent and grounded. Not afraid to stand up for what they believe in and their teachers let them – its part of the mutual respect that is so valued here. It's cool to be clever and to be responsible. Timid girls tend to blossom, and enjoy – as one parent put it – the slightly Victorian approach to structure and boundaries. Not many of the hair flickers in Starbucks in Hammersmith will be from Godolphin, and one old Dolphin – also a current parent – pointed out that it's fine for girls here to have chunky thighs and to use the wrong hand cream. Old Dolphins include Nigella Lawson, Davina McCall, actresses Kate Beckinsale, Jemima Rooper and Samantha Bond, writer Sarah Dunant, Professor Dame Susan

Greenfield, architect Julia Barfield and singer Sophie Ellis-Bextor.

Entrance: Competitive – about 500 each year apply for 110 places. About a quarter from state primaries, large number from central London preps – Pembridge Hall, Bute House, Thomas's – over 100 schools. Member of group 2 of the North London Consortium of girls's schools that set common maths and English exams. All girls are interviewed twice. 'We place a lot of emphasis on school report and interview,' says head. 'We are trying to get at potential, do they have the ability and willingness to think for themselves – are they teachable?' Adding how depressing it is when they ask what they do in their free time and are told that most of it is taken up with tutoring. A pretty high standard of raw ability is required if they are to keep up with the fast pace of lessons. Siblings will be turned away if not they're not up to it.

Exit: A small number – about 10 per cent – will leave after GCSE to go to eg Westminster, or boarding schools – Marlborough, Wycombe Abbey, Cheltenham Ladies ('but we bring in at least that number,' says head).

After A level or the IB almost all go on to the most selective universities; 13 to US in 2014, rest to Oxbridge, Bristol, Edinburgh etc.

Money matters: A development director raises funds, particularly for bursaries. School will make every effort to ensure that no-one has to leave because their family has fallen on hard times. One or more music scholarships at 11 and music and art scholarships in the sixth form.

Remarks: A stimulating school that does its job well. Produces independent, confident (rather than arrogant) girls that are looked after but appear to be looking after themselves. An excellent choice for your busy daughter who loves to join in.

Hawkesdown House

27 Edge Street, London W8 7PN

Independent • Pupils: 145 • Ages: 3–8 • Non denom • Fees (per term): £4,695 – £5,395

Tel: 020 7727 9090
Fax: 020 7727 9988
Email: admin@hawkesdown.co.uk
Website: www.hawkesdown.co.uk

33

Head: Since 2010, Mrs Claire Renton-Bourne MA (known to the parents as Mrs Bourne), a Cambridge classicist and Nottingham theologian

(early 50s). She spent three years at Perrott Hill School in Somerset, tutoring scholars and heading the classics and RS departments. This led to

her fascination with theology and a Nottingham RE diploma, which she completed whilst deputy head at Knighton House in Dorset in 2001. Head there from 2004 continuing to teach classics. Her two children attended nearby Bryanston and one is now in PR and the other is training as a mechanical engineer. She is married to a civil servant; they have a bolt hole in Dorset where they escape at weekends and she can enjoy gardening, playing the piano, which she finds relaxing, and attend local church.

A self-possessed, thoughtful, articulate individual, 'More modest than many, quiet, sensible, not brash, calm and steady,' comment current parents. Other comments: 'Amazing Ms Bourne has the boys' best interests at heart 24/7. Parents are kept in the picture, communication is excellent and her door is open if there is a concern.' When questioned about the future, she replied, 'I love this school and am very happy.The longer I am here the more I can see the importance of my role in supporting the parents. I strongly believe in the importance of single sex education to 13.' Parents feel she is doing a great job and appreciate her advice and the links she has made with the next schools so that each individual is considered. As one American remarked, 'The head is diplomatic. She explained the English system, the general landscape and was particularly helpful regarding the next school.'

Entrance: There are two main entry points. The first is the nursery (16 places) and the second is reception, which is made up of two classes of 20.There are no open days; instead Mrs Bourne gives individual tours with prospective parents lasting about an hour with a follow-up chat in her office. This is key, as she sees if the aims and ethos of parents are aligned with the school. The boys are asked for an introductory session in the autumn when they are due. This is purely to see if the boy would be happy in the school and whether it would be the best place for him. Mrs Bourne and the head of early years provide a variety of activities for a half hour session in the nursery adjacent to the courtyard, with opportunities for outside play. Those hoping to join in year 1 upwards spend a morning in the relevant class and are assessed in literacy and numeracy before being offered a place. The pupils come from a wide spread of local nurseries. There are no bursaries, scholarships or sibling discounts on offer.

Exit: Most to established London prep schools including: Colet Court, Westminster Under, Sussex House, Wetherby Prep, St Phillip's. Others choose to board at a range including Caldicott, The Dragon, Summer Fields and Papplewick. Most boys leave after year 3 but some go after year 2 to Latymer, Colet Court or Westminster Under.

Remarks: The school was founded in 2000 by Mr and Mrs Loveridge and is part of a family group. This includes Devonshire House School and Lyndhurst House, both also in London. It is named after Hawkesdown Hill, in Devon, familiar to the Loveridge family, and where an ancient, gigantic, defence earthwork fortress was built. A colourful painting of Hawkesdown is on view in the entrance hall, a reminder of the qualities the school promotes – tradition, charm, community endeavour – and a source of inspiration.

The school provides a traditional curriculum with emphasis on the basics with literacy and numeracy sessions most mornings. 'This is necessary as the demands of the next selective preps are still very traditional, including English written composition and comprehension at a sophisticated level.' Topics and daily routine are deliberately timetabled to cater for boys' interests and enjoyment. We saw evidence of solar system models, astronauts, aeroplanes, castles, and, in year 1, an imaginative life cycle display with very neat handwriting and illustrations, under the friendly eye of one of the few male teachers. Undoubtedly, once the wireless network is installed and running, the boys will also be able to enjoy more ICT opportunities across the curriculum than existed at the time of a recent inspection. One mother commented that having initially intended sending her son to a co-educational school, she now believes he would have suffered seated next to a girl with beautiful penmanship as boys have a definite rhythm of learning. 'They are,' as another parent acknowledged, 'wriggly'. That is catered for and understood completely by the staff at HH. French is taught from reception. No dedicated science laboratory, art or design technology rooms. The boys are prepared for serious entrance exams and given plenty of practice. 'The boys are not pushed too much and they have a good balance of work and play.' In year 1, for example, judo is added to the timetable with chess in year 2 and fencing by year 3. Violin, piano and singing lessons are available from year 1, as well as Mandarin, with plenty of after-school clubs.

'My son told me he had learnt all about Lord of the Rings from another boy at lunch.'

One drawback, commented on by some parents, is the lack of space for a playgound. During indoor lunch break in their classrooms, the top year boys we saw looked extremely happy in Connect heaven, constructing imaginative vehicles and missiles with great enthusiasm. Nevertheless, 'by the time the boys are in their final year they are big and notice the lack of space,' remarked one parent. They make use of Holland Park for PE in good weather, with football once a week, team games and formal matches arranged, and run around in Kensington Gardens enjoying plenty of controlled rough and tumble. Still, some boys, especially the older sporty ones, might find this frustrating. Judo is extremely popular, as are football, cricket and PE (no swimming). All boys play in fixtures against other schools at some point.

Young teachers and teaching assistants, some from abroad, are lively and enthusiastic and support the boys with different languages, an important feature as this school caters for international families. Pupil teacher ratios is approximately 8:1 with average class sizes of 17. Nobody has been on the staff for more than 10 years, but this is hardly surprising as it is a relatively new school.

The house system with its homage to royalty, Plantagenet, Windsor and Tudor, has been revitalised to excellent effect. Parents are encouraged to be involved and are welcomed, once a fortnight, to attend Friday assemblies in the packed main hall. Boys are awarded pen licences, house points and many awards for tying of shoe laces and ties, good manners at lunch time and community spirit among others. The skills encouraged are spot on for this age and there's always a loud cheer for the winning house. The boys are taught to be courteous and polite and they respect the staff who know them so well. The positions of house captain, vice captain and prefects merit special house ties, rather than the normal school tartan ties (which do look a little odd against the blue and white check shirts). The navy blue and red uniform including blazers and caps is popular, and several parents commented, 'the boys look so cute'.

An important duty for the house prefects is to ring the large bell outside the dining hall for lunch, serve food and clear up. One parent remarked just how great it was that the boys sat in houses for lunch. 'The younger ones look up to the older boys. My son told me he had learnt all about Lord of the Rings from another boy at lunch.' This social mixing may account for the ease with which the boys spoke during our visit. One recent newcomer was highly appreciative of the way he had been made to feel welcome and, a sensitive soul, had clearly benefited from another boy's support. Lunch is extremely popular, even more so since the arrival of a new chef who has a great following. Special themed meals, such as for Wimbledon (with strawberries and cream) and Independence Day, are a real hit with even the fussiest boys.

Parents tell us that pupils with SEN are well catered for because 'the school is small and there is plenty of support'. We saw happy boys with hearing aids and the sparky, young SEN coordinator supports form teachers, ensuring that individual plans are monitored carefully and reviewed. Setting in maths and English is realistic and understood:

'Kids quickly know where they stand'. A speech and language therapist comes in weekly and boys are offered High 5s sessions before beginning lessons as well as booster groups. TAs work with boys who need extra help. This is not the school for someone with disruptive behavioural problems or physical difficulties because of the school's layout, but emerging problems are dealt with in a caring way.

A thorough mix of English and international families with a number of bilingual pupils. Most parents live within walking distance of the school and many work in the financial sector. HH is reassuring to the many new to the English examination system; right from the start, it provides advice, support and the necessary preparation to give parents and pupils a very happy start in a caring, environment without undue pressure.

Hill House International School

17 Hans Place, London SW1X 0EP

Independent • Pupils: 960 • Ages: 4–13 • Non-denom • Fees (per term): £3,450 – £4,700

Tel: 020 7584 1331
Fax: 020 7591 3938
Email: info@hillhouseschool.co.uk
Website: www.hillhouseschool.co.uk

34

Principals: Since 2002, Mr Richard Townend FLSM (sixties), educated at Westminster and the Royal College of Music, and his wife, Mrs Janet Townend Cert Ed. Mr Townend is principal and headmaster and Mrs Townend is principal and director of admissions. He is quirky, humorous, clever and a passionate musician. She is terrifically busy. This is a huge school – just shy of 1,000 children, spread over several sites in London, all of which are small town houses and short on space: no wonder little children marching in crocodile in their brown and mustard uniform through the streets of Chelsea are as much a part of the scenery of this chic and expensive area as the Venus statue in Sloane Square. They spread into the space that's available.

Like Prince Charles, an old boy of the school, who is still waiting, Mr Townend had a long wait before getting his hand on the job that was always going to be his. The school was founded by his late father, the legendary Lt Col H Stuart Townend, whose image, influence and inspiration persist. The Colonel, as he was known to everyone, was 93 when he died in 2002 and ran the school as a tight ship right to the end. He died during half term, when Richard Townend took the reins. 'I had no idea how to run the place,' he confides, though this has to be a bit of an exaggeration, as his wife had been

the administrator under the Colonel. However the impression one gets is that his heart is really in his music – wonderful instruments all over the place, a harpsichord and clavichord in his flat, a splendid 456 pipe wooden organ in the main school and fabulous pianos and harps scattered throughout. 'I couldn't get up in the morning if I didn't play each day,' he says.

They regard their job as being to inspire the children – his disdainful intolerance of petty inspectors who worry more about the site of sick bays and the use of Tipp-ex in the register than the teaching and the evident happiness of the children is unashamed. Some may criticise this as failing to keep up with the times, but his exasperation at how he was questioned about the identity of his wife without a photocopy of her passport on record does invite the question as to which is the wiser approach.

Taking a different tack to his controlling father, he is already preparing his second son, Edmund Townend, for the eventual running of the family business and he is involved in the day to day administration of the school. His elder brother, William, is given the title of property bursar – his father wryly observed that this effectively means he unblocks drains. He is also a full time opera singer.

Each part of the school has its own head, known as heads of house.

Entrance: First come, first served at 4, but the school, famously, will fit people in if they possibly can and if they like them. At 6 a test in maths and English. Prospective parents are invited to turn up for a tour of the school on any morning without appointments. A pool of children are regularly on hand to show visitors round. When we visited, the front hall was filled with eager children waiting to escort equally eager, though slightly overwhelmed, prospective parents. Places occur at all stages. This is an international school – a lot of movement.

Exit: A wide and diverse spread – Mr Townend has no truck with parents who don't carefully assess the right school for the child and will not spare them his forceful advice. Nearly all girls leave at 11 to a range of London day schools, including state schools – La Retraite, Ursuline High and Lady Margaret's. The independent schools are those you would expect – St Paul's, Godolphin and Latymer, the two Francis Hollands, Queen's Gate and Queen's College, More House and Latymer Upper. A tiny few stay on to 13 – often to board at Wycombe Abbey, Downe House or Cheltenham Ladies'.

Most boys leave at 13, about half to London day schools and the other to board. A few leave at 11, and a tiny few to the Catholic state schools – the Oratory and Cardinal Vaughan. Chief destinations are Dulwich College, City of London, St Paul's, Westminster and a few to Latymer Upper and Portland Place. No special boarding favourites, but

Little children marching in crocodile in their brown and mustard uniform are as much a part of the scenery of this chic and expensive area as the Venus statue in Sloane Square

spread of top schools which includes Eton, Harrow, Charterhouse, Winchester and Worth. Most pupils get their first choice of school and always a cluster of scholarships each year. No preparation for any boys to leave at seven or eight – this is not expected nor supported.

Remarks: A tour of Hill House is unlike a tour of almost any other school and you get a real sense of what the hordes of children do each day. Rather like a line from Annie, little children everywhere, scampering around the rabbit warren of buildings. Each of the five sites is cramped and used to the max. The famously conspicuous brown knickerbockers and mustard cable knit woollies were designed as a uniform so the children didn't need to change for sport – no room for that kind of luxury. On our visit we spent much of the morning stomping around Chelsea and jumping on and off a Hill House mini bus (the school owns a fleet). The two girls who showed us round were whipped off mid tour to rehearse their end of term play. Mr Townend scooped us up and we then interrupted a class music

lesson in the organ room, while Mr Townend gave an impromptu in depth tour of each organ pipe.

As soon as you enter the main hall at the senior school in Hans Place you are transported to a 19th century boarding prep school. A smell of faded grandeur – oak panels, Latin mottos, a plethora of gold leaf memorial boards, listing among other things the four principles of the school, past head choristers, various awards and scholarships, as well as contributors to the life of the school. A sweeping staircase, piles of silverware and even an Olympic flag (the Colonel was also an outstanding athlete who competed in the 1930 Empire (now Commonwealth) Games and was in charge of housing for the 1948 London Olympics).

Hill House was founded by the Colonel in 1951 and his aim from the first was to create a genuinely international school which nurtured each individual child's talents. Glion House in Switzerland, the Hill House chalet, used to be a major feature of the education here and though less so now, it is still used for anything ranging from geography field trips, ski and hiking trips to trumpet tours. The signature oak panels in all the London sites are intended as a reflection of their Swiss residence. Photos plastered all over the walls – lots of smiling children as well as fabulous Swiss landscapes, some dating from the 1970s, vaguely reminiscent of a teenage bedroom.

The classes are unusually small, averaging 12 – just as well, as most rooms are too small for many more. At the top end of the school they get results – several scholarships, eg the King's scholarship to Eton and the top scholarship to Wellington, and almost all getting into their first choice school, partly, no doubt, as a result of Mr Townend and Mr

elsewhere if this is going to be a problem. Rave reports from some parents, on the other hand, about how the gifted and talented fare here. 'My child has been set alight – his previous school just didn't recognise his talents,' commented one parent. The school motto is: 'A child is not a vessel to be filled but a fire to be kindled'.

This ethos permeates the music, a central feature of the curriculum, as you would expect from someone of Mr Townend's pedigree. No grades allowed – 'that's just for the mothers to boast about with each other in the playground,' he retorts; instead the school owns more than 300 instruments, from tubas to harps, on loan for individual use: 'If a parent knew what a bassoon costs, they might not let their child play it,' explains Mr Townend. Thirty-two choral scholarships available to existing school choristers which enable them to attend residential music courses, often abroad. Parents enthuse about the whole school assemblies, which burst with music, that take place on Wednesday mornings in St Columba's, the Scottish Church in Pont Street – the only place suitable and big enough to fit the whole school.

Proper freshly cooked food at each site served in a civilised way, all children eating at long tables which magically appear at lunch time in some of the more cramped premises. No catering companies and no contract cleaners – in recruiting all his staff, from the brilliant head of music to the chefs (winners of the Tatler award for best school food in 2011), Mr Townend keeps his ears to the ground and if he discovers someone good he will poach them. 1950s style menus – no choice or puddings, but well prepared, and very fresh produce bought from Covent Garden market each day.

'If a parent knew what a bassoon costs, they might not let their child play it,' explains Mr Townend

---

Brennan's shrewd guidance as to which school is right for the child. Boys and girls taught separately from year 5 (though they continue to do music and sport together); Latin from years 6 to 8. French from the beginning – teachers are all French ('Preferably not Parisian – they have the wrong attitude,' comments Mr Townend). Girls can do Mandarin in year 6. Lots of antipodean teachers – 'they are so good,' remarks Mr Townend, though not all parents agree.

Small classes also allow for individual help when needed (we are assured) and specialist SEN support in years 3-5. Nothing more than mild dyslexia catered for here: you would be advised to look

Lots of exercise had by all – an hour of sport each day; Duke of York Square is their local playing field and where Field Day happens at the end of each summer term, when the four houses compete vigorously. Hyde and Battersea Parks are also used, as well as various local pools, halls and gyms, providing for a good range of physical activity – 24 sports, we're told.

The art teacher is a current parent and canny about entering the children into various art competitions – outside as well as within school. Lots of prizes are won and during our tour we were asked to choose our favourite painting of a flower from a wall where about 40 different flowers were displayed – not an easy task. Finally plumping for one, we were told, 'That child will win the prize this week'.

When we visited, the school had recently achieved an extraordinary coup in securing the purchase of the former Welsh Church in Radnor Walk. One of the advantages of not having governors nor any red tape, Mr Townend explained – they could pounce quickly. These graceful premises are now used as a theatre, gym, art gallery and ICT centre. A beautiful lofty space and to Mr Townend's delight, it also came with the church organ thrown in.

Parents here come from all over the world and all walks of life – a few Chelsea football stars send their children, as well as a large number of embassy families. Many more first time buyers than a lot of London preps, primarily because the fees are relatively low (an advantage of having such a large school). Alumni equally diverse, from Prince Charles to Lily Allen. If a family needs help with fees, arrangements can be made but, as with so much here, no formal structures in place. Once you sign up, the deal is that you leave the education and the running of the school entirely to the school. No PTA (Mr Townend is as scornful of the

motives for joining one of these as he is about the motives for doing music grades). Quite the contrary – parents are positively discouraged from becoming involved with the everyday life of the school.

For all the apparent chaos, a huge amount of work is put into the children by a dedicated and loyal team of teachers, games staff, music teachers (all real musicians, points out Mr Townend, many of whom are old friends of his), caterers and cleaners, all of whom embrace the eccentric ethos of this family run school. It is a long day so everything can be packed in. The oldest boys stay until 6pm Monday to Thursday and 1pm on a Friday (a range of after school activities are offered on Friday afternoons).

An overwhelming buzz of creativity and energy here, but if you are looking for calm, controlled order, with 'yes sir, no sir' boys and girls, this is definitely not the place for you.

Holland Park School

Airlie Gardens, Campden Hill Road, London W8 7AF

State • Pupils: 1,335 • Ages: 11–18 • Non-denom

Tel: 020 7908 1000

35

Email: admissions@hollandparkschool.co.uk
Website: www.hollandparkschool.co.uk

Head: Since 2001, Mr Colin Hall BA PGCE (early 50s). What he inherited was a disenchanted fiefdom, with low attendance, low academic performance and more than its fair share of inner-city problems. 'Standards are not high enough,' lectured Ofsted crisply, and 'behaviour is unruly'. Since his arrival,

Mr Hall, an energetic terrier of a man, has worked 14-hour days and six-day weeks to transform the school into one of Britain's 'most improved'. A recent Ofsted described Hall's leadership as 'inspirational' – and few would disagree.

Mr Hall attended Durham Wearside Grammar School, read history at Sheffield, followed by a PGCE at Cambridge. Started out as a history teacher, before transferring to English at Thurston Community School (now College) in Suffolk, then at Harrogate High School in North Yorkshire. Rose rapidly through the management ranks, firstly as director of sixth form at King Edward VI Morpeth, in Northumberland, then deputy head at Cheney School in Oxford. First headship was Longford Community School in Feltham, Hounslow, a tough inner-city school, where he quickly drove up GCSE results from 16 per cent A*-C to 40 per cent before being headhunted for Holland Park. The school he joined was on the verge of special measures and it soon became apparent that Mr Hall and existing staff were not on the same wavelength. 'My job involved assisting people's passage to places where they might flourish,' is his velvet-glove description of those 'ugly' times. His own views are clear and consistent, 'Adults run the school. That's what makes it a safe and agreeable place to be'. Describes his job as an obsession: 'I'm not good at the work-life balance. This is a passion, the best thing I could have ever done with my life'.

Academic matters: In 2014, 86 per cent of pupils got 5+ A*-C at GCSE including English and maths and 34 per cent of GCSE grades were A*/A. Has a banded intake, with four bands selected on the basis of verbal and non-verbal reasoning before entry. All are then re-assessed in the middle of their first term and setted for each subject. It's clearly a method that works, but some students find it creates a 'them-and-us' mentality. The quality of the teaching is strong and the dedication of staff unquestioned. 'I'm looking for robust teachers, open-minded, passionate about what they do, with an energy beyond their subject,' says Mr Hall. 'If children love a subject, it's because of the person who's teaching it.'

Pupils have nothing but praise for the staff. 'The teachers are really, really dedicated,' said one sixth former. 'They'll stay in school till 8 or 9. Even on their birthday. They never take a day off.' Teacher development is very much part of the programme. Younger staff observe their more experienced colleagues and can take specialist

---

The corridors are polished, the reception ornamented with fresh-cut flowers and the pupils themselves, in smart grey suits, would do credit to any independent school brochure

courses at the weekend for aspiring leaders. 'Once you've found them you want to hook them,' says Mr Hall. Preparation and monitoring are meticulous. Classrooms are laid out in advance of lessons. 'It's about rigour and order' – and that applies to students, who all have chic student planners for parents to sign weekly.

The school has a humanities specialism and English is its lead subject. The approach to the curriculum is relentlessly innovative. Latin is on offer for GCSE and A level. Dance, music and drama taught as separate subjects in years 7 and 8. Modern languages are French and Spanish ('We tried Italian and German, but they didn't root'). GCSE is a three-year programme, in which most students will already have acquired their 5+ A*-C grades by the end of year 10 ('They can see the end point more quickly'), leaving year 11 to focus on a wider diversity of choice including early A level study.

Sixth form is now, as always, primarily academic, with some very small classes ('It's like a free private school,' said one pupil). At A level in 2014, 76 per cent A*/B, 45 per cent A*/A. English and maths most popular A level subjects.

Parents cannot praise SEN highly enough. Some 220 pupils on the register of emotional and learning needs, overseen by the SENCo and 15 teaching assistants in specialist accommodation.

Games, options, the arts: Hall wants Holland Park to be a 'life-transforming institution' and has worked as vigorously to develop the extracurricular as the academic. Art rooms are large, light and lively. Highly praised director of dance, collaborates with several dance companies including English

National Ballet and English National Opera. Poet Simon Armitage is a friend of the school, as is the writer Alan Bennett (one of its houses is named after him). Music, with new teachers and increased funding, is an ever more popular choice at GCSE and pupils have performed at the Royal Albert Hall.

The school has its own art gallery and produces a range of music, dance and drama events, one particular highlight being an annual Shakespeare play performed by members of the school's Leadership Team and English department.

Sports facilities in the school are exceptional, including a 25m competition swimming pool and extensive specialist multi-surface outdoor spaces. Sport is important (and recognised by a Sportsmark award). 'Sport can build up or destroy confidence,' says the head. Rugby, rowing, indoor cricket nets for the winter, Duke of Edinburgh are order of the day, and a summer tour to Ampleforth College in Yorkshire is one of the highlights of the sporting calendar.

Amongst the wide range of clubs available, sports fans can do football, rugby, cricket, judo, baseball, gym and swimming. An annual garden party celebrates outstanding sportsmanship. School trips, too, are seen as a foundation pillar of the education and are underwritten by a £1m trust, enabling for example, every child in year 7 to visit Stratford (for Romeo and Juliet and dinner in a restaurant), year 8 to Rome, GCSE historians to Berlin and Auschwitz, A level geographers to Iceland and Sicily. 'The trust enables us to benefit the children of families who don't have those kind of resources.'

Background and atmosphere: The original school building was designed by the architect of the Royal Festival Hall, Sir Leslie Martin, and, built at the then astonishing cost of £1m, it opened in 1958 as one of London's first purpose-built comprehensives. The school, set in eight leafy acres of London's most costly square footage, has always been controversial and Kensington locals weren't entirely happy with its arrival. Naturalist Peter Scott (who claimed the children would frighten away nightingales), John Betjeman (who worried about the trees), and the High Commissioner of South Africa (who feared for his garden parties at nearby 'High-end') were only a few of those who inundated The Kensington Post with their concerns. At the time, the feeling was that the school would 'reduce Campden Hill to Earl's Court'. Early fears, however, were soon confounded. The school quickly attracted high-profile, left-leaning pioneers convinced that state education was the answer for a more egalitarian age.

Celebrated former peer and socialist minister Tony Benn transferred his two oldest sons from Westminster and Charles Jenkins, son of Labour cabinet minister Roy, joined the sixth form from

Celebrated former peer and socialist minister Tony Benn transferred his two oldest sons from Westminster and Charles Jenkins, son of Labour cabinet minister Roy, joined the sixth form from Winchester

Winchester. Hardly surprising, then, it was soon dubbed 'The Eton of comprehensives'. In the '60s and '70s, became increasingly progressive and undoubtedly cool (Anjelica Huston was a pupil, as were the children of the Marquess of Queensbury), but the 80s and 90s were not so kind, and cool turned to chaos.

Today, its pristine, £80m, light-filled classrooms are once more an oasis of well-ordered calm. The corridors are polished, the reception ornamented with fresh-cut flowers and the pupils themselves, in smart grey suits, would do credit to any independent school brochure. 'The environment,' says Mr Hall, 'is part of an attitude, a landscape for learning. It transmits that we care about young people and, as a result, students want to work hard and feel they belong.' Certainly students are proud of their school – 'It's a shining hall of hope,' said one; 'a fantastic place to be,' commented another. The school makes no apology for its utterly aspirational approach, or for the drive, focus, passion and high standards on which it insists.

Pastoral care and discipline: Where once mayhem, now tranquillity, and pupils higher up the school notice it most. 'When I came here it was completely chaotic – now it's an incredible school,' said one year 12 boy. 'There is a very special thing about the school, an openness and willingness,' says the head. 'Pupils behave with good grace and enthusiasm.' They definitely feel comfortable here. 'It's very close knit, like a family. It looks after the kids and cares about how you are,' says one. The head aims to create a safe and secular, humanist community and instil a sense of spirituality. 'We live in such a ready culture – we don't want to replicate what happens out of school'. Pupils meet weekly in their house (Anderson, Baker, Bennett, Chappell or Seeley) for assembly, and listen to choral music and poetry – 'not because its of use in exams, but because it takes them beyond their everyday passions'.

Praise is very much part of the mix and an annual awards dinner, Perfect Tense, recognises outstanding achievements, attitude and contributions during the year. Award winners' portraits ornament the corridor walls. Vertical tutor groups

exist for a better understanding across the years ('and less bullying,' said one pupil). Behaviour is good – 'students are friendly and welcoming and express pride in their school,' said Ofsted.

Pupils and parents: From a vast range of ethnic backgrounds (90 languages spoken). Fifty per cent speak English as a second language, about 10 per cent are refugees, mainly from Somalia and Eastern Europe. Around 50 per cent are actually English by origin and language but, as was the original intention, investment bankers ('we felt the head was a great leader, a visionary person. We took a gamble, but we're delighted with it') and intellectuals (Will Self) are once more happy with their local state provision.

Entrance: Around 1,400 apply for 240 places. Banding tests are held in November/December. The school operates a sibling policy, then distance from the gates. Makes every attempt to ensure parents understand that if you live more than a mile away, your chances of entry are slim. Last year 60 appeals produced only one extra place. There are 24 Art Aptitude places each year; applicants sit an aptitude test and are subject to different entry criteria.

All sixth form applicants, internal and external, are interviewed by a deputy head, who leads

the sixth form. Places offered on the basis of a school report and predicted grades. A*/As required at GCSE in the subjects the student wants to study at A level: 'It's not absolutely rigid – some students are bored at GCSE'. Year 11 students the school wants to retain are wooed with 'an extra bit of love and a series of suppers'.

Exit: A large number leave post-GCSE – 71 per cent in 2014 – for sixth form/FE colleges with different curricular offerings or work-based training. Whilst the school is totally comprehensive, the sixth form is 'an unashamedly elite institution' demanding A*/A GCSE grades. Lots of sixth form leavers to London universities eg Imperial College, King's College, Queen Mary and UCL. Others to Oxbridge (two in 2014), Nottingham, York, Warwick, Edinburgh, Manchester and more. All have one-to-one guidance

on university choice and a programme of visits, with time and effort put into personal statements and developing 'cultural capital'.

Money matters: Now an academy, but retaining its very close links with the Royal Borough of Kensington and Chelsea, it remains the area's flagship comprehensive school. Always well funded by the Royal Borough, this is now matched by funding from the EFA.

Remarks: A school which has gone rapidly from 'could try much harder' to 'outstanding' (Ofsted), under a dynamic and inspiring head. Now, once more, a model cosmopolitan, inner-city comprehensive. Suits those, according to one student, who are 'hard-working and opinionated, who strive to do their best. It's not for someone with a blasé attitude'.

John Betts Primary School

Paddenswick Road, London W6 0UA

State • Pupils: 237 • Ages 4–11 • Non-denom

Tel: 020 8748 2465
Fax: 020 8746 3571
Email: admin@johnbetts.lbhf.sch.uk
Website: www.johnbetts.lbhf.sch.uk

6

Interim head: Steve Owen, education commissioner and adviser at Westminster City Council, is in charge whilst a new head is appointed.

Entrance: Over-subscribed. Priority given to children in care, those with statements of special educational needs, siblings and proximity to school (cut-off point is about a third of a mile from school as the crow flies). Occasional places become available further up school but are quickly filled. Waiting list in operation. Some 15 per cent speak English as an additional language.

Exit: Approximately half to independent schools. Popular private schools include Latymer Upper, St Paul's Girls', Godolphin and Latymer, Notting Hill and Ealing and Emanuel. State favourites are West London Free School and Holland Park.

Remarks: Housed in a dark, Victorian, listed building in Hammersmith: forbidding from exterior but classrooms are surprisingly light and welcoming. Stunning new block recently added comprising of a reception classroom, library and ICT room, each with huge French windows opening onto playground. Playground is big enough to play a game of netball, though no fixed play equipment and a

bit grey. Redevelopment of playground is next on the agenda. Voluntary-aided school. One class per year of 30, with one 'bulge year' of 60.

English, maths and science taught to a high standard and foreign language teaching taken seriously. French taught from year 2 and Italian from year 3. Excellent reports about how nurturing the school is for pupils with special educational needs. All children are screened for dyslexia in year 2 or at point of entry thereafter. PTA partially funds four hours a week of specialist learning support. School employs a whole raft of support programmes. When we visited, numerous small groups of children were dotted around school being given individual or small group support. Currently 32 pupils are identified with some form of additional educational need; five pupils have statements. Gifted and talented pupils well catered for through extension work and master classes at local secondary schools. Masses of tutoring from year 5 onwards for those heading for independent sector. Parental peer pressure palpable as 11+ approaches.

Drama and music are strengths of the school. Annual performances, led by top year, are of an exceptionally high standard and are eagerly anticipated. Every child in school is involved. Recent performances include Oliver!, Beauty and the

Beast and Lion King. In addition, year 5 performs an annual play in French and year 1 performs songs in French with local French nursery. School choir is thriving with over 50 members. Children are encouraged to join the borough choir and Saturday music school. Instrumental music lessons given out of school, run by borough. Band and orchestra currently not running, which one parent believes is 'an issue.' High standard of artwork throughout school. School takes part in a variety of inter-school sports events and uses nearby Ravenscourt Park for training. Extra sports coaches recently taken on. Cricket, football, skittle ball and netball all on offer. Pupils swim for three terms in total. Although some parents critical of lack of sports provision – 'not well organised,' commented one, and described as 'an afterthought,' by another – school does provide more than the national curriculum requires.

Residential school trips for year 6 to Isle of Wight and year 3 to Buckinghamshire with a focus on team-building. School subsidises pupils who cannot afford to go. Varied selection of clubs available before, during and after school. Science, gardening, drama, chess, athletics, football and art are currently popular. No limit on the number of clubs a child can do.

On-site kitchen with delicious hot meals on offer. Compulsory school lunch for all pupils to make it financially viable. General consensus that food is 'amazing.' One child claims that the best thing about school trips is the sandwiches which the school makes.

Parents are very involved, through hearing reading, accompanying day outings, giving linguistic expertise in International Week, attending

General consensus that food is 'amazing.' One child claims that the best thing about school trips is the sandwiches which the school makes

celebrations and fundraising. PTA described as 'brilliant': huge amounts raised each year which go towards subsidising workshops and other projects on head's wish list. Fairly affluent families with only 15 per cent of pupils entitled to free school meals. Parents have high expectations and are not afraid to voice their opinions. Prize giving has been contentious in recent years with some parents feeling that the school gives out too many cups, leaving a minority without. No wraparound care available on site but a walking bus at the end of the day to an aftercare service based at nearby school is a godsend for families where both parents work.

A small, traditional establishment with old fashioned values. Feels like a village school, in the heart of Hammersmith. One current parent feels it is a great school for hard working children, though possibly not as good for those who are less academic and in need of plenty of physical activity. Others disagree and feel it is the best primary school in the area where 'children feel safe because expectations are made clear. You know your child is going to get a thorough grounding at John Betts.'

Kensington Prep School

596 Fulham Road, London SW6 5PA

Tel: 020 7731 9300
Fax: 020 7731 9301
Email: enquiries@kenprep.gdst.net
Website: www.kensingtonprep.gdst.net

Independent • Pupils: 295 • Ages: 4–11 • Non-denom
• Fees (per term): £4,835

7

Head: Since 2003, Mrs Prudence Lynch MA PGCE (mid 50s). Hails from Guernsey, studied psychology at St Andrew's before going to Goldsmiths to do her PGCE. She has two grown up sons and is a proud and committed grandmother. A zany, thoroughly modern head, from her boldly stylish dress sense to her dropped vowels and upward inflection at the end of her sentences. She also brings a wealth of experience to the job – previously head of juniors at Notting Hill and Ealing, a sister GDST establishment,

via Colet Court, where she initiated the SEN department, taught study skills, maths and 'thinking', a passion of hers. Here she teaches philosophy for children, which is 'too wonderful for words', where they discuss things like 'Is it helpful to have an unrealistic ambition?' or 'Is it ever right to kill someone?' She relishes encouraging them to think and listen to each other. 'Girls need to be as good as men at thinking up fresh ideas and taking risks. Spoon feeding is not going to solve a credit crunch no one has ever experienced before,' she says.

Keen to inject an element of risk to the very safe school she inherited. While she accepts that not every child can achieve anything they want, she firmly believes that it's better to go for the thing you can nearly do rather than the thing you know you can do. Otherwise what have you learnt? 'I, too, am a risk taker,' she says.

A touch scatty – efficient administration is not one of her strengths, something remarked on by parents – and she freely admits that she forgets things all the time, while hastening to add that there are enough efficient administrators around her to make sure the school doesn't drop any balls. She is a head with something much more to offer,

---

Head swiftly replaced the drab grey tunics with the cheerful electric blues and reds – 'I wanted it to be fun for them to get dressed in the morning,' she says

---

however – vision, a big heart and a huge sense of fun. 'I love playing,' she says, as she shows us her latest acquisition – a black rag doll that sits, rather incongruously, among the array of toys and clutter on her desk. Determined to counter the intense pressure felt by parents here and elsewhere in the

'ruthless' London day school system and trying to ensure that the girls still have 'dream time' and still enjoy their childhood. How refreshing.

Entrance: At 4+ more than 200 applicants for 44 places. Put your daughter's name down any time up to December prior to entry the following September. Assessments in January. Girls are seen in groups of five or six and assessed during play. 'With a heavily oversubscribed school like this one there isn't an ideal fair way of doing it'. Also an official entrance point at 7+ – register any time up to September the year ahead, but the number of places varies and may be only as few as two. Occasional places do crop up – keep trying. Expects most siblings to join the school, but reserves the right to say no if it is felt to be in the child's interest.

Exit: Almost all to what parents here consider to be 'the top' London girls' day schools – Godolphin and Latymer, Putney High, Francis Holland and Queen's Gate. Most popular boarding school Wycombe Abbey plus one or two to Cheltenham Ladies', Downe House, Heathfield, St George's Ascot and St Swithuns. Lots of scholarships – music as well as academic.

Remarks: Housed in a former Marist convent on the corner of a busy junction of the Parsons Green neck of the Fulham Road, the school occupies a wonderful space. Wide corridors, large windows, spacious high-ceilinged classrooms, broad staircases – institutional but brightened with loud colourful murals of, eg, clowns and kites. A wonderful library in the

former chapel, with stained glass windows, high beamed ceiling, some sturdy oak tables softened by comfortable sofas and beanbags – a soulful place to work and read.

The playground stretches into the distance complete with tennis courts, slides, colourful springy tarmac and a snazzy bandstand where they hold popular summer concerts. When the whole school is out here it doesn't look crowded, just a sea of bright colours (head swiftly replaced the drab grey tunics with the cheerful electric blues and reds – 'I wanted it to be fun for them to get dressed in the morning,' she says). At the ring of the bell all girls freeze in silence before filing obediently into their correct line ups – that's what they're like here, law abiding and conscious of the school values. They couldn't fail to be – they are prominently displayed throughout the school, the positive balanced with the negative, 'Do listen, don't interrupt'. (They sometimes trip up on this one – our guides, a case in point, who were bubbling over in their desire to please and enthuse about their school.)

A GDST with a difference. It stands alone, so doesn't benefit from the resources that come with having a senior school attached. No bursaries at all and fees are a bit higher than at other GDSTs. But the no-nonsense high academic standards you would expect, combined with affluent and demanding parents, make this one of London's most competitive girls' schools. 'We are good at fast-paced education,' says head. Parents here feel

DT and photography. Thursday morning is 'thinking time': 'What would it be like to have legs like jelly?' A whole afternoon dedicated to music and drama, another to music and art. We saw innovative teaching – the younger children on all fours marching round the room barking numbers one to 50. Computers everywhere and laptops widely used in every classroom. Year 6 create TV programmes as well as cook canapés, in addition to doing all the marketing and costing associated with the project.

Resident SENCo manages learning support, which is part of the package until key stage 2, from when it's organised on the same model as visiting music staff. Children can dip in and out or have more structured support over a period of several years, maybe just to boost their understanding of maths or to tackle a more serious problem like dyspraxia. However only mild to moderate learning difficulties can realistically be accommodated here. Mrs Lynch abhors the label 'gifted and talented' – 'they're far too young. It implies there's something rigid about who you are'. She infinitely prefers everyone to be stretched through lots of differentiation in class and the open-ended activities they do so well here.

French from year 1. 'Not mega,' says Mrs Lynch, 'but you get your "êtres" and "avoirs" and more formal stuff at the top to help those who go on to do CE elsewhere'. A relaxed taster of Latin in the final year. Class sizes of about 20, maximum 23. Young, (almost entirely) female staff who tend to stay for a long time. Only two or three men, including the recently appointed and much praised head of music, who has introduced a junior orchestra and won't stand for any waiting lists for girls who want to learn an instrument. 'We'll just get more teachers'.

Parents largely local – the Caffè Nero opposite is bursting at eight am with yummy Fulham mummies sipping lattes and testing their pretty

---

'The big freeze' had the whole school interpreting and creating. The result: swathes of tin foil around the school as well as a smashed mobile phone

---

hugely lucky if their daughter makes it through the assessments at 3, but we heard reports of a number of children getting tutoring further down the line because they want to ensure results. Our view is that this pressure doesn't necessarily come from the inside. A number of parents here want a seamless transition to schools they regard as being the best and are not always prepared to accept it if they are told their daughter may not be up to it.

Head does her best, and the curriculum is broad – lots of open homework and off piste whole school activities to stimulate thinking skills and collaborative team work through the year groups. 'The big freeze' had the whole school interpreting and creating. The result: swathes of tin foil around the school as well as a smashed mobile phone. Lots of interdisciplinary projects using art, daughters on their timetables. Dads very present in the school, too, helping with reading and on the parents' committee, 'We like to encourage that,' says Mrs Lynch. Lots of clubs – football run by a Chelsea FC player currently very popular, also bridge, Mandarin, Spanish cookery, craft, lots of music, as well as a host of others. School likes to keep a close eye to make sure girls don't do too much. 'Food amazing,' gushed our guides. Mango and orange red smoothie caused great excitement as we were shown the bright yellow and green

dining room in the bowels of the building. Lots of trips, including a choir tour to Belgium, trips to France, Cornwall and the Isle of Wight.

A vibrant place in every respect. Girls here are earnest and keen, immensely privileged with impeccable manners. A quirky eccentric, whether she is fiercely bright or not, could get lost here (school refutes this – 'we are absolutely about inspiring quirky girls as much as the more conformist') but a wonderful start for your robust all-rounder.

Knightsbridge School

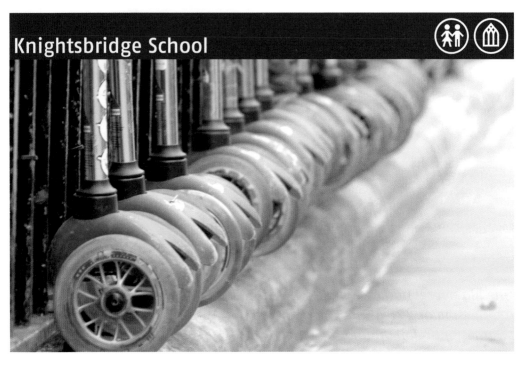

67 Pont Street, London SW1X 0BD

Independent • Pupils: 370 • Ages: 3–13 • Non-denom • Fees (per term): £5,408 – £5,755

Tel: 020 7590 9000
Fax: 020 7589 9055
Email: registrar@knightsbridgeschool.com
Website: www.knightsbridgeschool.com

36

Head: Since 2006 (when school first opened), Mr Magoo Giles (mid-40s). Previously head of Garden House Boys'. When he discovered the highly impressive building in Knightsbridge he decided to found another co-ed school in the community. So, backed by a huge amount of energy and enthusiasm, that is what he did. A natural organiser, not a teacher, he believes his ability to lead comes from his parent's nurturing, his education within Eton's hallowed walls (or more probably the famous playing fields) and his training and service in the Coldstream Guards. Parents say he may not be an academic but is

an excellent manager and a real leader. Has built up an administrative/advisory team to fill in any gaps in his experience and knowledge and to cover all contingencies. Perhaps his biggest coup was to bring in Robin Badham-Thornhill, retired ex-headmaster of Summer Fields, as head of development. His links with top senior schools and knowledge of the preparation needed to get into them is indisputable.

It would be hard to find a more passionate head; he wants all his pupils to be as enthusiastic about their education as he is. He wants them to be all-rounders and have a good sense of community. He believes strongly that all parents should be involved and participate in the huge range of extracurricular and charity fund-raising activities. Parents say 'his personality at the top goes right down the school', ' he sets a great atmosphere' and that he's 'a perfect role model for the kids'. Don't believe anyone could keep their hair up when Magoo is about. Does not teach but writes stories which he tells to the children, having created large painted MDF models of the characters. Not afraid of innovation, constantly looking for new ways to motivate, including some mind-blowing, parent-involved fund-raisers. Says likes to keep an open mind – might even introduce PYP, if it looked the right way to go. In deciding on a name for the school chose Knightsbridge School, not only because of location but also because of the initials KS. All children carry concertina cards around in their pockets. The school code, a reminder list of things they must do: 'I will treat others as I would like to be treated' etc and, most important, 'Keep smiling because smiling is contagious'. That's the spirit of the school. That's Magoo.

Entrance: Registration is followed by an informal interview with parents and child, who also spends a day at the school in the relevant class. Beware – your child will only be accepted once you have discussed the day together and all given it the thumbs up. Magoo only wants enthusiastic, interested children in his school. Nursery class for siblings only. Still some spaces at senior levels, but reception lists closed for several years to come.

Exit: A few leave at 7+ or 8+ for eg Westminster Under or Colet Court. Most popular 11+ destinations inclulde Francis Holland SW1, Queen's Gate and More House. Recent 13+ leavers to Charterhouse, King Edward's Witney, Harrow, King's Wimbledon, Portland Place, Bloxham, Emanuel, Latymer, Dulwich College, St Paul's, Shrewsbury, Marlborough.

Remarks: A school with great potential. After six years, feels well-established and an exciting place to be. Children and staff alike are eager and enthusiastic and, judging by results, seem to be getting it right. Could fly pretty high.

Originally the Hellenic College until it closed down in 2006, the ideal situation for a new school. Did not require an enormous amount of reconstruction. On five floors including basement, where lunch is served by smiling domestic staff. 'Pretty good food – sometimes pizza; Thursday's pudding day, otherwise it's yoghurt and fruit'. Lovely bright art rooms at the top. It's a bit of a ramble up and down different staircases, but children say it really doesn't take long to know your way around. Wonderful photographs and creative works displayed all over.

In the science room, when we visited, eager be-smocked children clustered together excitedly as a sheep's head was passed round – 'here, you have the eye now!'

Formality is definitely not the name of the game. Teachers are called by their first names with an added Mr or Miss in the junior school; they do acquire surnames for the seniors but, we ask, is Mr Magoo ever Mr Giles? Classrooms contain happy, interested children listening to their teachers, not necessarily sitting quietly but totally absorbed. In the science room, when we visited, eager be-smocked children clustered together excitedly as a sheep's head was passed round – 'here, you have the eye now!' Parents say children really love it and will excel because they 'want to go to school, want to learn, want to do their homework'.

A team of young, motivated teachers, average age about 30, ensure that all lessons are fun, interesting and stimulate a desire to learn. Class sizes no bigger than 18, average is more like 15. Location

tends to mean varied nationalities, so different languages abound. All learn French from nursery, a second language from reception and the top seniors learn Latin. A variety of others taught and all cultures explored but no doubt about basic Englishness. Parents love this and say 'best blend of British school system with international flair' and 'play hard, work hard for juniors; work hard, play hard for seniors.'

All children informally screened for learning difficulties in reception, formally in year 1, and any necessary help given from then on. Parents say communication lines always open, never any problem making contact – teachers and head always accessible. Also school stands behind every policy document – 'what you see is what you get'. Extra English support available for those who need it, but good understanding is essential to get a place at the school.

Good facilities and all mod cons – two computer suites, interactive white boards everywhere, laptops galore. Lovely light, well-stocked library. Excellent music facilities, with rooms for individual lessons. Orchestras, choirs, theatrical facilities with a great stage where all perform. Fully-equipped gym and big school hall for daily assemblies. It's all there.

No outdoor play space, but uses St Columba's Church Hall across the road for breaktime and Burton's Court (Royal Hospital) for sports. Two buses take the under 5s to sports grounds and centres. The rest walk – not unusual in London.

Some parents feel perhaps this is the one drawback, but the variety available is enormous and children are encouraged to try everything. The majority of the sports they will find at their public schools are here to be tasted – if they don't like one, they can try another. Good familiarisation and confidence builder for when they move on. Some parents love this, others wish they would concentrate on the competitive side a bit more. All know it is something they are working on and have total confidence that a perfectly balanced programme will evolve. Fencing and swimming given particular mention as outstanding. Matches in the usual sports played against other London day schools, and at weekends once a month matches against prep schools for the seniors. These will grow as the school expands.

Exceptionally strong parents' association which, hopefully, will continue to help the school in a meaningful way without interfering with the management – that belongs to the head and his expert team of advisers. An entrepreneurial school which is continually thinking up new ideas to stretch its pupils, expand their horizons and involve the whole family. As the head suggests, most children skip into school into school every day and walk slowly out of it. It is one of the happiest schools we have seen. Parents say: 'Good rounded education, strong academics, high quality teachers, not intimidating and not exclusive.'

Lady Margaret School

Parson's Green, London SW6 4UN

State • Pupils: 720 • Ages: 11–18 • C of E

Tel: 020 7736 7138
Fax: 020 7384 2553
Email: admin@ladymargaret.lbhf.sch.uk
Website: www.ladymargaret.lbhf.sch.uk

8

Headteacher: Since 2006, Mrs Sally Whyte BA French and Russian, PGCE NPQH. Formerly deputy head at Dr Challoner's High School in Buckinghamshire and assistant principal at Exmouth Community College in Devon. A charming, cheery lady who undoubtedly has the school firmly under control and clear plans for the future – Ofsted praised the 'exceptional capacity of the recently formed senior leadership team'. 'This is a lovely school to be head of,' she says.

Academic matters: Traditional, rigorous teaching produces invariably good results (English was rated outstanding by a recent Ofsted subject inspection) – 'we're now fully staffed with excellent teachers'. Everyone – except the few girls with statements of

special educational needs – takes a foreign language to GCSE and RE is also compulsory. In 2014, 75 per cent of girls got 5+ A*-C grades including maths and English; 38 per cent of grades were A*/A. English literature, history, mathematics, biology, chemistry are the most popular A level subjects. Art and design subjects also have a very strong showing. The sixth form is expanding with a new state-of-the-art building which has allowed the introduction of new subjects at A level, including economics, psychology and music technology. In 2014, 33 per cent A*/A grades and 67 per cent A*/B grades at A level.

Missed an 'outstanding' rating in the latest Ofsted inspection because of variable progress between subjects and year groups – the most and

Very strong sense of community, happy atmosphere, tightly regulated; parents comment that it has the feel of an old-fashioned girls' grammar school

least able have tended to make the best progress. The head, however, is beefing up the systematic monitoring of each girl's academic progress so no-one should be overlooked in future. 'They add tremendous value in a lot of cases,' said a parent, 'as long as the girl is not resistant to having value added.'

The girls with SEN – mainly dyslexia – are well looked after, with excellent targeted support. Very few with behavioural difficulties – they would be likely to struggle in the traditional, closely-regulated environment. 'Parents tend to realise that if their daughter's not going to be able to cope here, it's not right for her to come.'

Games, options, the arts: Art and textile design are popular and successful A level subjects, with a high proportion of A grades, and quite a few pupils go on to art college. Plenty of impressive art on display. Music 'permeates the whole of the school' and large numbers learn instruments. Plenty of ensembles and choirs –- a musical production such as Annie or Oliver! every other year. Inter-house music, debating and drama competitions. But performance space is limited – no drama studio or theatre and no drama GCSE or A level.

Not ideal for the sports-mad child – facilities on-site are limited to some tennis/netball courts and a gym (yoga, basketball and dance amongst activities on offer), though older girls use the local sports facilities. Netball, rounders and football matches – 'we play and achieve well'. Amazingly, 15 girls took GCSE PE in 2012 and four took it at A level.

Background and atmosphere: Has its origins in Whitelands College School, founded in 1842. In 1917, when Whitelands was threatened with closure, the second mistress, Miss Enid Moberly Bell, and other school staff 'rescued' a large number of pupils, who joined the new Lady Margaret School, named after Lady Margaret Beaufort, mother of Henry VII, founder of St John's and Christ's Colleges, Cambridge.

The school is in three listed Georgian houses facing leafy Parsons Green, with a gym, hall, impressive technology block, classrooms and landscaped garden beyond. A £6 million programme to expand school to accommodate four-form entry now underway and will include new classrooms, larger dining facilities, improved accessibility etc.

Very strong sense of community, happy atmosphere, tightly regulated; parents comment that it has the feel of an old-fashioned girls' grammar school.

Pastoral care and discipline: A traditional school with a strong Christian ethos and pastoral imperative

that includes taking on girls with health and social problems. A parent commented: 'They have an impressive record of nurturing.' Strict about uniform, homework and manners, and everyone takes part in collective worship in the mornings, 'though the Muslim and Jewish girls I know feel extremely valued,' said a parent. A very few short term exclusions, virtually none permanent. 'The vast majority come here wanting to work, get exam results and have fun.' The PHSE programme covers careers, study skills, citizenship, sex, drugs, alcohol etc.

Pupils and parents: The intake reflects the surroundings of this very leafy part of south west London. The revised entrance system has changed the make-up of the school. 'But there's still a critical mass of well-supported, compliant girls,' said a parent. Incredibly committed parent body, plenty of whom could have afforded to go private. Some impressive fund-raising goes on – the latest summer fair day raised some £20,000. Pupils strongly supportive of each other, confident, lively. OGs: Janet Street Porter, Jill Saward, rape law reform campaigner.

Entrance: Sixty-seven places (called foundation places) are reserved for girls who have been to a C of E church on a regular basis. The other 53 are open places. The main criterion is walking distance to the school. Everyone takes a maths and English banding test and is placed in band 1 (top

25 per cent), band 2 (middle 50 per cent) or band 3 (lowest 25 per cent), with places allocated in those proportions. A few places go to those with an SEN statement and looked after children. Very oversubscribed – over 500 applicants each year for the 90 places. NB You must complete and return both the local authority common application form and the school additional information form.

Those hoping to go through to the sixth form must have at least six A*-C grades at GCSE, including B grades in the chosen A level subjects; mathematics, languages and sciences need A grades. An increasing number of girls join the sixth form from other schools.

Exit: A few don't make the grade to go through to the sixth form and some go off for a wider range of courses – 'we offer quality but not quantity'. Nearly all sixth form leavers go on to university, over 40 per cent to the élite establishments over the past five years (fourth comprehensive in the country on this basis), including five to ten a year to Oxbridge.

Remarks: Small, traditional, friendly church school with high standards and family atmosphere in a quiet green setting. The social mix is changing but, in this part of London, it will always attract a high proportion of bright, hard-working girls, and the head is not letting the school rest on its laurels.

Latymer Prep School

Linked school: Latymer Upper School, 287

36 Upper Mall, London W6 9TA

Independent • Pupils: 160 • Ages: 7–11 • Non–denom • Fees (per term): £5,072

Tel: 0845 638 5700
Fax: 0845 638 5732
Email: registrar@latymerprep.org
Website: www.latymerprep.org

9

Head: Since 2001, the genial Mr Stuart Dorrian BA, erstwhile long-serving head of English and of lower school in the senior school who was persuaded to take over the prep, principally with the aim of upping the academics. He is a real enthusiast and clearly relishes his domain – its lovely main building, its river setting with the light that floods the place and the children who come to him naturally and easily. He still teaches some sixth form English and drama to his year 3 – so, a very nice job all in all.

Entrance: Roughly 150 compete at 7+ for the 40-odd places. They take an exam, half are invited back for

some science-related activities and team-building exercises and observation. Around two-thirds are boys.

Exit: Almost all move into the senior school, though 'entry not guaranteed'.

Remarks: Main building is the beautiful 1800s villa, Rivercourt House, which overlooks the river and is full of light. Retains cornices, elegant staircase, pilasters, columns and decorative panelling and is a privileged environment for small children to learn in. Strange 1930s building on the other side of the

small garden with maritime motifs, crinkle-crankle wall and outside spiral staircase now – once a writing studio – now The Seahorse Drama Studio. A further building, Latymer House, accommodates more classrooms, food tech, cookery and IT. It is all neat and cosy, though not over-endowed with outside space, and makes for a delightful prep.

All subjects are taught by specialists – we like that. A good little library, a large art-room at the top of the school in which we enjoyed clever printing and an imaginative project on the art of WWI. Photography thrives, music tech is offered and we saw lively work across the curriculum. All learn Italian for four years and, in year 6, they start French to prepare them for the senior school. Mr Dorrian insists that the years of Italian are not lost – 'they prepare them for the deep structures of Latin languages' – but it seemed a little illogical to us, as they can only pick up Italian again much higher up the senior school. We saw relaxed, absorbed, happy and confident little ones, clearly quite at home and busily learning. SEN support much praised by grateful parents and, in fact, we witnessed a one-to-one lesson focused on structuring and sorting and a very absorbed pupil with a lovely smiley teacher. Well worth trying to get Theo and Tilly in at seven here – probs solved until UCAS forms and student loans.

Latymer Upper School

Linked school: Latymer Prep School, 286

237 King Street, London W6 9LR

Independent • Pupils: 1,180 • Ages: 11–18 • Non-denom • Fees (per term): £5,770

Tel: 020 8629 2024
Fax: 020 8748 5212
Email: registrar@latymer-upper.org
Website: www.latymer-upper.org

10

Head: Since September 2012, Mr David Goodhew. Read classics at Oxford and previously deputy head of Durham School. He inherits a school in good heart and a considerable investment of trust that he will maintain its new-found spirit.

Academic matters: Results have steadily improved, though Latymer has yet to achieve as highly as its intensely selective intake would lead you to expect. A levels in 2014 saw 75 A*/A grades, with 33 per cent at A*. GCSEs were 89 per cent A*/A.

Newish curriculum looks both worthily innovative and imaginative, though some chafe at the lengthy double lessons – now 90 minutes long. 'It's fine if it's your favourite subject, but if it isn't…' Designed to improve educational value in general with, it is hoped, knock-ons for results which, while good, remain a notch short of stunning. A few parents of the brightest feel that Hawking Minor is less than stretched, but this may change now. Most teachers highly praised and much admired. Sixth form teaching seen as especially good – along with excellent careers and university advice: 'My son's tutor made all the difference'.

Parents enthuse about the learning support department, which is 'excellent and run by two most wonderful women'. 'My son can go before school, during lunch break or after school,' one told us gratefully. 'We don't pay for this extra help,' another acknowledged. 'And my daughter can take her homework or anything else she needs help with.' School reckons on around 10 per cent needing some kind of support, mostly dyses, a few ASDs; will lay on help in year 7 for temporary EAL if needed.

Games, options, the arts: Sport is notable and famed throughout the western (London) world! On-site provision is limited, though sports hall, fitness suites, pool and two tarmac courts find nesting room here. New sports hall under construction. Main school games take place 15 minutes away in Wood Lane and the lack of on-site facilities offers no impediment to the school's legendary prowess. Rowing and football are particular strengths, but all pursued with vigour and success.

It has few competitors, being the only co-ed with an academic reputation for miles around. The school of choice, therefore, for the educated middle classes, from fat cats to media types on short contracts

Four good-sized studios pump out impressively free and imaginative art across the media, and similar creativity informs the lively work done in DT. Very professional jewellery made in silver smithing club; two lasers, a furnace and a brazing hearth, even an anvil, enable skill and experimentation of a high order. 'We prepare them for a future in architecture, product design or engineering,' we were told. But also, 'it can be a fantastic release to heat something to 1000º and beat the hell out of it.' Quite! All take DT, art, music and drama to end of year 9 and then, somehow, choose. Music is powerful, with any number of bands and ensembles large and small in wildly various musical modes – from Latin to chamber choirs and a full orchestra. Outstanding standard overall. Likewise drama – taken seriously and executed professionally.

Lunch hours are packed with activities and all pupils – especially the first three years – encouraged to take on as much as possible. Quite

astonishing range of extracurriculars on offer – we counted nearly 100. Good range of outside speakers. Everyone drools over the trips. 'Amazing – far better than at my last school,' enthused a recent arrival. 'I've been everywhere – fantastic trips to South Africa, Egypt, Argentina.'

Background and atmosphere: You could miss it, crouching unobtrusively behind a low, gothic arched wall on the south side of the rather dingy King Street between Chiswick and Hammersmith. It occupies a rectangular plot between King Street and the roaring A4 into London (you don't notice the roar, we are told, after a month or two) under which runs a cunning subway, through which the children troop to the prep school, the sports hall, pool and, rather surprisingly if you're not quite sure where you are, the River Thames. The Latymer boat house nestles underneath (opposite the St Paul's Boys' one) and the school is a rowing powerhouse. The main building dates from 1890 (hence the red-brick gothic); smart newer buildings abut it now and the old tarmac car park has recently been reborn as an attractive 'piazza', popular for chillin'. Other on-site outside space is minimal but no-one is given much time to miss it.

The school began in 1624 and boasts a tablet commemorating founder Edward Latymer (a wealthy puritan, who pledged funds on his deathbed to educate and feed 'eight poore boies') – set into the outer wall, in piam memoriam etc. Old style main hall, complete with honours boards, WWI and II memorial tablets (always heartbreaking), stained glass and large portraits of former heads. Brown glazed tiles very much set the tone in the main building – smooth wood and big windows more the

and three floors of science, plus small lecture theatre. A pint pot here now accommodates a quarts-worth of space – cleverly done.

The site has been softened in recent years by planting with a design sense lacking hitherto. Spacious sixth form common-room reminiscent of an airport lounge with TV, sofas and vending machines. Sixth form also have a rather swish café bar – open to others too, but it oozes cool that would be wasted on the young. Dining hall serves excellent food, though lunch time is a crush. Organising 1,100+ pupils in this limited space inevitably results in log jams and queuing at all changeover times, but it's pretty good-humoured and everyone shrugs.

Pastoral care and discipline: Considerably improved under previous head – but then it needed to. Parents applaud. 'My son keeps being late and they make him stay in – which I approve of'. Veteran parents who have witnessed the last years' changes concur. 'The discipline is stricter now, which is right because things quickly get out of hand'. Some older pupils chafe under what they see as a harsh régime. 'If I didn't have to come to early registration, I could have an extra half an hour in bed, which would be of real educational value,' one cherubic sixth former vouchsafed, earnestly. 'They're very anal about stuff

---

> *'We prepare them for a future in architecture, product design or engineering,' we were told. But also, 'it can be a fantastic release to heat something to 1000º and beat the hell out of it.' Quite*

---

mood in the good new buildings. Performing arts centre, connected to older arts building by two glazed bridges, has enhanced provision in all subjects, especially music. Good-size, flexibilissimo studio theatre. Block with ground floor library (exemplary – has the feel of a top quality municipal resource but is exceptionally well-stocked and, when we visited, was stuffed with silently working pupils, who genuinely did not look as if they'd been bribed) like that,' a friend chimed in – while parents rejoice behind the cornflake boxes. School discipline is pragmatic and effective – 'Drink, smoking, drugs and bullying? We have them all, and anyone who says they don't is lying through their teeth'. Has expelled and will expel pupils if drugs are brought into the school, and the good of the school as a whole will always prevail. Likewise with bullying – 'we have an open culture here. The bully thrives on silence and fear. If a child is feeling belittled or upset, there is always an avenue he can go down.' And it's not just words – pupils say it really is like that now. Much praised system of older pupils mentoring the younger ones. The sixth formers sense a real change when they reach this elevated state – 'The staff really make an effort to get to know you and work with you... I've had endless individual help'. Boys and girls now wholly integrated and it feels like a proper co-ed – 'You don't ever feel the boys have been there longer,' a sixth form girl affirmed.

Pupils and parents: West London and fringes – most from within 30 minutes' travel, though a recent influx from the Kensington end of things. It has few competitors, being the only co-ed with an academic reputation for miles around. The school of choice, therefore, for the educated middle classes, from fat cats to media types on short contracts. At 11, around half come from state primaries – providing local tutors with most of their annual income. Parents praise much-improved school-home communication. 'They always get back to me quickly'.

Several actors among its famous alumni – Hugh Grant, Alan Rickman, Christopher Guard,

Imogen Poots, Mel Smith, Gus Prew; also heavyweight musos Walter Legge and Raphael Wallfisch, plus Pete Townshend's dad, who was expelled; a few notable sportsmen plus politicos Kulveer Ranger, Keith Vaz, George Walden, the Beeb's Joshua Rozenberg and local MP Andrew Slaughter. Also Heston Blumenthal, Dr Hilary Jones and Lily Cole. Appealing mix on Old Boys' nights, no?

Entrance: Most of the school's own on-site prep come up. Around 50 per cent from local primaries. Some 800 candidates for the 130 places at 11+ – boys slightly outnumber girls. Usual English, maths, reasoning and interview. At 13+, around 45 sit for the seven places on offer. At 16+, around 185 candidates for about 50 places. School requires minimum four GCSEs at A including the subjects to be taken in the sixth.

Exit: Everyone pays tribute to the careers and uni advice. Oxbridge, Manchester, Bristol and London are top choices. Increasing numbers to Oxbridge, US and other top international unis. A few annually to art, music or drama schools, otherwise medics, economists, engineers and linguists.

Money matters: Getting increasingly generous. Around 70 pupils on 100 per cent bursaries and more planned.

Remarks: Summed up by a year 13 girl – from the first cohort of girls to go all through. 'It's a really academic school, but not just academic – it's a real all-round school. I've loved it. I've had a ball.'

The London Oratory School Junior House

Linked school: The London Oratory School, 291

Seagrave Road, London SW6 1RX

State • Pupils: 80 • Ages: 7–11 • RC

Tel: 020 7385 0102
Fax: 020 7381 7676
Email: admin@los.ac
Website: www.london-oratory.org

11

Headmaster: Since 2007, Mr David McFadden, head of The London Oratory School in its entirety.

Entrance: Admits up to 20 boys at 7, up to 10 of whom are choristers. All applicants tested for general academic ability and for music aptitude; potential choristers also tested for choral aptitude and suitability. Priority to practising Catholics who

attend Mass frequently, baptism before 6 months, helping in church etc.

Exit: Nearly all move up to senior school.

Remarks: Not a separate school but a separate wing: the junior house, with four classrooms, a choir room and several practice rooms, as music is everything here (all recently refurbished). Officially it

is part of the senior school, but it is the part which takes under-age boys (7-11). Unofficially, it operates rather like a choir school in a cathedral school – only without the boarding. In that respect it is unique – the only state choir school. For potential applicants, who must be of at least average ability, musical promise is the only criterion which counts here, once you have demonstrated your Catholic credentials – all the boys have musical potential. Entrance tests in academic and musical aptitude.

Not all boys are in the Schola – some just follow an instrumental course. The Schola sings every Saturday evening in the Brompton Oratory. Junior house boys play every instrument you can name under the care of innumerable peripatetic teachers of high quality and use all the senior school facilities. They tour, record and give stunning concerts. A super start in life for your musical, Catholic, motivated little boy.

The London Oratory School

Linked school: The London Oratory School Junior House, 290

Seagrave Road, London SW6 1RX

State • Pupils: 1,380 • Ages: 7–18 • RC

Tel: 020 7385 0102
Fax: 020 7381 7676
Email: registrar@los.ac
Website: www.london–oratory.org

12

Headmaster: Since 2007, Mr David McFadden BSc MA (50s), a round peg in a circular hole. An Old Boy, began his career here, thence to Australia, where he spent 20 years teaching and, ultimately, headmastering. His previous two schools were Aquinas College and the Christian Brothers' College in Fremantle.

Mr McFadden retains an Aussie twang with a characteristic Aussie candour and relaxed confidence which we found engaging and reassuring. He has a clear sense of his school and what he wants to do there and, while paying tribute to his long-serving and much-admired predecessor, made pretty radical – and generally approved of – changes in his first, fast-moving year. It was not a honeymoon. He has been extraordinarily busy, engaged, among much else, in a huge consultation process to find out what the school community sees as priorities for change. This led to an impressive and

The Schola is a choir of professional standard: three visits to Rome in as many months, including representing the Vatican in Al Gore's LiveEarth initiative

far-reaching strategic plan – a massive agenda of 'things to do'.

Boys, parents and staff enthuse: 'He's very involved'; 'He's exceptional.. dynamic.. very approachable'; 'He seems to know what you're thinking.. and (most importantly) the lunches are heaps better'. We can't think of many heads we know who better fit their posts and we look forward to a further flourishing of this unique institution.

Academic matters: Parents and boys attribute the results to good teaching, high expectations and the discipline which, though too strict for some, clearly pays dividends. Teaching is assuredly excellent in general, though with some serious failings here and there. Excellent showing in English Baccalaureate, as already long established that all pupils take mathematics, English, three separate sciences and MFL for GCSE and a very significant proportion study history and/or geography. Languages do exceptionally well here – refreshing in a boys' school; especially heartening to see German thrive. A level results in 2014, 67 per cent

A* – B and 43 per cent A*/A grades. At GCSE, 84 per cent of pupils got 5+ A* – C grades including maths and English; 49 per cent A*/A grades.

Parents and pupils pay tribute to the 'challenging' curriculum, which makes a virtue of teaching beyond the syllabus, and to the efforts of the staff, who see strugglers individually and dollop out support and encouragement. The less academically able are offered a sixth form course in advanced business – a hybrid of two A levels and an AS, leading to qualifications in business and computing, a practical alternative to a sixth form college course for those who can't bear to leave. Classes felt by some to be too big, especially at sixth form level. However overall standards are high, high, high, to the extent that, in the recent Sutton Trust report, it was ranked top amongst all non-selective state schools, second amongst all selective state schools and 30th amongst all schools, including the independent schools.

SENs catered for – attracts standard numbers of the usual spread of needs: a few with Asperger's but no other ASDs at time of our visit. In-class help along with withdrawal where appropriate. Wheelchair-friendly and SENs seen, in general, as just part of life.

Games, options, the arts: Outdoor space is in short supply and boys are bused to Barn Elms – a round trip of not much less than an hour. Rugby is big here, with six teams in the first form alone and more than 20 in total – becoming more available to all. Mr McFadden speaks of 'heart and hand' – seeing the development and nourishment of all parts of a pupil as central to his education. Rugby

played mostly against the independents and at weekends, so a big commitment for the privileged few. Weights, water polo, rowing and basketball are other main activities at present; also a good, well-used, on-site, 17m pool. World Challenge has more participants than any other school in the country – state and independent – and sends boys on exciting, self-financed trips of a lifetime. Also popular is D of E. CCF perhaps the biggest in any state school, both army and RAF – tours, camps and expeditions of all kinds. Lots of sixth involved in community work – helping at local schools and care home, at soup kitchen on Saturdays, at the offices of a local charity etc.

Music is very big, fuelled by those who come up from the Junior House, all of whom have exceptional aptitude. Some 600+ pupils learn at least one instrument. Bands, choirs and orchestras thrive and are well-housed in the arts centre. The Schola is a choir of professional standard and considerable significance in the world of RC – and secular – music: three visits to Rome in as many months, including representing the Vatican in Al Gore's LiveEarth initiative. They record for films and TV and are regarded with deserved respect. They were one of the main choirs at the mass for the beatification of Cardinal Newman on the Papal visit to Britain.

School's on-site arts centre is an impressive asset and includes stunning 300-seat galleried theatre in which full scale shows are mounted – Pirates of Penzance in production when we visited. Good display spaces – a stimulating photo show by member of staff was good to see, along with a vast Paolozzi Brutalist sculpture. Pupils go on to study

Background and atmosphere: Founded by the Oratorian Fathers, 145 years old. It moved to its present site and buildings – in the lee of Chelsea FC's massive stadium – in the 1970s and has worn surprisingly well. Some rooms and corridors, notably in the sixth form areas, are dilapidated but, in general, the place was imaginatively designed and feels looked after. We liked the brick courtyard with its lead flashing. Newish block provides English department classrooms, learning support rooms and a function room to aid parental involvement. Has the look of a less than well resourced independent school, but the faces of the boys and staff belie that – an air of engagement and pride, a sense of collaborative energy and achievement which transcend the physical shortcomings and lack of space in some areas.

Some clearly unsatisfactory aspects – lunch (now good and with vegetables, though no sandwich option) is eaten in house rooms, which are also used for teaching after the metal grilles are rolled down and the servery disappears. Some year groups have no social space to speak of and are cramped and crowded. The large sixth form common room doubles as a fencing salle. Much of the school has a rather austere feel, which you couldn't describe as 'monastic' and, therefore, perhaps, good for the soul. We felt it to be bleak when we visited but, since then, the paintbrushes have been out and more displays put up, which must lift the spirits. Recent extension to and major refurbishment of main teaching block.

The chapel, opened in 1992 by Basil Hume and dedicated to St Philip Neri and St Edward the Confessor, is simple in design and has a warm and gentle feel. Major ceremonies held in the famous, huge, Italianate Oratory Church in South

> *Has the look of a less than well resourced independent school, but the faces of the boys and staff belie that – an air of engagement and pride, a sense of collaborative energy and achievement*

art/art history or architecture at prestigious institutions. But art/ceramics/DT etc not much in evidence – more of their efforts around the school would help the ambience and encourage les autres. No photography or textiles on offer, though both are available in extracurricular clubs.

Lots of overseas trips in the holidays – foreign exchanges, cultural and historical visits. Rugby tours to far flung places and singers and instrumental players performing far and wide.

Kensington. The Catholic ethos underlies all aspects of the school but not obtrusively or obsessively – it is simply a given and central also to Mr McFadden's plans to develop the community involvement of the school. Long-standing commitment to local primary schools and charities – such as SURF and the SVP soup kitchen – with sixth formers carrying out voluntary work and the music department involved in outreach programmes.

Pastoral care and discipline: Discipline is acknowledged to be tight – rules are strict and enforced strictly. Any mobile phones spotted on the premises will be confiscated and have to be collected by parents. Eight boys were expelled or left in Mr McFadden's first year after two cannabis smoking incidents. 'You need a clear-cut policy, but you have to have a listening ear and heart.' The approach is 'compassionate', but zero tolerance for physical violence – automatic suspension for anyone who tries to sort a problem by 'raising a hand against someone else'. House system encourages friendships between the year groups and boys in the sixth can mentor those younger who need support over a subject or a problem. Parents warmly praise the staff for their pastoral care, especially the deputy heads – of whom one has been in the school for 20+ years since the start of her career and the other who is a past pupil of the school. Head keen to grow the 'heart and hand' of each boy – to integrate his learning into what his life is about, both individually and in terms of his service to the community.

Pupils and parents: From a vast geographical area, most London boroughs, inner and outer – some leave home at 7.00am to come here. Over 50 languages spoken at home; serious Roman Catholicism

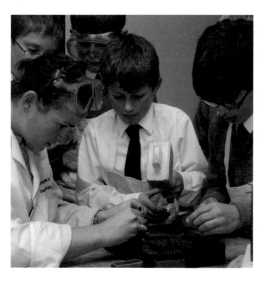

the only – but unifying – common denominator. Parents are warming to head's drive to involve them in all ways – social, educational and practical. Parents' groups for sports, music and food and more to follow. Reports are now termly and home-school contact far more a normal thing, though some complaints persist of parents not being kept in touch. Children appreciate the knock-ons of greater parental involvement and find it supportive and helpful. The boys themselves are relaxed, friendly, ambitious and hard-working. Classes are head down and concentrating. We heard no raised voices, saw few inattentive faces. Pupils have a sense of pride in themselves and in the school which one would wish to see replicated everywhere. The only boy who wouldn't like it there, we were told, was someone who didn't want to involve himself.

Sixth form girls are no mere modern import designed to boost results. They date back to a link with a girls' school in the 19th century and were incorporated into the sixth in the 1950s after a merger. Their numbers are small but, says head, 'They add so much to the school'. It was good to see girls and boys out and about in the lunch hour clearly in relaxed friendship and at ease – no cattle market or points system here. Notable former pupils include Simon Callow and Haley Atwell. Oh – and David McFadden.

Entrance: Simpler than hitherto, but heart-sinking for anyone other than an assiduously practising Roman Catholic family. In fact, don't bother to apply unless you are a pillar of your local church and known to your priest, who will have to vouch for your bona fides – both pupil's and family's; early baptism and Catholic primary education both essential. Admission process involves completing the school's Religious Inquiry Form and a local authority Common Application Form. Eight hundred plus apply for the 160 places. Junior House boys transfer automatically and parents praise the seamless transition. Sixth form also over-subscribed. Forty places for girls attract 200 applicants and, again, the RC credentials are what counts, plus 'expected performance at GCSE and suitability for an A level course which will be sought from each pupil's current school'. Likely applicants are invited to a 'course suitability meeting'. Girls join from Sacred Heart – virtually the whole year applies – Gumley, the Ursuline Convent and a few from Lady Margaret's.

Recently subject to another damning report from the Office of the Schools Adjudicator, which found it to have broken over 100 aspects of the schools admissions code over the last two years, using its entry system to cherrypick a disproportionately privileged and white pupil population. This, the latest of several reports with similar findings, requires the school to change its admissions policies 'as quickly as possible'.

Exit: Most (around 75 per cent) stay on after GCSE; almost 400 in sixth form. Regularly wins Oxbridge places covering the range of disciplines (10 in 2014). Otherwise to good universities everywhere to read everything. Refreshingly few silly subjects pursued

– these pupils have been properly taught and sensibly advised.

Remarks: Much that is excellent, but also much potential for building this school – in bricks and mortar terms as well as educationally and spiritually. Destined for stardom.

Lycee Français Charles de Gaulle

35 Cromwell Road, London SW7 2DG

Independent · Pupils: 2,469 · Ages: 3–18 · Non-denom · Fees (per term): £1,628 – £3,408

Tel: 020 7584 6322
Fax: 020 7823 7684
Email: inscription@lyceefrancais.org.uk
Website: www.lyceefrancais.org.uk

Proviseur: Since 2012, Mr Olivier Rauch. Degrees in history and geography from University of Lyon as well as Agregation (French civil servant educational leadership qualification). Previously head of lycée in Rabat and a lycée in Toulouse (which included a preparatory programme for the prestigious Grandes Ecoles). Started career as a history and geography teacher. Married, with three grown up children who live abroad.

Urbane and distinguished, he is confident in his preparation, knowledge and previous experience of running large French lycées, yet a touch of humility makes for easy conversation. He's also head of the three satellite primary feeder schools.

One of his major concerns is the launch of a new school in Wembley in 2015. He and his leadership team are working on the bigger problem of how to redistribute London's French school-age children into satellite French schools, and how to use the space this would free up at Charles de Gaulle – more student lounges, common areas and specialist classrooms. However he knows families worry how the inevitable change in location for some might affect them.

Another goal is to assess the anomalies between the French baccalaureate and A levels that seem to impede his leavers' entry into some British university courses (medicine for example). And if that weren't enough, he's also planning the school's centenary in 2015.

Parents comment that discipline has improved since head's arrival – he thinks this may be a result of his close communication with students via the student council.

Academic matters: Lycée Charles de Gaulle is the premier French school in Britain and one of the largest in the world. The raison d'être is to provide French education leading to the French baccalaureate, regarded by many as one of the most robust school-leaving qualifications there is. With many dual national French-English families enrolled, the Lycée also offers GCSE and A levels.

The French model has the following divisions: maternelle (reception and year 1), primaire (years 2-6), college (years 7-10) and lycée (years 11-13). In primaire and college, the school offers the French curriculum in French. From the final year of college (year 10) students either move over to the British section to do GCSEs and IGCSEs followed by A levels or continue through to the French baccalaureate. Parent perspectives on the Lycée vary significantly depending on their own cultural expectations of what constitutes a school education, but most parents seem to feel that overall the kids are well taught, learning lots, enjoying the challenge and loving the school's international community.

Primary class teachers do everything (including art and PE), specialists support IT and music. The quality of the art is down to the creativity of the teacher but we've heard of some great stuff with cross-curricular projects and older classes partnering with younger ones. Parents say there's 'frequent assessment and evaluation' so a struggling child is quickly identified. A primary parent with British school experience describes the French

With the French and Francophile population growing daily, it seems that the entente cordial is alive and well in this petit coin of London

system as 'less flexible, but of high standard.' Class sizes are about 28, with an assistant in each class. Classroom arrangements are fairly traditional, with desks in rows, though we saw some more varied arrangements.

College is another story. Some students entering college come from schools where the entire enrolment is less than the year group they are joining. Students move around for different lessons in what one parent described as an 'anonymous teacher environment.' Students have advisers whom they see for maybe 30 minutes per week and there's no expectation of pastoral care on the adviser's part. They monitor pupils' progress through frequent assessment and parents are kept informed. The problem is that it's public knowledge, so if you are bottom of the heap everyone knows, which can take its toll on the self-esteem of less confident adolescents. The survivors – and there are plenty who thrive on the mounting pressure – develop strong independent skills and learn to manage their time and work successfully, attributes French parents expect to see.

The French curriculum is followed in the French section for the oldest students (confusingly called the 'lycée'). In year 12 there are three French baccalaureate pathways: economics and social science, literature and science, where the subjects studied vary as does the number of hours devoted to each. The word is that there is pressure from both school and parents to go down the prestigious science route. Because so many students are fluent in English, many do a GSCE in English within the French bacc stream.

The international version of the French baccalaureate (which follows the French bacc curriculum but has more courses in English and leads to the same official French bacc exams) has recently been introduced, so it's too soon to evaluate. (Not to be confused with the IB diploma). Students join this programme in year 10; transfer from this programme into the British section is only available in year 12 and depends on availability of space. No 'bacc-light' – this programme reputedly demands an even heavier time commitment than the regular bacc.

The British section offers the GCSE/A level pathway. Students must be fluent enough in English to manage. Discipline is also an issue – nobody with a rap sheet gets in. Occasionally this route is apparently recommended for students who may not succeed with the French bacc.

Year 10 pupils do a wide range of about 10 courses, including French of course, but also a third language (pupils are spoilt for choice – Italian, Spanish, German, Arabic, Russian, Greek and Latin on offer). French IGCSE exams are compulsory, which pleases parents, though there seem to be some questions about timing with kids sitting exams too early.

In year 11 students generally drop one or two subjects as they get into their AS level and A level subjects. Parents rave about the maths, chemistry and physics, but suggest that those interested in the arts tend to look elsewhere (French education is not noted for intellectual autonomy or commitment to creativity, which are fairly fundamental for art). French and PE are compulsory until year 13;

Urbane and distinguished, he is confident in his preparation, knowledge and previous experience of running large French Lycées, yet a touch of humility makes for easy conversation

from 2015, A level French will be taken in year 13.

Deciding which route to choose – French bacc or British A levels – can be daunting. Those opting for the British tend to be dual nationals, non-French who joined the Lycée because their kids were in a French system and Anglophile French families setting down permanent roots in the UK.

The appeal of the French bacc is its strong global reputation, with its slavish commitment to developing intellectual rigour. But it's hard work, rigid, requires lots of memorisation and absorbing of new information. 'The French system crams knowledge into your brain – and we know the brain is a muscle that can be stretched,' says one French parent.

But some French students aiming for a UK university question the need to do the full-blown bacc when they can focus on more specialised A levels. Plus it's no secret that class sizes in the British section are smaller (about 12 compared to 28 to 30 for the French section) and the teaching style is more conducive to project work, class discussions and debates.

The French bacc classes, 'no wishy-washy child-centred approach,' are more traditional, 'cruelly elite' in a 'sink or swim' learning environment. 'Teachers instruct with minimal empathy. You listen and absorb the learning, which can be

a challenge for students with strong personalities inclined to engage in debate and, God forbid, challenge the teacher.' Then there is the matter of 'loyalty to French heritage.' If they move to the British section some families lament the move away from the French educational tradition, even though it may be the right decision educationally. British section kids have more time for extracurricular activities. Places in the British section are competitive; with the Lycée full to capacity, expansion of this programme seems unlikely. But more French students are considering the advantages of the A level university pathway, so there are more applicants than spaces.

Ongoing discussion amongst parents about A level results. The small size of the A level cohort means there are limited courses offered and timetabling clashes can prevent kids from taking the courses they want, leading some frustrated families to change schools after GCSEs. It has also been suggested that some French parents whose children are in the British section have a hard time overcoming the 'pedagogical cultural divide' between the French and British systems; they simply don't understand the flexibility that British teachers have in delivering the curriculum.

The governance and management structure of the Lycée is naturally focused on the French curriculum. For a British deputy head, finding a way to sit within that institutional culture is undoubtedly a challenge. Although the policy of rotating the head makes sense for Lycées worldwide, it probably has an impact on attention to GCSEs, A levels etc in the British section. Each new head has to get up to speed with the whole (and for them, anomalous) British programme, along with all the other challenges of running such a large institution. It's a steep learning curve for even a top educationalist.

French bacc results are excellent, above the French national average. The overall 2014 pass rate was 98 per cent with 104 distinctions out of 264 candidates.

A levels are by comparison less impressive, with 56 per cent A*/A grades in 2014. French A level results could be more impressive, given the context, although the school points out that students only have three hours a week for French and take the exam a year earlier than other schools. GCSE results show 65 per cent A*/A grades in 2014. Parents think this differential in results between the French bacc and A level has been taken on board by the head.

Although French nationality, language and heritage is the common denominator here, some kids are not completely fluent in French. It's full immersion, so if a child isn't capable of fully functioning in French by the age of 5, parents say they'll struggle when reading and writing begins. Others move their children out as they get older because parents lack sufficient French language to fully support them – unless they have a French-speaking nanny at home to sustain the French speaking day and supervise homework. English as a second language is taught from primary, with some setting for levels in consideration of the native speakers. In college, students are streamed for English. Other languages are available but no mother tongue instruction other than French and English.

For students with special needs, the educational psychologist and speech and language adviser recommends what sort of specialist might help manage the student's learning (dyslexia is not uncommon) but the school itself does not provide much support in-house. School has disabled access in all but one building but the logistics of the daily timetables and student movements mean that students with mobility challenges would struggle here.

Many teachers (average age early 40s) are civil servants, with professionalism and benefits for which French teachers are renowned. Forty-five per cent have been at the Lycée for more than 10 years.

Games, options, the arts: On Wednesdays, primary classes end early but extra activities like cooking, crafts, IT, sports and games are offered. Human Rights Club, Justice in the Heart and House of

---

Over the years the Lycée has spread. If approaching the area during pick-up you'll think you've alighted at the wrong end of Eurostar

---

Students are student-led activities the British and French section students do together, but French section students have less time to devote to these.

Curriculum-related residential trips abroad include India, Berlin (history), Paris (Comédie Française), Greece (classics), Venice (Italian), New York (art), Moscow (Russian). Compulsory work experience programmes in years 10 or 11 are organised by parents.

A few hundred students do sports, many on Saturdays at the sports facility in Raynes Park, competing against London schools and schools abroad. There's a school sports day but parents warn: 'Don't expect to get a ribbon unless you place first, second, or third..' Music is popular, with ensembles, orchestra or choir to choose from.

Background and atmosphere: School was founded to serve London's French population, but also to further France's 'mission civilisatrice' – making French culture and education available to the

Brits. During the Second World War it became the home of the Free French and the head sits in the office once occupied by General de Gaulle, so the school's name has meaning. British section was created 60 years ago to offer the French programme in English, but the differences in the French bacc and A levels meant that a marriage was not practical, so the British section sits within the organisation as a 'stand alone'. Over the years the Lycée has spread and now occupies a city block across from the Natural History Museum. If approaching the area during pick-up you'll think you've alighted at the wrong end of the Eurostar.

Part of the AEFE (Agency for Teaching of French Education Abroad), the Lycée is one of more than 100 overseas schools directed by the Ministry of Education and is governed by a committee including the French ambassador and other diplomats. Heads are rotated, with posts lasting up to five years. British section is managed by Kelvin Zane, dapper ex-deputy-head of a London comprehensive, whose fluid command of French has enabled him to adapt to this large French organisation. His UK experience is invaluable when it comes to matters such as child protection and Ofsted.

Facilities have been renovated to absorb increasing student numbers – a combination of inter-connected new build and Victoriana and using lots of cheerful colours. Buildings open out at the back to play area shared by all ages. Parents say 'it looks confusing, but the kids figure it out in a day or two.' Primary is in a building shared by upper classes on the top floor. There's a large hall for dramatic and musical performances, music and art rooms; PE is outside in the central yard, at local sports facilities or own grounds in Raynes Park. The yard has large canopies with seating areas to provide all-weather cover; no indoor play area.

A large library mushrooms over several floors, separated into college and lycée sections. Classrooms have desks in traditional rows. Computers in the libraries, study rooms and computer lab, but not much evidence of technology inside the classrooms.

Lunch is served in a bright, clean cafeteria. Youngest have their own lunch room; lunch is compulsory unless there are extraordinary dietary needs. Varied three course menu looks just short of Cordon Bleu by usual school standards. Considering that the chef turns out more than 2,500 meals a day, the food looked and smelled very appealing; fish always on offer for those with Kosher or Halal preferences.

School also boasts an impressive medical centre, staffed with sympathetic nurses and a full-time doctor. Parents are happy with home-school communication, and it's easy to have a quick chat with the primary teacher at dismissal. The formal

Parents prefer this more realistic reflection of society to the rarified atmosphere of economic privilege that they associate with many London independent schools

communication cycle is 'front loaded' with year-group parent events at the beginning of the year; after that it's up to parents to seek out the teachers – but they'll be in touch if there's a problem.

Pastoral care and discipline: With such an enormous student body, parents' reports are mixed. Some parents insist the kids 'don't get lost, are well looked after,' while others say that once in college 'students are a number and their teachers hardly know them.' For students joining college, the school tries to put them in classes with three designated friends to ease the culture shock of coping with the sheer scale of the Lycée. This is less a concern for rising Lycée primary students already familiar with the environment.

Playground attendants are a prominent French feature – supervisors keeping an eye on everyone. College students may leave campus provided they have parents' permission (most don't); in the top years most go out for lunch. A nifty school diary is issued to track home-school communication; the back cover has every student's photo, identification and timetable so anyone trying to slip out can be identified and sent back to class.

The children are cheerful and polite; primary teachers remind them about the importance of greeting people respectfully. No lockers – backpacks are stored here and there. No reports of any significant behaviour issues; everyone knows what is expected. If students fall short, they may be given more homework or required to attend school on Saturday. School psychologist offers counselling for students. Secondary school year group leaders have offices in their own sections of the school, with a secretary to manage the 300 or so kids in each level.

Parents warn that drop off and pick up can be stressful. By staggering start and finish times the school manages the flow of traffic pretty well under the circumstances. But parents need to be prepared for the possibly overwhelming feeling of chaos and confusion at the start.

Pupils and parents: The French connection is the common denominator. Eight-eight per cent French nationals with at least one French parent, 22 per cent dual nationals (British/French), six per cent British. Other nationalities include Canadian, American, Italian, Spanish, Lebanese, Moroccan and Russian. Many parents are in London on short-term assignments – diplomatic, financial services, media, industry. The generously subsidised fees (not available in the British section) widen the socio-economic net, attracting families who may not normally aspire to private education. Parents prefer this more realistic reflection of society to the rarefied atmosphere of economic privilege that they associate with many London independent schools.

Students come from all over – some with long commutes on public transport – but they feel it's worth it. In some cases the main wage-earner commutes to France or travels internationally but the family has chosen to stay in London in order to keep the kids at the Lycée.

The APL (parents' association) organises after-school activities, raises funds, supports the athletics programme and serves as a sounding board for issues of community interest. Some non-French speakers say it's difficult to become involved. Eclectic list of 'vieux garcon et filles' includes Jacqueline Bisset, Natasha Richardson, Gyles Brandreth, Lady Olga Maitland, Roland Joffé.

Entrance: Registration process begins around April of the entry year, with decisions sent in early May. Highly over-subscribed, entry is described as 'a nightmare, haphazard and chaotic.' Families normally apply to other schools as well; some start off elsewhere to await an offer. There's a priority list of criteria: children of French diplomats, siblings (in primary only), children from another official French school (locally or abroad), including students following the CNED (the French distance

learning programme), then any miscellany of Francophones fortunate to get in.

Siblings trump everything else in primary so families bank on getting one tiny first foot in the door, knowing the others are pretty much a shoe-in. One French national tells us she put her children on the waiting list from the earliest time allowed. Her eldest was unsuccessful but a few days after the term began the younger one was offered a place, posing a dilemma for managing two-school runs simultaneously. When she explained this to the school, they somehow magicked up a space for the second child.

Best tip for locals is to transfer from one of the official AEFE Ecole Homologuée nursery schools such as Ecole le Hérisson, L'Ecole des Petits (Fulham) or La Petite Ecole. Feeders for primaire entry include the annexe schools – Wix (Clapham), South Kensington, Ealing and Fulham. Year 7 feeders include Ecole Jacques Prévert, L'Ecole Bilingue, L'Ecole des Petits and L'Ecole de Battersea. For year 10 (British section) and year 11 (French section) it's the Bilingual College in Kentish Town (CFBL). Beware though – not all schools with emphasis on French language are official AEFE schools, so check the Lycée's website if you're banking on this as your golden ticket. Families do move on so vacancies arise mid-year, but school always refers to the waiting list. According to one successful mother, 'this is the only hope for a local family wanting their child to go to the Lycée' and requires strategic planning of Napoleonic proportions.

No admissions testing and once a child is in, parents have no worries about future entrance exams such as 11+ or CE.

Exit: The Lycée prides itself on its careers department, with advisers specialising in UK, US and French universities. Careers counselling begins in year 11; a major careers forum involves experts and university reps from three continents. Some parents feel more coordination is required to rationalise the Lycée exams and Oxbridge and Russell Group entrance criteria, and more focus needed on writing UCAS personal statements.

Roughly one quarter go to French universities, with 10 per cent of bacc graduates gaining entry into the Grandes Ecoles. British destinations include Oxbridge (six places in 2014), Manchester, Bristol, Essex, King's College London, Southampton and Surrey; American destinations include Rhodes Island School of Design, Virginia, McGill, Santa Clara and NYU. A few do gap years.

Money matters: A 50 per cent AEFE subsidy (except for those in the British section) makes for bargain tuition by London standards. Some welfare grants and bursaries – and APL has been known to rally when a family falls on hard times.

Remarks: This is a huge institution yet parents say children are happy, well taught and love the cultural diversity. The waiting lists are testimony to the school's overall success. With the French and Francophile population growing daily, it seems that the entente cordial is alive and well in this petit coin of London.

Mander Portman Woodward (MPW)

90–92 Queen's Gate, London SW7 5AB

Independent · Pupils: 600 · Ages: 14–19 · Non-denom · Fees (per term): £6,552 – £8,391

Tel: 020 7835 1355
Fax: 020 7259 2705
Email: london@mpw.co.uk
Website: www.mpw.co.uk

38

Principal: Since 2010, Steven Boyes BA, MSc, PGCE (mid-40s). First became principal in 1997 and now back at the helm after four years, during which he was working on a number of development projects for the MPW Group. Read geography and English at Lancaster University before going on to do a master's degree in management sciences. He has subsequently published articles on aspects of physical geography and is a textbook reviewer for two publishers. He was a senior A level examiner for over a decade and is a serving inspector for the Independent Schools Inspectorate. Was appointed chairman of the Council of Independent Further Education (CIFE) in 2010. Married to a lawyer, Melanie, with two children. A former county level squash player, he still plays a variety of racket sports and golf. Other hobbies include collecting crime novels and political biographies and crosswords.

Buzzy but relaxed atmosphere, with staff and students on first name terms, no dress restrictions and a lack of petty rules

Academic matters: You can take or retake GCSEs and A levels here, in one or two years or even a over a term. You can also come in for after-school private tuition, for a week's revision course at Easter or for extra Oxbridge preparation. Never more than eight in a class and those retaking in a year are taught in a different group from those in the second year of a course. Will run courses for single students but with half the normal teaching hours – 'If you're being taught one-to-one you whizz through the syllabus'. Some GCSE students are studying A levels at the same time; 34 per cent A*/A GCSE grades in 2014.

A staggering range of 43 subjects in any combination at A level – from ceramics to geology to statistics. The 'reassuringly expensive' fees fund a high enough ratio of staff to students to provide a genuinely personalised curriculum, with staff willing to set extra practice work when necessary or go over tricky subjects with individuals after lessons. 'And because the classes are so small, they can stop and explain anything you don't understand,' said a student. In 2014, 66 per cent A*/B grades and 37 per cent A*/A.

MPW stands or falls by its exam results and university places and a high proportion of staff are also public examiners – 'this can be a double-edged sword: great expertise but sometimes too great a focus on exams'..

Students get plenty of timed tests and exam practice. Parents are kept up to date with twice-termly reports and can also log in to see test results, what homework has been set and whether or not it has been done – 'particularly useful for those who are overseas'. They are also encouraged to pick up the phone to personal tutors whenever they have a query. 'They put themselves out to be helpful,' said a parent.

Helping students get into Oxbridge was MPW's original raison d'être, and it has added medical, veterinary, dental and law school applications to its expertise. Indeed, it publishes books on these and several other related subjects. It provides interview practice, seminars and specialist preparation for university entrance tests, plus detailed guidance on completing UCAS forms. 'The director of studies was very helpful over my son's personal statement,' said a parent. 'I didn't get involved at all, which was such a relief.'

Historically, SEN help was not high on the agenda. But the principal has appointed a head of academic support – 'I didn't want to ghettoise particular learning difficulties' – who is a qualified educational psychologist. Staff are trained to use academic support plans and set appropriate targets for students, such as always writing down verbal instructions. 'We're not an SEN school but I think everyone is getting something out of having a SENCo. It is a growing area of need'.

University of London International Foundation Programme now offered alongside A level courses.

Games, options, the arts: Offers fine art, ceramics, photography, textiles and graphics, separately or combined into a single A or AS. Art, textiles and ceramics studios, graphic design suite, two dark-rooms and a well-equipped history of art library. Organises two exhibitions each year, with work by ex-students at art college or university on display alongside pieces by current students and staff, and helps those aiming at art college to put a portfolio together. Art historians visit Florence or Paris as well as local galleries. Strong links with the University of the Arts London – speakers come to meet students every year.

A donation from a grateful ex-student now at Cambridge has re-equipped the theatre studies studio, used for extracurricular activities such as yoga as well as examination practicals. The Winter Ball is becoming an institution.

Sport is not a major part of college life, particularly in the sixth form, where it is voluntary – GCSE students have one compulsory and one voluntary session a week. However, free membership to the nearby gym is extremely popular and there are enthusiastic football and rugby teams. Netball is, by popular request, another option.

> '*Too often schools divide up the pastoral and the academic. Our tutors are a one-stop shop for parents – the buck stops with them.*'

Background and atmosphere: Founded in 1973 by three eponymous Cambridge graduates to offer small group A level retake and Oxbridge entrance tuition. Now greatly expanded, with sister colleges in Birmingham and Cambridge, it occupies three listed stucco buildings in smart South Kensington, where enviably large sums have evidently been invested in facilities and decoration.

Buzzy but relaxed atmosphere, with staff and students on first name terms, no dress restrictions and a lack of petty rules – 'You're not going to be told to do your tie up or tuck your shirt in here'. 'Everyone's very friendly,' said a parent, 'and my son really likes all his teachers – they treat him like an adult.'

Activity days at the start of term (e.g. study skills day, film school day) encourage students to get to know each other in an informal setting. Likewise communal activities such as bowling, ice skating, a college ball and in-house events such as an annual spring festival celebration. General studies programme of extracurricular options includes a college drama production, debating, chess playing and other choices designed to help the students feel part of a community and see each other outside the classroom.

Pastoral care and discipline: 'I feel they're actually concerned about you,' said a student, 'which I never felt at my last school.' Personal tutors, who have a light teaching load, are responsible for students' work and welfare – 'Too often schools divide up the pastoral and the academic. Our tutors are a one-stop shop for parents – the buck stops with them'. Parents are full of praise – 'They are very open to any kind of discussion. And unlike his previous school, we get lots of communication'.

Despite the relaxed atmosphere, strict about turning up on time and getting work done. Registers are taken at the beginning of each lesson and the registrar is liable to phone absconders' parents, even if it is 3am where they are. 'It is very difficult not to work here. We are a very disciplined place. We give masses of homework and you get a lot of feedback. The students always say that MPW stands for "makes people work".'

Will expel for 'any involvement with drugs on or off the premises', violent behaviour or even persistent smoking in the vicinity (fair to say that groups of illicit cigarette smokers were conspicuous by their absence). 'If you're clear about boundaries most will push it as far as the limit, then stop. Parents never say we didn't warn them.'

Pupils and parents: Virtually all from independent schools, around two-thirds from UK. GCSE students tend to be recent arrivals from abroad – 'lots of foreign students come in by chauffeur,' commented a parent – or those who have had differences of opinion with their previous school. A level students may have outgrown boarding school, lost confidence in their previous school or had medical problems. An increasing number transfer into the upper sixth after disappointing AS results elsewhere. Plenty of diplomatic and business families.

Entrance: By interview. Will never take anyone who has been expelled for drug-taking, but will consider perpetrators of long-term low-level misdemeanours or one-off mistakes. GCSE applicants take English and maths tests: those applying to join year 11 may be advised to go into year 10 to build up their skills or English fluency. A level applicants generally need at least six grade Cs at GCSE, with Bs in their A level choices, but can retake English or maths if necessary alongside AS levels. Those whose English is not fluent can study EFL alongside other subjects until they catch up.

Exit: Some 80-90 per cent of GCSE students go on to the sixth form. Around five per cent a year to Oxbridge – three in 2014 – and up to 10 per cent to medical/dentistry/veterinary schools – 'as a non-selective school we do very well across all subjects. We have good connections with medical and dental schools, and they know we know what we are talking about when we recommend a student'. Around half to Russell Group universities.

Money matters: Scholarships and bursaries of up to 100 per cent at all levels by competitive exam.

Remarks: Relaxed, collegiate atmosphere combined with a strict attitude to attendance and work. Small classes, great flexibility, plenty of communication with parents and a strong emphasis on what it takes to pass exams and get into university.

The Moat School

Bishops Avenue, London, SW6 6EG

Independent • Pupils: 90 • Ages: 11–16 • Fees (per term): £8,783

Tel: 020 7610 9018
Fax: 020 7610 9098
Email: office@moatschool.org.uk
Website: www.moatschool.org.uk

13

Headteacher: Since February 2013, Miss Clare King (30s). Has only taught at The Moat, where she started as an NQT and received accelerated promotion. Previously director of studies and deputy head.

Academic matters: Small classes (approx 10) and a learning support assistant ensure each child is given attention, especially during the first three years of secondary school. Education is broad – pupils taught lots of communication and study skills alongside literacy and maths. They are weaned off the extra help during the two year GCSE syllabus but by then class sizes get even smaller. Each pupil is issued with a laptop and helped to manage this responsibility by having convenient lockers to store them in between lessons (an example of the practical solutions to problems of organisation for dyslexics).

'A good range of subjects,' according to pupils, who all aim to leave with at least five GCSEs, though no language or classics teaching. All sit maths, English and science (many sitting additional science), but creativity high on school's and pupils' agenda since popular subjects are business communication, design technology, drama and media studies. The year groups and classes are small and so results vary each year, but of the 20 children in the GCSE year, 20 per cent or more leave with at least 5 graded A* – C GCSEs. Considering almost every child ends up with access arrangements that often include a scribe or a reader, this is no mean feat, but clearly The Moat is not a school for those primarily seeking academic results. Everything taught as kinaesthetically as possible – we saw a paper ball being thrown from teacher to pupil and back while being questioned – to help keep focus, keep energy levels high and pupils on their toes. Media studies and business studies are popular GCSE subjects – partly because they are ideal for visual learners with plenty of ICT input, but also because of 'brilliant' teachers. Teachers clearly working together – staff meetings, socialising, eating together, extra training – all evidence of a good staff team. Specialist subject teachers are trained in specific learning difficulties and share good practice via cross-curricular learning. For example, vocabulary is extended with a 'word of the week' programme that is used in all lessons. Concentration problems associated with

School achievements include productions in West End theatres as part of competitions (including Shakespeare for Schools)

learning difficulties eased by having regular break times rather than endless and confusing lesson changes. With many practical solutions to pupils' learning difficulties, stress is removed from the equation allowing for calm, purposeful teaching.

Because all pupils have specific learning difficulties and all teachers are trained in special needs, individual pupils are not withdrawn from lessons for extra literacy but instead an integrated Skills for Learning programme takes the form of small, cross-age range groups, who are mentored in literacy skills three times a week throughout their school life, working on specific areas of weakness. Occupational therapist available and two speech therapists work with individual children but also teach language and communication skills throughout year 7. Speech therapists run 'Talk About'

sessions in small groups to discuss how to speak in public, how to present oneself, how we make other people feel; these culminate in an outing to practise skills in public. Pupils particularly appreciated 'the chance to go out' and the female students especially liked their separate sessions and 'having time to talk about girl things'.

Games, options, the arts: Practical subjects predictably popular – science, media studies, music, art, PE. Drama a large part of the school curriculum with all children taking part in productions in one form or another. School achievements include productions in West End theatres as part of competitions (including Shakespeare for Schools). Sport encouraged but it is definitely not a competitive school and sport is 'more about keeping fit than winning'. Usual range of sport takes place in the playground – no large playing fields, though some rowing and yoga too, and tennis courts across the road. Music for GCSE but also plenty of individual music lessons – drums, saxophone, guitar, piano etc. Facilities for composition as part of music technology in GSCE. Gorgeous art all over the school includes collaborative and fine art (and lots of visits to galleries) but also wider design technology and resistant materials, and even film making. On our visit we saw very practical wood turning and food technology lessons – skill-based practical activities that suit pupils who have lots to offer, allowing for achievement outside the strictly academic spheres. Extracurricular activities are not an after-school option but each day ends with an hour of a chosen extension activity such as quilting, drama, cricket, debate, sport. DofE and residential school trips

each year, as well as much-loved day trips related to school studies (theatre, galleries, museums etc).

Background and atmosphere: Food is cooked on the premises and staff join students for lunch with vegetarian option and salad bar (only used by teachers according to one pupil), though predictable complaints by pupils about food – not enough, not enough choice, too many vegetables. Pupils and staff may eat together but the fact that no first names are used for teachers is indicative of clear boundaries and rules which include zero tolerance of bad behaviour. This helps keep the school calm and stress free, critical for many academically fragile pupils. Many choose to stay inside and read magazines at break rather than play football. Not really enough 'chilling' space, according to pupils, and especially for the girls who are in the minority anyway and who want to be outside but not standing around avoiding footballs.

The building is practical but dull, some areas clearly in need of a refit. This fits with the ethos of the school somehow – practical solutions and purpose more important than image. Even the terminology used is unambiguous – each morning starts with a 'gathering', Friday's gathering is for giving merits to pupils and sharing successes. The year book is called The Keep, as pupils hold on to these at the end as a memory of their school life. Pupils say they are 'respected for who we are, not how we look'; 'it is what's inside that counts'; and what is inside the school is respected and respectful pupils and staff, working together to achieve.

Pastoral care and discipline: Behaviour and control are evidently an important part of what is taught and learned at Moat House. Clear boundaries and sanctions intended to assist with the teenage problem of organisation and lost property that is exacerbated by dyslexia and dyspraxia. Friday litter detention for loss or carelessness with laptops. After three warnings for misbehaviour students are sent to the Referral Room, a reflection sheet is completed together with staff following the misdemeanour to work out what happened, why and whether an apology or other action needed. A serious offence (physical violence, swearing) or three referrals leads to consequences that range from weekend detention to temporary exclusion. Pupils need to be 'persuaded to behave appropriately', but if not, then it is not the right school for them. Pupils we spoke to found sanctions fair, but explained that 'it didn't happen much'. Understanding their own thinking and learning styles and self-reflection are encouraged and a school counsellor is available for children who are referred or who ask for time to talk.

Pupils and parents: Pupils come from far and near making socialising outside school tricky. Eighty per cent have statements and are paid for by local authorities from all over London. They are all dyslexic but come from a wide range of backgrounds and there's no one type – sporty, academic, shy, drama queens – all sorts sharing a common tolerance. They need to be bright enough to manage the expectation that they attempt GCSEs but academic achievement is not the only goal. Parents say there is plenty of communication and regular reviews, with open access to teachers – many of whom assist parents by emailing homework or notes directly if pupils can't organise their homework alone. All parents we spoke to raved about the teachers. Concerns by parents over lack of consistency in homework being dealt with by a

> *Everything taught as kinaesthetically as possible – we saw a paper ball being thrown from teacher to pupil and back while being questioned – to help keep focus, keep energy levels high and pupils on their toes*

review of the entire homework policy and strategy – showing some openness to criticism – and parents felt that their suggestions were acted upon. The school council is active and pupils use this as a conduit for change. Students say, 'Teachers come to you if they see you are struggling and don't wait for you to ask or put your hand up'. Many famous patrons act as role models of achievement, including Richard Rogers, Jeremy Irons, Ruby Wax.

Entrance: Entrance by way of careful review of a pupil's reports. The head will also take a view when the child comes in for an 'acquaint' day, and if the school feels they can support the child they will take them in even if reports are poor. Primarily a school for a child with dyslexia or dyspraxia, many also have expressive language difficulties. Many more interviewed than taken on because a good match needed in such small classes. Most mainstream primary schools, but also we met several from Blossom House and some from Fairley House in year 9, though late entry to the school a real disadvantage since the preparatory learning that takes place from year 7 all builds towards good learning skills for GCSE.

Exit: The school ends at GCSE; some parents and pupils expressed the desire for the school to continue to sixth form, but at present 75 per cent of pupils go into mainstream sixth form colleges or schools rather than supported placements and so the need is not there for this provision. It's a credit to the school that they are able to wean the pupils off special support. No data re where every child goes after sixth form but school suggests that about a third go on to higher education.

Money matters: The Constable Educational Trust set up the school in 1997 and continues to run it (one remaining founder governor). They are about to open two new primary free schools which, while not for dyslexic children specifically, will work towards early identification of learning difficulties. This is evidently not a wealthy school, it relies on charitable donations and fundraising efforts. Money used for education rather than capital projects – no stinting on school trips and outings or staff:pupil ratios. All credit to a school that spends money on pupils rather than buildings – though the buildings are ready for some input too.

Remarks: This special school is remarkably conventional in many ways – discipline, high behavioural expectations, solid learning leading to GCSEs in usual range of subjects. What is unusual is such innovative and integrated teaching. This reviewer found it a joy to see alternative ways of learning and teaching employed to such good effect.

More House School (London)

22–24 Pont Street, London SW1X 0AA

Independent • Pupils: 210 • Ages: 11–18 • RC • Fees (per term): £5,500

Tel: 020 7235 2855
Fax: 020 7259 6782
Email: office@morehouse.org.uk
Website: www.morehouse.org.uk

39

Headmaster: Since April 2014, Amanda Leach, previously deputy head. BSc from Liverpool and PGCE from Exeter; began her career at Cranbrook School in Kent, then a year teaching English in Rome before moving to Uffculme School in Devon to teach science. Joined More House in 1998 and appointed deputy head in 2008. Married with two young daughters. Her husband teaches PE and she has been a keen hockey and squash coach, as well as leading expeditions abroad, so life outside school tends to revolve round sport and the outdoors.

Academic matters: A broad spectrum of ability here, including many girls who would sink without trace in larger, more ruthless environments. 'I'd never passed a maths exam before I came here,' said a dyslexic sixth former, who now has a clutch of top GCSEs and the offer of a good university place. With such a small year group (usually fewer than 30), GCSE results variable. Thirty-eight per cent A*/A grades in 2014.

Everyone learns French, German and Latin in year 7, and can take up Spanish in year 8 or 9. 'We choose German because it's good to have a language that most come to fresh. They often find it easier than French and the year 7 activities week in Germany gives them a substantial immersion in German language and culture.' Everyone studies RS to GCSE, but no obligation to adopt a Catholic viewpoint – 'my daughter's an atheist and really enjoys RS. She doesn't have to pretend to have particular beliefs'. Three ability groups for maths, English and languages from year 7.

A level subject groups are often tiny, always fewer than 10 and sometimes one-to-one – 'we have a moral obligation to run a subject if a girl wants to do it. We're about encouraging them to find out what they want to do with the rest of their lives, so we won't tell them they can't study geography, for example, because they're the only one signed up'. The subject range is necessarily narrower than in larger establishments but encompasses five languages, including Latin and Arabic, RS (very popular), drama and textiles. In 2014, 23 per cent A*/A grades at A level and 39 per cent A*/B.

Well set up to help those with special needs. 'We're successful because they're not regarded as the mad relative to lock away – staff are well aware of their needs. A school like ours resolves these issues easily because once we have taken them on, we see it as our job to educate all our pupils to the highest level irrespective of their needs – it's our ethos to care for all of them'. As well as individual help for those with learning difficulties and ESOL lessons for girls whose English is not colloquially fluent, the school now offers weekly lessons with a visiting speech and language specialist.

Games, options, the arts: 'We've always had a massively strong tradition in the creative and performing arts.' Art is conspicuously successful; all three art teachers are also professional artists. Artwork of great quality, from life drawings to an intricate ballgown, lines the corridors. The sixth form has its own art and textile room on the top floor, complete with skeleton, and quite a few go on top art and design schools, eg St Martin's, London College of Fashion.

Music is also very strong. The school is too small to field a full orchestra, but girls from year 7 learn composition from a visiting specialist teacher. They play in ensembles and perform in the many school concerts each year, such as a 'fabulous' performance of Mozart's Requiem at the

A broad spectrum of ability here, including many girls who would sink without trace in larger, more ruthless environments

Cadogan Hall. The school is known particularly for its choirs, with an annual international singing tour. 'They rehearse really hard. It is clearly a professional music tour rather than a school trip with a bit of singing'. A sixth former described her tours as 'the best memories I'll take away from More House'.

Drama is increasing in profile, with a whole school play each year alternating between straight play and musical, eg Twelfth Night and Pirates of Penzance. 'We have so much fun,' said a pupil. School hall used as theatre, dining room, assembly hall and space for house competitions; also a dance/drama studio.

Pupils are unlikely to choose the school for its sport, but offers PE GCSE and A level, 'as well as the concept of exercise being a part of healthy living'. School fields a hockey squad for the London Youth

Games, running is popular, girls visit Hyde Park and Cadogan Gardens for lessons and play in inter-school competitions. 'We don't work on an élite squad approach to anything – we encourage everyone to take part.' Fencing and dance are optional extras.

Activities week every year, including D of E, and school trips to, eg, Russia – 'we went on the Trans-Siberia overnight. It was eye-opening'. Sixth formers enthuse about the 'great fun' they have at the Berkeley Dress Show, traditionally the inaugu-

---

'We went on the trans-Siberia overnight. It was eye-opening.'

ral event of the London Season. The only outside space is a small courtyard but activities abound at lunchtimes, eg cooking, keep fit, arts and crafts and movie club, as well as sports clubs. 'You're always so busy,' say students.

Background and atmosphere: Named for the Tudor sage and saint, Sir Thomas More, the school opened in 1953 at the request of a group of Catholic parents. It moved to its present site in two adjoining red-brick panelled houses a few streets south of Harrods in 1971. Around 50 per cent of the girls are Catholics and mass is held in the school chapel and in the church of Our Lady of Victories down the road – 'but our Catholicism is about service – about how we treat people. We don't see ourselves as an evangelical outpost of the Vatican'.

Small, cosy and friendly, the school suits girls who value its nurturing atmosphere rather than those seeking the bracing winds of competition – 'London girls' day schools can have a reputation for ruthlessness and I came here expecting it to be like a scene from Mean Girls. But I found a family atmosphere – the girls have time for one another and so do the staff,' said the previous head.

House system is now a central part of school life, with all the staff below deputy head level attached to houses, which field teams in competitions – sport, drama, art, music and even English and maths. 'It gives you a sense of identity in the school,' said a pupil.

Pastoral care and discipline: Described by parents as 'a very caring school' – 'The girls really are treated as individuals, with things tailored to their own needs'. Minor skirmishes about skirt lengths, with girls being told to wear trousers if their skirt is too short – 'the war of the skirt,' as one parent described it – irritate some, who feel that discipline on such subjects has got stricter. But most girls want staff approval. 'Catholics do guilt well.

We always distinguish between the behaviour and the person. By investing in their self-esteem, you get girls who like themselves'.

Active leadership programme for the lower sixth, who act as mentors for year 7s and run the lunchtime activities programme alongside staff members. They also have their own private penthouse area with two cosy common rooms, kitchen with coffee machine ('our favourite toy'), IT suite, textile studio and other specialist teaching rooms.

Pupils and parents: A diverse lot, more international than Sloane. Many European and diplomatic families, with Catholicism as the draw, alongside London girls travelling in from Hammersmith and Hampstead.

Entrance: Part of the North London Consortium, with common maths and English exams. Interviews everyone in groups before the exams, including a series of lessons to give them a feel for the small school environment – 'I'm interested in what they find interesting, what they find difficult. We begin to build up a picture of their strengths and weaknesses before the exam, and we're very interested in potential as well as performance'. A large number of feeder prep and primary schools, including Hill House, Thomas's, Finton House, Our Lady of Victories and the Oratory primary. Worth trying for places higher up, as international families come and go.

Sixth form entrants are interviewed and expected to have at least five A*–C grades at GCSE, with B or above in their AS subjects.

Exit: Up to half leave after GCSE, to co-ed schools or abroad. After A levels, to a broad range of universities to do a broad range of courses and destinations ranging from Bristol to Chelsea College of Art to London Met. 'We don't see any one destination as better than another. We try to encourage girls to recognise that it is their life and think deeply about where will suit them best'.

Money matters: Various academic scholarships, some aimed specifically at Catholic girls, and exhibitions for prowess at art, drama, music or PE, which can be topped up by means-tested bursaries.

Remarks: Small and nurturing school with strong Catholic caring ethos, that does well by girls of a wide ability range. Ideal for those of a creative bent who do not feel the need to compete in the more ruthless worlds of many larger London day schools. 'It is a lovely school,' said a parent. 'My daughter is so happy there.'

Norland Place School

162–166 Holland Park Avenue, London W11 4UH

Independent • Pupils: 220 • Ages: 4–11 • Non-denom
• Fees (per term): £4,185 – £5,110

Tel: 020 7603 9103
Fax: 020 7603 0648
Email: office@norlandplace.com
Website: www.norlandplace.com

40

Headmaster: Since 2002, Mr Patrick Mattar LRAM MA (40s), a Brummie (though you wouldn't know it), educated at Solihull, one of four siblings all of whom are talented musicians and went to various prestigious music colleges. Came here in 1989 as director of music straight from the Royal Academy of Music. He says if he had gone to an academic establishment he would have been more of an arts/language person than a scientist. A six-year interlude at Wetherby from 1996, where he ended up being deputy head, before returning to Norland to run the school when he was only 36. Married with two young sons. His wife teaches at Sussex House, where several boys move on to from here each year. Works very closely with his bursar and with proprietor Sylvia Garnsey, who ran the school for 40 years. 'She gives me a loose rein but needs to know what's going on'. Since his arrival a huge number of building and structural systems put in place

With his background one would expect the school to be heavily weighted in favour of music (he confessed to being secretly delighted when asked by parents to do a recital to a packed Steinway Hall in Marylebone to raise money for an auction) but he stresses that equal weight is given to art and sports. 'I've never been one of those heads who thinks "I'm musical and therefore want the school to be musical,"' he says.

Very popular with parents, who comment on his approachable, natural manner and understanding of the children. He teaches years 3 through to year 6 – current affairs, reasoning and some Latin in year 6. He has a good feel for senior schools and

Unashamedly traditional – boys are in shorts, girls neat in blue and white checks, berets are worn in winter, boaters in summer

which would suit each child, but says he will be as involved as parents want him to be when deciding where their children should go. His quiet confidence brims with integrity. You would think ambition might be making him restless but he clearly loves the job – 'There's never a dull moment

– and my favourite part is the children: they're the easiest,' he grins.

Entrance: At 4-years-old. Not selective, so you need to get your child's name down as soon after birth as is feasibly possible – preferably on the day. Parents are given forms so they can apply before birth and deliver it on the way back from the hospital! If you don't get it in until your child is a week old, you will end up on the waiting list. Mr Mattar will make sure he sees all parents who have places, so they understand the ethos here and know what they're signing up to. Children come from a number of local nurseries including The Acorn, Miss Delaney's, Ladbroke Square, Strawberry Fields, Rolfes and Mynors – no particular feeder. Siblings won't automatically get places – they still have to be registered and will be given priority on the waiting list, but be warned: siblings of a daughter who has left early to go to, eg, Bute, is unlikely to be given priority. 'There's no point coming here unless you want Norland and want it all the way,' head warns.

Exit: Pupils progress to vast range of schools. Boys at 8+ to, eg, Westminster Under, Colet Court, Sussex House, Westminster Cathedral Choir School, Wetherby Prep, St Philips, St Anthony's, Fulham Prep and the odd one to board at, eg, Caldicott.

Girls at 11+ to St Paul's, Godolphin and Latymer (head points out that recently nearly half the year got in here – impressive for a non-selective school), Francis Holland (NW1 & SW3), Wycombe Abbey, St Swithun's, Downe House, City of London, Harrodian, Latymer Upper, More House, Notting Hill & Ealing, Oundle, Portland Place, Putney High, Queen's College, Queen's Gate, South Hampstead High and St Mary's Calne.

We were shown bird boxes that the year 5s were making for their gardens while others bubbled about growing chickens in incubators

Remarks: Founded in 1876, situated on bustling Holland Park Avenue in three town houses connected by a maze of corridors and staircases, giving it a very up and down feel, but with two small-ish playgrounds and a plethora of outdoor toys. Unashamedly traditional – boys are in shorts, girls neat in blue and white checks, berets are worn in winter, boaters in summer.

A definite flavour of 'old money'. Parents here are terribly discreet and reluctant to be drawn into talking about the school or each other. Increasingly families come from Shepherds Bush and Hammersmith rather than round the corner, as Notting Hill becomes more flashy. To the casual observer it appears very English – not much evidence of headscarves and only a few brown faces, though school anxious to point out that it does not select on any criteria at all. Families here seem grounded, wanting what's best for their children without being drawn into the competitive London day school fever which is more susceptible to brand rather than ethos. Lots of children here had parents and grandparents at the school. George Osborne and Hilary Benn are among the alumni. We witnessed excellent rapport between staff and pupils, which was confirmed by parents. Senior girls are natural, mature and responsible but humorous and not fawning.

A wide range of ability. Children assessed for SEN from reception, when any concerns are flagged up and watched. Mild to moderate SEN can be catered for, but children have to be able to make the benchmark each year. EAL is dealt with in class, help often given before school. From early in the morning teachers are on hand to support and stretch those who need stretching, but a charge is made for timetabled learning support lessons.

For the more able ('I try to avoid labelling them as gifted and talented,' says head) lots of opportunity to differentiate and split lessons for English and maths in years 4, 5 and 6, but not setting or streaming. The ethos here is that children support each other – 'everyone has different talents'. Specialist teaching for English, maths and science from year 4.

Two forms per year until year 3, when boys and girls divide. Boys then get their heads down to prepare for the 8+ and one form for girls from years 4 to 6. French is taught from the start, with a smattering of Latin from Mr Mattar at the end. 'We're very good at not pressurising the children,' says Mr Mattar, 'while still getting the results.' Humanities has had an injection of energy with the appointment of the dynamic and greatly loved Mrs Hart, who brings history vividly to the present with dramatic interpretrations of, eg, VE day. We saw an assembly littered with bunting, every child waving a flag (including the odd German one), a number of them wearing hard hats and 40s style headscarves and the whole school doing the Lambeth walk.

Nothing is done on a grand scale but we met with great enthusiasm for what is on offer – only one afternoon of sport a week: football and cricket for the boys, a bus ride away; netball and rounders for the girls. Two PE lessons a week happen in the playground and hall. Swimming from year 2 at Kensington leisure centre. DT is incorporated into art – we were shown bird boxes that the year 5s were making for their gardens while others bubbled about growing chickens in incubators. The atmosphere of grounded traditionalism is epitomised by the traditional desks in the classrooms which, when opened, not only reveal neat piles of books but also colourful personal displays – photos, glitter, magazine cut outs – decorated by each girl.

A good traditional London day school that prepares each child for the next stage beautifully and punches well above its weight.

Notting Hill Preparatory School

95 Lancaster Road, London W11 1QQ

Independent • Pupils: 300 • Ages: 4–13 • Non-denom • Fees (per term): £5,510

Tel: 020 7221 0727
Fax: 020 7221 0332
Email: admin@nottinghillprep.com
Website: www.nottinghillprep.com

41

Headmistress: Since September 2003, Mrs Jane Cameron BEd (50s). Married with three grown-up children. She had run the Acorn Nursery in Lansdowne Crescent for 25 years, and parents there encouraged her to translate its ethos of teacher/parent partnership into a prep school. Approachable, dynamic, greatly respected by parents and pupils, 'terribly hands-on and involved,' said a parent. 'Problems get sorted out very quickly because she'll invite you straight in to see her.' Another said: 'She is the backbone of the school. She brings a committed energy and a genuine passion in the joy of learning. She is an inspiration to us all.'

Entrance: Has two reception classes; younger children are offered a gentler introduction with some shorter school days. Automatic places for siblings; the rest are allocated by ballot – separate ballots for boys and girls and for September to February birthdays and March to August birthdays. Ballot is drawn in May, 16 months before date of entry. Highest waiting list places allocated to those who signed up soonest after birth. Those successful in the ballot are asked to pay a £1,000 deposit 18 months before entry. Places higher up by assessment. Some, mostly boys, join in year 7, and there are one or two bursaries a year available for children from state primaries. 'It was lovely to hear from a boy from one of the local high-rise estates [who had moved on to a top boarding school] that rowing was now his favourite sport.' Can cater for some specific learning difficulties and EAL.

Exit: About half the girls and a handful of boys leave at 11, moving on to eg Latymer Upper, Godolphin & Latymer, South Hampstead, Harrodian, Francis Holland; or to board at eg Cheltenham Ladies', Wycombe Abbey, Benenden, St Swithun's. Boys mostly stay on till 13, then head for eg St Paul's, Westminster, City of London, UCS; or board at eg Eton, Harrow, Charterhouse, Winchester. Boys and a few girls leave at 13 for co-ed boarding schools eg Marlborough, Wellington, Rugby, Bedales, St Edward's. Music awards from Latymer Upper, City of London Girls, Winchester and Wells Cathedral Choir.

Remarks: On the borders of achingly trendy Notting Hill (Hugh Grant expected to stroll idly by at any minute) and grittier Ladbroke Grove, with tubes on the Hammersmith and City line and cars on the elevated Westway forming the northern horizon, and

On the borders of achingly trendy Notting Hill (Hugh Grant expected to stroll idly by at any minute)

Portobello market just down the road. The school opened in 2003 with 57 pupils in a 1900s school building (currently owned by Campden Charities) which still has the painted brick classroom walls and high windows of a classic Victorian school. Some Acorn parents found out that the property was available, gathered shareholders, and moved fast to secure the lease, and the fledgling school was set up within a whirlwind nine months. 'We got a band of great teachers together, some of whom still work here.'

There's a large hall with stage for assemblies, plays and concerts; art room adorned with clay models, papier mâché shields and a cardboard violin; small library with comfy sofa. A painted timeline starts in the entrance hall with dinosaurs and continues up the stairs and through the ages.

The upper school building across the road, purpose-built and opened in 2008, is shoehorned into an intricate space where a Belgo restaurant once stood. Wood-clad, with whitewashed walls, rooflights and curved ceilings, it includes a basement dining/assembly/dance and drama room as well as classrooms, science lab, music and computer rooms for years 4 to 8. It looks out one way onto Ladbroke Grove tube station and Chicken Village fast food restaurant, the other onto wooded slopes that border the tube line.

'I feel passionately that I'd like our children to be educated in the true sense of the word, but we also have to manage preparation for very narrow tests at the end of the road. We do aim to light the fire rather than just filling the bucket.' Children from reception upwards encouraged to express opinions, with plenty of small group discussions. Philosophy4Children and de Bono Thinking Hats systems used to encourage enquiring, reasoning approaches to learning. 'There is a real onus on independent thinking and this seems to give the children an enormous self-confidence and sense of self,' said a parent. Practical, fun teaching; year 2 was investigating friction and gravity using toy cars and ramps of books during our visit. Kung Fu Maths, a NHP invention, sees children awarded 'belts' in assembly for learning tables, knowing number bonds, solving problems of increasing complexity. 'The teaching staff at all levels are extraordinary,' said a parent. 'Their talent, enthusiasm and dedication are an inspiration to the pupils'.

As children move into year 4 and the upper school building, the pace of learning changes too. 'The early years are particularly gentle and nurturing,' said a parent. 'When they cross over the road they graduate to a much more serious work ethic. It's a very successful symbol.' Another commented: 'You see a real mix between academic rigour and the fostering of imagination.'

Non-selective system means particular needs do crop up. 'If a teacher raises concerns, the SENCo will observe the child in class and suggest strategies. For the first two years, we will give extra support and keep watching. If it becomes evident we can't meet the child's needs we'll discuss it with the parents.' The SENCo can give one-to-one help at extra cost; speech and language and OT experts available to visit.

Music is a particular strength. The school has twice performed pieces written by the 'amazing, hugely enthusiastic and charismatic' music master at the Schools Proms at the Albert Hall – most recently The Eagle, based on a Tennyson poem. Some two-thirds of pupils play an instrument and many join the choir, orchestra or ensemble groups. Plenty of opportunities to perform, in assemblies, concerts, poetry recitals, school plays – Hansel and Gretel was under rehearsal during our visit. Art imaginative and inspiring.

Sport was the only area picked out as a weaker link in last ISI report; Jane Cameron acknowledges the challenges a new-ish school (and particularly a co-ed one) faces in setting up a fixture list. Football (boys' and girls'), rugby, netball, cricket and rounders matches played with varying degrees of success;

the swimming squad is apparently 'second to none'. Compact playground, so sport involves travelling: most matches, and many sports lessons, at the Linford Christie stadium; they also use the Westway Sports Centre and Kensington Leisure Centre.

Clubs range from Greek to chess to netball to lateral thinking; they make good use of London, with trips down the Thames, to a Hindu temple, to City Hall and the Olympic site; they go off to Normandy, skiing, on outdoor pursuits courses and field trips.

Much parental involvement, whether helping in the library, giving a talk on the nature of consciousness or on Leonardo da Vinci, giving a violin recital or running a crafts workshop. 'There is a constant stream of authors, musicians, journalists, actors and artists, not only dropping off and collecting their children, but generously volunteering their time and talent by speaking at assemblies and judging various competitions, such as poetry and public speaking,' commented a parent.

Great parental praise for the 'pervasive caring ethos' of the school. 'The NHP community is one in which the children show an enormous and unusual amount of empathy.' 'Every child feels valued, and different talents are truly celebrated. Children take great pride in the achievements of their peers, not only academically but in music, art and extracurricular areas.' 'Altruistic behaviour happens all the time. It is the way things work at NHP and what we treasure most.' 'We feel indebted to NHP for giving our children a love of learning, a sense of belonging and pride.'

Our Lady of Victories RC Primary School

Clareville Street, London SW7 5AQ

State • Pupils: 240 • Ages: 3–11 • RC

Tel: 020 7373 4491
Fax: 020 7244 0591
Email: sarah.mcbennett@olov.rbkc.sch.uk
Website: www.olov.rbkc.sch.uk/

42

Headteacher: Since 2007 Mrs Sarah McBennett BEd (forties). After university in Belfast, started her career in education and has taught children across the primary age range from reception to year 6. These days she is mainly managerial and tends only to teach to cover staff absences. Formerly head of primary section of an international community school in Jordan, then deputy at a large Catholic primary in Kent. Something of a whizz with the budget, parents tell us, she works extremely hard for the school and puts in many extra hours.

Committed and kindly personality, with an open door policy, always happy to spend time talking to parents, pupils and staff. Supported by a long-serving deputy head, school secretary and lively PTA.

Entrance: Pupils come from the parishes of Our Lady of Victories, Our Lady of Mount Carmel and St Simon Stock. Priority goes to baptised, practising Catholics; all applications must be supported by letter from the parish priest. Where possible siblings get priority followed by those living closest to

Younger horticulturalists grow many colourful flowers and shrubs

the school. Children attending the nursery are not automatically guaranteed a place in the reception class, which is always oversubscribed. Contact the school for occasional places in older age groups.

Exit: To state schools and independents in many different directions. Coeds St Thomas More, Holland Park, Emanuel, St Benedict's, Latymer Upper. Boys, London Oratory, Cardinal Vaughan, independents Westminster, St Paul's, Dulwich College and City of London Boys. Girls, Sacred Heart, Hammersmith, Gumley House, independents More House, Queensgate, Francis Holland, Godolphin and Latymer. A few to Catholic boarding schools eg St Mary's Ascot, Worth and Ampleforth.

Remarks: Very high standards across the curriculum continue to make this a successful and sought-after primary. All teaching is graded outstanding. Lots of attention to detail, personal successes, the pupils are encouraged to take pride in everything they do. Continuous assessment and monitoring ensure everybody reaches their potential, and those who need additional support are identified. Parents tell us enthusiastic staff always want to make sure the children really enjoy themselves and develop socially as well as academically. School aims to pick up SEN early; pupils are supported by differentiated teaching, specialist teachers and therapists in small groups or one-to-one. International clientele so lots of EAL tuition for those who need.

Tall Victorian buildings with lots of stairs, however, good-sized classrooms, beautifully decorated; the school has gold Artsmark. Displays show that even the tiny children have beautiful handwriting. Nursery and reception classes have been redesigned so 3 to 5-year-olds are taught in a large, open plan space with its own playground. French starts at key stage 2, other languages via clubs, year 6 have French penfriends and make an annual trip to Cannes. Sadly, Latin has disappeared from the curriculum. After-school verbal reasoning club in the run-up to 11+ exams. Inner city location means outdoor spaces are tight, but they are well-maintained and decorated with mosaics made by the children. Younger horticulturalists grow many colourful flowers and shrubs through the gardening club which they organise themselves.

The school has a Sportsmark; multi-purpose hall is large enough for short tennis, gymnastics and ballet lessons. Outdoor sports take place at Battersea Park; professional coaches, including ex-Middlesex cricketer, teach good range of team games. Specialist teachers for both art and music, pupils can have individual instrumental tuition on a range of five different instruments, and often join the young musician's performances at the Albert Hall. Enticing range of extracurricular activities, clubs, trips and special visitors; year 5 can complete their cycling proficiency certificates at school.

Parents say pastoral care is very good and inclusive, the weekly newsletter keeps everybody up-to-date with events and pupils are given a voice through the school council which meets regularly with the deputy head. Food is often on the agenda, as the school has Food for Life Award, everything is cooked on site and where possible locally sourced. Encouraged to be involved in the school community, parents run cookery classes, listen to readers and raise large amounts of money which go towards paying for improvements and equipment for the school as well as for outside charities. Catholic beliefs remain at the heart of the warm, family atmosphere of the school. First rate and first choice school for Catholic families in Kensington.

Pembridge Hall School

18 Pembridge Square, London W2 4EH

Independent • Pupils: 400 • Ages: 4–11 • Non-denom • Fees (per term): £5,820

Tel: 020 7229 0121
Fax: 020 7792 1086
Email: contact@pembridgehall.co.uk
Website: www.pembridgehall.co.uk

43

Headmaster: Since September 2012, Mr Henry Keighley-Elstub BA (Hons) PGCE (early 40s). Appointed in November 2011, succeeding Barry Evans who only served for five terms before taking early retirement. Fran Baylis acted as interim head while Mr Keighley-Elstub served out his notice at Wetherby Prep where he was deputy head. Educated at Eton and Leeds University, where he read classical civilization. He has taught history at Ludgrove, Cothill and Chesham Prep where he was head of department and also senior master. As well as this being his first headship, it is also his first experience of an all girls' school, and one that finishes at 11 years rather than 13. 'I was worried about that at first,' he admits, 'but now I barely notice, and communicating with an 11-year-old girl is equivalent to talking to a 13-year-old boy.' Married to Sarah who works at IBM ('I have no idea what she does', he confides. 'Perhaps she's a spy.') They have recently had a daughter.

Mr Keighley-Elstub, though slight of build, has an immediately warm, engaging and enthusiastic personality that makes even the stiffest person unfurl. His conversation is littered with verbs and adjectives like 'skip along' and 'groovy'. His upbeat chipper approach is directed at everyone. As well as the girls, the parents and the teachers it embraces the peripatetic music staff, games staff and the odd visitor. Despite being an Old Etonian with an unusually complicated name both to spell and pronounce

Parent volunteers and staff recently collaborated to run a very successful lettuce planting project for the UNICEF Day for Change

(think 'Keighly'), Mr Keighley-Elstub is remarkably down to earth. He attributes this to his Northern pedigree (his father was a Yorkshireman but practised as a GP in Wimbledon where Mr Keighley-Elstub grew up). His family used to turn up at Eton in a clapped out old VW, but 'that wasn't remotely embarrassing,' he avers. 'Eton's not smart at all. The greatest compliment anyone could pay me,' he continues, 'is to turn up to meet me in jeans.' If he weren't so refreshingly open you wouldn't guess it – he looks immaculate in his well-cut suit and playfully shrieks when he discovers the odd crisp on the floor in a classroom.

He loves music – his wife is a violinist and he has recently formed a staff choir. He is also an enthusiastic sportsman (running is his thing) and he is determined that the girls here start winning some matches for a change. He champions all departments – art, music, sport and drama – equally and works to get them all to enjoy working together rather than being at loggerheads as happens so often. He is relishing the challenges of his first headship and is not unaware of the benefits of running a school that is part of the Alpha Plus group. He talks of the wealth of resources available to him, from legal to financial as well as the supportive but 'hands off' nature of the governing body. Although ambitious with lots of energy, he is clearly here to stay for some time – 'I couldn't leave while there is still so much to do,' he says. 'I want to transform a good school into an outstanding one'.

Entrance: Names down at birth – 'but realistically that means within two weeks of birth,' says head. He is keen to dispel the myth that you need to plan a Caesarean and father needs to put the form through the letter box as the baby arrives. It absolutely makes no difference at all on what day of the month your child is born. They divide the months into thirds and take an equal number from each third. Non-refundable registration fee (currently £150) does not guarantee you a tour of the school. Personal tours with the head offered as soon as you are off the waiting list and offered a place (something Mr Keighley-Elstub has recently introduced – prior to his arrival tours with a member of staff offered at deposit decision time – close to starting). The competitive market (for children more than the schools) and wealthy catchment of West London means that parents don't blink at paying these sort of sums without even being given the chance to see the school before making a decision. The alternative to long waiting lists is a selection process at 3, and that would mean 'we may miss the wild wacky ones that add colour to the place,' says Mr Keighley-Elstub. Nevertheless, close liaison with feeder nurseries (he mentioned The Acorn, Rolfe's, Strawberry Fields, Minors and Ladbroke Square) to make sure girls will manage.

Exit: Plenty of scholarships, academic, sporting as well as well as musical and artistic, each year and fine boards in the upper school hall to commemorate them. A number of offers each year are made from the prestigious academic girls' day schools in London (10 from City of London Girls this year – none of which were accepted), St Paul's, Godolphin & Latymer, Francis Holland (Clarence Gate favoured by these parents more than Sloane Square), as well as the less academic like Queen's College and St James. Parents starting to show an interest in a refreshingly more diverse mixture of schools, The West London Free School for example, as well as North London Collegiate and South Hampstead. Boarding schools tend to the be of the all girls variety, Downe House, St Mary's (both Calne and Ascot), Wycombe Abbey, Sherborne, Benenden etc. Mr Keighley-Elstub encouraging boarding school – or at least opening the parents' eyes to it, as the international flavour of parents here tend to prefer the day options.

Remarks: Situated in a particularly leafy, white stucco square in Notting Hill Gate, the lower school is in a tall building a minutes' walk from an identical building containing the upper school. In between is Wetherby pre-prep – the boys'

equivalent – and also owned by the Alpha Plus group. In the basement of number 10 (the Upper School) is Minors Nursery – another Alpha Plus establishment: no wonder such direct communication about the character and ability of the girls can be made.

Round the corner in St Petersburg Place is the splendid St Matthew's Church where whole school assemblies take place each week. We joined a river of red blazered and straw boatered girls as they walked immaculately to the church. An overwhelmingly white collection of girls for such a multicultural part of London; they are international – American, Russian, European as well – but only about 10 out of 400 girls receive EAL help. Mr Keighley-Elstub described the ethos as 'lightly Anglican' but a very English education, which seemed to be requirement of even the most foreign of families.

Girls here are well spoken, eager to please and confident. Lots of awards and prizes and opportunities to speak publicly and take responsibility to build that confidence. We were particularly impressed with an astonishing game designed by a 10-year-old girl out of a cardboard box, which

We were particularly impressed with an astonishing game designed by a 10-year-old girl out of a cardboard box, which intricately displayed the planets and included chance and question cards which she had devised herself

intricately displayed the planets and included chance and question cards which she had devised herself. She then explained through a microphone how to play the game to an audience of about 450 people in the church, including parents as well as teachers and children.

Classrooms spacious, bright and airy with wonderful high ceilings and tall windows. Lovely wide corridors and staircases that seem to go up and up for ever. Lush red carpet (to match the uniform?) in the lower school, upper school mirrors the lower school but in blue. We saw some very impressive still life work in the very studio-like space at the top of the school, which had brilliant ceiling windows, creating an excellent space to be creative. Well-equipped science labs in the basement with a good old-fashioned full-sized skeleton in the corner. Super space in the basement for drama and productions with a wealth of colourful and imaginative

costumes and hats. All years get a chance to perform: year 5 do a Shakespearean medley, year 6 do their annual play in the local Tabernacle Theatre. Both buildings have large halls which double as dining rooms at lunch time. Wide choice of healthy cooked lunches and imaginative fruit (watermelon and pineapple – not just your regular apples and bananas). How refreshing not to see children eating packed lunches at their desks.

Healthy number of male teachers and the arrival of Mr Keighley-Elstub has seen barely any staff turnover at all. He feels proud of having injected renewed energy and purpose into the place and acknowledges that when he arrived there was a lot of reassurance to be done. Parents were rattled and there was a lack of direction. Those we spoke to referred to a terrible lack of communication. Many considered moving their daughters but remarkably few did, explaining that the pastoral care remained excellent throughout and they didn't want to uproot a happy child. Emphasis is now on communication – particularly with parents; improvement and consolidation of the academics; and improvement of sport.

Girls are starting to win netball matches now – and we were proudly told of how they beat Glendower recently. Netball and hockey played in nearby Avondale Park and Holland Park, athletics at the Linford Christie stadium in Wood Lane and swimming at the Porchester Baths. Plenty of inter-house matches so that everyone can have a go. Tennis as a club rather than a school sport, and rounders possibly on its way out. 'I don't see the point of it,' says Mr Keighley Elstub. 'It's rather a poor man's cricket'. He is very open to the idea of introducing football and cricket for the girls but so far there doesn't seem to be the demand. Several outside spaces in both buildings for fresh air between lessons and 'unless there's the threat of a tornado out they go,' says head, who can't understand why the girls have been treated with such velvet gloves in the past, with the mere threat of rain resulting in their reading inside.

Three classes of 20 in each year. Setting only in maths from year 3. Serious preparation for the 11 plus starts in year 5 but the groundwork is now being laid much earlier. Mr Keighley–Elstub teaches years 5 and 6 so he can give well informed advice about schools. He is not afraid to tell a parent if they are being overly ambitious academically but

will look at the whole child and advise which is the most appropriate school on that basis. Vast majority of parents here are in finance – though the odd one is glamorously famous, you wouldn't describe this as a trendy school. Mr Keighley-Elstub famously put a stop to the cashmere scarves – as part of the school uniform and supplied by a parent: this isn't the image he wants to nurture.

Large, busy, and traditional with a dynamic head, Pembridge Hall can only get better and better and could be an excellent choice for your enthusiastic daughter.

Queen's Gate Junior School

Linked school: Queen's Gate School, 319

125–126 Queen's Gate, London SW7 5LE

Independent • Pupils: 150 • Ages: 4–11 • Non-denom • Fees (per term): £4,950

Tel: 020 7761 0303
Fax: 020 7584 7691
Email: registrar@queensgate.org.uk
Website: www.queensgate.org.uk

Headmistress: Since 2013, Mrs Nicola Greenwood BEd Homerton, Cambridge, (French and education) who joined the school from St Cedd's in Chelmsford where she was head of Upper School (50-ish). Previous posts at Ipswich High Juniors where, for 17 years, she was head of KS2. Mrs Greenwood is clearly a popular appointment. She is highly experienced and approachable, very smiley, relaxed and fun. She has four children of her own including

twins and commutes daily from Colchester. Parents find it odd not to see her anywhere at all on the school's website.

Entrance: Around 100 applicants for each of the 23 places at reception. One 7+ competitive academic scholarship worth a third of an annual fee. Assessment morning with groups of 8-10 children given tasks and observed by the headmistress and other staff.

Exit: Around three-quarters to the senior school. Rest to a range of London good schools and a few to boarding.

Remarks: A few doors down from the senior school and an equally discreet entrance belies the warmth, fun and productive activity that goes on here. Up to 23 tots in the first two years – each in a good sized room with teacher and two teaching assistants. Happy, absorbed children are relaxed and busy in rooms that are stimulating without being frantic. Some older classes quite noisy with a buzz of activity but everywhere, even the art room, is orderly and purposeful. Quiet sustained work for the oldest girls who would change nothing about the school save its lack of outdoors and really like their friends. Rooms light and recently refurbished – and at a sensible temperature. Good sized hall – like the senior school, the old salon in grand architectural style. Good-sized library, well-used with a real, 'very hard-working', librarian shared with big sister school. Lots of multi-purpose spaces and facilities. Good IT suite.

Lots of music – choirs and an orchestra. Very lively art, we encountered 'Dragolina', an immense dragon being constructed for the coming Chinese New Year – and were glad to see good old-fashioned

We warmed to the sight of children spontaneously hugging their teachers (probably illegal!) A safe, cosy and well-structured start for your precious daughter

crayon work. Tastes of French, Spanish, German, Italian and Latin as the girls progress through the school. Fun but some parents query the purpose, 'they really don't know any French at all when they go into the senior school'. Teaching eg science done by senior school staff. By bus to sports facilities all over the place – ensures plenty of indoor and outdoor sports. Lots of lovely after school clubs three days of the week – 'So hard to choose, Mummy!'

Parents happy. 'It's traditional, though the new head is livening things up. It really suits my daughter.' Staff now mostly young and pretty international. We warmed to the sight of children spontaneously hugging their teachers (probably illegal!) A safe, cosy and well-structured start for your precious daughter. And once she's there, you could really forget about her education for the next 14 years and trust them to give her all she needs.

Queen's Gate School

Linked school: Queen's Gate Junior School, 318

133 Queen's Gate, London SW7 5LE

Independent • Pupils: 350 • Ages: 11–18 • Non-denom • Fees (per term): £4,950 – £5,850

Tel: 020 7589 3587
Fax: 020 7584 7691
Email: registrar@queensgate.org.uk
Website: www.queensgate.org.uk

45

Principal: Since 2006, Mrs Rosalynd Kamaryc BA MSc PGCE (50-ish). Petite, chic and with a lovely soft Irish voice, Mrs Kamaryc immediately comes across as the warm, calm and practical person to whom you'd want to entrust your precious daughter. A mathematician who still teaches – in her case, the bottom GCSE set. 'I just love teaching,' she says and 'counts it a privilege to walk the school' once a day.

Mrs Kamaryc has an impressive pedigree, this being her second headship. She began teaching in Scotland and spent 10 years as head of Wykeham House School, Fareham – via Forest School and Woodbridge School. Parents enthuse: 'She gives

terrific support to the girls,' we were told. 'She's extremely capable, a very safe pair of hands with a very clear vision for the school.' 'Very approachable though can seem a little shy.' Her catwalk walk at a school fashion show wowed everyone. 'She commands respect but she can kick up her heels too. She's fun.'

Academic matters: 'It punches above its weight academically,' one parent told us and the results bear this out. French, English, maths, art and geography shine brightly. Tiny sets at A level – often ones and twos – a rare privilege and at half the cost of the top

A lovely school for lovely girls in a classy and sophisticated milieu. Tiny classes, delightful teachers, charming friends, with a faint St Trinian's spicy edge

tutorial companies. They will run an A level course with one pupil and don't ditch the subject – or its teacher – if it has no takers in a given year. Art, French maths have biggest numbers. If a subject has more than seven takers they split the group. Some depts seen as better than others. 'English and history are very strong; art is amazing,' we heard repeatedly and 'though the teachers are all lovely, their actual teaching isn't always great – a little dull and uncreative sometimes.' But A level results are remarkable these days, 58 per cent A*/A in 2014 with a just a few at grade c or lower.

Good range of GCSE subjects for so small a school. Ancient history and classical civilisation, Latin and Greek and lots of modern languages available – and not just for native speakers. Good results in English, geography, French, drama, art – but no weaklings here (71 per cent A*/A in 2014). 'We chose it,' said a parent, echoed by more, 'because it is not obsessed by exam results.' 'It's not a hoop-jumping school.'

School has 1.5 staff on learning support team – much praised. 'Incredible support for my daughter's mild dyslexia. Possibly not for much else,' thought a parent, and this is borne out by the head.

Games, options, the arts: Parents glow and when you make it to the loftily-situated art dept you understand why. The main studio entrance is festooned with trompe l'oeil blue velvet curtains and abutted by a display of white paper insects; inside is a huge range of work, all demonstrating boldness, creativity and imagination. 'We do some gruesome stuff,' chortled the dynamic and experimental head of art as we gaped at the 'urban zombies', the girl under a blanket of fresh minced steak and various startling depictions of blood and vomit. It was reassuring to turn to the multi-coloured shoes on every step of the staircase, the cardboard relief masks, the fun, wit, skill of it all. DT even more surprising, facilities include a laser cutter, 3D printer and vacuum former. Products we saw included acrylic pencil and iPad holders and electronic dice. We warmed to a girl (flatteringly, given our age) mistaking us for a potential parent, who insisted on telling us: 'If someone wanted to do product design, they really mustn't go anywhere else.' Art and DT results from here are outstanding.

'Our drama teacher is so dedicated and lovely.' We interrupted a rehearsal of 'Darkwood Manor' – a bit of Gothic horror written by the girls, gory in their white and cicatriced faces, blood and masks. No theatre though a small semi-studio – 'we don't need a 100 seater theatre,' claimed a proud parent. Good music room with lovely Broadwood grand and reassuring number of real instruments plus

modern keyboards with headphones. Many learn instruments and school music is lively and popular.

Sports regarded as much improved during Mrs Kamaryc's tenure though almost all involves bussing hither and yon. 'We don't mind, it's not an issue,' parents feel, though some pupils we spoke to yearned for playing fields and pitches. It probably isn't ideal for your jumping bean, though on offer now are rowing, squash, fencing among others and girls love it all. 'We have 95 clubs,' we were told and a buzz of jolly fun activities and try-outs pervades the place. Some little sorrow that not everyone joins in with all this opportunity as fully they might.

Background and atmosphere: Queen's Gate is a smart, elegant road in anyone's book. You walk past this school and back again without knowing it's there, so discreet is its little brass name plate. 'It's a fantastic location,' gush Kensington mummies, 'just like a house.' And so it is – three houses, in fact, knocked together and inside – apart from the fabulous cornices, ceiling roses etc, it's yer actual rabbit warren. 'Yes,' nods a wise mummy, 'but good teaching can take place in a tent.' We lost count of the number of floors and semi-floors above the basement (ICT, lab, lockers and gym and still somehow redolent of the butler's clipped footfalls and scurrying maids). Some upper floor corridors are so narrow that we fear future generations of Tubby Tillies may get stuck. Not that we saw any such here, of course.

Main entrance hall embellished with wall-mounted bell, a set of gongs, a digital clock, fire extinguisher, staff pigeon holes, a vintage radiator, a vitrine bulging with silver trophies and a venerable wooden post box we couldn't open. All this somehow seemed to sum up the whole. Wonderful main hall confected from the two adjoining salons from the houses' glory days – newish wooden floor and matching brass chandeliers. No playground, just a couple of tiny roof gardens for the younger years. Otherwise, breaks are taken in classrooms – and these, on, admittedly, a dark January day, were some of the most overheated we have encountered. Pupils and staff were busily fanning themselves as the rude bell shattered the silence and doors opened. 'It does get very hot,' a youngster confided, 'and sometimes it gets very cold.' Black (for pupils and staff) and white (for pupils) dining rooms, wonderfully elegant and decidedly different. Food reckoned to be good – around half bring in their own. Some come for breakfasts which sounded more than worth sliding out of bed and down the road for.

Main library is a beautiful room with splendid polished oak tables and equally venerable stock in many cases (nothing wrong with that!) and a lovely place to work. Sixth form have surprisingly

spacious common rooms with sofas. Also a kitchen and a work room, but work decidedly not happening when we peeked in.

No uniform, most dressed perfectly sensibly though this feature of the school clearly stresses a few. 'Some girls bring in ridiculous designer bags,' one mum kvetched, but no-one looked especially coutured to us – though perhaps we are not the best judges. Certainly a divisive issue for some – though not exactly on an 'in/out of the EU?' scale.

Pastoral care and discipline: Everyone praises the pastoral care. 'They are very good at sorting out individuals,' one father told us. 'My daughter is very happy there.' Another praised the good relations between the girls, fostered by the staff and the care taken to build inter-year relationships. A third described the amount of extra time and effort put in by the teaching staff. A fourth said: 'My daughter feels there is always a teacher to chat to if she has a problem' – and so on. Each term has a 'pastoral day' and a trip to France in year 7 is 'brilliant for bonding us'. Very little sense of serious disciplinary problems being on anyone's radar.

Pupils and parents: Head stresses: 'We're a very English school with an international community. Many of our parents came here from overseas as students – and stayed. We are a Christian foundation but we celebrate all faiths and cultures.' Evidence was the great excitement – and splendid dragon we witnessed in preparation for the Chinese new year. Largest number of overseas nationals probably Italian, followed by French, Spanish, US, Aussies, Qataris and a few Russians. Much-loved by its Old Girls, many of whom are current parents; good supportive parents' group. Only, but repeated, gripe is that 'communications are not great' – a surprise to the school but something they are addressing.

Notable OGs include HRH the Duchess of Cornwall, various Redgraves, Sieffs, Guinnesses; Amanda de Souza, Jane Martineau, Nigella Lawson, Lucinda Lambton, Tracey Boyd, Aurelia Cecil, Trinny Woodall and Imogen Poots. Former head of MI5 Eliza Manningham Buller used to be on the staff.

Entrance: Most of the school's own junior school join the senior school. Around six applicants per place at 11+. Waiting list for all years, but occasional places occur so worth a phone call. A few in at year 12 but 'we are very selective' and A*/As at GCSE are a requirement. Head meets all prospective parents before anyone is tested on anything.

Exit: Almost all stay to A level. Of the 20 per cent or so who try pastures coed, boarding or state, some scuttle back tout de suite. Head says that she encourages them to 'be brave and look elsewhere' at this stage. You'd be brave – or rash – to move from so small and nurturing a community to a place where no-one knows a thing about you. Year 13 leavers go to a wonderfully eclectic bunch of good universities around the globe. Oxbridge is not uncommon, solid Russell group for most but

around a quarter much further afield. Art and art history, classics more common than science

Money matters: All 11+ entrants are automatic scholarship candidates and 25 per cent fee remission offered to high flyers. Art, drama, music and sports scholarships also available – apply on registering. Similar 25 per cent remission available to sixth applicants. Means-tested bursaries too, but no point in applying until a place is offered.

Remarks: A lovely school for lovely girls in a classy and sophisticated milieu. Tiny classes, delightful teachers, charming friends with a faint St Trinian's spicy edge. Not for you if you want gritty urban reality – except, perhaps, in the art room.

Ravenscourt Park Preparatory School

16 Ravenscourt Avenue, London W6 0SL

Tel: 020 8846 9153
Fax: 020 8846 9143
Email: secretary@rpps.co.uk
Website: www.rpps.co.uk

Independent • Pupils: 410 • Ages: 4–11 • Non-denom • Fees (per term): £4,997

Headmistress: Since 2013, Mrs Kate O'Shaughnessy BA QTS (thirties). Educated at Penistone Grammar School, Barnsley College and Trinity and All Saints University in Leeds. Started teaching career at Stag Lane First School, Collindale, then moved to Reddiford School, Pinner as specialist English teacher. Joined Ravenscourt Park in 2005 as senior leader and head of teaching and learning.

Progressed to head of upper school and then deputy head, a post she held for three years.

English is her passion and she enjoys 'the results of stimulating my pupils' imaginations and creativity and seeing this manifested in the quality and standard of their writing.' Her husband is site manager of a senior school and they have a young son. In her spare time she enjoys reading, going to the theatre, skiing and walking.

Entrance: Non selective, the September after a child's fourth birthday. It is vital to register a child on his/her first birthday. Can't be registered before. After that it is a lottery. Siblings get priority, then names are drawn randomly and places allotted strictly to ascertain an equal number of boys and girls.

Exit: Traditionally, to London day schools, but with changing local demographics, some parents now looking to send their children to top boarding schools. Therefore some boys are leaving early, although, as one parent said, 'this is not a light decision'. So, occasionally boys at end of year 5 to country prep schools or London day schools that go through to year 8 (Fulham Prep, Kings House).

Twelve scholarships in 2014. Girls headed to a wide variety of schools, including Godolphin & Latymer, Francis Holland, Clarence Gate, Notting Hill and Ealing High School, Putney High, Lady Eleanor Holles and St Paul's Girls'. Boys' choices included Hampton, Westminster Under, Colet Court, City of London Boys' and University College School. Some to co-eds like Kew House and Latymer.

Remarks: Parents said before we visited: 'Not a hot house', 'kind and nurturing', 'safe environment', and 'excellent communication'. We found no reason to argue with these comments. Teachers and children buzzed with enthusiasm, the atmosphere felt relaxed although each time we walked into a classroom work stopped, the children leapt to their feet, chimed 'good morning' and stood there until we left. This, apparently always happens and, we felt, emphasised the edge of formality at the school. However, everywhere we went we were made to feel more than welcome. Parents also feel 'there really is an open door policy'.

Founded in 1991 by Maria and Ted Gardener, former teachers, this school has grown and gone from strength to strength. Its most recent building, opened in September 2011, has enabled it to move from two-form entry to three, gradually adding 20 more children to each year. No problem filling the spaces. There is some feeling that it would, perhaps,

The atmosphere felt relaxed although each time we walked into a classroom work stopped, the children leapt to their feet, chimed 'good morning' and stood there until we left

have been better to have added two more years, thus solving the problem of boys leaving early. (They say this is not a problem!) But as rumour has it that the owners, London Preparatory Schools Ltd, will soon be opening a secondary level school not too far away, maybe there was a different agenda. Some parents feel perhaps too much emphasis on the business side, 'definitely an eye for profit above all'. For

instance: 'Why do we have to pay extra for lunch, when it is compulsory and our children are not allowed to bring a packed version?'

Fantastic facilities. The new building has enabled the top three years to move into nine bright new classrooms, colour coded per floor. 'We chose our own colours,' said our two of our guides proudly. And, 'look we've even got a lift but we can't use it without permission!' Splendid new science lab with all the latest equipment; a light bright art room displaying a friendship bench, 'to sit on when you feel lonely', being painted by the art club and, very exciting, including a kiln; a music room where children were reading notes displayed on an interactive white board – of course these abound; an ICT lab with a laptop per child, 'we're making our own websites'. Perhaps best of all, as far as our guides were concerned, was the new school hall/theatre: 'The choir sings from the balcony', 'we can learn to operate the light and sound'. All very impressive.

A tad more cosy, the rest of the school is housed in two buildings, with a separate good sized dining block. All food cooked on site and children served at their tables by catering staff. Most meals are hot, always healthy and compulsory unless a child has a dietary problem. As we walked across the large, mainly tarmaced playground, our guides pointed out equipment for active play (including balls galore) and soft area for the younger ones to climb, slide and play safely. We were later informed that there is an imminently scheduled building project to update the whole playground. Our younger guides proudly showed their fully equipped classrooms, interactive whiteboards and all. Children's work, art and otherwise, on display all over. All pupils appeared happy and relaxed, quick to say hello and answer questions. Unmissable code of conduct pinned up all over. Our guides were quick

to explain the provenance of the many badges they were wearing. As one parent said: 'Lots of smiley teachers, lots of smiley children, such a happy school!'

A reasonably varied curriculum, at least for the first five years. The importance of 11+ kicks in during the summer term in year 5 and children are given lots of homework for the holidays. From then on English and mathematics dominate until all entrance exams are over; afterwards lessons become theme based and more adventurous and relaxed children take part in a whole range of different activities, home and away. Recently, year 6s wrote traditional stories which they then read to the reception classes. The change of pace must work well because the majority of pupils get into their first choice of secondary school, parents having been well advised by the head, of course.

All pupils in years 1 and 3 screened for literacy and specific areas of difficulty. Parents informed of any problems and help given where necessary. Small group lessons focusing on literacy and motor skills, if needed, once or twice a week for half an hour. One-to-one help also provided occasionally, if absolutely necessary. 'No extra ever charged for special needs support'. Say they wouldn't normally decline a place to a child with pre-identified minor learning difficulties. A special needs room in each building. Teachers always available to talk to parents.

Extracurricular regarded as important and many different after school clubs, sporty, arty, intellectual, musical. The range changes from term to term. Several orchestras and choirs, individual lessons offered on a wide variety of instruments. Recently a year 3 boy scored one of the highest marks in the country for his piano exam. A full

Afterwards lessons become theme based and more adventurous and relaxed children take part in a whole range of different activities, home and away

programme of outings, cultural and academic, plus some residential trips for older children. All the usual charity fund raisers – luckily some parents take these very seriously and are happy to organise. They have already built one school in Burma and currently a major project is to raise sufficient funds to build another.

Redcliffe School

47 Redcliffe Gardens, London SW10 9JH

Tel: 020 7352 9247
Email: admissions@redcliffeschool.com
Website: www.redcliffeschool.com

Independent · Pupils: 170 · Ages: 3–11 · C of E · Fees (per term): £1,745 – £4,640

Headmistress: Since 2006, Mrs Susan Bourne BSc Hons (mid 50s). Read chemistry at Manchester University. Previously deputy head of the Old Vicarage School in Richmond and taught chemistry in both the state and independent sector. 'I still love teaching and teach the year 6 science lessons.' The sort of sensible woman you could rely on in an emergency, her calm demeanour permeates the whole school.

Married to a management consultant ('he's my anchor') with three grown up daughters (Latymer Upper, Queen's Gate and Godolphin and Latymer), she took time out while based in Geneva and Paris with a young family so knows what it's like to be a parent both at home and in an international setting. 'She really understands,' said one mother. Now lives in Richmond but escapes most weekends down the M3 to cottage in the New Forest where she and her husband sail their boat ('but only in calm weather!')

Entrance: Entrance to the nursery is first come first served but it is advisable to put names down within six months of birth. Places are sometimes available at the last minute due to parents in this area applying to lots of different schools, so it's worth staying on the waiting list. Entrance to the main school is by assessment and an interview with the head. 'When we assess children for entry to the main school, we are looking for more than just academic ability,' said Mrs Bourne. 'We are looking for sociable children who are going to be happy here. For example, I choose children who are comfortable when separated from their carer.' Most children go through to the main school from the nursery. Two mixed forms from reception to year 3, then one form of girls in each year.

Exit: Boys go at 8+ to schools such as Colet Court, Northcote Lodge, Wetherby Prep, Westminster Cathedral Choir School and Sussex House. Girls leave at 11+ to a mixture of boarding and day schools with Benenden, Putney High, Queen's College, Godolphin and Latymer and City of London being popular recent choices. Regular music, academic and art scholarships.

Remarks: This well-established prep school is situated on two sites on Redcliffe Gardens – a busy thoroughfare taking traffic from north to south London. Although it has expanded over the last few years and now has 170 pupils from nursery age up to 11, it still feels small and intimate.

The upper school is housed in the original main building which when you enter looks more like a rather scruffy family home than a school. The cosy atmosphere is continued in the head's office, where visitors sit on a comfy but rather shabby sofa. However, when you enter the classrooms it's an entirely different matter. The recently refurbished hall in the basement (which is also used as a dining room) is state of the art, and when we visited during morning assembly, a Mendelssohn concerto was being played through a brand new music system. (A different composer is studied each week). Children filed in and sat with their eyes closed so that they could appreciate the music. When the deputy head asked them what they were going to do that day, one girl replied 'have fun,' which summed up the attitude around the school. (The answer she was actually looking for was 'work hard!')

A new extension at the back of the school is light and airy, while the other classrooms upstairs, although a little cramped, have high ceilings and natural light. The top floor houses the music room where piano, violin, flute, trumpet, guitar and voice are taught by peripatetic teachers. Music is one of the school's strengths, with some children gaining music scholarships to their next schools. The school orchestra plays at school events such as the carol service and prize giving and there are concerts for parents and friends at least twice a year.

The lower school, at St Luke's church a quarter of a mile down the road, comprises five bright and well-lit classrooms in the basement of the church (one for nursery and two classes each of reception and year 1). A large hall is used for indoor sports and lunch (which is trolleyed down from the upper school kitchen), and is also the venue for whole school assemblies on Thursdays and Fridays which

parents are encouraged to attend. 'Sometimes it's standing room only as these have become such popular events,' explained the head proudly. Children use a specially designed play area outside, with climbing frames built on an artificial grass covering with toys and scooters available. 'We like to spend as much time outside as possible.'

The teacher to student ratio is high, with a maximum of 16 in each class. There are specialist teachers for music, sport, French and drama. Recent productions include Minibeast Madness by the lower school and A Midsummer Night's Dream by the upper school. Extra EAL lessons support children who require help (particularly when they first

'We used to finish early on Fridays to enable our families with country properties to leave London before the rush hour, but more and more are staying on to take advantage of the sports clubs,' said the head

join the school) and a learning support teacher sees a number of children (around 10) twice a week on a one-to-one basis to help with specific learning difficulties such as mild dyslexia (but this costs extra). Most of the staff are women (three have been there for over 10 years), with one male teaching assistant and a male PE teacher, and this does give the school (especially since boys leave at eight) a rather female atmosphere. 'We would like to recruit more good male staff,' said the head.

Food is cooked on the upper school site and there are themed lunches for events such as Halloween and Bonfire Night. 'Children who have left the school write back to say how much they miss the food.' Parents are regularly invited in to have lunch with the staff and the children. 'We always feel very welcome at the school,' said one mother.

Children are bussed to nearby parks once a week for sports – football and netball in the autumn term, hockey and tag rugby in the spring and rounders, cricket and athletics in the summer. Weekly swimming lessons all year round at Fulham Pools. They compete against other schools and also have their own swimming galas and sports days. On Friday afternoons school finishes early and children can take part in a wide variety of sporting activities from yoga to fencing. 'We used to finish early on Fridays to enable our families with country properties to leave London before the rush hour but more and more are staying on to take advantage of the sports clubs,' said the head.

Families are drawn from the local area – half the children have either one or two international parents. 'Most of the schools round here have a high number of international families,' says one American mother, 'but this school seems very British still.' Another mother commented: 'It's very down to earth for a prep school in this area and you don't need to worry if you turn up at the school gate in the morning with no make up on. No one will judge you.'

Former pupils include Daniel Radcliffe. 'He was a rather quiet boy,' said the deputy head. 'We never expected him to become famous.' But Redcliffe is nothing like Hogwarts, and all in all this is a warm and cosy school with a nurturing environment. The atmosphere feels somewhat cloistered and it probably wouldn't suit a boisterous child who likes to run around a lot. But this could be just the place for gentler, less confident children to flourish.

Sacred Heart High School (Hammersmith)

212 Hammersmith Road, London W6 7DG

State • Pupils: 820 • Ages: 11–18 • RC

Tel: 020 8748 7600
Fax: 020 8748 0382
Email: info@sacredh.lbhf.sch.uk
Website: www.sacredhearthighschoolhammersmith.org.uk

15

Headteacher: Since 1992 Dr Christine Carpenter BA PhD FRSA (early sixties). A formidable and much admired head, the girls speak of her with a mixture of awe and fear. 'She's scary,' said one. We attempted a formal visit but were rebuffed no reasons given. This report is therefore based on our own research and a tour of the school on one of the official open days.

The head clearly has a strong work ethic and devotes herself to her job with tireless energy. She held the chapel filled with more than 500 hopeful parents in the palm of her hand. Her blistering

authority is in no way diminished by her short frame, sensible hair, modest suit and shoes. A hint of her background can be discerned from what she wrote when campaigning to encourage more families to sign up for free school meals. Some families, she said, don't apply for free school meals because of the stigma attached to it. 'You should know that I, too, had free school meals because of my family circumstances,' she wrote. 'I don't believe this made me less successful or less socially adept – indeed, quite the contrary.'

If you ain't Catholic then don't even think about it. Even if you are, start to sweat if you haven't had your child baptised before she is six months old and you can't produce the baptism certificate of at least one parent

Girls commented on the quips Dr Carpenter has been heard to make when she sees a particularly short skirt: 'Does your skirt need an absent note, or is that a belt?' she has been known to remark, with some humour. She regards all her girls as 'the leaders of tomorrow' and so makes the nurturing of leadership qualities a priority. Leaders clearly don't wear short skirts.

Academic matters: Sacred Heart has been a specialist school in maths and ICT since 2005. New sixth form opened in September 2013 for 80 of school's own pupils moving up from year 11. Will admit up to 30 external pupils to sixth form from 2014.

Academic results are impressive, even for the upmarket intake. Dr Carpenter proudly explained that the school had outperformed the Oratory, equalled Cardinal Vaughan and come within the top 25 per cent nationally. In 2013 91 per cent achieved five or more A*-C passes at GCSE including maths and English. Forty-nine per cent A*/A grades.

We were told that science and geography were school's strong subjects. Girls can either do the more simple core science and additional science or opt for three separate science modules. Pupils perform exceptionally well in RE, as you might expect (the data shows that history and RS are the school's 'popular and strong' subjects). French also stands out, as well as maths and English. Spanish is on offer but no German or Mandarin. Latin by invitation only. A teacher is supplied by a charity, the Iris Project, and comes in once or twice a week to teach a handful of keen and lucky girls. Plans afoot to offer an exam in Latin in partnership with Latymer Upper. All credit to Dr Carpenter that she facilitates this – apparently she is a classicist herself. Good DT facilities, but sadly no cooking. Girls praised the music tuition and music is offered as GCSE subject.

Setting from year 7. The girls we observed in a history lesson were attentive but the class size – even once setted – approached 40. Most teachers are Catholic but many are not.

One person responsible for SEN. It wasn't clear how effective the provision is but it would appear from the prospectus that differentiation in lessons

– what one would hope for in any event – is the main kind of support available. Bearing in mind the large class sizes, a parent might be forgiven in worrying that her mildly dyslexic daughter could become 'lost.'

Games, options, the arts: Facilities not bad for an inner city state school, with four tennis/netball courts on-site (they can double up as rounders pitches too). School has a gym and dance studio as well as the use of Hammersmith and Fulham Health and Fitness Centre. Softball, basketball and volleyball on offer. Girls are kept active with at least two hours of PE per week and PE can be chosen as a GCSE subject. School has had some success in the borough in netball, hockey, rounders and athletics. After-school clubs include street dance, yoga, cheerleading, fencing, trampolining and football. There are inter-house competitions, the highlight of which is the annual sports day held at local playing fields.

The usual musicals take place annually – Little Shop of Horrors, My Fair Lady, West Side Story etc. Debating and public speaking (getting girls ready to lead) takes place after school, as well as sports and AS courses to stretch the brightest. A number of girls play musical instruments and there is a school choir and orchestra.

Busy art studio. 'Everyone loves art,' enthused one girl. We saw lots of pop art style self portraits, plastic neon jewellery and key rings crafted in DT. Plenty of opportunities to get involved with charitable work, such as raising money to support an orphanage in Zimbabwe.

Background and atmosphere: The school, or 'convent of the Sacred Heart,' is built on a site steeped in Catholic history dating back to the early 17th century. Four different orders of nuns have taught girls here for more than 300 years. The current Tudor styled buildings were built in the late 19th century. Sacred Heart was a secondary grammar school until 1976 when it received its first comprehensive intake. Since 2012 it has been an academy. To the uninitiated it looks rather forbidding, not helped by the fact that the impressive gates on Hammersmith Road do not yield to entrants, nor is there any sign to explain where the main entrance is. A number of prospective parents we spoke to were baffled at the lack of help in finding how to get in.

Once you do arrive within the redbrick walls (the entrance is on Bute Gardens by the way) there is a wonderful calm and peace, wholly unlike your typical state school, let alone your inner London state comprehensive. The site is leafy and well-kept and it's hard to believe that seconds before you were pounding round the hectic Hammersmith roundabout. You won't think for one moment, however, that you are anywhere other than a Catholic establishment. As soon as you go through the door you are faced with a huge mural of the crucifixion. The wide spacious corridors of the cloisters are similarly adorned with religious paintings and look out over a beautiful garden (only for year 11s and up). The chapel is simple and peaceful and the library well-stocked and imaginatively designed, with a 'traffic light system' to denote how quiet you need to be in different areas. The nuns have recently vacated, which has made room for the new sixth form intake. The school is currently busily spending an £8 million grant on a new building development to house science and sports over three storeys.

There's a canteen where girls can buy hot food and cold lunches are also on sale. Civilised place to eat, talk and relax.

Pastoral care and discipline: This is without question a strict school. From appearance (short skirts are not just the subject of corridor quips, but regularly feature in the head's letter) through to punctuality (your daughter will be in detention at lunchtime if she is even one minute late) and general behaviour, Dr Carpenter rules with a very tight rein. The good thing, we were told by one girl, is that pupils don't just get put 'on report' for bad behaviour, they might be required to see a member of staff regularly because they are feeling overwhelmed with work or struggling in some other way.

A peer mentoring scheme between year 7s and year 11s encourages the older girls to take a leadership role and also fosters good relationships between all years. Inevitably we heard tales of 'bitchy' behaviour, often a feature of all girls' schools, but obviously not tolerated by the conscientious and vigilant Dr Carpenter and her team.

Pupils and parents: To adhere to the strict admissions procedure, jump through the various hoops and keep within the tight deadlines, parents here have one thing in common. They are committed, determined and quite often strategic. It is the state school of choice for many families, not only in west London, but even as far as Islington (Tony Blair's daughter being the obvious example). Despite its 'non selective, fully comprehensive' label, girls here are overwhelmingly middle class (for an inner London comprehensive), white and with English as a first language. Far fewer children on free school meals than is usual in this part of London (fourth on the Fair Admissions Campaign list of the most socially selective state schools in the country). Reassuring for many parents. As one said to us: 'I feel happy to be part of a club of like-minded people who share the same values as me.' Old girls include Kathryn Blair, Pauline Collins, Patricia Hayes, June Flewett and Mel Martin.

Entrance: If you ain't Catholic then don't even think about it. Even if you are, start to sweat if you haven't had your child baptised before she is six months old and you can't produce the baptism certificate of at least one parent. Make sure your daughter attends an RC primary and then you might want to think about how close to the school you live. Applicants are banded – to ensure a 'comprehensive' intake – and sit a reasoning test as part of the admissions process. There have been instances of siblings failing to get in.

Exit: Vast majority go on to do A levels. For the first year of sixth form, 80 out of of 164 stayed on at Sacred Heart. Traditionally quite high numbers go to either Cardinal Vaughan or The London Oratory as well as Twyford C of E. The odd one to the independent sector including UCS, St Benedict's and Latymer Upper.

Remarks: An excellent, smaller than average, state school in the heart of London, if you are after a traditional education, are lucky enough to qualify and prepared to toe the very tight line, this may be the school for your daughter.

St Charles Catholic Sixth Form College

74 St Charles Square, London W10 6EY

State · Pupils: 1,200 · Ages: 16 – 19 · RC

Tel: 020 8968 7755
Fax: 020 8969 1061
Email: admissions@stcharles.ac.uk
Website: www.stcharles.ac.uk

47

Principal: Since 2002 Mr Paul O'Shea BA, PGCE (50s). Educated at a Kent grammar school, scholarship to read history at St John's Oxford, he went on to study at St Mary's Strawberry Hill for his PGCE. Started as a history teacher, later becoming head of department at Woodhouse School, now Woodhouse College. In 1994 he joined St Charles as vice principal. Cool, calm and collected, he is extremely well thought of by both staff and pupils, and encourages the whole school community to get along and work in partnership with each other. He leads a highly successful and inclusive college, with Catholic values at its heart. All other faiths are welcome who are happy to fit in with the Catholic identity of the college. Mr O'Shea still teaches citizenship

and is chairman of the London Citizens. He lives in North London and is married with two grown-up children, now at university.

Academic matters: Whilst around three-quarters of the students follow traditional A level courses, St Charles also offers BTec firsts, certificates and diplomas, vocational courses and foundation skills in English and mathematics. The college also offers GCSE retakes for those wanting to improve their grades. More able students can take the extended project qualification. Students are all taught to plan and develop their work alongside how best to manage their time. Being a rounded thinking individual is part of the college's mission: everyone

follows the compulsory general RE programme, which involves much critical discussion around the purpose and meaning of life through theology and philosophy. Students who are successful in completing the course gain the nationally recognised Certificate in Religious Investigation and Moral Reasoning. The school is well-known for added value, with seven per cent of A level grades A*/A in 2014 and 29 per cent A* – B; this is no mean achievement for a mixed ability college. Spread across two floors, the library provides quiet areas for working and a good range of books, multimedia, newspa-

---

Quite overwhelming feedback from staff that St Charles is a breath of fresh air, organised, and with a positive attitude across all disciplines really matter

---

pers and periodicals. Active and well-resourced learning support department provides assistance to students with a range of specific needs. The building is now fully wheelchair accessible. Intensive courses for students with English as an additional language are organised for small groups to ensure much personal attention.

Games, options, the arts: Impressive and modern sports facilities; sports block also incorporates new IT suites. Huge sports hall, four new indoor courts and fitness suite; students can also use the Birkbeck College sports ground for football and rugby. Basketball team have won the London Pioneers for three out of the last four years. Very strong art and design department puts on well-attended exhibitions, and a number of students go on to foundation courses at top London art schools. Drama and music are also popular and the school produces plays and musicals, with auditions open to all students. Film and media students are involved with projects run by the British Film Institute, enabling them to show and discuss their creative work with film and television professionals. Very enthusiastic and successful young enterprise team recently won Best Overall Company for North Central London. The college links up with other organisations to provide community outreach opportunities, be it helping older people gain ICT skills or mentoring other young people. Students can also become involved in the CitySafe initiative run by London Citizens, an organisation committed to improving young people's lives and skills and combating street violence.

Background and atmosphere: As you walk into the entrance hall, a peaceful and positive atmosphere is immediately apparent, the most inspiring design taken from Milan cathedral. Everywhere is spotlessly clean, and well cared for corridors positively shine. The college is named after St Charles Borromeo, a 16th century Italian archbishop who believed strongly in the redeeming powers of education. Founded by Basil Hume in 1990, it continues to go from strength to strength. Quite overwhelming feedback from staff that St Charles is a breath of fresh air, organised, and with a positive attitude across all disciplines really matter. The college is conveniently located in St Charles's Square, often referred to as 'The Little Vatican', due to the neighbouring Catholic primary and secondary schools, St Pius Church and a Carmelite monastery. Much about the college is designed around hope and inspiration, and a large amount of wall space is dedicated to portraits of students with accompanying testimonials and histories of their educational and career development. Interestingly, quite a few ex-students return to work at the college in both academic and non-academic posts.

Pastoral care and discipline: St Charles's continues to work very hard to ensure the best possible pastoral care and that every student feels part of the community. Everyone has a group tutor group under one of the pastoral managers which looks after their progress and well-being. There is a referral system for students with academic and/or personal problems. An outside agency provides both male and female counsellors who visit the school on a weekly basis. The full-time chaplain looks after the small but beautiful chapel, where daily morning prayers are said and a mass every Friday lunchtime. The chaplain is available to students on a drop-in basis. Whilst supporting students, he also organises voluntary work experience and charity work. Students are provided with a Code of Conduct, so everyone knows exactly what is expected of them in all aspects of college life and behaviour. Zero tolerance towards smoking, alcohol and drugs, all banned from the site.

Pupils and parents: Very diverse 21st-century London group of students, from all over the world, Portuguese, Filipino, Hispanic, Afro-Caribbean and Eastern European. About 80 per cent from ethnic minorities, many of whom are the first members of their family to have the opportunity to attend an A level college and go on to university.

Entrance: First priority goes to those with specific needs, then to students applying from four partner Catholic secondary schools, which makes up about 20 per cent of the intake. Other than that, fairly open access; students come from around 150 feeder schools. Everyone applying on time will be offered an interview to discuss their application and suitable course.

Exit: Approximately 75 per cent go on to university, others to art colleges or FE colleges to follow vocational training courses or apprenticeships.

Money matters: College raises some funds by hiring out the excellent facilities including the large hall,

indoor and outdoor sports areas and equipment, and spacious restaurant and catering area. The student bursary scheme provides grants for those in financial hardship while studying full-time.

Remarks: Some remarkable achievements happen here. Great place for motivated and hard-working young people from all walks of life who want to move on, regardless of previous achievements or background.

St James Junior School

Linked schools: St James Senior Girls' School, 335

Earsby Street, London W14 8SH

Independent • Pupils: 255 • Ages: 4–11 • Non-denom • Fees (per term): £4,610

Tel: 020 7348 1793
Fax: 020 7348 1790
Email: admissions@stjamesjunior.org
Website: www.stjamesjuniors.co.uk

16

Headmistress: Since 2009, Mrs Catherine Thomlinson, BA in English and history from Roehampton (40s). A St James' disciple to her fingers' ends, having spent almost all of her teaching career there after being educated at sister school, St Vedast (brief spell in South Africa before coming back to the fold). Two children, a son and a daughter, both of whom attended St James from age 4 right through senior school. A thoroughly lovely lady who radiates kindness, humanity and good humour, and

this despite having a shocking cold when we met. The study oft proclaims the head, we've found, and Mrs Thomlinson's was sparely but beautifully furnished, bright and calm. Amidst some exquisite pictures of quiet seas, a joyous tract reads, 'Let your light shine!' – and hers most assuredly does.

Despite her lifelong loyalty to the St James traditions, Mrs Thomlinson has not been afraid to modernise. She has pushed through substantial curriculum development, including DT,

French and dance; and both boys and girls now do cookery, woodwork and sewing. Introduced interactive whiteboards for upper junior classrooms ('a fantastic tool'), and is looking to bring these in throughout the school. Major development of EYFS provision, following criticism in 2010 inspection report. Parents report improved communication. Continues to uphold strong emphasis on speech, drama and music, 'because they really touch the emotional intelligence'.

Entrance: 'We don't take children on an academic basis,' says head, and accordingly there's no entrance exam at age 4; instead, the school holds informal assessments that involve meeting both child and parents, plus a report from child's nursery where applicable. Children of alumni and siblings have priority, as do those whose parents registered them early for a place. School looks for 'a certain confidence, and for children and families who value what we value'. Places higher up the school occasionally become available, and children who apply aged 7+ take assessments in reading, writing and mathematics to establish whether they're able to manage within the standard of the established class.

Exit: Junior girls stay until the end of year 5, when virtually all of them progress to St James Senior Girls, which begins at year 6 and is situated on the same site. Overwhelming majority of parents are happy with this. 'I'm very grateful that neither they nor I will have to face the 11 plus,' one mother of two daughters commented. This is just as well, since for girls to change schools at this point would be extremely difficult. Very occasionally, however, a girl may opt to do her final junior year elsewhere, and Bute House has been one such destination.

St James Senior Boys is out at Ashford (a very comprehensive coach service is provided by St James Schools), so boys stay on at St James Junior for their year 6 and can be prepped for common entrance to other senior schools at parents' request, 'but more and more boys are staying and going through to Ashford,' currently 88 per cent. Once again, it seems, parents appreciate the automatic entry. Where boys do go elsewhere, routes include Fulham Prep, Latymer Upper, Wetherby Prep, Hampton and Colet Court.

Remarks: A frieze of the goddess Athene gazes down benevolently from one of the foyer walls, and this may explain the air of gentle wisdom that really does pervade this unusual and admirable little school. It nestles quietly within residential streets, the outside resembling a monastery, with its high walls and expanse of sheer red brick, but the tableau through the security gate wasn't in the least forbidding. Children played cheerfully in a

pretty, cloistered courtyard under the eye of a watchful but serene-looking teacher, and the whole was framed by light and airy corridors – a preponderance of new glass giving a modern, clean balance to the Victorian charm of the original

---

'One of the reasons we send our children to the school is to learn early on to take a pause, allow the noise to stop.'

building. The atmosphere, as far as we could judge, was one of kindness and peaceful activity. Parents all confirmed this: 'It's a very happy place.' 'It's an extremely happy school.' 'A warm and nurturing environment.' 'My child has loved being there from the very beginning.'

The school's ethos places an unusually high emphasis on generosity, mutual respect and 'being the best human beings we can be,' and achieves this through a number of distinctive practices. Every lesson begins and ends with a 'moment of stillness'. Such moments 'give you that sense of ease and reflection,' says head. These pauses, as they're

known, are popular with parents and children: 'It gives you a chance to be still,' said a year 6 child, whose demeanour was courteous and mature beyond his years. Parents agree. 'One of the main benefits of St James is the peacefulness,' was one comment, and 'One of the reasons we send our children to the school is to learn early on to take a pause, allow the noise to stop,' was another.

All the children, even the little ones, learn Sanskrit, in accordance with the school's belief that the Eastern philosophies have much to teach us; and both children and parents insisted to us that this was one of the things they 'really loved' about the school. St James describes itself as 'multi-religious', and philosophy itself is a very important part of the curriculum. The school teaches a Socratic method of dialogue and questioning, and the children are taught to develop open-ended questions and to debate as a class ('No putting-down of others' opinions is allowed,' says head firmly). The school motto – 'Speak the truth, be generous and kind, be your best' – seems to mean more here than such saws do in other schools. St James's policy of teaching boys and girls separately, then bringing them together for social activities (break-times, lunch, productions, trips, etc) may also be a key factor in establishing such good relationships between the children. 'You can see the

boys, but you don't always have to be with them,' said a grateful year 5 girl, with which one of the boys countered, 'The girls think they're best, and we just get on with being even better.' We suspect this is amiable posturing: a number of parents confirmed to us that their child's closest schoolfriends included those of the opposite gender.

Academic performance is strong, with the standard of written work exceptionally high, both in content and accuracy – all the more impressive, given that the school's intake is not academically selective. 'I'm a great advocate for academic rigour,' confirms the head, adding, 'but I'm just as passionate about children finding out what they love.' All classes have weekly sessions in the well-stocked library, run by a dedicated librarian, and there are regular visits by children's authors. ('My son very quickly developed a love of reading,' reported a satisfied parent.) SEN provision is good, with about 30 EAL children cared for within the classroom set-up. We applaud the emphasis on using Shakespeare as a teaching resource at all levels, more so than in any other school we've visited. We saw verses from The Winter's Tale charmingly illustrated by the reception children, and read some excellent commentaries on Polonius's advice to his son ('To thine own self be true') by the year 3 boys. 'We love Shakespeare,' the head acknowledged. 'We did A Midsummer Night's Dream and The Tempest last year. And Mozart's The Magic Flute. We have a great cultural reservoir to draw on – why not give them the best material?' Why not indeed!

And in fact the drama on offer is very impressive, with all the children involved in at least one performance every year. 'We like big productions!' beamed a member of staff, before hurrying off to oversee preparations for Fiddler On The Roof, for which the school hired the Britten Theatre at the Royal College of Music because 'we like to be ambitious'. Previous big productions include My Fair Lady, The Railway Children and The Sound of Music. For in-house performances, the school's hall has been recently refurbished and hosts frequent verse-speaking, plus dance for both girls and boys as well as drama productions. Music is strong, with 70 children taking instrumental lessons at school on 'pretty much anything they want', and regular concerts, often featuring the school's orchestra. The children sing every day in assembly – repertoire by Mozart, Purcell and Vivaldi is popular – and have music lessons every week. Artwork of an astonishingly high standard adorns the walls, produced in the attractive and lightsome art room under the gaze of the stuffed menagerie up on the shelf: a goose, a grouse, a heron and a weasel.

All children have a period of games or sport every day, be it gym, dance, swimming or ball skills, and the upper juniors (years 3-6) go off-site once a week to Barn Elms to hone their skills at netball, rugby, cricket, athletics, cross country and the like. There are lots of inter-school competitions, and the children told us proudly about recent triumphs over Wetherby and Fulham Prep. Swimming is held in nearby Fulham Pools, and ISA golds and silvers have been a feature of recent years. St James Junior is a member of Forest Schools UK, with two of its staff trained as Forest Leaders, and there are many trips to Minstead Study Centre in the New Forest. 'I've been seven times!' enthused one upper junior boy, 'and I enjoyed it SO MUCH!' A varied programme of outings closer to home has encompassed museums, art galleries, theatres, and the usual London fare. Excellent range of lunchtime and after-school clubs includes guitar, yoga, cookery, gymnastics, model-making, archery, fencing, lacrosse and the perennially popular Mad Science Club. The head actively encourages all her staff to take up hobbies themselves, and the staff music band, we're told, is going from strength to strength. Use of ICT across the school has increased, although actual ICT lessons are still for year 6 only, so the boys get them in their final junior year, and the girls in their first year at the senior school. Children are 'encouraged to use ICT at home,' which may or may not be enough preparation for the increasingly ICT-based curriculum they'll face at senior school. But the junior school's stated priority is to develop clear cursive handwriting in its pupils, and from what we saw, they definitely succeed.

Food here is vegetarian, so that all the children can eat together, and is included in the fees. We were impressed by what we saw: a delicious-smelling vegetable curry, fresh bread being baked, home-made leek and potato soup, and lots of genuinely appetizing fresh fruit. The number of clean plates testified to its popularity with the young clientèle, and one solemn little girl was particularly enthusiastic about it to us as she lowered her elbow into her coleslaw. No problem, though – the lower juniors (years R-2) wear smocks down to lunch, which we thought eminently sensible.

All aspects of the pastoral care were rated excellent in the latest inspection report, which commented on the 'family atmosphere of mutual respect,' adding that 'the pupils thrive in the positive, caring environment' and are 'very well cared for.' The pupils concur. 'It's fun here,' 'The teachers are very kind,' 'Everyone is really nice,' 'You don't feel you have to be afraid of anything,' 'You can be yourself,' 'You can be proud of yourself,' 'The teachers are proud of us and they trust us,' were some of the many tributes we heard. This is all the more inspiring, given that the School of Economic Science, which founded the St James schools, attracted some very different comments from its embittered pupils a few decades back (see our entry on The St James Independent Boys' School).

But all that is history. St James Junior impressed us as such a kind and enlightened medium in which to culture young minds, that we occasionally had to remind ourselves that this was a school we'd stepped into and not a Botticelli painting. It was almost a relief to see one small boy aim a punch at another, to hear an indignant cry of 'I was first!' and to meet a teacher who was unmistakeably knackered after her morning's work. But these tiny wrinkles only served to throw into greater focus the sweetness and calm of this remarkable community. Not a school for budding Piers Morgans, we suspect. But who cares?

St James Senior Girls' School

Linked schools: St James Junior School, 332

Earsby Street, London W14 8SH

Independent • Pupils: 325 • Ages: 10–18 • Non denom
• Fees (per term): £5,400

Tel: 020 7348 1777
Fax: 020 7348 1717
Email: admissions@sjsg.org.uk
Website: www.stjamesgirls.co.uk

17

Headmistress: Since September 2014, Mrs Sarah Labram BA (40s), formerly deputy head (academic) here. A classicist with a degree from King's College London, she is totally imbued with the St James ethos: a former pupil and head girl, whose two daughters were both educated at the junior and senior schools. She joined St James in 1996 as a classics teacher and has risen through the ranks to become head of department and then deputy head.

Academic matters: Girls take the IGCSE in maths and all three sciences – for greater rigour. At GCSE, 62 per cent A*/A grades in 2014. Stunning success in physics, history and English and at least respectable

The 'art of hospitality' is taught to years 6 and 7 – cookery, but not as you might have known it elsewhere

everywhere else. At A level the 20 subject options now include theatre studies, Spanish and art history. Results creditable in most subjects – few grades below B – and English and maths impressive. In 2014, 86 per cent of A level entries were graded A*-B (59 per cent A*/A). School also offers EPQ to give students the opportunity to get deeply involved in a subject that interests them, to pull together learning from other subjects and to develop extended research and writing skills – all of which are hugely valuable preparations for university study.

But this is not a school to think of solely in these terms. The school's culture largely determines the extended curriculum. Sanskrit is continued for those who join from the junior school (introductory course offered to those joining in year 7) and available as an option at GCSE. Singing, dance and philosophy are taken by all and everything is taught from the philosophical perspective which underpins the St James schools' ethos. This approach extends to the LDD provision which is managed on the basis of an individual's needs, although the hope is that most pupils can work independently by the end of year 8. Thereafter, the SENCo sees girls individually or in small groups according to need – no withdrawal from academic lessons. The staff monitor progress with care. Strong gifted and talented provision.

Games, options, the arts: This is a compact city site so anything involving running takes place at the Chiswick playing grounds, a bus ride away. On site, they cram in netball, aerobics, gymnastics, health-related fitness and dance etc and off site lacrosse, netball, athletics, rounders and tennis are the main sports. They have their own adventure club – the St James Challengers – and D of E. Two good art rooms in which, largely, the trad skills are taught by much-admired staff. Visiting instructors add to the core curriculum and the school now has a kiln but no dark room. And no DT. One of the best schools we know at actually displaying its own pupils' art – everywhere and with style. Music is big here (again under charismatic leadership); everyone sings – we heard it everywhere; the whole school sings together twice weekly. Music seen as part of the spiritual education provided. Lots of individual lessons and good collaboration on concerts and productions with the boys' school – despite the distance. Drama popular and lively; new drama studio. The 'art of hospitality' is taught to years 6 and 7 – cookery, but not as you might have known it elsewhere: the thrust here is on sharing food and using it as a way of nurturing relationships. The sixth form cook for each other, have formal dinners with high profile guests etc. In year 10, all go on a residential week which focuses on 'becoming an adult' – life skills, presenting oneself at interview and being a responsible citizen etc. Much emphasis on community service.

Background and atmosphere: Founded, along with its sibling junior school and senior boys' school, in 1975 by the School of Economic Science (see the review of the senior boys' school for background and history), the girls' school and junior school moved to their impressive modern accommodation in 2001. The outside is daunting. The main gate, within sight of Olympia down a quiet side road, is encased in uniquely secure architecture – grilles, grids, gratings and entry phone. If you happen to be a billionaire or high profile political refugee, you will deposit your daughter here in the mornings, confident that the bad world will be kept firmly outside.

The junior and senior schools co-exist happily and it is rather nice – if surprising – to come across classrooms full of 6-year-olds as you cruise around the corridors. Nonetheless, the schools are finding, as was inevitable, that both need more elbow room. School has planning permission to build a new sixth form centre in a nearby park, which will free up space for a larger library, another science lab and expanded classrooms. The place is in good nick – lots of white-painted corridors, blue carpets, good wall displays and useful noticeboards. The sixth form have privileges – eating in the staff dining room, for one – and responsibilities which are taken seriously.

Classrooms, while not quite providing the 'beautiful environment' aimed at, are orderly and well-kept and all now have whiteboards and projectors. The library is clearly too small and a new library is part of the building plan. Outside space is limited though care has been taken to provide little trellised alcoves for quiet chat around the tarmac playground. A sense of cheery collaborativeness abounds – girls look relaxed and happy and appreciate their unusual school. Staff, according to parents, 'always smile and are friendly'. 'Silence, stillness and meditation' are important – everyone has a few moments for these at the start and finish of each lesson. The food is vegetarian and the tables are laid invitingly – hot home-cooked food plus fresh fruit, salad, bread and cheese.

The boys' school move to Ashford has provided much-needed expansion space in a very attractive position. But while the arrangement presents opportunities for the St James schools, there may well be difficulties now that the family of schools is spread over a wider geographic area. How families wanting the St James brand of education for their boys, girls, juniors and seniors will adapt remains to be seen. Nevertheless, we hear that so far the majority of the junior boys are still transferring to the senior boys' school. Senior boys and girls also enjoy a good number of extracurricular activities together.

Pastoral care and discipline: Highly praised. Pupils like the mentoring system and the 'strong bond'

they feel to many teachers. Younger pupils are assigned sixth form prefects as mentors, sixth formers have form tutors. 'Your mentor is your friend – they always give you someone who doesn't teach you – you go to her with any problems – not just academic ones.' School relies on the 'very strong programme of education' to guard against the usual teenage problems. 'We emphasise strengthening a girl's social conscience and confidence..if you present with difficulties we will help you so long as you are not harming the rest of the community.' On bullying, 'we keep working at it.. stressing the importance of unity and not harming each other.'

The school's strong spiritual ethos underpins the disciplinary side but girls don't feel it's thrust down their throats. A parent expressed the general view – 'we like the way they approach education – they believe strongly in the spiritual side of it – it doesn't invade life but they look at the whole development of the girl and believe that the academics will follow.' Who wouldn't fit in? 'Someone who is only out for themselves wouldn't find themselves in their natural environment..our girls are gentle on the outside but inwardly strong and independent – they are women of some integrity.'

Pupils and parents: Mixed as befits its west London location. Unsurprisingly, given the influence of 'the wisdom traditions of east and west', the school has an appeal to families with Asian backgrounds who make up around a fifth. Some of the staff are members of the School of Economic Science, some are ex-pupils, but a large majority of the pupils are now from families who have no direct connection with the SES. Some pupils come from great distances – at least for the first five years – though most are relatively local. Former pupils include actresses Emily Watson and Sasha Behar and novelist Laura Wilson.

Entrance: St James Junior pupils move seamlessly through – NB at year 6 – and, at present, given that they share the site, this is much easier for girls than for boys, who head off to Ashford. Main prep feeders are Pembridge Hall, Orchard House, Chiswick and Bedford Park, Glendower, Ravenscourt Park Prep, St Nicholas Prep, The Falcons School, Bute House, Garden House, Kew Green Prep, Thomas' Battersea and Thomas' Kensington. Some also from St Mary Abbots, Barnes, Belmont and Fox primary schools. A few join at year 6 but main intake into year 7 when around 175 apply for around 25 places. School is part of the North London Consortium so tests in maths and English. School's own reasoning test day also includes activities in baking, art, drama, dance and chemistry. A few come in at year 12.

Exit: Currently around 30 per cent leave after GCSEs; some to co-eds, often to colleges, occasionally to board or to nearer home. A pity as the sixth form classes are small – one-to-one in some cases – the teaching is good and nothing beats the continuity of staying where you are known. Some gap years. Thereafter to a range from UCL and SOAS to the Prince's Drawing School. An increasing number are pursuing science degrees and over the last three years a third have left to study science of some kind. Many pursue careers in which they contribute to the community. Four to Oxford in 2014 – two to study Sanscrit.

Money matters: The school operates a means-tested bursary scheme. All current and future parents may apply. Future parents need to be registered with the school. This is not a rich school so don't look for masses of help.

Remarks: If the high moral tone appeals and you enjoy the repetition of words such as 'fine', 'wise' and 'beautiful' you have achieved Nirvana here. A tiny, peaceful school offering what many parents dream of.

St Paul's Girls' School

Brook Green, London W6 7BS

Independent • Pupils: 745 • Ages: 11–18 • C of E • Fees (per term): £6,958 – £7,479

Tel: 020 7603 2288
Fax: 020 7602 9932
Email: admissions@spgs.org
Website: www.spgs.org

18

High Mistress: Since 2006, Ms Clarissa Farr MA PGCE (50s), who previously spent 14 years at Queenswood, the last 10 as head. She has also taught English in Hong Kong, in a Bristol comprehensive and in a sixth form college in Farnborough. She is married to a sports journalist and has two teenage children.

As the established incumbent of one of the most exposed headships in the land, she exudes an elegant, intellectual confidence that could intimidate nervous potential parents and pupils. 'She seemed aloof initially,' said a mother, 'but she's much warmer when you get to meet her.' As a parent commented, 'You could easily get the wrong impression of her – she seems like a cut-glass ladies' college type – but my daughter really likes her.' 'Mine is really scared of her,' admitted another, 'but I noticed that the head girl and her team are all very relaxed with her, and they all clearly value each other's opinions.' Another added, 'She's always around, she knows them all by name. And my daughter says she'll sometimes give her particular look that makes you feel very important – as if you're the one person who matters.' By all accounts always present at school events, 'even the little drama club productions'.

Academic matters: Pretty close to unbeatable. School can afford a lofty disdain for league tables as it is always at or near number one (nearly 55 per cent A*s and more than 91 per cent A*/A grades at A level in 2014; over 93 per cent A*s at GCSE). The common claim to prioritise a broad education is undoubtedly justified here: many parents chose the school amidst a plethora of offers from other London powerhouses for this very reason. 'It really does feed a broader intellectual curiosity,' said one. Another commented: 'The teaching is second to none – exciting and stimulating. The teachers really get the children and make the most of them.'

Those few with special education needs often have coping strategies in place before they arrive, but the school is well set up to help. 'They've been astonishingly good at responding to my daughter's

As the established incumbent of one of the most exposed headships in the land, she exudes an elegant, intellectual confidence

needs, and put in plenty of support for her,' said a parent, 'so it hasn't been too much of an issue. But they have made it clear that she is expected to meet the standards of the school.'

Tight group of almost entirely academic subjects at GCSE and A level, which includes Italian, Chinese and Russian in the wide range of languages, though with relatively few takers at A level, and the recently added government and politics and theatre studies A level. Maths is by far the most popular A level subject, as one would expect, with a fairly even spread between the runners up biology, chemistry, English and history.

The school considered offering the IB but decided against it. 'We decided that A levels are a more flexible instrument – you have time to do things outside the curriculum that are not measured, and you can be a specialist or a generalist. It also gives more time for the bespoke Paulina unique co-curricular opportunities.' These include the Senior Scholarship project, which sees girls between years 12 and 13 carrying out projects with titles ranging from 'Is There Beauty in Chaos?' to 'Visualising Polytopes in 4 Dimensions'; and the Friday lectures from luminaries such as Shami Chakrabarti from Liberty and documentary maker

Michael Cockerell on his latest work, The Life of Boris Johnston.

Games, options, the arts: With a legacy of Gustav Holst as first director of music and in-house composer, music has always been exceptional. Indeed, the recently renovated music department and singing hall – 'where Holst and Miss Gray [the then high mistress] listened to girls singing' – are an important nerve centre of the school. There are orchestras, music ensembles and choirs open to all, but the symphony orchestra and senior choirs are by audition only and perform at astonishingly high levels.

Art, too, is high profile. When we visited, the impressive coursework for the school-directed art GCSE course was on display in the hall. 'Art here is very special,' commented a student. The top floor art rooms include a terrace with a panorama of the London skyline where girls learn about architecture. There are spaces for digital art, animation, ceramics, sculpture and print-making as well as painting and drawing. DT is a GCSE option only as part of art and design (a school-designed course), but an example of the talent was an impressive pupil-designed bus shelter that adorned the entrance drive when we visited.

Drama has perhaps been a poorer relation in the past. 'Music and art have always been great strengths,' says Ms Farr, 'but theatre studies is my

With a legacy of Gustav Holst as first director of music and in-house composer, music has always been exceptional

second subject, and it struck me that drama had not developed to the same level, so we have evolved a separate drama department.' It is a successful GCSE and A level option (though a mother commented that she was unusual in encouraging her daughter to take two arts subjects at GCSE: 'Lots of parents only want their daughters to do academic subjects'.) The purpose-built Celia Johnson Theatre hosts several annual school plays, with smaller scale productions in the drama studio. Students devise and direct their own plays, including the year 12 Colet Play, which has been performed at the Edinburgh Fringe on several occasions. Girls also join in St Paul's Boys' School productions.

Lacrosse is the main sport, with 7.30am practices for team players ('they all love it, so it's fine', commented a less devoted pupil), international tours and players often making county and area squads. The school also competes successfully at sports including netball, basketball, rowing, cross country, fencing and swimming. However, there are opportunities for the less talented too, with teams down to D and E in the lower years. 'My younger daughter is in a team even though she's rubbish,' said a parent honestly.

One parent commented: 'It's very inclusive. There's choirs and orchestras anyone can be in, and the same from drama and sport.' Amidst so many very talented girls, however, some of the younger ones in particular can take time to gain confidence and find their niche. 'My daughter plays an instrument but hasn't been asked to take part in anything so far. She and her friends like singing, but they found the choir too highbrow. And they were very disheartened when none of them got through to the second round of auditions for the school musical.' Another parent said, 'There are huge opportunities, but it's up to them to make the most of it.'

Huge numbers of clubs, seminars and trips: writing courses, physics and maths competitions, conferences in Paris, museum visits in St Petersburg, dance shows and debating competitions. 'The girls get caught up in the energy of the place,' says Ms Farr, and a parent commented, 'My daughter always comes home having done amazing things.'

Background and atmosphere: Some 400 years after John Colet founded St Paul's School 'for the children [not girls, naturally] of all nations and countries', the Mercers' livery company, guardians of his estate, decided girls were also worthy of an education and set up SPGS. Its red-brick main house, designed by Gerald Horsley, with marble-floored corridors, and panelled and galleried great hall, has a gracious, traditional and peaceful feel. 'But if you go in at break time it's very buzzy,' said a parent. 'They're all running round the hall, there's music blaring out.' Lack of uniform gives an informal air, with most girls dressed in ubiquitous jeans or shorts and tee shirts.

Ms Farr recognises that the school has an undeserved reputation for being 'very formal, starchy, cold, highly competitive, ruthless and unforgiving'. But once families join, she says, 'they find it's much friendlier than expected, and more informal. We like to do things in a friendly, collegiate way.' Parents agree: 'It's a much more normal place than you'd think from its image. It's much nicer from the inside than from the outside.' 'They really care about the individual.'

Impressive admin: 'It's really well run, which means a lot to us,' said a mother. 'Induction week in particular is brilliantly organised. They told the girls what would happen, and it did. They're very accommodating and very professional.' Another said, 'Unlike at my son's school, I don't feel I have to stress about homework and deadlines. I leave it to them.'

Pressure to achieve tends to come from highly-ambitious girls and their families rather than from the school. However, some feel that the school could do more to mitigate anxieties. 'Success is taken so seriously that it sends out a message of pressure,' said a parent. 'Lots of girls really worry about how they are going to do in school exams.

The food, said a pupil, is 'amazing. I feel as I am eating in a restaurant every day. Food is important to Paulinas.'

You can feel very unsuccessful if you aren't brilliant.' Some parents of younger girls feel the homework can be overwhelming. 'It tends to take much longer than intended because they're perfectionists,' said a year 7 parent. 'She and her friends take all evening doing homework.' 'I don't know how they cope if they miss anything, because lessons move at such a fast pace,' said another.

'We had the preconception that you had to be pretty, funny and clever to fit in here,' said a mother. 'But my retiring daughter has come home beaming from day one.' Another said that her daughter has found it tough: 'It took her a while to make friends. Coming from a state primary was particularly hard from a social point of view. But she's already gaining in confidence. They make the girls feel really proud of being there.'

Girls are encouraged to take the initiative. 'If you come up with an idea, the school will back you up and support you all the way,' said a sixth former, citing the in-house second-hand clothes shop, housed in a restored Victorian coal cellar that previously acted as a junk room, set up and run by students to raise money for local charities.

Pastoral care and discipline: 'I like to think it is a kinder school than it was,' says Ms Farr, who has increased the emphasis on the pastoral side. 'We have clear boundaries but lots of room for independent expression. We treat the girls like adults as soon as possible.' 'There's a marked lack of rules,' agrees a parent. 'There's a respect and a feeling of equality between teachers and girls.'

Some of these highly-ambitious girls do succumb to eating disorders or other expressions of teenage angst, but the school is very conscious of the problem and encourages a relaxed approach to eating. The dining room has recently been refurbished and the food, said a pupil, is 'amazing. I feel as if I am eating in a restaurant every day. Food is important to Paulinas.'

Small tutor groups of 12 girls keep the same tutor for two years in the lower school and three

'Our admissions process is a very careful, solemn business. We try to make it humane as well as thoughtful, and we discuss every candidate in detail.' The school optimistically asks parents to state if their daughter has been tutored, 'though we know they will answer what they think we want to hear.'

in the middle school. The sixth form has a vertical system to enable those in different forms to share experiences. The sister scheme sees girls from the middle and upper schools help new girls settle in, and two year 13 girls are attached to each lower year group, available for mentoring and encouragement. 'The sixth form isn't hived off in its own area but is very much part of the school. The girls are role models and figures to look up to for the younger ones.' 'Very approachable' school nurse.

Pupils and parents: Intellectual, ambitious, often multi-national families. 'I sometimes feel that my daughter's in a minority having two English parents. Lots of girls speak a second language fluently.' From a range of backgrounds – journalists and artists, academics and scientists, with a large proportion of bankers and lawyers ('You can spot those with bursaries,' said a parent wryly, 'because their dads aren't bankers.') Largest single cohort from Bute House, which regularly sends up to 20 or so girls here; the rest from a wide range of preps and primaries across London and beyond.

'There is a view that you must be super-confident to succeed here,' says Ms Farr, 'but girls vary here as much as anywhere. We do have a place for sensitive, quieter girls, and we enjoy the challenge of bringing them out. However, some parents still don't feel that their daughter is tough enough.' Parents agree that eccentricities are well tolerated. 'Of course the top dogs are the cool girls,' said one, 'but you can be a total geek and it's not a problem.'

Old Paulinas include (amongst many) Harriet Harman, Shirley Williams, Carol Thatcher, Stephanie Flanders, Rosalind Franklin, Rachel Weisz, Imogen Stubbs, Marghanita Lanski, Dodie Smith and Rachel Johnson.

Entrance: A computer-based test in November, aimed to be tutor proof and to identify 'girls with intellectual potential', deselects around 20 per cent of applicants. 'There's a vast industry preparing girls for St Paul's, and we don't want to miss bright sparks who haven't been tutored.' The rest take maths, English and comprehension exams in January, with those short-listed invited back for interviews. 'Our admissions process is a very careful, solemn business. We try to make it humane as well as thoughtful, and we discuss every candidate in detail.' The school optimistically asks parents to state if their daughter has been tutored, 'though we know they will answer what they think we want to hear'. They are trying to increase the proportion of successful state school applicants (currently around 15 – 25 per cent), and run a series of enrichment days for gifted and talented year 4 and 5 girls from local state primaries. Parents are given information about bursaries and encouraged to attend an open evening. 'We don't positively discriminate, but we do try to see through disadvantage.' The school is clear that it is looking for a particular type of girl. 'Our girls devour intellectual material very quickly. Those who want to work at a slower pace will be happier elsewhere.'

Exit: No-one is asked to leave because of poor academic performance (though they might reconsider someone who showed a lack of interest in learning). 'We make an undertaking to see them through, and every year we take through one or two girls whose GCSE performance is less than starry.' Minimal numbers leave after GCSE (a few are tempted off to co-ed sixth forms, particularly Westminster). Vast majority stay the course and move on to do mostly solidly academic subjects at a very narrow range of top universities. Around half get Oxbridge offers; seven or eight a year go off to study liberal arts at Yale, Harvard and other Ivy League universities; virtually all the rest to Durham, Edinburgh, Bristol and the London universities. The school is investigating European destinations, but no-one has been tempted across the Channel as yet.

Money matters: Four music (£100 a year and free music tuition) and four academic (£250 a year) scholarships at 11+; various art, music and academic scholarships at 16+, all worth £250 a year. The school aims to fund 20 per cent of girls through its means-tested bursary programme – 'we would like to feel that any girl from any setting could plot her way here' – and staff visit likely families at home to ensure they are not running a fleet of Ferraris from a multi-million pound mansion. Those on 100 per cent bursaries also receive a grant towards music or PE lessons, school trips, textbooks and travel.

Remarks: Unmatched environment for girls who thrive on hard work and have an appetite for intellectual experiences. 'What is on offer is exceptional. They have so many wonderful opportunities.'

St Philip's School

6 Wetherby Place, London SW7 4NE

Independent • Pupils: 110 • Ages: 7–13 • RC • Fees (per term): £4,600

Tel: 020 7373 3944
Fax: 020 7244 9766
Email: info@stphilipschool.co.uk
Website: www.stphilipschool.co.uk

48

Headmaster: Since 1990, Mr Harry Biggs-Davison MA (mid-fifties and bearing a passing resemblance to Daniel Craig). Educated St Philip's, Downside, Fitzwilliam College, Cambridge, where he read geography. Immediately returned to St Philip's to teach games in 1978 and has stayed ever since. Married with two grown up sons, his wife, Anna, is an invaluable part of the teaching team as the SENCo and with her own year 4 class. Head speaks of the school (his school) with enthusiasm and pragmatism, and of the boys and his staff with insight, pride and affection – and a healthy dose of good humour. When asked about St Philip's in the post-Biggs-Davison era (not that this is yet on the cards), expresses his hope that he will have a successor in the pipeline, 'in plenty of time', so that the inevitable disruption will be kept to a minimum.

Entrance: Boys come from local pre-prep and primary schools and most live within three miles of the school. Entry is into year 3 (10 boys) and year 4 (10 boys). School over-subscribed at both points but so far the temptation to select purely on the basis of

ability has been resisted. Priority is given to brothers of current pupils and to Roman Catholics. After that, references from schools and observations made during an activity afternoon form the basis of any decision to offer a place. The head is well aware that for some parents St Philip's may represent a fall back option; understandably he prefers to offer places to boys and parents for whom it is a firm favourite. It's hardly a gamble; there are plenty of parents who simply like what they see so the school does not need to change its modus operandi.

Exit: At 13+ roughly half to London day schools and half to boarding schools, including St Paul's, Westminster, Harrow, Wellington, Downside, Ampleforth, Radley, The Oratory (Reading), The London Oratory, Charterhouse, Eton, Worth.

Remarks: A school with few pretensions and a big heart, St Philip's feels like a large, slightly unconventional family. It reflects the best of Roman Catholicism; the religious ethos that underpins the day-to-day life of the school produces genuine

A school with few pretensions and a big heart, St Philip's feels like a large, slightly unconventional family

humanity and flexibility in the education of the young boys for whom it caters. The boys themselves are confident, polite and enthusiastic and willingly engage with any interested adult.

The number of pupils is generally steady at around 110 and the average class size is 20, while the ratio of pupils to full-time staff is 7:1. About 80 per cent of pupils have British passports but many have dual nationality with numbers from Europe and South America. However, this does not mean that the pupil body is a transitory one and most stay from beginning to end.

Mr BD says happily that there is 'room for eccentrics here', and we saw evidence to support this, although 'quirky' might be a fairer description. Staff are a good mix – many are young, several have been there for years, even decades. Stable staffing has not led to stagnation; teaching we observed was dynamic, technology is used to good effect across the curriculum but without sacrificing the rigour of more traditional methods. The balance seems just about right. In a year 8 Latin lesson boys were highlighting words they had problems remembering, followed by a session based around a series of pictures to assist those who were visual learners. The image of a shouting clam (clamo – to call, shout) or a vampire sinking its teeth into its victim's jugular (neco – to kill, slay) certainly seemed to do the trick.

Music has a high profile; more than half learn at least one instrument. The young director of music is one of the country's top organists: he has played the organ for the Pope and is credited by Mr BD for the number of music scholarships and exhibitions won recently by St Philip's pupils to eg Ampleforth and Winchester.

Differentiation in the earlier years and streaming in year 8 enables effective teaching across the ability range and impressive results at 13. Learning support is offered both inside and outside the classroom for the relatively few boys with mild learning difficulties. School accepts that life is not always easy for some children, often through no fault of their own, and sensitive, expert counselling is also available for those perceived to be in need. Head says parental expectations are managed through trust and 'not being too dogmatic'. He admits they are 'having to raise the bar', but some parents we spoke to expressed concern that the academic push does not come early enough for the pre-tests and opportunities are missed.

School housed in a red-brick Victorian building cleverly arranged to best accommodate pupils (and staff). Science and ICT are situated on the top floor, 'the only purpose-built part of the school'. Sport takes place off site at Barn Elms playing fields (which are currently being redeveloped in what Mr BD claims is 'an exciting fashion') and at Fulham Pools. The parents' association is very active and, allegedly, organises 'the best match teas in London'.

The outdoor space into which boys spill enthusiastically at break and lunchtime is something of a gem: a garden rather than a playground. It is an oasis of green with fruit trees, climbing roses, shrubs, flowers, vegetables and herbs. The boys play games around and within the vegetation as well as in the slightly more open areas where table tennis tables and badminton nets are erected. There are quiet corners for the quieter boys and plenty of staff on duty or simply outside because it's a great place to be. Mr Biggs-Davison admits that 'by year 8 the boys are outgrowing the space', but, of course, that is exactly as it should be.

Servite RC Primary School

252 Fulham Road, London SW10 9NA

State • Pupils: 240 • Ages: 3–11 • RC

Tel: 020 7352 2588
Fax: 020 7351 4024
Email: info@servite.rbkc.sch.uk
Website: www.serviteprimaryschool.co.uk

49

Executive Head Teacher: Since 2002, Mrs Kathleen Williams BEd NPQH (early 40s). Has spent all her teaching career in borough of Kensington and Chelsea. Previously deputy head of St Mary's Primary, Ladbroke Grove. Married with a young child, who (she hopes) will soon be a pupil here. 'I couldn't think of my son going anywhere else. I want him to have the grounded education which

Servite provides,' she says. Loves theatre, opera and all things musical. Friendly, capable and calm; an experienced pair of hands. Servite works in partnership with less serene local schools, in order to help raise standards and strengthen leadership. Head is ably supported by associate head teacher, Claude Gauci, who takes over the reins when she is out nurturing other schools. They make a robust team. Head admits that teaching is a demanding profession, but 'we're lucky. It's a privilege to be part of this happy school.'

Entrance: At 3 to nursery but a separate application is required for entry into reception. If they don't meet the strict criteria, then nursery children don't make it through to reception. Over-subscribed: approximately 60 apply for 30 places in nursery and 140 vie for 30 places in reception. Ever-decreasing catchment area (currently about half a mile). Pupils come predominantly from World's End estate and Earls Court. Priority given to baptised, practising Catholics who worship next door at Our Lady of Dolours. Occasional places further up school, though pretty rare due to low pupil mobility. V few non-Catholics. School currently at full capacity with 30 pupils per class.

Exit: Not a feeder for one particular school. Vast majority go to local Catholic state schools, including Cardinal Vaughan, Sacred Heart, St Thomas More and London Oratory, as well as a handful each year to Chelsea Academy. One or two go down the independent path, usually to Queen's Gate on bursaries. No special preparation given for 11+ and school seems to have escaped fanatical tutoring which goes on elsewhere in final years. A breath of fresh air.

Remarks: This successful school is tucked away behind an unprepossessing façade on the Fulham Road, opposite Chelsea and Westminster Hospital. Surprisingly spacious once inside with large, light classrooms and three playgrounds for different year groups (the one for the smallest children particularly colourful and welcoming). Impressively large hall which transforms into a dining room, gym and theatre and boasts sophisticated lighting and sound equipment.

Head believes Servite offers a broad education, which encourages self-confidence and independence. Children are well prepared for life at secondary school by the time they leave. 'Servite

Paul Canoville, first black player for Chelsea, regularly visits the school as part of its programme to promote positive attitudes towards racial diversity

gave my daughter the firm foundations on which to build,' said one grateful parent. Parents value the close association with the church which backs onto the playground. Pupils visit on holy days and every week one class celebrates mass there. Only three school rules –follow instructions; use kind and helpful words; keep hands, feet and objects to yourself. Pupils seemed to be adhering to these when we visited, though last rule appeared hardest to uphold.

Significant proportion of male teachers now. Staff consists of dedicated long-servers whose average age is 40. Appear devoted to the school and appreciate its family feel. 'They go the extra mile,' says head, 'and attend events at weekends such as school family mass with parents. No matter where the teachers live, they come to these events and the parents really appreciate it.' New teachers aren't taken on if they won't make a strong commitment to the school, beyond the classroom basics. Palpably strong relationships between teachers, parents and pupils. 'We have an open door policy,' says head, 'but within a structure. Not mayhem! Boundaries are set in a respectful way and issues are dealt with quickly.' One parent said, 'The school is professional but understanding'. Problems tend not to fester for too long.

Academic standard has been raised and school now boasts impressive results. Able children are extended through creative writing groups and extra maths support. Some bright sparks achieve level 6 in maths. Links fostered with Imperial College and Royal Institution to extend knowledge and develop understanding of science. Spanish,

Fantastic, carved Viking longboats on display and amusing portraits done by pupils of the staff line the stairs

School reflects the international, mixed community in which it finds itself. Head comments that many pupils come from, 'poor, working families, where parents are often in domestic service.' Many families struggling but tend not to be on benefits. One in five pupils is entitled to free school meals. Roughly 60 per cent has English as a second language. Many pupils hail from Philippines, South America, East Africa and Western Europe. Main languages spoken at home are Spanish and Tagalog. Extra language support catered for through small targeted group work and some one-to-one support on offer. Parents happy with speedy progress made by those with limited English on arrival. 'Now you wouldn't know which ones were behind with English when they started,' commented one.

Fantastic, flexible wrap-around care on offer but school admits it's hard to sustain at a competitive price. Includes breakfast at start of day as well as tea, activities and opportunities to do homework at the end of the day. Children can be looked after from 8am-6pm. Parents aware they are lucky and are the envy of other schools nearby which don't have extended care on-site.

Impressive range of sport on offer and given as taster sessions. Netball, football, athletics and swimming taught either on site, in Battersea Park or Chelsea baths. Dance and gym compulsory. A wide assortment of clubs including taekwondo, yoga, zumba and street dance. Football, drama and cooking currently very popular. Parents pay for these. Good use made of the local community and has strong links with neighbouring Chelsea Football Club. School participates in 'Educate through Sport' initiative and an English reading programme offered by the club. Paul Canoville, first black player for Chelsea, regularly visits the school as part of its programme to promote positive attitudes towards racial diversity.

Excellent use made of its central London location. 'You name it, we've been there!' says associate head. From designing apparatus for Cirque du Soleil acrobats to jump over in the Albert Hall to PGL visits to Weymouth, the pupils have fun here. Parents pay for school journey, but school helps those who are genuinely struggling to meet the cost. School payment plan in operation and parents encouraged to save for trip on a weekly basis.

Impressive art, drama and music. Annual art show to which parents are invited. Fantastic, carved Viking longboats on display and amusing portraits done by pupils of the staff line the stairs. Christmas nativity put on by youngest children and year 5 performs The Passion at Easter. Two nights in July are devoted to a musical production, generally led by year 6 leavers, and about which parents rave. Years 1-6 learn a class instrument, including ocarina, violin and ukulele. Currently 75 taking one-to-one lessons in piano, violin or guitar.

Effective communication between school and parents via weekly newsletter. Parent Council is parent-led and discusses initiatives such as school meals and uniform. Money raised by PTA tends to be spent on travel expenses for school journey, restocking library and equipment for playground.

School lives by its motto: 'Learning to love and loving to learn.' Family feel to the place. Children skip in each morning and enjoy their time here. On the day we visited, ambulance sirens blared incessantly on the road outside while the children danced around merrily in the playground, totally oblivious to the noise and fumes that engulfed them.

Above all, a welcoming school. No wonder head won't be considering anywhere else for her son.

Sussex House School

68 Cadogan Square, London SW1X 0EA

Independent · Pupils: 180 · Ages: 8–13 · C of E · Fees (per term): £5,610

Tel: 020 7584 1741
Fax: 020 7589 2300
Email: registrar@sussexhouseschool.co.uk
Website: www.sussexhouseschool.co.uk

Headmaster: Since 1994, the engaging, cultured Mr Nicholas Kaye MA ACP, Magdalene, Cambridge English graduate followed by music research (youthful 60). Whilst deputy head here, following a brief spell at Asra Hawariat School in Addis Ababa, of which he is a trustee and fund-raiser, the opportunity arose to acquire the school from the Vernon Trust, which he seized with typical energy, creating an independent charitable trust. Sussex House has never looked back, going from strength to strength, achieving the recent accolade of Best Prep School award. Parents admire this 'erudite man' and the boys sum him up as 'diverse, really talented, passionate about music, poetry, architecture, and a playwright'. His study/Victorian parlour is crammed full of book shelves with leather-bound volumes and novels by past Old Cadogans, an ornamental pianoforte ('The best pianoforte is the concert Steinway in the ballroom,' remarks the head) along with a cornucopia of porcelain, potted plants, objets d'art, furniture, rugs and oriental carpets illuminated by wooden lamp stands with large lampshades.

As one might expect in this very traditional institution, there are school photographs, house shields and embroidered banners made for the Jubilee and carried in procession on special occasions such as the annual All Souls' Day Requiem at St Mary Magdalene, Little Venice, which we attended. Conducted by Mr Kaye, this was an uplifting service in which the Sussex House choristers sang exquisitely. Mr Kaye enthusiastically teaches 10 periods to the top years with a focus on creative writing and literature. All the parents we spoke to agreed 'he has an excellent rapport with the boys'. One parent remarked, 'The headmaster has a key role in setting the tone of the school. Even more amazing is the fact that he sees the best in every child and gets the best out of every child.' Another commented, 'He teaches the sixth English in his study and they appreciate their elevated status. The sessions are challenging, quite adult, like an Oxford tutorial'. He is very ably supported by his PA/registrar who firmly declares, when questioned on the future, 'We are certainly not ready to hang up our boots yet!' And fortunately they show no signs of it.

Entrance: At 8+ and only later if there happens to be a place available. Thirty-six pupils are selected on the basis of a rigorous, competitive entrance examination in English, maths, reasoning and interview. Strong English is a key requirement and there are no boys in the school with EAL requirements; however, it does cater for up to 23 boys on the SEN register who are given support without additional charges. Parents suggest, 'Not a school of mixed ability, although mild learning difficulties such as

dyspraxia are dealt with'. Prospective parents are all given a personal tour by the registrar, meet the headmaster and are invited to a special evening led by members of the sixth form. The majority of boys live within a few miles of Cadogan Square. Regular

---

We heard a talented 9 year old play the violin with incredible skill and learnt he is also a valued member of the football team

---

feeders are Garden House, Eaton House, and other central London pre-preps. There are no sibling discounts on offer but bursaries and scholarships are available according to need and are up to the full remission of fees in cases of genuine need.

Exit: Majority to Eton and Winchester, some to Harrow, just under a third going to London day schools such as St Paul's and Westminster, with some major academic, art and music scholarships in recent years.

Remarks: Mr Kaye chose the aspirational school motto 'Lead me to the rock that is higher than I', and, as he explains, 'This implies a journey, which unlike climbing Everest, is never complete'. Unusually for a day school, there is an Anglican school chaplain who leads important services in the local church which acts as the school chapel.

This is a distinctive, remarkable school which is unashamedly academic. After being greeted by gowned school marshal, Sergeant Khim Sherchan, formerly of the Gurkhas, you are ushered into a grand Norman Shaw arts and crafts town house with William Morris wallpaper, stunning fresh flower arrangements, a realisation of Morris' tenet 'Have nothing in your house that you do not know to be useful or believe to be beautiful'. Parents who would prefer something more modern and spacious, where boys can let off steam at break times kicking a ball, should look elsewhere. Up the wide, ornate mahogany staircase is the ballroom, which provides a venue for daily assemblies, lessons around polished tables and tea time concerts. These concerts are an example of how every effort is made to encourage budding musicians at all levels. The music is stunning and every year concerts with a professional orchestra take place at the Cadogan Hall along with an annual musical at the Fortune Theatre. We heard a talented 9 year old play the violin with incredible skill and learnt he is also a valued member of the football team. One parent we spoke to remarked, 'The school is small enough so that each boy finds a niche.' Creativity abounds and is an intrinsic part of life at Sussex House along with its nurturing approach, and why many parents choose it over other top prep schools. As a parent commented, 'The wonderful drama is performed in the West End, giving unparalleled opportunities for this age'.

During our visit we saw some excellent architectural models in the making, in readiness for the annual exhibition with the theme of Iconic Chelsea. The clubs and art lessons include opportunities to do pottery and oil painting as well as making use of laptops for presentations about artists. The subject specialist staff are long-serving and popular with their pupils. All the boys we met commented on how the staff are prepared to give up their own time to help individuals. The boys themselves are a superb advertisement for the school: intelligent, polite, lively, responsive and articulate. 'They are confident without being arrogant,' commented a parent, adding candidly, 'That is not to say that they are not sometimes boisterous, and need careful handling in this confined space by their form teacher and/or the deputy head.' They are given Stars for rewards and Stripes for punishments. The sixth formers are prefects and wear gowns unless they fall from grace and are no longer allowed to wear a gown: a great incentive. They have opportunities to exercise at Battersea Park at least twice a week, and A,B,C,D, teams regularly play fixtures against other schools. The school day includes regular walks to Nicholls Hall for gym, fencing and music. Fencing is excellent here and the school magazine The Cadogan records many sporting achievements and activities, as well as superb poetry. The classrooms for younger boys still house old-fashioned lacquered desks, which are confining, and it is important to be aware that break times are spent inside the school, which would not suit all boys.

Average size of classes 18, with 12 in the top year when a scholarship group is formed. The curriculum is carefully tailored to suit the needs of individuals who will sit various school examinations. Mr Kaye would love to have a six day week, 'but that is not possible', as so much is packed in: orchestra practice and Greek before school, for example. As there is no dining room or kitchen, boys must bring packed lunches; 'not ideal,' state parents, but lunch time is a social occasion with the form teacher followed by numerous, popular clubs including architecture and discussion group. One ex-parent remarked on how 'well-rounded SH boys are', and that out of 250 boys at Eton in her son's year, three of the 12 chosen for the Eton debating competition were SH boys. The boys we chatted to would love to play rugby, but revel in football alongside options such as fencing, tennis, cricket, golf and swimming. They appreciate the spacious new science laboratory and find the art they do inspiring.

For those parents seeking a Summer Fields in central London, Sussex House fits the bill. Parents agree, 'It really does prepare boys for boarding at 13+ and gives them a wonderful, well-rounded platform'. It is not surprising that so many Old Cadogans hold the school with great affection. They include novelists Edward St Aubyn, Jason Goodwin and Richard Mason, along with actors Daniel Radcliffe, Jasper Britton, and Christopher and Jay Villiers, composer Michael Csanyi Wills, and many more recorded in the annual, very impressive magazine.

Thomas's Fulham

Linked schools: Thomas's Kensington, 352; Thomas's Clapham, Thomas's Battersea, see *The Good Schools Guide: London South*

Hugon Road, London SW6 3ES

Independent • Pupils: 400 • Ages: 4–11 • Non-denom • Fees (per term): £5,038 – £5,640

Tel: 020 7751 8200
Fax: 020 7751 8201
Email: fulham@thomas-s.co.uk
Website: www.thomas-s.co.uk

19

Headmistress: Since school opened in 2005, Miss Annette Dobson BEd. Trained at Homerton College, Cambridge and has SpLD postgraduate certificate. Taught at North Bridge House before joining Thomas's Clapham, where she worked for 10 years, latterly as head of the lower school. Highly regarded by parents, who feel she has guided the school well through its growing years. Approachable and relaxed, children and parents alike find her easy to talk to. Has succeeded in creating a happy school with a relaxed atmosphere despite the solid drive behind everything that is going on.

We didn't discover what the boys do while the girls pirouette. Maybe they are out kicking balls around?

Entrance: Selective at 4. Assessment in January before September entry. Sociable, confident children preferred. Must be able to cope and take what the school has to offer. Head personally sees all possible pupils. Sibling policy. Best to get children on waiting list as early as possible. Occasional places further up the school when potential pupil will spend half a day with peer group to see if he can cope. From year 3 assessment of academic potential and letter from previous school essential.

Exit: No preparation for 7+ or 8+ so majority move at 11. About a third transfer to Thomas's Clapham and Battersea for their last two years, some boys having done the pre-assessment test for eg Eton, King's Wimbledon and St Paul's Boys. At 11+ Ibstock Place, Francis Holland, Godolphin & Latymer, Emmanuel, Downe House, Kew House, St Paul's Girls, Putney High, Wimbledon High, Whitgift etc. Numerous academic and other scholarships (nine in 2014).

Remarks: A busy, buzzy school that packs a huge amount into each day. A place where parents say their children are exceptionally happy and never say they'd rather be at home! Possibly not for the very timid but somewhere that does seem to build a child's confidence in himself. We looked for the flaws but couldn't find them.

The newest of the four Thomas's preparatory schools in South West London, it has, perhaps, the youngest team of teachers we've met. Average age early 30s, passionate and imaginative, a good mix of male and female, they help create a generally happy atmosphere and a school full of enthusiastic children. Our guides, two of the most self confident 10-year-olds ever, led us round excitedly pointing out the things they really like and introducing us to their school. Different coloured staircases, painted in house colours, took us up and down, around and about, in and out of classrooms, laboratories, music rooms, art rooms, everything a child needs to stimulate interest and a hunger for education.

Parents say, 'they work them very hard', 'they are really driven', but these are parents who want their children to succeed. Work hard, play hard seems to be the ethos. For the top year, the Michaelmas Term is heavy on homework. Two 11+ practice papers at weekends together with other revision. But they take this in their stride, it's only for one term. They are being taught about competitiveness. This work ethic builds up slowly as they move through the school. Lots of play and fun at the bottom, lots of work and fun at the top. Streamed in maths from year 3 and taught in different groupings in year 6, depending on whether they are doing 11+ or not.

Teachers find different and innovative ways of getting them to learn. For instance, as you move from one classroom to another, you could come

across a subject-based quiz challenge on a board. Find the answers to the questions, put them in a coloured envelope and gain points for your house. Our guides were thrilled by this. Yet 'my son never felt pressured,' says a parent, 'but they still man-

---

Find the answers to the questions, put them in a coloured envelope and gain points for your house. Our guides were thrilled by this

---

aged to stretch him gently and bring out the best in him'. Another parent said, 'my child finds learning to read a bit of a struggle but it never worries her. Teachers boost her confidence and she thinks she's the best in the class!'

The theatre, as in all Joanna Thomas's schools, is very much a focal point. Loads of drama on the curriculum with a major production a year for each age group, as well as several clubs extending the experience for those who want it. To see the photographs of the becostumed children is to gasp in admiration. Ballet is compulsory for all children in reception and for girls in years 1 and 2. We didn't discover what the boys do while the girls pirouette. Maybe they are out kicking balls around?

Music also strong (parents say 'fantastic'), four choirs and various orchestral ensembles. A wide variety of individual instruments played, some to grade 5; lessons timetabled on a rotational basis but practising has to be done at home. 'Their performances are wonderful,' we were told, 'not just run of the mill; there was a lovely group of five boys drumming at a recent concert'.

Originally late Victorian school for 1000+ children; later, part of Chelsea College of Art and Design; the airy rooms and tall windows result in bright classrooms throughout. Light pervades. Largish school hall, doubling up as gymnasium, where assemblies are held twice a week either by year or for the whole school, when, we gather, it becomes quite a squash. Dining area canteen style. Pupils come in year by year, gobbling down food as fast as possible to let the next lot in. Some overflow into the school hall. They all say food is delicious and they like the choice. A parent said, 'the chef is a genius'.

Good playground space (recently redeveloped) divided into two sections for older and younger pupils. Lots of ride-on equipment for the little ones alongside good soft landing area with slides, climbing equipment and some very popular toadstools. Outdoor play in most weathers is regarded as essential at least twice a day.

Parents say sport top notch. Mostly in South Park opposite and round the corner in Hurlingham Park. Some busing in the top years. Lots of matches, inter-house, inter-Thomas's and against similar London schools. Several clubs to learn non-run-of-the-mill sports as well. The huge variety of clubs is extraordinary, covering indoor activities as well as sports (Hip Hop and Mandarin recent additions) and there is one for homework, phew. Green initiative against being driven to school means large piles of scooters and bicycles by the back gate – must be fun sorting through them at going home time.

Mild cognitive problems dealt with and extra help brought in if necessary. One-to-one tuition available at an extra charge. Systems seem to be in place for identifying potential problems though one parent felt they could possibly have spotted her child's earlier. 'All our pupils speak English', they say, even if some need a little extra help. Eighteen different languages are spoken in their homes, though. Also extra co-ordination for the gifted and talented with occasional higher level classes. Parents kept informed of progress, via email.

Systems in place to prevent any suggestion of unkindness to others. Parents say children 'really do care and want to be kind'. Worry boxes in each classroom. Older children have sessions working with the younger ones, keeping barriers down. New

---

Large piles of scooters and bicycles by the back gate – must be fun sorting through them at going home time

---

'values-based education' includes silver unicorns for live school values alongside golden unicorns for work and effort.

Generally good communication all over. Parents say open door policy and can talk to teachers any time. New all singing and dancing parent portal, just launched, tells everything that is going on and answers all queries. So no excuses for forgetting violins or games kit now.

Thomas's Kensington

Linked schools: Thomas's Fulham, 349; Thomas's Clapham, Thomas's Battersea, see *The Good Schools Guide: London South*

17–19 Cottesmore Gardens, London W8 5PR

Independent • Pupils: 360 • Ages: 4–11 • Non-denom
• Fees (per term): £6,666 – £7,333

Tel: 020 7361 6500
Fax: 020 7361 6501
Email: kensington@thomas-s.co.uk
Website: www.thomas-s.co.uk

51

Headmistress: Since 2012, Miss Joanna Ebner BEd MA PG Dip Couns Cert FT NPQH (40s), previously head of The Royal School, Hampstead (now absorbed by North Bridge House). A north Londoner by background, educated at North London Collegiate, Homerton College, Cambridge, and the Institute of Education, started teaching at Primrose Hill Primary School in Camden. She then went on to take a postgraduate diploma at the Training Institute of Family Therapy and City University and combined her teaching with a role as a school counsellor at South Hampstead High School. Once her children were of school age, she had to choose between teaching or counselling and teaching won. She returned to teaching at the North West London Jewish Day School, a primary school in Willesden, followed by a successful stint as deputy head of the junior school at The Hall, Hampstead.

After completing the NPQH (National Professional Qualification for Headship), she was appointed head at The Royal School, Hampstead in 2006. The mother of three teenage children (two

Not for the shy, withdrawn type: the pace is fast and the endless opportunities need to be grabbed with both hands

girls and a boy), she has also managed to fit in co-authorship of Counselling in Schools and contributed to the Girls' Schools' Association's best-seller, Your Daughter, as well as their My Daughter website.

Entrance: School full of large families, mainly from Kensington and Chelsea, with a few from further afield, Brook Green and Notting Hill Gate figuring highly. Mostly within walking, or at any rate, cycling distance. School keen to discourage motoring. Very over-subscribed, so best to get on

list as soon as possible after birth. Assessments in November before 4-year-old entry in September. Sibling priority but not guaranteed. 'We must feel child will be able to cope.' Occasional places further up the school, so always worth asking.

Exit: About a third, mainly boys, to Thomas's Battersea, many already with conditional places at top schools. Parents say, despite sameness, children find it quite hard to break into, and the move across is tough, but also say good step up and preparation for bigger school. Otherwise a few leave at 7 and 8, but not prepared for these entrance exams, and the rest at 11+. Mainly to senior London day schools – Francis Holland, Godolphin and Latymer, Harrodian and Latymer Upper amongst others.

Remarks: A busy, happy, international school where children learn to love learning and have fun at the same time. A cosmopolitan place, reflecting the changing face of London, where the 'be kind' ethos seems to work and children and teachers alike are exceptionally supportive of each other. Not for the shy, withdrawn type: the pace is fast and the endless opportunities need to be grabbed with both hands. But there is a world of education to be had in the grabbing.

A school on three sites with very little outdoor play area, so much use is made of local tennis courts and the park. Tall Kensington buildings, with several staircases meandering in and out of bright, smallish classrooms and learning areas, give a comfortable old-fashioned feel, but teaching and facilities bang up to date. Parents say 'wonderful, local, cosy school'.

Lower school housed in an entire unit of its own. Bright classrooms, own hall, dining facilities, library, IT, music and art rooms. Go round the corner to the preparatory school for pottery. Also have own outdoor play area; presumably, as has historically been a school for a long time, neighbours are used to it and don't mind a little noise. Space for planting and growing too. A teaching assistant in each class. A gentle, friendly place to start.

Pace speeds up on the move to the preparatory school and setting begins in maths. Specialist teachers, so classrooms become subject-based and much more moving around. Teachers enthusiastic and relaxed, average age mid-30s, a third have been at the school for more than 10 years. Good male representation. Particularly high quality reading and writing. In recent national competition to write to the Prime Minister, a year 4 boy was runner up. Small outdoor area, for quiet study only, so mid-morning break in classrooms with quick race around neighbouring tennis courts to expel surplus energy. Lunch takes place in converted Leith cookery school round the corner. Fantastic ultra-modern kitchen and cafeteria-style service. Dining area doubles up as gym with plenty of equipment. This building also contains exciting, purpose-built theatre for all those ambitious, glitzy productions. Seats 80. Also used for lectures, concerts and as extra play space, probably much needed on wet winter days. Two music rooms as well. Around 40 per cent learn an individual instrument, currently up to grade 4.

Sport perhaps less successful although does take up 20 per cent of the timetable. Lack of playground and size of school not helpful, and for boisterous boys it is not perfect, although school has worked hard to raise the profile of sport, including PTA sports reps. School says 'when we play schools of similar size, we have been very successful' and 'in running and swimming we are right up there with the very best'. Some parents feel this does not help with integration when they move across to Battersea at 11+. Lots of bussing to various different grounds and sports centres, as at their sister schools, and several sport-based after-school clubs. Having said that, the top classes can go for a 3k run in the park before school, and sports scholarships to senior schools are not unknown.

Assistant head also head of learning support. Sympathetic, trained and highly experienced. Makes sure all staff are well informed and the youngest pupils are properly monitored so problems can be picked up early. 'Must know how to spot and observe.' Good relationships with local dyslexia centre and occupational therapists. One-to-one support and laptop training when necessary. Makes sure specialist sports staff also aware of problems. Feels that school culture helps: 'sympathetic and calm'. Approximately a third exposed to language other than English at home. Plenty of help with speech and writing.

Parents say communications excellent and 'teachers very approachable and seem to really care', 'children really supportive of each other'. As at all Thomas's schools, loads of expeditions and outings, but here anything not involving overnight stay is included in the fees. Huge variety of after-school clubs including athletics in the summer. Lots of charity projects too. These children are really encouraged to help others.

Westminster Tutors

86 Old Brompton Road, London SW7 3LQ

Independent · Pupils: 45 · Ages: 14+ · Fees (per term): £6,666 – £7,333

Tel: 020 7584 1288
Fax: 020 7584 2637
Email: info@westminstertutors.co.uk
Website: www.westminstertutors.co.uk

52

Head: Since 2007, Ms Virginia Maguire BA MLitt (40s). Was previously director of studies at David Game College, and lectured at a Thai university for five years, publishing articles on sociolinguistics and aspects of Thai culture. She read English at UCL and gained distinction in her MLitt in English Studies from Strathclyde University. Her own mother took her A levels at Westminster Tutors. As well as running the college, she acts as SENCo, teaches English and delivers the PSHE programme.

Academic matters: This is a tiny organisation with some 50 pupils altogether, most of whom are taking or retaking A levels. The retakers – who may be there for a term or a year – are often high achievers who narrowly missed a place at a top university, and may be adding on another A level to improve their chances next time. Those who come for the full two year course tend to be attracted by the very individual attention. 'A lot of students who haven't coped well in a big school setting do well with us.' There is also a very small number – some five in all – taking or retaking GCSEs.

In spite of its size, the college offers a wide range of subjects, ranging from Greek to law to physics, by dint of having a large pool of freelance tutors it can call on, many of them Oxbridge graduates. These may be students working on PhDs, musicians, writers or experienced teachers moving towards retirement who want to keep their hand in. 'I will try to find someone to teach anything – I keep an eye out for what we are likely to need.' A large proportion of lessons are one-to-one, and each student has an individual timetable: drawing these up to suit teachers and students is a fiendishly complicated exercise.

Around a third of students have special needs of one sort or another, mostly dyslexia. The one-to-one system also copes admirably with, for example, the very bright girl with Asperger's who likes being immersed in two-hour-long lessons, and the boy with ADHD who works best in short bursts, including supervised homework sessions. 'It's like having one's own private tutor,' said the parent of a pupil who had floundered elsewhere, 'but in a friendly college setting.' 'My daughter's motivated at last,' said another. 'She's actually keen to go to school and to get on with her homework.' The school has links with an educational psychologist, and will adapt teaching according to her reports, but cannot cope with severe behavioural problems.

Exam results are highly creditable for such a mixed, totally non-selective intake. 2014 saw 73 per cent A*-B, 41 per cent A*/A at A level.

The college also offers private tuition for mature students who, for example, want to study medicine and need science A levels, helps with common entrance exams, and specialises in preparing outside students for Oxbridge, medical and law school applications. The head originally set up Uniprep as a separate company, but it is now merged with the college. She specialises in medicine and dentistry preparation plus LNAT, and her Oxbridge graduate tutors provide preparation for

'It's like having one's own private tutor,' said the parent of a pupil who had floundered elsewhere, 'but in a friendly college setting.'

their respective degree courses. The college also runs half term and holiday revision courses. 'We work very well across the spectrum from special needs to very bright.'

Games, options, the arts: Art and photography are both A level options. Students visit the linked David Game College in Notting Hill to use its facilities, either joining an existing group there or forming their own. A 'wonderful art teacher' provides enrichment classes as well as taking history of art students for fortnightly gallery visits. The college is handy for the South Kensington museums and for theatre trips.

Sport is not a high priority, but the college does field a five-a-side football team, and weekly sports sessions are held at Chelsea Leisure Centre on the King's Road. One ping-pong table – being used as a desk when we visited. Because of lack of space and facilities, the college cannot offer drama, dance, PE or media studies courses.

Background and atmosphere: The college was founded in 1934 and is one of the oldest tutorial

colleges in the country. It is now one of the David Game group of colleges, which includes some 25 institutions in the UK and overseas.

It is based in two adjoining townhouses near South Kensington tube, and most of the space is decidedly compact. Staff and students share a common room. 'We're really small so we all mix in together.' Library, IT room, physics room and biology practical room that decidedly resembles a small kitchen (chemistry students use the labs at David Game College in Notting Hill).

Pastoral care and discipline: All students have personal tutors – one of these 'is brilliant with way-ward boys: we give him the younger ones who need to be constantly chivvied'. But the head is the personal tutor for the A2 students, supporting them through UCAS, as well as being the main point of contact for all parents. 'If parents have any concerns they always deal directly with me.'

Non-attendance at any lesson is swiftly followed by a phone call – first to the student then, if they don't reply, to a parent. But otherwise the atmosphere is informal: 'We're not oppressive about rules. It's easier to have a cooperative environment'. Students organise dinners or parties, with the head boy and girl in charge of younger pupils; only over-18s are allowed to drink alcohol. Bad behaviour unlikely to go further than a recent incident of older students placing bets for younger ones at a shop down the road. 'A warning is usually as bad as it gets. If I'm cross they know why.'

Pupils and parents: Eclectic mix of those with special needs and others who have not thrived in the rough-and-tumble of larger, more traditional establishments, combined with high achievers who come for the expert teaching.

Entrance: By interview with the head. 'We talk about what they are doing now, what they are hoping to do, their university goals. I look at their results so far and their school reports. But we're non-selective academically, and my main criteria are whether they are going to be happy, suit our way of teaching and fit into the college. We don't want to upset the harmonious atmosphere here.' She will not take students who have been expelled elsewhere for serious behavioural problems, drug or drinking offences, but will probably turn a blind eye to one-off misdemeanours, and rarely turns people down. 'But sometimes I can sense attitude problems, and I might not be so encouraging about them coming here.'

Exit: Over 95 per cent to higher education, ranging from anthropology at Durham to nuclear engineering at Birmingham and dentistry at King's College

London. Advice is always geared towards finding a course appropriate for the student. 'Some students are not suited to university, but I would always try to direct them to some sort of higher education. I try very hard to find a course that's right for them, which may have a very practical bent for someone with severe dyslexia.'

Money matters: As one would imagine, the one-to-one staff:student ratio does not come cheap. However, fees are comparable with other tutorial colleges that have much larger classes. Up to four A level scholarship places. A few statemented pupils funded by LAs.

Remarks: Has developed a niche providing one-to-one teaching for gifted students with special needs, and also helps prepare potential medics and Oxbridge candidates. The rest come because they are attracted to the cosy, friendly, supportive atmosphere, 'and you can be sure they getting the best chance to achieve,' commented a parent.

Wetherby School

Linked school: Wetherby Preparatory School, 210

11 Pembridge Square, London W2 4ED

Independent · Pupils: 250 · Ages: 4–8 · Non-denom
· Fees (per term): £6,170

Tel: 020 7727 9581
Fax: 020 7221 8827
Email: learn@wetherbyschool.co.uk
Website: www.wetherbyschool.co.uk

53

Headmaster: Since 2008, Mr Mark Snell BA PGCE (40s). Busy, enthusiastic, hearty, noisy, ebullient, much loved by boys and parents alike. Passionate about education. Deputy for two years before taking over as head. Read business studies at University of Westminster before going to Brighton University to get his teaching qualification. Taught at Eaton House the Manor and Westminster Under before becoming head of maths at King's College School, Wimbledon, Junior where he stayed for five years. Teaching is definitely 'in the blood' – his wider family own Mowden School in Brighton and Ludgrove in Berkshire. Married with two young children, lives in Wimbledon, where his wife teaches maths at King's College School.

Has, according to parents, made the school 'more touchy-feely' or 'a bit more chilled without affecting standards'. 'All the staff like him and the boys think he's their best friend'. But they still respect him and would not dream of doing something of which he did not approve. One child's father jokingly called him 'Mr Smell', which so horrified his son he told him off severely. Another parent told us 'he is a mixture of charm and strictness, he gives

---

A notice on his office door reads, 'Stop. Smile before entering or do not enter!' That says it all

---

children boundaries with humour'. Teaches maths to the older boys and helps out with the younger ones. Believes you need to teach in order to know the boys properly and really does appear to know boys and parents inside out. Holds open staff meetings so that all can have their say. Believes teachers should be the core guidance in future planning although he will always make the final decisions. Determined that school should be a happy, fulfilling, jolly place – 'I am really here for the kids and I'm scared of silence'. A notice on his office door says, 'Stop. Smile before entering or do not enter!' That says it all.

Entrance: Non-selective, so get on the waiting list fast – at birth is strongly recommended. Staggered throughout the year so ages properly mixed. The majority live locally, although one parent said that the net seems to have spread further round London these days. Some spaces occur at other times for the lucky ones. Lots of multi-national families but speaking English is regarded as a necessity.

Exit: About a third to Colet Court and Westminster Under and 40 per cent to Wetherby Prep, with the remainder split between the other London day schools and boarding preps.

Remarks: No longer the glitzy glam place of yesteryear, now a busy, buzzing, caring, cosy school where all boys are exceptionally well prepared for the next stage. They are not only taught how to learn but also how to be kind and the importance of good manners. Yet they have an enormous amount of fun at the same time. 'Just the right balance,' say parents.

Young (average age 32) teachers who parents say are 'superb' and 'relate to the boys, enthuse them and have a very good rapport'. The head has rejigged the timetable so that the serious lessons – maths and English – are in the first two periods of the morning. These are structured classes when the boys know that they have to work hard. All other lessons are holistic and cross-curricular, partly to make them more fun and relaxing but also to introduce different styles and ways of learning. Speaking and listening is an important part of the curriculum in years 1, 2 and 3. A teaching assistant per class. Three mixed ability classes per year. Maximum number in each 21. Classrooms quite small but all bright and jolly containing happy, chatty children working informally at different levels. No 'silence in class' here. EYFS directive means that reception classes are now much more play based. 'No bad thing', says the head, 'but we do build in some structure because we feel it helps the children intellectually when they enter year 1'.

Good music. Over 50 per cent learn an individual instrument. Several choirs and bands which regularly perform externally. Art and DT now perform a much larger part in the school as is indicated by the number of masterpieces decorating the walls, some showing exceptional talent for such young children. Unexciting library, with rather bare shelves, also contains computer area. ICT taught in half sized classes. Interactive whiteboards everywhere.

No outdoor play space but parents don't seem worried. All younger children have 15 minutes twice a day running around in the communal square and the upper school also have four activity sessions a week. The previously rather formal annual sports day has, apparently, been transformed into a jolly, fun day for all, 'now a wonderful and relaxed time'.

Exceptional SEN support and pastoral care. Secure system in place for spotting boys with even minor learning difficulties. Parents are involved from the beginning and all necessary help is provided. Unless this is one-to-one or specific, it is regarded as part of the service. One parent with a boy who was desperately lacking in confidence said it was 'awesome' how they helped him build it up. Another one, with a dyslexic child, was full of praise for the way they handled his difficulties. 'Golden Rules' encourage honesty and gentleness amongst the boys.

Parents say, 'a small, charming, smarty pants school which nurtures boys and sets them up with a baseline for life'. 'Our three boys are totally different yet all are doing well and love it.' 'At Wetherby they are not going to let anyone fall through the crack.' 'Really teaches children rules and gives them pride in their education.'

West

Borehamwood
Watford
Bushey
Barnet
M25
M1
Rickmansworth
Edgware
Hatch End
Burnt Oak
Pinner
Colindale
The Hyde
Kenton
Harrow
Brent Cross
Ruislip
Denham
North Wembley
South Harrow
Ickenham
M40
South Ruislip
Brent Park
Wembley
Kilburn
Northolt
Uxbridge
Harlesden
Hillingdon
Maida Vale
Greenford
M25
Iver
White City
Hayes
Southall
Shepherd's Bush
South Ealing
Kensing
West Drayton
Hammersmith
M4
Chiswick
Harlington
Brentford
Kew
Cranford
Fulham
Isleworth
Barnes
Richmond
Hounslow
M25
Twickenham
Richmond Park
Feltham
Ham
Staines
Wimbledon
Bushy Park
Kingston
Sunbury-on-Thames
New Malden
Morden
M3
Surbiton
Worcester Park
Weybridge
Esher
1
2
3
4
5
6
7
8
9
10
11
12
13
14
15
16
17
18
19
20
21
22
23
24
25
26
27
28
29
30
31
32
33
34
35
36
37
38
39
40
41
42

WEST

BRENT

1. JFS 410
2. Maple Walk School 425

EALING

3. Drayton Manor High School 381
4. The Ellen Wilkinson School For Girls 385
5. Montpelier Primary School 430
6. North Ealing Primary School 435
7. North Primary School 441
8. Notting Hill And Ealing High School Junior School 448
9. Notting Hill And Ealing High School 449
10. St Benedict's Junior School 455
11. St Benedict's School 456
12. Twyford Church Of England High School 470

HARROW

13. Harrow School 398
14. The John Lyon School 412
15. North London Collegiate School Junior School 436
16. North London Collegiate School 438
17. Orley Farm School 452
18. St Dominic's Sixth Form College 460

HILLINGDON

19. ACS Hillingdon International School (Junior Section) 369
20. ACS Hillingdon International School 371

21. Glebe Primary School 387
22. Haydon School 403
23. Little St Helen's And St Helen's Junior School 420
24. Merchant Taylors' School 426
25. Northwood College Junior School 444
26. Northwood College 445
27. St Helen's School 462

HOUNSLOW

28. The Arts Educational School (London) 375
29. Belmont Primary School 378
30. Gumley House Convent School 389
31. International School Of London – Junior 405
32. International School Of London 406

RICHMOND–UPON–THAMES

33. Hampton Court House (Junior School) 390
34. Hampton Court House (Senior School) 392
35. Hampton School 394
36. The Lady Eleanor Holles School, Junior Department 415
37. The Lady Eleanor Holles School 417
38. The Mall School 421
39. Newland House School 433
40. St James's Catholic Primary School 465
41. Twickenham Preparatory School 468
42. Waldegrave School 475

An introduction to West London and its state schools

Brent

Gritty Brent with its huge ethnic mix is largely famous for Wembley Stadium. Even Brent Cross shopping centre is in neighbouring Barnet. The leafier northern part of the borough hosts JFS qv , the extremely popular secondary school that is the largest Jewish school in Europe. It moved from Camden to a purpose-built site in Kingsbury in 2002. Islamia Girls School, in Brondesbury, is rated as outstanding. Kingsbury High and Queen's Park Community schools are good local non-faith schools. Ark Academy in Wembley is a new all-through school. Due to open in 2015 is a new 11 – 18 Lycée, which will no doubt affect the demographics of the area.

One of the best-rated primary schools is North West London Jewish Day School. St Joseph's and Our Lady of Grace are popular Catholic primary schools, whilst Malorees is an outstanding non-faith school, as is Oakington Manor School in Wembley, which has its own centre for children with speech and language difficulties.

Ealing

Ealing, a sprawling west London borough, comprises Acton and Ealing to the East, Greenford, Northolt and Perivale to the North and Hanwell and Southall to the West. It is the fourth most ethnically diverse borough with 55 per cent of residents coming from an ethnic minority. This is reflected in the make up of the schools. An influx of residents (there are large Polish communities, particularly in the north in Greenford, Perivale and Northolt, as well as Somali residents in Acton and Hanwell, and Indian communities in Southall) has resulted in most of the primary schools expanding from two form entry to three and in some cases four. The question many are asking is how the secondary schools are going to meet the greater demand for places.

One of the most popular secondary schools at the moment is Drayton Manor qv. Residents describe it as structured and old fashioned with good results but perhaps lacking a creative edge. The more arty child may be better suited to Brentside High, a modern site with shiny new facilities. Elthorne Park remains top of many parents' list – despite receiving a disappointing Ofsted report recently. The site is spectacular for an inner London comprehensive, with endless playing fields at the back, and excellent outside facilities. Results here are impressive too. Cardinal Wiseman (Greenford), Greenford High (Southall) and Twyford C of E High School qv (Acton) come out top on the results table but Elthorne is hot on their tails.

Twyford's reputation is phenonomenal. Parents are prepared to move mountains (by which we mean dedicate themselves and their weekends to the local church) in order to get their children in here. We agree, it is good, and probably worth the sweat, particularly shining in music and languages. One to watch is the new William Perkin C of E (also Church of England and linked to Twyford – they have the same executive head and board of trustees). Situated in a relatively deprived area of the borough, the main admissions criterion is proximity to school (rather than, like Twyford, years of church-going and brass-polishing). Will it ever be comparable to its sister school?

Practically all primary schools are good, some outstanding. Popular primary schools include Derwentwater, Berrymede and the Ark Priory in Acton, Fielding (which as its name suggests is lucky enough to have a lovely field rather than just usual bricked playground), North Ealing qv (known for good results) and Montpelier qv in Ealing, and Hobbayne, Mayfield and Brentside in Hanwell. Southall alone has 18 primaries, including one Sikh faith school. North Primary qv and Havelock are considered to be outstanding and the rest, with one or two exceptions, good. In contrast Perivale has only three primaries, one of which, St John Fisher, is Catholic and outstanding. In Northolt and Greenford (19 schools between them) ones to consider are Vicar's Green and Gifford.

Harrow

Harrow, with Hertfordshire to its northern border, is undoubtedly one of the leafier of the London boroughs, dotted with small detached and semi-detached houses and a good proportion of garden-for-money, though the affluent areas of Harrow-on-the-Hill (home of the eponymous Harrow School qv), Pinner and Stanmore contrast with more deprived areas such as Wealdstone. It is extremely diverse ethnically and religiously, with a large Indian population. Nower Hill High and Whitmore High are the top rated secondaries along with the girls' Sacred Heart Language College. St Dominic's Catholic Sixth Form College qv has an excellent record. Around half of its students are Catholic, nearly all the rest Hindu or Muslim.

It has several high-performing Catholic primary schools eg St Anselm's, St Bernadette's and St John Fisher. The Moriah Jewish Day School does well too. Popular non-faith schools include Grimsdyke, Pinner Park, West Lodge and Whitchurch Junior – and Newton Farm, in the news in 2013 because its maths and writing Sats results were disallowed due to 'maladministration'.

Hillingdon

Hillingdon sits right on the western edge of London, a mix of green belt land and residential suburbia, with the Metropolitan line providing a quick link to the centre. Haydon School qv in Northwood is one of the most popular secondaries (specialises in languages and applied learning, with lots of BTec options), alongside Bishop Ramsay C of E in

Ruislip, Douay Martyrs Catholic school and Vyners, both in Ickenham, and Queensmead in Ruislip.

Amongst the primary schools, Catholic St Swithun Wells, Sacred Heart and St Mary's all perform well. Other popular primaries are Whiteheath Junior, Hillingdon primary, Oak Farm Junior and Breakspear. Guru Nanak Sikh Primary Academy, half of whose pupils enter the school knowing little or no English, is vastly oversubscribed.

Hounslow

Hounslow, which abuts the Thames at Brentford and includes Osterley Park and Syon House, is a gateway to all roads west. Heathrow airport is a major employer (and the source of much flight noise), and the population is very diverse, with large numbers of families speaking English as an additional language.

Gumley House qv, in a Queen Anne house surrounded by lovely grounds, and St Mark's Catholic School, are popular faith-based schools. So is the Green School (girls, C of E) in Isleworth. Heathland School in Hounslow is a high-performing co-ed school. Cranford Community College takes large numbers of disadvantaged children, the vast majority from ethnic minorities, and is rated outstanding.

Belmont primary qv caters for an affluent area of Chiswick and gets some seven applicants for each place. Spring Grove, Grove Park, Blue C of E and Chatsworth are other popular primary schools, as are St Mary's RC schools in Chiswick and Isleworth.

Richmond-upon-Thames

Straddling both sides of the Thames, Richmond's borough limits can confuse even locals (just as well they don't go in for drumming strangers out of town: they'd probably never leave).

But whether cosying up to Kingston (south bank) or Hounslow (north) however, schools suffer from the same overcrowding problem. The LA is tackling the problem, tacking on classrooms and building two new schools from scratch. Meanwhile, living as close as you can to the desired school (dustbin in playground ideal if has own postcode) has never been a better idea.

Richmond comprehensives, with the notable exception of Waldegrave qv, have until recently been no better than they should be and, in many parents' eyes, rather worse, given excellence of primary school performance that should give pupils a substantial head start. As the only single sex senior school in the borough, Waldegrave plunders the area's girls, boys currently accounting for approaching 60 per cent of pupil roll almost everywhere else.

What won't now wash is the old excuse about under-investment. Teddington (rated 'good' in last inspection) was one of last schools to secure funding for a complete multi-million pound rebuild and is drop dead gorgeous (even if so big that you can spend the whole lunch hour trying to find your friends).

There's been similar makeover for Twickenham Academy - historically one to avoid with GCSE results and reputation still lagging and considerable way to go before it tops ambitious parents' wish lists. Ditto Hampton Academy, this despite commitment from Swedish based sponsors who run both to effect Cinderella-style transformation.

More promising is all-through Catholic school, St Richard Reynolds, which was very controversially allowed to have voluntary aided rather than academy status, thus enabling it to give all its places to Catholic children. It opened its doors for its first intake (mix of reception and year 7 pupils) in September 2013 and is, it says, 'passionate about improving the life skills and chances for children created in God's image.' (Doesn't say anything about chances for those who aren't). Another north-west of the river comprehensive, Orleans Park, with excellent extracurricular list including after-school Mandarin, 'has come up a lot in the past year,' says local.

Developments on the way include addition of sixth forms to many schools - likely to impact on currently over-subscribed Richmond College, currently biggest post-16 destination.

Popular primaries north and west of the Thames are St Stephen's C of E, Archdeacon Cambridge's C of E and Hampton Junior, together with Collis, one of first to be surgically enhanced, now boasting indoor facilities so good that at least one envious visiting teacher had to be coaxed to leave for own less impressive establishment. Downsides headed by danger of low-flying helicopter parents (as well as flight path noise).

Following amalgamation of formerly separate infants and juniors departments, Stanley School, with head count of 700 plus, though worlds apart from quaint little village school, is academically very much on the up.

Borough-wide praise for staff, whose own enthusiasms translate into impressive extra curricular activity. St John the Baptist's head is a Shakespeare nut, busily abridging plays (three so far and counting) highlight so far a performance of Macbeth in nearby Hampton Court Palace. Hampton Hill, in contrast, excels at music – nine ensembles and four choirs including – wonder of wonders - one for boys only as well as audition-entry chamber group, while at Chase Bridge, also equipped with lovely new buildings, makes most of links both with army music centre Kneller Hall and Twickenham stadium (both nearby).

The icing on the cake? Securing dream catchment area to allow seamless primary to secondary move. Good bet, for those with daughters and deep pockets, is Twickenham Green, pairing Trafalgar at primary level (spiffing buildings, horribly oversubscribed, par for the course) with one of UK's top small comprehensives, Waldegrave Girls.

ACS Hillingdon International School
(Junior section)

Linked school: ACS Hillingdon International School, 371

Hillingdon Court, 108 Vine Lane, Hillingdon, Middlesex UB10 0BE	Tel: 01895 259771
	Fax: 01895 818404
	Email: hillingdonadmissions@acs-england.co.uk
Independent · Pupils: 210 · Ages: 4–11 · Non-denom	Website: www.acs-england.co.uk
· Fees (per term): Fees (per term): £3,327 – £6,637	

20

Head of School: Since 2012, Linda LaPine; from the USA; BA (Urban Studies) State University of New York; MPS (master professional studies, special educational needs), Manhattanville College, New York; teaching and principal certification. She was a special needs teacher in New York, also in private practice, before going abroad to International School of Tanganyika, American School in Singapore, Anglo-American in Moscow as deputy head, most recently International School of Panama as director. Now as head of a school that is part of a larger group of four, she devotes most of her time to running Hillingdon, while collaborating with the other ACS heads and board developing programmes and policies for the ACS schools group.

In her words, she came into a good school with no major issues to resolve. After significant developments at ACS Qatar, Egham and Cobham, Hillingdon likely to be the next candidate within the ACS schools group for capital investment, so Ms LaPine is working with colleagues to determine what that might be: strengthening of curriculum, technology, internationalism and/or use of the outdoor environment. 'I am not aspiring for ACS Hillingdon to be a "magnet school", I just want to provide an overall inclusive educational programme that is a based on a strong school community. Academics are priority, but it's also about the overall family experience, the kids being comfortable and happy, and every child feeling important.' Two daughters attending the school. On contract till 2015.

Entrance: Non-selective; will admit pupils they feel they can serve and will benefit from the programme. Admission based on previous school records and testing scores, family statements and references from previous school are preferred, though the admissions director understands that

369

for last-minute summer transfers these are sometimes difficult to obtain. Additional assessment or writing samples may be requested. Decisions to admit pupils to grades 5 and above with diagnosed special educational needs are made in consultation with the specialists. It is sometimes possible – and recommended – that prospective pupils spend a day in the school. Predominantly expats at the school with about 17-20 per cent turnover, so usually hope of a place. Pupils are admitted throughout the year. Occasional waiting lists. No deadline but apply by end of March for a better chance of being successful. They are sympathetic to the sibling issue and do their best to accommodate the entire family (and we spoke to families who were highly complementary about the school's efforts in this, and the admissions staff in general).

Exit: Students generally leave because of family moves. Very few leave to attend other local schools: most continue on to ACS Hillingdon's middle school.

Remarks: American-style curriculum with international add-ons, including language and cultural studies up to grade 2, which parents help to run, then multicultural weeks, including Spanish, in grades 3-5 organised by the PTSA (Parent Teacher Student Association). The early childhood programme is a nice blend learning-through-play and structure, supplemented by specialist teachers for music, art and PE, and cultural classes.

Parents like the fact that the primary principal is very much around in the classrooms, engaged with the kids and monitoring progress. One of the few complaints is that some feel that homework

---

There are revolving student art exhibitions in the head's office (a proud primary pupil was taking a photo of this to send to his grandmother)

---

is somewhat inconsistent, with more in the lower school than in the middle school. (The school says it has a coherent homework policy published in its handbooks). Plenty of up to date technology, including iPads issued by the school.

Language and cultural studies expose the youngest ones to languages represented in the school community. A different language and culture is featured each month, and children learn when basic phrases, explore traditions and sample food.

The NLE (Native Language Enrichment programme – an ACS Schools feature) provides mother tongue instruction. The school funds one hour after-school classes for a minimum of three pupils of similar ages and levels (if fewer than three, the school helps find a tutor but classes are paid by parents). Parents say they'd like to see more, and it can be difficult to enthuse children about taking the mother tongue when their chums are doing 'fun' after-school activities, so they may revert to Saturday schools.

Lots of monitoring and MAP tests to track progress (MAP means Measures of Academic Progress – a data-led approach originated in the US).

Learning support teachers available at no charge, but in grades 5-12, a student must have a current ed psych report or be in the process of obtaining one. Decisions to admit students with learning issues is partly dependent on the current case load, to ensure they get the support they need.

EAL classes have specially trained teachers, aiming to help each pupil acquire basic vocabulary and vocabulary relevant to classroom topics. The youngest ones have full-immersion English, with specialists either working alongside them in the mainstream classroom, or withdrawing them for one-to-one or small group support.

After-school and some lunchtime clubs for all ages. A popular Saturday sports programme for all ages features basketball, tennis, football and baseball.

Student art work everywhere, including revolving exhibitions in the head's office (a proud primary pupil was in the office during our visit taking a photo of this to send to his grandmother) and in the centrally located Bridge Gallery. Primary music takes place in the main mansion – in a stunning room with high ceilings, sculpted crown mouldings, cornices, coving and massive windows overlooking the gardens, surely one of the most elegant primary school music rooms on the planet. Many kids (from grade 4 upwards) take private music lessons during the school day. Hillingdon's Got Talent is hugely popular amongst the whole school community. In fact, parents described the overall arts programme as 'phenomenal'. Internationalism is celebrated with lots of support from the PTSA multicultural committee and events such as International Spirit Week. Lots of trips locally (starting with a grade 4 camping trip) as part of the curriculum.

Parents like the fact that each section of the school is in a more or less in self-contained area. Pre-K and K have their own self-contained pavilion (a calm oasis on the day of our visit) with a small library and colourful outdoor play area behind the main house overlooking the gardens.

ACS Hillingdon International School

Linked school: ACS Hillingdon International School (Junior section), 369

Hillingdon Court, 108 Vine Lane, Hillingdon, Middlesex
UB10 0BE

Independent • Pupils: 385 • Ages: 11–18 • Non-denom
• Fees (per term): £6,637 – £7,350

Tel: 01895 259771
Fax: 01895 818404
Email: hillingdonadmissions@acs-schools.com
Website: www.acs-schools.com

21

Head of School: Since 2012, Linda LaPine; from the USA; BA (urban studies) State University of New York; MPS (master professional studies, special educational needs), Manhattanville College, New York; teaching and principal certification. She was a special needs teacher in New York, also in private practice, before going abroad to International School of Tanganyika, American School in Singapore, Anglo-American in Moscow as deputy head, most recently International School of Panama as director. Now as head of a school that is part of a larger group of four, she devotes most of her time to running Hillingdon, while collaborating with the other ACS heads and board developing programmes and policies for the ACS schools group.

In her words, she came into a good school with no major issues to resolve. After significant developments at ACS Qatar, Egham and Cobham, Hillingdon likely to be the next candidate within the ACS schools group for capital investment, so Ms LaPine is working with colleagues to determine what that might be: strengthening of curriculum, technology, internationalism and/or use of the outdoor environment. 'I am not aspiring for ACS Hillingdon to be a "magnet school", I just want to provide an overall inclusive educational programme that is a based on a strong school community. Academics are priority, but it's also about the overall family experience, the kids being comfortable and happy, and every child feeling important.' Two daughters attending the school. On contract till 2015.

Academic matters: Take a deep breath before you try to penetrate ACS's patchwork quilt curricula. Start with American-style pre-K – grade 4 with international add-ons including some IPC (International Primary Curriculum) units, language and cultural studies to grade 2, then Spanish plus PTSA (Parent Teacher Student Association) led multicultural weeks (grades 3-5); IB Middle Years Programme with Spanish or French, followed by the last two years of high school with the IB diploma, a fair range of AP courses (11 on offer), high school honours (which is really just 'regular' level, meaning not IB or AP), or a combination thereof.

So it combines American school roots with academic programmes, legacies of previous ACS International Schools leadership and drawn from the experiences of the sister campuses – sewn together, with some added layers of internationalism appliquéd on top to embellish the whole work of art. Parents seem happy with what's on offer, and kids are moving forward successfully in their various academic paths. IB average in 2014 was 34 points.

There are two full-time counsellors in the High School at Hillingdon alongside an IB co-ordinator. School provides counselling on course selection and university and career planning – beginning in 9th grade. Students who are less likely to be successful with the full IB are given some early guidance, leaving it up to the student and family to decide whether to go for full diploma or certificates. About 60 per cent of students go the IB diploma route.

Plenty of up-to-date technology is apparent throughout busy tech labs, with ample use of interactive whiteboards and smart TVs. An Apple school, students from grade 1-12 have iPads issued by the

---

There's been a proposal from the kids for a sleepover in the mansion to see if there's any truth to the rumour that Hillingdon Court is haunted

---

school. The IT team includes three 'integrationists' who work with teachers to integrate technology into the classroom. The IT team is available for students and even parents who need minor repairs or tech support.

The NLE (Native Language Enrichment programme – an ACS schools feature) provides mother tongue instruction. With a minimum of three students of similar ages and levels, languages are supported by classes funded by the school (if fewer than three, the school helps find a tutor but classes are paid by parents), scheduled after school for one hour each week. The idea is to maintain reading, writing and oral proficiency; typically on offer are up to 10 languages including Spanish, French, Dutch, German, Arabic and Japanese taught by native speakers. Parents appreciate this but say they'd like to see more, and it can be difficult to enthuse children about taking the mother tongue when their chums are doing 'fun' after-school activities, so they may revert to Saturday schools. At IB level, the provision ramps up as mother tongue language A courses (Japanese and Dutch currently offered).

Lots of monitoring and MAP (Measures of Academic Progress – a data-led approach originated in the US) tests to track progress.

EAL specialists support pupils in regular classes to help each student acquire basic vocabulary and vocabulary relevant to classroom topics. Beginner non-English speakers are accepted up to grade 7; after that some proficiency in English is required. For middle school EAL is scheduled during French and Spanish classes.

Faculty made up of some 17 nationalities, roughly one third each British and US, the remaining from Canada, Australia, New Zealand plus other countries. Average staff age is 40s, and some have been there for quite a long time; average tenure is 7-10 years. The teacher to student ratio is 7.5 to 1. Maximum class size is 20, average 14.

Games, options, the arts: After-school clubs (and some activities offered during lunch) for all ages range from crafts to Model United Nations, Duke of Edinburgh, International Schools Theatre Association, National Honour Society and scouts to sports; there are even middle school magic and Lego robotics clubs. A popular Saturday sports programme for grades K-8 features basketball, tennis, football and baseball. There's been a proposal from the kids for a sleepover in the mansion to see if there's any truth to the rumour that Hillingdon Court is haunted. All suggestions obviously considered!

Quite aside from one parent's comment that sports may not be this school's strong suit, ACS Hillingdon has the highest uptake of the three UK ACS schools: 70 per cent of the students do extracurricular sports. Staff say it's not so much about winning and victory as it is about getting involved, having fun and being well-rounded. But despite all that fun and well-roundedness, the riot of banners and plaques prominently displayed in the gym are testimony to plenty of winning over the years. Recent notable achievements include boys' rugby, basketball and tennis, and girls' basketball and softball. Kids participate in the usual international school sports fixtures, travelling to other countries for tournaments. Sports fields are out in Iver Heath, about a 12-minute bus ride away; an impressive double gymnasium and tennis courts are on-site.

Student art work is exhibited everywhere including revolving exhibitions in the head's office (a proud primary student was in the office taking a photo of this to send to his grandmother), and the centrally-located Bridge Gallery. Most music activities (including lots of music tech and a recording studio) are based in Harmony House; primary music that takes place in the main mansion – in a stunning room with high ceilings, sculpted crown

It combines American school roots with academic programmes, sewn together, with some additional layers of internationalism appliquéd on top to embellish the whole work of art

mouldings, cornices, coving and massive windows overlooking the gardens – surely one of the most elegant international primary school music rooms on the planet. Many kids (grades 4-12) take private music lessons during the school day, and various musical ensembles are available for middle and high school students. Hillingdon's Got Talent is hugely popular for the whole school community. In fact, parents described the overall arts programme as 'phenomenal'.

When compared to other local international schools, community service at ACS Hillingdon seems a bit more focused on fundraising for good causes rather than hands-on action. That said, IB students do projects at an orphanage in Bulgaria (running several years now), help in a local nursing home, and also do volunteer activities within the school.

Internationalism is celebrated with lots of support from the PTSA Multicultural Committee and events such as International Spirit Week. Lots of trips locally (starting with a grade 4 camping trip) and abroad as part of the curriculum; middle school trips to Spain or France take place on alternate years linked to the language programmes.

Background and atmosphere: Located in a residential pocket of Hillingdon, a west London suburb on the former estate of Lord Hillingdon, the original Victorian mansion was used during the war as nursing home. Modern buildings added onto the lovingly maintained 19th century house are a bit at odds with the beautiful proportions of the house, but do accommodate the school's many classes and activities.

Entrance through the manned security gates leads to a morning room conservatory, the reception area, a splendid ground floor entry room used for various meetings and events, the admissions office in a beautiful wood-panelled study, and music room and the high school library – several of which overlook the manicured gardens. The aim has been to give the kids access to these beautiful reception rooms, and not to restrict them to the modern parts where most of their classes now take place. The fact that the head's office is not in the auspicious rooms of the original house, but more

centrally located at the heart in the school, says something about the school's values.

Lots of nice bright classrooms, generous space for art rooms, numerous science labs, music rooms. Two areas for drama (the auditorium and a smaller mirrored dance or drama rehearsal studio); two libraries, one each for primary and middle/high school, both located in the mansion.

Each section of the school is in a more or less in self-contained area, which parents like. Beyond the gardens are some outdoor sports grounds and tennis courts, and somewhere out there two vegetable gardens tended by students.

Though the school has won awards for its healthy catering, kids say the lunch room food is 'okay'; but parents love the touch fingerprint payment system as well as the school's flexibility, so kids can buy there or bring their own lunch without the need to handle money.

Hillingdon is one of four ACS International Schools (three in UK, one new one in Qatar), governed by a board of independent, non-executive directors (who typically have international and UK experience across a range of areas including education, finance and law). According to the school's website, the board 'supports the development and the day-to-day operations of the schools'. We interpret this to mean that they support the ACS leadership team that meets regularly and consists

of the managing director, the heads of finance, marketing, HR, and Ms LaPine and the three other ACS heads.

Pastoral care and discipline: Positive feedback from everyone, including parents, about the strong sense of community. The counsellors are reportedly excellent at helping students integrate into the school and families to cope with the transition to a new country and school, particularly at the primary school level, in addition to supporting the usual issues such as relationships, self-esteem and behaviour. They've also developed with teachers a cyber-safety programme for kids and parents, starting with the youngest children. No mention of serious behaviour issues; good home-school communication; teachers are responsive to emails.

Pupils and parents: About 40 nationalities: 34 per cent US, 14 per cent British, and, among many others, a recent increase in families from the Middle East. Parents are made up of a good many corporate expats (particularly finance and pharmaceuticals, many based at Stockley Park), US embassy and other diplomats, and private entrepreneurs, and the international diversity is part of the attraction, according to many parents we spoke to. Some of the British students are repatriating from abroad

and prefer to stay in the international school environment with its more relaxed and varied teaching approach. As is true in other London international schools, total annual turnover is lower than one might expect: about 17-20 per cent. Families (including staff kids) are staying longer.

A super-active PTSA organises events for parents to socialise and get acclimated with London, and also works with the school to make sure all new families are contacted. Buses are available and covers a wide net: from Maidenhead and High Wycombe to the west, Watford and Amersham to the north, central London to the east, and

Holistic soul-searching about this American international educational institution may well lead to some interesting developments in the years to come

Heathrow and Windsor to the south. It's a combination of door-to-door or pick up point, and a very good late and late, late bus service is appreciated by families whose children get involved in after-school activities. (Pre K and K students are not allowed to take the late buses.) Forty per cent of the school's kids are bussed from central London. Parents love the availability of this service, but suggest parents consider realistically the likely travel time.

Entrance: Non-selective; will admit students they feel they can serve and who will benefit from the programme. Admission based on previous school records and testing scores; family statements and references from previous school are preferred, though the admissions director understands that for last-minute summer transfers these are sometimes difficult to obtain. Additional assessment or writing samples may be requested. Academic English required for non-native speakers to enter grades 8-12, assessed through a test that can be sent abroad to the current school to administer. Decisions to admit students (grades 5-12) with diagnosed special educational needs are made in consultation with the specialists. It is sometimes possible – and recommended – that prospective students spend a day in the school.

Exit: About 40 per cent of students go to North American universities (eg Boston College, Brigham Young, NYU, Notre Dame, San Diego State, Emory, American in the US, McGill, Uni of British Columbia in Canada); about 40 per cent go to UK (UCL, Royal Holloway, LSE, Warwick, Bath, Lancaster, Edinburgh,

King's). A handful go to countries such as Japan (eg Waseda, Keio), Australia, Germany and Denmark (eg Technical University). Most of the UK applicants are IB students, though some AP candidates as well.

Money matters: ACS Hillingdon is privately owned by a for-profit corporation, fee-supported with no endowment. The school relies on income from fees, with surpluses reinvested in the schools to maintain high standards; it is evident that there has been continued investment in the school facilities.

Limited need-based financial aid is available from the ACS Foundation. No big development and advancement programmes; the PTSA does fundraising activities to support school programmes and events.

Remarks: This is a happy, internationally diverse school that is ticking along nicely. The newish head with her strong international school pedigree and a special interest in curriculum is bound to bring some changes to the programme once she's had the opportunity to do the prerequisite observation, research and consultation. She'll no doubt want to preserve the positive features of the school. Some holistic soul-searching about this American international educational institution may well lead to some interesting developments in the years to come.

The Arts Educational School (London)

Cone Ripman House, 14 Bath Road, London, W4 1LY

Independent • Pupils: 205 • Ages: 11–18 • Non–denom • Fees (per term): £4,627 – £4,920

Tel: 020 8987 6600
Fax: 020 8987 6601
Email: pupils@artsed.co.uk
Website: www.artsed.co.uk

29

Headmaster: Since 2012, Mr Adrian Blake (40s) BEd MAPgDip NPQH. Formerly the director of teaching and learning at Arts Educational Schools since 2009. Started his career as lecturer in performing arts at NESCOT followed by director of thinking and learning and advanced skills teacher at Greenshaw High School, before becoming assistant principal at Lambeth Academy. He is also education consultant for Kestrel Visual Learning and for BEST Education on a range of educational topics.

Academic matters: 'Arts Educational School is not a stage school. The academic emphasis in the school is equal to the vocational importance and the aim is to produce well-rounded, interesting and interested young people who have the confidence to perform both on stage and in the classroom.' This might come as a surprise to visitors who are surrounded by leotards and leggings, girls' hair scraped into buns, choruses and piano rehearsals booming out of each room. But the complex timetable is firmly balanced.

At GCSE, everyone takes biology and chemistry, along with two Englishes, maths (setted from the off), French and three options from a number of blocks – art, dance, drama, geography, history, music, science and media studies. The head of modern langs speaks seven languages himself and would find teachers for any language a pupil wanted to take. In 2014, 79 per cent of pupils got 5+ A* – C grades at GCSE including English and maths, and 34 per cent of grades were A*/A. The academic corridors look much as anywhere, and good displays on historical topics make a reassuring change from the glitzy pictures of past productions elsewhere.

School now runs two parallel courses in the sixth form: a trad A level course along with classes in dance/drama/music, or two ASs and two As plus a foundation course in musical theatre, which is now an accredited BTec. More pupils are choosing to stay on and a number of new students come in at that stage. Ten AS/A level subjects offered – including philosophy, history, photography, maths, history

of art and media studies, plus the musical theatre course. Creditable results – 56 per cent A*/A grades and 69 per cent A*-B grades at A level in 2014.

Games, options, the arts: On admission in year 7 pupils choose to major in either dance or drama – but both groups have classes in both subjects. Sport is offered three or four times a week at the nearby sports centre but, as one parent said, 'the school is so full of energy and they do so much physical activity, neither of our children feel locked in or

> *This might come as a surprise to visitors who are surrounded by leotards and leggings, girls' hair scraped into buns, choruses and piano rehearsals booming out of each room*

worried about the lack of outside space' – which is just as well as there isn't any and you'd be wise to go elsewhere if you need to get seriously muddy twice a week. Everyone dances their socks off, and yoga, stage combat and dances like hip hop also use up surplus energies. Vocational courses include spoken voice, audition technique, text in performance, choreography, dance of all kinds and music.

Music is impressive – loads of individual lessons, good resources – now with excellent facilities for music tech. Everyone has music twice a week. Four choirs, various instrumental groups including a jazz group, and many pupils have private music lessons too. Everyone performs all the time and it is most refreshing to go into a studio and see 13-year-olds of both sexes improvising without self-consciousness – no blushful hanging back here. Three major productions a year – aided by professional wardrobe, stage management and set-building staff – and every corridor has racks of costumes just waiting to be donned. Pupils help on the backstage side and learn about the technical aspects of production, as well as acting for camera. Production values are professional and exacting. Unlike at stage schools, however, pupils are not encouraged to have agents and to take off long periods for professional work – school life and work come first. However, film producers do drop round to choose children for roles – some in major productions, some in ads.

The art rooms are a quiet relief and art is a popular GCSE and A level here. Work is varied, colourful and clever. Sixth form now has eight new laptops for photographic work – very popular. Plenty of trips to concerts and galleries.

Background and atmosphere: It's a long, three-storey, plain red brick building, unimpressively occupying about 100 yards of prime Bedford Park along the Bath Road in pricey west London and surrounded by leafy roads housing TV executives in semis which go for £2m++ apiece. Inside it's a different world – once you are past the new turnstile and security system – and security now stops you at each corridor, for which you need an ID card. Plain corridors, plain rehearsal rooms – dozens of them, which all look much the same to visitors, apart from some being black and curtained and others bright and light, but clearly have very different feels to the students, eg 'that's where I do tap; I couldn't think of acting in there,' etc.

A proscenium arch theatre, lots of storage space for costumes and sets, a good-sized, adaptable studio which mimics 'fringe' conditions – everything is geared to preparation for the outside reality. Students look bright-eyed and busy – you cannot tread water here and drown quickly if you try. Parents rave about 'the positive energy of the place'. Little recreation space – the sixth form has space which acts as a common room but that's it and no outside. Little time for traditional teenage bickering here – 'it's very friendly and you have to work together,' says sage 12-year-old student.

A good canteen and good food, though not cheap. Most pupils eat a hot meal at lunchtime – lots of pasta, always a vegetarian option and all prepared on site by unusually friendly staff. Good salad bar. Breakfast daily from 7.45 – a good idea, considering that some pupils commute from as far as Kent or Reading. It's a long day, especially for dance students – 8.30am-5.30pm.

The school shares a building and facilities with the schools of acting and musical theatre. So the foyer and common areas are full of creatively dressed and coiffed students who mingle indistinguishably from the sixth formers. Lots of hugging and kissing and a real sense of cooperation and mutual support. Local area is moneyed and attractive. Lots of development going on: new studios and classrooms, IT suite, smartboards throughout, ramps and lifts, main theatre completely refurbished to West End standards (thank you, Andrew Lloyd Webber Foundation), plus a brand new film and TV studio.

Pastoral care and discipline: Ambiance is energetic and purposeful and the emphasis is on self-discipline. Few, having got here, would want to jeopardise their place, and few drop out though some, obviously, realise after a while that the life of a performing pro is not for them. Carefully structured tutorial system. Students are remarkably focused and learn quickly that success isn't easily won. Drugs, cigarettes and alcohol are seldom a problem at the school because the students are too

busy and committed to their chosen courses to have time for such things. Clear policies on all these sins.

Pupils appear to love their teachers – 'they aren't "showbiz" – they're here to help us with technique,' 'my daughter's science teacher is a hero to her – even though she's not at all into science,' 'the teachers are all so friendly – I mean, not too friendly but just, well, lovely and they are brilliantly supportive,' 'my second daughter isn't into performing but her sister is so happy there, it seemed unfair not to send her too and the academics – more her thing – have been excellent.'

Pupils and parents: From a huge radius round London and very mixed in all ways: the common denominators are talent, a willingness to work, enthusiasm – and parents who can afford the fees. Some sixth formers from far afield are put up in local digs. Very beautiful and talented young people who may have stars in their eyes but definitely feet on the ground.

Many parents are in the business and appreciate the school's values – 'the performances are always professional.. an excellent training for young aspiring actors and it is most emphatically NOT a stage school and all that implies,' we were told. 'I wish I'd gone there,' mused one noted actor. Former pupils include Julie Andrews, Sarah Brightman,

Darcey Bussell, Martin Clunes, Joan Collins, Leslie Crowther, Janie Dee, Nigel Havers, Cherie Lunghi, Will Young, Glynis Johns and loads and loads of others. Lots of high calibre thesps among current parents – all clearly loving the school.

Entrance: By audition. Pieces prepared for audition depend on which course you are applying for, eg dance solos, drama monologues, sung or instrumental pieces. Then participation in unprepared workshops and classes. Tests in English and maths. Don't come along seeing yourself as the next soap star or Billy Elliot: 'We're looking for team-workers'.

Exit: Some 40 per cent leave post-GCSE to study at institutions that offer the science subjects at A level or to larger, non-fee paying schools. Majority of sixth form leavers go on to study at drama schools and dance schools in the UK and overseas, including ArtsEd, LAMDA, RADA, Drama Centre, Rambert, The Central School of Speech and Drama, Bristol Old Vic Theatre School, Mountview Theatre School,

Trinity Laban Conservatoire of Music and Dance, London Studios, The Urdang Academy, New York Film Academy. A few stay on and join the degree courses in the same building. Some to other degree courses at eg Royal Holloway, Birmingham University.

Money matters: No government or local authority help. The school has a bursary fund to help existing pupils and is currently looking at ways of increasing it. Various charitable trusts might help an existing pupil in case of collapsed finances but the bottom line is, you'll have to find the fees – which are very reasonable given what is provided.

Remarks: For those who are serious about the work involved in performing arts – with the accent on the work. It's huge fun, but you need energy, commitment and camaraderie. Now with excellent academic teaching too. If you can cut the mustard at audition, you'll have a ball.

Belmont Primary School

Belmont Road, London, W4 5UL

State · Pupils: 480 · Ages: 3-11 · Non-denom

Tel: 020 8994 7677
Fax: 020 8742 7866
Email: office@belmont.hounslow.sch.uk
Website: www.belmontprimaryschool.org.uk

30

Head: Since 2010, Ms Verity Coates MA PGCE (late 40s). She has been in various roles at Belmont since 1996, including deputy head from 2005. She graduated with a degree in mathematics from Newnham College, Cambridge in 1987 and after a PGCE at York and a brief spell at a London primary school she worked abroad in Africa. On returning to England in the mid 90s, she started as a class teacher and SEN coordinator at Belmont and is fiercely loyal to the school.

Keen to press her commitment to state education, she appeared anxious about Belmont being perceived as the middle class answer to independent schooling. Tight-lipped when challenged on the question of Sats results and the high numbers of pupils who have private tutoring – she is determined that her staff too get some credit. Quite right too.

Entrance: Preference given to siblings. Next in the pecking order are those who live within the Primary Admissions Area – 'catchment' to you and me. In recent years, even living in the catchment has not guaranteed a place at the school. Children

in public care and those with medical/social needs come high up in the pecking order. After that – don't even try. Very over-subscribed. Parents are known to rent property within the area just to qualify, and then..? More hope from year 2, however, as a steady trickle leaves to go to prep school/move out of London. Places are snapped up, though, and school tends to be full all the way through to year 6.

Exit: About half to Chiswick School, although the numbers are decreasing with the advent of competition in the area. A clutch to West London Free School and Hammersmith Academy as well as the usual numbers to Twyford, Lady Margaret, Gunnersbury and the Green school. The rest (about 20 per cent) to local independents, including Godolphin and Latymer, Notting Hill and Ealing High, Latymer Upper, Hampton, Ibstock Place. The occasional one to Colet Court at 8 as well as at 11.

Ms Coates asks for a financial contribution for the school reports required for entry into such schools. Lots of outside coaching during years 5 and 6 to prepare for independent school entrance exams.

An abundance of facilities – from musical instruments, playground play equipment, books and materials to the brand new stage for dramatic performances

Remarks: The reluctance of the head and her staff to welcome us to look round this super, over-subscribed, well-funded state primary (or indeed respond to our messages) bemused us – especially considering that Belmont is one of the most successful and popular state primaries in West London, with seven applications for each place.

The sunny, enthusiastic (and overwhelmingly white for this inner London area) pupils bubbled with enthusiasm and love for their school as they showed us round. An abundance of facilities – from musical instruments, playground play equipment, books and materials to the brand new stage for dramatic performances. Results are excellent, showing much higher than expected progress between key stages 1 and 2 and a quarter of pupils in their final year sitting the optional level 6 in reading and maths.

The school caters for an affluent corner of Chiswick and the catchment area is becoming ever tighter. Families from sumptuous houses in the Bedford Park area can no longer expect to get a place. Were it not for the council accommodation on the school's doorstep, you might not get the social mix one would expect in an inner London state primary school at all. Head keen to give precise statistics: 52 per cent of pupils from minority ethnic groups. In any event, a first impression of faces in the playground is that there is an unusually high proportion of white middle class kids. Those who would not come under the umbrella of middle class or British tend to come from Eastern Europe, a few affluent UK residents from say, Canada or Sweden. This ain't your typical London primary.

This big bustling school is housed in a large, three-storey brick building that benefits from the high ceilings, large windows, well proportioned rooms and wide corridors typical of Victorian buildings of its kind. A generous refurbishment programme has resulted in shiny polished floors and child-friendly primaries and pastels (plenty of aqua and primrose) painted on the walls – helping the building to fall firmly on the side of happy, cheerful school rather than gloomy Victorian mental institution.

Far from being the rabbit warren of most independent schools in the area, Belmont is beautifully mapped out, with two classes at either end of each spacious floor, each one charmingly named after fruit – apples, pears, cherries. The main hall in the middle space between classrooms is used for play (reception and year 1 – lots of dressing up and imaginary play goes on here), assemblies (years 2 and 3 on the middle floor) and drama and gym (years 5 and 6 on the top floor). As well as the classrooms, on the fringes of the hall there are yet more rooms – housing musical instruments galore (drum

kits, pianos, flutes, various percussion), two well-stocked libraries, two ICT suites (the juniors have the luxury of one computer each, one between two for the infants) and dedicated SEN provision. Teaching up to the end of year 2 is mixed ability. Setting in maths and English arrives in year 3. Two sets – the higher being slightly the larger and having, therefore, up to 32 children to the lower set's 28-ish. The upper set has just one teacher, no classroom assistant being needed with these children because, of course, they are motivated and keen to learn. We couldn't see much problem with the lower sets either.

About 20 per cent of children identified as having special educational needs but a very small proportion of these have statements (nine pupils). One of these on the autistic spectrum, no one currently in the school with Down's. School has coped in the past with more severe special needs, but children must be able to climb stairs.

About a quarter of pupils don't have English as a first language (about 43 different first languages other than English recorded) but no marked difference in the performance of these children – credit to the school. Dedicated part time EAL teacher as well as SEN coordinator with a team of teaching assistants give support in the class room. Sats results in all subjects are at least 10 per cent above

Photographs on display suggest a high level of dramatic productions, much supported by parents, many of whom are 'in the arts'

local and national averages and are far higher by year 6. Those with EAL needs are seen individually or in small groups for as long as necessary, until they are up to the general standard. Teaching assistants support individuals, pairs or groups under the supervision of the SENCo. A reading recovery teacher sees individuals who, by year 1, are falling behind – with 'fantastic' results. When we visited, there had been a relatively high turnover of staff (head assures us that this is a result of career progression, maternity – no reflection on the school). Five male teachers – always a bonus. Years 3 to 6 have 40 minutes of French weekly. Everyone has two hours of physical activity weekly.

All classes have class music lessons and learn singing with a specialist teacher. In addition to class music, many learn individually – often more than one instrument. Recorder is offered to the whole of year 3 and there is a choir. Swanky staging facilitates an annual production from year 6. Other year groups, sometimes working together, also put on shows each year. Photographs on display suggest a high level of dramatic productions, much supported by parents, many of whom are 'in the arts'.

Good sports provision. A school sports partnership linked to Chiswick School and an outsourced sports programme (football, netball and athletics) in addition to members of staff teaching sport. On Friday afternoons here there is 'enrichment time', when for 30 minutes children can choose from a wide variety of activities, from Glee Club to comic making. Strong after-school club provision. These include, as well as the sport and music, Big Bang Science and Doughlightful – a clay modelling activity.

The locality is certainly urban – school is on a crossroads with Sainsbury's and Starbucks opposite, lots of residential streets and light industry all around, near the tube and on a bus route. But once inside, the enormous playground creates a safe, comfortable and peaceful environment. The Belmont Home School Association – PTA to you and me – raises between £20,000 and £30,000 each year. This has helped make the playground ever more luxuriant, with designated spaces for quiet reflection, a wilderness garden, covered areas for performances with costume boxes, lots of bike sheds, a super climbing wall painted by parents and plenty of gardening boxes replete with flowers, herbs and plants.

At playtime out come the toys (from hula hoops to skipping ropes, racquets and balls) and the place is filled with the sound of happy laughter.

The early years spill out beautifully into carefully designed outdoor play areas, secure from the rest of the large playground. The nursery is particularly roomy and attractive – 52 places with sessions of a maximum of 39 children, an à la carte choice of mornings or afternoons or a combination of whole days and half time sessions. Three large rooms, own toilet facilities and a large kitchen area ('mummy sometimes comes in to help us cook', said an excited 3 year old) as well as access to the hall and library. Few chic little independent nurseries provide as much as this. Everyone eats in the school canteen and the number of pupils having cooked lunches delivered by the borough increases all the time. The rest bring their own.

Ofsted hasn't done a full report since 2007, when school was judged 'outstanding'. Head is greatly aided by a posse of 'liberal middle class' parents only too eager to help in all areas of school life, including arranging fundraising events to enable disadvantaged pupils who might not otherwise be able to afford to take part in trips etc. She is aided, too, by an excellent governing body, as well as by a good relationship with her local authority. A very small number of exclusions in previous years, but none for some time. A proper and well-understood system of sanctions. Also an established homework system with extension work on the school website for those who want to push their offspring further – this school is working on all fronts.

Many parents commented that they were sometimes frustrated by the blank wall that meets their follow up questions on their child's progress and

results. 'Teachers can be cagey', remarked one parent, 'which makes me nervous. I might be surprised'. If you can cope with this and a certain complacency ('we don't need publicity', remarked the head at one point), then this is a no brainer – an excellent state school with most of the advantages of an independent school without the fees.

Drayton Manor High School

Drayton Bridge Road, London, W7 1EU

State • Pupils: 1600 • Ages: 11–19 • Non–denom

Tel: 020 8357 1900
Fax: 020 8566 1901
Email: adminoffice@draytonmanorhighschool.co.uk
Website: www.draytonmanorhighschool.co.uk

Head: Since 1994, Sir Pritpal Singh BSc MA FRSA, educated at Highgate School and London University, where he read chemistry (mid-50s). Previously deputy head at Cranford Community School, prior to which he was head of chemistry, head of science and head of year in various other comprehensive schools, mainly in London. His own schooling (DMHS has academic links with Highgate) and, perhaps, his current school's early history as a grammar, underlie his approach, and grammar school virtues seem subtly to strengthen this non-selective comprehensive. Premier league football clubs could learn from Sir Pritpal's career. Put a good man in a moderately-achieving school and let him get on with it for long enough to find a vision, amass the means and expertise to realise it and then build on it. The high-flying Drayton Manor High of today is the result and Sir Pritpal – along with numerous other honours and awards – was knighted for services to education. Supported by many long-serving staff, notably the senior deputy head – here since 1983 – he is relaxed, candid, softly-spoken, smiley, winning in manner, and, though wholly on top of 'initiatives' and the latest government plans, is refreshingly free of edu-speak.

His tenure has not been without controversy. In 2008, he went head to head with Ealing Council over admissions. Accused of trying to select middle class children, the school was vindicated and the result is an admissions policy which allows children to come to Drayton Manor if it is the nearest school to their

---

Excellent and popular food – a particularly wide choice and reasonably priced – though we wondered about chocolate peanut butter cheesecake

---

home. See below for explanation of what seems obvious. In 2011, the school was granted academy status. The attempt to seek parental opinion was only a partial success – very few replies. 'I like to think it was that they trusted us,' remarks Sir Pritpal, somewhat beadily and probably correctly. Those parents who do involve themselves are appreciative – 'he runs

a tight ship... his staff are happy and, mostly, they stay... he is always there at parents' evenings and events ...'. This last is significant as some 'superheads' more or less disappear from the day-to-day life of their schools. Staff likewise pay tribute – 'he has added to the culture of the place and made it what it is today; it was hard work, especially on standards and behaviour. He took us back to the fundamentals and it has worked'. Drayton Manor struggled for decades but now, under professional management and sound educational principles, it is giving the local independents real competition.

Academic matters: Now outperforms other Ealing state schools and some of the local independents at A level – this reflecting, but only to some extent, the height of the academic bar to A level courses. Thirty A level subjects on offer plus extensive Wednesday afternoon enrichment programme which includes EPQ and citizenship courses worth half an A2.

Latin survives at GCSE with excellent results, though struggles at A level; German also battles on; best language results in French at GCSE and A level. Separate sciences at GCSE with exemplary results – much parental praise for staff, also in history and English. Starry A level results in government and politics, history, English, media and further maths. Overall, results impress – 61 per cent A*-B grades at A level, with 30 per cent A*/A, in 2014. A few non-A level sixth form courses available for those who don't make the grade at GCSE – site and facilities don't allow for more. At GCSE in 2014, 63 per cent of pupils got five plus A*-C including English and maths, with 23 per cent of grades A*/A.

Setting in maths from year 7, in science and languages later on. Enlightened approach re setting – 'We don't have an ideology – we look each year at what will work best' – and parents praise the flexibility of pupils moving up and down as appropriate. Library not huge for the size of school – good stock of popular fiction plus smallish, though interesting, stock of subject books. Parents say, 'I've got a lot of time for all the teachers – they require grammar school standards: our children have achieved even more highly than we had hoped, due to them'; '˜They like lively discussion to promote learning.'

Around 20 per cent have some type of SEN: support is rigorous, systematic and professional under head of inclusion. Good links with primaries, baseline assessment on arrival, SENCo involvement with subject and class teachers and constant target setting and monitoring make for unusual progress. Thirty-four statemented children, 290 on school action or school action plus; eight with an ASD, 157 with MLD or SLD and 61 with behavioural or social difficulties. EAL support offered on a withdrawal or in-class basis, mentoring, masterclasses, tracking. Inclusion centre takes children on a last warning and is staffed by 'our best teachers', who offer individualised teaching to 'develop positive behaviour for learning' – a narrow curriculum, taught in small groups in 'a nurturing environment'. Those identified as gifted and talented are monitored by the intervention department, who check they are sufficiently stretched and challenged.

Games, options, the arts: Great range of sports, much success. Sporting ambition fostered in teams and individuals. Lots of showings in the higher levels of Middlesex tournaments and beyond – boys' 1st XI won the Middlesex Cup; both girls' and boys' football teams reached English School national finals last year. Netball and dance also outstanding. On site provision of numerous hard courts and field supplemented by nearby pitches – the best for a state school in Ealing, we are told. New all-weather surface in the offing. Lively drama, culminating in the key stage 3 expressive arts festival (art, music and drama) every summer including the inter-house drama festival, the Shakespeare Schools festival and the school production attended by many of the feeder primaries as part of the transition programme. A good idea. Art is produced by an enthusiastic minority but we were not wowed by what we saw; most work, however, to be done on music where the talent has yet to be harnessed and developed. 'We're determined for it to be of the highest standard – we are working very hard behind the scenes,' says the head, acknowledging the problem. However, a flautist is part of the National Youth Orchestra and has performed nationwide. Food tech, DT and textiles all

with specialist provision. New arts building – the Sir Montague Sharpe Building – opened in January 2014. Lots of trips and visits – we are particularly pleased to see London theatres featuring prominently. Also, impressive range of speakers from the Big Outside.

Background and atmosphere: Began life as a grammar in 1930 and has the solid, handsome building you'd expect, though now supplemented by later blocks of varying quality around the central piazza – tastefully developed in recent years during multi-million developments, including large scale refurbishments to buildings and sports facilities and new science labs. Outstanding is the Frances Moore Building, named after much-loved deputy head. Impressively broad corridors. Venerable trees, well-tended shrubbery beds and a few hanging bas-

Everyone is included in awards, not just high achievers but those who've made progress. The ethos encourages aspiration

kets greet the visitor, and the reception area is more friendly smiles than forbidding security measures. Pupils are well-turned out, the place is in good nick and we saw little litter. Classroom after classroom was engaged in orderly and seemingly quiet, collaborative work. Few eye-catching displays – though some good blow-ups of current pupils are an attractive feature – little to distract and a purposeful, no frills approach pervades the school. Lots of IT; trad school hall used for productions and gatherings.

Good new-ish dining hall with new caterers and excellent and popular food – a particularly wide choice and reasonably priced – though we wondered about chocolate peanut butter cheesecake! All foods prepared on-site using fresh ingredients – healthy options predominate. Sixth form have a common room for each year – spacious, well-used and appreciated. Pupils have a cleaning rota! Some sense that house system is underused and that pupils have little idea what those outside their immediate circle do. The head sees the truth in this and says, 'we're on to it.'

Pastoral care and discipline: 'We've had one smoking incident on site in the last 10 years,' says the head. One or two permanent exclusions or 'managed moves' annually for persistent disruptive behaviour. Very rare drugs incidents – 'they know that if they do that they jeopardise their own future'. Good structured pastoral care system, mentoring, buddying, quick pick-up on problems. We heard no reports of bullying not jumped on and dealt with. 'Care, courtesy, consideration and integrity come before anything else,' says the head. Staff call each other 'sir' and 'miss' as they pass in the corridors. Parents praise the inclusive atmosphere – 'everyone is included in awards, not just the high achievers but those who've made progress. The ethos encourages aspiration'. Also appreciation of the disciplined approach – 'they are hot on punctuality and attendance' – and the efficient staff-home communication. Uniform and sixth form dress code seemingly adhered to – though they don't look like automata either. Much in place to guide towards post-school life though some students felt it needed to start earlier and be more pro-active. Again, Sir Pritpal, wonderfully

undefensive in the face of criticism, sees this as something he is happy to address – new careers coordinator now appointed.

Pupils and parents: From a very narrow chunk of Ealing these days as the school's popularity and reputation have grown. With a catchment area that takes in everything from the neat Edwardian terraces opposite, the detached grandeur of the Victorian houses a few hundred yards to the east and the council estates of west Ealing and Hanwell, the mix could not be richer. A vast range of backgrounds – 57 different home languages spoken and 34 per cent have English as second language. Lots of after-school classes, notably in ESOL and English, offered to parents alongside other support classes. Pervasive culture of aspiration melds and blends and whatever background you came with, you leave with a sense of your own potential. Notable former pupils include Lord Justice Sir Michael Fox, Martin Rowlands, artist/producer Steve McQueen, Jay Kay, Rick Wakeman and 'if I hadn't been a footballer I'd have been a virgin', Peter Crouch.

Entrance: Vastly over-subscribed. Lots of siblings. Usual local authority criteria apply but the court case won in 2008 means that children will gain a place at Drayton Manor if it is the nearest school to their home. In practice this means that if you live a mile from the school but it remains the nearest school to home, then you will have priority over children who live half a mile away but have other schools from which they can choose. Some 50 per cent come from five local primaries – Drayton Green, Hathaway, Hobbayne, Montpelier and North Ealing. Odd disparity in local population and in other local schools means that all years have more boys than girls. Entry to the sixth form depends on five good GCSEs including English and maths as well as other stipulated grades depending on your choice of A level – most subjects requiring Bs at GCSE. These requirements apply to existing students and to applicants from outside.

Exit: Around a third leave after GCSEs – to employment or vocational courses elsewhere. Virtually all sixth form leavers to university – four to Oxbridge in 2014; several vets, medics, dentists and pharmacists; quite a few engineers; Brunel, Queen Mary's, Westminster and Sussex popular.

Money matters: An annual £10 contribution is asked for.

Remarks: Get clear about the admissions policy and move house. This is about as good as it gets.

The Ellen Wilkinson School for Girls

Queen's Drive, London, W3 0HW

State • Pupils: 1,450 • Ages: 11–18 • Non–denom

Tel: 020 8752 1525
Fax: 020 8993 6632
Email: office@ellenwilkinson.ealing.sch.uk
Website: www.ellenwilkinson.ealing.sch.uk

4

Headteacher: Since March 2014, Ms Rachel Kruger, previously acting head. She joined the school in 2012 as deputy head. South African born, she is a maths and music graduate and a trained opera singer.

Academic matters: In 2014, 68 per cent of students got 5+ A*-C grades at GCSE including English and maths (29 per cent of exams with A* and A grades). English, sciences, languages (including Arabic and Latin) all strong. A specialist maths and science college – a healthy proportion take maths, biology and chemistry A level (increasing numbers opting for physics with plenty of A grades). Arabic, further maths, psychology and philosophy are recent additions to the A level choices. In 2014, 39 per cent A*-B grades at A level and 16 per cent A*/A grades. Several vocational options at level 2 and 3, including business studies, travel and tourism, health and social care and ICT. Runs maths and science taster sessions and masterclasses for feeder primary schools, with excited pupils trying out practical experiments in real science labs.

Some 50 per cent of students speak English as a second language – EAL support is excellent. 'Most speak English enough to be understood. The difficulties arise with subtleties of language – maths terminology, for example.' So both English and EAL lessons focus on the specifics of language, and learning foreign languages can help with sentence structure. Drama is particular helpful for some girls who get little conversation practice outside school because their close female relatives do not speak English. Literacy catch-up programme in year 7 for those who need it, plus personalised online reading programme. Study support available instead of a second language in year 8, and option support higher up supports learning throughout the curriculum. Good SEN help, in and out of the classroom. Extracurricular gifted and talented enrichment activities. Scores very well on value-added basis, and is probably the best-performing Ealing school that does not select on academic or religious grounds.

Games, options, the arts: PE facilities have been transformed by new sports and performing arts building. Plenty of outdoor space, with grass and all-weather hockey pitches and netball/tennis courts. Sport is popular and high on the agenda – 'Because we're an all-girls school it's cool to be sporty'. Successful basketball and netball teams, lots of clubs, eg dance, trampoline, badminton,

ultimate frisbee, inter-form matches. 'We do competition here. We celebrate people taking part but we reward winners too. Students need to be resilient.'

Art studios ablaze with papier mâché, silk screen printing, life model drawings. The (smallish) canteen is decorated with exotic designs created during the year 7 arts and crafts day. Everyone does drama in years 7 and 8 and a fair number carry on

---

'We do competition here. We celebrate people taking part but we reward winners too...'

---

to GCSE and A level. Plenty of performance opportunities: monthly concerts, Christmas musical extravaganza, school musicals, year 12 pantomime, orchestra, rock band, choirs and the wonderful Ukulele Ladies.

Gardening is a popular club – paths are lined with daffodils and crocuses, flowers bloom in brightly painted pots, herb gardens and vegetable gardens. Other clubs include Amnesty, debating, chess, film. Students go on geography field trips, D of E, language exchanges; they take part in mock bar trials, science, technology and maths challenges, debating competitions, classes with visiting artists, musicians and actors.

Background and atmosphere: Named for Mancunian Ellen Wilkinson, who was a Labour MP during the '20s, '30s and '40s, one of the leaders of the Jarrow March in 1936, and became the first female Minister for Education in 1945. The school sits amidst comfortable, leafy, mock-Tudor suburbia, though few pupils live in the immediate vicinity. Brick buildings, mostly one or two storeys high, flanked by grass and flower beds planted by the gardening club, with a tube line running behind a high wall round the edge of the playing fields. New sixth form centre and study rooms, library and resource area.

The only all-girls state school in Ealing. 'This makes them unselfconscious: they're happy to sit and make daisy chains in the summer, they're keen on science and sport, they're very appreciative of each other. They don't grow up quite so quickly.'

Pastoral care and discipline: Well-ordered. Girls are put in one of four divisions – similar to houses – and stay in these throughout their time at the school. 'It's like having a smaller school within a bigger school, with a family feel.' For some girls from difficult backgrounds, school is the most

stable aspect of their lives, and discipline is based round 'catching them being good'. Learners of the Month are celebrated, awards for perseverance and commitment. Most are well-behaved girls, who give the school a good name. A member of the audience during a recent class trip to the National Theatre wrote to the school to praise the exemplary behaviour of its students.

Pupils and parents: Great ethnic mix, with around 20 per cent white, 20 per cent black, 20 per cent Asian and 20 per cent Arabic. The rest come from a variety of backgrounds, eg Polish, Chinese. Most of the well-heeled residents in the immediate vicinity patronise independent schools, though several Japanese girls from the local enclave have been choosing it recently in preference to their community's school. The catchment area tends to spread along the local tube lines and bus routes.

Entrance: Increasingly oversubscribed, with over 600 applicants for 216 places. Priority to siblings, looked-after children and those with specific medical or social needs. Then 10 per cent from linked Ealing primary schools. Other Ealing primaries get next preference, with the remaining places filled by those living nearest. In practice, this probably means less than two miles away.

About 40 girls from other schools join the sixth form each year, with a baseline of 5+ A*-C GCSE grades for A level courses, including Bs in their A level subjects. Those who don't make the grade can take level 2 courses.

Exit: The 30 per cent or so who leave after GCSEs tend to go to mixed sixth forms or colleges, or follow vocational courses elsewhere. A few high-fliers are lured by scholarships to local independent schools.

Sixth form leavers mostly go on to university, with a trickle to Oxbridge, but some potential students find it socially alien and the majority stays in London. Imperial is particularly popular; as are SOAS, Kings, Queen Mary, Royal Holloway and Brunel; recent others include Liverpool, Leeds, Lancaster, Sussex and Anglia Ruskin. Biomedical sciences, business and law figure highly, with English close behind.

Remarks: An increasingly successful and popular school. Huge social and ethnic mix, egalitarian traditions. Stable staff, nice girls, few discipline problems. For many pupils it is a haven and a springboard to academic success.

Glebe Primary School

Sussex Road, Ickenham, Uxbridge, Middlesex UB10 8PH

State • Pupils: 440 • Ages: 3–11 • C of E

Tel: 01895 671951
Fax: 01895 674143
Email: glebe@hgfl.org.uk
Website: www.glebe.hillingdon.sch.uk

22

Headteacher: Since 2006, Mr Nick Alford BA PGCE NPQH (mid 40s). Previously taught in Weston-super-Mare, then at schools in London for 10 years before moving to Glebe Primary.

Married to a teacher (who is deputy head at an independent school). 'We talk a lot about education and compare notes,' he says. Young son attends nearby state primary school. 'I did think about him coming here,' he told us, 'but if he ever got picked to be in a school play or for the school football team then parents would always think it was because he was the head's son.'

A cheerful down-to-earth chap who admits to being a long suffering supporter of Plymouth Argyle. His other passions are cricket and music (The Smiths and The Beatles).

Parents praise him for being very approachable. 'He's always in the playground in the morning and knows every child's name,' one mother told us. 'It means he can spot potential difficulties before they become a problem.'

Entrance: For nursery places apply direct to the nursery and for the school apply through the local authority.

Exit: One or two go to the independent sector and a few to local grammars, but the majority head to Vyners School in Ickenham or Douay Martyrs.

Remarks: Set in the deepest London suburbs (Ickenham tube is near the end of the Piccadilly and Metropolitan lines) and built in the 1970s, the school caters for a mixed intake. Ten per cent of pupils come from military families stationed at the local RAF base and often only stay or a short time. Most pupils are drawn from the local area but the catchment area has shrunk in recent years as the school has grown more popular. 'When I first started as head I used to see some local children walking away from Glebe to a primary school further away which had a better reputation,' said the head. 'But now I'm proud to say that those children are now coming back to Glebe and even transferring from the other school.'

Sats results are above the national average but the most recent Ofsted report found that 'more able pupils have not always done as well as expected.' However the head told us that this point has been addressed 'through setting and focus groups for more able children over the last few years' and as a result, level 5 Sats results have risen to well above the national average. There is a joint project for gifted and talented pupils with a neighbouring school and Glebe recently won the Hillingdon Maths Challenge. School also has links with nearby Brunel University – for science and PE lessons.

The school's go-getting motto is 'We can and we will!' and first impressions reminded us more of a private school than a state primary. Photos on the wall of the head boy, head girl and house captains show the ambitious nature of the place and the head told us that he was keen 'to replicate some of the best aspects of independent schools, such as widening opportunities in sports, music and introducing a house system and prefects.'

Much of the games teaching is delivered by a specialist sports coach. Sports include football, netball, cross-country, athletics, cricket and tag rugby (supported by an enthusiastic year 6 teacher). The school takes part in inter-school competitions and recently won the Uxbridge football competition.

All children get the chance to study a musical instrument. This starts in year 2 with recorders and free tuition on the keyboard from year 4. Parents can pay for tuition in violin, cello, clarinet or flute if they want their children to take music exams. Two guitar clubs after school and when we visited we saw a group of year 4 children strumming away

confidently. School choir performs regularly in different concerts, including one at the 02 Arena. 'The music provision is wonderful,' said an appreciative parent. Former pupils include TV presenter Sue Cook and London 2012 athlete Julia Bleasdale.

The school is a regional centre for those with impaired hearing. The SRP – Specialist Resourced Provision for hearing-impaired children – has two teaching areas and a speech therapy room. Each classroom has a Soundfield system, amplifying the sound of the teacher's voice. There are places for nine hearing impaired children and the school employs two specialist teachers of the deaf. All the children are on the roll of their mainstream class and school aims for them to be taught in class alongside their hearing peers, with support if necessary.

School has just moved into a brand new two-storey building, to great parental relief, and will at last be able to serve hot lunches.

Parents are very supportive and reckon the school has a strong nurturing ethos. 'It feels like a little village school and it has a very caring environment,' said one. 'All the children are aware of each other and support each other.' Another told us: 'I wouldn't hesitate to recommend it to anyone. I feel that I struck gold when I found Glebe.'

Gumley House Convent School

St John's Road, Isleworth, Middlesex TW7 6XF

State · Pupils: 1,190s · Ages: 11–18 · RC

Tel: 020 8568 8692
Fax: 020 8758 2674
Email: general@gumley.hounslow.sch.uk
Website: www.gumley.hounslow.sch.uk

Headteacher: Since 2012, Mrs Ewa Kolczynska, previously deputy head (early 50s). A no-nonsense character who had reams of experience at six other schools before joining Gumley House. Read English at London University and then did a PGCE at King's. Originally from Poland, moved to London at the age of 7, not speaking a word of English. Educated at St Augustine's, Ealing and still lives in Ealing. Husband is a teacher turned education consultant. One grown up son.

Hobbies include theatre, reading, opera (her father was an opera singer). She also loves dancing whenever she gets the chance. Parents find her very approachable. 'She's such a lovely person and is always there if the girls or parents need to talk,' enthused one parent. 'She has a great sense of humour,' said another.

Academic matters: For a non-selective state school, very good results. Compares extremely favourably with local and national averages. In 2014, 53 per cent A*-B and 23 per cent A*-A grades at A level. At GCSE, 84 per cent achieved 5+ A*-C grades including English and maths (36 per cent A*-A grades). Designated as a high performing specialist school and has a languages specialism. First school in the borough to teach Mandarin (taught all the way through from year 7 to 13).

Very committed to special needs provision. Two fully qualified teachers and 14 learning support assistants. SEN catered for include physical difficulties, learning difficulties, ASD, dyslexia, Down's Syndrome. To make sure they miss nobody, school's policy is to screen for literacy at the start of year 7 and organise support as appropriate – literacy

Superbly equipped library in former chapel (just the place for inspired contemplation) and sensational octagonal assembly hall

tuition, in-class support, reading clubs or monitoring as appropriate. Wheelchair access throughout the school seen as part of ethos. 'We encourage concern for the disabled, the marginalised and the needy,' says the school. Sixth formers involved in helping younger pupils.

Important links with world of work. School's director of global learning and communication organises science and enterprise projects with Imperial College, where girls compete with other schools. 'We want to prepare our students fully for the commercial and globalised world,' she explains. The school's motto is Vive Ut Vivas (live that you may have life) and the school extols this to the full with partnerships with schools in Africa, India and Singapore.

Games, options, the arts: Netball, hockey and athletics very strong – school regularly wins all local tournaments. Eight tennis courts, all-weather surface hockey/football pitch set in spacious 10 acres. Dance and fitness studio (very popular) and two drama studios. Thriving orchestra (has performed at European venues) and plethora of private instrument lessons on offer. Annual art exhibitions, drama productions, poetry festivals – some of which are open to the public.

All extracurricular clubs (including science, debating, languages, geography, drama, art and sport) are free. The only extras parents have to pay for are LAMDA classes and private music lessons – 'but we do have money available for those on free school meals,' says the school.

Background and atmosphere: Founded in 1841 as a school and convent by the Faithful Companions of Jesus. The Queen Anne house, surrounded by lovely grounds, creates a peaceful oasis in west London. Superbly equipped library in former chapel (just the place for inspired contemplation) and sensational octagonal assembly hall for whole school events. 'The school even has its own cemetery which is unique,' said one parent.

Pastoral care and discipline: School prides itself on discipline. Truancy is very rare and school/home links are strong. Distinctive uniform – 'the colour brown is so unflattering, though,' complained one mother, although the head commented: 'The uniform can be brightened up by the striped blazer.'

Strong emphasis on religious, spiritual and moral formation of pupils. Very supportive staff. Two part-time counsellors (who make up one full-time post) and two pastoral managers support the heads of year. 'We have a zero policy on bullying but if it occurs we have very clear procedures and it's dealt with justly,' explained the head. Special IT system to detect internet bullying. Peer mentors are trained to help younger students and look after the year 7 students particularly well.

School offers great support for students coping with exams. One mother told us that when her year 10 daughter was finding the workload difficult her head of year organised relaxation classes for any

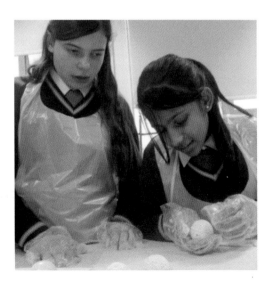

girls who were feeling stressed. 'It's not just about results,' she said. 'They really make sure that the whole person is happy.'

Pupils and parents: The catchment area covers a wide area of west London (from Southall to Twickenham) so a broad mix of intake and 63 feeder schools. Majority of girls from Hounslow and Ealing, with others coming from Richmond, Hammersmith and Fulham, Hillingdon and even Southwark. Sixty-four languages spoken – main one is Polish. Parents are asked to make a voluntary contribution to the school's development fund each month.

'My vision is of a Gumley family,' enthused the head, pointing out that many former pupils send their daughters to the school. Parents concurred. 'Even though there are over 1,000 girls at the school, it doesn't feel that big and you feel that your child is looked after,' one parent told us. 'I can't recommend it highly enough,' said another.

Entrance: Non-selective academically at the age of 11 – but girls and their parents must be practising Roman Catholics (baptism certificate and written proof required from parish priest) and must attend Mass every Sunday. Other entrance criterion is distance from school. School is heavily oversubscribed but places sometimes come up for non-Catholics so it's worth getting on the waiting list. Open policy for year 12 (including boys – there are currently nine in the sixth form) but students need to have five A* -Cs at GCSE and Bs in the subjects they wish to study at A level (for maths A*/A recommended).

Exit: One to Oxford in 2014 (to read medicine); others to a range including many top universities eg maths at St Andrew's, architecture at UCL, theology at Durham, mechanical engineering at Birmingham. Some students go for gap years or apprenticeships.

Remarks: A very caring school in lovely surroundings that achieves good results. Well worth a visit.

Hampton Court House (Junior School)

Linked school: Hampton Court House (Senior School), 392

The Green, Hampton Court Road, East Molesey, Surrey KT8 9BS

Independent • Pupils: 110 • Ages: 3–11 • Non–denom • Fees (per term): £3,857 – £4,747

Tel: 020 8943 0889
Fax: 020 8977 5357
Email: sarah@hamptoncourthouse.co.uk
Website: www.hamptoncourthouse.co.uk

34

Headmaster: Since 2012, Guy Holloway MA (Cantab). Studied at King's College School, Wimbledon, before reading English at Peterhouse, Cambridge. He is a passionate educationalist, fascinated by how children learn and the vastly different approaches to education across the world. For several years he was a volunteer with Save the Children UK, working with disadvantaged children aged 6 to 12. He spent many years in Paris, first at the international PR firm, Burson-Marsteller, and then at the Ecole Active Bilingue, where he was head of English in the section Britannique, teaching A level and preparing his first students for Oxbridge, whilst simultaneously creating chaos in the section Française, teaching his beloved classe de seconde.

He was part of the 1993 founding team which opened the Harrodian School, where he was director of studies.

He has run Hampton Court House (junior and senior) as a single school since 2012. He leads a weekly seminar – a comprehensive history of music course for all children in years 1 to 8 – and teaches GCSE psychology.

His interests include piano, record collecting (vinyl LPs of 1950s and 1960s), concert-going, foreign travel, languages, mathematics (statistics), chess, film directing, and theatre (has directed over 30 plays).

Entrance: At 3 into the nursery via informal interview with child and parents. Head looks for families who will be in sympathy with school's aims and ethos and will tell them if he feels they aren't. Into pre-prep via reading and interview. Likewise into the prep – looking for potential, a capacity to think and imagine rather than the crammed and tutored child. At 10, the children are tested more conventionally in English and maths.

Exit: As some come in, some go out. Still thinks of itself as a prep and some 11 and 13-year-olds sit for other schools at this stage –although school says the vast majority now stay on. Leavers head to a range of schools, including Surbiton, Westminster, Kingston Grammar (very popular), Bryanston, and The Lady Eleanor Holles School.

Remarks: It's a magic place and little children must be wowed to have the run of the stunning old house, its gardens, sizeable pond, outbuildings – and all in one's home clothes too. The educational principles warm the heart. The 3Rs predominate – hooray! – in the early years, but discrete subject teaching starts early too and everyone learns Latin from year 5 right through to CE. Language learning is a fundamental. French is taught through teaching other subjects (such as mathematics and humanities) in French – from day one and by native speakers 'with perfect accents.' All children who go through the prep emerge as at least competent, if not fluent, communicators in French. One hears it as one passes down corridors – spoken, chanted, sung, from room after room. Spanish also lively and enthusiastic and Mandarin taught from year 5.

Art, drama and music seen as central to education in its broadest and deepest senses and divinity is taught very much with an eye on the art it has inspired. Music seen as exceptional by everyone. IT now well provided for with a designated room full of Macs with big screens. We watched a class of happy 9-year-olds working on music animation programmes. Some on-site sport but swimming etc a ride away.

Little children must be wowed to have the run of the stunning old house, its gardens, sizeable pond, outbuildings – and all in one's home clothes too

Garden a wonderful asset for outdoor play (tree climbing allowed in moderation) and early years have their own dedicated garden, also used as an outdoor classroom.

Continental teaching methods are important here – head impressed by, for example, maths as taught in Hungary and Poland and incorporates principles derived therefrom. The academic staff are multi-national – around half from abroad and many more with overseas experience. Internationalism flavours the wider curriculum and prep school children learn about major world figures, eg Leonardo da Vinci, Dante, Mozart and great European dynasties, eg the Hapsburgs and the Holy Roman Empire. Science takes a Socratic approach – discussion is as important as experimentation.

Unusually flexible about keeping children down a year or bumping them up one – in consultation with parents. This can work exceptionally well, especially in a case of mild bullying, exceptional aptitude or slowness, but can also have adverse consequences and be a problem if the child wants to move elsewhere.

SEN provision, previously reportedly 'well-meaning,' now tightened up and 'outstanding,' as far as Ofsted is concerned (they praised IEPs). Provision for more than mild dyses may need careful enquiry. Not that caring, dedication and attention to individuals are lacking – it's just that in this haven of the love of learning, one can,

maybe uniquely, appreciate officialdom's insistence on policies, systems and strategies. Certainly some parents, seduced by the trumpeted ethos, flee after a while, scared off by the realities of the place. Not a school for the conservative, the conventional, nor those who snuggle down of an evening with health and safety reports as bedtime reading.

Hampton Court House (Senior School)

Linked school: Hampton Court House (Junior School), 390

The Green, Hampton Court Road, East Molesey, Surrey KT8 9BS

Independent • Pupils: 100 • Ages: 11–16 • Non-denom • Fees (per term): £4,997 – £5,457

Tel: 020 8614 0857
Fax: 020 8977 5357
Email: admissions@hchnet.co.uk
Website: www.hamptoncourthouse.co.uk

35

Headmaster: Since 2011, Guy Holloway MA. He studied at King's College School, Wimbledon, before reading English at Peterhouse, Cambridge. He is a passionate educationalist, fascinated by how children learn and the vastly different approaches to education across the world. For several years he was a volunteer with Save the Children UK, working with disadvantaged children aged 6 to 12. He spent many years in Paris, first at the international PR firm, Burson-Marsteller, and then at the Ecole Active Bilingue, where he was head of English in the section Britannique, teaching A level and

preparing his first students for Oxbridge, whilst simultaneously creating chaos in the section Française, teaching his beloved classe de seconde.

He was part of the 1993 founding team which opened the Harrodian School, where he was director of studies. He runs a weekly seminar – a comprehensive history of music course for all children in years 1 to 8 – and teaches cultural studies to years 10 and 11.

His interests include piano, record collecting (vinyl LPs of 1950s and 1960s), concert-going, foreign travel, languages, mathematics (statistics),

chess, film directing, and theatre (has directed over 30 plays).

Academic matters: Languages, the arts, civilised values and culture reign here and it is a UNESCO associated school. If you want your child to be a linguist, to study academic subjects with values attached, to learn about art, music and to develop individual interests in a liberal, relaxed atmosphere, you'll probably love it, particularly if your offspring is bright, motivated and responsive to opportunities. At GCSE, an admirable range of options for so small a cohort includes five languages – old and new. We watched an attentive and large class of year 11, seemingly all girls, doing psychology.

In 2014, 51 per cent of GCSE grades were A*/B, nine per cent A*/A. The emphasis is on self-motivation, if you don't want to work no one exerts much pressure – and this may also be true of some pupils' families.

School says, however, that things are changing here – 'more discipline and rigour', while keeping the 'ethos of happiness', and clearly the intellectual and cultural values will not be sacrificed to a galumph up league tables – and grace à Dieu for that. But Latin and the languages, art, music – all acknowledged to be superb – flourish and Mandarin has recently been introduced. IT now well-provided for with a designated room full of Macs with big screens, and the school is recognised as a lead school in computer science. Teachers – many from abroad – provide intellectual clout.

School very accepting and inclusive of SENs. SEN department consists of a SENCo who comes in three days and as needed plus two others, one trained and the other very experienced. They work in small groups or one-to-one, as best suits the child. Nineteen per cent of pupils on SEN register – mostly mild to moderate dyslexia but school will support ADHD and dyspraxia. Ofsted praised good use of IEPs. Invitingly crowded and well-stocked, smallish and recently refurbished library with views over the park.

Opening a sixth form in September 2015 – to be led by former Westminster head Tristram Jones-Parry and with lessons running from 1.30pm to 7pm.

Games, options, the arts: Arts are strong, strong, strong and part of the feel of the place. Art seen as anything but a discrete subject – rather very much part of the philosophy that underpins the educational approach. Delicious things like the band kit set up in the old ice house in the garden, music everywhere – around half the pupils take individual classes and everyone throws themselves into drama and art. Music department comprises professional, practising performers (an impressive list) and children here are clearly exposed to the best. Several

of the ones we spoke to had performing ambitions and clearly no shyness about such things prevails here. This confidence also evident in the manner of the children as they move around the school and address each other and the staff.

School says a newly appointed head of sport is leading a focus on football, netball and athletics, with fixtures throughout the school. D of E is taken up by 90 per cent of year 10 cohort and year 10 and 11 pupils do Young Enterprise. Lunchtime sports clubs and after-school activities are available every day.

Background and atmosphere: Built in 1757 by the gloriously named George Montague Dunk, second Earl of Halifax, the house is stunning. Its entrance hall – as pictured on the prospectus – has to be seen, columns, gallery, ceiling fireplace 'n' all. To say nothing of the view over Bushy Park, the proximity to Hampton Court itself and the fabulous neighbouring houses on the little lane one drives down to reach the gate. The lake, grotto and ice house in the garden were added in 1771 and, when his lordship died, the house was left to his mistress, Mrs Donaldson, and, on her death, to their daughter. Nice work if you can get it. The house then passed through a succession of tenants and, in 1871, was sold to Marmaduke Blake Sampson, city correspondent of The Times and Argentine consul in London. He built the picture gallery, later a ballroom and subsequently concert room. Then a further century of lettings and sales – among them to the tea-planting Twinings – until, in the 1980s, it became a Save the Children home for refugee Vietnamese boat children. You couldn't make it up.

The school began in 2001 as a pre-prep and prep but, as the first pupils got to leaving age, it seemed natural to continue into the complex realms of senior education. Ofsted recognised the school as 'good, and increasingly outstanding' in 2013.

Children of all ages mix and mingle – lots of hugging in break time, which we liked. No uniform, though 'you have to look presentable' – and they do: rather more here than in many uniformed schools where the rules are stretched to the scruffy limits. The teachers too – some in suits, others very casual, but no-one pushing at the boundaries. Happy parents love the 'warmth and liberality of the ethos – it's just what we wanted. Not perfect but so much better than a hothouse.'

Pastoral care and discipline: Discipline is expected to come from within rather than be imposed. School's philosophy is a belief that all – pupils and staff – should be treated equally and with respect. Politeness and good manners are insisted upon and bullying, we are told, is not countenanced, though some parental feeling that, on occasions when it occurs, the bully is accorded rather more TLC than the bullee. School aghast at this allegation, but reports of bullying not adequately dealt with reached us more than once. On the other hand, we learned of other such incidents which were swiftly and sensitively sorted.

Children who need space and air can breathe here and find they do want to learn. We witnessed a cheerful confrontation between a teacher and a genial but recalcitrant fifth former on our visit – amicable and polite, but clearly a conflict between equals rather than one in which authority was firmly exercised. Children with a more mature understanding of personal relationships will think they've come to heaven.

Pupils and parents: Popular with French families for its commitment to French. School does not claim to be bilingual from year 5 upwards – with the breadth and transience of the school population it could hardly be by senior stage. Pupils from a 30-mile radius – school bus collects and deposits. Attracts the unconventional, the liberal, the arty. Lively Friends of HCH have outings, balls and shopping events to support both school and a Sri Lankan orphanage.

Entrance: Via interview with candidate and parents, plus maths and English tests. Head must be satisfied that the pupil and family are in sympathy with the school's ethos and approach. From Cameron House, Hill House, Wetherby and local juniors.

Exit: As diverse as you could imagine. Leavers to Kingston Grammar, UCS, Hockerill Anglo-European, The Brit School, Hampton, DLD, Bryanston, Halliford, Westminster, Hurtwood House, Latymer Upper, Richmond or Esher Colleges, Wellington, Eton, City of London.

Money matters: Up to three scholarships – academic, music, arts – annually, worth 10 per cent of fees max – all 11+ candidates automatically entered.

Remarks: Ideal place to grow and learn for those who will thrive on the relaxed and civilised values of the place. Historically seen as a refuge for those who couldn't get on elsewhere – sometimes the obstructive or wayward – but now more selective, though the head will continue to take on those with something to offer that may not be conventionally academic. And so he should.

Hampton School

Hanworth Road, Hampton, Middlesex TW12 3HD

Independent • Pupils: 1,200 • Ages: 11–18 • Non-denom • Fees (per term): £5,585

Tel: 020 8979 5526
Fax: 020 8783 4035
Email: admissions@hamptonschool.org.uk
Website: www.hamptonschool.org.uk

36

Headmaster: Since September 2013, Mr Kevin Knibbs MA (early 40s), previously principal deputy head. Educated at King Edward VI Grammar School, Chelmsford and read history at Oxford (won two football blues). Was head of lower school and senior master at Bolton School Boys' Division before joining Hampton in 2007.

Has helped the Hampton U15 football team to national success and keenly promotes rugby at the school, including the building of the new all-weather pitch and strengthened links with the London Wasps.

Firmly believes that academic success flows from a balanced all-round education in a

supportive, unpretentious environment and says his ambition is to enable boys to grow into well-rounded, happy individuals who aim for personal success while supporting those around them.

Academic matters: A consistently tip-top performer locally with already good results moving onwards and upwards. At GCSE, number of A*/A grades has been rising markedly – 87 per cent in 2014 – putting the school amongst the top independent schools in the country. At A level in 2014, 93 per cent A*/Bs and 71 per cent A*/As keeps the school in the top 25 – without anyone being asked to leave after GCSE (and very few choose to), so no large intake of high-flyers into the sixth form. The in house Hampton extended project qualification now forms an important part of the broad sixth form enrichment programme. Although the school is no slouch on the Oxbridge front, with 25 offers in 2014, many parents see the absence of a hothouse atmosphere as a strength (and one of the reasons why they choose the school). Wide range of subjects on offer with plenty of take-up in languages and science subjects.

IGCSE science and maths are taught – no coursework and more testing. Some boys take one or two GCSEs early. Setting is organised to ensure that no boy is in the bottom set for all subjects – 'No Hamptonian should, nor does, see himself as a bottom set boy,' explains Mr Knibbs. Year 7 boys choose between French, German and Spanish. Latin is compulsory until year 8. The launch of Mandarin is a proven success.

Average class size on entry is 23/24, though the size of teaching groups is often much less, with nine or fewer for German GCSE not uncommon. Sixth form sets are in single figures to low teens. A modern extension houses English, technology and art, and the myriad of machinery and art equipment gives the impression of being very well used, as are the various IT suites. All boys can now access their computer-based work files from home. A state-of-the-art teaching block, the Atrium, houses 11 fully-equipped classrooms and an additional biology lab. All classrooms have Apple TVs and digital projectors and most staff and many pupils have iPads.

The library is welcoming, open even in the holidays, and extremely well-stocked. Careers advice has a high priority and is impressive (although one parent bemoaned lack of advice for A level choices) with efforts being made to think more globally.

Ideal for high calibre all rounders, but don't think of sending toffs, tremblies or tearaways

Plenty of females on the staff. Average age of staff 37 and they are top drawer – plenty of Oxbridge graduates and PhDs. Several old boys also to be found in the staff room. Turnover never out of single figures.

Special needs are catered for free of charge through a head of learning support, but the school is cagey about how many boys or how much work this entails – delve deep if you want to send an SEN boy here. Provision for children with English as an additional language is negligible.

Games, options, the arts: Sport is very strong: 16 current boys have won international honours for England or GB at nine different sports. All the necessary facilities are on site, apart from the new boathouse shared with neighbouring girls' school, Lady Eleanor Holles (LEH), a mile or so away. Each boy chooses the sport he wants to play – a key success factor, according to the school: 'The boys taking part are there because they want to be and there are none who don't, which makes for higher quality sessions'. All sports spawn international players.

The ideal school for a budding Beckham: unlike most private schools, football is a major sport here with the U15 and first XI often winning the Independent Schools Football Association Cup. Have also twice won the inaugural ISFA Fair Play trophy in recognition of on field conduct and respect for officials. Rugby has taken off in similar leagues recently with the first XV having won the Esher President's Cup and the inaugural U18 Topflight International Schools' Shield, and the first XI having been named Rugby World Team of the Month. New all-weather pitch is apparently a 'unique facility' as accredited for football and rugby. Rowing is big, big news – one of the leading UK schools (check the

provenance of the Oxbridge Blues next Boat Race day). Notably strong in cricket, the first XI winning the 50/40 league for several consecutive years. But not all brawn and no brain – chess thriving: up to four teams playing matches each week.

Music takes many forms and can be at a very high level. Has recently had its first BBC Young Musician of the Year finalist, now at the Royal College of Music on a full scholarship, and three organ scholars in residence at Oxbridge, as well as several choral scholars. Plenty of light-hearted groups and joint performances with LEH each term

---

Parents can breathe a small sigh of relief – girls may be nearby but not a shop or pub in sight. Superbly spacious grounds

---

too. Drama productions sometimes shared with the girls but often all-male affairs. The recent 450 Hall (it actually seats 400 – built to celebrate the school's 450th anniversary) was designed as a centre of excellence for the performing arts and is an exceptional facility both for the school and for use by the outside community.

The list of co-curricular activities is so long that you wonder how they can all be fitted in, especially since most boys, reliant on the school coach service, go home promptly at 4pm. The answer is the extended lunch hour – where plentiful and reportedly high quality food is served over a long enough period to fit around all the clubs. In addition to all the extracurricular activities, a very popular lunchtime programme of eminent speakers – politicians, businesspeople, academics, media figures and famous old boys: Dr David Starkey is on the list of speakers as well as Jeremy Paxman, Zac Goldsmith, Iain Duncan-Smith and John le Carré, and don't forget Tara Palmer-Tomkinson. The boys who are busy at their sports clubs don't know what they're missing!

Similarly, so many trips and activities in the holidays you wonder if the boys ever see their families. Beware – all these jolly jaunts are not included in the fees. For those desirous of helping their fellow man plenty of opportunities for helping in the local community, as well as links with African communities in Uganda and Malawi. Jointly with LEH won first place in the Barnardo's People Recognition awards for their Saturday activity club for children with disabilities – all the result of a huge commitment from the staff to the wider curriculum.

Background and atmosphere: In the heart of suburbia surrounded by houses and other schools. Parents can breathe a small sigh of relief – girls may be nearby but not a shop or pub in sight. Superbly spacious grounds; buildings not an architectural gem though well-maintained and constantly being updated. Loads of outdoor space – quads, gardens and playing fields which many boarding schools would envy. Interiors are light and airy and remarkably tidy – even the corridor outside the rowing ergo rooms presents kitbags in a long, neatish row. The sixth formers are proud of their common room with its own café selling vital sustenance at break time and a flatscreen TV tuned to Sky Sports.

Claims to be the first school in the country to go 'climate neutral' through off-setting emissions caused by its daily running. Climate Care, the link company, offsets through projects including renewable energy and energy efficiency schemes in Southern Africa and India and forest restoration in Uganda. Has its own bore-hole for irrigation of its playing fields, solar panels and a wind turbine. Continues to raise pupils' awareness of climate issues – the boys conduct regular audits of the school's energy consumption.

Formerly a state grammar school (went independent in 1975); about 50 per cent of the pupils come from state primary schools, and is fully committed to a large 13+ entry from prep schools. Many of the parents were not independently educated and definitely not a school for Hooray Henrys, although within school the boys look the part in blazers and ties (even in the sixth form). However the minute they leave the school gates the shirts become magically untucked and the ties unknotted – these guys know the meaning of 'grunge'. A marriage here of public school ethos and London lads.

Proximity to Lady Eleanor Holles is supposed to provide 'the best of both worlds' – single sex teaching means that monosyllabic 14 year olds are not intimidated by garrulous girls, but 'The boys certainly know what girls are,' says the head. The two schools have audited their joint activities with a view to expansion. Hampton has also established sixth form management courses with Surbiton High.

Pastoral care and discipline: New boys at 11 are given as much help as possible to settle in with their peers – an overnight team-building exercise is very popular, with boys returning 'raring to go'. Similar jaunt for 13+ entrants. Mentors from the upper school are allocated to newcomers. New boys are closely monitored and any who are found to be struggling with work or organisation given special support and help with study skills. Counselling is readily available; a parent whose son had an extended illness felt that staff went the extra mile

to ensure an efficient return to school – 'He was even met at the door by the head of year'.

Assemblies celebrate a range of achievements – concentration on success is more important than telling the boys what they have done wrong and exceptional work is presented to the head. Stringent illegal substance policy – expulsion is a serious threat.

Pupils and parents: No obvious Hampton boy but, if you want your son to be kept busy, here is an environment to suit all sorts. 'Like most things in life, it's what you put in that counts,' says one parent, 'and most people in the Hampton community both give and consequently receive a lot – it might not be the right school for a boy if he's not the type to roll up his sleeves and join in.' Delightfully suburban – no smart cars, champers and party frocks here on prize-giving day but a nice mix of keen mums and dads from a wide range of backgrounds. All faiths represented and celebrated, according to the head. Huge west London and Surrey catchment area bolstered by the extensive school coach network shared with LEH. Socially, neither the boys (nor LEH girls!) complain about bussing, but parents take note – it's not cheap, and be prepared to spend hours in the car at weekends to pick up and deliver from far flung friends' houses. Once a Hampton boy, always a Hampton boy – contacts with ex-Hamptonians are strong.

Entrance: Two thirds come at 11 (mostly from state primaries) and one third at 13, from more than 200 schools. (Denmead School is part of the same foundation but is no more 'tied' than any other.) Majority of 13+ candidates are pre-selected at 11, then need 65 per cent at common entrance. Four applicants for every place at both 11+ and 13+ entry.

Advance place exam available for 10 year olds to avoid the scramble at 11, but boys who don't make it early are encouraged to re-sit with no prejudice. Both the 11+ and 13+ pre-tests consist of three papers: maths, words and reasoning, English response and composition. Locally, the tests are perceived as demanding – according to the school, 'The entrance exam is designed to identify innate ability rather than to test what has been taught or coached'. The local private tutors, who make a tidy sum coaching for this and other school exams, would no doubt disagree. Acceptance is based on school's own exam, interview and school report combined with an age allowance. What is clear: it is not enough just to be academic – the school also assesses 'a pupil's likely positive contribution through good behaviour to the aims, ethos and co-curricular life of the school'.

Acceptance at sixth form is based on at least six GCSEs at A or A*, interview, school report, personal statement and written assessment.

Exit: Hardly any leave after GCSEs. Almost all sixth formers to top universities or medical schools. In 2014, 25 Oxbridge offers, though not all the brightest choose to apply – school is relaxed about this. UCL, Bath, Bristol, Nottingham, Durham and Exeter all particularly popular; increasing numbers to US, often on academic or sporting scholarships; also Dublin, Belfast, Sydney, RADA and Central St Martin's.

Money matters: Academic, all-rounder, art, music and choral scholarships. Means-tested bursaries.

Remarks: A super outward-looking school keen to preserve its strengths (not about to go co-ed), but ready to embrace change if it will further educational achievement. Ideal for high calibre all rounders, but don't think of sending toffs, tremblies or tearaways.

Harrow School

5 High Street, Harrow on the Hill, Middlesex HA1 3HP

Independent • Pupils: 830 • Ages: 13–18 • C of E • Fees (per term): £11,530

Tel: 020 8872 8007
Fax: 0208 423 3112
Email: admissions@harrowschool.org.uk
Website: www.harrowschool.org.uk

13

Head Master: Since 2011, Mr Jim Hawkins MA (40s). Educated at King Edward VI Camp Hill School for Boys in Birmingham and read maths at Brasenose College, Oxford (he was a year above David Cameron and knew the PM slightly). Did PGCE at Oxford before first teaching job at Radley – perfect combination of teaching maths and coaching rugby and rowing. Head of maths at Forest School in Walthamstow, then deputy head at Chigwell School. Prior to Harrow he was head of Norwich School for nine years – 'a fantastic school in a beautiful city.' Norwich went co-ed during during his headship but there are 'no plans' whatsoever to follow suit at Harrow. 'We are very happy as we are,' he says firmly.

Proud of the fact that Harrow enables boys to enjoy being boys. With a plethora of activities from dawn till dusk, he reckons the school suits 'the kind of boy who wants to take the opportunities we offer and throw himself into things.' He says education at Harrow goes 'way beyond the exam syllabus' and that there's 'no better place for the really bright boy with a strong attitude towards life and learning, the sort of boy who is going to contribute and soak everything up.' School sends loads of boys to Oxbridge but head is equally proud of those who 'work jolly hard to get their As and Bs. They are some of our great successes.' When we asked who the school wouldn't suit he was unequivocal. 'It wouldn't suit someone who wanted a sixth form college sort of experience. Harrow is a highly organised, very busy school and it's very clear what the demands are.'

Dynamic, focused and urbane, with dashing good looks. Still keeps his hand in at the chalkface by teaching 'a bit of maths' to the youngest boys at the start of the academic year. 'It's really nice to have 40 minutes when you are focusing on something entirely educational,' he says. 'The key thing as a head is to find ways of interacting with the boys. Without that you lose touch with reality.' He makes a point with having lunch with boys and in the 'beaks' dining room' when he can. Very sporty – he rowed for Oxford's lightweight crew

Charles I rested here while preparing to surrender and little inclines have memorable names like Obadiah Slope

and was captain of Brasenose rowing. Ran the 10-mile Long Ducker, school's annual charity race from Hyde Park to Harrow, in 90 minutes, though laughingly admits that the director of studies did a faster time.

Loves his job, although he admits 'the highs are very high and the lows are quite challenging'. Says there are three main educational areas he wants to develop. First is the 'super curriculum' to encourage academic scholarship above and beyond the timetabled curriculum, research, independent thinking and university-style learning. Second is to look at preparing boys even better for university – he's already appointed a five-strong universities team with specific knowledge of Oxbridge, medicine and the US universities – and third is to concentrate on 'leadership and service'. School is already very active in local community (links with primary schools, tea

parties for elderly, projects with Mothers Against Gangs charity etc) but head would like to do more. 'We want the boys to understand that leadership and service go hand in hand,' he says.

Wife Zoe is an artist and they have a young daughter. They live right in the heart of the school (along with their newly acquired cocker spaniel puppy) and regularly invite boys for breakfast – 'bacon butties and croissants.' Enjoys music, sport, reading and the theatre.

Academic matters: Teachers, parents and the boys themselves describe Harrow as an 'academic' school. Harrow's results don't appear in league tables – head says he's fed up with the 'one-dimensional snapshot' they deliver – but results are impressive. At A level in 2014, more than 26 per cent A* grades and approaching 56 per cent A* at IGCSE. IGCSEs taken in English, French, German, Spanish, history, geography, maths, as well as biology, chemistry and physics. Drama and PE introduced at GCSE this year. Thirty-one subjects on offer at A level – all the usual, plus business studies, government and politics, history of art, music technology, photography and th eatre studies, with a range of languages. Maths is the most popular subject at A level, with nearly two-thirds taking it. Half the boys do four subjects at A level rather than the usual three (one boy recently did nine). Sixth form electives are a recent innovation for sixth form pupils – a chance for boys to experience university-style teaching in specialist areas. Cerebral subjects on offer include programming, the history of western art, the greats of European philosophy,

psychoanalysis and its impact on European culture, and financial mathematics.

Dazzling array of languages on offer – French, German, Spanish, Italian, Russian, Turkish, Polish, Japanese, Arabic and Chinese. All three sciences are compulsory at IGCSE. School has its own observatory with three telescopes and astronomy offered as a GCSE. At GCSE classes range between 14 and 20 pupils while at A level the average is 8.5 and none are greater than 12. School caters for mild dyspraxia and dyslexia. One-to-one help given off-timetable, at no additional cost. Dedicated band of teachers (or 'beaks' as they are known at Harrow) includes many writers of scholarly books. Women make up 19 per cent of staff.

Games, options, the arts: There's no doubt about it, Harrow is a very sporty school, with hordes of teams regularly trouncing their opponents. Sport played five afternoons a week, 32 sports on offer and director of sport encourages even the less enthusiastic to 'have a go' at something. Main sports are rugby, soccer, cricket and Harrow football. The latter is played with a pork-pie shaped ball which absorbs the wet and can be propelled by any part of the body. Even though it's played in the depths of winter and is a very muddy affair the boys love it and only wish more schools played it (Harrow is the

only one). When we visited pupils were counting the days till their Harrow football match against an OH team. Last year lots of their fathers had played and there was even one grandfather in the side – 'but we were very careful with him.'

Vast expanse of playing fields, sports centre with indoor climbing wall, weights room, 25m pool and sports hall, courts for tennis, rackets and squash, nine-hole golf course and Olympic-sized running track. School boasts national champions in rackets, fencing, fives and judo, two boys playing rugby for England and number of cricketers play-

The latter is played with a pork-pie shaped ball which absorbs the wet and can be propelled by any part of the body

ing at national and county level. The mother of a gifted sportsman was full of admiration for the way the school nurtured her son's sporting talent whilst keeping him focused on his academic studies and helping him achieve stellar grades. 'The school sees each boy as an individual and were very supportive and flexible,' she told us.

Head of music admits that when he arrived eight years ago there was a perception among rival directors of music that Harrow was 'an old-fashioned school where little value was placed on music and the arts.' To his delight he found the reverse was true and there's a 'wealth of musical talent.' Half the boys learn musical instruments and 50 per cent of these achieve grade 8 or better by the time they leave. Practice sessions timetabled for younger boys. Loads of orchestras, choirs and strong tradition of singing (see below). More than 100 concerts a year, with recent performances at the Royal Albert Hall and Royal Festival Hall. Steady stream of boys to top universities and conservatoires to read music too.

Excellent Ryan Theatre seats 400 and is used for school and professional productions but annual Shakespeare productions take place in the beautiful arts and crafts Speech Room. A huge, wood-panelled half-moon, it boasts authentic Globe-style staging and seats the entire school. Wonderful art and, befittingly for a school where photography pioneer William Fox Talbot was a pupil, photography. There's no lounging around with nothing to do at weekends either – scores of extra curricular activities to choose from, everything from the Alexander Society for boys interested in military history to the Turf Club for horse racing fans.

Background and atmosphere: Harrow is one of only three all-boys, full-boarding schools left in the UK (along with Eton and Radley). Boys have been educated here since the 13th century but the school was founded in 1572 under a royal charter granted to local farmer John Lyon by Elizabeth I (Lyon's, the newest boarding house, is named after him). The aim was for the school to provide free education for 30 local scholars, a number later increased to 40 by the governors. School sits in picturesque Harrow on the Hill, surrounded by 400 acres and with panoramic views across London – of it, yet remote from it, as we said last time. On a clear day you can see Canary Wharf from the head's study and it's just 25 minutes by tube to Green Park. Visitors to the undulating school site take note – flat shoes are a must.

School is steeped in tradition and history. The 17th century Old Schools contain the beautiful Fourth Form room, with names carved into every inch of panelling, from Byron to Robert Peel. It's also where Professor Flitwick's charm classes were shot in the first Harry Potter film (lots of tourists gazing admiringly when we visited). The stunning Vaughan Library, designed by architect Gilbert Scott (he also created London's St Pancras Station) has chess sets on tables and stays open late during exam periods. War Memorial Building commemorates the 633 OHs who died in the First World War. You can't help but be profoundly moved by the Alex Fitch Room, an Elizabethan wood panelled room with stained glass windows and a Cromwellian table, given by a grieving mother in honour of her 19-year-old son after he died in the First World War. She asked that it should be used for the purpose of boys meeting their mothers and that a light should always be left on over her son's portrait. Plaques and memorials commemorating quirky events are everywhere. Charles I rested here while preparing to surrender and little inclines have memorable names like Obadiah Slope, wittily named after Trollope's unctuous Barchester Towers character.

Harrow Songs are legendary. No Harrovian, either past or present, fails to mention the strength of feeling they engender and the lump in the throat they provoke. Songs have been an important part of the school since 1864, when the head of music wrote the first song, and they are considered to be 'a unifying force.' In November each year the whole school assembles in Speech Room in honour of its most famous alumni, Sir Winston Churchill, for the Churchill Songs. Like rival Eton, school has its own jargon. 'Skew' is a punishment, 'tosh' is a shower, 'tolley up' is permission to work late and so on.

Pastoral care and discipline: Pastoral care is meticulous, with highly structured system of resident housemasters, assistant housemasters and matrons. Harrow's 12 houses are integral to the school and boys are fiercely loyal to their own house. Some houses are regarded as stricter than others and parents we spoke to said it's important 'to pick and choose carefully.' One of the houses – West Acre – was recently the subject of an ITN documentary series, following the life of the school for a whole year. Housemasters in post for 12 years and as well as doing most of the admissions assessments each gives their house its character and reputation. They also work round the clock – 'at the beginning of every term I say to my wife "see you at the end of term",' one housemaster told us with a grin.

We visited two very different houses – Druries, which dates back to the 1790s and is a maze of charming nooks and crannies, and the ultra-modern Lyon's, or the Holiday Inn, as a few wags have nicknamed it. 'It's the best piece of real estate around here,' joked one boy, hugely appreciative of its light, airy, five-star rooms. 'There's room for us to move around and not cause too much havoc.' Each house has common rooms, games rooms (kitted out with plasma TV, pool and table tennis tables), garden and 'yarder,' an area where boys can run off steam and kick a ball about. Two boys sharing is the norm in the first year but by year 11 (or

Boys can make toast and heat up soup in their houses – 'and the more ambitious make Pot Noodles,' said one boy

even earlier) they get their own room, complete with desk, shelving, computer and, occasionally, en-suite shower. All pupils' names etched on wooden house boards, with head of house's name picked out in gold. Boys can make toast and heat up soup in their houses – 'and the more ambitious make Pot Noodles,' said one boy. We trust he was joking. Meals are eaten centrally and food gets a firm thumbs-up – from us too, if the lunch we had with sixth formers was anything to go by. Boys are allowed to go out for a meal with their parents on Sundays but there's no weekly or flexi-boarding. Two weekend exeats in the autumn and spring terms and one in the summer.

Harrow takes a pragmatic approach to technology and social media but the boys are so busy there isn't much time to sit around and play computer games. Pupils understand that bullying is 'completely unacceptable' and head says that it has plummeted, 'not down to zero, but pretty close.' School does a bullying survey every winter and housemasters, year group tutors, matrons, two school chaplains, health education tutors and school psychologist pick up on most things. Discipline is clear and firm but the place feels pretty relaxed, with boys knowing exactly where they stand. 'You are given freedom but if you abuse the freedom you would be punished,' one boy told us. Zero tolerance on drugs and use or supply in term-time or holidays means expulsion. Anyone found with spirits suspended and warned while smoking is handled through 'escalating sequence of sanctions imposed by housemasters.'

Smart uniform of dark blue jackets (bluers), grey flannels (greyers), white shirts and ties, plus, of course, Harrow's infamous boaters. Boys wear them or carry them and either love them or loathe them. They're allowed to write their names and draw pictures on the inner rim and spray them with varnish to protect them. Members of Philathletic Club (school's top sportsmen) get to wear bow ties. Sunday wear is black tailcoat and the whole kit and caboodle.

Pupils and parents: Pupils come from all over and school is proud of its 'broad and varied intake.' We said last time that it's the sort of place where a Yorkshire farmer's son will be sharing a room with the offspring of a City banker – and it still holds true. Between 10 and 15 per cent are progeny of OHs, while 20 per cent are from overseas (some

ex-pat, others from vast range of countries – 40 at last count). Twenty-five with EAL requirements. Most boys are C of E but there's a 'significant' RC community. Small numbers of all other main faiths or none.

The boys we met were engaging, appreciative of the fine education they get and very proud of their school. 'It doesn't give you a sense of entitlement, just a great responsibility to give something back,' one boy told us, while a sixth former who'd joined from a state school at 16 said that he'd been 'pushed and challenged' and that there was 'a lot more opportunity for debate' than at his previous school.

Parents reckon the school suits all-rounders who work hard and like sport. 'It's very disciplined and the boys are busy all the time so they have to be organised,' one mother said. 'There isn't any time to get up to any mischief and the boys are really tired by the end of term. There's a real camaraderie about the place and the boys make life-long friends. I can't fault it.' Another reckoned that even though it's 'strict,' any boy would thrive at Harrow, as long as they can cope with being in a large school where they won't necessarily be 'king pin.'

Long and distinguished list of former pupils – seven former prime ministers (including Sir Robert Peel, Lord Palmerston, Stanley Baldwin and Sir Winston Churchill), 19th century philanthropist Lord Shaftesbury ('a towering figure – we refer to him a lot,' says the head), Jawaharlal Nehru, King Hussein of Jordon, Lord Cardigan (who led the Charge of the Light Brigade), General Sir Peter de la Billière, plus countless other men of military renown (20 holders of the Victoria Cross and one George Cross holder). The arts and sciences are equally well represented, with a dazzling list of luminaries including Lord Byron, Richard Brinsley Sheridan, Anthony Trollope, Terence Rattigan, John Galsworthy, Cecil Beaton, Edward and William Fox, Richard Curtis, Benedict Cumberbatch and James Blunt, plus Crispin Odey (one of the UK's most successful hedge fund managers), Julian Metcalfe (founder of Pret à Manger), cricketer Nick Compton and Tim Bentinck (better known as David Archer).

Entrance: Very competitive. Around 600 apply for the 160 places on offer at 13. Prospective pupils are assessed at the start of year 7, through tests, interviews and school reference. Offers are made – subject to CE or scholarship exams 18 months later. Sixty per cent expected at CE. 'Some weight' given to sons of OHs and boys' siblings – 'but brothers don't automatically get in,' said a parent. Boys arrive from more than 100 regular feeder schools. All-boys' boarding preps like Caldicott and Cothill top the pack but others from a myriad of co-ed and day schools.

Total of 24 new pupils a year into the 340-strong sixth form. Candidates need at least seven or eight A*/A at GCSE but many will have straight A*s. Candidates write a CV, plus letter to the head explaining why they want to come to Harrow, and take tests in their proposed A level subjects. The best attend a day of interviews and assessments.

Exit: Ninety-nine per cent to university – 22 to Oxbridge in 2014 and most of the rest to Russell Group. Significant number opting for Ivy League universities in the US and other top international institutions.

Money matters: School has given franchises to Harrow Beijing, Harrow Bangkok and Harrow Hong Kong, with a fourth likely to follow in the next few years. These are all successful enterprises carefully monitored by Harrow and also fund generous bursary schemes at home.

Wide range of scholarships and bursaries at 13 or 16. School offers means-tested bursaries of up to 100 per cent of fees to pupils who win a scholarship of any sort. Up to 30 scholarships a year for academic excellence, music, art or talent in a particular area (normally worth five per cent of fees). There are also Peter Beckwith scholarships for gifted and talented boys whose parents can't afford to send them to Harrow. Two awarded each year to boys aged between 10 and 13 – these can cover fees at a private school from the age of 11 and Harrow fees from 13.

Remarks: Parents looking for a top notch, blue chip, full boarding, all boys' school will be hard-pressed to beat Harrow. This is a school on top of its game.

Haydon School

Wiltshire Lane, Eastcote, Pinner, Middlesex HA5 2LX

State • Pupils: 2,010 • Ages: 11–18 • Non–denom

Tel: 020 8429 0005
Fax: 020 8868 8213
Email: info@haydonschool.org.uk
Website: www.haydonschool.com

23

Headteacher: Since 2006, Robert Jones (mid 40s). Read economics at LSE and taught in Hong Kong for four years before returning to the UK. Moved to Haydon in 1999 and quickly moved up the ranks to become assistant head, then head. Married to drama teacher. Two sons – one grown up, one at primary school. Originally from Manchester, he's a huge Man United fan and looks rather like an ex-professional footballer himself. Still plays football and coaches Ascot United under 7s (his son plays for the team) and keeps fit by running a number of half marathons each year.

Academic matters: Specialist language and applied learning college. Seventy-one per cent of students achieved at least five A*-C grades including maths and English at GCSE in 2014 (25 per cent A*/A grades). Language provision is excellent, with students starting off with French and Italian or Spanish and German. Options for taking on further languages (such as Mandarin and Latin) higher up the school. 'Around 100 opted for Mandarin this year,' says the head proudly. Forty per cent take two foreign languages at GCSE.

More than 30 GCSE or BTec options. 'We want to offer as broad a curriculum as possible,' explains the head. Applied learning specialism allows the school to offer a wide array of courses, from Greek to construction. 'There is a broad range of subjects offered,' one parent told us.

All KS3 teaching (apart from maths and technology) is in mixed ability groups. 'We believe this gives all of our students the best possible chance of achieving their best,' explains the head. Parents like the fact that class sizes are around 25, but some would prefer more streaming. 'At present in year 7 there is streaming just for maths,' says one parent. 'I would like to see this extended to other key subjects such as English and science as is practice in other local schools'.

At A level 47 per cent A*/B (22 per cent A*/A) in 2014. Again, a wide choice of subjects available. Parents praise the quality of teaching and particularly the revision lessons offered around exam time.

We were very taken with the pool table and primary colours in the rather groovy sixth form common room

---

Students need six GCSEs at A*-C (including maths and English) to study four A levels. Those who do not have a minimum of a C in English or maths are able to retake these and can study three A levels.

Twenty-two statemented students. One SENCo and a team of learning support assistants support these pupils. There is also a special centre where students can be taught in small groups. When we visited we met a group of students learning to express their emotions through making Star Wars masks.

Games, options, the arts: School has scored successes in a host of sports – at both local and county level. Particular strengths are rugby, rounders and indoor athletics and there is even an ultimate frisbee team in the sixth form. New sports hall.

Haydon has benefited from new facilities in recent years, including £5 million art and design building and £2 million music and performing arts centre (three music rooms, drama studio and music mixing room. plus one-to-one teaching rooms). School has two orchestras, jazz band, samba band and wide variety of other music groups. Four big concerts a year as well as annual musical or play.

Thriving art department achieves excellent exam results. Students can study art, textiles and photography at A level. Lots of school trips too – to France, Germany, Italy, Peru and Swaziland.

Background and atmosphere: School is situated on the edge of the Northwood Hills in Pinner, with spacious playing fields. Rather nondescript 1950s buildings – originally two grammar schools that merged in 1977. Lots of building work going on when we visited.

Food in the sixth form café is so good that the staff choose to eat there. Food in the canteen for the rest of the school has less favourable reports but new caterers were about to be appointed when we visited so this will hopefully improve. Some of the toilets need a little TLC but these are in the process of being refurbished. 'The boys' changing rooms are a real state,' one student told us, but we weren't shown these on our tour. We were very taken with the pool table and primary colours in the rather groovy sixth form common room though.

Pastoral care and discipline: A new positive reward system has recently been introduced. 'The reward system is a great motivator,' one parent told us. "My child strives to get good news notes, commendations and other rewards.' Meanwhile a year 8 student said: 'I really look forward to the awards assembly. It's a way of showing how hard we are working.' One of the top awards means pupils get a special lunch with the head (mums sadly aren't eligible to compete for this award).

Students excluded for threatening behaviour or repeated disruption in lessons (four permanent exclusions last year). Parents are happy with school's approach to behaviour. 'I have always found that a high level of discipline is maintained from the minute the children arrive at the school,' said one. When we visited, students seemed well behaved and friendly.

Pupils and parents: 'Haydon has a really good reputation round here,' a student told us, 'and all my friends at other schools wish they were here.' The school offers both pupils and parents a chance to voice their opinions – parent voice group meets four times per year.

Entrance: Most students live locally (within a mile or so to the school). Admissions criteria are: children in public care, then siblings, then children living nearest to the school, then employees' children. An additional 60 students join in the sixth form.

Exit: A quarter of pupils leave after GCSEs – for college, other schools, apprenticeships or employment. Around three-quarters of sixth formers to university, and about a third of these to top universities eg Southampton and Nottingham, including one or two a year to Oxbridge (none in 2014).

Remarks: A friendly comprehensive that really does cater for all, with strong vocational courses as well as the more traditional A levels – all taught to a high standard. 'I would have no hesitation recommending Haydon,' said one parent. 'I feel my children are lucky to attend the school.'

International School of London – Junior

Linked school: International School of London, 406

139 Gunnersbury Avenue, London, W3 8LG

Independent · Pupils: 140 · Ages: 3–11 · Non-denom
· Fees (per term): £5,833 – £6,900

Tel: 020 8992 5823
Fax: 020 8993 7012
Email: mail@ISLLondon.org
Website: www.ISLLondon.org

32

Head: Headmaster Huw Davies, MA (Oxon) PGCE from University College, Worcester. Has extensive experience as a former deputy head, IB diploma coordinator and higher education advisor, as well as being a governor of a sixth form college in West London. Has taught history and theory of knowledge at diploma level and is a member of Llafur – the Welsh History Society.

Entrance: Rolling admissions allows pupils to apply from all over the world, year round, although there are waiting lists for some year groups. Apply before Easter to improve chances of admission. Admission is determined by previous records, a teacher reference, student and family questionnaires. Interviews are always welcomed. No testing (English language

Many organisations, not to mention a few world leaders, could learn a lot about fostering global understanding from this school

is assessed after admission); pupils with special educational needs should provide diagnostic assessments so school can decide whether it can properly help them. Will take non-English speakers with good academic report. During interviews there's a lot of discussion about the mother tongue programme and the possible fees for this service.

No official sibling policy, but parents say they make an effort to ensure all children in a family get a place. Admissions director gets high marks for his thoroughness, efficiency, responsiveness and care, and he can tell you about every pupil in the school. Though on first impression he may appear somewhat diffident, with his many years' experience working with ISL families, 'he knows his onions'.

Exit: Around 75 per cent move to senior school.

Remarks: The school teaches the IB primary curriculum. Specialist teachers for music and PE; art is taught by class teachers. Plenty of class assistants. The major draw is the 'terrific' mother tongue programme, which may cost extra depending on numbers; if a new child's language is not on the list, they will try to find a teacher. EAL support is also strong.

A gentle introduction which does not include pushing reading at an early age. This suits families coming from countries where academic learning begins at age 6 or 7. However, other parents comment that while they're very happy at ISL, the range of English fluency may mean a lesser academic pace and rigour than in other independent schools.

Engaged and cheerful children everywhere we went. A parade of pupils with yummy sandwiches headed to the dining hall, leaving behind open exercise books in their classroom with individually written recipes for 'my favourite healthy sandwich' (part of their health living unit using hands-on IBPYP approach); the youngest children ate and chatted while teaching assistants circulated attentively.

Parents are generally happy with home/school communication. Some say that whilst staff seem to address issues they raise, they don't always keep parents in touch with the follow up. The parent of a young child was surprised when parents were not invited to accompany children to see the classrooms on orientation day. Parents new to the IB may struggle if they don't attend the parent education events provided by the school.

With families coming from so many different national education systems, everyone has their own idea about the 'right way' to do things. Managing these expectations and helping children adapt is part of the ISL challenge, and for the most part, parents report they do a great job.

The school has clearly won over the hearts and minds of its many international families. Many organisations, not to mention a few world leaders, could learn a lot about fostering global understanding from this school.

Linked school: International School of London – Junior, 405

---

139 Gunnersbury Avenue, London, W3 8LG

Independent • Pupils: 365 • Ages: 11–18 • Non-denom • Fees (per term): £6,900 – £7,866

Tel: 020 8992 5823
Fax: 020 8993 7012
Email: mail@ISLLondon.org
Website: www.ISLLondon.org

33

Head of School: Since 2009, Mr Huw Davies, Oxford University MA (PPE) PGCE. Has long experience at ISL: previously deputy head, IB diploma coordinator, higher education advisor, history and theory of knowledge teacher. Generous with his extensive IB knowledge and experience, is an IB consultant to prospective IB schools and often on authorising teams for IB schools worldwide. A man of few words, he comes across as an archetypal British ex-history master, yet he clearly has a foot firmly in

the international education world. Parents did not have a lot to say about Mr Davies; he is possibly more engaged in the behind the scenes day-to-day school management and the big-picture strategic jobs (school refurbishments, increased capacity for growing demand, mother tongue programme etc); delegating more of the 'front of house' interactions to his teachers and principals.

Academic matters: The school offers the IBPYP, IBMYP, IBDP continuum. Some high school students opt out of the full diploma, earning instead an ISL high school diploma. There's a good selection of IB courses, with more online through Pamoja Education.

Primary students have specialist teachers for music and PE; art is taught by class teachers. From middle school, specialists teach art, drama, music and PE (through grade 10). Strong level of support in primary classes with plenty of assistants for classes that can number up to 20.

The major draw for every single family we spoke to is the 'terrific' mother tongue programme. It may cost extra depending on numbers, but mother tongue classes are offered primary through to high school with about 16 IB languages leading to the added advantage of a bilingual IB diploma. If a new child's language is not on the list, they will try to find a teacher. EAL support is also strong.

Some primary parents prefer the slight 'delay' in reading for younger children when compared to the local English schools. For families coming from countries where formal schooling begins at the age of 6 or 7, ISL's gentle introductory literacy approach at age 5 is more comfortable. However, others comment that while they're very happy at ISL, the range of English fluency may have an effect on the academic pace and rigour compared with other independent schools.

Laptops are lent to students and kept at school, so away from school students access their work online. Interactive whiteboards or smart TVs in many classrooms. We noticed there weren't as many students 'connected to devices' as in seen in other London international schools – for better or worse.

Engaged and cheerful children everywhere we went. A parade of primary students with yummy sandwiches headed to the dining hall, leaving behind open exercise books in their classroom, with individually written recipes for 'my favourite healthy sandwich' (part of their health living unit using hands-on IBPYP approach); youngest children eating and chatting while teaching assistants circulated attentively; middle school students debating the value of democracy and advantage of a student council that can organise fun activities in preparation for an upcoming assembly; CDT students sawing away at wood; art students busily tidying up their room to head to the assembly...everyone looked settled and at ease. Great esprit de corps apparent from fact that the entire secondary participate in assemblies.

IB results steadily rising in recent years; average point score in 2014 was 33; just under half earned bilingual diplomas, far above the international average.

Parents generally happy with communication with the school. There's good overall consultation. Some say response to emails are occasionally inconsistent: while issues raised in an emails seem to be addressed by staff, parents aren't always kept informed of the follow up. The parent of a younger

---

ISL is a rabbit warren of hallways and stairwells with every nook and cranny utilised – the staff room, practically in the rafters, is a hive of energetic teachers planning and conversing in umpteen languages

---

child was a surprised when parents were not invited to accompany children to see the classrooms on orientation day. Parents new to the IB curricula sometimes may struggle if they don't attend the parent education events provided by the school.

With families coming from so many different national education systems, everyone has his own idea about the 'right way' to do things. Managing these expectations and helping children adapt is part of the ISL challenge, and for the most part, parents report they do a great job.

Approximately 90 teachers, average age is early 40s, with several part-time language teachers. About 15 have been there for over 10 years.

Games, options, the arts: There's a mix of after-school clubs, though some primary parents would like to see more, and juggling after-school pick up can be tricky if a younger sibling has nothing to do. Usual international school sports such as volleyball, football, basketball and tennis, and triathlon offered too, with international tournaments. Primary PE and sports take place on site in the hall, small playground, or neighbouring park. Secondary kids go to a nearby sports centres or the park. Weekly swimming for all up to grade 10 at Brentford Leisure Centre. One parent suggests ISL may not suit the 'uber-athlete'; 'it's fun and competitive to a point, but for serious athletes, families join local sports clubs.'

Private instrumental lessons schedule during the school day, with ensembles practising after school. ISL takes advantage of London as a vast field trip opportunity; early in the year there's a week when nearly everyone from grade 4 vacates the school for three to five day trips. Some incorporate team-building to integrate newcomers; in the middle years they're language-related (Beijing just added). Only the youngest and the IB students (except those on a biology trip) stay behind. Primary parents tell us that the idea of sending their 9-year-olds off on a residential trip 'takes some getting used to'.

Many community service opportunities on offer by school and students also organise their own. One returned to her native India to volunteer in a school for the summer. ISL has work experience programme for all grade 9 students; the school

---

A man of few words, he comes across as an archetypal British ex-history master, yet he clearly has a foot firmly in the international education world

---

helps organise, or parents and students find their own placement. Though they're a bit young to work, it can inspire their thinking about what IB courses they may select. For one student it also led to summer job opportunities and a gap year project after graduation.

Background and atmosphere: A secondary school founded in north London in 1972, ISL was one of the first authorised IB diploma schools in the country. The school merged in the late 80s with the International Community College, a primary school founded by the Marakem family, becoming a full 4-18 school and moving into a former Catholic school on the North Circular Road in west London. The school is still owned by the Makarems, who recently opened schools in Qatar and in Surrey (buying Shell's former Dutch school). The group is managed by Amin Makarem, the founder's son, who oversees the leadership team of the three schools. Parents say the ISL's quite independent of the other two; not much inter-school activity at student level apart from some sports competition between the Woking and Surrey, but we hear more collaboration is planned.

The building would not win any architectural prizes, but it is undergoing a major refurbishment to modernise and make more it attractive. The primary is located in an annex rented from the next-door church; the school reports that it has no plans to relinquish this space even when the refurbishment is completed. ISL is a rabbit warren of hallways and stairwells with every nook and cranny utilised – the staff room, practically in the rafters, is a hive of energetic teachers planning and conversing in umpteen languages – a very positive vibe.

The school definitely needs sprucing up; it's not easy to see any rationale to the arrangements of secondary school classrooms or corridors and public spaces. Possibly due to building works under way, the school can feel cramped and disorganised. The head and school leadership team are considering how to reconfigure the classroom arrangements once the refurbishment is complete.

The primary lunch room is uninspiring, and the play area out front is basically a hard surface to run around and play a few ball games on, though as a result of the construction the kids are going to the park more, which is a lovely treat and very handy. The school is protected by secure gates.

There's a two-level art room and a photo lab, a great CDT classroom, functional science labs of a certain age, a useful multi-purpose hall, a library (which will be relocated after the refurb) and lots of multi-use classrooms of various sizes. Middle and high school students share classrooms and primary share some of the language and specialist classrooms; primary parents reassure us that it's a happy family atmosphere, and of course the teachers are always supervising youngsters as they move through the building.

But the likelihood is that if a family visits ISL for the first time after seeing other international schools in the area, the facilities and environment may not quite measure up. One parent said that when they first drove up to the school, 'we could have cried', but having got past that, it was their first choice school, and they are very happy there. Despite the tight spaces, the students are friendly, polite and seem to move through the building in a pretty organised fashion, and it bodes well for world peace if kids of 50+ nationalities can get along so well in these relatively cramped quarters. The strong message coming from parents is 'don't be put off by first impressions'.

The school is aware of its limitations, hence the renovation programme. They are also always on the lookout for suitable additional space, and if the appropriate solution were found, they might relocate the IBDP to its own centre. Families considering ISL may bear this in mind, and that other schools in urban London face similar challenges when planning ahead.

Grades 11 and 12 may leave campus for lunch, early years eat in their classrooms, and everyone in between eats in the dining canteen. Parents we spoke to say their children prefer to take lunch from home over the optional lunch programme booked termly. Door-to-door bus service is available; with growing London traffic problems, they strongly recommend that families choose from neighbourhoods like Kew, Chiswick or Ealing.

Pastoral care and discipline: The strong sense of community provides a solid foundation for the behaviour and discipline in the school, which is of course guided by the IB Learner Profiles. The school handbook directs parents to home room tutors for everyday matters, or the divisional principals, with more serious or school-wide concerns then directed to the head. Some less IT-savvy parents seem to be having some teething problems with a new online communications system. But their main concern is the welfare of their children, and as one happy parent said, 'at ISL children are treated like royals.' No big discipline worries came to our attention.

Pupils and parents: Possibly the most international school in the city if not the country; ISL's students come from 55 countries – the largest single group representing only 13 per cent. It creates a fertile conditions for developing open-mindedness and international understanding for students, as well as parents and faculty. With many dual-national families, some kids hold as many as three or four passports. Parents love this environment where 'if you speak several languages, you're not unusual'.

Parents are also drawn to ISL by its smaller size and the friendly and approachable staff, who they credit with helping children settled in so easily and comfortably, knowing 'how to manage the adjustment for children coming from very different school systems'. Teachers are approachable and deal with new children individually (and also help parents with tips to manage the family transitions). At ISL, this is more than marketing hype.

We hear that families interact socially outside of school; ISL parents believe that having their children learn to understand peers from of all backgrounds is a huge advantage. Parents of older

---

But their main concern is the welfare of their children, and as one happy parent said, 'at ISL children are treated like royals.'

---

students report that their children meet at weekends, and most are happy for them use public transport to arrange this; week nights are spent at home with their noses in the books.

Very active PTA; many families regard the school as the heart of the community. They plan outings and orientation activities for new parents. Parents arriving mid-year are welcomed with newcomer's events and even English language lessons. One parent told us of a group of families who regularly take weekend trips around the UK. Another

said she sometimes feels there are more activities for parents than for the kids. PTA got praise from everyone we spoke to.

Most are expats on temporary assignment in the UK, many based at the nearby Brentford business park or growing hub of international companies in Hammersmith, or one of the many embassies. A number live within easy distance of the school, which makes managing the social life a bit easier and parents know one advantage in living away from the centre of London is that their money goes further – bigger houses, bigger gardens.

Entrance: Rolling admissions allows students to apply from all over the world, all year round, although there are waiting lists for some year groups. Apply before Easter to improve chances. Admission is determined by previous records, a teacher reference, student and family questionnaires. Interviews are always welcomed (required for IBDP). No testing (English language is assessed after admission); students with special educational need to provide diagnostic assessments used to determine whether the school can properly serve the student. Non-English speakers with good academic reports are admitted up to Grade 10. During interviews there's a lot of discussion about the mother tongue programme and the possible fees for this service.

Although the school does not comment on a sibling policy, parents say they make an effort to ensure all children in a family get a place. Admissions director gets high marks for his thoroughness, efficiency, responsiveness and care and he can tell you about every student in the school. Though on first impression he may appear somewhat diffident, with his many years' experience working with ISL families 'he knows his onions'.

Exit: About 70 per cent go to UK universities, although more now applying to American universities. Some return to their home countries and ISL has a long history of helping students find the right fit in a wide range of countries – an important consideration for families. Even students who earn the ISL High School diploma gain entry into UK universities. Very occasionally, a student may leave ISL to pursue A levels. The largest numbers have gone to Edinburgh, Oxford, Warwick, UCL, King's, Imperial, St George's Medical School and Queen Mary; overseas destinations include Tokyo Science University, Kyoto University, Keio McGill, Technical University of Budapest, University of Chicago, University of Texas, Bocconi Milan, and Ecole Superieure du Commerce. An impressive list, but parents are advised to ask the school specifically about the more recent successes.

Money matters: No scholarships as such as most pupils have corporate support, but school will keep a child in extreme circumstances if a family financial problem arises.

Remarks: A school with a solid academic track record that has clearly won over the hearts and minds of its many international families. Many organisations, not to mention a few world leaders, could learn a lot about fostering global understanding from this school.

JFS

The Mall, Kenton, Harrow, Middlesex HA3 9TE

State · Pupils: 2,055 · Ages: 11–18 · Jewish

Tel: 020 8206 3100
Fax: 020 8206 3101
Email: admin@jfs.brent.sch.uk
Website: www.jfs.brent.sch.uk

Headteacher: Since January 2008, Mr Jonathan Miller BSc MA NPQH (late 40s). Educated at Carmel College and Imperial College London, he has been at JFS for many years. A former head of chemistry and head of science, he was responsible for planning the school's timetable and IT strategy when it relocated to Kenton, also deputy head. Articulate and highly respected, considered even handed, even tempered and level headed, well able to preserve the happy balance which exists between pupils of a wide range of religious observance within the school.

Academic matters: A very large comprehensive that compares favourably with many grammar schools in terms of results. In 2014, 48 per cent of A level grades A*/A and 79 per cent A*-B, while 90 per cent of students gained 5+ A*-C grades including English

and maths at GCSE, and more than 49 per cent of grades were A*/A.

New pupils are admitted into 10 accelerated or mixed ability tutor groups and all subjects are set by ability in year 8. Both upper and lower ends are given unusually strong support. The gifted and talented have accelerated classes from year 7, while the large special needs department – with over 80 statemented children – has its own suite, six special needs teachers and six permanent teaching assistants. Those struggling at the bottom of the middle band are perhaps the least well served. Ofsted commented that less able students make slower progress than others. French for all in year 7, Spanish for all from year 8. IT bang up to the minute, with interactive whiteboards in every classroom. Science, too, unusually well equipped with 15 laboratories.

First-rate, highly sought after, academic sixth form with around 550 pupils, housed in its own discrete space (though with some lessons taught in the main school). Large expansion of the curriculum at this point, with applied art (including photography and graphics), economics, business studies, psychology, sociology, childhood studies, theatre studies, media studies, politics and critical thinking added to the GCSE basics. Masterclasses, too, for the 25 or so Oxbridge candidates, including some pupils from neighbouring boroughs.

A core of long-serving staff provides some outstanding teaching in all subjects. 'A child who wants to work could not receive a better education anywhere in the country,' said one mother, whose son recently left for a top-flight university. Teaching is carefully monitored, with videoing of lessons – prides itself on its continuing professional development and places the training of teachers from a number of teacher training institutions high on its agenda: about a third of its trainees stay on as teachers, so few problems with recruitment.

Games, options, the arts: Outstanding range of facilities, which include 14 acres of playing fields, two sports halls, a dance studio and a multi-gym for students and staff. Games lessons focus on athletics, ball games, gymnastics and dance.

Strong music department – all students take music in years 7, 8 and 9 and about 15 per cent also take instrumental lessons with visiting staff. Ten practice rooms, keyboard laboratory, recording studio, two specialist classrooms, plus music masterclasses. Large auditorium which seats 900, plus a concert hall for 450. Amphitheatre for outdoor concerts and performances. Five interconnecting art rooms, plus a sculpture terrace. Media studio with professional standard film and television equipment and an editing suite. Well-equipped library.

Annual reading festival and poetry competition. Excellent range of school trips, including Poland (for sixth form Holocaust studies), Israel (year 9 residential scheme), Prague, Strasbourg, Flanders and Paris. Duke of Edinburgh, Young Enterprise. Kosher kitchen with a healthy and balanced diet – no other food can be brought into school.

Background and atmosphere: The largest Jewish comprehensive in Europe, has a particularly distinguished history and tradition. Founded originally in the East End in 1732, it had, by the 19th century, become the largest school in the world, with 4000 students, mainly poor Jewish immigrants. Bombed in WW2, it was re-built in Camden Town in 1958, but by the time it transferred to Kenton in 2002 the accommodation had, in the words of its previous head, become a 'cesspit'. Perhaps previous head Dame Ruth Robins's most significant

achievement was guiding the complex negotiations which secured the large and leafy site in north-west London and overseeing the design and building of the new school, with its light, modern buildings, wide curved corridors and state-of-the-art technology. Has a strong family feel – often parents, grandparents and even great-grandparents are former pupils – with an outstanding sense of continuity, community, warmth and commitment. The social side of school life is particularly prized by parents and most students enjoy coming to school and make life-long friends.

Pastoral care and discipline: Blue and white uniform, which meets the demands of the most Orthodox – so girls in skirts with arms covered, respectful necklines and 'no ironmongery', boys with heads covered with skull caps (albeit some only when they see the head approaching).

In such a large school, the organisation of the pastoral side is of vital significance. On entry, the intake of 300 is subdivided into 10 groups of 30. Each student joins a tutor group and is assigned a tutor – who stays with them throughout – a year manager and director of studies, so three adults looking after every child. Also buddy and peer-men-

Has a strong family feel – often parents, grandparents and even great grandparents are former pupils – with an outstanding sense of continuity, community, warmth and commitment

toring systems. The ethos is strict, determined but kind. Discipline is certainly not a major issue, with quiet and orderly classrooms. Famous detention room – Room 17 – for any persistent offenders and a designated behaviour team to deal with transgressors. 'One or two per cent take up all the time, but I don't know of a single child we haven't turned around,' said the previous head.

Outlook and practice is Orthodox and one of the key aims is to further Jewish values. Very strong Jewish studies programme – 'outstanding,' says Ofsted – and all take GCSE in religious studies. Modern Hebrew and Israel studies are included as part of the Hebrew education programme. Accelerated GCSE in modern Hebrew. Daily services, led by students. Wonderful light, purpose-built synagogue with delicate stained glass windows, where volunteers teach additional Jewish education to the most Orthodox.

feel comfortable here if you didn't want your child to be involved with the Jewish experience. Indeed, for some non-practising parents, it offers a religious opportunity they feel they can't provide at home. 'We're not observant,' said one mother, 'and one of the nicest things about the school was that it enabled my son to have a bar mitzvah.'

Entrance: Some 700 applicants for 300 places. In 2009, following a much-publicised court case, the applications process altered and it was forced to abandon the principle of giving priority to those children who are Jewish according to the religious principles stated by the Chief Rabbi. Instead, in common with other Jewish schools, it now gives priority to those who meet a test of religious practice. Parents for year 7 places have to provide a certificate to testify to synagogue attendance, evidence of a formal Jewish education and/or of family activity in the Jewish community. Places awarded on a points system, which also applies to siblings and external applicants for the sixth form. Those applying for admissions should study the criteria carefully.

Exit: Around 10 – 15 per cent leave after GCSEs. Of those who stay on for sixth form, a sizeable majority go to top universities. In 2014, 16 to Oxbridge (a school record), with Leeds, Bristol, Nottingham, Nottingham Trent, Birmingham and Manchester the most popular destinations.

Recent downgraded by Ofsted from 'outstanding' to 'requires improvement' – largely due to concerns about behaviour, sanctions and attendance.

Remarks: An outstandingly well-run comprehensive, with a warm and well-ordered atmosphere, in bright and spacious modern buildings – though currently criticised by Ofsted about pupil behaviour. Ideal for those looking for a strong education within a secure environment and Jewish cultural tradition.

Pupils and parents: A very broad spectrum of religious belief, from 'those considering rabbinical studies to those who've never seen a candle lit on Friday night'. Nonetheless, you would probably not

The John Lyon School

Middle Road, Harrow, Middlesex HA2 0HN

Independent • Pupils: 600 • Ages: 11–18 • Non–denom
• Fees (per term): £5,386

Tel: 020 8515 9400
Fax: 020 8515 9455
Email: enquiries@johnlyon.org
Website: www.johnlyon.org

14

Head: Since 2009, Miss Katherine Haynes BA MEd NPQH, a mathematician (40s). Miss Haynes was the first woman to be appointed head of an HMC, boys only, school – a notable milestone. Previously head of maths at Warwick School, prior to which she held the same post at Edgbaston High. This is a

look-you-straight-in-the-eye-plus-firm-handshake head, one whose palpable intensity of purpose masks, you feel, warmth and a sense of fun. She is articulate, forthright, focused. 'What a school provides needs to match its location...I want teaching that is dynamic and energetic, that enables boys to learn in the way that is best for them.' She is realistic about the physical limits of the school site – 'It's a question of going with what we can do rather than "what if?"' Perhaps less visible about the school than her popular and relaxed predecessor, Miss Haynes initiated a crackdown on 'standards' and discipline from day one – clearly a bit of a bombshell for some but appreciated by most. All recognise that 'she is keen to do good things with the school'...'she is going to up its game' ...'she's obviously keen to do her best'. Whatever uncertainty and scepticism might have rippled through the school on her appointment, it sure as anything isn't there now and parents, staff and boys look puzzled at the idea that a woman in the job is unusual. She took on an interesting school at an interesting time – boys' only day schools are thin on the ground these days. In her hands, John Lyon is a school of which north west London is going to sit up and take notice.

Academic matters: Mainstream trad curriculum. Maths much the most popular A level subject with majority getting A*/As. Chemistry, history, religious studies and economics also with good uptake and results mostly in the A/B band. Biology more of an A-C spread. Few modern linguists – nothing unusual there in a boys' school – though Spanish now an ab initio option with French which may strengthen both. School also offers psychology, drama and music tech at this level. In 2014, nearly half A*/A grades at A level, 61 per cent at GCSE. Maths IGCSE taken and results are impressive. All three sciences also very strong. The Englishes

now IGCSE and get mostly A*/B. Latin & Roman Civilisation taken by year 10 pupils with strong results. German now, sadly, dead. No obvious weak areas. Able to take advantage of big brother school up the hill, ie Harrow, for individual language specialisms among other perks. IT hitherto seen as integral to learning in general and not as 'a sub-

---

Drama clearly lively and popular – possibly not unrelated to the fact that girls from several chic local schools compete at auditions to play opposite the boys

---

ject' but this is changing – all take it in the first two years – no shortage of computers about the place – and an A level in the subject is 'probably on its way'. No DT, though – simply not possible given the constraints of the site and, seemingly, no pupil or parental pressure to bring it into what otherwise might be seen as a natural home.

Learning support dept works in classroom and via withdrawal. Around 60 on the register at the time of our visit. Mainly assists dyslexics and dyspraxics – of a mild to moderate kind – and has boys on the ASD spectrum too. Site is a bit up and down but most is accessible and wheelchairs are 'not impossible'. We grilled many parents and boys and no subject is seen as weak – most staff, in fact,

praised for the support they give. Library full of PCs and much fiction. Somewhat eclectic stock otherwise and what appeared to us an unusual cataloguing system.

Games, options, the arts: Drama clearly lively and popular – possibly not unrelated to the fact that girls from several chic local schools eg St Helen's, Northwood College and North London Collegiate compete at auditions to play opposite the boys in big, well-appointed, productions. We witnessed some younger boys improvising with none of the coyness and self-consciousness common elsewhere at this age group. Provision is good – two studios and the big hall, though no performing arts centre here – no space. Parents enthuse about productions. Music also exceptional despite unglamorous accommodation – school musters all manner of ensembles and boys play a great range of instruments. Good to see, alongside the bands and R and B, a motet choir and string ensembles. Music tech growing. 'The standard of music and drama is amazing,' a parent told us. 'The last concert was so moving I came out in tears.' Art in a series of studios and some good displays of pupil work here and there in otherwise rather uninspiring corridors. Good to see art done by staff on display – and not just by art staff. Sports hall – though not of the cavernous size found elsewhere – and provision otherwise is good – impressive fitness centre, excellent pool, playing fields up and down the hill and much borrowing of Harrow's fields and pitches also enhances opportunities. Cricket an exceptional strength. Lots of popular expeditions – sporting, educational and charitable – classroom building in Uganda, India and Vietnam occasioned particularly zesty response – along with mountaineering in the Alps.

Background and atmosphere: It's tucked into a winding road on the Harrow hill, still reminiscent of the quiet leafy village this must have been. Harrow School dominates the hill and its fields and structures abut John Lyon's, but this is a happy brotherly co-existence, and the cadet school benefits in many ways from the senior. School sits on the edge of two conservation areas, which concentrates creative thinking as far as development is concerned. The main school building is Victorian gothic. One small new-build – under the 'estate strategy' – enabled it to change its designation from housing economics and dining to become a new sixth form centre. It includes a dedicated sixth form work space with state of the art IT facilities, as well as a space for relaxation. Pretty arts and crafts villa now the admin hub. Most corridors, painted white under fluorescent lighting and with municipal carpet, are pretty stark. Good-sized school hall, with picture windows and views on two sides. The site is not spacious and few buildings delight the eye but it doesn't feel crowded – partly because of the surrounding pitches and fields. Limited space means that the population has to stay at more or less its present size – the relative smallness of the school seen by all as a great attraction. Parents are united – 'everyone knows everyone – they all mix, older and younger, especially on the school bus and all are very accepting of each other'... 'sport and drama means they make good friends across the age groups'... 'because it's small they get a lot of individual attention and that develops and strengthens their confidence'. Three-quarters eat school food which, reportedly, 'could be better' and assuredly needs a more comfortable home. Atmosphere is healthily but not aggressively male – good number of women teachers probably helps. Parents pay tribute – 'the school is very good at bringing on their confidence'... 'it's academic but not pushy'... 'it's an academic school but people aren't separated into geeks and jocks'. 'not cliquey...everyone is treated equally'... 'good at parent-teacher contact'. 'My son is very happy there.'

Pastoral care and discipline: All lessons start and end with boys standing for the teacher – we approve. Year 13 boys are peer mentors for the younger boys – trained and monitored by professional school counsellor. Clear disciplinary structure – detentions and brief suspensions sort most problems and these are mostly related to late work or behaviour. Two exclusions since Miss Haynes's advent – both for unacceptable behaviour. Drugs/smoking/drink infringements seemingly unknown. Bullying managed by prevention so very little goes on. Self-discipline is the ethos and it seems to work. Pupils clearly proud to be here.

grades needed in A level subjects and a decent spread of good grades overall.

Exit: A range of subjects and universities – economics, IT, business, engineering, biomedical sciences and dentistry loom large. In 2014, five medics and one dentist. UCL, King's, Manchester, Durham, Nottingham, Birmingham and Bristol all popular. Lots, seemingly, reapply post A level results – better matching their results to their choice of course, perhaps, and school offers good support.

Money matters: Good number of bursaries – all means-tested. Scholarships worth up to £2,000 remission of the tuition fees in academics, sports, art & design, music, drama and all-rounder. If you have a gifted son and no money you could get a fabulous deal here.

Remarks: Solid, sound and sensible. Deserves to be far better known.

Pupils and parents: Huge ethnic and social mix reflecting the local area. Thirty-odd home languages. Around two-thirds a mix of Asians – mostly Indian. All seemingly mix and co-exist with the school needing to do very little to help it along. An overall ethos of work and collaboration does all that's needed. Most live within two miles of the school but they do come from further afield into eg Ealing, Hounslow, Watford and Bucks. Five bus routes. Noted Old Boys include actors Julian Rhind-Tutt and Timothy West, writers Geoff Atkinson and Liam Halligan.

Entrance: Main feeders at 11+ are Alpha Prep, Reddiford; at 13+ St Martin's, St John's, Quainton Hall, Clifton Lodge. At 11, c60 places and c40 at 13. Heavily over-subscribed at both levels. Selection via exam – an online test and an essay at 11. Then an interview with some mental maths. At 13, exams in maths, English and science plus optional papers in eg history, geog or RE. Plus interview. At 16 there are additional places and well worth applying. A

The Lady Eleanor Holles School, Junior Department

Linked school: The Lady Eleanor Holles School, 417

Burlington House, 177 Uxbridge Road, Hampton Hill, Middx TW12 1BD

Independent • Pupils: 190 • Ages: 7–11 • C of E
• Fees (per term): £4,750

Tel: 020 8979 2173
Fax: 020 8783 1962
Email: junior-office@lehs.org.uk
Website: www.lehs.org.uk

37

Head of Juniors: Since 2011, Mrs Ffion Robinson BA MA PGCE (30s). She came from King's House boys' prep, where she had been assistant head. Prior to this she taught at The Pointer School in Blackheath. Both her degree and PGCE were taken in her native Wales – she is a Welsh speaker – and like many prep school teachers, she can turn her hand to many things. She still teaches each class once a week – maths, history, RE, English and guided reading. 'I love the creative subjects,' she says, 'and it's great to keep my hand in the classroom'. Quietly enthusiastic and plainly delighted with her job, she is smiley and efficient. Parents, similarly, are quietly confident that this is a good appointment and thank heavens their daughters are pupils here.

Head of whole school is Mrs Heather Hanbury (see senior school entry).

Entrance: School's own entrance tests in English and maths at 7+ and interview. About 48 places. Only about two girls trying for every place, but don't be fooled – the older they get, the faster the ride, so best for tots who seem exceptionally bright and eager to learn. Pupils come from lots of primaries and many from pre-preps like Athelstan House, Denmead and Jack and Jill.

Exit: Sensible system for moving from junior department to senior department. 'I was concerned that preparation for the 11+ entrance exam dominated the curriculum. We were creating all this inevitable anxiety and a division between the two parts of the school. Now the junior department girls are assessed on the basis of their classroom work and school exams and offered a guaranteed place in year 5. The very small number who are not offered

Then there are the adored 'hedge homes' – little dens in the hedges abutting the brook separating the school from the grounds

such a place are given lots of support and extra help to prepare for tests to other schools and they may still sit our exam if they wish'. Those who wish to try for a scholarship also sit the entrance exams, along with the outside applicants.

In effect, around 80 per cent go up to the senior department. Others go to eg Tiffin Girls, St Paul's Girls and Latymer Upper.

Remarks: Inside, you can still see relics of the attractive old house at the heart of the school. Outside, it is a somewhat forbidding three-storey block with a one-storey extension in unattractive brick and PVC windows. However, unlike preps elsewhere, it has lovely outside space – real space. A super garden area with excellent climbing frames and other apparatus, courts and pitches, much of it, of course, shared with the senior school. Then there are the adored 'hedge homes' – little dens in the hedges abutting the brook separating the school from the grounds. Apparently the girls use pebbles for money and run these little domestic havens just as they would their brick and drainpipe equivalents.

Inside, everywhere is carpeted – it makes for quiet corridors and a civilised feel. Classrooms are airy and light, while classes are attentive and absorbed. Girls look a treat in their grey/red/blue tartan skirts and red sweatshirts. A sense of purpose and concentration pervades the school and we saw much to delight and impress. We especially liked the cross-curricular approach to much of the teaching – something that plainly inspires the girls. If they learn about the ancient Greeks they make Greek vases. If they learn about Rio de Janeiro and Brazil, they make carnival masks. Arts and crafts throughout are unusual and clever. We particularly enjoyed the silhouette work and girls enthused about the animated films they make using their own clay and cut-out models.

The library, though inviting and piled high with books, is small and barely adequate for this number of girls. Trips to interesting places – including a local Gurdwara and the National Archives at Kew to look at Victorian prison records (after which they 'used metaphors to write poems as if we'd been in prison'). This is imaginative and lively teaching of the kind we don't see everywhere. Terrific sports (great preparation here for the legendary sporting culture of the senior department) and lucky girls use many of the older girls' facilities. Good traditional hall for productions, assemblies and younger girls' gym, and they use the wonderful senior school theatre.

The school food (eaten by most) is 'brilliant' and the place hums with happy learning. 'We let little girls be little girls,' says the head reassuringly. 'People are kind here,' one year 6 girl confided. 'If someone is being bullied they go to a friend or a buddy, but it doesn't happen much'. 'There's so much for them to do,' a parent enthused. 'My girls just love going to school'.

The Lady Eleanor Holles School

Linked school: The Lady Eleanor Holles School, Junior Department, 415

Hanworth Road, Hampton, Middlesex TW12 3HF

Independent • Pupils: 680 • Ages: 11–18 • C of E
• Fees (per term): 4,750 – £5,800

Tel: 020 8979 1601
Fax: 020 8941 8291
Email: office@lehs.org.uk
Website: www.lehs.org.uk

38

Headmistress: Since September 2014, Heather Hanbury, previously head of Wimbledon High. MA Edinburgh, MSc Cambridge in geography then land economy (40s). A breath of fresh air with experience in the 'real world' prior to teaching – spent nine years working in various management consultancy roles in the City, then as a corporate fundraiser. She was always told she should teach ('and resisted it because I don't like to do the expected'), eventually had a change of heart and took a PGCE with the express ambition to become a head. 'I always wanted to run things,' says Mrs Hanbury. 'I like making organisations efficient, effective and happy.' Began her teaching career at Blackheath High School in 1996, quickly rising through the ranks to head of sixth form, before moving on to Haberdashers' Aske's School for Girls thence deputy head of Latymer Upper School. She hums with energy, is quick to smile and laugh and is intent on injecting some fun into school life.

Academic matters: Few do education better and it's done via thrilling, not drilling. Committed to

A levels rather than the IB or Pre-U, the school ups its academic offering at the top end via the AQA Bacc and the Extended Project Qualification, plus an enrichment programme. Maths the most popular A level. Relatively few take modern languages despite exemplary results – German flourishes here as nowhere else we know. Good range of new sixth

---

She hums with energy, is quick to smile and laugh and is intent on injecting from fun into school life

---

form subjects – eg classical civilization, psychology and economics (in which virtually all get A*/A). 2014 saw 74 per cent A*-A grades. GCSEs similarly outstanding – 95 per cent A*/A with less than one per cent below a B grade. Grown-up attitude to all subject areas exemplified by the regular Focus newsletters published by the school – excellence aimed for across the board. A culture of enquiry and exploration fostered throughout.

Few with more than mild learning difficulties here, though SEN support is embedded and SENCo is abetted by a specialist who's in school four days a week. One-to-one when needed and lots of support. Seriously good school to consider if you have mobility problems or are wheelchair-bound – flattish site, lifts and wide corridors, plus can-do approach.

Games, options, the arts: Legendary for sports and the facilities here are second to none for a girls' day school. Some parents choose the school on the strength of the sports – academics, what's that? Lacrosse the main winter game and played to win – which they do. We heard about the first lax team's match against the first rugby team from Hampton – sounds a hoot. Rowing also a speciality – a welcome rarity in a girls' school. Sports tours to eg Barbados and America. We visited at a time when the arts were surviving in annexes and temporary accommodation, pending the unveiling of a splendid new performing arts building with theatre and purpose-built or cleverly converted space for art, drama and music, which opened in 2013. This meant the rehoming of sixth form common rooms and other amenities and involved a considerable – though highly desirable – upgrading all round.

Drama here is seen as 'brilliant', music is exceptional – The Holles Singers were BBC Youth Choir of the Year recently. We enjoyed the art we saw – particularly the ceramics – although we felt that far more of it could be displayed around the school.

Some parents choose the school on the strength of the sports – academics, what's that?

Also lively textiles, but only to GCSE. The extracurricular life of the school is exceptional – especially so for a day school. Parents enthuse – 'there are so many opportunities – a huge amount going on all the time'.

Background and atmosphere: The school was established in 1711 under the will of Lady Eleanor Holles, daughter of John Holles, 2nd Earl of Clare. This makes it one of the oldest girls' schools in the country. It began life in the Cripplegate Ward of the City of London, then moved to other premises in the City till 1878, thence to Mare Street in Hackney (that building now houses the London College of Fashion). The current school, purpose-built and designed in the shape of an E, opened in 1937. Such a long history is scarcely uncommon in many of our great public schools but rare in girls' schools. A palpable pride underpins the place – made more palpable by the great 300th anniversary celebrations of late 2011. The staffroom has seen many distinguished names. They include Pauline Cox, former head of Tiffin Girls', Margaret Hustler, former head of Harrogate Ladies' College, Cynthia Hall, former head of Wycombe Abbey, and Frances King, former head of Roedean, who all taught here.

Very long, horizontal, featureless and functional, the two-storey main building doesn't delight the eye but then again, it doesn't offend it either. Inside, the corridors are wide, the rooms are light and everywhere is well-kept. The place is somewhat hospital-like with its lengthy corridors and polished wood floors. The pupils insist though that 'the thing that brings it alive is the girls' – which is fair enough. Excellent sixth form centre features small teaching rooms – ideal for a history seminar or session on poetic form. The sixth form library somehow exemplifies the whole. It's light, overlooks the pitches, is exceptionally well-stocked and has neat tables for study and rows of PCs. But while the stark white walls (one, admittedly, temporary at the time of our visit) allow for no distraction, it's pretty Spartan and cries out for more display. Big main library, again well-stocked, especially with classic and modern fiction.

Focused and purposeful atmosphere. Girls are well-turned out in grey uniforms and the sixth formers look fresh and neat in casual dress. A sense of order pervades throughout, including the monitoring and assessment of pupils' progress. Parents praise the ethos of the place. 'It's cool to be clever and cool to be good at sport,' said one, while others told us: 'It's a real all-round school. You've got to be bright to get in. They don't mince their words and you've got to keep up. They expect a lot from the girls from an early stage – they have to take responsibility for themselves. If you don't turn up for a practice, you don't stay on the team'. Strong links with Hampton School – the boys' school just across the playing fields. They share a boathouse, coach service and drama. Girls take a typically pragmatic attitude – 'it's very helpful in debating – it makes a huge difference having to do it in front of boys as well,' they said.

Pastoral care and discipline: House system going great guns. 'It expands the range of extracurricular activities and the opportunities for leadership and taking responsibility'. The girls themselves enjoy getting to know older and younger pupils and the houses make for greater cohesion and community. This is continued through outreach work and the increasing involvement of alumnae. Much praise for the pastoral care system – a clear structure and everyone knows who to go to. All heads of year have

Seriously good school to consider if you have mobility problems or are wheelchair-bound – flattish site, lifts and wide corridors, plus a can-do approach

their own offices. Good system of buddying, and a feeling that no transgressors would get away with it for long. No noteworthy sins of the drink/drugs/fags kind and minor bullying problems are dealt with swiftly. A culture of openness means that it's all right to tell someone if you're not happy. Academic monitoring also praised. 'They've always recognised that my daughter has potential – the teachers are patient, encouraging and they've helped her to reach the point of realising just how well she can do,' one parent told us. Everyone likes the food – a huge range of options.

Pupils and parents: From a wide area – Acton to Woking, and all points in between. Families are

They expect a lot from girls from an early stage – they have to take responsibility for themselves. If you don't turn up for a practice, you don't stay on the team

mostly professional and clever and increasingly ethnically diverse. Lots of parents have boys at Hampton – a good mix. The common denominator is a valuing of what this school offers.

Entrance: Around a third come up from junior department, the rest from schools like Newland House, Twickenham Prep, The Study, Bute House, Holy Cross Prep, Kew College. Girls come from as many as 40 different schools, including a wide range of primary schools. Four to five applicants for each place. Tests in maths, English, non-verbal reasoning and a general paper. School also sets its own exams for sixth form applicants. No GCSE hurdle here. 'We trust our judgment,' say staff, who look at exams, interviews and reports from current schools. Grateful parents of girls who came through 11+ selection are impressed by the process. 'It was by far the most individual interview system,' one told us. 'It was slick and in 20 minutes they seemed to have learned everything about her'.

Exit: Relatively narrow range of universities, perhaps resulting from word of mouth and established traditions. Over recent years, on average, 80 per cent to Russell Group universities. Destinations include Oxbridge (8 in 2014), Durham, Bristol and London. A couple to Trinity College Dublin and the USA. No limits to what they study – good courses in everything. Notable old girls include Lynn Barber, Charlotte Attenborough, Carola Hicks, Annie Nightingale, Saskia Reeves, Jay Hunt and Gail (University Challenge) Trimble.

Money matters: Drive underway to increase the number and value of bursaries. Means-tested and reviewed annually. Academic scholarships worth up to 10 per cent of fees at 11+ and sixth form level. Arts scholarships up to 10 per cent, plus free instrumental tuition.

Remarks: 'It's been just what we hoped for,' one mother told us, while an imminent leaver sighed happily, 'I've enjoyed every day'.

Little St Helen's and St Helen's Junior school

Linked school: St Helen's School, 462

Eastbury Road, Northwood, Middlesex HA6 3AS

Independent • Pupils: 260 • Ages: 7–11 • C of E
• Fees (per term): £3,424 – £3,910

Tel: 01923 843210
Fax: 01923 843211
Email: admissions@sthn.co.uk
Website: www.sthn.co.uk

24

Headmistress: Dr Mary Short

Entrance: At 3 or 4 by observation and interview. At 7 by tests in English and maths and interview.

Exit: Usually a smooth transition from LSH to the juniors and from juniors to seniors. Very few to local state grammars, boarding or competition: 'I asked my daughter if she would like to look at other schools; she looked at me like I was bonkers.'

Remarks: 'Makes learning exciting, with no pressure', to quote a parent of her 4-year-old – gets crisper as they get older of course. The nursery, Little St Helen's, and the junior school are all housed in buildings around this beautiful site and share many of the facilities of the senior school. Some buildings have more inviting exteriors than others; however each has bright, airy classrooms, excellent, thoughtful displays and exhibited artwork, libraries, gyms, good-sized halls or studios and is well-resourced. Much given to heartening mottoes: 'Enter with an Open Mind', 'Reach Higher than Your Dreams' – an improvement on the school's Latin one, which is an odd combination of conquering, crosses and daisies.

Lots of ICT, good DT and everyone tries out three languages before they move up to the senior school. All do ballet, PE, music and speech and drama as part of the curriculum. Happy atmosphere, lovely bright uniform, civilised loos and teachers who say 'ladies, will you please take off your shoes now' to a crocodile of receptive 6-year-olds.

A teacher and teaching assistant to each class in Little Saints plus a newly-qualified TA, some teaching assistants in junior school. 'I think these girls are so lucky,' sighed the registrar wistfully as we strolled. 'We are the lucky ones,' replied a passing teacher.

The Mall School

185 Hampton Road, Twickenham, Middlesex TW2 5NQ

Independent · Pupils: 320 · Ages: 4–13 · C of E
· Fees (per term): £3,427 – £3, 978

Tel: 020 8977 2523
Fax: 020 8977 8771
Email: admissions@themallschool.org.uk
Website: www.themallschool.org.uk

39

Headmaster: Since 2011, Mr David Price, BSc (environmental science) MA (school and college management) PGCE (40s). Worked in a conservation unit for a few years before starting his career in a state primary school some 20 years ago. This is his eighth year at The Mall, where he has been head of juniors and director of studies. Previously he was head of English and deputy principal at Latymer Prep and before that taught at Melbourne Grammar School in Australia, where he lived with his family for three years.

Seems to be doing well in this, his first, headship. Obviously knows the school inside out and so has been able to leap straight into action – no root and branch reformation, rather a gentle reorganisation in a few areas. Physically and procedurally, he's been tidying up the place and has improved the management structure, appointing a senior tutor for years 7/8 and a head of the 'middles'.

Tremendously affable, he has an open-door policy for staff and parents and consults widely before deciding anything, but he will always have the final word and is prepared to put his foot down where necessary. 'He's really personable, but don't cross him,' advises one parent. Parents generally seem to appreciate the fact that he's 'one of us' and 'a family man'. He lives locally with his Australian wife Lindy and two school-age children (a son at The Mall, and an older daughter), and 'he totally gets where we are coming from,' said a mother. 'He's got the same concerns as we do and I've got nothing but praise for him,' agreed another.

He's quite a stickler for the rules and likes things neat and organised – that includes the boys and their uniforms, and he's not above manning the school gates himself to check that all is shipshape. A precise person who believes that standards must be maintained in all areas and if you bother to have a policy you should follow it through. He's strict, but not feared – 'I would say the boys like him and have a lot of respect for him,' said one mother. 'He's easy to speak to,' confirmed our young tour guides. Not remote and office-bound, he still fits in some RS teaching, runs breakfast meetings with parent reps and attends all the concerts and sports matches. 'I think he's dynamic and wonderful,' said one fan. 'Nothing is too much trouble,' said another.

Out of school he enjoys walking, cycling and socialising, plus frequent trips to visit family in Australia.

Entrance: Non selective at reception, it's first come, first served – register two years ahead. A DP innovation has been to invite boys joining in September to spend time at the school during the previous summer term. 'We obviously have a look at them and see reports from nursery, but it's not an entrance test,' he says. These infants join one of two mixed ability classes. Joiners thereafter will be assessed in English and maths, and anyone joining after year 4 will be additionally assessed in French and science. Almost self-selects because of its reputation as an academic school, although DP is keen to move away from possibly harsh connotations associated with that reputation. But even so, the bottom 25 per cent of pupils at The Mall end up in the top half of the national average. No dedicated feeder; The Mall takes from over 20 local pre-schools and nurseries including Jack and Jill, Sunflower, Windsor, Pavilion, Maria Grey and De Lacey. Scholarships available for outstanding candidates joining at 7+ or 8+.

Exit: No links to any one school, but does have a close relationship with neighbouring senior

It's heads down every day as soon as the boys arrive, with assembly timetabled for just before lunch, so the work is done when the boys are at their freshest

school, Hampton, whose head is on Mall board of governors. Typically two-thirds of leavers go to Hampton, Kings College Wimbledon, Westminster and St Paul's. 'It varies according to parental mood and which senior school is flavour of the month.' Others to St Georges in Weybridge and Reeds in Cobham and a handful to board. Boys are expected to stay to 13+ so are not really prepared for 11+ exams, though a few do leave then, usually for a grammar school place.

Remarks: A well-established prep which knows exactly what it has to do and achieves more.

Things start gently, with reception and year 1 pupils based in a separate building, five minutes from the main school, on a fairly busy, semi-residential road; you can't drop off on site or outside, need to park up and walk. Parents like the fact that their little ones are physically separated from the older, bigger boys; 'I think it makes it easier for them as they start,' said a mother.

The infants' building is a converted Victorian vicarage, with two reception classes downstairs and two year 1 classes upstairs – maximum 22 in each class, generally around 18. Not masses of space for 80+ little boys, but neither are they jammed in. Bright classrooms enlivened with colourful displays. Lessons we saw were very settled and children seemed happy and focused. There is lots of topic-based work eg on space, where we saw some inventive designs for 'a planet unlike Earth'. Each class teacher has a full-time classroom assistant and there are specialist teachers for music and swimming – both strengths of this place, of which more later. Homework twice a week, spellings once a week and reading every night. Boys needing extra help with work will be peeled off for extra tuition with SENCo – no stigma, no extra cost at this level, but you will be charged higher up the school. Also a charge for help with EFL, but school says boys generally catch up quickly, typically within a term or so.

There's one large room, not grand enough to be called a hall, but where the whole infant school can gather for assemblies. Year 1 eat their packed lunches here too – no hot meals for infants – and reception pupils eat their lunch at their desk. Sounds messy, but school says it works.

Some nice touches outside – a bird box/camera and raised beds where the boys can plant – go some way to compensate for limited outdoor space including a sadly under-used grassy area ('little boys and grass don't mix,' said school).

Generally the atmosphere is relaxed, but not sloppy. All staff expect and receive respect – for example, the boys will be asked to re-enter a room if they have not entered it properly. 'I like the place and the pace here,' said one mother. 'It's perfect for little boys, with quite a lot of play-based learning in the early years as they improve their fine motor skills, then things hot up as they move through the school.'

From year 2 the boys move to the purpose-built main site, with 7+ entrants joining in year 3. Everyone automatically transfers to the senior section from year 4 (ages 8 to 13) to take up the common entrance curriculum. Years ago boys would be asked to leave if they did not make the grade – all that changed under the previous headmaster and Mr Price shares this same philosophy. 'I am here to get the less able boys through too and I like to see a wide range of abilities.' To this end school has a series of strategies to help and support the less able and is very keen on early intervention, 'the earlier the better'. Then in senior school there is a director of personalised learning, who develops individual plans. DP is also setting up a programme for non-academic scholarships and Mall pupils have already had some success in winning music, art and all-rounder places. Lots of mocks and target-setting, overseen by newly introduced 'academic tutors', aim to ensure early detection of anyone not working up to their capability. Currently 26 boys with SEN, mostly mild dyslexia and dyspraxia. 'From year 4 parents can pay for additional support if they choose', says school.

That said, academics is the focus here – no bones about it; that's why most parents choose The Mall in the first place. It's heads down every day as soon as the boys arrive, with assembly timetabled for just before lunch, so the work is done when the boys are at their freshest. Streaming and setting at the top of the school – in year 7 an accelerated class is introduced, from which come the scholarship boys, while the other class goes at 'ordinary pace'. In the past three years Mall pupils have won 18 senior school scholarships and over 40 prizes for performance at CE. Well over half The Mall's pupils achieve A* and A scores in their CE.

'It's a very good all-round school, but its USP is the learning environment – they have got it just right,' said a father. 'The all-round atmosphere is extremely conducive to learning,' agreed a mother. 'As we looked around it felt like we had come home.

It's all brilliant from the get-go and I like the drive in this place. They let boys be boys, but also push them to do their absolute best.'

Parents seem to share an unerring confidence in this school and trust it to do right by their sons. There is an orderly, comfortable atmosphere and the boys are well-prepared for their CE. The ongoing tests and plenty of exam practice mean that the boys are so au fait with the whole procedure that it's no biggie when the important ones come around. 'They are totally familiar with what's expected and almost relaxed about it,' said a mother.

There is a fair amount of homework, including holiday homework – building up so that by year 7 there's about an hour a night, 1.5 hours by year 8. Teaching is strong across the board so it is invidious to pick stand-out subjects – 'Really it's all good,' chant parents – but suffice to say French ('extremely well-taught' by native speakers) history and music all mentioned time and again. All year 2 boys play recorder to get them ready and interested and 140+ boys go on to play instruments – we saw boys having great fun drumming and composing. There is also an 80-strong choir – 'It's one of the nice things about a single-sex school,' says one parent. 'Boys are simple creatures and follow what others are doing, so they don't see singing as "girly".' Plenty of chances to perform via regular productions – DP plans for the standard of school concerts to be even better. 'I think he just wants the boys to practise more,' said one mother. 'To make the shows a bit more polished'.

Facilities generally on a par with similar London day schools, with some outstanding features. There's a splendid theatre, a sublime swimming pool and a new sports hall. There are two full games afternoons each week and although school is lacking in lush grounds, it is but a short skip and a jump to the bosky expanses of nearby Bushy Park for football, rugby and cricket. There's

---

Mothers' Day breakfast designed to tug at the heart strings – each boy paints a picture of his mother which he presents to her along with a red rose

---

not so much athletics or tennis and some parents feel sport is not taken as seriously as at some other schools in the area – with the exception of swimming where the U10 team are IAPS national champions. But most agree that it does 'well enough' for their sons and praise 'smashing' sports staff. 'I wouldn't say it's for a very sporty child,' said one. 'It doesn't have the focus that it does in other schools, which irritates some of us'.

Not masses of extracurricular activities on offer, though there's all the usual art, DT, chess and of course a swimming club – it would be criminal not to make the most of their gorgeous pool. Offering of clubs has been beefed up to include computing, karate, judo and science. Some of the clubs are at lunchtime as it's already quite a long day (8.25am – 4pm) but school has to balance this against the fact that many Mall parents are both working and would appreciate their sons being able to enjoy a longer school day.

Apparently there's no such thing as a typical Mallian: 'We prefer them to remain individuals,' says DP. But he will concede uniformity in that they are confident ('not arrogant' he stresses), well-mannered and well-rounded young men. 'I think they are all quite different really,' agreed one mother. 'And I like the way they are encouraged to develop their own interests and skills'.

Staff have good relationships with the boys – good humour abounds, house points (plus or minus) moderate behaviour and are delivered with some theatrical flourish by school deputy. Head says there is something in The Mall's DNA that promotes good staff/pupil relationships here,

bringing out the best in everyone. 'I'm continually impressed by the conversations we can have with them at a very early stage,' he says. Boys are encouraged and taught how to speak confidently in public and to vent their opinions though lots of debating activities. Pupil council and prefects' programme are all part of promoting leadership qualities in the boys. But they are equally encouraged to embrace sentimentality on occasion, such as the Mother's Day breakfast (DP imported the idea from Australia) designed to tug at the heart strings – each boy paints a picture of his mother which he presents to her along with a red rose after reading her a poem – most mums cry.

There's a fairly cosmopolitan mix of families here with a wider diversity of cultural backgrounds than seen in other preps in this area of south-west London – Asian, Chinese and European boys in the mix. 'I think it's fantastic that The Mall has such a varied population – it's not the rarefied exclusively white intake typical of schools around here,' says one mother. School minibuses run in the morning from Kew, Osterley and Kingston, other pupils from Hounslow, Isleworth, St Margaret's, Richmond, Twickenham, Teddington and Hampton.

Friendly bunch of parents – busy PTA does lots of fund-raising but has recently changed its focus to include more social events to get people together. Class reps effective and take the role seriously.

Parents say they feel welcome in school and well informed. Lots of good advice about 'where next?' and DP has introduced a 'future schools information evening' to boost this area. The place is very upfront, it's easy to get to see staff and DP has introduced the Clarion call text communication system which parents have been crying out for. 'They've always been great if I've had a problem,' said a parent. 'There's always a nice atmosphere and I feel very comfortable talking to them,' said another.

School runs a good and thriving thrift shop for uniform. Overall parents feel extras are relatively small, not many super-expensive ones, but neither is much available for free. Because The Mall is a small school there are not a lot of big expeditions and sometimes not enough takers to make an expensive jaunt viable. But that's not to say the boys don't get about; there's a year 3 residential trip to PGL Marchants Hill, older pupils to York and France, plus the occasional sports tour.

In all a happy, high-achieving academic school displaying a kinder attitude than of old – trying to be more inclusive. A settled, focused, organised place, which does exactly what it says on the tin.

Maple Walk School

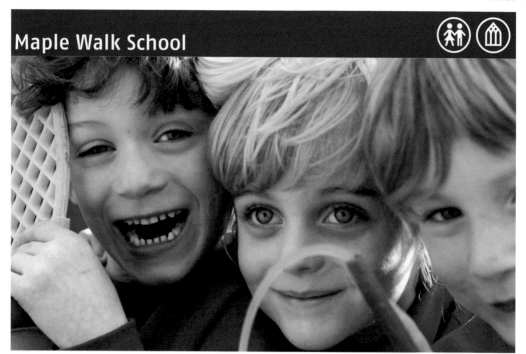

62a Crownhill Road, London, NW10 4EB

Independent · Pupils: 200 · Ages: 4–11 · Fees (per term): £2,590

Tel: 020 8963 3890
Fax: 020 7799 6688
Email: admissions@maplewalkschool.co.uk
Website: www.maplewalkschool.co.uk

Headmistress: Since 2012, Mrs Sarah Gillam, previously head of the now defunct White House Prep School in Wokingham. Her 30-year career includes two middle school headships and one head of junior science. She has a BEd from Homerton College Cambridge and is married with three university-age daughters.

Entrance: Non-selective intake of 40 at reception stage. Siblings get preference, then in order of registration – waiting lists for several years ahead. For spaces higher up the school, the head meets the parents and the child has a trial day in the relevant class, 'to check that they will fit in socially and academically'.

Exit: To a wide variety of schools, including Francis Holland, Aldenham, Notting Hill and Ealing, Channing, John Lyon, Queen's College, Portland Place and North Bridge House in the private sector, and St Marylebone, Hampstead School and West London Free School in the state sector. Younger children have also gained places at, amongst others, Wetherby Prep, Notting Hill Prep, Bute House and Sunningdale Prep.

Remarks: The New Model School Company (NMS) was set up by Civitas (but is now an independent entity) when research identified a gap in the market for a low-cost chain of not-for-profit independent primary schools. Maple Walk was the first NMS school, starting in a rented room in a sports centre off Ladbroke Grove in 2004 with one teacher, two pupils and school materials stored in a trunk. A year later the fledgling school of a dozen pupils moved to the upper floor of a church hall off Kensal Road. In September 2009 the school – by now with classes up to year 4 – moved to its own purpose-built premises in Harlesden, which have impeccable ecological credentials: a sedum roof, solar panels, a ground source heat pump and a rainwater harvesting system, plus a no-car travel plan. It has added a form each year and now has a full complement of 200 children.

The education is traditional, with reading taught by phonics, French throughout, history taught chronologically. A strong emphasis on politeness and courtesy, with every child shaking their teacher's hand at the beginning and end of the day. The first Ofsted report, written in 2008 when the school was still in temporary accommodation, is surprisingly lukewarm, but the previous head was sanguine about it: 'The weaknesses were mostly to do with paperwork and correct materials. We were able to address the areas they highlighted while we were still there.' Indeed, a recent Independent Schools Inspectorate report praises the 'good' teaching standards, 'excellent' personal development and 'outstanding' relationships between parents and school.

Certainly parents are happy. 'They seem to be getting a very good grounding,' said one. 'They have really nice teachers who know the children well.' 'They're doing incredible work,' said another. 'I think it's outstanding.' The head's after-school secondary transfer club introduces exam techniques to older children, and the year 6 class teacher 'is very experienced at secondary transfers'. 'They do their absolute best to make sure they are well prepared,' said a parent.

The school can cope with mild SEN – 'we don't assess children coming into reception, but we do ask parents to be honest and transparent and we may talk to their nursery if we have any concerns'. One-to-one literacy and numeracy assistance at extra cost; some children get speech and language support outside school.

An emphasis on children becoming confident public performers: the annual Craigmyle poetry competition (named for the charitable trust that paid for the new site and building works) involves everyone from reception upwards reciting a poem by heart, and there are public speaking competitions, music concerts and drama performances. 'The children are very confident,' said a parent. 'They have nice manners, they can talk to adults, they look you in the eye.'

The school's outdoor space includes playgrounds for infants and for juniors – with a climbing frame purchased by parents from Ebay – and a football/netball court with climbing wall (also funded by the PTA, Friends of Maple Walk). The gardening club grows vegetables in tiered beds and a butterfly/bee-friendly area is in concept. The children learn to swim at a local pool and try out a different sport each half term. A dance group – 'the youngest by a long stretch' – came third in the Dance Challenge UK national finals at the Cadogan Hall.

This is a low-cost, no-frills school, which depends on plenty of parental involvement. The PTA has raised funds for part-time specialist dance and sports teachers, and parents have donated computers, including a suite of Netbooks that travel round different classrooms. Parents run clubs and help organise book weeks, art extravaganzas – 'delicious organised chaos' – and cultural celebrations. The school is a Christian one, with weekly religious assemblies and nativity plays, but all faiths are welcome and Jewish and Muslim parents come in to talk about their religions.

Despite the low fees, it is still very much a white, middle class demographic – albeit mostly journalists, artists and musicians rather than bankers and lawyers. However the school is building links with the local state primary school just down the road, with shared activities, teacher training, netball and football matches. Now the school has its own settled base in a very diverse area, it hopes to attract a wider social and ethnic mix of families.

Parents cite the 'village school' atmosphere as one of their main reasons for choosing Maple Walk. 'There's a nice, cosy, community feel,' said one. 'I liked the fact that it is small, pioneering and affordable,' said another. 'It's a really vibrant, eclectic community.' Parents emphasise how happy their children are – 'mine will look back and feel they've been part of something really special and exciting'.

Merchant Taylors' School

Sandy Lodge, Northwood, Middlesex HA6 2HT

Independent • Pupils: 890 • Ages: 11–18 • Non-denom • Fees (per term): £6,017

Tel: 01923 845514
Fax: 01923 835110
Email: admissions@mtsn.org.uk
Website: www.mtsn.org.uk

25

Head Master: Since 2013, Mr Simon Everson (late 40s). Previously head of Skinners' School in Tunbridge Wells. Studied at Cambridge and Nottingham, has masters' degrees in English and philosophy and has taught at state and independent schools and a school in Japan. Married to Ginny, a psychotherapist who specialises in treating victims of domestic violence and supporting children in foster homes. His outside interests include prehistory, philosophy, running and travel.

Academic matters: Ideal for the curious free-thinker with a deal of self-motivation. A rare breed, an academic school with a wonderfully cool feel; understands there is more to academic excellence than great exam results but achieves top notch performances anyway. No specialism, just tries to do everything to a high standard and adamant it is not an exam factory or hot-house. 'There is so much else to do, we're more rarefied'. Boys take a number of IGCSEs (English, science and maths) and go beyond the syllabus. Consistently outstanding results: 67 per cent A*/A and 94 per cent A*/B at A level in 2014. At GCSE, 91 per cent A* or A. No weak subjects. All boys study French and Latin in years 7 and 8 and begin either German, Italian, Spanish or classical Greek in year 9. French, German, Spanish offered at AS and A. English offered as three different A levels (lang, lit, and lang and lit). Maths and further maths popular at A level, geography increasingly so. Biology very good, and new head of physics upping the ante by introducing dynamic elements such as electronics and robotics. Bright bunch, a number take the sought-after extended project qualification (EPQ) though head confessed, 'I get the ones who teach me. It stretches them but they rise gloriously to the challenge.' Recent introduction of drama A level and GCSE illustrative of way school listens, 'They consult with us and very much run the school for us, which is a real honour.' Drama A level may seem incongruous in such an academic setting, but one recent alumnus who gained a place at Imperial to read medicine, in part because, in addition to starry science, panel impressed with his A level drama.

Emphasis on encouragement and inspiration not pressure and perspiration. 'You go to the gym to work out, and to school to work yourself out,' say staff. Introduced hour-long lessons to ensure sufficient time to explore, pause and reflect. 'Just when a lesson might be getting difficult or dull, teachers have the knack of lighting the touch paper and bringing back to life. They work us hard but they care and make learning exciting. They're always happy to help, whenever and however.' Parents equally enthused: 'My boys buzz with enthusiasm when they come home from school. The teachers understand boys and know how to structure lessons to suit inquisitive boys.'

Learning support not a traditional métier but, says school, 'We're getting better, fast.' Asks parents to be up front about learning difficulties: 'If we don't know, we don't know what we are dealing with and precious time may be lost'. One parent felt support was in danger of becoming too thinly stretched, another that school is not always swift at detecting difficulties, but praised the way they meet the needs of both child and family once they're apparent. 'As soon as I met the head and staff I realised they would go the extra mile to help my son.' Views every teacher as a teacher of specific learning difficulties with support available to anyone. Caters for boys with physical difficulties, including wheelchairs. Those with identified needs are monitored and helped; one off or regular, but strictly no withdrawal. Work towards self-help; one boy heading to uni requested a book on Asperger's to better understand his condition and how to explain it to others. Extra time and use of laptop not unusual, but here, even lowest maths sets pursue maths A level and are oft rewarded with top grades. Enrichment for Oxbridge (16 offers in 2014) focuses on feeding a passion, not spoon feeding.

Games, options, the arts: Boys enjoy rough and tumble, 'They are like puppies, they need to be let out for a good run around', say staff, and run around they do. Not a macho rugby school, boys confessed, 'Often we seem to be half the size of our competitors but we still try to give them a good run for their money.' Hockey big and getting bigger, thanks in no small part to charismatic England coach on the staff. Keen to find something for everyone – both on and off the sports pitches. Tries to ease boys out of their comfort zone: 'Sometimes they simply lack confidence.' Range of sports extends beyond cricket, basketball, athletics, swimming, tennis, soccer, badminton, croquet, cross-country, golf and shooting. Super facilities include sports hall, cricket nets, heated indoor pool, all-weather hockey pitches, athletics track, lakes for sailing and windsurfing, tennis courts, squash, handball fives courts, assault course and fencing Salle. Director of sport as pleased with a good, gutsy performance from E team as those in top squads achieving national recognition. Pros coach all teams. Believe most important thing is

Unlock your daughters, these are the good guys – charming, amusing, entertaining and self-effacing – the ideal dinner guests

taking part and having a good time but enjoy winning too! Moral attitude to sport – no truck with swearing or arguing with the ref and unbending insistence that, win or lose, they do so with grace.

Serious charity work, includes long-term, on-going, outstanding work with Phab – residential Care Week held annually and funds raised throughout the year. Head openly enthused and inspired by boys' enterprising and benevolent spirit and visibly glowed as he recounted numerous anecdotes of their generosity, including recent competition win (first prize in Bank of England competition) and their insistence that the cash prize be donated to one of their charities. Myriad of community activities, links with Harefield Academy plus weekly sports sessions and reading with youngsters from local state primary school; 'We shared an end of term concert: that really cemented the relationship between the schools.' Excellent music with orchestras, swing band, jazz bands and every kind of ensemble. Concerts throughout the year with recitals galore and performing opportunities for all. Plenty of drama; technical side revered, 'Productions are amazing; expect fireworks, bangs, flames and fun,' said one boy; another commented, 'There is so much humour, not just in the plays but in the school, perhaps that's what sets it apart', though added hurriedly, 'We're serious when we have to be or when it is inappropriate not to be.' DT popular, with good and imaginative teaching; boys involved in design of new DT building, art equally impressive. Merchant Taylors' Diploma being introduced: will provide formal recognition of co-curricular activities.

Background and atmosphere: Founded in the City of London in 1561 by the Worshipful Company of Merchant Taylors and Linen Armourers, it was then the largest school in the country. Moved in 1933 to current impressive 250-acre green belt site, with exquisite formal gardens and spectacular protected area for wildlife, including a lake that is home to herons, swans, moorhens plus countless interloping fowls. Feels like a cross between a boarding school (which it once was) and an Oxbridge college: unhurried calm, timeless beauty but oozing with purpose and discovery. Lush, manicured playing fields outside, plus core of (listed) buildings, with a dominant Deco angularity, pay homage to superb facilities inside, including newish library and information centre, politics and economics centre, entrance hall and sixth form common-room. Boys confided: 'Sometimes we wander round the grounds and just explore the school; it's an exciting place with nooks and crannies.'

Pastoral care and discipline: Criticisms few and far between. 'We live in a perfect bubble. They set you up for uni and are so caring and supportive we worry we might not be equipped for the bad things life might throw at us.' Vertical tutor system popular with most staff, who enjoy getting to know a mixed bag of boys well, but mixed reports from parents, boys and moles. 'Not all teachers are born tutors, some are naturals, others take time to grow into the role but when they get it right, the tutor is almost an extension of your family, wonderful.' Christian services held in the chapel, but other faiths welcome with a Muslim prayer room, Jewish society, Christian discussion group and three much-praised whole school assemblies. Lunch important – head insists all boys dine together; no packed lunches but all reasonable dietary requests catered for. Expulsions rare, school is good at giving second chances but not at any price: 'Sometimes it becomes clear that we simply are not the right place for a child.'

Pupils and parents: Unlock your daughters, these are the good guys, charming, amusing, entertaining and self-effacing; the ideal dinner guests. Lots of social entrepreneurs who take moral responsibility seriously, are quietly competitive but will ask 'how can I help you?' not 'what will you do for me?' Boys are acutely aware of their privileged education and humbled by it, saying, 'you won't find any pomp, plums or fat-cats wearing silly hats.' We certainly loved their sense of fun and the gallant

way they responded to gentle teasing; no airs or graces, 'School doesn't try to mould us, they find out what's best for us, they adjust. I guess we do too, because we want to. Importantly they don't try to make us tick boxes.' Parents say boys are 'down to earth, grounded with a healthy degree of humility and tolerance.' Staff agree, adding, 'They respect others, sometimes they lack edge and aren't good at pushing themselves forward.' Others comment on

Plenty of drama; technical side revered. 'Productions are amazing: expect fireworks, bangs, flames and fun,' said one boy

the friendly rivalry, with each boy wanting to be just a little better, achieve a little more, than his friends.

Broad appeal to Bucks, Herts and London sets but with a touch of Goldilocks – Bucks think school rather urban, London a bit in the sticks and Herts just right. Ethnic mix reflects the area, roughly 35 per cent Asian, 65 per cent white, many faiths including Christian, Muslim and Jewish. Increasing numbers from London for the ethos, lakes and space, including first time buyers and dual income families. Parents say school is wonderfully inclusive: 'We have friends of all races and faiths and our boys do too.' Another volunteered their enthusiasm for the carol service: 'It is a Christian service but boys of all faiths take an active part and parents and siblings join in'. Parents very involved with school and encouraged to attend events and take part in committees, which, according to our moles, eliminates parents' moans and whinges. Revered old boys' network. 'I love the fact that my friends all do very different things to each other and to me,' said one OMT. Famous alumni include Sir Edmund Spenser, Clive of India, Titus Oates, Samuel Palmer plus, more recently, Reginald Maudling, Lord Coggan (Archbishop of Canterbury), Nobel prize-winning medic Sir John Sulston, the sculptor Lynn Chadwick (whose work graces one of the many manicured lawns), comedian Michael McIntyre (who left when his family fell on hard times and could no longer afford the fees) and Conn Iggulden (author of Dangerous Book for Boys).

Entrance: Competitive. Good mix at 11 between state and independent schools including from Radlett Prep and Reddiford. Odd state school refugee at 13 but vast majority from independent schools: St John's, St Martin's, Northwood Prep, Durston House, Orley Farm, York House, Gayhurst, Chesham

Prep and Davenies, Trevor-Roberts, Devonshire House, Lyndhurst and others. Buses from everywhere. Huge surge in demand for year 7 entry, year 9 constant. Average IQ of 121 (equates to pass mark for Bucks grammar schools) but accepts those as low as 105 and does a great job with them. Adamant they are not seeking statistics or grade point averages; want boys with an interest or passion, whose presence in the school will help others get a good deal out of it. For 11+ entry, register by November 30 preceding the January exams in English, maths and verbal reasoning. Boys who do well are asked to return for interview. At 13 need to be registered by June a year in advance, with interviews in autumn preceding entry. School's own exam in all CE sub-

Allegro not andante, hits the high notes with ease, in a lively-paced, vibrant setting; tingling with team-spirit, sparkling with wit

jects with scholarships divined from outstanding performances. Scholarship candidates who do well are invited back for further interviews. Sixth form places by examination in March – candidates must register by December 31 and will be tested in the subjects they wish to study, followed by interviews. 'My child loved the interview, that's when he decided he really wanted to go to MT'. Uses interview to gauge level of interest and engagement, get boys off script, attempt to delve under the skin of those who have been tutored to the hilt, see what lies beneath; can they cope with the unfamiliar, do they have a passion, are they enthusiastic?

Exit: Virtually all stay on to sixth form. In 2014, 16 to Oxbridge, rest to a broad range of academic subjects at Russell group and other top universities – lots to London unis, others to Nottingham, Warwick, Birmingham, Durham and Bristol. University and careers advice a strength with each sixth former assigned to a senior head of department who acts as his university adviser. Work experience – some of which can be done abroad – is highly developed and includes a companies link.

Money matters: Keen to attract parents from all walks of life whose son's life would be enriched by attending MT. Honorary academic scholarships as per Oxbridge (20 at 13 and 10 at 11); scholars receive status plus enriched programme. A clutch of music, sports and all-rounder scholarships at 11, 13 and 16. Music scholarships include two up to 25 per cent of fees and up to two music exhibitions (worth up to one tenth of the fee.) Additional music awards, covering the cost of tuition of up to two instruments, also available. Hopes to fulfil school founders' dream whereby up to 200 boys receive some sort of means-tested financial assistance up to 100 per cent of the fees; used the 450th anniversary to launch 'Forward to our Roots' appeal.

Remarks: A premier league school of quiet confidence and substance with room for the erudite but not for ego. Produces bright, happy, savvy boys with a caring and compassionate outlook. Provides a truly rounded, high-octane education in a friendly, unstuffy, and surprisingly stress-free environment. Allegro not andante, hits the high notes with ease, in a lively-paced, vibrant setting; tingling with team-spirit, sparkling with wit, infused with emotional intelligence.

Montpelier Primary School

Montpelier Road, Ealing, London, W5 2QT

State · Pupils: 670 · Ages: 4–11 · Non-denom ·

Tel: 020 8997 5855
Fax: 020 8810 6702
Email: admin@montpelier.ealing.sch.uk
Website: www.montpelierschool.net

Headteacher: Since 2003, Mr Am Rai (mid-40s). BA in sociology, Birmingham Poly, MA in educational management and administration at University of London, Institute of Education. Married, two children. Very experienced head who had already worked in seven London state primaries prior to his arrival at Montpelier. He had been twice seconded

to rescue failing schools. And you can see why. He is a man of very clear vision and sound, liberal educational principles. He is highly articulate, straightforward and frank in conversation. In two hours' conversation, we were wearied by no jargon, no pseudo-academic parroting, no political posturing – so refreshing. There is no disguising Mr Rai's

confidence and his ambition – both personal and, more overtly, for his pupils. The results are there for all to see. Montpelier's most recent (2012) Ofsted – with only two days' notice – achieved a full house of grade 1s. His results top the borough's and top most other boroughs too. The children are stimulated, creative, challenged, smiley and rewarded. A very good head.

Entrance: Oversubscribed at all levels but high turnover among local international community means that occasional places at all stages are not uncommon. Up to 200 apply for the 52 nursery places; 500 for each place in reception. All managed by Ealing LA and, if you have no special circumstances, you need to live up close and purposeful if you are to get in. And families increasingly swap their large homes in less well provided for bits of the borough for flats round the corner from this school.

Exit: Some leave for local preps at end of year 4. Of the majority, around 30 per cent go to the local hotshot comprehensive – Drayton Manor HS. Around 15 per cent to Ellen Wilkinson HS – the local girls' comprehensive. The rest either to local RC or CE high schools or to the local independents – Notting Hill and Ealing, St Benedict's, St Augustine's. Increasingly, some to the Tiffins, to Bucks, Berks or Middlesex grammars, to St Paul's Boys' or Girls', Latymer Upper or John Lyon, and some parents even move house after their bright buttons gain places there or at eg Henrietta Barnett. No disaster schools in the area – another good reason for coming here.

Remarks: Sited on a corner of two quiet, tree-lined roads and adjoining a pretty park. The surrounding streets are similarly well-appointed, orderly and solidly middle class – this is suburban bliss, though the North Circular grinds along only a couple of hundred yards away. The nearest schools are all independent and, not surprisingly, they are the chosen destinations for a sizeable minority of Montpelier leavers.

Three connected school buildings, and only one – due for renovation – makes the heart sink. The latest (2009) is a clever extension housing reception and admin. Infants and reception on ground floor – makes sense. Four playgrounds with good play equipment though not over-provided with soft

---

The surrounding streets are similarly well appointed, orderly and solidly middle class – this is suburban bliss, though the North Circular grinds along only a couple of hundred yards away.

flooring. Reception classes have integral loos, so no tots trailing down corridors. No overheated classrooms here – though we visited on a dull January morning and no class feels over full, despite 30 in each and staff. Windows have replaced doors wherever possible – school has a light and open feel. Reception in large classroom with a teacher, a nursery nurse, a student teacher and a teaching assistant. Corner with fresh fruit and drinks available all day for whoever feels inclined. 40 per cent bring food from home but the school lunch menu – outside caterers – looked varied and appetising.

Infants' classes full of quiet, concentrated activity – seven or eight things going on in each room – water, measuring, building, weighing, word work, writing etc. Every class has a whiteboard and IT used imaginatively round the school – connecting people and activities and joining things up. Learning legacy boards provide testimony to what has been learned during the term. Monitoring and appraisal embedded into everything – each child has her own targets for the core skills and a list of 'I Can' statements to keep parents abreast of what has been mastered and what still needs to be done. This complemented by the clever use of iPads by teachers who photograph work and load it onto a parents' portal so that latest work can be admired at home.

Lots of imaginative cross-curricular learning: displays everywhere are evidence of lively thinking and teaching. Year 2 work on portraits looked at what portraits can teach us rather than being merely an excuse to draw ourselves. Super project on Medusa – each child had made a 'Wanted' poster with clever text – and another class displayed illustrations of The Lady of Shalott with sensitive use of quotes. Oxford Reading Tree used throughout with

In two hours' conversation, we were wearied by no jargon, no pseudo-academic parroting, no political posturing – so refreshing

built-in encouragement for parental participation and each child has weekly guided reading session to build comprehension skills rather than just skimming speed. A good hall/gym, a nice little library – properly used for lending and reading – two IT suites, art room, and every class has an art week in which they can drop everything else and experience sustained and concentrated work on a project of their own. Unusually strong music – 150+ learn an instrument in or after school – and school provides child care for siblings until 5.00pm to facilitate music activities. Everyone has an afternoon of sport weekly. Not much but better than many.

Remarkable amount of support given to those who need extra help with eg language, writing task or maths. We saw one-to-one sessions and numerous small groups in all available spaces. Also, for those with an SEN to whom – until recent changes in government SEN provision, at least – school has given exemplary support. And organised time made to equip those who arrive with no English with key words and skills. As socially diverse as any school in the capital. Around 55 per cent speak a language other than English at home – huge range of languages and cultures – among which highest proportions from the Middle East and Japan, then India and various bits of Europe. Families include a lot of 'corporate nomads' ie those with three or five year contracts who stay and are relocated anywhere on the globe. After school language (French, Spanish, Arabic, Mandarin) and many other clubs.

The first thing that strikes you on an ordinary school day is how quiet it is and how class after class of 30 diverse children work absorbedly and happily together. In this highly organised school – and it is a large primary by any standards – children look relaxed and secure and, even amongst the smallest, there is a sense that school is about learning. Few behavioural problems – jumped on smartly when they occur. Head 'will exclude if a child is spoiling the lives of other children', but no-one excluded for bullying in eight years prior to our visit.

Parental talk of 'the warm community feeling', express gratitude that 'the children are looked after well and are happy,' and pay tribute to the truly multi-cultural ethos – 'all faiths and beliefs are celebrated'. Very active PTA and lots of community activities eg annual international food fair and remarkably effective fund-raising summer fête.

Most staff – many are young – highly praised. Head is seen as dynamic and approachable by some and by others as remote and over-protective of his staff. No-one, however, wishes they had sent their children elsewhere, and none would dispute that he has made a stunning success of a school which, before, had been content to be good enough. 'We judge things by the happiness of our children,' asserts head wisely.

Newland House School

32– 34 Waldegrave Park, Twickenham, Middlesex TW1 4TQ

Independent • Pupils: 405 • Ages: 4–13 • Non-denom • Fees (per term): £3,395 – £3,795

Tel: 020 8865 1305
Fax: 020 8744 0399
Email: admissions@newlandhouse.net
Website: www.newlandhouse.net

40

Headmaster: Since 2010, Mr David Alexander BMus Dip NCOS (early 50s). Previously head of Norland Place School and Haddon Dene School. Warm, welcoming and with a good sense of humour. Very kind and doesn't have a bad word to say about anybody. Justifiably proud of his charges. 'Our 13-year-old boys are a delight, as are our 11-year-old girls. I'm very proud to know any of them. I like what the school has done for them.' Parents say, 'What you see is what you get. Pupils and parents respect him but he knows how to laugh too.' Believes one of his main jobs is to steer parents towards the right school for their child: he wants his pupils to be at the top of their game at their senior schools. The children adore him because he's such fun: he is currently keen for the school to buy a boat which can act as a floating classroom on the Thames. Holds a commercial flying licence and commands a reserve RAF squadron at weekends. Mr Alexander selects the head boy and head girl by deciding which pupils he would most like to have lunch with.

Entrance: Over-subscribed – best register your child as soon as possible after birth. Two main points of entry: 4+ and 7+. At 4+ entry is on a first-come, first-served basis, with siblings given priority. Forty places available at this stage and a waiting list in operation. Once at the pre-prep, a place is guaranteed at the prep school. At 7+ pupils are tested in English and maths. Assessments take place in November for entry into the school the following September. Twenty more places available at this stage. Academic and music bursaries available – up to 50 per cent of fees, negotiated on a yearly basis. Ten per cent discount for third sibling when all are in school together.

Exit: Predominantly private day schools, including St Paul's, Hampton, KCS Wimbledon, St. George's

College, Reeds, Surbiton High, Wimbledon High and Lady Eleanor Holles. A couple each year head for boarding schools such as Marlborough and Wellington. Girls leave at 11 and boys at 13. Girls can stay on to 13, but don't. 'It would be a leap of

---

Currently a group of senior boys is investigating the effect of tyre pressure on the environment and presentations have been made to MPs

---

faith' says head. Consistently high number of academic, sports, music and all-rounder scholarships. Head puts this down to outstanding teaching and the fact that the children are in a happy environment and so want to learn.

Remarks: The pre-prep is run by the approachable and calm Tracey Chong. All-female staff ('by coincidence') give it a homely air. Building very tired-looking but there are plans afoot for a major refurbishment before a possible move to a new site bang next door to the main school. Pupils venture across the road to main school for ICT and games.

'We're very much one school despite being on two sites', says head. 'The teachers at Number 11 (the pre-prep) are lovely and smiley and it rubs off on the children,' says one parent.

Classes at the prep are mixed ability, maximum 20 children. Lessons are lively and fast-paced with specialist teachers for PE, art, music and ICT from the start. Separate sciences taught from year 4. Children set for English, French and maths from year 5. Days are long, especially for those who start with the full cooked breakfast on offer at 7.30 am.

Once the girls leave at the end of year 6, the boys are placed in two mixed ability classes and one small scholarship set; vacancies left by girls are not filled. Greek on offer to potential scholars. Parents love the fact that children get so much individual attention at the top of the school. 'A real strength,' says one. Children are well-prepared for 11+, 13+ and scholarships. As the head puts it: 'We are a preparatory school. It's our job to prepare them for the exams for entry to their next schools.' Parents report that a massive amount of coaching goes on in the final years, of which the head is critical. 'It's not necessary. We are all fighting a coaching culture but people get sucked into it.' Head gives out CE results to boys as they sit around a camp fire on the year 8 trip to Wales. 'A lovely touch, and the boys never forget it. It's a gesture typical of the school,' says one parent.

Classrooms are spacious and light, with traditional wooden desks arranged in neat rows. Impressive ICT suite, tablets about to be introduced but head keen this shouldn't be a gimmick. The school enters a huge number of national and international competitions with frequent success. Recently won three World Maths Day trophies, out of a total of five awarded to UK schools. DT department is the envy of other schools and recently assembled a car for the Shell Eco-Marathon that achieved a mileage of 1,000 miles per gallon. Currently a group of senior boys is investigating the effect of tyre pressure on the environment and presentations have been made to MPs.

Plenty of choirs for each year group, new pop choir for year 7/8 boys is thriving. Several hundred individual instrumental and singing lessons take place every week. Lots of bands, ensembles and orchestras. Children have recently taken part in performances at the Kingston Music Festival and concerts at the Barbican with the London Symphony Orchestra.

Art clubs include weekend activities where parents can become involved. Local artists exhibit and sell their work in the reception area and include a couple of inexpensive pieces so that children can buy a picture if it catches their eye.

Sport is a real strength of the school. Boys play rugby, football and cricket; girls play netball, rounders and hockey. Swimming, cross-country and athletics also on offer and even more sport possible through numerous after-school clubs, including golf at neighbouring club. Main playing fields are five minutes away by mini-bus; two multi-purpose, all-weather courts and four cricket nets on site. Lots of tournaments and matches mean everyone gets the chance to compete.

Full-time head of SEN. Head believes 'a good learning support culture enhances what you do'. Provision for mild dyslexia, dyspraxia and dyscalculia, though not the place to send a child with severe difficulties.

Many long serving staff. Head did away with 'teaching' and 'non-teaching' labels when he arrived. 'We're all teaching the children in different ways,' he says. One satisfied parent commented that staff were 'prepared to go the extra mile for the children.' Teachers are lively, good humoured and passionate about their subjects. Two gap year students help with sport and a French assistant teaches conversational French.

Parents are typically hard-working professionals. 'The school reflects the local community and lots of the children arrive at school on foot or by scooter,' says head of pre-prep. Active PTA raises substantial funds, half money raised goes to charity, the other half to the school – recently paid for a climbing wall. Activity-based wrap around club from 7.30am to 6pm.

A competitive, purposeful and demanding school which has retained old fashioned values (the pupils call the head 'Sir' and scramble to their feet when an adult enters the room). Pupils are challenged on all fronts and, as one parent put it, 'By the time the children reach year 5, they are

Children can buy a picture if it catches their eye

under pressure to perform. It's not a soft school but, for the right child, there simply isn't anywhere better in the area.' One mother felt that 'it's not for the retiring child. I think they'd get trampled underfoot.' The head disagrees and feels the school caters for all personalities and abilities as there is so much on offer and so many chances to shine.

North Ealing Primary School

Pitshanger Lane, Ealing, London, W5 1RP

State • Pupils: 590 • Ages: 3–11 • Non-denom

Tel: 020 8997 2653
Fax: 020 8991 7609
Email: admin@northealing.ealing.sch.uk
Website: www.northealingprimary.co.uk

6

Head: Since September 2014, Sally Flowers, previously deputy head. She joined the school as assistant head in 2011.

Entrance: Wider catchment area now due to three form entry but pupils still need to live within a mile of the school to get a place.

Exit: Majority go to Brentside High, a few others to Drayton Manor, Ellen Wilkinson, Twyford and Cardinal Wiseman. A handful each year to grammar schools. One third go private – St Augustine's, Latymer, St Benedict's, Notting Hill and Ealing and John Lyon.

Remarks: Hidden away behind the main road, the sunflowers and flower tubs welcomed us in as we walked across the playground to the school entrance. The school is divided into three main areas. Reception and nursery classes are housed in a bright and airy modern building at the back of the site where outdoor classrooms are covered for use in all weathers, allowing free flow between back and forth. 'The children are so lucky to have a new building and they love being able to explore inside and outside,' enthused one parent.

Years 1 and 2 are in equally bright classrooms and at the end of their corridor is a dedicated music room. There is also a hall where we observed

The sunflowers and flower tubs welcomed us in

new reception children doing a movement class. 'Bend knees!'

Children are also separated at play time: nursery, reception and year 1 all have their own separate playgrounds. Years 2, 3 and 4 have the back playground and years 5 and 6 are at the front. The school even has its own garden which backs on to Pitshanger park.

Years 5 and 6 are housed in the old part of the school (100 year old Victorian building). Classes

> *There is also a tidy classroom competition each week where the school cleaners choose the tidiest class and their prize is to go first at lunch*

here a bit cramped but bright wall displays, eg a display about the local Brentham estate in Victorian times, make them feel welcoming and warm.

Key stage 2 children are set for maths and we observed an able and talented maths group being taught in the library, preparing for the Primary Schools Maths Challenge. Around a third of year 6 students achieve level 6 in their maths SATs and results in reading and writing are among the best in the borough. 'We saw a great improvement in our reading levels after we introduced guided reading in 2011,' explained the deputy head.

Music and drama are particularly strong, with the school choir taking part in local music festivals. Children can learn the recorder in key stage 2 and there is also the opportunity to study the violin,

cello or guitar. Each year the head directs the year 6 production; last year it was Bugsy Malone. 'The standard of the drama is really high, thanks to the head's passion for theatre,' explained one parent.

Sports are also very high profile, with a glass cabinet bulging with cups in the school reception. Netball, football and all the usual sports teams win prizes each year. There are numerous sports clubs before and after school most days. 'The head is very keen on keeping fit and his enthusiasm rubs off on the kids.'

Very active PTA organises regular quiz nights etc. 'As well as raising money, these events are a great way to meet other parents.'

Hot dinners are cooked on the premises – half the children have school dinners and half bring packed lunches. The school has a healthy eating policy – no sweets or chocolates are allowed in children's lunch boxes. 'We don't check the staff room though,' quipped the deputy head. Senior staff are on duty at lunch time and there's a staggered system so that no one has to wait too long. There is also a tidy classroom competition each week where the school cleaners choose the tidiest class and their prize is to go first at lunch.

All the usual EAL, SEN and inclusion provision. Anti-bullying guidelines are adhered to and there is a buddy system where older pupils support younger pupils.

Former pupils include Peter Crouch and Honor Blackman.

A very friendly and welcoming local school that achieves excellent results.

North London Collegiate School Junior School

Linked school: North London Collegiate School, 438

Canons, Canons Drive, Edgware, Middlesex HA8 7RJ

Independent • Pupils: 300 • Ages: 4–11 • C of E
• Fees (per term): £4,966

Tel: 020 8952 1276
Fax: 020 8951 1293
Email: office@nlcs.org.uk
Website: www.nlcs.org.uk

15

Head of Junior School: Since 2003, Mrs Jo Newman BEd (50-ish). Came from Fairseat, Channing's junior school. 'They've got our lovely Mrs Newman,' they told us. She is bustling, bright-eyed, thrilled with her school and proud of her charges, who smile sweetly and confidently at her. Popular with parents and just about everyone.

Entrance: Vastly over-subscribed at 4+, when group and individual assessments (no reading/writing, mercifully) result in the allocation of 40 places. At 7+, maths and English tested, but only eight to 10 places for the armies who turn up. Most continue from first school through to lower school until they are 11.

Exit: Around 90 per cent continue into the senior school. Parents of those who the school perceives might not make the grade are alerted early and helped to look elsewhere.

Remarks: Shares the glorious site with its big sister but has a bright one-storey modern (1995) building of its own, divided into first and lower schools. Good stable staff – 16 have been at the school for more than 10 years – retain their enthusiasm and clear enjoyment of their bright and bubbly charges. Two form entry – first school class size of 20 and 24 in the lower school, each class having its own teacher and TA. Rooms are spacious and airy – room to move, not found in more central London preps.

Our tour was full of pleasures – inside and out. We liked the bright displays everywhere, the sense of orderliness and the little loos – so important – with their fish motifs. We loved the Montgolfier

> *We applaud the garden club, Friday's Golden Time and the Three Bears' cottage with bed, kitchen and mirror*

balloons, an imaginative undersea montage with fishing nets, lobster pots and portholes and some lively nascent DT sculptures – thank heaven for kitchen roll tubes and egg boxes! We watched reception miming seed planting to a tape, and saw that

not all were fully engaged in this – perhaps still learning to listen? We did wonder whether artistic endeavours might not be over-directed, but the vivid year 2 Kandinsky–influenced houses seemed more relaxed. We applaud the garden club, Friday's Golden Time and the Three Bears' cottage with bed, kitchen and mirror.

Overall, facilities are good – designated science, IT and art rooms plus a good-sized hall and libraries for both parts of the school, the lower school one being particularly inviting, with a lovely display of 'antique book covers' when we visited. The girls also enjoy the senior school's sports facilities as well as the senior girls themselves – several come down to help. Specialist subject teaching from year 5, and we were impressed by the school's introductory courses to languages: Spanish in year 3, German in year 4, Chinese in year 5 and French in year 6 – good fun and sensible. No children currently with statements but around five per cent with mild SEN – catered for by school SENCo; most leave for the senior school no longer needing much support.

Parents, for the most part, enthuse – 'It's a lovely school and Mrs Newman and the staff are very kind.' Girls make good friendships and positive relationships are encouraged at every stage. Any complaints are taken seriously and resolved as soon as possible. The ethos – of discipline, a non-competitive striving for one's personal best and stimulation which is also fun – is very much that of the senior school, and the junior branch, in every way, equips its young alumnae to seize the opportunities they will be offered in the next exciting stage.

North London Collegiate School

Linked school: North London Collegiate School Junior School, 436

Canons, Canons Drive, Edgware, Middlesex HA8 7RJ

Independent • Pupils: 770 • Ages: 11–18 • C of E
• Fees (per term): £5,875

Tel: 020 8952 0912
Fax: 020 8951 1391
Email: office@nlcs.org.uk
Website: www.nlcs.org.uk

16

Headmistress: Since 1997, Mrs Bernice McCabe BA MBA PGCE, (a glamorous mid-50s). Had exemplary, if not wholly predictable, credentials for this top job in girls' independent education. An English graduate, she spent 23 years teaching in the state sector and was appointed to her first deputy headship in 1986 at Heathlands School, Hounslow. Her various responsibilities there helped her gain the expertise needed for the effective running of a modern school and she took her MBA during her first headship at Chelmsford County High, which, under her seven-year tenure, became one of the country's leading state schools.

She teaches all year 7s – an excellent principle and one that all heads should practise, in our view. She is not interested in drilling or ranking girls, 'We have no class positions, no prize-giving except when they leave.. I want the staff to find out what the girls are good at and develop their potential, not just teach them to jump through hoops'. She lunches with her Big Six – the committee of sixth form girls who act as a conduit between her and the school community. She fosters a democratic

community, which is generally appreciated and comfortably taken for granted now.

Clever, charismatic and good company. Also stunningly pretty and elegant – clearly a role model in all ways for her girls, who appear to adore her: her dark red nail varnish is imitated by half her sixth form. She is relaxed, dedicated to education in its

Art practised joyfully by many – as the super paintings and other exhibits round and about demonstrate: witty, fluid in style and imaginative

truest sense and committed to sharing what she and her school has with the wider world, notably with those who teach or learn in the state sector. Hence her directorship of The Prince's Teaching Institute, a high calibre residential project to reinvigorate subject teaching in schools and re-inspire the teachers. At NLCS she is, clearly, very much in charge and the regime is benign, respected and popular. It is also now a long-standing one. 'She is simply wonderful,' say parents in unison.

Academic matters: Second to none and, as with all truly top schools, it is achieved through a preparedness to teach beyond the curriculum and celebrate the pleasures of learning for its own sake. Offers the IB in tandem with A levels and an increasing number of Pre-Us; the IB is now taken by up to a third of the year. The IB points score is 'phenomenally high' – an average of more than 42 points per pupil in 2014 and four students achieved the maxi-

---

A smart meeting place with coffee and snacks, patronised by sixth form and staff and all very cool and chic: 'It's like going out of school with a friend.'

---

mum 45 points. Top IB school in the UK for last eight years. A level results are as good – 87 per cent of subject grades A*/A and 98 per cent A*/B in 2014. The curriculum has no surprises, though it is good to see a healthy Greek contingent at A level and five modern langs too – French, German, Russian, Spanish and Italian. Mandarin now an option for the sixth. RS is popular, as are biology and chemistry, but maths and English are way ahead of the rest in terms of take-up. I/GCSE results impressive – nearly 99 per cent A*/A in 2014.

Long-serving, sensible, deputy head is i/c SEN. No current statements and a very few with special needs. Of those, most are mild dyspraxics and some use laptops and have extra time in exams. No withdrawal from classes or in-class support. SEN here mostly means even more gifted and talented than the rest, and the latest inspection report paid tribute to the individual help given to these, as well as to dyspraxics and the use of IEPs where appropriate. School's philosophy was articulated by past head – 'Everyone matters' – and now, in Mrs McCabe's words, 'I try to do everything I can to put them in charge of their own destiny'.

Games, options, the arts: The endless playing fields and superb facilities – with which no other London girls' school can compete – inspire sporting enthusiasm and prowess. Options abound – riding, scuba and golf along with the trad games. Lacrosse especially successful (school has players in national squads) but cross country thrives too. Art practised

joyfully by many – as the super paintings and other exhibits round and about demonstrate: witty, fluid in style and imaginative. Music is celebrated and many play to top standards. Good music tech. Very good music hall with gallery – light and inviting. Grand pianos seem to breed here. Numerous ensembles, choirs, tours and concerts and much success in major musical competitions, festivals etc – as you'd expect from girls with this amount of creativity, energy, opportunity and encouragement.

The performing arts centre (PAC) is a superb facility. Its auditorium seats 350, with a removable floor over an orchestra pit and, helpfully, it is connected by corridor to the music school. Drama, always good here, has now a tremendous buzz – everyone can take part on or backstage and productions are numerous and exciting. Good drama studio in use for smaller productions, exam work, lessons etc. The PAC has a café/bar which the girls talk about almost more than anything else – a smart meeting place with coffee and snacks, patronised by sixth form and staff and all very cool and chic: 'It's like going out of school with a friend'. The roof terrace, with benches and view over the whole estate, is another great place for coffee and chat and the sixth form love it.

Vast programme of complementary activities. Parents pay tribute to the imaginative and high-calibre opportunities and the girls look almost

bewildered by the range on offer. 'You have to prioritise – there's too much to do; you just can't do everything'. Debating especially popular – we enjoyed ads for forthcoming meetings, eg 'This house would die young', 'This house would be a boy', 'This house would ban violence in entertainment' etc – many of them pinned onto noticeboards which line the rather stark staircases, reminiscent of a students' union in which everyone has opinions. Charity work a priority, though we aren't sure when they find time to do it and so much of it.

Background and atmosphere: Venerable and unique – no other school in the history of girls' education in the UK has such significance. It was founded by Frances Mary Buss in 1850 in Camden and set the standard for ambitious, forward-looking education for girls on a par with the best of that offered to boys. In 1939 – remarkable foresight or luck? – the school moved to Edgware. It acquired the former estate of the Dukes of Chandos – of Handelian fame – then comprising a splendid, late 18th century house, now the school's central building (recently refurbished), and 30 acres overlooking formal gardens and down to Canons Park. The original ducal palace – Canons – was demolished in the 1740s after the financial collapse of the first Duke. Perhaps, in his distress, he

would have been glad to know what an excellent site for a girls' school his domain would become.

The main building – housing the offices, sixth form centre and some teaching – is elegant outside and impressive inside – wood panelling, grand

---

Outsiders must goggle at the lime tree avenue, the grand aged cedar tree, the sizeable reedy pond, formal gardens and sheer glorious green space

portraits of former heads, some of them the prime movers in girls' education in their day, archival photographs, stucco and cornicing. Later built additions range from functional and boring – eg the main teaching block – to inspired and enlightened. This last is especially so of the library – a fine building full of light and cleverly constructed on four storeys. It is also as well-stocked and managed as you'd expect here. About to start building a large indoor extra-curricular space and an extension to house extra classrooms and labs.

You reach the school either via a walk from the tube across the park or by a meander down Canon's Drive – all large detached houses, much mock Tudor and with more than a whiff of Wisteria Lane. The road goes only to the school or the park so a sense of entering a wonderfully secluded world. And secluded, safe and stimulating it is, though what is provided here hardly excludes the outside world – true partnerships with schools elsewhere (notably in Zambia and in Dagenham): reciprocal visits, educational collaboration, mutually informative and enlightening both ways. And Mrs McCabe's Prince's Teaching Institute also informs the school's ethos and daily life. Outsiders, though, must goggle at the lime tree avenue, the grand aged cedar tree, the sizable reedy pond, formal gardens and sheer glorious green space, overlooked by the very pretty main house.

Food served in huge lunch room is clearly terrifically good – girls don't usually worry about ODing on school food but it's clearly a temptation here: masses of choice and high, high quality. The atmosphere overall is collaborative, enthusiastic and relaxed. Lots of male staff – many of them young – and the average age of staff here is only 32. Old Girls will raise several eyebrows at all this. We can't recall visiting another all-girls' school and finding quite this kind of relaxed self-confidence – normal in the best boys' and co-ed schools. 'My fundamental belief,' says head, 'is that anything is possible for the girls – it's about stretching, enrichment, passion.'

Pastoral care and discipline: Classes are uniformly orderly, relaxed and full of concentrating faces. Relations between staff and girls are clearly warm, especially so in the sixth form, and girls pay tribute to the time and individual care their teachers give them. A noticeable cachet to sixth form life here – the girls move into the upper rooms of the charming old main house, they don't wear uniform and they chat on easy terms with staff. They are also given responsibilities for younger girls, often running clubs for them. This fosters a healthy bonding between the years and probably contributes to the tiny number of leavers post-GCSE. Strong tutor system throughout. No major problems within last five years: 'They're very sensible,' says head. Lots of collaboration with boys' schools –Eton, Harrow, Winchester and Whitgift – socially and in extra-curricular activities. Occasional bullying dealt with firmly and parents are 'pleased with the approach'. 'The girls know where they stand,' says Mrs McCabe.

Pupils and parents: Multi-ethnic, multi-faith, multi-brains – we spoke to no two pupils from the same ethnic or geographic origins. In common is a desire to learn and share the fun of doing it here – along with a fair bit of cash, though bursaries help (see below). Notable Old Girls' list is uniquely long and impressive – see Wikipedia. But, for starters: Barbara Amiel, Alice Beer, Eleanor Bron, Tanya Byron, Gillian Cross, Fenella Fielding, Margaret Fingerhut, Helen Gardner, Stella Gibbons, Susie Orbach (expelled), Myfanwy Piper, Anna Popplewell, Stevie Smith, Marie Stopes, Judith Weir, Rachel Weisz and Anna Wintour, along with a great many useful types – doctors, civil servants, scientists, artists and academics.

Entrance: At 11+ by exam in maths and English and interview. Forty-four come up from the junior school and a further 60 places for the 550 who apply. Don't despair – someone has to get them. Junior school children are not in competition for their places – they take the exam like everyone else and, if a chance of them not thriving in the senior school, they will have been warned and helped well in advance. At 16+ by exam in their A level subjects and by interview – around 80 applicants for 25 places.

Exit: Most go through to the sixth form and Mrs McCabe stresses: 'No-one is ever prevented from going into the sixth form. Once the girls are here we never write anyone off'. Later, Oxbridge is the norm (30 in 2014) – along with UCL, Bristol, LSE and the best of the rest, including quite a few at Ivy Leagues, notably Harvard. They do solid subjects – lots of medics – at the top places and, unsurprisingly, do well.

Money matters: Lowish, we feel, for what is offered here and a generous number of valuable bursaries available. Means-tested but offering between 10 and 100 per cent of fees. Scholarships up to 50 per cent and can be held along with a bursary. Music schols too.

Remarks: Possibly the best advertisement for girls-only education in the country.

North Primary School

Meadow Road, Southall, Middlesex UB1 2JE

State • Pupils: 420 • Ages: 4–11 • Non-denom

Tel: 020 8571 7749
Fax: 020 8574 0629
Email: admin@north.ealing.sch.uk
Website: www.northprimary.co.uk

7

Headteacher: Since September 2010, Mrs Rebecca Hastings BSc PGCE NPQH (late 40s). Studied at Leicester University, PGCE at the West Sussex Institute of Higher Education, worked in primary schools in London – Camden, Hackney and Harrow – where many pupils have English as an additional language and come from areas of social deprivation. Assistant headteacher, acting headteacher for two years, associate head in a school facing challenging circumstances. One daughter at secondary school.

Passionate about learning: schools are a place of learning for children, staff and parents/carers – makes extracurricular activities available to children and their families. School has a responsibility to provide quality learning experiences for all children, a curriculum that is engaging, to ensure every child achieves the best they can.

Entrance: Admissions handled by the London borough of Ealing – the usual criteria apply. Main feeder is Grove House Nursery. No one except looked-after children will get into the early years from out of catchment; a waiting list for all years. Key stage 2 applicants may have more luck – entrants (often new arrivals from abroad) in the later years.

Exit: Most go on to Villiers HS, some to Greenford HS, a few to Guru Nanak or Cardinal Wiseman. A handful each year try for the Berkshire grammars or Tiffin schools – around seven or eight get in.

Remarks: We went as sceptics but came away converts – and in love. Twenty-two languages are spoken at home by these children – mostly Punjabi or Gujerati, though significant numbers of Singhalese children and Somalis too. According to social deprivation statistics, school's population is in the top 80 per cent. Also has significant numbers on School Action or School Action Plus, though not huge numbers with many SENs other than EAL. Ninety-eight per cent of pupils speak English as a second language, but English unifies the school and everyone is open and friendly. We were struck by the clear and helpful delivery of the teachers – they mean children to understand, back up their words with helpful body language when needed and everyone learns. We were impressed with every class we went into – and we went into them all.

SATs results are astonishing – especially given this intake and the fact that children come at all stages with little or no English. Everyone except a few SEN pupils reaches level 4 or higher in English – this is extraordinary and is achieved, in part, by determined individual catch up sessions with those who fall behind or arrive with little English. In both science and maths, 90+ per cent get level 4. Large

We were impressed with every class we went into – and we went into them all

percentages at level 5. This puts it way ahead of comparable schools, both locally and nationally. Not that it teaches to the test – teaching has to be good from reception onwards, not just year 6. This is a lead school for good practice in EAL provision and the induction process for each new child is meticulous. Has translators and resources in all its main languages and works hard at involving parents. We were touched by the care taken to instruct each new child in, for example, how to ask in English for the loo.

So – a modern, purpose-built jewel in Ealing's crown? Hardly. The core is an 1851 schoolroom, still in remarkable nick and surmounted by the original bell tower, complete with pullable bell chain – still used on special occasions. Later add-ons are solid and functional and make for a well-structured, two-storey building overall. We have yet to see a tidier, cleaner school – everywhere is freshly painted in bright but not garish colours, and we spotted not one piece of litter in our entire visit. Children are proud of their school and it shows. Outside is just tarmac and apparatus, but well marked out for the younger children and reasonably spacious, with railings separating the older children from the tots. Older children have a tarmac football pitch. The school is in a quiet residential nook at the east end of Southall close to an old village green and

with some splendid older buildings round about, reminding one of the village this once was.

In every classroom the children were attentive, engaged and absorbed. Every inch of wall space has excellent displays – pupil and teacher-made – all helping to structure and illustrate the work in hand. Everyone can see at a glance what the term's syllabus and aims are in all curriculum areas. Corridor displays on everything from black history to symmetry, musical notation, bridges and forces. Boards for improvement, achievement and attendance encourage everyone. Community project volunteers have provided imaginative murals here and there – we especially liked the Aztec drinking fountains. Excellent new ICT suite is an exciting addition and each class has a whiteboard. Resources are carefully used. The key stage 2 library is better-stocked than those in many senior schools we know and as inviting and orderly as everywhere else in this welcoming, safe-feeling school.

All classes are orderly and inviting. Most seem well ventilated and comfortable, but a few look rather crowded and were decidedly too warm. What goes on in them is consistently impressive. Reception and year 1 children work purposefully in small groups but all together in a big sectioned room with teachers and support staff and, seemingly, concentrating so busily that they need little regulation or control. We enjoyed a year 2 French class taught by a native speaker with a mouth-watering unison recitation of the constituents of une salade. A year 5 class was working on rhetorical questions and a year 6 class writing 'recounts' of events and being given demanding literary objectives – which they seemed to relish. Both key stages have good-sized, airy halls and we warmed to the way children really spoke out in rehearsal of their Easter assembly.

G and T children are well-catered for by a designated teacher, who provides 'challenge boxes' for each class, brings in graduate volunteers and runs a chess club and newspaper club exclusively for these children. Lots of other clubs for everyone.

Their ensemble containing instruments from every bit of the globe is a major investment but at the heart of the ethos

Most children with SpLD are supported in class. Part-time SENCo and TA will take children individually – some have a differentiated curriculum. An Alexander Technique teacher comes in on occasions. We saw a lesson taken by a supply teacher with an entirely attentive class. Each child is

assessed every half term for progress in reading, writing and maths.

Music is big here: won the local Rotary's best ensemble award several years running – their ensemble containing instruments from every bit of the globe is a major investment but at the heart of its ethos. Good ceramics and a collection of musical instruments made from recycled materials which included a beautiful harp. The little garden is eagerly worked on by the children, who grow vegetables from seed – and then eat the results in the school's canteen. The home-cooked food is a good mix of the trad and the healthy – we drooled at fisherman's pie, Asian pasta and chunks of fresh oranges. Parents are helped to continue the healthy eating approach at home and encouraged to involve themselves in all activities. Many do. The school's annual fête – the mela – along with its concerts and shows are huge events, and several parents help in class. Children look good in white shirts, grey trousers and scarlet cardigans.

A model for primaries everywhere.

Northwood College Junior School

Linked school: Northwood College, 444

Maxwell Road, Northwood, Middlesex HA6 2YE

Independent • Pupils: 265 • Ages: 3–11 • Non-denom
• Fees (per term): £3,107 – £4,142

Tel: 01923 825446
Fax: 01923 836526
Email: admissions@northwoodcollege.co.uk
Website: www.northwoodcollege.co.uk

26

Head of the Junior School: Mrs Hina Thaker

Entrance: At 3+ into the nursery via observation and little tasks, ditto at 4+ into reception. Forty-eight places at this stage. At 7, via maths, English, reasoning and interview – up to 10 new places at this stage.

Exit: Nearly all to senior school.

Remarks: Junior school in three buildings on same site as senior school. The early years centre, home to 80 nursery and reception children, is a super building, sensitively conceived and completed. Sensory garden, excellent playground, and lots of lovely touches and thoughtful additions – wellies for rainy days, masses of well-integrated IT, colourful toys, space, cookery, a beautiful library. We loved the collage on the life cycle of a hen and the display about the Philosophy Bear who 'likes to look at things carefully and ask questions'. Years 1 and 2 in Vincent House, 3 and 4 in junior school – both attractive, small scale houses. All safe, well-maintained, full

of impeccable and attractive displays. Parents are thrilled – 'My daughter was so shy – they've really brought her out..They're so caring and nurturing'; 'They take the child and encourage her to be the best she can, but according to their own character – they don't have to fit a mould'.

School is pioneering 'thinking skills' and they approach this seriously from nursery onwards via 'cognitive development programme', plus f/t director to coordinate it. We were seriously impressed – junior school pupils feel empowered and the results are tangible. School held a recent Dragons' Den event – with high profile 'dragons' – and even juniors' projects were taken seriously.

Girls venture out into college grounds for science experiments and maths trials; they tap dance, play chess, learn K-Kwon-Do or do speech and drama. Food exceptional – home-made soups and yogurts, lots of fresh everything; everyone above nursery eats school lunch, which is included in the fee.

Majority of parents British Asians, with moveable contingent from local NATO base.

Northwood College

Linked school: Northwood College Junior School, 445

Maxwell Road, Northwood, Middlesex HA6 2YE

Independent • Pupils: 560 • Ages: 11–18 • Non-denom
• Fees (per term): £4,982 – £5,022

Tel: 01923 825446
Fax: 01923 836526
Email: admissions@northwoodcollege.co.uk
Website: www.northwoodcollege.co.uk

27

Head Mistress: Since January 2009, Miss Jacqualyn Pain MA MA MBA PGCE NPQH (50s), a theology and philosophy graduate and a most experienced head. Two previous headships, both impressive – Henrietta Barnett 2000-2005, St Albans High 2005-2008 – prior to which she'd been deputy head at Northwood. She'd had no intention of leaving St Albans until Mrs Ruth Mercer, her predecessor at Northwood College, was appointed to the headship of Godolphin and Latymer. Miss Pain, who believed 'so strongly in the ethos of the school – that it does so well by every kind of girl' – couldn't resist coming back and is a round peg in a spherical hole, if ever we saw one. 'The school has changed, of course,' she admits cheerfully, 'because schools must move on, but the underlying principles are the same and I passionately believe in them.' Highly competent, understated, relaxed, elegant and popular, she is quietly but enthusiastically building on the energetic modernisation initiated by Mrs Mercer. She likes cats and chocolate. Northwood College, too long the unsung school in this well provided for part of the world, is lucky to have her back.

Academic matters: Takes a spread of ability – but well above the national average. Value-added very strong here so you should achieve your potential, whatever it is, and not feel pressured while you

Recent Dragons' Den event – with high profile 'dragons' – even juniors' projects were taken seriously

do it. Your 10 A*s pupil happily coexists with your artsy, mathematical struggler and both feel good about themselves. This is very much the Northwood ethos and the one Miss Pain was keen to come back to and strengthen.

At GCSE, all take two Englishes, maths, a language, three sciences; options include art, classical civilisation, drama, Latin and Greek, home economics, RE and textiles. RE is the star subject – taken by most with exemplary results; maths (IGCSE) and English pretty good too. 2014 results saw 67 per cent of subjects taken achieve A*/A. At A level, maths, economics and RE impress. Maths, the sciences and psychology are popular. Tiny numbers for history and English (though good results), reflecting the science orientation and aspirations of the school's current core constituency. The same is true for languages, but scope for new-ish HoD (a French and Mandarin specialist) to boost numbers and broaden curriculum. Much to be done here, especially in increasing the uptake at A level of a broader range of subjects – parents as well as girls will need to be convinced – and the school, in fact, offers an admirable range. In 2014, 75 per cent A*/B grades and 38 per cent A*/A.

Most mild SENs managed in lessons with occasional extra temporary support and withdrawals. Can cope with mild ADHD and Asperger's along with dyses. Older parts of site not really set up to accommodate serious motor difficulties, though will adapt where possible.

School is pioneering 'thinking skills' and they approach this seriously from nursery to sixth form via 'cognitive development programme', plus f/t director to coordinate it. We were seriously impressed – junior school pupils feel empowered and the results are tangible. School held a recent Dragons' Den event – with high profile 'dragons' – and even juniors' projects were taken seriously, to the extent of possible commissions from the commercial world outside. Clever stuff, integral to the overall ethos of the place and a real selling point.

Your 10 A*s pupil happily coexists with your artsy, mathematical struggler and both feel good about themselves

Games, options, the arts: It's got the lot – in miniature, in some cases. Yer actual sports hall, of course, plus 25m pool –and everyone swims all year. Pitches and courts abut the main campus and most girls are keen. Some parental feeling that more effort is needed and girls should be pushed harder. Performing arts centre cleverly shoehorned in, and now providing good drama studio, range of music teaching/practice rooms and much-used recital room. No room here for grand theatre or concert hall, but assembly hall does as well and, though hardly glitzy, has all a good school needs. Art is enthusiastic – painting, modelling, textiles, principally. Music likewise, enthusiastic – 50-strong orchestra, jazz bands and lots of fun had in staging productions – more Oliver! than Othello. Forty-nine page booklet details all the extracurricular activities from the physical (trampolining, badminton etc) to the cerebral (think club, puzzle club, chess) to the fun (book club, bridge, life drawing etc etc) – good stuff. 'Fabulous' trips – 'we went to Brazil for a month on World Challenge' – and closer to home, eg Regent's Park theatre, and good in-school events, eg African drumming evening.

Background and atmosphere: Founded in 1878 in Endsleigh Gardens, Bloomsbury, with around 25 boarders and a few day girls. Headmistress, Miss Buchan-Smith, who had modern ideas about the importance of the extracurricular as well as the curricular, and was concerned about the unsavoury influence of the Euston area on her girls, moved the school to Northwood in 1893. Interestingly, this area – now leafy, prosperous and safe as £1m+ houses can be – was, in 1871, described as 'a destitute district near Moor Park'. But the coming of the tube, a few years later, changed all that and made Northwood a jolly useful commutable suburb, which it remains. In 1893, the present, late arts 'n' crafts red-brick with leaded lights building was opened for 20 boarders and two day girls; the next door Briary accommodated little boys. Boys long since gone, but touching tribute paid to their presence – especially to those who went on to fight and fall in the two wars: school still lays an annual wreath at Ypres.

More land has been acquired, more buildings built and the school is now a nest of attractive, disparate edifices, centred on a couple of tennis courts, which make a kind of quad. To the side of the school are the pitches and playing fields – the overall feeling is one of a slightly crowded campus made up of pleasant, purpose-built or acquired blocks forming a cosy community. Despite the somewhat cramped feeling, it is a surprise, in a quiet residential street, to find it there at all. The latest additions – the early years centre and the performing arts block – are notable assets, in terms both of their additional provision and imaginative design, which cannot, here as elsewhere, be said for the few, lesser, 1960s architectural indiscretions.

Cosy, civilised library in old, converted, vaulted gym. Excellent string of sixth form studies – each shared by five/six girls – for private work in free periods (boarding ended in 1990). Exemplary displays everywhere. Good dining room, cafeteria system, food exceptional – home-made soups and yoghurts, lots of fresh everything; everyone above nursery eats school lunch, which is included in the fee. A formal partnership with the nearby John Lyon Boys' School enables collaboration on curricular and extracurricular matters, to the considerable benefit of both communities – a sensible and enlightened move begun by Mrs Mercer and Kevin Riley, former head of John Lyon, and continued by its current head, Katherine Haynes.

Part of the Girls' Day School Trust (GDST) since November 2013 and combined with Heathfield School for Girls in September 2014. A most unusual move – it is rare for schools to join the GDST family, although Heathfield was acquired by the Trust in 1987. The school is continuing with the same head

Boys long since gone, but touching tribute paid to their presence – especially to those who went on to fight and fall in the two wars

on the same site and all Heathfield girls were promised places – requiring ingenuity and creativity as the Northwood College site is not generously endowed with space. But we are promised exciting and imaginative developments and will watch with interest.

Pastoral care and discipline: Year heads and form tutors handle most pastoral matters. Tutor changes annually. Discipline seldom a problem here – one minor recent drugs incident. Girls feel involved in decisions – 'Miss Pain really wants to hear from us – our ideas about what can be improved,' we heard. 'The girls do as well as they do here because of the way we nurture them,' says Miss Pain, and

parents concur. Overall sense of a relaxed, orderly community in which little disturbs and everything encourages.

Pupils and parents: As you'd expect in this cosmopolitan, well-heeled suburb: majority are British Asians – mostly Hindus – and Christians and sprinklings of everyone else. Little need for EAL. Contingent from local NATO base makes for movement in and out and enriches the mix. Five

This area – now leafy, prosperous and as safe as £1m+ houses can be – was, in 1871, described as 'a destitute district near Moor Park.'

extensive coach routes bring in girls from Ealing, Edgware, Kenton, Gerrards Cross and Radlett. Proximity to the Metropolitan line makes tubing it easy. Sense of community, and devoted parents from all backgrounds pitching in to support. Former notable pupils include judge Dame Margaret Booth and actress Sue Holderness.

Entrance: At 11, via the exams set by the North London Consortium, to which the school belongs, plus online test and group interview – 30 places. One out of three girls who apply usually gains a place, many off the waiting list.

At 16, conditional on GCSE results, plus online test and interview – 20 places. Occasional places do occur in other years – particularly on account of NATO personnel coming and going, so always worth a call. 'We're looking for girls who will fit into the school,' says Miss Pain. 'We're academically selective but not narrowly exclusive – we want people who will benefit from an all-round, holistic education.'

Exit: Nearly all stay on to sixth form. Majority go to a range of Russell Group and newer universities; one to Oxford to read physics in 2014. School produces an extraordinary number of pharmacists and a good number of dentists; otherwise anything from art to retail, English to – well, pharmacy.

Money matters: A few means-tested bursaries – up to full fees. Also scholarships for academics, art, music and sport.

Remarks: The parents have it: 'My daughter has been given opportunities and she's flourishing'; 'Northwood has given my daughters so many opportunities'; 'It was the best decision we ever made'.

Notting Hill and Ealing High School Junior School

Linked school: Notting Hill and Ealing High School, 449

26 St Stephen's Road, London, W13 8HH

Independent • Pupils: 310 • Ages: 4–11 • Non-denom
• Fees (per term): £4,083

Tel: 020 8799 8484
Fax: 020 8810 9947
Email: enquiries@nhehs.gdst.net
Website: www.nhehs.gdst.net

8

Headmistress: Since September 2013, Mrs Silvana Silva BEd (forties). Previously deputy head for 11 years. Married with one son (reading chemistry at Warwick). Has been at NHEHS since arriving in 1989 as a young teacher, has 'absolutely loved every minute' and worked her way up the ranks. She covered the previous head's maternity leave thee years ago confidently and with complete success. Well known to pupils and parents and completely committed to the school and to each girl's individual success and happiness. The school's open door policy, approachability and sympathetic ear to concerns seem in safe hands here.

Comfortable with the GDST ethos. Clear educational vision – 'our job is to spark an interest in learning,' she says. Wholly committed to single sex education. 'Girls tend to have low self esteem and aren't risk takers,' she says, determined to inspire them with confidence and encourage them to learn interactively and independently. A great rôle model for budding young girls.

Entrance: Heavily oversubscribed and fiercely competitive – about 100 applicants for 40 places. Assessed just before fourth birthday – three staff will work with four children for an hour and half. 'We want to see how they play and how they interact. We're looking for inner confidence and self assurance,' says the head. 'It's not about knowing your ABC or how to count to 2,000 – we can teach them that.' Very flexible before assessment – will reschedule for illness; takes into account what a child's previous experience has been. But no budging after assessment and no sibling policy – it was the talk of Ealing when a child with four older sisters who had been through the school was refused a place. At year 3 (age 7) eight places and usually 30+ applicants. They sit papers in English, maths and verbal reasoning, plus interview for those who have done well enough. Other than these two entrance points it's very rare for the occasional place to come up, but it does happen.

Exit: Almost all to senior school – informed in year 5 if eligible, then do exam in January of year

6, primarily for the purpose of setting in senior school and to award academic and music scholarships (usually a handful of these). Help is given to the (very) few who are not up to it (these will nor-

Funky lavatories decorated in bright girly colours – lots of pinks and purples reminiscent of a Vue cinema

mally have left at seven anyway) – they are placed at, eg, Heathfield and Northwood College. Tiny few to St Paul's or Latymer Upper – tends to be for a specific reason – eg proximity to home or availability of scholarships.

Remarks: All the hallmarks of a GDST – excellent delivery of the curriculum, thorough assessment of children, down to earth professional parents. Bright spacious classrooms – lots of windows and impressive displays in corridors as well as in classrooms, some of the best (and most genuine) we've seen. Large playground with imaginative places to sit and to play – gazebo with benches, round tables and chairs, assault course, springy colourful tarmac and netball hoops. Separate playground for reception where the little ones can spill out to play with sand, Wendy house and puppet theatre. Funky lavatories decorated in bright girly colours – lots of pinks and purples reminiscent of a Vue cinema. The senior school is 100 yards to the rear, younger girls share their swimming pool, netball courts and dining room and perform the odd concert in the grand West Wing auditorium, but otherwise it's a separate entity.

Always near the top in the league tables. Wouldn't suit a child that isn't up to it academically: if she can't keep up she may find herself excluded – even in the playground, reports one parent. (School surprised at these reports and keen to deny them.) Year 1 class teacher doubles up as SENCo – a few on the dys–strata and some with mild Asperger's. They can have extra help at a cost – not the school to send your daughter if she has serious learning difficulties. As for the gifted and talented – 'all girls here would be given that label,' says the head – and she clearly knows. The particularly brilliant (about four in each class) are catered for with differentiation and extension exercises – 'it helps that they can bounce off each other'.

Good discipline and pastoral care. Girls are taught right from the beginning to wait their turn and to respect others, but do have fun and are encouraged to participate. Our guide proudly related the teaching behind the catch words, THINK ('Is it truthful, is it helpful, is it inspiring, is it necessary, is it kind? If not, don't say it') and TAG (tell person how you're feeling, ask them to stop, get help from an adult). It clearly sticks.

You can do almost anything from Mandarin and chess to yoga and gardening in spare time but the music is particularly strong. Ninety per cent of girls learn a musical instrument, one third of the school is in the main orchestra. Impressive carol concerts in St Barnabas. Larks and tone deaf given equal attention – the hugely committed head of music holds 8.00am sessions in the week for the enthusiasts, of which many.

Most parents working professionals – ladies who lunch thin on the ground. Children of BBC types, lawyers and doctors come mainly from the local area, but a fair number prepared to travel the distance from Shepherds Bush and Ruislip – determined to get their daughter an excellent education from four to 18.

If your daughter wants to work hard and play hard, this is an excellent choice.

Notting Hill and Ealing High School

Linked school: Notting Hill and Ealing High School Junior School, 448

2 Cleveland Road, London, W13 8AX

Independent• Pupils: 580 • Ages: 11–18• Non-denom• Fees (per term): £5,250

Tel: 020 8799 8400
Fax: 020 8810 6891
Email: enquiries@nhehs.gdst.net
Website: www.nhehs.gdst.net

9

Head: Since 2008, Ms Lucinda Hunt BSc ARCS PGCE (Oxon) (late 40s). Formerly deputy head at St Paul's Girls, read physics at Imperial. Striking, clear-sighted and determined, enjoying a meteoric career in education with a year's secondment at Goldman Sachs to boot. Working in a bank reinforced her appetite for teaching – 'when profit is the motivator the bottom line is that it's dull'. In the early years of her career she taught science, maths and geology in Australia and France. Well versed in the ethos of GDST (and very happy with it) – a period at Putney High and eight years at Wimbledon High, where she rose to head of sixth form.

'I'm not afraid to rock the boat if it needs rocking,' declares Ms Hunt, but adds that she is no Hazel Blears and will only make changes that are needed. Quick as a flash, she has fearlessly cut swathes through the existing management structure. At the same time she is well tuned to the relatively gentle spirit of the place – 'that indefinable quality that makes a school different from the others, despite the fact that we all say the same sort of things,' she explains. One of her aims is to open up the windows and doors – 'at the moment not enough people know what we're about'. Parents agree and some comment on poor communication about the day to day. She starts with her own door which, unlike that of her predecessor, is always open to staff and pupils alike. The best thing about the job is the 'wry, intelligent' girls, she says, despite the fact that she doesn't teach any. The energy that she brings to the place is tangible. Here's someone whose influence is restoring the school to its former status as one of the best girls' schools in west London.

Academic matters: Once again, 2014 results were league-table topping. At GCSE 90 per cent of results were A*/A while at A level 69 per cent were A*/A and 92 per cent A*/B. This is a very high level of achievement indeed. Subjects taught are wide ranging, including philosophy of religion and ethics, and psychology. Maths and geography strong. Chemistry and biology also popular as well as drama, history and English. Year 12s choose a general studies option, can range from jewellery making or music technology to Russian, Mandarin or Ancient Greek. Mandarin compulsory in year 7,

They emerge articulate and confident, full of west London sophistication, but without the trendy, street-wise demeanour characteristic of their peers in more high profile schools in west London

which they learn alongside a European language. Class sizes large for an independent school – maximum 30 in years 7-9, average 22 in years 10-11. A lot of young teaching blood – Ms Hunt asserts the usual turnover you would expect in every London school. Twenty per cent have been at the school for more than 10 years, one third men. Pupils speak of the commitment of the staff and generally feel well supported.

Ms Hunt reluctant to be drawn into specific learning difficulties – wary of labeling, she explains – but five to 10 per cent of children are eligible to have extra time in exams and school is becoming

more adept at identifying who should be screened. The SEN teacher will go into lessons to work with individuals. No extra charge for any extra support. School proud of its success with one girl with serious visual impairment who went on to read English at Durham University. 'The term "gifted and talented" could describe almost every girl in the school,' says Ms Hunt. These are catered for with the various activities that take place during the school week including whole school assemblies. Parents praise an inclusive approach to academics – girls in lower sets are not ignored as 'dunces'.

Games, options, the arts: As with most suburban schools, space has always been at a premium, and this school now has little outside space. In September 2013, however, it unveiled a massive and beautiful new building at its heart which includes a huge, subterranean sports hall, big hall for assemblies and concerts, good-sized studio theatre and large dance studio. Four Astroturf pitches, swimming pool and tennis and netball courts also on site.

For hockey, rounders and athletics girls can run or be bused to nearby sports grounds. Not known, hitherto, for its sporting achievements – 'but girls get plenty of physical activity,' one parent told us and the new build looks set to transform opportunities. Mutterings among some that if their daughter is not in the tennis team they are left to play among themselves. Ms Hunt keen to introduce some less conventional individual sports for which you 'don't have to get undressed (so many girls just prefer not to)' – fencing currently riding a wave of enthusiasm; other innovations may follow.

Drama jolly good fun. Music well provided for – orchestras, choirs and ensemble groups, with about half the school playing a musical instrument; school will accommodate the few who want to do it at A level. The choir has performed in Tuscany and in Venice and planning is now under way for a tour to New York. Plenty of trips abroad for the non-musical too – recent trips have included a classics expedition to Rome, an art history trip to the museums and galleries of New York, geographers to Barcelona and Iceland, history trips to Russia, Germany and the battlefields of northern France, physicists to Cern and a sixth form trip to China led by the economics department. French students go to Paris and Spanish ones to Andalucia. Lots of enthusiasm for debating – whether it be competing against other schools in debating competitions or Model United Nations events. Duke of Edinburgh awards – most girls take bronze, over a third take silver and a thriving gold award group in the sixth.

Background and atmosphere: Founded in 1873 – the oldest of the Girls' Day School Trust schools.

Moved from Notting Hill to its present site in a large house (grand entrance with columns) in a broad Ealing residential avenue in 1931 and a number of features of the original building moved with it.

People we spoke to commented, rather blandly, on the warmth and friendliness of the school: Ms Hunt attributes this partly to the intimacy created by the leafy central quadrangle that connects the old with the new – lots of meeting and greeting as girls pass each other on stairs. Refurbished and much extended dining room with a bright, airy feel and plenty of space.

Newish sixth form centre in a separate building on the south west corner of the main site – a listed modernist building that had been a children's home, lying empty since 2006. It was gutted and converted into a bright, modern, airy building with seminar rooms, common room (with the obligatory leather sofas), multigym, café and outside terrace.

Strong community sense around this school – current pupils often the daughters or granddaughters of Old Girls and their annual OG bash always a sell-out.

Pastoral care and discipline: Girls are noticeably well behaved around the school – some of the quietest entrances in and out of assembly that we have seen anywhere. Head acknowledges instances of bullying (a good sign – it's the ones who deny any at all that one has to look out for). New area of concern, not just here, is the opportunity for students to use cyber space to make each others' lives difficult. Ms Hunt well aware of this and ready to take on the challenge. With her modern, forward-thinking approach, if anyone born in the early '60s can meet that challenge, she is your woman. A few worrying reports from parents about having nobody to go to talk to about pastoral issues ('Don't want to be nuisance and worry the head – she's got enough on her plate'), but encouraging signs that school is onto this and attempts are being made to plug the gap.

Pupils and parents: Families more modest than you would find at most London independent schools – typical GDST parents: professional, ambitious, looking for value for money but not prepared to compromise on their daughters' education. It's a local school – but some come from as far as Richmond, Perivale, Harrow and Greenford to the west and Notting Hill to the east. Cosmopolitan (particularly Asian), community – reflective of the local area. Lots of doctors and dentists, chartered surveyors, but creative types too – record producers, fashion journalists, business consultants. A wide range, ethnically, culturally and economically.

Girls here are focused but enjoying life. Not so pressured as their contemporaries in more central schools – they can work hard without being cowed by expectation and league tables. We saw lots of initiative – girls writing scores for musicals, scripts for witty renditions of the Theseus and Ariadne myth and choreographing amusing Michael Jackson dance routines for mythical monsters. They emerge articulate and confident, full of west London sophistication, but without the trendy, street-wise demeanour characteristic of their peers in more high profile schools in west London. OGs include Angela Rumbold, writer and TV presenter Bettany Hughes, BBC children's presenter Angellica Bell and Blue Peter's Konnie Huq.

Entrance: Competitive consortium examination in maths and English plus interview. About half come up from the junior school, the rest from west London state and independent schools. Most go on to the sixth form. External sixth form applicants have interviews in their potential A level subjects and sit a general paper; They are expected to have

obtained A*/A grades in their chosen A Level subjects, with A or above in the majority of their other GCSEs. For the occasional place in the senior school girls are tested according to their age and stage.

Exit: Now losing far fewer after GCSE. Why go elsewhere with these results and facilities? Each year a number of girls go to Oxbridge, some win scholarships. A lot read sciences – and not just medicine. History, politics and English are also popular. Bristol, Manchester and Nottingham favourites at the moment.

Remarks: A well run, efficient GDST school that does exactly what it says on the tin. Your daughter will get a very good, balanced education here. Oversubscribed, and no longer in the shade of other schools of its kind. The dynamic Ms Hunt has been busily making the school her own – without altering the relatively relaxed, down to earth friendliness of the place.

Orley Farm School

South Hill Avenue, Harrow, Middlesex HA1 3NU

Tel: 020 8869 7600
Fax: 020 8869 7601
Email: office@orleyfarm.harrow.sch.uk
Website: www.orleyfarm.harrow.sch.uk

18

Independent • Pupils: 495 • Ages: 4–13 • Non-denom • Fees (per term): £4,107 – £4,747

Headmaster: Since February 2013, Mr Tim Calvey, previously an art teacher and propelled from the deputy headship at a moment's notice after

the abrupt and bizarre resignation of Mr Mark Dunning, who had been an unexceptional head for seven years. Mr Dunning left after what the school described as an 'error of judgement'. Evidently, after some years' attrition with a departing member of staff, Mr Dunning expressed his feelings, weakly disguised in an acrostic-style sentence, in a newsletter to parents. Nothing has got Harrow and Sudbury buzzing quite so loud since the young Lord Byron led a revolt against the headmaster at the place up the hill.

Entrance: Virtually all enter at 4 though occasional other places crop up – more since the recession. From 40+ nurseries and none. Some 165 applicants for 60 places. Good-sized entry again at 11+ when the girls and some boys leave – around 30 applicants for 13 or so places. School keeps waiting lists at all stages. Assessment via observed activities and games – all age-appropriate. Previous head was confident that the process picks out those for whom Orley will work; later tests (parents say there are lots) attest to this – 'we know what is expected of an Orley Farm pupil and we want the children to be happy. We'd be doing them a great disservice if we took them and they couldn't cope with, enjoy and flourish in the life we have here'. Pupils concur. 'You do need to have a natural drive and everyone is really trying to push themselves,' one young man told us. 'We all want to succeed.'

Exit: Breadth again – to a creditable range of schools and many scholarships (impressive 46 in 2014, including several to each of John Lyon, St Helen's and Northwood College). Most boys to Merchant Taylors', others to St Paul's, Habs, Aldenham, John Lyon, Harrow, Hampton, Westminster, Charterhouse etc. Girls to Habs, Godolphin & Latymer, North London Collegiate, Northwood College, Notting Hill and Ealing, St Paul's Girls, St Mary's Calne, Aldenham, St Helen's, Cheltenham Ladies', Wycombe Abbey etc.

Remarks: You won't find a parent or a pupil who doesn't think the options and opportunities here are outstanding. The teachers, likewise, are warmly praised – 'our teachers are interactive,' an earnest

---

Drama – previously limp – now burgeoning under much-lauded new teacher and productions clearly zing

year 8 boy told us. 'They don't act as "teachers" – superior: they're there to help you.' 'The school is very good at finding out what you're good at and helping you get better at it,' another affirmed.

Broad academic curriculum, all heading for 11+ for girls and 13+ for boys, though one or two girls are to be found in years 7 and 8 – either joiners or stayers. French and Latin for all and Greek comes in as a taster for the soon-to-be leavers. Twenty children per class and fewer in sets for maths and English. Specialist subject teachers in music, drama, ICT and PE from pre-prep up and for science, French and Latin later. Previous head doubled the number of classroom assistants, all

of whom support English and maths. Some sense among parents of the less able that they have to really push themselves to keep up – witness one remark worth quoting from a year 6 boy: 'We were given an IGCSE maths paper – it was an insult to my intelligence'.

Full-time learning support teacher plus part-timers assist those who need it – mostly mild dyslexics. All support given in class or in small groups elsewhere. Eighty pupils on learning support register at time of our visit – 45 on school action plus. Not an easy school for those with mobility problems – very narrow corridors and up and down site. Outside tutoring is common – not because of deficiencies in the school's provision: more likely to support English when the home language is something else or because life is very full-on at Orley and the quieter ones may just need that bit of one-to-one to boost confidence. So parents feel, anyway.

All do DT and art – good studios for both. We were especially impressed by the range and quality – real imaginative breadth and care in execution too. Lovely models of early airplanes, Masai shields, mosaic tiles and more. Displays changed termly and with respect for the work. Carousel system for these subjects and some pupil grouses that not enough time to complete DT projects before you have to move to your art term, but with so much on offer and different curriculum requirements it's easy to see why some things have to give. Drama – previously limp – now burgeoning under much-lauded new teacher and productions clearly zing. Music a jewel in Orley's crown – 90+ per cent learn at least one instrument, the concerts cause grown men to weep with joy and music scholarships abound.

Privileged sports – can any prep in a London borough claim such riches? Forty acres, gym and sports hall, pool and Astroturf and far more on offer than in most London preps. Sports praised by everyone – the only problem being that Orley is big enough to field C, D and E teams, but they'd have no-one to play against. It's hard cheese for the also-rans and some complaints that the less than starry don't have such a good time. Expeditions week is a big thing here – a regular annual programme which takes everyone from year 3s up out everywhere, from mid-Wales mountaineering to 'total immersion' in a château. Wildly popular – and included in the fees. Plus tours and trips of all kinds everywhere – the optional trips taken in the holidays can be very expensive if your child is keen but your pocket isn't.

Orley, again unusually, has a purpose-built home – an attractive, two/three storey long red-brick house nestling at the foot of Harrow-on-the-Hill, all quiet leafiness and shady detached residences. It began in 1850, in two houses, one of which was the model for Trollope's Orley Farm, so the school was named after that. The aim was to prepare boys for the big school up the hill. By the turn of the century the school had outgrown the old house so a new one was commissioned, and in 1901 the present building was proudly opened. Its first head was 47 years in post. Since then it has grown and four buildings now surround the central quad, providing excellent sports, arts and teaching provision. The main building – with its top floor all narrow corridors and very reminiscent still of the boarding that went, finally, in 1984 – is all good-sized rooms, well-supplied and organised. Three libraries – stocked mostly with fiction. Pre-prep rooms all have integral loos and cloakroom. Good dining room with very appetizing food – eaten by all. Breakfast club from 7.45am. Lots of pretty gardens and outside space with adventure playground and play equipment. It looks and feels like a well-appointed village school. £11m refurbishment programme ongoing.

Thriving house system – pupils like it as they get to know all year groups and school encourages this (older children escort younger ones hither and yon and help with reading etc). 'It's like a very, very, very, very big family,' said one girl. Any problems to the form teacher – 'The teachers are very good at helping you if you are new. You're assigned a partner to look after you, and they do.' Classrooms all quietly buzzing when we visited – not all silent, thankfully, but purposeful and a sense of self-control at work rather than teacher-control. We heard no teacher shout.

School hotting up on eco matters – car share system for parents, tree planting project, annual school clean-up etc. Good home-school communications in that all staff have voicemail and email accounts available to parents and children have diary to be signed by home and school, but 'not always working as efficiently as it should,' we were told. Family backgrounds as mixed as you'd expect in north west London – many languages spoken at home, all blend easily at school. Former pupils of note include Lord Butler (former Cabinet Secretary), Anthony Horowitz and the late Simon McCorkindale.

'My children are all so different but they've all been happy there,' a parent said, and others concurred. Previous head delighted us when he extolled the virtues of a schooling which is about far more than exams and results – 'the world is changing fast. There are opportunities out there that we can't even imagine. That's why giving them breadth is so important.' We agreed and we await developments now that this visionary is head no more.

St Benedict's Junior School

Linked school: St Benedict's School, 456

5 Montpelier Avenue, London, W5 2XP

Independent • Pupils: 290 • Ages: 3–11 • RC • Fees (per term): £2,440 – £4,070

Tel: 020 8862 2254
Fax: 020 8862 2058
Email: enquiries@stbenedicts.org.uk
Website: www.stbenedicts.org.uk

10

Headmaster: Since 2005, Mr R G Simmons, BA, the second secular head.

Entrance: Non-selective at 3 or 4.

Exit: Almost all to senior school on site; a few on occasion to Merchant Taylors', Cardinal Vaughan and London Oratory.

Remarks: Junior school housed in very large, very attractive Victorian red-brick building across the playground from senior school (playground shared

but times staggered so tinies not swamped by six foot rugger types). Playground also encloses new small area for tots. Building recently and carefully extended to provide lovely, light new hall and classrooms. New rooms include excellent new ICT suite with modern low tables and matching chairs and inviting, comfortable library overlooking the abbey and lawns. Interactive whiteboards in every classroom and well used. Leafy Ealing far more apparent here – super trees with space to grow and local family homes just across the way. Excellent displays everywhere – really interesting, too, on stone carving, perspective, shape and colour. A good orderly feel with happy, confident-looking pupils in a school recently commended in ISI report for excellent music and ADT. Pastoral care, too, clearly exceptional. A super start for your son or daughter and big school just across the playground. New nursery housed in super refurbished Victorian house just down the road. Last Ofsted inspection rated the early years foundation stage provision as outstanding.

St Benedict's School

Linked school: St Benedict's Junior School, 455

54 Eaton Rise, London, W5 2ES

Independent · Pupils: 810 · Ages: 11–18 · RC · Fees (per term): £4,620

Tel: 020 8862 2254
Fax: 020 8862 2199
Email: enquiries@stbenedicts.org.uk
Website: www.stbenedicts.org.uk

Headmaster: Since 2002, Mr Christopher Cleugh (rhymes with rough) BSc MSc (late 50s). Read chemistry at Hull. Resonant Liverpool accent ('I prefer Everton,' he says), he grew up and taught on Merseyside until he came here. Educated at St Mary's Crosby, where he returned as a teacher for 17 years (by the time he left he was deputy head). Went on to become head of St Anselm's in Birkenhead for eight years, before moving south to run St Benedict's, which felt fated: 'I remember the day I saw the advert,' he says. Married with two sons and two daughters – his wife is head of a Catholic primary school in Acton, his first grandchild is a pupil in the junior school here. Utterly unpretentious and forthright, Mr Cleugh is a keen sports fan and loves his cricket and football. Warm and humorous, one nevertheless detects steel beneath the avuncular surface.

Only the second lay headmaster since the school was founded, Mr Cleugh is a practising Catholic and a firm believer in co-education – 'in the modern world it's the right way forward. It's a co-ed world out there and this is the natural preamble to it,' he says, adding that there's 'all sorts of nonsense about which environment produces the best academic performance, but at the end of the day it's nothing to do with single sex or

co-education – it's the way they're taught and how you instil confidence and self discipline.'

You know where you are with this head, who is not afraid to risk unpopularity for the good of the community, and is a man of quiet but total convic-

---

Rugby is huge (they don't play football, nor do they row, and it's not the place for your son if he's mad about ballet)

---

tion. Knows, and knows about, all his pupils, and has a sensitive understanding of their concerns.

Much loved by parents and pupils alike – 'he's always around'; 'easy to talk to'; 'makes time for everyone'; 'you can talk to him about anything – he never makes you feel uncomfortable' is the resounding message. Mr Cleugh unequivocal too about his favourite thing about the job – the children.

Academic matters: Respectable results, especially bearing in mind the school is not highly selective academically. Seventy-four per cent A*/B grades at A level in 2014, 36 per cent A*/A. However, a starry place in league tables is not what they're about, Mr Cleugh is keen to point out, and what he cares most about is that each child fulfils his or her potential. Among the 74 per cent who got A*s, As and Bs there would have been a number who would have fallen by the wayside in a more pressured environment. A good range of GCSE subjects on offer with everyone taking RS. RS curriculum largely RC in content and other faiths learned about in PSHE. History, maths and chemistry most popular subjects at A level. In 2014, a disappointing 20 per cent A*/A grades at GCSE. Modern languages reasonably popular and take place in language labs in the £6.2 million development.

Wheelchair access throughout the school (lifts and ramps) means they have been able to accommodate a number of children with severe physical disabilities. Three children in the school currently have statements, including one with cerebral palsy and one paraplegic. 'As long as I feel they would be happy I will take them,' says head, who is keen to emphasise his inclusive approach. Full time SENCo who occasionally withdraws pupils from lessons but prefers to provide in-class support as well and extra time pre- and post-school. Lots of support given to children with their organisational skills and the SEN room provides a useful base for children who need more help. Very positive noises from parents about the caring and supportive approach of the school to a whole range of special needs.

At the other end of the spectrum, a Gifted and Talented Coordinator runs a programme through the curriculum, but also does a lot outside.

Excellent ICT facilities. The subject is well taught and IT skills used extensively in other areas including art and music.

Games, options, the arts: Rugby is huge here. It's the main winter sport for boys (they don't play football, nor do they row, and it's not the place for your son if he's mad about ballet) and school recently ranked the top rugby school in the country (currently slipped to fourth but we suspect not for long). Tours to Dubai, Japan and New Zealand. Girls as keen to perform well as the boys. Netball tours to Sri Lanka and Barbados. Full size Astroturf pitch. Cricket, athletics, rounders and tennis in the summer. School uses 14 acres of playing fields in Perivale about a mile away and plays hard, winning more than losing. Games staff everywhere – proper professionals in their matching coaching kit.

On-site sports hall, sparkling multi-gym and fitness centre as well as fencing salle and dance studio. Fencing a major sports option with regular fixtures against other schools. Basketball, volleyball and yoga are also offered.

Less than world-class pupils appreciate the school's attitude to sports – 'everyone's given a chance,' said one in heartfelt tones, having

experienced the 'if you're not in the first team you're nobody' syndrome elsewhere.

Music strong and there's a huge variety – a symphony orchestra, lots of singing – four choirs (strongly influenced by the Abbey choir), jazz band, big band, swing band, string ensembles and brass groups. (Almost) everyone gets involved at some stage and one parent remarked on how well talent is spotted and nurtured. Excellent facilities, three grand pianos and lots of uprights in tip top condition. An IT lab is dedicated to music, posters of Led Zeppelin and the Beatles decorate the walls, lots of computers equipped with piano keyboards.

Exciting art. Intensely imaginative, disciplined and creative sculptures are dotted around the school and spectacular oil paintings adorn the reception area. IT facilities dedicated to art in the attractive one-storey modern art/DT block. Before – and after – school study supervision in the library on offer, and over 80 clubs which include karate, history society, CCF, D of E, Saint Vincent de Paul charity fundraising, debating and current affairs. One boy keen to point out that if you want to do something new, school will make it happen.

Background and atmosphere: Founded in 1902 by the monks of Downside Abbey, St Benedict's is the only Benedictine day school in the country. Its sister schools are Worth, Downside and Ampleforth

which, like St Benedict's, have all relatively recently started to take girls all the way through. (There have been girls in the sixth form here since the 1970s, from year 7 since 2008). The Roman Catholic faith is evident in every aspect of the atmosphere and the environment of the school, its publications,

---

Modern Cloisters development – stunningly light and bright with a large window in the shape of a cross taking up most of the ceiling

---

its ethos, yet almost half the pupils in the senior school are not Catholic. Eighty-five-ish per cent are Christian including those from other denominations, and you will find Muslims, Sikhs, Hindus, and Jews. The only condition is that they must respect the Catholic faith and take part in the regular masses that take place throughout the school year.

The buildings are a mix of un-gloomy Victorian red-brick and various 20th century extensions, additions and blocks – some of which are wearing better than others. The Cloisters, a stunning development costing £6.2 million, is the first thing you come to as you enter the school and has the same contemporary feel as some of the underground stations on the Jubilee line. Smooth concrete walls, aesthetic balconies, quadrangles and colonnades, an imaginative foil to the glorious abbey, which is situated across the playground and adjacent to the junior school. Whole school mass is said in the warm and totally unforbidding abbey, but smaller class mass is said in the intimate chapel in the modern Cloisters development – stunningly light and bright with a large window in the shape of a cross taking up most of the ceiling. New art block and sixth form centre planned for 2015.

A generation of trust in the Benedictine ethos of respect for each other, and an unquestioned local reputation for quite exceptional pastoral care, have been battered by a storm of revelations, the most recent relating to 2007. See the website for the report of an inquiry, commissioned by the school's trustees and conducted by Lord Carlile (who we rate as unquestionably independent). The school tells us that it has fully implemented his recommendations. It is now fully independent of the Abbey Trust; the governing body has a lay majority and a lay chair, whilst three members of the monastic community are governors and another three work at the school. It regularly reviews its safeguarding and child protection policies.

Against that background, parents and pupils pay tribute to the trouble taken over the smallest worry, and pupils feel supported and secure. Advent of girls throughout has also contributed to modernisation and a sense of opening up.

Pastoral care and discipline: Very strict – until the sixth form all children carry around a yellow card – reminiscent of the traditional satis cards (short for satisfecit – has he done enough?) in order that their behaviour – good and bad – can be constantly monitored. Parents are kept in the loop, they sign it each week and house points are affected. However, it's not inflexibly strict – 'first and foremost I'm a parent – I know children can get it wrong sometimes,' is Mr Cleugh's humane approach. Regular parent forums on, eg the dangers of ICT at home, 'I would ban Facebook if I had my way,' Mr Cleugh exclaims. He likes to keep the sixth form in at lunch time (though they can go out). There is so much to do here,' he says, 'plus there are a few too many muggings in Ealing'.

Pupils and parents: 'Pupils in state schools think we're posh but Latymer kids think we're common,' a sixth former told us. You don't get many posey trust fund kids here. Solidly middle class but a genuinely wide range of parents, a number of single mothers and families who have made huge sacrifices to get a good education for their children. A number of parents talked of how supportive the school was – not just of their child but of the family as a whole. One boy commented on how no one is arrogant about money – the influence of the abbey means that everyone feels welcome. Mostly local. Some come from as far afield as Barnes or Holland Park. Just over 50 per cent are Catholic.

One girl we spoke to was keen to mention that girls are not treated as second class citizens, attributing it to the fact that there have been girls in the sixth form for over 30 years. There are good inter-year relationships. Mentoring schemes where the older ones help out with the juniors and whole

---

One boy commented on how no one is arrogant about money – the influence of the abbey means that everyone feels welcome

---

school involvement in drama and music. Pupils here are extremely courteous and mature. Old Priorians (the official title for former St Benedict's pupils) include Julian Clary, Lord (Chris) Patten (who also sits as an advisor on the governing board), Peter Ackroyd, Declan Donnellan, Andy Serkis, Professor Denis MacShane MP and poet/songwriter Labi Siffre,

---

It's not inflexibly strict – 'first and foremost I'm a parent – I know children get it wrong sometimes,' is Mr Cleugh's humane approach

---

as well as plenty of rugby players, including Hugo Ellis and Joe Simpson of Wasps.

Entrance: (Practically) all start at 11 – though school will still take the occasional few at 13. Ninety-six places, 40 of which go to the children coming up from the junior school (almost all transfer automatically). Entrance exams in maths, English and verbal reasoning. Most interviewed. Looking to discover what the child will give back to the school. Sixth form requirements – a minimum of six GCSEs at B or above and Bs in A level subjects. A number of people join in the sixth form from local girls' schools looking for a more inclusive approach.

It's no longer true that if you don't get in anywhere else you will get a place at St Benedict's. Although Mr Cleugh is keen not to be too selective, as numbers rise priority will have to be given to Catholics and siblings.

Exit: Virtually all sixth formers to good universities and to an impressive range of courses – no stereotypes here. Two Oxbridge offers in 2014; others to eg Bristol, Nottingham, Durham, Exeter and Leeds for subjects ranging from aerospace engineering to theatre performance. Some 20 per cent leave after GCSE to go to eg Latymer Upper, Catholic state schools or sixth form colleges.

Money matters: About half a dozen on 100 per cent bursaries, lots of others get help. 'Once a child is in if a parent falls on hard times we will do our best to help them,' says Mr Cleugh.

Limited number of academic scholarships at 11+ and at sixth form – up to 50 per cent fees and can be augmented by bursaries.

Remarks: We said, 'A wholly unpretentious, good, solid school with sound values that is never going to squash your child into a box. Exactly the school for your brightish but quietish child who would sink in a larger, or tougher, environment. An honest, hard-working place with a gentle and loving approach', and we still think that that is a fair description. Although there are still occasional ripples from its troubled past, the school is now a very different place.

St Dominic's Sixth Form College

Mount Park Avenue, Harrow on the Hill, Middlesex
HA1 3HX

State • Pupils: 1020 • Ages: 16–19 • RC

Tel: 020 8422 8084
Fax: 020 8422 3759
Email: registrar@stdoms.ac.uk
Website: www.stdoms.ac.uk

19

Principal: Since 2013, Andrew Parkin. Educated at St John's RC Comprehensive School and Queen Elizabeth Sixth Form College in Darlington. Studied music at Durham and Cambridge and started his professional career in London at The St Marylebone Girls' School. Went on to be deputy head teacher at Sion Manning Girls' School in Kensington and then St Augustine's High School in Westminster. He is a keen amateur musician and is chairman of the BBC Symphony Chorus.

Academic matters: Very wide range of courses – some 30 subjects available in more-or-less any combination. Maths much the most popular subject, with chemistry, biology and economics close behind. Impressive results: 66 per cent A*-B grades and 33 per cent A*/A grades in 2014. Option to change subjects in the first week or two if you really

Students do sponsored walks and sleep outs, work in soup kitchens, volunteer on a Catholic farm, go off to work in a school in Uganda

loath psychology or have just developed a passionate interest in Italian. A level 3 BTec in business studies is the only vocational course on offer, but those of a less academic bent can take a BTec in travel and tourism or engineering, or a lower level business studies BTec, at the Sacred Heart and Salvatorian sixth form centre down the road.

Nearly everyone does an extended project. 'They have a free choice of subject, but it makes sense to relate it to a subject they may do at university, and gives something to talk about at interview.' Large numbers of aspiring medics, so the college runs a programme of BMAT preparation and mock interviews. Excellent university and careers advice. 'We're realistic and honest, and allow no poverty of aspiration.'

The Study Plus learning support centre is staffed by a manager and three assistants. Some drop in from time to time, whilst others, often identified

at initial interviews, are assigned one-to-one help. 'Some resent it at first but soon don't want to be taken off the list.' Student mentors train to offer help with specific subjects eg chemistry and maths.

Games, options, the arts: Sports hall completed in 2010 includes a multigym and hall for badminton, table tennis and five-a-side football, with its use juggled between A level PE students and general recreation. Sport is not compulsory, but the new hall 'has increased motivation and attendance. We've been pleasantly surprised that participation rates have been very high.' On the morning of our visit the multigym was full of (mostly) young men working out – many of whom, we were told, would not normally have come to college so early. The only outdoor space is a five-a-side football/netball court, but the college fields football (girls' and boys'), rugby, netball and cricket teams. It also offers opportunities for cheerleading and street dance for those less competitively inclined.

Small numbers do music A level, but many keep up their instrumental skills, and play in the termly concerts. Top floor studios show sophisticated artwork and fashion creations, and several each year go on to art and design courses. No college drama productions, but theatre studies students showcase their devised pieces.

Volunteering and fundraising are important parts of the ethos. 'Charity efforts spring up out of nowhere.' Students do sponsored walks and sleep outs, work in soup kitchens, volunteer on a Catholic farm, go off to work in a school in Uganda, join a pilgrimage to Lourdes. 'There's an ethos of respecting other people and helping the wider community,' said a teacher.

Background and atmosphere: Opened in 1979 in what had been St Dominic's Independent Grammar School for Girls, run by Dominican nuns. Sits on a hill above a leafy, gated estate of substantial houses with large gardens that could have strayed from the Chilterns, with views across the west London fringes to Ealing. By the entrance to the site is the chapel, a peaceful and atmospheric building with lovely stained glass, 'the heart of the college'. Assemblies and introductory talks take place here, as well as morning masses, and Muslim students use a side room for prayer.

Planning permission is not easy to come by here – it can take up to seven years – but the college has gradually developed most of its open space and is well off for indoor facilities (remodelled library, ICT suite, music and art rooms) if not outdoor. No common room, but students gather in the canteen, and can work in the library, which has a mezzanine floor with a row of computers.

Faith is a major part of the deal here. Mass is held every week, tutor groups take it in turns to choose readings, everyone studies RE. 'We want our students to develop on an academic, moral and

> On the morning of our visit the multigym was full of (mostly) young men working out – many of whom, we were told, would not normally have come to college so early

spiritual level. We want them to critically examine their faith, to mix with people from other faiths and hear why it is important to them. It makes a tremendous difference to what we can offer and how they develop in later life.'

About 50 per cent of the staff is Catholic, but all teach RE and buy into the ethos. 'It's a very happy place to work,' said one. Prayers are said each morning and each tutor period. 'It is a moment for thinking outside oneself – a lovely sharing moment.' Very good relationships amongst staff and between staff and pupils. A student commented: 'The staff are so committed and positive.'

Pastoral care and discipline: The atmosphere may be relaxed, with staff and students on first name terms, but students are under tight control. Electronic registration for every lesson means that everyone is accounted for: the pastoral team phones parent and student if the student is not in by 10am. Effort and achievement grades given every six weeks. 'Our monitoring is much more frequent than they have time to do in schools. All our staff are focussed on the sixth form – not on settling in year 7s or helping year 9s choose GCSE subjects – and we're very good at it.'

Zero tolerance for drugs or violence. No drugs problems for many years – 'why would they do it here?' The rare offenders usually withdraw, 'and we support them to move on elsewhere'.

To mitigate severe government funding cuts, college has increased student numbers, and lengthened the day – now 8.30am – 4.25pm – to accommodate the extra students without increasing class sizes.

Pupils and parents: About 50 per cent Catholic, most of the rest Hindu or Muslim. Homogeneous in that all take their religious faith seriously and may talk about it at interview. Also tend to be serious about academic life, since the college offers virtually no vocational courses, and there is a high level of competition for places amongst non-Catholics in particular. Mostly from Harrow, but some from further afield from a wide range of schools.

Entrance: About 30 per cent from the two partner schools, Salvatorian College and Sacred Heart Language College. Students from these schools are guaranteed a place providing they get at least five A* – C GCSE grades including English language (applicants from elsewhere must get at least seven) and meet the individual subject requirements. These range from a C in English for religious studies to an A in maths for further maths. Priority to Catholics, then other practising Christians, then other faiths: applicants other than those from the partner schools must provide a reference from their priest/imam/rabbi, and fill in a form about their own religious commitment. Successful non-Catholic applicants are those with the highest predicted grades. Everyone is interviewed, mostly to check that their chosen subjects correlate with their future ambitions.

Exit: Around 90 per cent to higher education. University of Hertfordshire very popular, as are many of the London universities, Nottingham and Warwick. Law and medical/biomedical subjects tend to top the tables. Fewer Oxbridge applicants than one might expect given the calibre of students (five offers in 2014, for subjects ranging from medicine to PPE), largely because so many are prospective medics aiming at the London teaching hospitals.

Money matters: Free if you're under 19. Excellent and enlightened system of bursaries for students and staff to fund specific projects and trips.

Remarks: Greatly sought-after college in pleasant leafy location with high academic standards and a strong Catholic ethos of care for each other. 'A lovely place to work and study,' say staff and students.

St Helen's School

Linked schools: Little St Helen's and St Helen's Junior school, 420

Eastbury Road, Northwood, Middlesex HA6 3AS

Independent • Pupils: 1,120 • Ages: 3–18 • C of E
• Fees (per term): £4,977

Tel: 01923 843210
Fax: 01923 843211
Email: admissions@sthn.co.uk
Website: www.sthn.co.uk

28

Headmistress: Since 2011, Dr Mary Short BA PGCE PhD (early 50s) – did her PhD, in the politics of budget-setting in the 1920s, at Cambridge. Has taught undergraduates at Cambridge and pupils at independent schools including St Paul's Girls, City of London Boys and Haberdashers' Aske's Girls (deputy head). She has teaching in her blood and is married to a fellow teacher. Apart from history, likes walking, bread-making and travel. Aims to up the academic performance, partly by 'reviewing the admissions process to more accurately identify academic potential', but more by curriculum reviews, consistency of aims, better monitoring of performance, peer review of teachers, that sort of thing. Good relationship with her top-notch governors.

A smile of measured mischief, and a fascination with bringing the best out of each pupil. Her eyes light up when describing how the school is going about sorting out one of her more troublesome charges. 'Is quietly powerful', says a parent, 'I really really like her, and so do the girls.'

Academic matters: Not the top of the highly competitive North London academic tree, but no slouch. Lots of male teachers, lots of teachers who have had other professional lives before or even during teaching. Every pupil we talked to had at least one teacher they found truly inspiring. Pupils describe the atmosphere as 'competitive but collaborative': in maths, for instance, where randomly chosen pairs of girls help each other to tackle problems and be the best pair in the class.

In 2014, 56 per cent A*/A at A level, 81 per cent A*/A at GCSE. Good range of subjects in the sixth. The overwhelmingly popular subjects at this level are the sciences, maths, economics and history, with maths results particularly strong. Physics as ever with girls the slightly weaker relation, but school working hard to encourage and take-up is growing – the Heath Robinson Club is clearly popular and interest in engineering is strong. The cuttings that adorn the corridor walls in the science department are totally fascinating, and would repay an hour's dawdling. Average IB score of 41 in 2014.

Way ahead of the government on the EBacc: have been doing it for years, with a strong emphasis on having a second language. Tendency to do art and/or drama as the 'free' choices. Highly IT literate: great facilities and teachers who know how to use them. Students are able to: complement their

---

Not in hock to the league tables, but plenty of ambition for its pupils, academically and otherwise

A level programme with the 'St Helen's Portfolio', which comprises additional qualifications such as the European Computer Driving Licence; take up modules offered by the Open University; continue with languages they have studied to GCSE or acquire additional languages or study further mathematics; also recognises CCF, D of E, other clubs and societies

Thoroughly sympathetic to SEN, from the headmistress down. Everyone is screened at 7 and 11 for potential educational difficulties. 'We then discuss with parents how we can make it better.' One teacher qualified to support pupils diagnosed as dyslexic and school is planning to appoint a head of learning support in the coming year. School can and does support autistic spectrum difficulties, mild dyslexia and dyspraxia, mild speech difficulties and children with hearing impairments. Currently focusing on better provision for those who struggle with numbers – some children have extra help with maths. 'All take iGCSE maths – we have no intention of becoming a specialist centre for dyscalculics, but do want to become much more effective at picking up those who struggle with number work before they become paralysed by algebra!' Support, but not separate teaching, for those who have English as an additional language. Some 100+ children currently identified as Gifted and Talented and supported with 'differentiated work schemes and activities'.

Games, options, the arts: The huge surprise for anyone visiting St Helen's and who, perhaps, has only seen it behind its sedate hedges and modest perimeter walls, is the unbelievable amount of space it has. Acres of playing fields, courts and pitches extend in all directions and you begin to realise that most of this end of Northwood is St Helen's! A vast new sports complex and superb, seemingly endless pool, in a stunning new building, in enthusiastic use. Lacrosse, netball, tennis, athletics, badminton and rounders all popular and many other games and activities available

including pilates, aerobics, fencing and trampolining. Lots of success – representation in lacrosse, swimming, cross-country and netball county teams and much success for school teams in all these sports plus athletics and rounders at impressive levels. Supports those who excel (and need time off for national teams) and has no beef with those who prefer music (but still have to do games).

Art, D&T and drama housed in the June Leader building, named after school's outstanding, and aptly named, head of 20 years (1966-1986), the great builder of the school, both in physical terms and in terms of the quality of education and values promulgated here under her uniquely humane regime. First rate art – teachers are real artists, teaching combines strong basic skills such as life drawing with experimentation, breadth and understanding. D&T bubbling and well taught if not as jazzily equipped as some (though there is CAD and a 3D printer). Dance and drama (some joint with Merchant Taylors') much enjoyed, especially in the context of the annual House Arts festival. It is good to see the arts so strong in a school whose spirit is essentially academic. The Centre is a new multipurpose space for the performing arts and sport (converted from the existing gym).

Music – with real musicians with flourishing musical careers as teachers – going from strength to strength with numerous orchestras, choirs and,

bands. The jazz band has made a CD, the huge choir tours abroad annually, there are many and varied opportunities for performance in school and the wider community, including regular concerts at St John's, Smith Square, London. The majority of girls play at least one instrument.

Collaboration with Merchant Taylors' also in CCF. D of E and Young Enterprise also popular. Visits from profs, writers and theatre companies. Successes in debating, maths and physics Olympiads, technology competitions. Lots of trips – Madrid, Kobe, Ypres, Berlin, CERN, Kew, Rome, House of Commons, Paris, British Museum, galleries.

Underlying ethos of opportunity, progression and support. Hundreds of things for pupils to try and, when they latch on to one, the school will find ways of allowing it to be taken further – as far, indeed, as the girl can go.

Background and atmosphere: Founded at the end of the 19th century with a vision of education for the whole child to which it still holds dear. A spacious school, trim and imaginative grounds, relaxed, not at all authoritarian. Dark green uniform up to 16; conservative freedom in the sixth.

Strong Indian, Tamil and Jewish (a strong JSoc and well-established links with the local synagogue) contingents, but absolutely no sign of segmentation or separation among the pupils, and parents report

> *Hundreds of things for pupils to try and, when they latch on to one, the school will find ways of allowing it to be taken further*

that it's like that with the ones they bring home too. Watch them swirl around you at break time and wish the world could be like that. Strong relationship with Merchant Taylors', already noted, supplies all the male element the girls want, and no more.

Notable absence of the unhealthily thin. Eating is a social rite here – you stumble across snacking groups all the time. School encourages this with decent breaks, delicious cookies and time enough for lunch.

The junior school is an integral part of the whole. Situated centrally, it is natural for girls here to stay the course – now from 3 to 18 – and continue to feel that it's all in the family. Longworthe, one of the former boarding houses, is now used for before and after school care in which pupils with busy parents can spend a long day – breakfast and tea included and quiet places for prep and recreation.

Nicely decorated rooms for sixth form relaxation and study (much studiousness observed).

Pastoral care and discipline: Each individual teacher is expected to notice and to care how their charges are, and to react supportively and promptly to any sign of trouble. As a result, while teachers talk of all the usual friendship and family problems, the girls seem hardly aware of them, and prefects do not see dealing with social ills as a significant part of their remit. Relationships within houses, year groups and tutor groups all seem close, giving girls a variety of communities to turn to.

Staff/student relationships palpably cordial. 'A lot of our teachers are role models,' said one sixth former. 'They are so kind and helpful and it doesn't just stop in the classroom. They will keep helping you achieve what you want to achieve.' A younger pupil agreed, 'and', she added, 'you just have to be friendly here because everyone is. The teachers are so sweet – they really look after you – there's always someone to talk to and problems are sorted out really quickly.' 'Never a door closed, they always have time for you'. The same applies to the San, with its welcoming Sister, and the two school counsellors (called Confidential Listeners).

Clear sanctions policy. System of warning and detention cards. MP3s/mobiles illegal in school time. No drugs incidents in living memory. The occasional foolish misdemeanour is dealt with individually but 'sanely. It's never public, it's not about humiliation – ever.' You're allowed to slip here.

Pupils and parents: Resilient, personable, happy, chatty girls who 'know who we are and why we are here', and whose attitude to problems is to 'tackle not buckle'. Alongside, that is, a deep-rooted conservatism: wary of the poetry shelves in the library and reluctant to take gap years (although the pupil we talked to whose ambition was to be an inventor was thought eccentric, she was still very much one of the girls). The head 'hopes to encourage greater risk-taking'.

Northwood is prosperous, with lots of large detached houses. Girls come from wide area – good coach service covers Beaconsfield, Elstree, Barnet, Amersham, Ealing, Hemel Hempstead and points between.

Old Girls' network huge and devoted. St Helen's inspires great loyalty. Alumnae include Patricia Hodge, a great supporter, Vanessa Lawrence (director general Ordnance Survey), Lady Lowry, Luisa Baldini, Penny Marshall and Maria Djurkovic.

Entrance: School part of North London Consortium which shares tests at 11. First point of entry is at 3 into Little St Helen's. At 11, exams in English and maths; around 300 apply for 50 places – not too terrifying as lots apply elsewhere but school is increasingly candidates' first choice. Junior school girls have to sit the exam too, but none have failed in recent years.

Interview and reference from current school as important as scores. 'Aim is to explore potential and to ensure that girls will be able to take full advantage of the curriculum and wider opportunities the school has to offer,' says the school. As ever true but never spelt out, parents should remember that they are on show too.

At sixth form, 'places are available for girls who the school considers will benefit by the educational programme offered and who will enjoy becoming members of the school community. We don't fix the number of places.' You need seven plus GCSEs at B+. Some leave along the way – around 10 leave at 11 for state system, boarding or (few) other local independents. A few leave after GCSEs.

Exit: Around a fifth leave post-GCSE. All sixth formers to higher education. Handful to Oxbridge annually (two in 2014), otherwise a wide spread of universities and courses (Bristol and Manchester popular). About a third science related: strong bias to medical, biological and engineering courses, with a high proportion of dentistry and medical offers in 2014. Careers advice considered by the girls to be top notch, and in general they have a much clearer idea than usual of what courses they would like and what careers they might pursue afterwards.

Money matters: Range of scholarships and means-tested bursaries. Bursaries awarded annually and are either awarded to girls whose parents could not otherwise meet fees or to girls whose families are experiencing temporary difficulties.

Remarks: Thoroughly impressive. Not in hock to the league tables, but plenty of ambition for its pupils, academically and otherwise.

St James's Catholic Primary School

260 Stanley Road, Twickenham, Middlesex TW2 5NP

State · Pupils: 680 · Ages: 3–11 · RC

Tel: 020 8898 4670
Fax: 020 8893 3038
Email: info@st-james.richmond.sch.uk
Website: www.st-james.richmond.sch.uk

41

Headteacher: Since January 2013, Mrs Clare Webber BA PGCE NPQH. Read history at university. Comes from a commercial background and spent time in recruitment, then became a full-time mother when her children were young. Has two sons, now both at university. Both her grandfather and father were heads – 'so teaching was in the blood'. Taught at the school for 12 years, followed by promotion to deputy and then acting head.

Charming, with a good sense of humour. Loves her job, takes her responsibilities very seriously and says the main challenge for her now is 'to continue to be an outstanding school'. One parent told us: 'We're very lucky to have her. She's fantastic'. Huge amounts

of energy – keeps fit with boot camp before school and enjoys regular trips to the V&A. Very visible at school events and in the playground at break time. Not a head who hides herself away in her office.

Entrance: At three to nursery (52 places) and four to the main school (90 places). St. James's is a Roman Catholic school serving the four parishes of St James (Twickenham), St Francis de Sales (Hampton Hill), St Margaret (East Twickenham) and St Theodore (Hampton). Priority given to those baptised within a year of birth who are devout, practising Catholics. Siblings given priority. Heavily over-subscribed, with more than two applicants for every place.

Occasional places become available in higher years, though there isn't huge pupil mobility. 'We don't lose many pupils further up the school, only if the families relocate', says the head. 'We certainly don't lose them to private schools'.

A place in the nursery does not automatically lead to a place in reception – 'though it is very rare for this not to happen'.

Exit: Between 20 to 50 per cent to independent schools. Hampton Boys' is popular and 'girls go everywhere', including Tiffin Girls' School, Gumley House and Waldegrave. One mother commented that many parents have chosen historically to go down the independent school route due to the dearth of good state secondary schools nearby – 'especially with the Oratory having reduced its catchment area'. That looks set to change with the new St Richard Reynolds Catholic High School in Twickenham starting to be an extremely popular destination.

Remarks: Head describes the school as having high academic standards, coupled with a strong Catholic ethos. 'Faith is central to what we do here', she told us. 'It is made explicit to parents. If you are a Catholic teacher, part of teaching is a mission as well as a job'.

School is large, spacious and well-run. Housed in fairly new accommodation in a leafy cul-de-sac. Light classrooms with generous windows and colourful displays abound. Two huge halls, well used for sport, dance, plays and assemblies. Glorious outdoor space where children can let off steam. Climbing frames, trees and quieter areas for those in need of tranquillity. Plenty of greenery surrounding the school. Rolling playing fields at the back and local golf club on the other side give the school a distinctly country feel.

School is at full capacity, with three parallel classes of 30 children from reception up to year 6. Children very engaged and focused when we visited and some impressive manners in evidence.

Symphony orchestra, three choirs (chamber choir is by invitation only), two rock bands and about half of key stage 2 pupils have private music lessons

Very strong academically. Rigorous analysis of progress and attainment of each pupil at each stage. Head aware of the importance of pupils becoming independent thinkers and thinking skills now embedded in the curriculum.

Small turnover of staff with a respectable number of long servers. Specialist teaching for art and some games. Masses of lesson observations going on – at all levels – to maintain high standards.

Head believes that sport is a vital part of the curriculum and it is taken seriously here, with the school competing at a high level. Recent borough athletic champions and 12 children competed at the national swimming championships in Sheffield – 'a great achievement', says the head, 'as they're normally dominated by private schools'.

Football, netball, rugby, cricket and tennis on offer. Reciprocal sharing of swimming pool and games pitches with The Mall, prep school next door.

Music is strong. A symphony orchestra, three choirs (chamber choir is by invitation only), two rock bands and about half of key stage 2 pupils have private music lessons. Musical events arranged with local schools and there are opportunities to perform at the Barbican in the London Symphony Orchestra's Discovery Series.

The art department definitely holds its own. Head is excited that, as part of the Take One Picture scheme, pupils have been selected to exhibit their work at the National Gallery. 'I can't wait to go', she says.

Number of children requiring learning support is quite small. Limited number with IEPs but one-to-one help is on offer for those in need. 'Our special needs children make exceptional progress and are very well provided for', says head. Full-time SENCo and part-time learning support staff. George Tancred Centre is based at the school and caters for 10 children with moderate autism. Regular opportunities for these pupils to be included in lessons at the main school but they can withdraw back to the centre when activities become too distracting. Their playground is separate from, but adjacent to, main school. The pupils with autism are 'very much part of our school', says head. Pupils from the main school can choose to visit and play with the children from the centre at break times.

No wrap-around care on offer but plenty of before and after-school clubs, so the school day can be extended to help working parents. A variety of tastes catered for at clubs – football, cricket, basketball, French, Spanish, Italian, Jamming Together

> *Head is excited that, as part of the Take One Picture scheme, pupils have been selected to exhibit their work at the National Gallery. 'I can't wait to go', she says*

and ballet. Basketball is currently very popular. Plenty of school trips on offer. Year 6 get a week in Norfolk and year 5 head for Dorset as part of the history curriculum. Day outings include visits to art galleries and RHS gardens at Wisley.

Children at St James's are expected to work hard. Lots of homework from reception onwards, culminating in a couple of hours a night by year 6. Parents are generally supportive of this. Some tutoring goes on at the top of the school – head is relaxed, as long as it does not become excessive.

Significant number of bilingual children – mostly Spanish, French and Italian. Parents are welcomed into the school and appreciate the open-door policy in place. Head knows most of the families well and believes parental involvement in the school is invaluable, either on trips or within the classroom. 'We'd be mad not to include them', she says. Parents are a fairly affluent, middle class group, reflecting the local area. Minuscule percentage on free school meals. Very active PTFA raises £30,000 annually. Money recently spent on the early years garden and subsidising school trips.

School has an excellent reputation in the local neighbourhood and parents feel lucky to have secured their child a place. At the start of the day, hordes of children in jolly yellow and grey uniforms race along the pavements on scooters. Ongoing problems over road congestion outside, however, and local residents aren't always happy. As one parent put it, 'it's a big, busy primary school. In the morning, the traffic can be horrendous'. Head encourages less driving to school and has even gone so far as to employ number-plate recognition surveillance for repeat parking offenders.

This is an outward-looking school that offers an excellent academic education in a nurturing Catholic environment. Ably led by an inspiring head and with high expectations of pupils, staff and parents, it's impressive on many fronts.

Twickenham Preparatory School

Beveree, 43 High Street, Hampton, Middlesex TW12 2SA

Independent • Pupils: 275 • Ages: 4–13 • Non–denom
• Fees (per term): £3,225 – £3,490

Tel: 020 8979 6216
Fax: 020 8979 1596
Email: office@twickenhamprep.co.uk
Website: www.twickenhamprep.co.uk

42

Headmaster: Since 2005, Mr David Malam BA Southampton (history), PGCE King Alfred's College, Winchester (40s). Has been at the school for 15 years, having joined as a history teacher, then deputy head for years. Before that taught in junior and first schools in Southampton (unusually including a year in a reception class) and at Lagos International School in Cyprus, teaching ages 7-16.

He's very popular with pupils, gets to know them all well and is warm and funny around them. 'They are very fond of him, but also really respect him', says a mother. 'He has natural authority and never needs to shout; has a great gift with children', says another. 'He's better with the children than with parents', says a third. 'Personally I agree it's all about the kids, but lots of parents seem to want indulging and he's not good at that side of things'. However, those that know him best say he is 'an excellent headmaster'.

He's a great sports fan, especially football and squash, and he has also played chess at a high level. Lives locally, married, with five children who he has, or has had, at the school. 'He treats them just the same as anybody else, they're not his favourites', said our year 6 tour guides confidently.

Entrance: Non-selective at reception, and while perhaps not necessary to register at birth, think about it by a first birthday. Although it behaves and sounds like a church school, there is actually no religious requirement in the admission criteria; if you are happy with the ethos they are happy to have you. That's not to say school will say yes to everyone; you've got to fit in socially, behaviourally and academically. Largely a local intake. Other places are occasionally available and subject to assessments in English, maths and reasoning. Bus service runs from Richmond and Twickenham. Aims to maintain its 50:50 ratio of boys: girls

Exit: All over, especially, at 11, girls to Lady Eleanor Holles, Surbiton High, Wimbledon High, Sir William Perkins, Kingston Grammar, St Catherine's. At 13+ boys to Hampton, Halliford, Reeds and St Georges. A few to St Paul's and King's College Wimbledon. Usually a healthy number of scholarships.

Remarks: A popular co-ed prep which prides itself on its positive, family atmosphere and strong Christian ethos. Non-selective, so not packed with academic boffs, but it's no place for a slouch either – increasing numbers of scholars attest to

the academic thrust here in recent times. Not as pressured a place as some Surrey schools, but still seriously ambitious for its children, who are indeed going on to win places at the county's top senior schools. Carefully guided by Mr Malam, Twickenham Prep children will not sit many entrance exams – no more than two or three. 'The eight or nine some do is ridiculous,' he says. 'It's unnecessary; we know our children very well and therefore know which school will suit them best'.

Specialist subject teaching from the off in French, ICT, Music and PE. By year 4 all teaching is subject-specific, with pupils moving from room to room for their lessons. No streaming, but setting for maths from year 4. Latin for most girls from year 5 and for boys when they move onto the common entrance programme. French for all, with a little bit of Greek and an introduction to Spanish for those up to it. Nice small classes, typically of 18. Homework is reasonably low key; 'I don't see it as a means of destroying family life,' says Mr Malam. Starts gently with some reading and spelling up to year 2, then one to two homeworks a night, reaching 40 minutes a night by year 6. Thrice-weekly homework clubs similarly take the pressure off family time.

Pupils seem well-engaged with their lessons, and the school's atmosphere is calm and purposeful. ISI inspectors judge teaching here to be always good, and sometimes outstanding, with provision

to 5 off site. Year 7 and year 8 boys pick up squash and badminton too.

Nice extracurricular clubs, including music and movement, historic adventures and sewing for pre-prep, and touch-typing, table tennis and knitting for prep pupils. Wrap-around pre- and after-school care. Mr Malam, and therefore his school, is a big fan of the Mind Lab (thinking abilities and life skills) programme which is timetabled as a weekly lesson. Typically the children will play strategy games and learn about lateral thinking. The idea is that this work makes pupils more adaptable and less easily phased when encountering a new problem for the first time. Mr Malam seems to have converted parents, who praise the programme. 'At first I thought it was some sort of hideous team-building exercise beloved of large organisations, but in fact it does get the children thinking in a different way', says one. 'They think they are just playing games, but really they are learning. And with all the verbal and non-verbal reasoning involved in many entrance exams these days, it does seem to give them a great basis for working things out'.

A recent fund–raising auction of promises saw one boy's family successfully bid for him to take over as headmaster for a day

for children with learning difficulties or disabilities said to be 'excellent'. However, it is not the place for a more serious special need, and none of the LDD children currently on roll are statemented.

Music is something of a strength here – there's a large choir and 80 per cent of pupils are swept up for music lessons and get plenty of opportunities to play and perform. Sport is often a bugbear in a small-ish set up like this one – on-site practice space is limited and it's hard to beat some of the larger schools in the area. But on the plus side, the school does have use of Hampton Football Club's facilities, which are directly behind it, and has notched up some major tournament wins of late. Parents appreciate the fact that the school's approach is inclusive, with all the children getting an opportunity to play competitively if they want to, with C teams fielded if necessary. Swimming from years 1

More mind games come in the form of chess – another Malam passion – or 'obsession' as one mother wryly observed. The school has built up quite a reputation as IAPs champions, English Schools national finalists and borough champions. Grandmaster Daniel King works with the school, involving up to 50 of the children regularly, with up to 30 of them going on to play for school teams.

Parents view the school as very strong pastorally – again ISI say its provision in this area is 'outstanding'. The school is a really nurturing place; welcoming and warm, a gentle and kind environment with no sharp edges. Watchwords for the pupils are 'calm, courteous, courageous and considerate'. 'And they don't just pay lip-service to those words, they really count for something here,' says a mother. Discipline not really an issue – teachers use positive reinforcement ('Praising a child who is doing well has quite an effect on a child who is not doing as well themselves', says Mr Malam). Losing or winning house points an equally effective device here.

And as you'd expect from a 'Christian' school, bible-based religious education is taken seriously here and children say prayers together. There's no affiliation to any one church, but close links with nearby St Mary's Church of England church where the children visit for Christmas and harvest services. Assemblies are Christian-based, with a bible story/theme and a moral message. School has its own hymn book, teaches Lord's Prayer, hosts visits from local Christian community and other faiths.

But that's not to say that the families at this school are all regular worshippers or indeed even Christian – several we spoke to were in fact agnostic or atheist or practitioners of another religion entirely – but obviously these parents share a willingness for their children to be taught about Christian values. 'We don't believe in ignorance of other religions and so have people in to talk about other faiths and cultures too', says Mr Malam. 'Generally I find our parents want their children in a school where they at least understand the ethos, rather than put them into a more secular environment.'

Attracts professional and business-type families, mostly local from Teddington, Twickenham, Sunbury and St Margaret's. The name Twickenham Prep is actually something of a misnomer, as the school is actually in Hampton – it was originally on Twickenham Green and chose to retain its by then well-established name when it relocated in 1992. Set in unexpectedly peaceful and leafy location behind a busy road, the main school building, Beveree, was once owned by John Blow, King's Musician to Charles II, and is grade II listed. Overall not masses of space, despite major extensions, but school makes the most of what there is and has sectioned off some space for a well-used amphitheatre and an adventure playground.

And, lest it all sound too unruffled and worthy, the children also have great fun along the way. A recent fund-raising auction of promises saw one boy's family successfully bid for him to take over as headmaster for a day. He took a lesson, spoke to staff, was included in an interview and allowed to introduce some of his own for-one-day-only initiatives. These included arranging for an ice-cream van to visit at the close of school and awarding headmaster's commendation certificates to genuine supporters of Fulham football club.

Increasingly strong academically, it's offering its happy and settled pupils a good all-round education, generally allowing them their pick of all the best local day schools. Holding its own in an area packed with competitive offerings. Not pressured or pushy, rather kind, inspiring and creative.

Twyford Church of England High School

Twyford Crescent, London, W3 9PP

State • Pupils: 1,400 • Ages: 11–18 • C of E

Tel: 020 8752 0141
Fax: 020 8993 7627
Email: lwelch@twyford.ealing.sch.uk
Website: www.twyford.ealing.sch.uk

12

Executive Head Teacher: Since 2002, Ms Alice Hudson MA (Oxon), (40s) educated at Slough Girls' High and Leighton Park, then St Hilda's, Oxford, where she read English. Previously deputy head at Brentside HS, also in Ealing, and prior to that taught at Central Foundation Boys', Islington and Maria Fidelis, Euston. Joined Twyford in 2000, first as deputy, then acting head and appointed head in September 2002. Married to Michael Lyon. He works for the Bank of England ('more public servant than banker,' she says). He is Roman Catholic, she and their four children are Anglican. Her eldest daughter was given a place at Oxford to read modern languages having completed the sixth form here; her son also attends the school.

'The first five years were Herculean,' she says, 'cleaning out the stables'. (She comes from a family of classicists and her conversation is littered with references to the ancient world.) There was the thorny issue of a divided community: the haves and have-nots. The crude observer would put it in plain black and white terms – the churchgoing but poorer and underachieving black community as opposed to the playing-by-the-book, aspirational and privileged white community. Ms Hudson takes a more sophisticated approach. 'The cultural

If there is a demand or a talent, the school will make it possible to follow that talent and achieve the potential

capitalisers and disenfranchised,' she elegantly puts it, 'overlaid with typical inner London under-achievement issues connected to socio-economic disadvantage, race and gender'. Whichever description you prefer, Ms Hudson was determined to 'harness the diversity of the student/parent body'. 'Exclusions were high,' she continues, 'and I didn't want to exclude, but to sustain a positive culture.' She proudly announces that she has now achieved three of her original goals: fixed behaviour and attainment, fixed cohesion, fixed aspiration. An intelligent and sensitive woman, she explains she learnt from watching the children; 'you have to read your institution,' she says.

During her tenure she has introduced a public school style house system (there are seven houses named after cathedrals, including Truro, York and Canterbury), a process of electing head boy and girl, the new post of school chaplain (allowing her to employ high calibre teaching staff who are not necessarily practising Christians), Latin and geology. Ms Hudson is a team player and her team consists of all the staff, all the students and all the parents.

Refreshing to see the head of a challenging, big state comprehensive not just running a business but also a passionate educator, lover of youth, life and learning. Not always the case in this inspection and results driven age. Parents and pupils admire her quiet authority (you could hear a pin drop in the assembly she took when she stopped mid-flow to say, 'distressed to hear three people talking', looking directly at them across the packed school hall). This, combined with more than a superficial knowledge of all the pupils as well as their parents, her infectious enthusiasm, disarming modesty, and striking physical presence – 'Miss Hudson is every-where,' says one admiring 15 year old – and her sensitive awareness of every nuance, all contribute to making her an outstanding head. Lucky school.

The only flicker of concern is whether her eye will be taken off the ball as she combines her work here with executive headteachership at William Perkin, a free school in north Greenford which opened in September 2013. Operations at both schools are 'directed strategically from the centre'. Ofsted, reporting in May 2012 (unsurprisingly, rating the school 'outstanding' in all categories), also picked up on this concern among parents. Ms Hudson is channelling an enormous amount of energy into the project but if there is anyone who has more passion to spare and who has the team building skills to pull off her vision, she is your woman. Again, unsurprisingly, Ofsted agreed.

New associate head teacher since September 2013 is Karen Barrie, previously deputy head at the school for nine years. She is a mathematician with a degree from Manchester.

Academic matters: Results just get better and better in this, academically, non-selective school. In 2014, 69 per cent A*-B and 37 per cent A*/A grades at A level. Top ability students complete extended project – mostly with A*s. Maths results exceptional. Choices include economics, music tech, photography (very successful), psychology, sociology. Biggest improvement is in sixth form – head's especial baby – 'it's a reliable place for your high-achieving child.. we chase them much more in the sixth form', but the less academic well supported too. In 2014 GCSE results saw 86 per cent of students achieve 5+ passes at C or above (including English and maths), with 46 per cent A/A*grades.

ICT (we saw loads of computers) a developing area though head refreshingly cheery when asked about the poor showing of interactive whiteboards; 'the most important interactive resource in the classroom is the teacher', she observes. Head sees wisdom in steering the less academic to the practical and creative which 'can be studied alongside A level', so double AVCE in ICT popular along with other more vocational subjects. Visual arts are a considerable strength of the school with significant numbers of students going on to art colleges.

Twelve per cent have SLD or SEN ('disproportionately high number of children with statements,' remarks Ms Hudson, 'skewed towards the severe end'). About five per cent of these including those

with autism (across the spectrum) and Down's syndrome. All pupils are well supported, either by regular staff or from outside. 'They will be valued and survive here,' says head, 'and parents are also

---

Everyone stays to watch the big matches. Another of Ms Hudson's community–knitting devices

---

given support – we have very good home-school links.' Although 280 pupils have EAL – first languages in this very ethnically mixed area Gujurati, Punjabi, Arabic and Urdu – no one needs additional help in English.

Since she arrived there has been a tremendous push on languages and it became a specialisation (along with music) several years ago. 'We identify potential linguists in year 7, accelerate them in French and, in year 8, give them a choice of German and Spanish.' The person responsible for the language programme 'is a zealot' she says. All children have to learn to speak the language, not just from text books, and there are numerous exchanges, to China as well as to the obvious European destinations. Latin is taught once a fortnight and pupils can also choose to do it after school. It's not just a hobby, but also a GCSE option. One girl we met who moved here from the Middle East achieved an A* in GCSE Arabic at the end of year 9. If there is a demand or a talent, the school will make it possible to follow that talent and achieve the potential. Other GCSE options include food technology and electronics but DT has been temporarily paused. Setting in most subjects (including science, maths and languages from year 7, English and the humanities from year 9). From year 9 boys and girls are separated in the top two sets in English. There are at least eight sets straddling seven forms plus a tiny nurture group for the extreme special needs. Parents remark on the fluidity of movement between sets, 'you don't just get labelled as 'D' set.' Pupils can sit the more rigorous IGSE in maths and science (Harrow school provides support with this). RE very much a feature of everyday school life and supported in the sixth form by two conferences each year, often with outside speakers on moral or spiritual topics. Curriculum taught on an alternating two-week cycle, which some find confusing at first, but they get used to it.

We heard some mutterings about the SEN department not always picking up strugglers (without statements) as fast as it should nor providing the continuous support needed. We wonder whether the major advances at the upper end of the ability range are sufficiently matched by rigorous attention to those who are finding work hard. There is no doubt that the formidable Ms Hudson, with her passionate eye for detail, would not like to give less than her full attention to everything, but it's a question of priorities. Expectations are undoubtedly high. Referring to one boy, who happens to be of African/Caribbean descent, who recently achieved eight A*s in his mock GCSEs, Ms Hudson says, 'unless he achieves 10 A*s when he sits the exams, we will have failed him.' When it comes to academic achievement, Ms Hudson comments, 'The big issue is that although we are doing well as a comprehensive state school, an independent school would be expecting those results. We need to push beyond.'

Games, options, the arts: Remarkable playing fields (albeit rented, not owned), well-concealed along this urban high street site. Netball especially strong here, but you can choose to play hockey, tennis, football, cricket and basketball too. Inter-form competitions are a major event. Everyone stays to watch the big matches. Another one of Ms Hudson's effective community-knitting devices. Dance and athletics popular. Rugby coached by pros from London Wasps. Consistent successes in many sporting areas and representation in borough and regional levels. Thriving art, and stunning music (some parents confessed they wished sport was given as much emphasis as music). The church influence from gospel to choral

When we visited we witnessed a potential Rumer, singing from the heart as she accompanied herself on the piano

---

filters through at every level. A main orchestra plus smaller groups and ensembles present opportunities for lots of live performing. At every assembly there will be live music. When we visited we witnessed a potential Rumer, singing from the heart as she accompanied herself on the piano. Music and music tech facilities impressive and well-used (including the state-of-the-art audio-visual recording studio). Drama is popular and lively and as well as smaller studio performances throughout the year the main event is the massive whole school production that takes place in February. The King and I and Oliver! have recently been performed and one parent commented on the enthusiasm and commitment of her usually shy and recalcitrant daughter while acting as one of the boys in Oliver!

There is a good work placement programme, though we heard some talk of the aspiring white middle classes with lots of contacts in the world of media and law etc getting plum placements while the less advantaged among the black community ended up working in the charity shop in Shepherd's Bush. School keen to point out that there is support (large data base with useful leads, past placements etc, plus an 'Aspirations' conference run annually which invites successful black professionals and entrepreneurs to speak about their work), but the students have to take initiative to tap into that support. The pushy ones are sorted by the end of Lent term, the more lackadaisical are scrabbling around for something a week before they have to start towards the end of the summer term. You can take a horse to water and all that. Pupils enthuse about the number and quality of trips and expeditions – everywhere from St Petersburg to the New Forest for every activity imaginable – photography to water skiing. Lots of charity work.

Background and atmosphere: School tucked behind rare bit of green along the Uxbridge Road. Main building, grade 2 listed The Elms, an elegant, early Georgian house, built 1735, well-preserved and sensibly painted in blues, houses the admin and offices side of things. A diverse mixture of less distinguished and pretty scruffy later blocks, A, B, unaccountably then D and M, house rest of school. Rather alarmingly nicknamed 'The Cage' is the large central piece of tarmac surrounded by fencing where 650 pupils line up in alphabetical order each morning. A logistical challenge in a disciplined corporate environment, at Twyford C of E high school it's like sliding a knife through butter. Some attractive modern buildings have emerged organically, including a wonderfully peaceful chapel, a contemporary and refreshingly un-institutional cafeteria (more Café Nero than trad school cafeteria), state-of-the-art performance centre, creative media suite with radio station and refurbished music areas.

Black uniform with white shirts creates somewhat sombre impression but most pupils look tidy (head strides around, not averse to pointing out, amicably, 'shirt!' to any wearer of stray shirt tails) and overall impression is of a good-humoured, confident mix of the boisterous and the purposeful. No uniform for the sixth. Huge ethnic diversity – 52 per cent from non-white British backgrounds, of whom the largest number from Afro-Caribbean families; Asians make up next biggest group. Christian principles in practice evident in staff's approach to all aspects of this richly diverse community. While Anglicanism predominates, all churches and faiths are celebrated and explored here and everyone feels part of the school. Two minutes' daily silent reflection before lessons – 'everyone is quiet', said a sixth former. 'Faith has a big profile here', says head. 'We place a high premium on formal acts of worship.' Everyone attends a termly communion service and there is a weekly voluntary one. Assemblies are inclusive but have an unashamed Christian bias. 'The key to inter-faith issues,' believes head, 'is to be clear about what one's standpoint is.' She talks of the validity of each individual's own 'faith journey'. 'Spiritual matters are neither embarrassing nor taboo here' – a big claim but it feels legitimate. Pupils, though seldom deferential, respect teachers – there is a good working relationship between staff and pupils at all levels. 'They stretch you as far as you can go – but not beyond what you can do,' reflected one sixth former.

Pastoral care and discipline: Well-established system of form tutors first resort though pupils able to talk to whichever member of staff they choose. Heads of year back up the tutors and pupils have regular meetings to check on targets, progress, happiness. Chaplaincy team also available. Interaction between ages encouraged – actively by sixth form mentoring of younger pupils and system of form reps. School recently mixed up tutor groups in the sixth form to avoid tutors having particularly strong bonds with the 'home grown' students and less good ties with the newcomers. School council much appreciated – 'It has a lot of power over changes and we can meet the governors,' we were told. Few serious problems – most pupils feeling

that offending in school time and on school property 'not worth it' and seemingly a bit immature, though usual crop of minor misdemeanours.

Pupils and parents: As above, huge ethnic mix, Christianity being the unifying principle though 30 places reserved each year for those from 'other world faiths', and Christianity itself taking in Russian/Serbian/Eastern Orthodox along with other denominations. Pupils come from wide geographic area – Brent, Hounslow, all over Ealing and further into town. Most, though, from Christchurch junior school, half a mile away, and nearly 50 other primaries. More boys than girls, though this not generally perceptible. Princes and paupers here – all social strata represented and cheerfully interrelate.

Entrance: Now here's the rub. To get in you not only have to be practising a religious faith but have all the badges and medals to show it too. As the school becomes ever more oversubscribed, an increasingly complex pecking order is developing based on family's attendance at and commitment to church for at least five years (you can't just turn up and be counted, we're talking about assisting with Sunday school, running the church fête etc – though this is now under review following a ruling from the Schools Adjudicator), along with home's distance from school. Worth checking this out in detail before losing your heart to the place. No-one is fooled by rapid conversion when your child is in year 6 – though it is still – widely and unsuccessfully – tried. Thirty places for pupils from other world faiths or no faith, where the family is committed to the idea and principles in practice of 'faith', and 10 music places.

Sixth form, hitherto less stringent, now oversubscribed 11:1. They must be getting something right. For external places in the sixth form students must meet individual entry criteria for courses as set out in the sixth form prospectus (minimum usually a B with one or two exceptions) and must be in sympathy with aims and objectives of a C of E school.

Exit: Some 30 per cent leave after GCSEs. Vast and creditable range of courses and universities. They break new records for Oxbridge offers each year – nine in 2014. The increasing uptake of the extended project has resulted in glowing feedback of pupils' performance in interview and an increasing offer of scholarships.

Remarks: This is an outstanding school. Don't make the mistake of thinking it's anything other than a highly successful inner London comprehensive, however, with all the challenges that entails.

Waldegrave School

Fifth Cross Road, Twickenham, Middlesex TW2 5LH

State · Pupils: 995 · Ages: 11–16 · Non-denom

Tel: 020 8894 3244
Fax: 020 8893 3670
Email: info@waldegrave.org.uk
Website: www.waldegrave.richmond.sch.uk

43

Headteacher: Since 2006, Mrs Philippa Nunn, BSc from UCL in zoology, MA in educational management from Greenwich, PGCE and NPQH (40s). Appointed a National Leader of Education in 2011. Married with two daughters at local state schools. Was previously head of the Holt School in Berkshire, an all-girls 11-18 comprehensive. Started teaching science in 1987. Currently teaches ICT.

A calm, glamorous presence. Parents are all big fans. 'She's fantastic. She's a real person. Very approachable. As a mother of two girls she really understands.' Some staff have been teaching here for more than 25 years, which 'adds strength to the ethos of the school'. Introduced a house system to promote a greater sense of loyalty and belonging and to enhance student leadership opportunities.

A keen sports enthusiast, she plays hockey at Teddington, tennis and real tennis are passions. She's also training to become an Ofsted inspector.

Academic matters: Consistently achieves good results in English, maths and science GCSEs. French, history, art, drama, RE always good too. The success rate in A*-C grades is well above the regional and national average; 83 per cent got 5+ A*-C grades including maths and English in 2013, and 47 per cent of grades were A*/A.

Top of the Sunday Times Parent Power list for 11 to 16 schools for four years. 'But this will change with the introduction of the new sixth form in 2014,' explains the head.

Quality of teaching is excellent. 'They're all so dedicated. I can't fault them,' says one parent. Achievements are recognised at assemblies throughout the year and at Celebration Afternoons at the end of the year. High academic standards are expected and some parents say that there is pressure on the students to get good grades. 'My daughter had to do French GSCE when she didn't want to do it as the teachers knew she would get a good grade.'

But provision is made within the curriculum for all abilities, and modest acts such as helpfulness to the school or to others are duly acknowledged and rewarded. Lessons are given in broad ability tutor groups initially, but setting for maths, science and languages occurs early on in the first years. In subsequent years, setting in other subjects if appropriate. All are entered for 6-10 GCSEs; some do 13 after discussion with parents and staff. Short course subjects such as ICT and PE well subscribed with good results.

Appointed as one of the first 100 Teaching Schools, and is also a National College for School Leaders National Support School. Designated area in an independent learning centre for gifted and talented girls and those with other special needs. With an incredible cultural diversity (43 different languages), EAL support is strong, even offering a lunchtime club for all age groups.

On the subject of lunchtime, a great deal is compressed into a very short 35 minute break: careers advice, ICT, rehearsals for choirs and bands, puzzle club, homework clubs. Similarly, lots of before and after-school activities. A breakfast club at 8.00am every morning with badminton on offer at the same time for the more energetic. After school up until 4.00pm – choice is much more varied with a high take-up rate.

New sixth form opened in September 2014.

Games, options, the arts: Good range of sports offered – rounders, tennis, volleyball, athletics, rugby (with the Harlequins). Classes in the fitness suite, cricket, rowing (linked in with Walbrook Rowing Club) and table-tennis. Hidden from view from the road is a huge outdoor green area with tennis courts and marked-out running track.

School regularly wins regional netball leagues and was recently the Middlesex hockey champion. Also borough winners at netball and rounders. Running club is popular with 40 girls doing a 5k run twice a week with four teachers before school. (The head attempts to join them once every half

---

When we visited we were blown away by the bird sculptures made in art lessons, inspired by their sister school in Madogo, Kenya

---

term). Head positively oozes enthusiasm, listing her school's sporting achievements. Another of her aims is to improve participation in sport. Gymnastics is strong – both a multi and traditional gym on site. A dance studio was funded through the National Lottery.

Extra opportunities include bridge, drama, study skills, chess, art, music theory, ICT, choirs, rock bands and full orchestra. Art and music are both strengths. Year 7 all learn the recorder and in year 8 they get the chance to play the ukelele! When we visited we were blown away by the bird sculptures made in art lessons, inspired by their sister school in Madogo, Kenya.

Drama is strong with four classes choosing GCSE. A big production every alternate year and an annual joint production with Hampton Boys' School.

After-school clubs also include extra languages, eg Mandarin GCSE and there's even an astronomy club which parents can also attend. These cost extra but the pupil premium funds places for those who qualify.

Background and atmosphere: Original 1930s building has been added to over the years. Science labs are housed in newish block and brand new sixth form building opened in 2014, housing new sports hall and dining room. Outside play area transformed with money from the PTA with an outdoor theatre and landscaped surroundings. Food freshly cooked on site, and a biometric system for payment. Some girls take sandwiches. 'I don't want them having a slice of pizza and a muffin every day,' explained one parent.

The girls themselves give this school a buzzy atmosphere. A former pupil remarks that 'all girls is a positive rather than a negative.'

Pastoral care and discipline: No real behavioral problems. First years are invited to spend a day in the school to find their way about and practise their journey to and fro – puts a stop to later excuses about buses being late. They also start the term a bit earlier before the older ones arrive. Prefects help out with the younger ones, organise charity events, welcome visitors and play an important leadership role in the school. Each tutor group elects a representative to attend the school council, which in turn represents the school at the Richmond School Student Council. All good training ground for debating and public speaking.

School is honest about bullying and admits that, like the poor, it is always with us. However, stringent efforts made to put an end to it. Girls, staff and parents exhorted to report any incident straight away and assured that something will be done.

Pupils and parents: Although the school has no religious affiliation, the majority of the pupils are Christian. More than 25 per cent are from an ethnic minority. All come from the surrounding borough of Richmond, which is known nationally for its high level of professional parents. A local parent declares it to be the sort of school where 'decent folk will be prepared to break all sorts of rules to get their daughters in.' New (mixed) sixth form will make this school even more desirable.

Entrance: Fully comprehensive intake. It is the only all girls' state school in Richmond so is always over-subscribed. Much to the head's relief, all admissions are dealt with by the local authority. Despite clear and rigid guidelines about admissions policies there are always appeals. Sibling policy includes stepsisters, half sisters and adopted sisters living in the same household. A percentage of their intake includes those with special needs and those in public care or who are deemed by the LA to have a particular need. Most girls will have attended local primary schools in the borough.

Six places are available each year for those with speech and language difficulties or those on the autistic spectrum.

There are 240 places in the new sixth form (120 in each year) and 40 of these places are for boys. Majority of places will be taken by existing students with 5 A* – C grades needed at GCSE with Bs in the subjects students want to study to A level.

Exit: In the past students have gone to Richmond Sixth Form College, Esher College, Strodes College or to sixth forms of independent schools. This will all change with the new sixth form and the majority of girls remaining at the school to study for A levels. 'We hope to be sending students to Oxbridge and the Russell Group universities,' explains the head.

Remarks: A really buzzy school. 'It felt more dynamic than the other schools we visited,' said one parent.' This school has so much going on that you're a lucky girl if you manage to get a place here. Now with the new sixth form you're even luckier!

North

Barnet

Enfield

Haringey

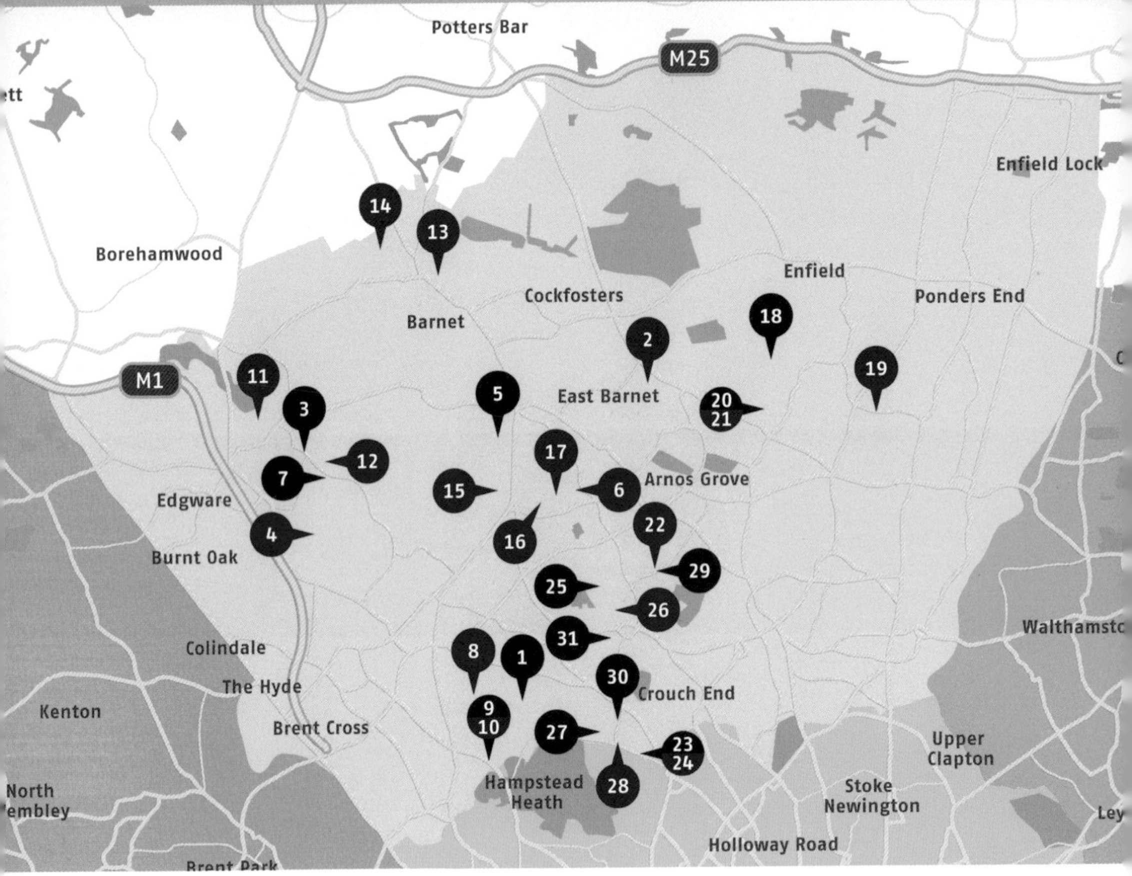

NORTH

BARNET

1 Annemount School 487

2 Ashmole Academy 489

3 Belmont Mill Hill Preparatory School 494

4 Copthall School 503

5 Dwight School London, Lower School And Kindergarten 506

6 Dwight School London (Upper School) 508

7 Grimsdell, Mill Hill Pre-Preparatory School 515

8 The Henrietta Barnett School 516

9 King Alfred Lower School 525

10 King Alfred School 526

11 Mill Hill County High School 533

12 Mill Hill School 536

13 Queen Elizabeth's Girls' School 548

14 Queen Elizabeth's School, Barnet 552

15 St Michael's Catholic Grammar School 557

16 Woodhouse College 564

17 Wren Academy 567

ENFIELD

18 Keble Prep School 523

19 The Latymer School 529

20 Palmers Green Lower School 541

21 Palmers Green High School 543

HARINGEY

22 Alexandra Park School 485

23 Channing Junior School 497

24 Channing School 498

25 Coldfall Primary School 501

An introduction to North London and its state schools

Barnet

Barnet, which stretches from Hampstead Heath to Hertfordshire, is leafy and suburban. It includes Hampstead Garden Suburb, founded in the early 20th century by Henrietta Barnett, whose eponymous school in Central Square is one of the most sought-after in the country. The idea of the Suburb was to have houses for a range of incomes and gardens for every single person. So houses range from tiny upwards, some Georgian but many Tudorbethan, with flower and tree lined streets. Highgate village is quietly residential with a rural feel, and Highgate and Hampstead golf courses near by.

As with Henrietta Barnett School qv (girls), Queen Elizabeth School qv (boys) also regularly attracts more than 10 applicants per place; the other popular grammar school is St Michael's Catholic Grammar qv. Mill Hill County High qv awards a quarter of its places on aptitude (24 technology, 24 music and 12 dance). Non-selective Ashmole Academy qv, Queen Elizabeth Girls qv, Compton, Copthall qv, Wren Academy qv (50 per cent church places) and Finchley Catholic High also do well, as does Woodhouse sixth form college qv. Hasmonean High is for orthodox Jewish children and JCoSS a cross-communal Jewish school.

Lots of faith primaries here too including Monkton Hadley C of E, St Mary's C of E, St Theresa's and Sacred Heart Catholic schools. There are several primary schools for orthodox Jewish families, including the Independent Jewish Day School and Menorah Primary. Popular secular primaries include Brookland , Garden Suburb and Moss Hall Infant and Junior Schools, Foulds, Monkfrith, Manorside and Northside.

Enfield

Enfield is on the northernmost edge of London, with the M25 dividing it from Hertfordshire and Epping Forest to the east.

It has over 100km of rivers and waterways, and copious parks and green space. It also houses the Chickenshed theatre, home to the largest youth theatre in Europe.

Its best known school is The Latymer qv, a co-ed grammar school, which attracts over 2000 applicants for 186 year 7 places. It will generally make offers only to those in its 'inner area' postcodes, which include parts of Waltham Forest, Haringey, Hackney and Islington as well as Enfield. Good non-selective secondaries in the borough include Southgate and the rapidly improving Highland School.

Walker primary in Southgate is top of many local parents' primary school lists, as are Chase Side, Eversley and Firs Farm. St George's RC, St Paul's C of E and Our Lady of Lourdes are among the most popular faith schools.

Haringey

Hilly Haringey is bordered by Highgate Golf Club in the west and the Lea Valley in the east. Its westerly wards include some of the most prosperous – Crouch End, Muswell Hill and Highgate – and its easterly wards some of the most deprived.

Fortismere qv, at the top of liberal, intellectual Muswell Hill, has long been the comprehensive of choice for those fortunate enough to live close enough. Alexandra Park School qv, its constricted site given an air of greenery by neighbouring Muswell Hill golf club and Durnsford Park, is gaining rapidly in popularity, as is Highgate Woods.

The more westerly areas in particular abound with excellent primary schools: Tetherdown qv, Rhodes Avenue qv, Coldfall qv, Coleridge, Muswell Hill, St Michael's C of E and St James C of E. Several have expanded in recent years to cope with huge demand, but catchments are often rather less than half a mile.

Alexandra Park School

Bidwell Gardens, London, N11 2AZ

State · Pupils: 1,430 · Ages: 11–18 · Non–denom

Tel: 020 8826 4880
Fax: 020 8888 2236
Email: office@apsch.org.uk
Website: www.apsch.org.uk

22

Headteacher: Since 2008, Mr Michael McKenzie MSc PGCE (early 40s). Educated at a comprehensive in Birmingham, he read chemistry at Nottingham, then did his teacher training at The Institute of Education. Head of year at William Ellis School in Camden, head of sixth form at La Swap, followed by deputy and associate head at Beal High School in Redbridge. Familiar and comfortable with the school's ethos before he applied, as the founding head had been his teaching mentor. Finds his pupils 'very entertaining, thoroughly enjoyable' and they (and their parents) feel he is a relaxed and positive addition. 'He's always about and knows a lot of the kids by name. He's very on the ball,' said one mother. Married, no children.

Academic matters: Alexandra Park's motto is 'success for all' and the school pulls off the very tricky achievement of being a successful London comprehensive welcoming the full range of abilities and social spectrum. 'Unlike other schools round here, it doesn't pick and choose. It's very inclusive,' says one parent. The intake may be all-encompassing but the academic values remain traditional. 'We don't play any games with the curriculum,' says the head, and the school is notably strong on core

subjects. 2014 results at GCSE: 72 per cent got 5+ A*-C including English and maths, with 33 per cent of grades A*/A. Most pupils take 10, including all three sciences. Spanish, French and Mandarin standard languages with Turkish also an exam option for GCSE and A level. Classics also a popular option with more than 120 pupils studying this at GCSE and A level

Has specialist status as a science and maths school and an international school. More than 200 students last year had the opportunity of studying in partner schools in France, Spain, South Africa and China. Mandarin on the curriculum here and is more than token – students can spend time on an immersion course in Beijing, with 30 studying the language pre-GCSE, a dozen or so in the sixth form.

A National Teaching School, indicating the importance the school places on appointing the best practitioners and ensuring they receive the latest training.

Some setting from year 7, depending on the department head – so maths and science are setted, English is not. Arts and media studies – unsurprisingly in this heartland of the media classes – are notably good so, to counterbalance the trend, has opted for a specialism in science and maths, with a dramatic upswing in results. Good vocational curriculum, with BTecs in sport, business, art, salon services and catering, some taught at the College of North East London. 'It means children who might have been less engaged have something positive and interesting to do, and those taking academic exams have the space to focus,' says one parent.

Strong gifted and talented programme – pupils take early exams in maths, statistics, astronomy and classics. Also notable SEN support under dynamic head of special needs, with additional support in year 7 for those who've not yet achieved the

---

Aspiring Nick Faldos can daydream their hole-in-ones gazing out from the classroom onto Muswell Hill golf course

requisite level in maths and English. Some parents, however, feel the extreme ends attract the bulk of attention: 'I think it would be quite difficult to get support if your kids come in the middle,' said one. 'You have to be very proactive.'

Popular sixth form – in 2014, a creditable 30 per cent A*/A grades and 61 per cent A* – B grades at A level; 32 subjects on offer – strongest include English, French, physics and 'a really happening' history department.

Games, options, the arts: Busy, busy, busy. Specialist music and drama with a media suite and dance on offer. Last year's huge, all-encompassing drama production of The Wiz attracted a cast of 260 kids and staff. Energetic visual arts with A levels in photography, art and product design, plus a creative and media diploma for those wishing to work on large-scale projects. Both BTec and A level music. School choir, with an international schedule. Trips a big feature, with 116 different excursions last year, including a three-week exchange to Beijing, geography in Iceland, French in the south of France, art in Madrid, politics to Washington and design in New York.

Though relatively limited on-site space for sport, games spill over into adjoining Dunsford Park and plenty of variety to suit all tastes. Basketball, football (Newcastle United striker Nile Ranger used to star in the APS team), cricket and netball are main sports, but judo, aerobics, tennis, badminton, wrestling, rugby and golf also part of the offering (aspiring Nick Faldos can daydream their hole-in-ones gazing out from the classroom onto Muswell Hill golf course). Online student newspaper. Eclectic range of after-school clubs includes

knitting, astronomy, fashion, pursuit cycling and cheerleading. 'Kids come up with the ideas,' says the head. Good careers advice with visits to universities and higher educational conferences. State-of-the-art sixth form centre, with study centre and purpose-built social space.

Background and atmosphere: Local parents lobbied the local authority to create a new school in the area and APS was eventually founded in 1999 on the site of a former FE college. A relatively constricted site, which feels more spacious due to the surrounding greenery of Muswell Hill golf course and Durnsford Park. The original mix of pleasant brick buildings, some from the 1950s, some from the 1980s, have been joined by a sleek modern extension (winner of a 2006 Civic Trust Award) and the sixth form centre.

Parents unanimous on the remarkably welcoming atmosphere – 'Everyone from the lady on the gate who checks uniform to the school receptionist makes you feel at home'. Even the police officer seeing kids onto after-school buses does it with a smile. Parents also enthuse about the school's multi-culturalism and inclusiveness ('They really try to be for everybody') and genuine concern ('It's far more nurturing than some of the other local comprehensives'). But concern is not cosseting

– 'My children came from quite a sheltered primary school, but I feel they've learnt to cope with life here and to cope with London'.

Pastoral care and discipline: Traditional values apply. 'Kids need firm boundaries and it's important for the school to set them,' says the head. 'We expect them to be at school, on time, in uniform, ready to work.' Smart red, grey and black kit is strictly enforced. 'There used to be a gang who wore their uniform in a special way and that's now all ended,' said one parent approvingly. Behaviour in general is good and school hopes to keep it that way by instilling a sense of responsibility. 'We're training pupils to choose to do the right thing.' Misdemeanours promptly and firmly dealt with – 'When my son got into a fight, there was absolutely no messing. They threw the rulebook at him'. Drugs not a notable issue. 'It's bizarre -' says the head, 'at a previous school we had an incident every week. Here perhaps they're more savvy – or more mature.' Weapons, too, conspicuously absent.

Year 7 has its own 'transition manager'. Pupils remain in the same tutor groups for five years with a director of studies for each year. Also supported by learning mentors and counsellors. About 40 pupils with statements of special needs have mainly cognitive rather than behavioural difficulties and the school copes well with autism, Asperger's and Down's. Communication between parents and schools clearly a strong point – 'All my emails, however trivial, get answered promptly'.

Pupils and parents: Wide social spread, from the comfortable middle-class suburbs near the gates to some of the most deprived kids in the country – 'a high proportion on the cusp of social needs'. Middle classes tend to dominate the PTA, which runs endless jumble sales and bazaars and is strongly involved in the day-to-day running of the school, but the kids themselves mix well. Very supportive parents – 'Parents helped set it up and want to make it work'. The school's popularity has reduced the catchment and the launch of another new school to the east is likely to make the intake more socially homogenous.

Entrance: Around 1500 applications for 216 places. Usual priority to looked-after children, those with statements of special needs and siblings, then distance from the gates, which is now less than a mile. A bulge from adjoining high-achieving primary Rhodes Avenue, as well as from Bounds Green, Our Lady of Muswell, Bowes, Coldfall and Hollickwood.

Majority of existing pupils continue into sixth form. Sixth form of 340; 80 per cent come up from year 11, the rest from other local schools. Open access, provided courses are available and attendance and attitude good enough. External applicants for A levels should have at least five GCSEs A*-C, with Bs in A level subject choice.

Exit: Some 30 per cent leave after GCSEs. In sixth form majority apply to university; destinations in 2014 included Oxbridge, Edinburgh, Bristol, Imperial, King's College London, UCL and Manchester.

Money matters: Training school and academy trust status bring in extra funding.

Remarks: A notably welcoming place for children (and adults) from a large swathe of the borough. Not an academic pressure cooker but a school with high standards for all.

Annemount School

18 Holne Chase, London, N2 0QN

Independent • Pupils: 100 • Ages: 2+ –7 years
• Non–denom • Fees (per term): £2,650 – £4,800

Tel: 020 8455 2132
Fax: 020 8381 4010
Email: headteacher@annemount.co.uk
Website: www.annemount.co.uk

Headmistress: Since 1993, Ms Geraldine Maidment (50s), previously head of Hilltop Nursery in Hampstead. First teaching experience was as an English teaching assistant in Vienna, during her University College London year abroad, whilst studying German and history of art. Worked at Sotheby's before teaching at Basset House School. A widely travelled linguist (she speaks five languages), she has visited and attended schools in many different countries. During a two-year sabbatical in Colorado, she did a master's in child and family studies at Denver University and joined a school board concerned with social and emotional issues of school age children. Has also been on UK local

government committees related to early years and works as an educational consultant for pupils who need schooling advice at any stage.

Has two grown up daughters and five step-grandchildren, who have all attended Annemount. Parents say: 'She's very on the ball and intelligent.' 'She's not going to be your best friend,' commented one (another 'begged to differ, especially over a 2005 Lynch Bages'), 'but she's incredible with the children'; 'She's very strict, but in a good way'; 'She's very good at explaining what is going on and how we can help.'

Entrance: Main intakes into the nursery (2.75+ years), kindergarten (3+ years) and reception (4+ years). Two classes of 16 or so in each year group. Both parents are expected to come on the school tour: 'I tell them you're making the biggest decision of your life for your most precious possession. You both need to be involved'. More or less first come first served into the nursery classes, with preference for siblings. Assessments for kindergarten upwards: 'They must be able to fit in socially and behaviour-wise, and they must be able to cope. Our classes are very busy, and the children need energy and stamina'. Discourages applications from families who live further than about four miles away – 'Children shouldn't spend hours a day sitting in a car'.

Exit: Some move at 4 or 5, but most at 7, to local independent schools, eg Habs' Boys' and Girls', Belmont, Highgate, Channing, South Hampstead High, St Margaret's, UCS, North London Collegiate, City of London Girls', St Mary's and Lyndhurst. A few to local state primaries, eg Garden Suburb or Brookland.

Remarks: One of a quiet street of large, brick-built early 20th century houses in the midst of leafy and wealthy Hampstead Garden Suburb. The school, with small but bright and colourful classrooms, was built by grateful parents for the previous ex-governess owner, who was head until she died in 1993 at the age of 93. Large garden, divided into a nursery playground with Wendy house and grassy area and a playground for the older children with a climbing frame, sand table, sports equipment, planting areas and gazebo.

Inevitably, its ultimate raison d'être is to prepare the children for 7+ exams, but this does not overshadow school life – 'People feel we really understand children, their stages of development and their needs'. The early years concentrate on personal and emotional development: learning to listen, developing good social awareness and independent thinking skills – 'We encourage them to be well organised, plan ahead, problem solve'.

A broad curriculum with lots of practical emphasis. Cookery is used to learn maths, debating helps with language, chess with strategy and problem-solving, sports with coordination. Reception had just finished making its own playdough when we visited, another class had taken photos of the other houses in the road and made models of them, and in another were newly-hatched chicks. In year 2 children choose a project they present to the class – which can be on anything from Nelson Mandela to Arsenal. 'By the time they have heard about all the different projects, they know a lot about a lot of things.'

Children are assessed for developmental delays from an early stage and outside help may be recommended for anything from a lack of pencil control to poor social skills. 'We have a good bank of respected practitioners, and interventions work particularly well when they are very young. We recommend them to protect children's self-esteem and help them reach their potential.' Probably not ideal for a very boisterous child, or for one who cannot cope with change. 'We have had fantastic success with one or two Asperger's children, but this is not generally the place for them. We offer places if we feel we can fully meet the child's needs. It is most important that children's school experiences shouldn't be stressful.'

Teachers a mix of youth and old hands – 'Some have worked with me for over 20 years, and we're like a family. We're more pedagogues than teachers'. Praise from parents: 'The children really love my daughter's teacher and want to please her'.

Children have plenty of opportunities for, and find great delight in, taking responsibility as head boy, head girl or a member of the school council, which has regular lunches with the head. Many performance opportunities too, in concerts, plays and poetry recitals – 'We like to celebrate the arts'.

Strong emphasis on all matters green: composting, reusing, exercise, healthy eating. Lunch boxes must contain 'real food': nothing processed or ready-wrapped. We saw children tucking in salmon risotto, sushi, tortillas and pasta salad. 'Seemed annoying at first,' said a parent, 'but my daughter is talking about why certain foods are good for you and why some are not, and how she feels when she eats something too sugary.'

Unusually wide range of extracurricular activities for a pre-prep. Around a third of the children learn the violin at school – 'It gives them zillions of study skills, such as concentration and perseverance, and those who keep it up tend to do exceptionally well academically'. Everyone does dance and drama, gym and swimming, French and

> *Lunch boxes must contain 'real food': nothing processed or ready-wrapped. We saw children tucking in salmon risotto, sushi, tortillas and pasta salad*

computing; also a very active and serious co-ed football team. 'When the children leave they have a whole breadth of experiences that stand them in very good stead later on.'

The head brought back with her from the States a belief in strong links with parents and the local community. Parents report lots of emphasis on getting together as families for meals and outdoor activities. The school runs parent education sessions, social events and plenty of whole school initiatives such as sponsored walks. Parents and grandparents come in to lead assemblies, help with topics, accompany school trips to anywhere from Hampstead Heath to the British Museum, talk about their jobs or hobbies. The PTA organises charity events, picnics and parties, and arranges school visits by theatre groups and farm animals.

'It's a very warm and friendly place,' said a parent. 'My daughter has thrived here and our experience has been brilliant. They do a nice mix of activities and she's really excited about learning.'

Ashmole Academy

Cecil Road, London, N14 5RJ

State • Pupils: 1,460 • Ages: 11–18 • Non-denom

Tel: 020 8361 2703
Fax: 020 8368 0315
Email: office@ashmoleacademy.org
Website: www.ashmoleacademy.org

Head Teacher: Since 1997, Mr Derrick Brown MA MBA DipEd – degree subjects psychology and business. Formerly a scientist, but changed career when he realised it wasn't all about 'filling pretty liquids into tubes. It was actually quite isolating and I'm a people person.' He was advised at the time to become either a teacher or a prison governor. He opted for the former. Prior to headship at Ashmole, he was vice principal at Leigh City Technology College in Dartford and then senior deputy at Cranford School – both schools much the same size and diversity of Ashmole and in comparable outer London suburbs.

Recently turned 60, but 'nowhere near retiring... I wouldn't know what to do with myself'. Quietly spoken, serious and tirelessly focused on getting things done, an outstandingly successful head. His drive and determination stem from his own 'not great' secondary school education which prompted him to challenge the state school system – in this case to turn a bog standard local comp into one with all the academic benefits of a private school education, without the fees. As he says: 'Why should only a privileged few have these opportunities? I want to make it available to all kids.'

Mr Brown vowed when he started at Ashmole to make an immediate impact on results; 'It was a fairly average performing school with not very high aspirations.' He took a hard look at the areas that were lacking and the following year results were already up by 10 per cent; 'I created partnerships with parents, worked on the discipline and talent scouted good teachers.' His 'football manager's mentality' of never being satisfied, and always something to improve on, has awarded Ashmole the title of 'super-state' school according to the Evening Standard.

One gets the feeling that this head has little time or inclination for many hobbies. With two grown up children of his own, any extracurricular activities he may pursue are of the more 'unusual' kind – which currently he says is re-vamping an old wreck he bought – (we're presuming he means property) Although there's no resting on laurels for this head, he has already consolidated Ashmole's reputation as a provider of comprehensive education at its best.

Academic matters: This school hasn't been awarded the title of super-state for no reason. As the head says: 'Every subject excels here, no subject is weak.' Ofsted outstanding – it has managed to sustain many years of exceptionally high results. Strong value added. Entirely non-selective, so the results

---

No chance of getting lost here. The only confusing things are the different coloured named staircases, like the 'orange staircase,' which in fact is blue

---

are impressive. Way ahead of the other non-selective schools in the area. 'There are no tricks here – all the students come from the local community.' Anyone can do well here, we were told – boys, girls the less motivated, 'everyone exceeds their personal best.' Classes are setted in main subjects – 'mixed ability doesn't work except in certain areas', says the head.

In 2014 78 per cent achieved five or more A*-C grades at GCSE, including English and maths, 37 per cent A*/A grades. A levels 30 per cent A*/A and 61 per cent A*-B grades. French is popular and there's a very strong exchange link with the twinned town

of Le Raincy, a suburb just outside Paris. Spanish and German are also offered at GCSE and A level, but less popular.

Students are closely monitored and undergo assessments after every half term. The head says: 'If we see underperformance, we can intervene and work with the child individually to make them improve.' However, one parent we spoke to disagreed. 'Ashmole is a great school if you are the academic, studious type. However, if like my daughter, you don't fit the mould, you're going to have more of a struggle there.' Teachers are also closely monitored and parents feel that there is quite a high turnover, although the school says it is similar to most London schools. But if this is the case, it is not an unhealthy state of affairs anyway, according to the head. He says: 'A stable school with no turnover can be a recipe for complacency and disaster.'

A third of the school has English as an additional language – support in place to make sure they progress, either through extra help or (mostly) in-class intervention. Around a seventh have some kind of SEN – about 1.5 per cent with statements. Learning support is located within own area, providing adequate space that caters for all needs. The weakest 30 students drop languages after year 8, taking BTec business instead, although this varies every year. These students have extra help with the basics.

Able, gifted and talented pupils – those who have all round ability across the core subjects of English, maths and science (around 1 in 4 students at Ashmole) – have their own programme designed for them. This bespoke Ashmolean programme involves a variety of activities which 'encourage aspiration,' whether this be by visiting higher education institutes or learning through Firefly, the

> His 'football manager's mentality' of never being satisfied, and always something to improve on, has awarded Ashmole the title of 'super state' school

---

school's virtual learning environment. However, one unhappy parent called it an 'exclusive' club and a very 'rigid' system; 'most students who are on the programme come on it straight from primary school and there seems to be little movement.' She also said that much is made of the G&T students and the privileges offered to them, which makes the other students feel less worthy. Another parent disagreed, saying that her child has been 'on and off the programme many times according to her grades.'

Games, options, the arts: The opportunities are plentiful and the facilities wonderful. Huge floodlit Astroturf court, playing field, sports hall and separate studio for dance, aerobics and net sports, but no pool. Outdoor table tennis on offer, which proves to be a very popular lunchtime activity. Outstandingly successful in both boys' and girls' football and this year alone saw the boys' football team winning the Barnet Cup and the girls' team reaching the semi-final of the Middlesex Cup. Rugby also a biggie and the year 8 rugby team won the Barnet Saracens tournament this year. One parent told us: 'Even if your child is not the academic type, the sports on offer can give them the opportunity to shine.'

Much acclaimed music department. Amy Winehouse was a former student (although head, who was here at the same time, says: 'Amy left us quite early on to join the BRIT school'). Having a music specialism, they are able to employ the very latest technology. Music scholarships on offer to help those with talent develop their skills, and an increasing number of pupils take individual music lessons. A full range of extracurricular music programmes also on offer, including an orchestra, jazz band, chamber string group, junior string group, brass band, senior wind ensemble, Latin rock band, two choirs and show band for the annual school musical.

Drama popular – big, well-equipped studio and major musical production each year. Standards are high – this year saw a 'fantastic' production of Hairspray. Impressive art studios and some astounding individual pieces of art. The school has its radio station and two recording studios. Plenty of lunchtime and after-school clubs, including film club, debating societies, mad for books club, Philosophy, homework clubs and numerous language clubs. Enrichment groups offer a choice of cultural, entrepreneurial and environmental activities. 'The options here are great,' a sixth former told us. 'We're bombarded with courses and clubs which enrich us as people.' He was not wrong.

Background and atmosphere: This is a different school, quite literally, from the Ashmole of yesteryear. It had survived in pretty dire conditions for years but, on his arrival in 1997, the head organised the sale of six acres of school land and began a visionary building programme with the proceeds. Design of new buildings the result of collaboration between the school, a very pro-active parent committee and the architect. Re-homing happened in 2004 at a cost of £14m. The result is a bright and spacious, well-mapped-out building 'which is easy to navigate,' one parent told us. All subjects

grouped into their own sections and everything immaculately labelled. No chance of getting lost here. The only confusing things are the different coloured named staircases, like the 'orange staircase,' which in fact is blue. The head told us: 'When

---

Design of new buildings the result of collaboration between the school, a very pro–active parent committee and the architect

we designed the building we wanted to colour group it into sections so, for example, meet at the orange staircase, but this wasn't DDA compliant for partially sighted people, so everything has to be kept white and blue.' Lifts are also available for students with disabilities.

Large, wide corridors with beautiful wall displays, seriously impressive artwork and a convivial atmosphere. As we progressed from section to section we witnessed quiet classrooms (with the odd exception), with atmosphere that encourages work and discourages messing around. 'We have a policy at this school that lessons should be silent, unless they require a discussion. It helps to keep the class focused.' We also noticed a lot of reading going on – by individuals in the canteen and elsewhere. The head told us that he insists every student carry a book of their choice around with them. 'There is no such thing as doing nothing,' he said. 'One can always read.'

Set in 28 acres of land in quiet, residential Southgate, the outside of the school is none too shabby either, especially for a London comprehensive. Plenty of outdoor space. Remarkably free of litter and immaculately kept lawns, outdoor classroom and environmental area, fully equipped with wooden table and benches. So much excess land that plans are under way to create an Ashmole primary school on the premises. 'There is such a lack of primary schools in the area, it makes sense,' says the head. We say: Start booking your kids in now.

The new sixth form block, kitted out with its own Starbucks, was opened in July 2014. This has been many years in the waiting, has taken £1.3 million to raise (through fundraising events and tightening of the old school purse strings), two contractors and various other obstacles. One student told us: 'It's so exciting, I'm just upset I'll only have one year to enjoy it.'

Pastoral care and discipline: Big on discipline. 'Not for the free spirit,' one mother told us. Strict adherence to their uniform code expected – no exceptions or students will be asked to go home and change. Lo and behold: if pupils are caught outside the school premises with a shirt hanging out, they will be seriously reprimanded, sometimes even face a detention. Mobiles, too, are strictly forbidden, except for the sixth form – confiscated immediately if found and, to add to the humiliation, parents have to go in to school and pick them up. While this has been a bone of contention with many of the parents, who like to get hold of their kids after school hours, others feel it is a good thing. 'If nothing else because there have been some phone thefts in the area, but muggers know not to bother with Ashmole kids as they never have phones on them,' one parent told us.

Zero tolerance of drugs, weapons and violence – on or off the premises. Much has been done to combat bullying, which has clearly been a problem at Ashmole in former years (as in many comprehensives of this size). CCTV cameras operate along main corridors 'to monitor any deviant behaviour that may occur' and when the new building was designed head specifically requested wide, open spaces free of 'little cul-de-sacs,' where vulnerable students could be cornered. As Orwellian as this may sound, bullying is now virtually non-existent and parents are very grateful.

Disruptive or abusive pupils are sent to the individual learning room, where they are under supervision, have no contact with their friends and hate it. Two or three days there usually does the trick, but head will exclude for serious offences – roughly five permanent exclusions a year. 'We just

---

'I wish I had bought on Cecil Road years ago. Houses must be worth a fortune now,' one parent sighs

---

can't let a disruptive child continue,' he says. 'They are given community service and various other deterrents, but if they are hell bent on being disruptive, they're out.' The result of this is a school in which pupils feel secure and comfortable and everyone knows the score.

Each key stage has its own learning mentors and key stage managers whom pupils know they can go to if they feel the need. Parents aren't so convinced. One parent we spoke to said: 'It's not always made clear who we should be speaking to, or emailing. I have left messages on several occasions and no one has responded. I think the communication between parents and year heads could be improved.' However, for the most part, parents and students we spoke to seemed extremely happy with

---

'There is such a lack of primary schools in the area, it makes sense,' says the head. We say: Start booking your kids in now

---

the school. One sixth former told us: 'I've loved every minute of this school. The sixth form is like a big family, even for external students.'

A large amount of interaction between the year groups, encouraged by the cultural and charitable activities.Pupils feel they have friends in all years. Charity work plays a vital part in the general ethos of the school and every year students and staff raise thousands of pounds for a variety of good causes. Overall, the school has a general sense of self discipline and a fostering of civilised behaviour.

Pupils and parents: Vast ethnic mix, as you'd expect from the Southgate area, though more Cypriots – Greek and Turkish – than anything else. Main religion is Christianity of all sorts, the second is Islam. Mostly working parents, but a supportive and hard working PTA makes big contribution to the school's development. Pupils are cheery, ambitious, focused and involved. Notable former students include; Amy Winehouse, former S Club 7 member Rachel Stevens, musician Stephen Sidwell, goalie Mark Bunn, Oscar winning producer Mark King, The Feeling lead vocalist Daniel Sells and Channel 5 tsar Sham Sandhu.

Entrance: More than 1,100 apply for the 232 places – of which siblings will take around 80. You'll get in if you have a sibling there, are a looked-after child or live very close – otherwise no chance. 'I wish I had bought on Cecil Road years ago. Houses must be worth a fortune now', one parent sighs. Up to 20 music aptitude places; these pupils, along with others who show talent, are placed on the music scholarship programme.

Exit: Around 15 per cent leave after GCSEs, mostly for vocational courses elsewhere. The rest need to get Bs in the subjects they wish to study for A levels to stay on in the sixth form. Around half of sixth formers to top universities; generally a few to Oxbridge and several medics; others to places like Durham. Warwick, London Universities, Nottingham, Leeds. Science, law and humanities are popular too.

Remarks: Slick, sensible and effective. Check out the housing market.

Belmont Mill Hill Preparatory School

Linked schools: Grimsdell, Mill Hill Pre-Preparatory School, 515 and Mill Hill School, 536

The Ridgeway, London, NW7 4ED

Independent • Pupils: 415 • Ages: 7–13 • Non-denom
• Fees (per term):£5,207

Tel: 020 8906 7270
Fax: 020 8906 3519
Email: office@belmontschool.com
Website: www.belmontschool.com

Head: Since 2004, Mrs Lynn Duncan BSc PGCE. Taught for 14 years in the state sector, then moved to boys' independent school Durston House for the next six years. Following this, she became deputy head of Belmont then head three years later. Married with two grown up sons, she is partial to a bit of hill walking and foreign travel (particularly anywhere with a rainforest).

Down-to-earth, matter of fact and approachable. Even in her 10 years of being at the school (and many years of being in the education sector), she remains as enthusiastic about her job – borne out of the fact that her children delight her and she 'marvels at the energy of our pupils when they come into school.' One parent commented how 'protective of her staff' she is, which can sometimes lead to disagreements with parents. However, another parent told us that the head is very inclusive with parents – welcomes their feedback and 'takes on board any grievance we may have.' Annual coffee mornings are held for parents to fire any questions to Mrs Duncan and 'she will answer them directly.'

Whilst the head points out that parental expectations are the same in both the state sector and the private sector, the stark difference, she says, are the facilities on offer, which give her and her staff more opportunity to be 'hands on.' She is currently a serving inspector for the ISI.

Retiring in July 2015.

Entrance: Automatic entry from pre-prep (Grimsdell) to prep (except in some very rare cases). This accounts for two-thirds of the school's intake. For external candidates, there are two main points of entry into the school – 7+ (year 3) and 11+ (year 7). Occasionally there are places available in other years – these are called 'chance vacancies'. Heavily oversubscribed from external candidates, so each expected to take reading, creative writing and maths tests together with a reference from their previous school.

Exit: Most, if not all, Belmont students continue on to Mill Hill School, although all have to sit the CE exam (for setting purposes. It is not a qualifying exam for entry). 'Children for whom Mill Hill is not the right school will leave at the end of year 6; once in year 7, the children have a place at Mill Hill at 13+ conditional on continuing good work ethic and good behaviour.' One parent felt that the fact that Belmont goes up to 13 is a massive advantage. 'At 13 they are desperate to make the next jump and are confident to do it. They are not little 11 and 12 year olds floundering around.'

Remarks: Established in 1912 following the success of its senior school Mill Hill, Belmont Junior House opened its gates with one student – Harold Pearse Soundy. By the summer term 1913, it had 12 pupils. Originally a boarding prep for boys, it has been a day school since the 80s and co-ed since 1995.

Situated on the relatively quiet part of Mill Hill's Ridgeway, the school is in an enviable location – set back from the road and flanked by large houses, beautiful greenery and a stone's throw away from the small but popular Belmont Farm. Hard to believe that a 25 minute train ride will take

---

Another commented incredulously that 'We've been to play other schools that don't even have their own cricket grounds' – which made him feel very lucky

---

you to the centre of London. Harder still after meandering through some 35 acres of parkland to the rear of the school – taking in the panoramic views of the Totteridge Valley. Undoubtedly the school's selling point, the grounds and its facilities are impressive for a London-based junior school.

For a sporty child, this must be their nirvana. The grounds host seven rugby pitches, 10 football pitches (of various sizes to accommodate different age groups), three cricket pitches, five cricket nets, five rounders pitches, two Astro mini hockey pitches, six Astro tennis courts, six netball courts, a fully equipped gymnasium and a small dance hall. Finally, a 1500 metre woodland cross-country course known as 'The Oti' (in memory of a former student who died of sickle cell anaemia). Pupils also have the use of the brand new 25 metre indoor swimming pool at Mill Hill School for swimming lessons and clubs. As one parent told us, 'Forget this school if your child has absolutely no interest in sport; they'll be unhappy', commenting that it is the most disciplined department in the school.

Outdoor facilities also include a large wooden adventure playground, a variety of large established games including a giant chessboard, for children to use during break and lunchtime, and a gardening area where pupils tend seasonal plants and flowers. We spotted a little recycling area and

then learned that Belmont has been awarded the much coveted Eco-Schools Green Flag Award.

After the spectacular exterior, the interior of the school comes somewhat as an anticlimax. The original eighteenth century house acts as the main entrance to the school and houses the function rooms, main reception area, staff rooms and the head's office. Whilst this has been tastefully refurbished (with the original beautiful winding staircase acting as the centrepiece), several of the classrooms on the upper level seemed on the cramped side and lacking in imagination. The science labs (in the Cloister Block) and the gymnasium particularly struck us as archaic and in need of a refurb.

That said, the Jubilee Hall, which accommodates most of the lower school classrooms, the dining/assembly hall and the head of lower school's office, is modern and airy. The school has a genial vibe, perhaps because it is not as formal as some of the other Independent schools we have visited. Colourful and interesting displays of student work adorn the corridors, and the pupils we witnessed, whilst not particularly noisy, were 'spirited'.

Belmont pupils 'speak with confidence, whether in a classroom discussion, reading in an assembly or conversing with adults' said their most recent ISI inspection. This was particularly evident on our tour when we met with school's council members – a bunch of 8+ year old boys and girls who were bright, articulate and bounced off each other like the future spokespeople they may one day become. They were confident, polite and hard pushed to find anything negative to say about the school. One bemoaned the fact that lunch should be better organised, whilst another commented incredulously that 'We've been to play other schools that don't even have their own cricket grounds' – which made him feel very lucky.

A Belmont child is a busy one. School opens at 7.30am for optional breakfast, and from there on in, a cascade of activities barely allows for an oxygen intake. Fifty clubs are on offer during lunchtime and after school, so if elastic or kicking a ball ain't your thing – why not try ancient Greek? Or perhaps origami, Dead Poets Society (we presume without Robin Williams), jazz band, Belle Plates or Bollywood dance, to name but a few. Popular after-school activities include chamber choir and horse riding. Fabulous trips (including a history trip to Venice) are offered from year 6 and above.

Clearly time is set aside for the curricular stuff, as results are well above national expectations. This, we are told, is achieved through 'excellent teaching', (ISI 2012), a broad curriculum that includes French from year 3 and Latin from year 6 and smallish class sizes. Teachers have annual performance reviews and their planning is monitored termly. No sluggards allowed here. A couple of parents we spoke to said that academia across the Foundation has definitely been stepped up a notch since Dr Luckett (head of Mill Hill school and chief exec of all three schools) came on board. One parent told us: 'Belmont was always more of a nurturing school, but the goalposts seem to be constantly changing and you feel like you are kept on your toes the whole time.' In Mrs Duncan's view, 'High academic performance is our number one target.'

A cascade of activities barely allows for an oxygen intake. Fifty clubs are on offer, so if elastic or kicking a ball ain't your thing – why not try ancient Greek?

Sats abolished in favour of continuous assessments from year 3. Most pupils are expected to continue through the Foundation, although places at Mill Hill are not unconditional. Any early problems, academically or behaviourally, are usually flagged up whilst the child is at Grimsdell school (the pre-prep), so there are 'rarely any surprises.' Mrs Duncan says that because Belmont is part of a Foundation of three schools, it is important to look at the bigger picture. 'If we didn't feel a child could cope, we wouldn't allow them to progress to year 7.' Although, she adds, these cases are few and far between.

The school has a small learning support department and is happy to accommodate children with mild cases of dyslexia and dyspraxia. Anything more severe, and 'we're not the school for them.' Small groups of gifted and talented children are arranged across the years, and most are prepared for the 11+ and 13+ scholarship awards.

Belmont is a Christian foundation based upon the principles of 'religious freedom'. Chapel services are obligatory, because if you start pulling pupils out, 'you lose the ability to say we can work together', says the head. However, the school's pupils represent a wide range of faiths and cultures, so chapel services and assemblies are inter-denominational.

During our tour, we noticed the school undergoing current building works – six new classrooms, two science labs and a 'state of the art hall'. Shortly after our visit, we discovered that Belmont, along with the other two schools in the Mill Hill foundation, is merging with the Mount School for girls in September 2014 (hmmm). School insists, however, that it 'is not planning a permanent expansion. We may have to, in the short term, absorb some Mount girls across the year groups, but there is no plan to make the school larger than current in the future.'

The imminent merger came as a great shock for parents who were informed by email, with no prior warning. One parent said: 'I bought into the Foundation of what it is today and not what it is about to become.' She expressed concern about how and where 100 new girls will be placed across the three schools. On the positive side, it may go some way towards evening out the currently boy-heavy ratio of pupils throughout the three Mill Hill schools.

Channing Junior School

Linked school: Channing School, 498

1 Highgate High Street, London, N6 5JR

Independent · Pupils: 240 · Ages: 4–11 · Fees (per term): £4,910

Tel: 020 8342 9862
Fax: 020 8348 3122
Email: fairseat@channing.co.uk
Website: www.channing.co.uk

23

Head: Since 2008, Mrs Louise Lawrance BPrim Ed (mid 30s). She left her native South Africa some 15 years ago and taught at state schools in Burton-on-Trent and Kennington before going to GEMS Hampshire School, where she worked for seven years, the last three as the head of the pre-preparatory school. Clearly immensely proud of her school and her girls, she seems to know each one and they chat to her happily and informally – a pleasure to behold. Also proud of her staff – 'we're very lucky. We're able to attract fantastic teachers and everyone is hugely talented in one area or another.' Appreciated staff are happy staff and make happy children. Back from maternity leave – her son was born in January 2014.

Entrance: Register as soon after birth as you like but no questions of lists closing at 12 months or whatever. Tour round the school with the head and then assessment at rising 4 in groups of 12 to spy out teachability, capacity to listen, collaborate, obey instructions. Wisely, tots are seen in two age-related groups so no panics if EmmyLou is an

August baby. Call-back of the most likely – there are only 24 places for a list of 250+ applicants. Offers made on the basis of potential – don't cram them with numbers and letters.

Exit: Eighty per cent progress to the senior school. Others opt for boarding, state sector or leave because their families are relocating.

Remarks: Housed opposite the senior school on the other side of Highgate Hill, the junior school occupies Fairseat (formerly the home of the Lord Mayor of London and backing onto the green charms of Waterlow Park), named in honour of said Lord Mayor Sir Sidney, who donated the park to the nation. And a jolly nice house it must once have been – memories linger in fireplaces, cornices, and a sense of gentlemanly solidity. And very fine views too. In 1927, it became part of the school – originally a boarding house – until boarding went in the 1960s. It communicates a relaxed and civilised ethos and this is reflected in the manner and conduct of its girls who are open-faced, relaxed and articulate. Top floor is where Mrs Elliott, senior school head, lives during the week and knowledge of this, too, must contribute to homely atmosphere.

Good displays everywhere and lots of colour. Much into 'thinking', as so many are now and with an encouraging board which poses questions such as 'What colour is Happiness?' Lots of expensive Apple Macs, excellent library in which intent reading was happening when we popped in, and especially pleasing was the thoughtful cross-curric-

> *Lively art – we loved year 1's charcoal drawings of bears – each one different, each one full of individuality*

ular work we met at all levels. Thinking clearly being done here – and not just by girls. Birds were being studied by year 3 and they make bird boxes in DT, assemble data bases of bird stats (maths), import clips of birdsong (IT) and make pictures (art), write instructions on feeding and caring for birds (English) and look at birds and habitat (biology). (This GSG

writer – an English teacher – was once upbraided by a pupil when she cited a Latin derivation – 'you can't know about Latin – you're an English teacher!' No such nonsense at Channing, we can tell.)

Exceptional music – 105 weekly music lessons and all orchestral instruments on offer. Really inviting large music room with ancient beams. Music and drama much praised – 'they are astounding – I am amazed by what the teachers can get out of the girls'. Lively art – we loved year 1's charcoal drawings of bears – each one different, each one full of individuality. Orderly but not obsessively tidy. Smiley faces. Quiet, concentrating classes.

Good outside space – and super outlook. Five courts, tarmac space, fields. Nature walk, bees' nest and fox's den! Good adventure playground with tower, fireman's pole, climbing wall, obstacle course and safe surface – oh to be 7 again! Multipurpose hall – assemblies, quick turnaround for dining (very yummy food) and PE space.

Parents happy too. 'We're thrilled to have found somewhere that really cares about the girls.' 'The school makes the girls aware of how much they have to offer.' 'I can always go in – the school is very friendly to parents.' 'My daughters love art, reading and music – they are so happy there.' 'It doesn't pressure the girls.' 'It's such a sensible school.'

Channing School

Linked school: Channing Junior School, 497

Highgate, London, N6 5HF

Independent • Pupils: 560 • Ages: 11–18 • Non–denom • Fees (per term): £5,340

Tel: 020 8340 2328
Fax: 020 8341 5698
Email: admissions@channing.co.uk
Website: www.channing.co.uk

24

Headmistress: Since 2005, Mrs Barbara Elliott MA PGCE (early 50s), a Cambridge linguist. Taught previously at St Albans Girls, St Columba's College (boys), East Barnet comprehensive, Aberdeen College of Commerce and Haberdashers' Girls – an impressively varied career. She is relaxed, engaging, sophisticated, capable, retaining a faint Lancastrian directness in her voice; the proud mother of four sons and someone who clearly relishes the charge of so many 'lovely' girls. Has a very level-headed view of her school – 'It's an intellectual place but we're not ferociously competitive. Everyone can try everything – they're not stopped from doing things just because they're not good at them.' 'Mrs Elliott is wonderful' is pupil and parental consensus.

Academic matters: Trad academic curriculum – everyone takes two Englishes, maths, science and a lang at GCSE; popular options are art, business and communications, geography, history and Spanish. Exceptional results in English lang and additional science; more than 85 per cent A*/A grades overall in 2014. Teaching reckoned excellent across the curriculum and nice small classes.

Again, no surprises at A level – 20 options, economics well-established and exceptionally successful; the teachers are examiners and 'they know how to deliver'; 92 per cent A*-B, 62 per cent A*/A in 2014. Apparently, the first girls' school to offer an AS in financial studies. Other popular subjects are English and maths, but no slouches among the disciplines. German, Latin and Greek survive, art flourishes and science numbers are highly respectable – clearly no fitting a mould here.

Staff very much given their head to choose the syllabuses they feel best suit their pupils – IGCSEs now taken in English, sciences and languages – and encouraged to pursue their own continuing education, always a good idea. ICT embraced enthusiastically with suites of Apple Macs and girls produce 'unbelievably sophisticated presentations and assemblies.'

No one with a statement but around 22 girls with an IEP, all supported by additional learning co-ordinator. Most have mild dyslexia or processing difficulties. Everyone screened on entry but 'our classes are so small the staff pick up quickly on any problems.' No withdrawals and girls 'access guidance and support' in lunchtimes and breaks. Wheelchairs would be difficult here as main school building is on five floors with narrow stairways and no lift. Apparently no-one hitherto with an ASD – 'so far they haven't applied.'

Games, options, the arts: Most done on site – PE mostly in the main school hall, has courts and pitches and new multi-use games area, though the girls also walk to Parliament Hill and Stanhope fields for broader pastures. No cavernous sports hall yet – major building project in progress to provide a new sports hall, music school and performing arts theatre – but good multi-gym and, all in all, no deprivation of facilities.

Lovely relaxed art studios at the top of the building with unique views right across London. Textiles, computer graphics, dark room, printing, drawing and painting – all with a rare freedom and sense of exploration. We saw no prescribed, formulaic work here – much inventive and witty. We liked, especially, the sculptures made out of white straws – a brilliant skeletal snake and a very scary skull. Music reportedly exceptional; lots learn individual instruments and are genuinely enthusiastic

---

School now appoints its own 'poet laureate' – not, we understand, rewarded with the traditional butt of sack but £200 to spend at High Tea of Highgate

---

– sixth formed their own A Capella choir recently, just for fun. 'They have wonderful instrumental teachers,' enthuse parents. 'They fasten onto what an individual child could be good at and nurture it.' Drama a major school preoccupation – good, lively productions with mass involvement, also studied eagerly up to GCSE and A levels.

The Highgate location is a dream for luring in visiting speakers – in the week we visited had played host to Carol Ann Duffy and Kazuo Ishiguro. Diane (Kindertransport) Samuels was writer-in-residence at time of our visit and school now appoints its own 'poet laureate' – not, we understand, rewarded with the traditional butt of sack but £200 to spend at High Tea of Highgate: sounds good. Clubs galore,

very much following the current enthusiasms of girls or staff. 'It's whatever we've got and,' says head, 'whatever you want. If there's an appetite for something we're very happy to run it.' Sixth form girls would like more opportunities, they told us – once-weekly enrichment classes enliven their studies but, seemingly, they have immense appetites for new things and could take more. Duke of Edinburgh Award pursued with as much gusto as everything else – 14 (out of 38) year 13 girls taking the gold award when we visited. Lots of charity activities which combine do-gooding with fun. 'The school really promotes initiative,' girls told us.

Background and atmosphere: Occupies a considerable frontage along Highgate Hill, yards down from the shops and easy-peasy if you live anywhere in this chic and desirable London village. In 2010, it celebrated its 125th anniversary and has a fascinating history. Founded in 1885 by a Unitarian minister and two of his congregation – daughters of a banker and Egyptologist – for the education of the daughters of Unitarian ministers, it remains the only Unitarian school in the country. Unitarianism, which originated in Hungary, fosters liberalism, religious tolerance and democracy and its tenets still inform the school's atmosphere today, though Unitarians themselves are thin on the ground. The present head of RE is a female Unitarian minister.

'Never forget,' reads the text over the sixth form centre, 'life is expecting much of you and me.' Thus said Miss Matilda Sharpe, one of the founding sisters

'If I come up against a sticky problem, I will sometimes look at what the Unitarians said,' says Mrs Elliott. The school was named after an American – William Ellery Channing – who, Mrs Elliott informed us, 'has a lot of useful things to say about education and women's rights, and the school always listens to extracts from his lectures on our Founder's Day in early July'.

The main building itself is attractive internally, though a rabbit warren away from the few spacious rooms – you go up and down narrow staircases and through little corridors that must take some time to learn. Plenty of remnants of the gentlemen's houses the school buildings once were – good marble fireplaces, elegantly paned windows and cornicing here and there – but it feels cosy and homely and lively displays of girls' art everywhere which warm the heart as one scurries along.

Library is housed in a good, light room overlooking the High Street – modern furniture, airy and well-stocked. We loved the ceramic models of shops on the High Street behind the librarian's desk. Three other buildings on site house the main hall, classrooms, the sixth form centre with kitchen and separate canteen – we have never seen so many coffee mugs anywhere – IT suite, gym/theatre and sports facilities.

Reasonable amount of outside space given village location, and a rather tragic small garden with a greenhouse and chicken run. But we did visit in late November – 'If you come in the summer it's amazing,' girls assured us. And Mrs Elliott confirms that the organic garden and chickens have fed the real appetite the girls have to become 'greener'.

Pastoral care and discipline: House system recently reintroduced here as elsewhere – always a giggle for this ancient writer, who recalls the abandonment of such things in the '60s when they were seen as reactionary and divisive. 'We love it!' bubble the girls. 'You meet so many girls in other years and it's such a good way to get everyone more friendly' – competitiveness here is clearly less than ruthless. Palpably friendly relations between staff and girls and a relaxed and collaborative feel pervades lessons. Girls evidently glad to be here and seldom rock the boat. 'My daughter had a problem,' a mother told us, 'and the school was magnificent. I cannot speak too highly of how they dealt with it.'

Pupils and parents: Mostly local but they come from all over north and central London as well as Herts and Middlesex. Predominantly white middle class, but a good sprinkling of everyone else too and everyone melts and blends happily together.

Old girls include Baroness Cox, Peggy Vance, Tanya Moseivitch, Harriet Sergeant, Eileen Hulse and Princess Sarvath of Jordan.

Entrance: In addition to the 20-odd who come up from the junior school, takes 60 external candidates at 11+; around 350 apply via the North London Consortium of Schools' entrance exams. About 120 places offered. Joiners from all the local preps and primaries – from around 100 schools. Head or member of senior team meets all prospective parents. At 16+, minimum of six Bs needed including A*/A in A level subjects. Well worth trying for a sixth form place here and many do. Occasional places occur and school keeps a list of hopefuls whom they contact and assess as appropriate.

Exit: The majority stay at for the sixth form but some leave for co-ed or boarding schools, state schools or sixth form colleges. Thereafter, to top universities – in 2014, law and classics at Cambridge, physics at Oxford, choral and music scholars at both, lots of medics, and academic degree courses at Bristol, Durham, Edinburgh and predominantly Russell Group universities. Some to USA and Europe too.

Money matters: Academic and music scholarships up to 10 per cent of tuition. Bursaries up to 100 per cent of fees – means-tested.

Remarks: 'Never forget,' reads the text over the sixth form centre, 'life is expecting much of you and me.' Thus said Miss Matilda Sharpe, one of the founding sisters. Its gentle exhortation characterises this school in which all is relished, much achieved and nothing forced. A parent told us, 'They get their Oxbridge places but in a different way.' Hard to imagine a better start for an outgoing, lively-minded girl.

Coldfall Primary School

Coldfall Avenue, London, N10 1HS

State • Pupils: 680 • Ages: 3–11 • Non–denom

Tel: 020 8883 0608
Fax: 020 8442 2189
Email: office@coldfall.haringey.sch.uk
Website: www.coldfall.haringey.sch.uk

25

Head: Since 1996, Evelyn Davies (50s). Ms Davies is one of life's 'superheads', a woman who has taken a 'bog-standard' primary and transformed it into a star act with an 'outstanding' Ofsted, three-form entry and very happy parents. Most find her open-minded and approachable. 'I had an idea', commented one, 'and she immediately said "let's have a chat about it".' Hard working and well-organised, she gets things done. 'She's not ticking boxes, she really gets involved in the nitty gritty'. An active opponent of testing, testing, testing, she's even been to parliament to protest, winning the admiration of her local MP ('if I were the minister for education I would grab Evelyn Davies and put her as his key adviser. That way our children would be well educated in every sense of the word').

Entrance: Places given out using the standard local authority formula: children in local authority care, followed by special educational needs, siblings and

distance from the gates. Recent expansion means a bit of leeway for those living a few streets away.

Exit: A primary whose catchment fortunately straddles the borough's two highest flying comprehensives. The largest chunk of year 6 proceed to Fortismere, just next door. Sizeable (and growing) slice to Alexandra Park, down the road. Enviable success rate too, in grammar school entrance, then in dribbles to a wide range of local and distant establishments.

Remarks: This meticulously run school has everything going for it. Teaching here is enthusiastic and thorough, with staff constantly looking to improve performance. Academic standards are high and virtually every child reaches the government targets, many far exceeding them. Though the school has an 'unusually high' number of children with special needs, both those who struggle and those who excel are provided with plenty of booster classes. Not all parents, however, feel difficulties are necessarily dealt with sympathetically. 'Our son has considerable problems', said one, 'and we found the attitude very inflexible'. Behaviour is good and positive performance (particularly regular attendance) rewarded (classes compete enthusiastically for attendance teddies).

Facilities here can only be described as exceptional for a London primary. The original, large, low-lying Victorian schoolhouse, once a secondary school, has now been joined by a sleek, modern addition, providing extra classrooms and a new gym. Expansive grounds boast country-like playing fields,

---

One enthusiastic parent recently organised an entire week of dance with over 60 workshops and professionals imported from the West End

---

as well as two large and notably well-equipped playgrounds kitted out with basketball and netball nets, table-tennis tables and sheltered cabins. Pupils also benefit from the school's own allotments and nature trail, as well as access to nearby Coldfall Woods.

Sport played enthusiastically and successfully. Two hours of PE weekly overseen by a qualified sports coach and training approached with professional efficiency (gymnasts, for example, use flip cameras to study performance). Both boys and girls triumph in borough-wide competitions, boys

winning recent golf and football championships, girls excelling in football and netball. Pupils also qualified for the London Youth Games.

Plenty of enrichment, in lessons and out, including chess (with championship-winning chess teams), French (taught by a native speaker), computer programming and cooking all part of the regular mix. Excellent range of clubs (including geology) and activities. Successful school choir has made appearances at the O2 centre and Barbican and one enthusiastic parent recently organised an entire week of dance with over 60 workshops and professionals imported from the West End. 'Things don't just happen here', said one mother. 'Everything is well planned and thought through'. Regular trips beyond the school gates include at least one visit to a museum, gallery and musical event for every pupil.

In the main (though not exclusively), parents are comfortably off Muswell Hill locals, so there's a good sprinkling of designer trainers in the playground, but this is low-key prosperity. Almost a third of pupils speak another language than English at home. Both mothers and fathers (plenty of the latter at pick-up time) involved in making the school a success. 'All parents', said one enthusiast, 'are given an opportunity to contribute, not just non-working mums'. Many arrive at weekends to help with the gardening, and the thriving PTA organises summer and winter fairs, weekly coffee mornings, a Valentine disco, quiz night, fashion show and organic vegetable scheme. Sizeable sums are raised for playground, computer and PE equipment. 'There's a real feeling that everyone matters', said one mother. 'The kids are really blessed'.

Copthall School

Pursley Road, London, NW7 2EP

State • Pupils: 1,045 • Ages: 11–18 • Non–denom

Tel: 020 8959 1937
Fax: 020 8959 8736
Email: enquiries@copthall.barnet.sch.uk
Website: www.copthallschool.org.uk

4

Head Teacher: Since 2005, Ms Jane Beaumont, BA (Oxford) PGCE (London University's Institute of Education). Started her career at Copthall as an NQT in the early 1990s and has not strayed very far since. Although she came into education 'late', she was assistant head/director of sixth form at Acland Burghley school for 10 years and deputy head at both The Compton and Fortismere schools. 'I live locally and that's very important. I know and understand the local community.' Her husband is head of a Redbridge comprehensive school.

Down to earth, forthright and likeable. Her abiding passion for the job is evident in the way she enthusiastically bounces through our meeting (metaphorically speaking), and is on top of all the facts, figures, statistics, Ofsted reports etc. However, it's not just about making the grade for this head – she also takes a genuine interest in the wellbeing of her girls. 'Around a lot', is what one of the parents told us. Another says she marvels at her dedication, 'she's always the last one to leave and will wait at the bus stop until every one of her students is safely on the bus.' One pupil told us, 'When she asks you how you are, you know it's because she really cares and it's not just meaningless words.

The product of a single parent family who went to 'tough schools', but got herself to Oxford University, Ms Beaumont says the experience 'has informed my career and made me passionate about the power of education to improve lives.' She is a firm believer in a strong educational background for a broad spectrum of pupils; 'I love the fact that Copthall is a genuine comprehensive school with children from all backgrounds and abilities. I find it amazing how ambitious most of them are in their learning, and we are here to get them to realise this ambition.'

Academic matters: In the top 20 per cent of schools nationally for student progress recently. All the more admirable when one takes into account that there are 60 different spoken languages at home and 22 per cent of students on free school meals (compared to 16 per cent nationally). Good solid results – in 2014, 56 per cent of pupils got 5+ A*-C at GCSE including English and maths (where value-added is very good), 22 per cent A*/A grades. Organises some learning by ability rather than age.

A good range of traditional and non-traditional options, including food tech, ICT, childcare, and a City and Guilds level 2 diploma in beauty therapy (equivalent of five GCSE grades A*-C). Wide range of A levels with maths, biology and chemistry all popular (as elsewhere, few opt for physics); psychology and sociology also get large numbers of takers. Over 40 per cent A*-B grades in 2014, 14 per cent A*/A grades. Non-traditional female subjects like sciences and technology are stronger than in many 'mixed' environments. This is something the head is very proud of – 'the fact that there is such a good uptake across the range of sciences, arts, humanities and technical subjects, allows us to have an unusually wide range of subjects offered at A level for a sixth form of our size.' Has leading practitioners for history, dance and business education.

Copthall has specialist business and enterprise college status and this is embedded across the curriculum: 'Our mission is that our students will leave Copthall prepared for the constantly changing world of work.' Plenty of opportunities to develop business acumen. These may include rais-

---

It has become a popular filming venue, which can add Call the Midwife to its recent list of credits

---

ing money for a World Challenge expedition (this year Malaysia), baking and selling biscuits or creating a new children's card game called 'Shuffles', enabling team members to develop production, finance and marketing skills amongst others. PHSE includes modules in personal finance.

The school is 'committed to educational opportunity and inclusion.' It needs to be – approx 32 per cent of students are on the SEN register. The SEN co-ordinator also liaises with outside agencies. One parent said, 'They're really on top of this. My daughter is dyslexic and she is offered a lot of support, including extra reading classes and a scribe for exams.' Reading is a priority here. The school analyses who is and isn't taking books out of the library. Actively encourages parents to read with their children, especially in families where English isn't the first language. Everyone is tested in year 7 – those in need get extra help in class or in small groups. Five teaching assistants manage year 7 and 8 pupils with complex needs who require full-time support.

Another says she marvels at her dedication, 'she's always the last one to leave and will wait at the bus stop until every one of her students is safely on the bus.'

Learning co-ordinators keep an eye on pupils' progression and those who are struggling with work and behaviour may embark on an intensive programme in the inclusion centre, which puts most back on track. The school has converted many parts of the building to make them wheelchair accessible. Two stair lifts and two wheelchair lifts have been installed and a number of classrooms contain height-adjustable furniture.

As with many large comprehensive schools, a healthy amount of self-motivation is required to succeed. One parent expressed concern about her daughter's education at the school: 'I do worry that pupils at the lower end of the spectrum could slip through the net.' However, she continues, 'in many cases the school's GCSE results don't reflect the hard work the teachers put in.'

Games, options, the arts: Plenty to do. A wide range of practical subjects on offer including art, DT and performing arts, with small classes for practical subjects. Good facilities and well-equipped DT and art rooms. Astounding pieces of art work on display in the art room, although some pieces which deserved to be mounted on feature walls were slightly hidden from view. (One student in particular could've given Dali a run for his money).

Strong on dance and drama. Great success in ballet and selected students have taken part in a programme with the English National Ballet (impressive wall displays of student performances). Drama very popular, too, with lots of performance opportunities in school and regular trips to theatres including the Old Vic, Sadler's Wells and Regents Park Open Air Theatre. The school runs a summer school for selected year 6 transfer pupils every year. The theme, purpose and pupils differ each summer depending on need, for example literacy and numeracy. Active and diverse music department with extracurricular

groups that include rock band, guitar club, a 'glee' choir and a year 11 a capella group.

Big on sports – perhaps inspired by the well known stadium down the road. GCSE PE is an option and as well as the traditional competitive sports, pupils are offered trampolining, Zumba, yoga, rowing, basketball and the option of cheerleading for the Saracens Rugby team,that now uses Copthall Stadium for its games. Own sports hall, netball courts and hockey pitches, with Copthall swimming pool and Power League Football Centre down the road. Links with local sports clubs are used to offer a wider sporting curriculum. Inter-form and inter-school matches, lunch time clubs, and keen sportswomen join Barnet sports clubs. Athlete and commonwealth medal winner Nadia Williams is an alumnus.

Background and atmosphere: Named for Copt Hall, the local 17th century manor house, opened as a grammar school in 1936 and merged with Woodcroft School in 1971. It became a girls' comprehensive in 1973 and operated as a single school on two separate sites, until extensive rebuilding enabled its amalgamation on one site in 1996.

Copthall is situated on the corner of two roads. Page Street is a leafy, pretty road with posh secluded houses and the promise of great things. Indeed, the facade of the school from this perspective is of an imposing brown brick building with a large feature window which sits in a decent forecourt. Turn the corner into Pursley Road and the picture changes. This is a very busy, nondescript road, redeemed slightly by the vast playing fields opposite the school. In the morning, one is faced with a sea of green, as the Copthall girls descend from the buses and make their way into the main entrance.

Enter the building from this side and you could be forgiven for thinking you had entered an NHS hospital. The reception area is large and airy, but sterile and very blue, with a large semicircular reception desk, where we almost expected to pick up our prescriptions. Above the waiting chairs, there is a large television screen with informative bulletins for students and a particular emphasis on healthy eating.

This school is a bit of a hotchpotch of the old and new, and we weren't really sure where one part began and one ended. The original part of the building is fairly dark with narrow corridors and high windows. There was a distinct lack of charm or character in this part of the building, which could partly be rectified by adding some personal touches – more student displays on the wall, a good injection of colour etc. Enter the school hall for a trip down memory lane. It probably hasn't changed since the 50s, which is intentional, the head assures us. This does lend a certain nostalgic charm to it and clearly word has spread as it has become a popular filming venue, which can add Call the Midwife to its recent list of credits.

On the positive side, a cash injection has allowed for some very nice elements. A pretty secluded courtyard where sixth formers can study or have some quiet time, a fully-equipped beauty salon for those taking the beauty course as an option, a superb, fully mirrored dance studio with a sprung floor, a large, well-stocked library and a decent sized (purple) business suite.

Students also took the initiative to design the façade of a new building a couple of years ago. They decided on a 'green vine' motif and had the brain-wave of turning each leaf into a national flag using different shades of green – representing the various nationalities in the school. The effect is a beautiful variegated pattern.

Plans are under way for the Copthall School expansion programme (12 new classrooms being built), and the school expanded by one form of entry in September 2014. One parent expressed concern about this expansion and told us: 'I understand the necessity for creating more school places, but I'm worried how the school will cope with getting even bigger, and how it will impact on the individual.' Indeed, it is hard to imagine how another structure could be cramped into this one site – the only plus side being that they may have to finally remove the demountables in the school's forecourt, which have well passed their sell-by date.

Pastoral care and discipline: Discipline a high priority especially with regards to uniform. One parent said, 'Have you met the head? Even I feel like straightening my skirt when she passes by.' Clearly Ms Beaumont has little time for nonconformists – the school prospectus says it all: 'students will be asked to remove nail varnish at a cost of 20p.. if students opt to have piercings (eg nose studs),

They decided on a 'green vine' motif and had the brainwave of turning each leaf into a national flag – representing the various nationalities in the school

this must be done at the beginning of the summer holiday, so they can heal and be removed for the start of school in September.' The result is a well turned out bunch of girls in a smart, dark green tartan uniform (a far cry from this editor's Copthall schoolgirl days). Any desire to out-individualise each other is done beyond the school gates.

One parent said, 'Have you met the head? Even I feel like straightening my skirt when she passes by.' Clearly Ms Beaumont has little time for nonconformists

Mostly nice, well-behaved girls (a couple of the classes we passed sounded a few decibels louder than possibly acceptable). Permanent exclusion rate is very low, averaging one a year. In most cases it is students who didn't start at the school in year 7. Strict on attendance and punctuality. The education welfare team works closely with the school to highlight the importance of this. An attendance of no less than 95 per cent a year is expected as is a prompt 8.35am start. Early school finish at 2.55pm (Gove would choke), but only a 35 min lunch break: 'We have a staggered lunch break to cater for four sittings so that students get a freshly cooked meal.'

Much has also been done to combat bullying, which in a school of 1,200 girls is almost a sad inevitability. Student services situated in the heart of the school is open to any vulnerable student throughout the school day. Peer mediation, buddying and anti-bullying council also help to protect more vulnerable pupils. Learning co-ordinators, many of whom are non-teaching heads of year, are employed specifically for the pastoral needs of students. One parent said, 'I had a child who was bullied when she first started the school, but it was dealt with promptly and sensitively and there are no issues any more.'

What the school lacks aesthetically, it certainly makes up for in its infrastructure. 'Inclusion' is a word used by many of the parents we spoke to. There is an admirable amount of information for parents, including informative weekly newsletters and three reports a year. One parent told us, 'we don't lack for information here.' A conscious effort has been taken to include parents from multi-cultural backgrounds who may find integrating a challenge. Ms Beaumont instigated a group last year for 30 parents which ran for 12 weeks and was completely funded by the school. As a result of its success, the plan is to make it an annual event.

Various incentives for students to perform are given throughout the year. The pièce de résistance is a Celebration Evening held at the end of the school year to recognise exceptional achievements in different subjects. One parent said, 'This is something my daughter really aspires to achieve and it motivates her.' Encouragement is extremely important, the head believes, 'if you get the pastoral stuff right, everything else will fall into place.'

Pupils and parents: A great ethnic and social mix with lots of middle class girls and those from tough estates – 'we don't have large numbers from any particular ethnic minority or social class, which gives us a nice breadth of views.' Parents mostly very supportive; very active PTA and parent governors – strong sense of parental inclusion. One parent told us, 'My daughter had the option of going to a selective school, but when we weighed it up we felt that Copthall provided everything she needed, academically and socially.'

Entrance: Heavily oversubscribed school – some 500 applications for expanded 210 places. Organised by the LA, with looked-after girls and those with particular medical or social needs first on the list, followed by siblings or those with a brother at their partner school Christ's College. Remaining places are offered on a geographical basis – generally less than a mile and a half away. Some 30 to 40 join the sixth form from outside.

Exit: Around 40 per cent of the year leaves after GCSEs, mostly for local colleges, many to follow vocational courses. Over 80 per cent of sixth formers to university (most of the rest to FE colleges), often one a year to Oxbridge. Others to study eg medicine at Manchester, history at Warwick and aerospace systems engineering at Coventry. Good work experience and careers advice.

Money matters: Barnet is officially viewed as leafy suburbia and thus not in need of urgent government cash for, eg, replacing portable classrooms. Stable staff, but turnover not helped by the fact that they can get inner-London weighting just a few miles south. Supportive parents help with raising cash.

Remarks: Good, solid, highly inclusive local school with a strong sense of community. Plenty of scope for developing a bent for science, languages or making a million at business, while picking up performing arts or food technology skills along the way. We hope its expansion will not dilute its ethos.

Dwight School London, Lower School and Kindergarten

Linked school: Dwight School London (Upper School), 508

49 Woodside Avenue, London, N12 8SY

Independent · Pupils: 180 · Ages: 2–11 · Fees (per term): £4,755

Tel: 020 8920 0600
Fax: 020 8445 0835
Email: admissions@dwightlondon.org
Website: www.dwightlondon.org

The Lower School Principal: Since 2007, Mr Matt Parkin BEd DipEd. Has taught in the UK, USA and Indonesia. Teaching football and swimming as a teenager helped him find his vocation. Married; likes going running with his Labrador dog ('though she is much faster than me').

Overall head of school is David Rose, previously head of Montgomery School in Germany and The British School of Houston, Texas, an ISI inspector, past chair of the London International Schools Association and an accreditation visitor for international schools.

Entrance: Mr Rose likes the phrase that Dwight parents use to describe the school: 'selectively inclusive'. Though most enter in September, expat families join throughout the year, as do children transferring from local state schools. Interview recommended (Mr Rose and Mr Parkin want to get to

know all of their students); this and a report from previous school only real requisites.

Exit: Most go on to the upper school to continue with the IB middle years and diploma programmes, but a few trickle elsewhere. Some expat families move on to other foreign assignments.

Remarks: The epitome of what an international school should be about. Year groups divided into two parallel classes with an absolute maximum of 20 in each. Lots of child-inspired batiks, pottery and art help create a vibrant atmosphere. IB learner profiles are displayed everywhere. IB primary years programme (IBPYP) well linked with the national curriculum, which keeps inspectorates happy and ensures children are well grounded with an international mind-set. All lessons in each half of term based around one aspect of the curriculum.

Playground not huge but much use made of local park for cross-country runs and scientific experiments plus compulsory swimming once a week at Trent Park

Specialist teachers for music, art, PE, French and EAL. Homework important and can be done at after-school club.

Kindergarten and reception based in their own little house, The Lodge, with its own garden for play. Half day and part time options are available and there's a wraparound care programme from 7.30am to 6pm for the lower school.

Years 2 to 5 in the main building have good sized, light classrooms with washing lines displaying student work. Each child has own drawer for storage. Computers everywhere. Media resource centres, a small library collection; great gym, which doubles up as the dining hall. Healthy food served from the kitchens next to it (where meals for the kindergarten are also prepared). Photos of all the year 6 student displayed in the passage with their personal blogs. Good music room and lovely art room. Year 6 has a separate and brand new eco-building with easy access to the specialist classrooms and playground.

Strong emphasis on pastoral care and exceptional provision for special needs, the Quest system, with good screening for dyslexia and related problems. (More needy students are referred to Holmewood School.) As in the upper school, the policy is to accept a controlled number of children with learning difficulties but not those with disruptive behavioural problems. Excellent EAL provision with an enthusiastic and dedicated teacher. Children usually become fluent within a year.

Playground not huge but much use made of local park for cross-country runs and scientific experiments plus compulsory swimming once a week at Trent Park. They also regularly use the school's own playing fields a short bus ride away. Lots of trips, visits and excursions as well. All year 6 students spend a week at an activity centre in Normandy (practising the French that they have been learning since they were 3) and some of them go on exchange to the Dwight School in New York.

About half the families are local north London. The rest are expats representing a mix of professions and embassies. Door-to-door bus service provided at extra cost extends to south to St John's Wood, Belsize Park, Hampstead, Golders Green – ask the admissions office about your area. There's a free shuttle service between their two campuses (Friern Barnet and Woodside Park) for parents preferring to drop off at one. Most families have an international background, usually one English-speaking parent. Nationalities include British, then Japanese (10 per cent), and then a complete mix of many nationalities.

Friendly, caring and kind are the adjectives we heard most from Dwight parents we spoke to.

Dwight School London (Upper School)

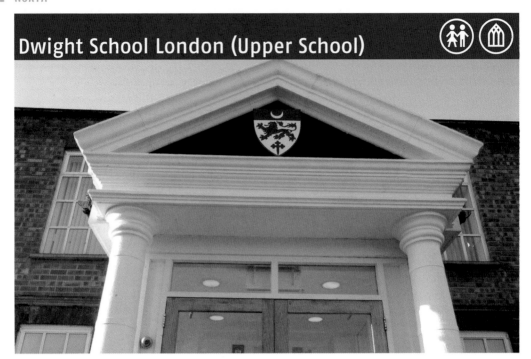

Linked school: Dwight School London, Lower School and Kindergarten, 506

6 Friern Barnet Lane, London, N11 3LX

Independent · Pupils: 250 · Ages: 11–19 · Non-denom
· Fees (per term): £5,275 – £6,130

Tel: 020 8920 0600
Fax: 020 8211 4605
Email: admissions@dwightlondon.org
Website: www.dwightlondon.org

Head of School: Since 2005, Mr David Rose (50s) CertEd BA MAEd LPSH. Married, with two adult daughters; his wife Vivienne recently retired as admissions director. Tall and distinguished, he looks the part of head of a serious school. He's had a long career in international schools, with headships in British international schools in Pakistan, Sweden, Cyprus, Germany and Houston. 'Totally approachable,' parents tell us, and by all accounts he knows all of his students.

The benefit brought by the long-term leadership of this confident yet somewhat self-effacing international educator is evident, and noted by longer-term families – notably the strengthening of the three IB programmes, and the improvement to school's culture of discipline. He's overseen renovation of some of the school facilities and the introduction of a new special educational needs partner school, and has raised Dwight's profile on London's international school map. Parents all describe him as a lovely, gentle person; he meets all the students at the time of application, and he regularly drops in to classrooms.

Academic matters: Runs the IB programme at all levels. In 2014, average IB point score 31 (out of possible 45). One or two students each year opt to take a Dwight High School Diploma, earning IB certificates rather than the full IB diploma. Average class size in upper school not normally more than 15.

Mr Rose was proud to announce that Dwight has been designated an IB Open World School – one of only seven worldwide. This means that students from other institutions may register to take IB diploma courses at Dwight through the Pamoja Online courses, which may appeal to local sixth formers who want to combine IB courses with their A levels. By having Pamoja Online courses available to Dwight's students, the course option are much expanded, and it enables students to experience the kind of online learning that is increasingly common at university level.

French is introduced in primary, Spanish added as an option in year 7. Other languages considered on request at additional cost. Computers and interactive whiteboards available throughout the school, yet on the day of our visit we did not see students working on these devices in any of the classes we visited. RE is not an IB subject, though religious and other cultural traditions are addressed through other areas of the curriculum, and parents tell us that there are opportunities to celebrate these in different ways. Photos throughout the the the school buildings depict many school trips, dramatic and music performances and community service activities, suggesting that a lot of learning is regularly extended out and about. After-school homework club for those who want extra help.

Parents receive a chatty weekly newsletter from the head, including updates on extracurricular activities available both to their children and themselves. Helpful and informative website.

Through the QUEST programme (at extra cost) the school can accommodate a range of learning needs, with the support of specialist teachers. The school has a sister school for more significant cases including statemented children.

EAL (also at extra cost) regarded as essential for children with two non-English speaking parents – two to five lessons a week, one to one or in a small group depending on needs. A mother tongue programme is available for Japanese pupils – the second largest group in the school (about 10 per cent) and some other languages (no extra charge is made if four or more students are in the same group and level). IB diploma students must be completely fluent in English. Language Heritage Day once a year sees everyone speaking their own language. Pupils of over 35 different nationalities, and full-time teachers of 15.

Parents say that what they like about Dwight is that it suits a great variety of children. 'I wanted a school where all of my children would be well served'.

Teachers are international and IB-experienced. They are always willing to help and respond quickly to any parent concerns. One parent tells us her child said that Dwight teachers must go through a 'humour test' – you have to have warm sense of humour to teach at Dwight.

Games, options, the arts: Games obligatory once a week for each year group – the school has its own sports field 10 minutes away by minibus and uses other local sports facilities. They compete not only with local and national schools but also with international overseas schools. Parents say they like the variety of sports on offer – not only the traditional ones but a wider range – rugby, football, basketball, track and field, sailing, ice skating… One Dwight student is representing London in the National Schools Swimming Competition.

Lots of after-school clubs. Strong music – about 15 per cent learn an individual instrument; there are rock, jazz and chamber groups. The choir has sung at London's 02 in Young Voices, and on the week of our visit, they were about to jet off to the US to perform with the Dwight New York choir at the Carnegie Hall. There is a music tech lab on a bright upper level that overlooks the music and art rooms below, and soundproofed rooms for individual tuition.

For the last period on Mondays, the pupils do mixed by year group community service projects. This helps to develop relationships across the ages, reinforcing the 'Dwight Family' concept.

Lots of outings to concerts, theatres and galleries as well as trips home and abroad. We saw photos from a science trip to Iceland, the Model United Nations Conference is popular, there's an annual exchange with the year 6 students at Dwight School in New York, and older students have been doing community service helping to build in Cambodian village. They raise funds, and roughly every three years students, parents and staff travel there to do volunteer work. The drama club was preparing to go to Cuba to study music and dance; while the year before the film club went to Hollywood! India is on the horizon.

Dwight London students are eligible to participate in the Dwight Global Leaders, a summer gathering of high school students from all over who come together at the Dwight Vancouver campus to

develop leadership skills and learn about social entrepreneurship. This programme features big name motivational speakers from the world of sport, education and business (for example Monica Seles and Michael Bloomberg) and it receives high praise from the families of students who have participated.

Background and atmosphere: The school originally founded in 1972 by Dr Stephen Spahn, chancellor of the Dwight School in New York. Previously known as Woodside Park and North London International School, the school has recently changed its name in a rebranding exercise to Dwight London School, to heighten awareness of its association with the Dwight family of schools that now has campuses on Vancouver Island, Seoul, and Shanghai. 'Dwight family' is a term used by staff and families alike. Dwight London has an advisory board of local parents and others who lend expertise and guidance and serve as a supportive sounding board for Mr Rose in the strategic planning of the school.

The school is on four sites in two locations. The upper school is in the former Friern Barnet Boys' Grammar School and in nearby Jubilee Hall. The main building has recently been refurbished and is clean, bright and welcoming, making very good use of light throughout. The administrative offices and faculty room share the same corridors as the

Many of these friendships endure and lead to exciting trips during the holidays to visit old friends who have moved on

classrooms, which must strengthen the sense of community. Every wall is full of original and creative student art and photographs, and there are posters with quotes from Gandhi, Martin Luther King and Nelson Mandela, who we learned are the role models for the three upper school student houses.

The individualised approach we heard so much about from parents was evident during our visit. One Spanish class had just two students; in a lively drama lesson, students were planning the direction and staging for a Dwight student version of a Chaucer play; art students in a large art room with plenty of natural light were working on sketches and prints as part of a unit on 'celebrations'; and the design technology lab was a hive of activity with students measuring and vigorously sawing away as part of a woodworking project (hopefully all the fingers survived). A painted wall is a legacy of one student's project on graffiti as an art form. It was easy to see why the parents rave about the quality of the arts programmes.

The Jubilee Hall nearby holds more classrooms, two science labs, the upper school library (closed for a few days when we visited, as the librarian was on a school trip) and a pleasant canteen open throughout the day (there are rave reviews for the new caterers), with a TV tuned into Sky News or the BBC. This looks out onto an outside playground where students engage in a bit of exercise during break or lunch, and a small world garden beyond with picnic tables and benches.

The school makes admits that conditions are a little crowded, and they are always on the lookout for new property in the area.

Pastoral care and discipline: Head has been credited with an improvement in student behaviour. The IB philosophy and emphasis on tolerance and global understanding is reinforced by the house system in the English tradition, with upper and lower school head boys and girls. Kids look tidy and seem happy, and although there is a uniform there are various options, so they can choose how casual or dressy they want to look. Parents love the small size of the school. 'It's a massive advantage. Everyone is known, everyone can shine and blossom.' It helps build self-confidence, and there's plenty of attention from teachers. As one veteran parent described it, 'The teachers really knew my son.'

Parents repeatedly assured us that they were not aware of any incidents of bullying, and the British ones in particular felt that the huge diversity of student backgrounds is a huge plus, with families inviting students home to share their family traditions during different holidays.

Pupils and parents: Dwight has a larger British student body than most other international schools in London, which seems to make it easier for international families to integrate into the local community. The impression from parents and from our visit is that there is relatively little sense of the 'expat bubble' in this international school. Long term families who joined the school in earlier incarnations (pre-IB) say they have been very pleased with the introduction of the full suite of IB programmes, and the interesting international experiences and friendships that Dwight's growing expat community brings. While they do see the turnover of families as a factor, many of these friendships endure and lead to exciting trips during the holidays to visit old friends who have moved on.

Parent Link works behind the scenes to support the school and organise the social events that are particularly helpful for new families. Parents can also volunteer in the school.

About half of families are local north Londoners. The rest are expats representing a mix of industries and embassies, though most live within less than 30 minutes away. Parents appreciate the expansion of the area served by the door-to-door transport provided by the school. There is also a free shuttle service from the local tube stations and the free inter-school shuttle facilitating drop off. Most families have an international background, usually one English-speaking parent. Nationalities primarily British, then Japanese, and then a complete mix of many.

Entrance: Mr Rose likes the phrase that Dwight parents use to describe the school: 'selectively inclusive'. In all of our conversations (with parents and staff), no one emphasised 'academic results'. Though most enter in September, since the school serves expats, there are students entering throughout the year. Interview and report from previous school only real requisites. Many come up from the lower school but others from other local schools or overseas.

Exit: University counselling programme in year 12, but it seems parents often start earlier, commenting they'd like to see a bit more attention to this area. Mainly to university, a lot London based but some overseas – eg recent admissions to Imperial College London, Edinburgh, Keele, Brunel, Reading, McGill, New York University, Columbia University.

Money matters: Tuition is marginally less than other international schools in London. Extras include school trips and activities such as Model United Nations or some after-school activities. Scholarships are available with testing in the early part of the calendar year.

Remarks: Dwight is a school where the education of the 'whole child' and the learning journey genuinely appear to be as important as exam results. As one parent said, 'When we visited other schools, it was a PR exercise where they told us about their tests, achievements, etc. At Dwight, they asked us about our children.' The school does all it can to provide each student with opportunities to pursue their individual interests, all within the IB context. 'It's a kind school.'

Fortismere School

South Wing, Tetherdown, London, N10 1NE

State · Pupils: 1,700 · Ages: 11–19 · Non denom

Tel: 020 8365 4400
Fax: 020 8444 7822
Email: office@fortismere.org.uk
Website: www.fortismere.haringey.sch.uk

26

Head: Since 2010, Mrs Helen Anthony BA MA PGCE (40s), previously head since 2006 of Central Technology College in Gloucestershire. Studied English at Liverpool and Keele, PGCE at King's College London. Had a number of teaching and leadership roles in London and Gloucestershire before joining Central Technology College, which was then one of the roughest boys' schools in the country. She brought it back from the brink of closure and transformed its rating to 'good' (Ofsted talked of a 'remarkable journey').

She has imported to very middle class Fortismere some of the tactics that had wrought improvements in her previous setting, such as a hard line on punctuality, attendance and litter. She clearly has a steely determination and is evidently not a head to be trifled with, though on our tour a pupil did not hesitate to buttonhole her to check she had signed a form for him. 'Very hard working and ambitious,' say parents. Mother of two daughters.

Academic matters: A large proportion of bright, motivated pupils and also a greater than average number of pupils with SEN, with a relatively small mid range. In 2014, 34 per cent A*/A grades at A level, with 66 per cent A*/B. Similarly strong at GCSE: 51 per cent A*/A grades, and 82 per cent of pupils got 5+ A*-C grades, including English and maths.

The previous head had introduced setting for every subject from year 7; this has been loosened, but school still sets early for maths and science, whilst English is taught in mixed ability classes. 'I trust my faculty heads on that, but they must show that it works.' Relatively low class size of 24.

Everyone learns French or Spanish in year 7 and promising linguists are offered Mandarin or German in year 8. They are encouraged to take two languages to GCSE; around 80 per cent of pupils take at least one. The top 60 per cent are encouraged to take triple science GCSE.

Teaching standards mostly very high with the odd exception, say parents. 'They expect of lot of the students – I think they push them very hard. They encourage and extend them, particularly with the personal projects in the sixth form.'

Reporting system to parents 'has improved. They tell you what your child's target is, what level they're performing at now and whether that's okay. I've mostly found teachers very responsive when I've emailed them.'

The sixth form admissions criteria are 'closer to a grammar school', with at least five B grades at GCSE required for A level, and As for certain subjects eg maths. The small number of vocational options, with five C grades at GCSE as a boundary, include music technology, ICT, business, media and sports science. School also teaches classical heritage and global perspectives Pre-U courses.

Maths a very popular A level, alongside his-

> *'I have to remember that parents don't just read the Guardian – quite likely they write for it too,' says the head*

tory (teaching dubbed 'exceptional' by parents) and English. Respectable numbers pursuing biology and chemistry, and – as one might expect in this liberal, intellectual area – philosophy, psychology, government and politics and sociology, though linguists disappointingly few.

'Amazing' preparation for Oxford, said a parent. 'It was all very low key, but there are several young Oxbridge graduates teaching at the school, and they ran workshops, put on seminars, did mock interviews, and put pupils in touch with other students who'd been through the process

recently. It was all there, but it was up to the kids to push themselves that much further.'

With its large, segmented site and high pupil numbers, possibly not the most suitable school for children with learning difficulties, but many choose it nonetheless, 'and we do a very good job with them'. Those with statements – and there are a relatively large proportion of these, mostly with autistic spectrum and behavioural issues – have their own teaching assistant. However, 'we try to keep away from TAs vecroed to children', and they are included in class work as far as possible, with small group sessions to help them develop independent learning skills. Linc team helps those experiencing learning difficulties – temporary or permanent. The secondary department of the Blanche Nevile School for deaf and hearing-impaired children occupies an impressive building on the site. Some of its pupils join in the main school activities.

Games, options, the arts: Fabulous new music block, with recording studios, composing and practice rooms, plus multi-use performance spaces, mirrors the importance of the subject here (though few take it to A level). Symphony orchestra, big band and several choirs; community choirs and orchestras include parents as well as children; hosts Saturday music school. 'We play a key role in the local community.' Head doesn't envisage the abolition of music aptitude places having any effect on the quality of music-making in the school. 'We have always had a lot of hugely musical students – it comes with the parent body.'

Impressive displays of art and fabulous photography coursework around the school on our visit, plus bright papier mâche aliens and rats created by younger year groups. Photography a popular A level and one can see why. Drama also 'massive'. 'We're a very artsy school. It's our natural default setting.' 'Fantastic' production of Little Shop of Horrors included the actual plant from the West End show; sixth formers regularly take productions to the Edinburgh fringe, and help with GCSE drama performances.

Sports stars used to hone their talents largely outside school, but sport has been bolstered by increased amounts of time in the upper years plus the introduction of Colleges, or houses, which run weekly inter-college competitions and encourage non A team players to get involved. However, parents report that it is possible for the less athletically inclined to avoid breaking into a sweat, and it is fair to say that reports of sports team triumphs do not feature largely in school newsletters. Sports hall, tennis/netball/basketball courts, acres of playing fields and 'very popular' table tennis tables. The head would dearly like the renovation of the 'stagnant' disused swimming pool to be her legacy, but financial constraints seem likely to stymie this ambition.

Another innovation is whole school enrichment sessions every other Wednesday afternoon, with a choice of 87 activities from yoga to cooking to science. All the staff, including admin staff, are encouraged to join in. An assistant head who was a dancer in a previous life runs a tap dancing club; the head runs a Born to Teach? training course for year 12, which includes planning and teaching lessons in primary, secondary and special schools.

Large range of trips includes 'brilliant and very well organised' week in Beijing for Mandarin speakers, exchange visits to France, Spain, Germany, Senegal and India ('though you do have to queue up at 7am with your cheque to get a place on the popular ones,' commented a parent), D of E, outdoor pursuits in the Brecon Beacons, ski trips, field trips and cultural visits. A steady stream of authors, scientists, politicians etc comes to give talks; librarian organises team of pupils to shadow Carnegie medal deliberations, reading and reviewing shortlisted books; teams enter debating competitions.

Background and atmosphere: Large site amidst leafy Muswell Hill Edwardiana has been the setting for a series of schools of all sorts, including private, state grammar and comprehensive. Fortismere was formed in 1983 by the amalgamation of Creighton and Alexandra Park Schools (another Alexandra Park School has since opened nearby). Site includes a hotch-potch of buildings from its various incarnations. North and South Wings linked by a quarter-mile pathway round the playing fields that can resemble a storm in the North Sea in inclement weather. Accommodation beginning to show its age, but bright and cheerful. Head has encouraged a multitude of notice boards – with college news, photos of trips, information on clubs.

Very much a community comprehensive with a relaxed atmosphere (subject to 'behaviour for learning' sanctions), and pupils strolling around in jeans and tee shirts. 'Proudly non-uniform', though with a veto on revealing too much skin or underwear. 'It's part of the ethos for children to be able to express themselves,' said a parent.

Pastoral care and discipline: Good transition system, with year 6s spending three days at the school in the summer term getting to know the site and teachers. Has recently introduced vertical tutor system, with 18 pupils of different ages from the same college in each group replacing old form tutor system. All staff – including admin staff – are tutors, 'which enables us to have small groups, and also increases student respect for non-teaching staff'. Mixed reviews from parents and pupils, some enthusiastic whilst others feel that the system needs time to bed in and become a tradition, and that they would prefer to spend the time with their peers.

Student leadership team, which includes head boy and girl and their deputies, has a meeting with the head each Monday. 'It has already had a real impact. They really challenge us about why we do things, and it makes me think about structures.'

Head's introduction of zero tolerance for lateness and absenteeism has shocked some families and delighted others, with one parent terming it 'draconian.' 'The behaviour here was good, but I thought it could be better,' says the head. 'If you are disrupting the learning of others, that is not negotiable. Parents complain, but when I tell them their child is stopping other people learning, they find that hard to justify.' She refuses permission for holidays in term time: 'We get a lot of poorly relatives

in far flung places towards the end of the Christmas and summer terms.' In response to pupils' requests for carrots as well as sticks, Vivo system gives house points for helpfulness, participation, tidiness etc and is widely reported in the newsletters.

Pupils mostly very happy and have good relationships with staff, but some parents feel that the pastoral system is variable. Some teachers 'do resolve your issues,' said a parent, citing the 'novel and interesting solutions' to stress suggested by her daughter's college head. However, 'I had a very unsympathetic reaction from the school to a family death. I found their policies very inflexible.'

'Fantastic' production of Little Shop of Horrors included the actual plant from the West End show

'They didn't seem to be sensitive to the needs of my younger daughter,' said another parent, whose children had joined from a different education system. 'I really didn't feel she got the support she needed, and I felt that no-one had an overview of the situation. I also had no response to a very carefully worded email about a pastoral issue that had upset her.'

Permanent exclusions rare, and usually for persistent defiance or repeated breaking of behaviour policies. Will swap recalcitrant pupils with other local schools. 'We're good at managed moves – they can be very effective.' Will also use outside providers such as local boxing and football academies for those who clearly need a different approach. 'We prefer to try something different before moving to permanent exclusion.' A parent commented: 'There are some wild and woolly kids, but they don't tend to disrupt classes.'

Pupils and parents: Largely affluent, liberal, middle class families – artists and musicians, writer and actors – plus quite a few looked-after children. 'It is a very political school. I have to remember that parents don't just read the Guardian – quite likely they write for it too,' says the head. These are mostly cool kids, relaxed and confident, proud to be at Haringey's most popular comprehensive. 'My daughters' friends are lovely,' said a parent. 'They meet up to study and all help each other.' Ex-pupils include soul singer Michael Kiwanuka.

Entrance: Takes 243 pupils into year 7. Those with an SEN statement naming the school – and there are many of these – will automatically get a place. Then priority to children in care, those with

particular medical, social or emotional needs, and siblings, with the remainder by distance, usually less than half a mile.

Takes 110 or so outside students into the sixth form, from state and independent schools. Requires 5+ A* – C GCSEs for vocational A levels and 5+ A* – Bs for academic A levels, with higher grades for certain subjects eg maths, from internal and external students. Those who don't get at least three D grades at AS are liable to be directed elsewhere.

Exit: Small numbers (around 30 per cent) move on after GCSEs, generally for more vocational courses elsewhere. Nearly all sixth form leavers to university: Sussex, Leeds, Manchester and Bristol the flavour of the moment; 10 to Oxbridge in 2014. English, philosophy, psychology, maths, law, geography all popular, plus a few medics and vets.

Money matters: Very active parents' association, the FSA, which underwrote the refurbishment of the sixth form centre.

Remarks: A popular and high-achieving comprehensive that successfully includes those with difficulties as well as extending the most able. Head's vision is for it to have 'an active mind, a finger on the pulse and a big heart.'

Grimsdell, Mill Hill Pre-Preparatory School

Linked schools: Belmont Mill Hill Preparatory School, 494 and Mill Hill School, 536

Winterstoke House, Wills Grove, London, NW7 1QR

Independent • Pupils: 180 • Ages: 3–7 • Non-denom • Fees (per term): £1,971 – £4,285

Tel: 020 8959 6884
Fax: 020 8959 4626
Email: office@grimsdell.org.uk
Website: www.grimsdell.org.uk

Head: Since September 2014, Mrs Kate Simon (early 40s). A current Grimsdell parent, Mrs Simon is no stranger to headship. Between 2002 and 2008 she was head of the junior school of the Royal School, Hampstead, and since 2008 was head of Girls' Upper School at Garden House School in Chelsea.

Entrance: Heavily oversubscribed, due in part to it being non-selective at age 3 or 4. 'I don't feel comfortable with failing children at that age', says the head. Most pupils come from within a five mile radius and there is a 'multi-cultural mix.'

Exit: The majority of pupils continue on to Belmont school. However, if the school feels that a child won't cope there, discussions about alternatives take place from year 1. 'We have to be realistic', the school says.

Remarks: Unfortunate name for a very pretty school. On a beautiful autumnal day, Grimsdell was the antithesis of 'grim'. Situated on Mill Hill's Ridgeway, but accessed via a small and very lovely private road, the school occupies the rather grand Winterstoke House. Originally a vicarage for the vicar of St Paul's and sold to Mill Hill School in October 1923, Winterstoke House was purchased to become a school boarding house to host some 42 boys.

The school became Grimsdell in 1995 – a newcomer compared to the other two schools in the Foundation. The reason for its formation was largely due to a Mrs Grimsdell, widow of an Old Millhillian, who bequeathed a large part of her late husband's estate to Mill Hill School. Following a request from the school governors, Mrs Grimsdell agreed that the benefaction be applied to create a 'much required' pre-preparatory school, and Grimsdell opened its gates. The school is situated adjacent to Mill Hill School but has its own grounds – not quite on the scale of the other two schools, but more than adequate for a pre-prep school.

This is a cute, cosy school. Nothing grand and pretentious, despite the impression given by its exterior. We were seated in a colourful and bright reception area with a large aquarium to gaze at while we waited to meet the head. Familiar sounds of over-excited kids emanated from one or two of the classrooms (and we were particularly struck by one over- zealous music teacher doing something very strange with her arms!)

All classrooms were light, airy and well equipped – particularly the Sunshine Room, which even in its name suggests something warm and nurturing. This is where pupils who need it go for extra one-to-one learning support. Specialist on-site teachers in music, PE and French are on hand and 4 to 7-year-olds have weekly keyboard lessons with a music specialist. The swimming pool at Mill Hill School is a great addition to the PE curriculum. Pupils use the theatre at Mill Hill School for concerts and performances. Cursive handwriting is taught from the start and we were quite amazed with the standard of year 1 handwriting displayed on classroom walls.

As with Belmont and Mill Hill School, Grimsdell's selling point is undoubtedly its idyllic surroundings. Pupils not only have access to 120 acres of beautiful parkland at Mill Hill school with its sports pitches, swimming pool and woodland, but they have their own great adventure playground and science garden to enjoy. A firm believer in the great outdoors, Grimsdell has its own Forest School. Each session has a theme and activities can range from mini beast hunting to fire building and cooking outdoors. With a school that states boldly in their prospectus, 'there is no such thing as bad weather, just bad clothing', you better be sure your little darlings have a healthy interest in outdoor pursuits. Forget this school otherwise – indeed discount the other two schools in the Foundation while you are at it.

Parents appreciate the expertise of the large Foundation, and the lack of pressure to take exams for future schools. One parent told us, 'Grimsdell is a secure and nurturing stepping-stone, which is illustrated by my own excited and eager children.'

The Henrietta Barnett School

Central Square, London, NW11 7BN

State · Pupils: 690 · Ages: 11–18 · Non–denom

Tel: 020 8458 8999
Fax: 020 8455 8900
Email: admissions@hbschool.org.uk
Website: www.hbschool.org.uk

Headteacher: Since September 2014, Mrs Del Cooke BSc MBA NPQH (50s), previously head of Sir William Perkins School in Surrey. Maths graduate with MBA in educational management, her broad experience covers the comprehensive system, sixth form college, adult education and boarding at Cranleigh, where she was head of maths, housemistress and finally deputy head. Interested in music, she plays a number of instruments, including self-taught

bassoon. A very likeable, approachable, relaxed lady. Married with three sons.

Academic matters: Consistently top or very near the top of the A level league tables, Henrietta Barnett seems to achieve that position without any of the obvious pressure found elsewhere. 'It's very uncompetitive,' said one parent. 'It's much more about collaboration and co-operation.' In 2014, 91 per

cent A and A* at GCSE, 80 per cent A*/A at A level. Dedicated band of long-serving teachers teach clever and motivated girls. Most do nine or 10 GCSEs, four or five AS, three or four A2s. Results strong across all subjects. A good range of languages. French and German for all in year 7, Latin for all in years 8 and 9. Plus ancient Greek and the recently added Spanish. The school has updated the curriculum in a number of other ways, bringing in drama in the early years and enrichment courses at A level. The bias at A level is currently towards maths and the sciences, though French and English have a healthy representation. The school wants to improve the balance. Godly amount of homework – 'But they're not driven hard. It's the engagement with other people that makes them think. They should be excited in the classroom.' Three form entry. Class size 24-31 in early years – with no setting except in maths – falling to 10-13 in the sixth form.

Games, options, the arts: Possibly not the most sporty school and certainly somewhat handicapped by its restricted grounds. However, new-ish large multi-purpose Astroturf court in the newly landscaped grounds for netball, hockey, football and volleyball. Four tennis courts, two polished but petite gyms, a new fitness suite with a range of exercise equipment and a variety of pitches available on the nearby Hampstead Heath extension. Two double periods of games a week, with a wide variety of exercise alternatives, including golf, swimming, rock climbing, orienteering, fencing, box exercise, yoga, Pilates and dance.

Has music college status (with English as a subsidiary). 'This is a very clear area of excellence and part of the majority of children's experience, which goes beyond subject teaching.' Very active music department. Specialist music house for peripatetic lessons, with its own music library. Eleven or 12 music groups meet each week, with teachers and pupils playing together. Music status brought new performance space, a music technology suite, a band room and a rehearsal space for rock music.

Previous head, with his wide experience of the independent sector, made a determined effort to broaden the extracurricular offering, with more drama, inter-school debating with local independent schools – 'The girls can be a bit shy and it helps to build up their confidence' – plus an artist-in-residence working on site all year. 'You need to work at building up confidence, self-esteem and achievement beyond the academic. They will all leave with good qualifications but we have to teach them how to make a success out of life.'

School trips, through each subject department, take every year group out once a year. French and German exchanges. Lots of day trips. Founder's week, held in the summer, provides an entire week of outings. Own field study centre in Dorset, which every pupil visits for one week during their early years at the school.

Background and atmosphere: Founded in 1911 by formidable social reformer Dame Henrietta Barnett, who wished to establish a school to educate bright girls regardless of their means. Housed in architecturally stunning Grade II* listed buildings by Sir Edwin Lutyens, the school sits, like a minor stately home, in a calm and soothing sea of green. The floors are polished parquet, the windows as high flying as the pupils, and the overall effect is of light and airy rooms straight out of an Angela Brazil novel. Nonetheless, parts of the building are fairly down at heel – the result of a long shared ownership with the local adult education institute. The school is gradually reclaiming the territory and buffing it up. 'The building is beautiful and the girls are very proud of it but it's not entirely fit for modern purpose.' A £7.5m government grant paid for the complete refurbishment of the science wing, and a music and drama school and art and DT centre. The school is now even more desirable.

Pastoral care and discipline: 'They're very well behaved and always do their best. Discipline is hardly needed here.' Polite and friendly girls are treated as adults from the word go, rules are explained and pupils tend to live up to the high expectations. Elected student council – which helps choose the head. Tutors in sixth form for groups of 10, seen individually to ensure problems, both academic and pastoral, are dealt with promptly. Junior and senior school have their own assembly halls for non-denominational assemblies, plus twice termly whole school assemblies.

Pupils and parents: Girls bright, curious, well-supported and very keen to learn. When the school was founded the intake was largely local but, since the arrival of league tables, the catchment has broadened considerably (now a parent-run bus service to cater for those who can't easily get here by the restricted public transport). Wide ethnic

mix – about a fifth Indian and a fifth white, the rest from serendipitous backgrounds. Well below average number on free school meals. Girls work unusually well together. 'There really are no cliques here,' said one parent with a daughter in the sixth form, but after-school social life is not necessarily as vibrant as elsewhere.

Entrance: One of the most competitive entrance tests in the country with 2000+ girls applying for 93 places. NB Register by late July. Verbal and numerical reasoning tests in September, and the top 300 are invited back for English and maths tests in January. 'It's fairly straightforward, but we do try to challenge the most able'. Pupils come from 50-60 primaries. A further 40-45 places (with approximately 100 applicants) in the sixth form with six A grade GCSEs minimum requirement plus As in intended A level subjects. Girls coming up through the school must also meet this requirement.

Exit: Around 10 per cent leave after GCSE to go on to larger (co-ed and/or independent) sixth forms. Twenty-five to Oxbridge in 2014. Lots of medics, dentists and biomedical scientists. Specialist UCAS adviser helps girls through their university applications and helps raise expectations of what can be achieved – 'We want to keep the blinkers off'.

Money matters: An active PTA and a parental support scheme to which many parents regularly donate.

Remarks: One of the top academic state schools in the country, providing a gentle, inspiring education in a wonderful setting for very clever girls.

Highgate Junior School and Pre-Preparatory Department

Linked school: Highgate School, 520

3 Bishopswood Road, London, N6 4PL

Independent • Pupils: 330 • Ages: 3–11 • Fees (per term): £2,620 – £5,555

Tel: 020 8340 9193
Fax: 020 8342 7273
Email: jsoffice@highgateschool.org.uk
Website: www.highgateschool.org.uk

27

Principal: Since 2002, Mr Mark James BA MA has been head of junior school. 'Parents love him,' one fan told us. 'He's involved in everything.' Another said: 'he's fantastic.' You get the idea. He's also head of admissions for the whole school and had

the task of transforming the boys' 7-13 prep into a modern mixed 7-11 junior school. Voila! Came from King's Wimbledon Junior where he'd been deputy head. An enthusiast and can-do character, he's just

the man to cheer everyone along during what will inevitably be a testing two years.

Mrs Diane Hecht DCE (fifties) has been head of pre-prep since 2010. Previously deputy head of St Columba's Junior School in Kilmacolm, she came south as two of her grown-up children had settled in London and feels that she has found a wonderfully similar school in Highgate. 'The girls here wear exactly the same tartan skirts as at St Columba's – it was meant to be!' Warm, efficient and enthusiastic.

Entrance: Oversubscribed – 350 try for the 36 places at 3+, 300 again for the 50 places at 7+. Sane and lovely pre-prep head admits that assessing two and a half-year-olds has to be on the arbitrary side, so do not be amazed if your astounding tot just doesn't astound on assessment day. At 3+ teachers observe them at play in groups, look for capacity to listen and follow instructions, general sociability – so don't make them learn their letters the night before. Assessing at 7 is easier – reading, writing and maths – but, again, the odds are not great. Other things count – siblings, school connections, where you live, parental statements on the application forms – but you can't wangle it. So have a Plan B, yes?

Exit: Nearly all go from the pre-prep to the juniors and nearly all go from there to the senior school. Plenty of warning given to those unlikely to thrive in the higher stages.

Remarks: The main junior school building will be smithereens by the time you read this. Whole school housed in Portakabins from January 2014 to December 2015, when they will take possession of a completely new and wonderful complex – judging by the plans.

Pre-prep separately, delightfully (and permanently) housed. Starts at nursery – 18 morning or afternoon tots in lively spacious space both inside and out with smiley, lively teachers. Whole school theme of colour and light when we visited and lots of attractive work on show. Glorious herd of Elmer elephants made from plastic milk cartons and coloured paper. Lovely singing – the most in-tune bunch of rising fives we've heard. An orderly, relaxed and friendly school. We saw much warm

---

Lovely singing – the most in-tune bunch of rising fives we've heard. An orderly, relaxed and friendly school

interaction between staff and small people and just wanted to stay and watch. Juniors have the whole school's fields and facilities to play with – a rare privilege. Excellent approach to emergent special needs – 'it doesn't matter whether they have a label or not, it's how you support them.' Full range of sensitive support, individualised learning, 'management' skills etc brought in when and where needed. Easy to understand why this is possibly the most oversubscribed junior school in London.

Highgate School

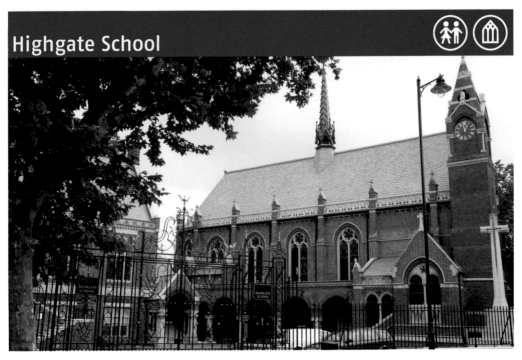

Linked school: Highgate Junior School and Pre-Preparatory Department, 518

North Road, London, N6 4AY

Independent • Pupils: 1065 • Ages: 11–18 • C of E • Fees (per term): £6,055

Tel: 020 8347 3564
Fax: 020 8340 7674
Email: admissions@highgateschool.org.uk
Website: www.highgateschool.org.uk

28

Head Master: Since 2006, Mr Adam Pettitt MA (late 40s). Oxford modern and medieval linguist. Taught French and German at Eton, Oundle and Abingdon and was second master at Norwich School, under Jim Hawkins, now head of Harrow – a formidable team. Has French wife and school-age children and is quite the most interesting, eloquent and thought-provoking head this veteran GSG reviewer has met in many a long school visit. Propelled by a sharply focused and incisively articulated moral and educational philosophy, Mr Pettitt is spare, brilliant and energetic. He must be an exacting – though supportive – man to work for. His pupils can only benefit from his firm commitment to outreach to schools and to those without their advantages, to placing an understanding of language at the heart of modern languages and to educational values rather than exams and results. The results will follow where this approach leads. Parents are unstinting in their praise. The most inspiring head we've met in years.

Academic matters: Head has a refreshing disrespect for the bodies deserving of it: 'You choose the exam board on the basis that it will have the least distorting effect on the way you want to teach' – bingo! IGCSEs now in English x 2, sciences, langs and history and many subjects now opt for the Pre-U as an alternative to A levels. This can only enhance the nature and quality of learning. English and langs the first to head this way. Mr Pettitt the 'de facto head of MFL' at the time of our visit so langs getting the oxygen they needed and number of takers is sure to rise. Mandarin now through to sixth form. Maths much the most popular A level and, with further maths, has impressive results. Also strong are English, art, Latin, all sciences and RS. Tiny numbers take theatre studies, Greek, classics, music – school does not offer music tech nor other popular 'modern' subjects eg textiles, psychology and loses a few post-GCSE on that account. Number of subject options (24) felt by some to be a little limited, given the size of the sixth form and some sixth formers would like more drama and art. However, good innovations include the 'knowledge curriculum' and 'critical method' courses. In 2014, 86 per cent A*/A at GCSE and 75 per cent at A level. Lively, student-led conferences. Mr Pettitt takes all criticism on the chin and, given that after his seven years in post (at the time of our visit) over 70 per cent of the staff are his appointees, this – as everything else – is fast developing.

Head's inclusive approach is just that: 'The quality of the way you learn is critical and every child's experience is equally important. Every day is important – I am most interested in the way each one of us teaches and learns.' IBAC – Independence through Buzz, Aspiration and Collaboration – the new acronym around the place. So this is not the school that was, nor the one people think they know. The fabric – see below – is radically changing and the character equally so. This is encapsulated

---

Terrific range of clubs (they include 'vinyl and philosophy,' beekeeping, LGBT soc and feminist society)

in the sane and sensitively individualised approach to SEN. The Victorian main building is not good for those with mobility problems though school says 'we will try to make it work by moving our routines and schedules as far as we can.' Director of learning support covers all three schools and is a renowned expert in autism. The support for all conditions and syndromes as they emerge is individual, tailored, supportive and 'concerned with management rather than labelling.' The very few with EAL needs are usually the very bright.

Games, options, the arts: Blessed with playing fields and space beyond the dreams of other London schools. If the educational philosophy and general zip in the place doesn't inspire you, the sporting facilities will. Girls' sport, some feel – school disputes – still catching up with boys'; football and netball still pre-eminent but plenty more on offer and played hard. Sports hall, pool, weights, Astroturfs, squash courts – it's all here. No country school could offer more.

Interior activities also privileged and currently being transformed by an enormous rolling building project that will add considerably to teaching space but also, it is hoped, to an eventual sixth form and arts campus. Drama and music thrive – many productions, concerts of all kinds and tours – art a little undemonstrative at the time of our visit but some lively colourful work around. Mills Centre provides studio and gallery space. Cultural life better displayed in the admirable school

publications – professional-looking periodicals on history, politics, science, theatre and thought written and produced by pupils. Terrific range of clubs (they include 'vinyl and philosophy,' beekeeping, LGBT soc and feminist society), trips, exchanges and tours – extracurricular is praised by many but not fully taken advantage of by all. 'I used to feel that some pupils' cultural references were limited to Arsenal: great though that club is, I want them to see and know so much more,' comments the head, happy to stress to parents that while these opportunities are on offer it is up to them to take them up.

Lots of charitable and outreach activities for both staff and pupils – several staff now working at local state schools as part of community partnership work. This very much part of the Pettitt ethos – outreach is not a box ticking necessity here but an essential part of what it is to grow into a valuing and valuable person.

Background and atmosphere: A school with an up and down history. Founded as the Free Grammar School of Sir Roger Cholmeley, Knight at Highgate, in 1565 – former pupils still known as Old Cholmeleians. Became Highgate School in the late 19th century – and no longer free. The chapel, undergoing terrific refurb at time of our visit, 'complete brick by brick restoration, new roof, stained

glass windows repaired and cleaned, apse painting restored etc; lighting and heating to render God's work less chilly and gloomy,' in Mr Pettitt's inimitable phrases – and main buildings are 19th century. Some impressive bits – old Gothic central hall with Norman arches, leaded lights, wrought iron balcony and cantilevered ceiling and splendid new Sir Martin Gilbert library in old assembly hall. A real library which, unlike so many schools' learning resource centres, actually has books in it, alongside all its rows of PCs, and an atmosphere to encourage concentration and study.

By the 1960s, the school buildings (some considerably less felicitous), including boarding houses, were spread over the heart of Highgate Village – the premier north London suburb whose denizens refer to it as 'the village' and who are, understandably, rather smug about living there. Charter Building adds new subject rooms in a five-storey glass cube. All very high tech – interactive whiteboards and PCs everywhere. The whole site is now a mix of the new, light, glass-bound, airy and stylish, and the old, rather shabby, small passages and dark areas along which school operates a clever one-way system – but all likely to look a great deal smarter and more coherent in the next few years. Much tramping up and down the hill between the main buildings and the Mills Centre, playing fields

etc and each day sees orderly crocodiles with professional chaperones trailing along.

School suffered during the 70s and 80s and took time to recover its reputation. Girls joined the sixth form in 2004 and year 7 in 2006, and the whole school is now fully co-educational and fully rehabilitated. A Christian foundation and an inclusive one, with multi-faith assemblies and speakers from different religions on a weekly basis. House system – 12 houses – but no fanatical exclusive loyalty to these, rather a friendly rivalry in competitions etc and designed to encourage the mixing of year groups. 'It's a family school,' a parent told us. 'Not everyone is terrifically academic, though they really make the scholars work. They are very encouraging to everyone.'

Pastoral care and discipline: We saw only absorbed and concentrating classes with lively teaching. Discipline, as pupils gratefully pointed out, is not dependent on the whims of individual staff but 'whole school,' ie you know what is coming to you at every level should you transgress. Very little transgressing these days and we have seldom seen so few uniform infringements – everyone is smart.

Small classes 'very well-monitored,' say parents. 'It's extremely well-run,' we were told. 'We are kept fully informed and have lots of email contact with staff,' another told us. 'The teaching staff are so enthusiastic and they really care about my children,' another enthused. Occasional loutishness clearly frowned on by majority of pupils who are a civilised lot. 'We have sent all our children there – they're so different academically and in their characters – but all have been happy.'

Pupils and parents: From a wide area of north and more central London, though most live near, if not within walking distance. 'Not ruthlessly elitist,' as one parent put it but lots of city lawyers, accountants etc with clear idea of what they want from the school. Pupils are friendly, happy and articulate. Most seem proud to be at the school and keen not to jeopardise their futures. Notable OCs include Rt Hons Charles Clarke and Anthony Crosland, Michael Mansfield QC, Johnny Borrell of Razorlight, Ringo Starr's son Zak Starkey of Oasis and The Who, Orlando Weeks of The Maccabees and DJ Yoda, Phil Tufnell, Sir Clive Sinclair, Alex Comfort, Nigel Williams, Sir John Tavener, Barry Norman, Gerard Manley Hopkins and Sir John Betjeman. Doubtless, Old Girl Cholmeleians shortly to make their marks.

Entrance: Wildly oversubscribed at every stage – on a scale we see most commonly with the grammars. Six hundred apply at 11+ for the 70 places available when the junior school pupils have been accommodated. At 13+, 180 compete for 25-30 places; tests and interviews in autumn term of year 7. At 16+, 120 for 30. At 11, around 60 per cent from state primaries and 40 per cent – mainly girls – from local preps. At 13+ mostly boys entering from the obvious preps – Arnold House, Devonshire House, The Hall, Keble etc.

Exit: Around a dozen, mostly boys, leave post GCSE to, mostly, Camden School for Girls, which has boys in the sixth. Around 90 per cent gain places at their first choice university – Bristol, UCL, Durham, Edinburgh and Leeds among most favoured; some now head to top US universities. Good numbers to Oxbridge each year – 23 in 2014. Economics, English and languages are popular subject choices.

Money matters: Scholarships – music and academic – at all usual entry points and now purely honorary. 'Much kudos, but not just to the particularly brainy but to those who exemplify scholarship (persistence, creativity, setting own agenda, leading learning in the classroom, originality),' stresses head. Bursaries up to the value of 100 per cent fees available each year and most go to those who get all or most of that amount. School makes extensive efforts via primary school visits etc to reach those who need to know.

Remarks: A new school in all but site and name – co-ed, modern, delivering a first rate education to the lively minds and limbs lucky enough to get in.

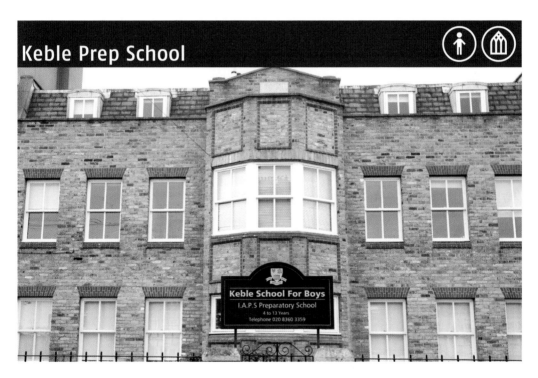

Wades Hill, London, N21 1BG

Independent • Pupils: 220 • Ages: 4–13 • Non-denom
• Fees (per term): £3,615 – £4,490

Tel: 020 8360 3359
Fax: 020 8360 4000
Email: office@kebleprep.co.uk
Website: www.kebleprep.co.uk

18

Headmaster: Since 2006, Mr Jed McCarthy (fifties). Studied maths and management at Queen Elizabeth College, London, PGCE at the Institute of Education, then worked in state schools in Brent. Left the profession to spend five years in industry, but realised he 'really missed teaching' and returned to Orley Farm, where he remained for 16 years (as head of maths, director of studies and deputy head). A quietly-spoken enthusiast, Mr McCarthy has worked determinedly since his arrival to build up the esprit de corps of pupils and parents and undoubtedly succeeded. Parents are lavish in their praise. 'He's always waiting at the gate and has a genuine interest in each boy,' said one mother. 'He's a very caring, very nurturing gentleman,' said another. Parents are also grateful for his availability and effectiveness. 'He's always ready to hear you out about any little gripe and he really gets things done.' Two grown-up sons.

Entrance: Register a couple of years before entry at four but pressure on places is not intense. The school is non-selective. Some new entrants from the state sector at 11.

Exit: A small exodus at 11 to high-achieving local grammar schools and comprehensives but head hopes to attract parents who understand the benefits of a school that runs to 13. 'I believe in 13 plus,' he says. At that age, Mill Hill and St Albans are historically the two most popular choices, but horizons are expanding – 'we are sending boys to Highgate, City, UCS, Westminster, St Edmund's Ware and St Columba's'. Wherever pupils go, the school does its utmost to ensure the best match between boy and school – 'we know the boys very well and recommend on personality'.

Remarks: A small school, which hovers at around 200 boys in all, so class size is reflectively intimate, ranging from 12-15 in two parallel forms. In the early years the school follows the national curriculum, with add-ons such as French, which starts in year 3.

Very much a traditional prep, it retains distinctive black and yellow blazers, formal good manners and neatly knotted ties. Boys still wear shorts in the warmer months and long hair is definitely frowned upon

The pace is accelerated and curriculum expanded as boys get older – 'we adapt it to the boys, easing into Common Entrance after 11,' says the head. Specialist teaching in music and PE in first two years, then further specialisation in art, ICT and French; by year 5, all subjects taught by specialists.

Enthusiastic teaching and boy-friendly approach. 'We try to make it very hands on,' said one teacher. 'We make models and castles.' Parents praise staff highly. 'My son is motivated, interested and enthused. It's a great credit to the teachers,' said a mother. 'The teachers are incredibly encouraging,' said another. In the past, the school has been criticised for not necessarily stretching the brightest, but the head has spent time, effort and money rebalancing that equation – 'and we're not finished yet'. A director of studies now has a clear brief and the brightest are given differentiated teaching in class and one-to-one support out of it. Boys are setted in English and maths from year 5, with informal setting in science, French and humanities.

The philosophy, however, is very much 'each child is an individual' and the struggling are equally well guided, with the full range of SEN support. The school deals comfortably with dyslexia and dyspraxia, mild autism and Asperger's. 'What I'm trying to do is not be the most academic school,' says the head, 'but to get all boys to expect more of themselves, set themselves higher standards and achieve them.' And parents confirm this is what happens – 'they really understands my son's strengths and weakness and really nourish him. I'm certain they meet all the boys' needs, even those at opposite ends of the spectrum'.

This is a small site and facilities are relatively restricted, though there is a French room and small science lab. Rebuild has brought more classroom space, a new science lab and an art room, allowing for relocation of the library, which had doubled as a music room. Limited space, too, for sports (though an attractive small gym), but games, played twice a week, are taken seriously. Rugby (re-introduced by the head), football, cricket and tennis are the main menu and a school minibus transports players to local and distant pitches. Rugby has put the school back on the prep school circuit. 'We mainly play other small local schools,' says the head. 'We lose more than we win, but we do play – and have tea afterwards.' Parents feel that even the sportiest get sufficient exercise and opportunity. 'A new PE teacher has invited a Tottenham scout to come to the school'. Numerous lunch-time and after-school clubs include puzzle club, movie club, Common Entrance drop-in club.

Has been going for 80 years, a lone prep school in an affluent suburban area of north London. Its aim now, as always, is to serve the local community, a community of small family businesses rather than City professionals. Many parents are first-time buyers. 'Our parents often want what they didn't have for themselves,' says the head. Many have Mediterranean roots (Turkish, Spanish, Greek, Italian, Cypriot) and a firm belief in family, and the school reflects those values with a strong family atmosphere.

Very much a traditional prep, it retains distinctive black and yellow blazers, formal good manners and neatly knotted ties. Boys still wear shorts in the warmer months and long hair is definitely frowned upon. Pastoral care is equally old school. 'We're looking for grounded, rounded individuals,' says the head. 'We cope well with all manner of children.' The aim is supportive rather than hothouse. 'We don't want to put pressure on ridiculously young. We want them to achieve, but not by testing to the eyeballs'. The mood is friendly and safe: 'If you're stuck on something,' said one boy, 'there's always a teacher to help you,' and the atmosphere is orderly and quiet, with bright noticeboards and well-run classrooms.

A 'big brother, little brother' scheme matches older pupils with younger ones – evident and unaffected warmth stretching across the age divide. On our visit, a boy at the top of the school, clearly revered by a recent arrival, praised his small friend for being able to tie his tie. Discipline is firm but certainly not draconian. 'Can you do it better?' is the gentle reproach. Pupils thrive on it. 'If I'm

honest,' said one undoubtedly honest young man in his final year, 'I love the school and I'm going to miss it when I leave'. Parents are equally positive. 'We chose it because it's very friendly and has a great identity that boys can relate to. I wish I could find a school for my daughter that is as good as this one'. 'We love the school. It's a home from home,' said another. 'My son looks forward to going to school every day.' Keble is not a wealthy or notably well endowed place, but is undoubtedly a happy and safe haven, where all boys are treated with respect and respond in kind. A very secure place to start your schooldays.

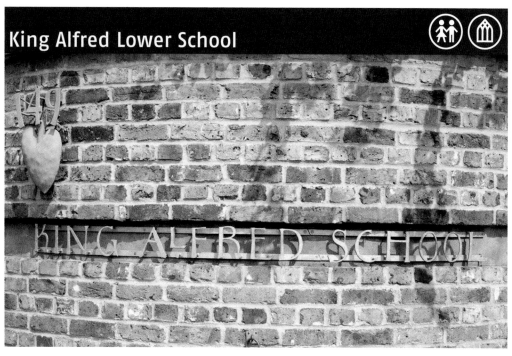

King Alfred Lower School

Linked school: King Alfred School, 526

Manor Wood, 149 North End Road, London, NW11 7HY

Independent • Pupils: 300 • Ages: 4–11 • Fees (per term): £4,397 – £5,066

Tel: 020 8457 5200
Fax: 020 8457 5249
Email: admissions@kingalfred.org.uk
Website: www.kingalfred.org.uk

9

Head of Lower School: Mr David Weale BSc PGCE

Entrance: For entry into reception at 4+, names are put down from birth. Date of registration in relation to the child's date of birth (over 200 apply for 40 places in reception) decides visit order. 'We go down the list'. Prospective students come for a two-hour visit and are observed by teachers to assess

children's readiness for the next stage of their education and 'whether the child is able to fully participate in and take advantage of the education offered by KAS'. Parents meet with the head and senior staff at the same time.

Entry for occasional places is also by waiting list order and the visits are half, full or two days, depending on age.

Exit: Majority to senior school.

Remarks: A gentle, liberal and progressive introduction to education, with first names, no uniform, no formal homework till the top of the junior school and no exams till the upper school. Non-selective; extra help for those at both ends of the spectrum. Lots of cross-curricula topic work.

Reception and Year 1 pupils start off in Ivy Wood, which used to belong to Anna Pavlova, across the road from the main school. Leafy site between Hampstead and Golders Green, with main school buildings round a village-like common. Den-building very much part of the experience and whole-year camping trips take place from year 4; top two years can join the annual school ski trip.

Visual and creative arts very important and everyone uses the well-equipped DT building, with impressive results. Lots of time for PE as well as outdoor play. All lower school classrooms have ovens for baking. Everyone learns drama and plays are performed indoors or in the outdoor amphitheatre. A small farm, complete with chickens, ducks and bees, an allotment and outdoor learning classroom.

Child-centred ethos; non-denominational; parents mostly on the liberal end of the spectrum, and from the surrounding wealthy suburbs of Hampstead, Golders Green, Highgate and Muswell Hill. High international contingent but low ethnic mix.

King Alfred School

Linked school: King Alfred Lower School, 525

Manor Wood, 149 North End Road, London, NW11 7HY

Independent • Pupils: 625 • Ages: 4–18 • Non-denom • Fees (per term): £5,056 – £5,301

Tel: 020 8457 5200
Fax: 020 8457 5249
Email: admissions@kingalfred.org.uk
Website: www.kingalfred.org.uk

10

Head: Since 2003, Mrs Dawn Moore (mid-40s) BSc MA (London) PGCE. Grew up in Nuneaton (daughter of a teacher), where she attended Higham Lane School, before proceeding to UCL to study genetics. PGCE at the Institute of Education, MA in education management at King's College, London. Started at King Alfred as a science teacher in 1986, recognising at once that this was somewhere she felt at home: 'On my first visit, pupils came up to me and said, "Hello. Who are you? Can we help?" They weren't afraid to talk to adults. It was so different from my teaching practice'. After having her two daughters (now in the senior school), she took a couple of years off. Returned as a part-time science teacher, then deputy head. 'There was no favouritism. I had to apply for every job'.

A warm, unpretentious enthusiast, completely committed to the school's ethos, Dawn operates an open-door policy and knows most children, from the tinies to the sixth form, by name. Parents see her as an intelligent, anchoring presence: 'Dawn is wise and good at putting your mind at ease,' said one. 'The head is lovely,' said another. A trained and practising schools inspector, in her limited spare time she loves reading and cooking.

Academic matters: A school where exams are famously not the only priority. Pupils sit no formal exams until year 10, although each subject has its own testing process to ensure students are ready for GCSEs. That said, prides itself on being able to teach to the highest standards – 'if a child can get four or five A*s, we'll get them there,' says the head. Pleasing results at GCSE (most pupils take nine), with 48 per cent A*/A grades in 2014; equally solid at A level, with 39 per cent A*/A and 66% A*/B. Exams may not be the main focus, but 'personalised learning' definitely is, and parents feel happy that every child is treated as an individual. 'We have no idea who the clever children are,' said one. 'All are special – they're not compared to one another.'

Not a vast range of subject choice at GCSE (curriculum languages French, Spanish and Latin); good variety at A level, with 24 options, and every attempt is made to accommodate any combination. The classroom approach, as with the whole-school approach, is relaxed. 'Teachers are not that strict,' said one senior school pupil. 'It can sometimes take quite a long time for lessons to begin, but you're still motivated to work.' Homework and marking, however, can be a bit too relaxed for some. 'The school believes that children should be children,' said one mother. 'I like the fact that it doesn't force

Teachers are called by their first name and pupils are expected to be self-disciplined, co-operative and self-motivated. Head sees the mutual respect between teachers and pupils as one of the key strengths of the school

them to do two hours a night, but sometimes I think they could push a little more.'

Sixth form particularly strong in the expressive arts (photography amongst the best in the country) and arts subjects (English, history); scientists generally find themselves in a minority. A few vocational options post GCSE (business studies and music technology. 'Some children are not ready to leave school at 16,' says the head.

Additional support is available for students with mild specific learning difficulties – individually, in groups or in class. Students are monitored throughout their time at the school. Teachers build up a picture of pupils' learning profiles and identify those who might require specific intervention.

Games, options, the arts: Known for its creativity and the strength of its visual arts teaching; all lower school classrooms have ovens for baking and the school has its own forge. Thriving drama, with theatre, 'black box' studio and masterclasses often given by parents who are themselves leading lights in the profession. There are two well-stocked libraries, one for seniors, one for juniors. Music is popular, with orchestras, band and ensembles of all kinds.

Sport played enthusiastically, but 'go, fight, win' is not what this school is about. 'We don't have a first 11 in each year – often we just have a mixed-ability team,' says the head. The spirit, however, is strong, and an eager crowd turns out to support the home team. As well as the usual ball sports, sails three (school-built) boats on Welsh Harp, the Thames and Norfolk Broads. Games aside, for a London school it is an outdoorsy place. The large central playing field is at the heart of the campus and even on the rainiest day is filled with fresh air enthusiasts. Considerable emphasis on self-sufficiency. Den building very much part of the experience and whole-year camping trips take place from year 4.

Extracurricular, too, is core. In the senior school, years 7-11 required to make their choice from a wide range of activities, from pottery to golf; sixth form options include screenwriting for films, emotional intelligence and Mandarin. Strong commitment to volunteering throughout, with pupils helping out at the local special school and raising significant sums for international causes (including building a school after the tsunami in Sri Lanka). Good careers advice (which kicks off in year 7) helps with GCSE and A level options and UCAS applications pre- and post-A level. As one might expect, green is high on the agenda – one of the first schools to introduce solar panels and recycling

bins. Delicious, exclusively healthy lunches with plenty of fresh salads, yoghurt and water.

Background and atmosphere: Founded by parents in Hampstead in 1898, original aim was to provide an education based on what was best for the child and encourage learning for its own sake. Part of the progressive movement, sees its kindred schools as Bedales in Hampshire and St Christopher in Letchworth. Moved to its current site, a leafy patch of north London opposite Golders Hill Park, in 1921, and has recently expanded, with a school building for the infants across the road from the main site at Ivy Wood, once the home of Anna Pavlova. Attractive, if compact, grounds, with a mixture of periods and styles (new fitness studio, music and drama block, lovely arts and crafts dining hall) grouped around a central village-like common. Star attractions include a wooded amphitheatre, an arbour (Squirrel Hall), formed from the sheltering branches of two ancient chestnuts, and a diminutive farm, complete with chickens, ducks and bees.

The original ethos – liberal, progressive, egalitarian, child-centred – remains core to the school's values today. Parents and pupils agree that the needs of each child are foremost. 'They try to act very holistically. They look at the individual and find out what makes them shine'. In many respects, too, operates as a large extended family, without the rigid age divide found elsewhere. 'It's a really friendly school,' said one year 9. 'Older kids look out for younger ones and you'll see sixth formers play with year 7s.' Most children seem to enjoy their time here. 'They skip into school every day,' said one long-time parent. 'Even after the holidays, they can't wait to get back.'

New Fives Court lower school building includes auditorium, cutting-edge art technology room with kiln and multi-purpose room for food science, rural studies and general science. ICT suite, learning support area and lower school library upstairs.

Pastoral care and discipline: Has always believed in minimal rules and flat hierarchy. Teachers are called by their first name and pupils are expected to be self disciplined, co-operative and self-motivated. Head sees the mutual respect between teachers and pupils as one of the key strengths of the school. 'We trust them to be sensible'. The expectation, too, is that wrongdoing is likely to be an accident. 'We enable children to learn from their mistakes. There are no quick sanctions. It has to be worked through. Equally there are few reoffenders'. Those who cross the line between liberty and licence – 'being irre-

---

Star attractions include a wooded amphitheatre, an arbour (Squirrel Hall), and a diminutive farm, complete with chickens, ducks and bees

---

sponsible in the science labs' or 'putting others in danger' –- are given a 'blue form' and sent to the head. Children can be devastated. 'I've seen 16-year-old boys cry,' said a member of staff. Offences too serious to talk through – inappropriate behaviour towards their peers, bullying – can result in suspension. Expulsion for drugs on the premises, but head can't remember the last incident, and the school has a 'huge' drugs education programme. 'The kids are pretty mature about sex and drugs,' said one parent. No uniform or dress code, but pupils tend not to push the boundaries, preferring standard-issue jeans and jumpers.

Four counsellors. 'We know what's out there and make it our business to be pro-active'. Help too from other pupils – peer mentoring, school 'Cits', pupils' council. The end result is a happy bunch of kids. 'I've seen other parents go through miserable teens,' said one mother with two teenage children at the school. 'King Alfred teaches them a lot of confidence.' Non-denominational – pupils of every faith and none.

Pupils and parents: An arts and media favourite, parents often choose it for its informality and creativity. 'They come from both ends of the spectrum,' says Dawn Moore. 'There are those who are so liberal they think we're conservative and those who are conservative with a small "c"'. Popular, too, with former pupils. New converts are often those who disliked their own, more traditional schooldays:

'I'd have killed to go to a school like this,' said one. 'They make it such fun.' Pupils, mainly from the wealthier suburbs of north London (Hampstead, Golders Green, Highgate, Muswell Hill), are confident and articulate and expect to be given equal weight as adults. Quite a large international contingent – Americans, South Africans, Israelis, Swedish, Germans, Spanish, Italians.

Entrance: Over 100 apply for a handful of places at 11. 'A lot of thought goes into the mix of classes'. Not highly selective at A level – four GCSEs minimum for those already in the school; at least five at grade B or above for 10 to 15 or so newcomers, with A*-B in chosen subjects. All candidates, however, interviewed to ensure they'll fit into the school culture.

Exit: Around a quarter or so leave post-GCSE. 'Some children have been here since they were 4 and it's quite a long time to spend at one school,' says the head. About 98 per cent to further education, a good chunk (8-12 each year) to art foundation, then to the full spectrum of universities. One to Oxford in 2014 (French and Portuguese), others to eg Birmingham, Bristol, Manchester, Sussex, York, LSE and Warwick.

Money matters: Though not particularly well endowed, attempts to keep fees as stable as possible while keeping facilities up to date. No scholarships, a small number (about four) of means-tested bursaries in year 7 and sixth form.

Remarks: A kind, liberal, creative school that suits the self-starter, the sophisticated and the artistic (pupils and parents). Will get the best out of most children, but possibly not ideal for those who require competition in the classroom or on the games field. Good, too, for the square peg and those who might find a more traditional environment oppressive. Not a school for parents obsessed with league-table position or those looking for children who jump to attention when an adult enters the room.

The Latymer School

Haselbury Road, London, N9 9TN

State · Pupils: 1380 · Ages: 11–18 · Non–denom

Tel: 020 8807 4037
Fax: 020 8887 8111
Email: office@latymer.co.uk
Website: www.latymer.co.uk

19

Headteacher: Since 2005, Mr Mark E Garbett (50s) MA (Cambridge) MEd NPQH. Plenty of experience in academically strong schools, including a previous headship at Stretford Grammar School, Manchester; five years at Skegness Grammar School and Royal Belfast Academical Institution; and a spell as head of maths at Framlingham College. All helps, though Latymer 'is much more selective, you're teaching very bright young people all day, every day, you've got to stretch them, you've got to be on top of your game to generate that respect that you know what you're talking about'. Head supported by three deputies and 82 full-time staff, all with degrees in their specialist subjects. A down-to-earth maths teacher who likes high standards, Mr Garbett 'still teaches two classes each year' and, in his fourth decade in education, loves the fact that 'I still get new questions' from students. He likes teaching and likes children, 'really important because just occasionally a parent comes across a teacher in a school and has this idea that that teacher doesn't like children. We can't have that here'. This helps with selecting new teachers: 'If I ask a teacher in an interview, "Do you teach chemistry or children?", I am really interested in their answer.' Since he has recruited around 60 per cent of the current staff since joining the school, child-friendliness level is evidently high. Head describes his position at Latymer as 'the best job in education – who would want to be secretary of state?' He finds the many opportunities to meet parents – at welcome evenings, parents' evenings, concerts, sports sidelines, one-to-ones – 'enjoyable, except for the time when I was foolish enough to volunteer to sit on a bucking bronco at an International Food Festival'. He fell off. Has two daughters, plays the piano, sails and runs.

Academic matters: Good GCSE results, making it the top performing school in Enfield borough and within the top six per cent in London, with 78 per cent A*/A grades in 2014. Pupils must choose a MFL from French, German (both very popular), Russian or Latin (not so popular) plus a humanity subject or religious education. ICT is not taught as a separate subject but incorporated across the whole curriculum.

Years ago a decision was made to reduce the number of GCSEs to nine to ease the stress on pupils and so that 'school life can be enjoyed for itself'. The recent introduction of triple GCSE science increases the number to 10 but head still thinks it important that academic success is not at the expense of 'a life outside school'.

At sixth form the school offers 'nothing apart from an unashamedly academic programme', so no vocational subjects here. The majority stay on at sixth form but another 50 join from other schools, so exam rates at 63 per cent A*/A and 84 per cent A*/B grades in 2014 are commendable. Having a larger than normal sixth form means the school 'can teach a big range of subjects, which smaller sixth forms struggle to offer'.

Parents agree that the school is 'very good academically' and it certainly makes plenty of effort to award academic achievement across all years. Year 13s are awarded in specialist subjects too, such as mechanics, statistics and government and politics. Pupils who do not gain a subject prize have the opportunity to be awarded either a Latymer Lodge or school prize for gaining a high aggregate at A level. There are also open awards for special achievements in spoken English, creative work,

We are told that the school's Amnesty International group is 'the largest and most active school group in the country'

instrumental performance, music composition and fieldwork. Prizes are awarded for service to the school in music, debating and service to the community, thus plenty of motivation to strive and to win here. 'They will take your child through the process and your child will pass the exams,' one parent stated confidently. Another said, 'I believe that both my children have been encouraged and guided to fulfil their academic potential. Classroom teaching is supported with a range of visits and activities to inspire as well as stretch.'

Where pupils have a special learning need, they will find help through one of the two SEN teachers, one of whom focuses on those who need extra support and the other on gifted and talented pupils. Around 350 pupils have EAL requirements and of the 29 pupils identified as having a special educational need just three have a statement.

Games, options, the arts: More than 17 different sporting activities offered (from athletics and badminton to volleyball and ultimate Frisbee). Notable achievements include winners of Enfield Schools Hockey Champions and Enfield Football Cup, alongside a number of other firsts, seconds and thirds in regional finals for netball, tennis and cricket. In year 10, when pupils have the opportunity to specialise, and at sixth form, they can also take squash, golf, swimming, orienteering and dry-slope skiing in addition to the normal range of sports on offer. The school encourages active lifestyles and rewards pupils' enthusiasm for sport with a number of awards that recognise outstanding achievement both in and outside of school. These include hockey, football (for girls, not boys), netball, cross-country, rounders, tennis and cricket. All pupils have the opportunity to spend a week at Ysgol Latymer (the school's outdoor sports centre in Snowdonia National Park in Wales) for activities such as hill walking, orienteering, climbing, abseiling and canoeing.

Latymer once had an art specialism and so the subject has a strong presence outside the department, with work on display around the school and contributing to cross-curricular subjects (for example, year 9s painted the background scenery for senior drama productions of My Fair Lady and Hairspray). Experts visit to do talks and run special workshops in oil painting and sculpture, and the department runs visits to the London Institute, Tate Modern and Tate Britain as well as to Barcelona and Paris. As a result, examiners have commented on the good grasp pupils have on contemporary artists.

Drama is supported by trips out and really plays out hugely in the big theatre productions that take place at the school each year: a main school production in November, a junior production in July, and the house drama competition every other year. The language and drama curriculums are supported by school journeys and exchanges through links with Russia, France and Germany; there have also been exchange visits with the Mwambisi school in Tanzania; other trips include geographers to Iceland, classicists to Italy, artists to New York, skiers to the French Alps, canoeists to the Ardêche, music to Austria, Belgium, Germany, the Czech Republic and other places in Europe; sports to Holland and Italy. Other destinations have included Nepal, India and Malawi, and every other year there is a sports trip to Barbados.

A quarter of the pupils learn a musical instrument at standards ranging from beginners to beyond grade 8. As pupils advance through key stage 3 they focus on 'practical music-making wherever possible', covering projects on classical, jazz, pop and world music, with regular assessment every half term. There are five orchestras ranged from grade 3 to post grade 8, a concert band and several choirs. They perform at school concerts and many are invited elsewhere, such as the National Festival for Music.

Latymerians enjoy a rich range of extracurricular activities that shape life at the school; parents value its contribution to their personal and social development. House, theatre and music productions; over 60 different clubs and teams run before, during, and after school, and at weekends. Clubs cover art, gardening, chess and more. There is an Young Enterprise group, an economics society, a Christian union and clubs whose sole purpose is to raise funds for less fortunate children in developing nations while pupils learn more about their lives. We are told that the school's Amnesty International group is 'the largest and most active school group in the country'. The LAFTA (Latymer Awards in Film,

Television and Advertising) is a fun and creative play on the Oscar-style awards ceremony.

Background and atmosphere: Tradition creates the atmosphere at Latymer. It was established in nearby Church Street in 1624 at the direction of Edward Latymer, a City merchant, who bequeathed certain property to trustees on condition that they were to cloth and educate 'eight poore boies of Edmonton'. His, and the 'generosity of the many others since', are remembered each year on the school's Foundation Day. Pupils are proud of this tradition and seem enthusiastic about the events that keep it alive. The school's motto – Qui Patitur Vincit (Who Endures Wins) – aptly sums up the spirit of the school, and is the title of the annual talk to the school (head's given it seven times so far and says it's a 'feat to bring a new twist to it'). The school moved to its present location in 1910.

On the day of our visit it seemed very quiet, apart from the hum and beat of instrumental practice (including drums) in the music department and a flurry of students preparing for the school's major production in the Seward Theatre downstairs. Built on three acres of land and flanked by 12 acres of playing fields, which separate the school from the main A10 road, it looks deceptively small from the front. There are a number of outbuildings around the main one, added at various times over the

Year 9s painted the background scenery for senior school productions of My Fair Lady and Hairspray

school's life and capturing its spirit of progress: the great hall (1928), which seats over 1000; the gymnasia and technical labs (1966); a performing arts centre (2000) and a sports/dining hall complex (2006). In 2010 the high-tech multi-purpose Seward Theatre (performance space, auditorium, media studio, art gallery and drama theatre) was opened. The school also has a number of rooms dedicated to specialist teaching, for example, a suite of 12 science laboratories, six fully equipped technology rooms, and specialist ICT rooms with wireless networks, an intranet and access to remote access learning. There is a large library, with separate learning resource and careers centres. Sixth formers have a large common room and quiet study area.

The school's traditional atmosphere is maintained by the old students' association (there is an old boys' football club and old students' badminton club). Ex-students are very much involved school life, participating in school events, contributing to lessons, presenting school awards and setting up special funds. There is a rich sense of celebration of the past: each year a whole school assembly is organised for the 'grand Act of Remembrance' in honour of Latymerians who died in the two world wars. They sing the national anthem, read from the Bible, listen to a talk about war life and have a 'blessing suited to a multi-faith audience' pronounced by a local reverend. There is a book listing war casualties in the library, which pupils proudly pointed out.

Pastoral care and discipline: The 186 pupils in each year are organised into six form groups, and each form group belongs to one of the six house groups. They remain in these groups throughout their school lives, meeting daily for registration and form periods, including, in the lower years, PSHE lessons delivered by the form tutor. Each year group also has a head of learning (first port of contact for parents concerned about progress) who, along with the deputy head of learning, also act as mentor.

House culture is strong. Each has a senior pupil to lead, democratically elected. Activities are organised by senior pupils and used to inject a sense of comradeship and teamwork across all year groups, and to make new year 7s feel fully inducted into life at Latymer. They do this via sports tournaments and various competitions such as cake-making, drama and music. 'Equally importantly', houses also 'operate non-competitively' to organise community service activities and to help raise funds for charity (one house group raised over £80 in 20 minutes for Water Aid by taping water bottles to themselves). Together, this creates 'a strong sense of coherence and team working' among pupils at the school.

Pupils are expected to abide by the school rules and the home school agreement they signed with their parents on joining the school, but the school views 'self discipline resulting from wanting to learn' as more important as a deterrent for poor behaviour. Although behavourial problems are rare and 'dealt with swiftly by the head of learning or form tutor', one parent did say she thinks the pastoral care side of things 'is not as strong as the focus is on the academic side'. However, other parents say pastoral care is excellent: 'Not only do my daughters experience excellent teaching, they also benefit from being at a school with a firm commitment to pastoral care. They feel safe, secure, confident and happy. While the academic side is challenging, it is not to the exclusion of everything else.' Another said she has 'always felt comfortable emailing teachers direct if I have a concern or question'.

Pupils and parents: Anyone and everyone who is 'very clever', though the school wisely lists acceptable postcodes in its admission criteria. This includes half from Enfield, plus some in Haringey, Islington, Hackney and Waltham Forest.

Entrance: Only those 'deemed capable of achieving higher grades of GCSE are considered' at this highly oversubscribed, selective school. Selection is by the NVR test as well as literacy and numeracy. A parent said 'it used to be harder to get into', but over 2,000 typically apply for the 186 places, so many are still disappointed. Priority is given to looked-after children and those who live in designated postcodes areas in the boroughs of Hackney, Islington, Waltham Forest, Haringey and Enfield. Offers also made to around 20 students who live in these areas and show 'exceptional musical talent and achievement' akin to grade 5.

At sixth form, 90 per cent stay on. An additional 50 places are allocated to pupils from other schools, bringing the size of the sixth form to 234. Sixth form is also oversubscribed with around 442 applications for these 50 places. Places are offered to students who achieve at least six GCSE grade As, including the subjects they wish to study at AS level; they must also pass the Latymer test and live in one of the designated postcode areas.

Exit: Around 95 per cent go on to university or other forms of higher education in music and art. The school does not 'push Oxford or Cambridge though plenty apply, and plenty get offers' (30 in 2014). UCL, Bristol and Nottingham also popular; courses include aerospace engineering, medicine, law, Chinese, Russian and Egyptology. Very few – one or two – leave to go straight into employment.

Money matters: The Latymer Foundation offers some financial assistance to pupils experiencing hardship.

Remarks: A peek back in time shows that some well-known former pupils like Baroness Claire Tyler (chair of CAFCASS and president of the National Children's Bureau), footballer Johnny Haynes and Sir Bruce Forsyth CBE all did well here. Pupils clearly still do. This is a zealously traditional school with a highly likeable yet firm-handed head and pupils who show a healthy balance between hard work and play. There is some effort to keep with the times but the head's view is that 'If it ain't broke don't fix it'. Ofsted has a similar attitude and in its last report described the school as outstanding.

Mill Hill County High School

Worcester Crescent, London, NW7 4LL

State · Pupils: 1,720 · Ages: 11–19 · Non-denom

Tel: 0844 477 2424
Fax: 020 8959 6514
Email: admin@mhchs.org.uk
Website: www.mhchs.org.uk

11

Headteacher: Since 2004, Geoffrey Thompson MA MBA (Ed) FCMI (50s). Formerly head of Duchess's Community High School in Alnwick, Northumberland. Educated at Campbell College, Belfast, then at St Catharine's College, Cambridge, where he read music. Started his teaching career at Langley Park School for Boys in Bromley, where he worked for 18 years, before moving to Norfolk as deputy head, then on to Northumberland. Though Mill Hill County has always been a school with high standards, his decade in charge has improved it significantly. 'Having a vision and a blueprint is not my way,' he says. 'You have a set of principles and good judgement, you make decisions with other people and the place grows organically.'

A dapper soul, whose own tie is always immaculately knotted, he has a dry sense of humour and a delightfully precise command of the English language. Married to a teacher (who also works in the school), he has two daughters and a son. Out of hours, he enjoys reading, particularly modern history, travelling and music.

Academic matters: Mill Hill County is one of the country's highest performing comprehensives. With 70 per cent A*/B at A level in 2013 and 79 per cent A*-C at GCSE including English and maths, this is a school which believes in an academic focus. Apart from a handful of vocational qualifications in ICT and media, the curriculum is traditional, with a good range of modern languages (Spanish, French, German, Latin) and a quarter of pupils taking all three sciences at GCSE. In the sixth form – the largest in the borough – the 33 subjects on offer include sociology, psychology, economics and dance. Maths and science, however, are the most popular options (with 10 groups for maths). Most sixth formers take four AS levels ('a few do five, but we don't encourage it,' says the head).

Teaching strong throughout (with regular awards for science, geography and maths) and most subjects provide plenty of enrichment. In English, for example, there are Shakespeare and poetry workshops, in DT, direct links with industry. An undoubted strength of the school is the focused attention it offers for all. 'Every child is taught to their own individual abilities,' commented one parent. For those at the top of the spectrum, there are two members of staff to encourage A level students to aim for A*s and Russell Group universities, while those who struggle to make the A*-C benchmark at GCSE are offered a one-year course in which to resit. At this juncture too, the school

---

A dapper soul, whose own tie is always immaculately knotted, he has a dry sense of humour and a delightfully precise command of the English language

---

participates in a Barnet-wide scheme which sandwiches vocational college training with English, maths and employment skills. Largest number of SEN pupils in Barnet with a department reflective of their very varied needs (including provision for the blind). A raft of teaching assistants provides in-class aid and specialist staff oversee classes and support students beyond. 'It's quite an operation,' says the head.

Games, options, the arts: The school prides itself on its extra-curricular offering, but there's little doubt that music is the jewel in the crown. 'There are few

local schools that can hold a candle to us,' says the head with legitimate pride. He himself rehearses all year 7s to appear in the Christmas concert and from time to time plays the piano at assembly or a duet alongside a visiting professional. Standards throughout are exceptionally high. Recently, for the fourth year in a row, the orchestra is performing a joint concert with the Royal Philharmonic ('you have to be quite good for the RPO to come and play with you,' says the head). Meanwhile the school band will feature alongside that of the Royal Air Force at the Watford Colosseum. Regular lunchtime concerts, major concerts twice a term, large-scale musical in the Easter term, plus an annual European tour for concert and jazz bands. A full range of other sounds, including gospel, African drum and steel drum. Boys participate as enthusiastically as girls – 'unheard of,' says the head – and one talented former pupil performs regularly at Ronnie Scott's.

In sport too, the school has become a 'force to be reckoned with,' particularly in boys' football and girls' netball. Basketball and rugby also on offer and table tennis played enthusiastically by all. Excellent facilities for sport include a range of pitches, three playgrounds, gym, sports hall and in summer, six-lane track and three tennis courts. Art thriving, with a weekly art club and life drawing workshop run by the Royal Academy for A level pupils. Numerous guest speakers and in-demand trips (languages to Barcelona and Normandy, politics to the US, annual ski trip) to inspire and raise aspirations. Good range of clubs run early morning and after school (which can be difficult for those who live at a distance), plus D of E, World Challenge and CCF (shared with nearby independent Mill Hill).

Background and atmosphere: Originally opened in 1931 as Orange Hill Boys' Grammar School, which then combined with matching girls' grammar in the 1970s. Merged again with Moat Mount School in 1984 to create Mill Hill County High School. The school, fringed by a good expanse of playing fields and forest, now sits on a hilly site with panoramic London views. There, however, the picturesque ends, with well-used buildings crammed together in an intricate hotchpotch to accommodate more students than ever. 'It is overcrowded,' said one parent. 'They're the victims of their own success.' Older parts of the fabric include some fairly basic Portakabins (which house dance and drama), but recent additions have provided modern labs, a sixth form centre, computer suites and an air-conditioned assembly hall. Seven new classrooms are currently under construction.

The lack of elbow room doesn't seem to detract from the upbeat mood, with friendly and positive staff (on the day the guide visited a member of the

office team was ringing up a local primary school to ensure a forgotten jumper was returned to its owner) and parents praise the general sense of well-being. 'The school is very good at communicating,' said one. 'They keep us informed and I have the email addresses of all my child's teachers.' Another was grateful for the empathy shown at a difficult time. 'They were understanding and supportive when we had family problems.'

Not the easiest school to get to. No tube nearby, which contributes to the mood of semi-rural calm but can be difficult for those wanting to arrive early or stay late for clubs or games. Mill Hill became an academy in 2011, but still works closely with Barnet Council, particularly in its responsibilities for Oak Hill, a successful facility for 32 emotionally and behaviourally disturbed children, four and a half miles away.

Pastoral care and discipline: One of the first things parents tend to mention is the uniform policy. 'They're very strict on uniform,' said one. 'Everyone looks very smart.' The head sees uniform as a means of setting the expectation bar. 'We're very clear about what we say and insist that what we say is done. We aren't repressive, but you'd be unlikely to see anyone with their shirt tails not tucked in or their ties not tied.'

The head also spends one lesson a week making surprise visits to a range of classrooms. 'That way, you see what's happening. You chat to the children, look at their books. It's a co-operative relationship, but you could potentially see those same children in another context behaving badly.' The insistent focus on behaviour, attitude and good manners undoubtedly pays off. 'Most people who come across our students have positive things to say.'

Pupils and parents: About half the school's intake comes from the leafy and prosperous suburb of Mill Hill, with its high concentration of professionals and business families, but the intake is certainly not uniform. 'There are quite a lot of deprived children and the ethnic mix is huge,' says the head. It includes significant numbers of families who originate from the Indian sub-continent, Asia and Africa. Only a few, however, 'don't speak excellent English.'

Entrance: Mill Hill has entrance criteria guaranteed to drive north London parents into a neurotic frenzy, with 240 places at 11 sliced up into small print sub-sections. Lucky locals can benefit from one of the 90 guaranteed 'geography' places. But distance from the gates is frighteningly close (0.8 miles in 2012). Siblings, too, are ensured a desk. After that the 60 places awarded on aptitude are split into: 24 for technology, 24 for music and 12 for dance. Technology is tested in two stages – a reasoning test in the summer term of year 5 whittles down about 1500 to 240, the second round (in abstract reasoning and maths) held in September cherry picks the rest ('it's harder than getting into Oxford,' jokes the head). Music equally competitive, with 389 auditioning last year. 'You can, however, play a snappy piece on the classroom xylophone and come out higher than a carefully coached

grade 4 violinist.' Dance candidates are selected by audition.

The large (and heavily over-subscribed) sixth form admits a further 40 to 60 pupils out of 600 applicants, with minimum entry requirements of six grade Bs at GCSE, including English and maths.

'You have to be quite good for the RPO to come and play with you,' says the head

Those wishing to study science and maths need As in their chosen subjects though, and most come garlanded with a string of A*s and As.

Exit: No one is ever asked to leave (except for disciplinary matters), but a fair few move on after GCSE to local sixth form colleges, independent and grammar schools. More than 70 per cent to university, the majority to Russell Group (the school has one of the highest representations here of any comprehensive in the UK). Nine to Oxbridge last year. Quite a number to drama and art-related degrees. A consistent trickle to the US.

Money matters: The transformation to academy status has released additional funds and these are now being used for building projects. Otherwise not rich, but not poor either.

Remarks: A cheerful, well-run school producing highly motivated, high achieving students. Exceptional music.

Mill Hill School

Linked schools: Belmont Mill Hill Preparatory School, 494; Grimsdell, Mill Hill Pre-Preparatory School, 515

The Ridgeway, London, NW7 1QS

Independent • Pupils: 650 • Ages: 13–18 • Non-denom • Fees (per term): Day £6,082; boarding £8,168 – £9,609

Tel: 020 8959 1176
Fax: 020 8201 0663
Email: registrations@millhill.org.uk
Website: www.millhill.org.uk

12

Headmaster: Since 2007, Dr Dominic Luckett BA DPhil FRSA (40s). Educated at the University of Leicester and Magdalen College, Oxford, where he did his doctorate in Tudor history. Taught at Harrow, where he became both head of history and

an assistant housemaster, then at Worth, where he was deputy head. He is a serving inspector with the ISI and on the council of the University of Leicester. Attracted to Mill Hill because it mixes day with boarding and because of its location in north

London. Married to Cara, a barrister, and has two young daughters.

A tall, softly spoken and sincere man who pauses before giving a considered response – a likeable head. 'He's very focused,' one parent said. He is under no illusion that the school still has a way to go academically before it can pit itself against other north London rivals, but says the foundations are there to make it a truly 'phenomenal school.' 'My job is to realise some of the potential this school has,' he told us. 'And I think we're getting there – we've already achieved the best A level results we've ever had this year. We're never going to be the most massively selective school, but we pride ourselves on having students with really lovely values, who may bring other things to the table.' That's why, he says, they interview potential candidates before seeing their exam results. 'If someone comes along for an interview and demonstrates they have extra strings to their bow – great at sport or drama for example – we may be a bit more lenient if they're borderline in their CE exam.'

The head's main objective is that each of his pupils feel really proud about being a Millhillian, and that he steers away from the school's reputation of being the 'back-up' school because they didn't get into UCS or Highgate. Says he would have given his right arm to have attended a school like this, having come from a non-privileged background with parents who had low academic aspirations. 'I know the difference a good education can make. I'm only where I am today because I got into the local grammar school, otherwise I could easily be working in the local Sainsbury's.'

Academic matters: In 2014, 45 per cent A*A and 76 per cent A*-B grades at A level. School's aim is to achieve each child's full potential while working in a way that makes them feel comfortable – 'for some, three Bs at A level is a real achievement, but others here get three, four or five As,' he says. Some children, too, require a lot of pressure to achieve and others buckle under pressure.

Twenty-four subjects on offer at A level, including Chinese, business studies and government and politics. One parent criticised the subjects on offer as limiting compared to other schools. 'My friend

---

The stunning and contemporary Favell building has a glass atrium – providing a light and airy home for seven departments

removed her child from the school to go to another sixth form as they didn't offer psychology as an A Level,' she told us. Good spread of languages offered at GCSE: French, Spanish, German, Greek and Latin, plus Portuguese and Chinese as extras.

Two of the learning resources on the campus are worth noting. The library (an 'innovative conversion' of the school squash courts) is a two-tiered, large, bright space, incredibly well stocked with books and a gallery for magnificent artwork by students. The stunning and contemporary Favell building has a glass atrium – providing a light and airy home for seven departments, including modern languages, history and geography. Also used for exhibitions and entertainment. Startlingly quiet classrooms (we had to check to see if there were students inside) surround the atrium on three floors. Well presented but scant student displays and artwork adorn the walls, encased in glass frames.

New science block is under way to replace the rather old-fashioned labs where Nobel-winning scientist Francis Crick once studied. (This doesn't seem to hold pupils back since Imperial College is a popular university destination).

Mill Hill takes in a reasonably broad spread of academic ability and aims to get the best out of each child by helping them to learn effectively. 'We're not a hot house,' says the head. 'We're never going to be the top academic school in the country, but we want to make teaching accessible and enjoyable and give children high expectations.' That said, we have some very bright children. It's a question of identifying what each child is capable of and providing what each child needs.

The school has limited facilities for SEN. Head is sympathetic but pragmatic. 'We have facilities in place to deal with mild to moderate dyslexia, but for anything more severe, we just don't have the resources in place.' All new entrants are screened for dyslexia and dyspraxia and are given extra time in the CE exam. One parent whose child is

moderately dyslexic said the school was 'helpful to a point,' but she had to fight for most things.

Games, options, the arts: Sport, sport, sport. A clincher for pupils and parents alike when choosing this school over others. Competitive and recreational sport has always played a big role at Mill Hill and with its expansive site it's easy to see why. Rugby and cricket are the two biggies here. As one parent told us: 'My son only agreed to come here because of the rugby.' The school established a reputation as a rugby playing school from the outset, and has produced a large number of international rugby players. Great facilities in which to play.

The school's cricket arena has been called 'one of the most beautiful grounds to play cricket in the London area.' To add to this, they have the services of a professional coach. Players are regularly selected to represent Middlesex and Hertfordshire and occasionally England. Girls too have done exceptionally well, representing both school (playing as part of the boys' team) and country.

Golf is another major sport here and is even incorporated into the timetable. They are the only school in London to boast a golf academy, (although ironically no golf course – pupils play at nearby Hendon). One girl has been selected for the England U16 girls' golf team. Tennis is very strong – one of the strongest schools in the south east.

Soccer, netball, hockey, cross-country and swimming (the school boasts a beautiful, new 25m pool) on offer. More adventurous pupils can try their hand at sailing, skiing/snowboarding, riding, clay pigeon shooting and Taekwondo (these incur extra cost). Mill Hill is also one of the few remaining independent schools to have an Eton Fives court. The shape of the court is modelled on the chapel at Eton (we thought it looked like a Roman gladiator chamber).

For non-sporty types (and they are seemingly few and far between), drama is very popular and taken by many at both GCSE and A level. With drama studio, theatre and large school stage, it is rare for a production not to be in rehearsal. House arts festival takes place every two years (alternating with a house music competition), with 10 plays performed over three nights. Many ex-students have become thesps of stage and screen. Art is strong and some of the art displayed around the school are amongst the best we've seen. This year saw the first inflatable sculpture floating around the studios. Good music facilities (specialised equipment for composition and recording) and in addition to curricular music, lots of opportunities to participate in a wide range of musical activities (chapel choir, string orchestra, jazz band and chamber music. Well-equipped on the DT side with 30 top-end computers and industry standard 3D printers.

A series of monthly lectures on a variety of topics – from classical history to journalism and politics (presenters include Jonathan Dimbleby and Terry Jones) are a popular and successful addition to the already crammed Mill Hill diary.

Thriving charitable work and partnership trips every summer; lower sixth form pupils have the opportunity to work for two to three weeks in a variety of educational projects with partners in Zambia, India and Nicaragua. Those taking part often talk about them being a 'life-changing experience.' As one parent told us: 'The school does exactly what it says on the box – there's something there for everyone.'

Background and atmosphere: Founded in 1807 by a group of non-conformist Christian ministers and city merchants, who placed their school outside London because of the 'dangers, both physical and moral, awaiting youth while passing through the streets of a large, crowded city.' Once peaceful and rural, The Ridgeway, where the school is situated, has become a busy and frustrating road (to be avoided like the plague at school pick-up). Nonetheless, it is still a very pretty part of the old Mill Hill village, laced with ponds and rambling cottages.

The school itself doesn't disappoint, with its handsome, neoclassical, pillared façade (BBC News website often uses a picture of Mill Hill School for articles about boarding schools). This is more like a stately home than a school, with pale yellow

They are the only school in London to boast a golf academy (although ironically no golf course – pupils play at nearby Hendon)

---

walls, marbled floors, pillars, plaques and elaborately framed portraits (most notably that of Mill Hill's former member of staff, James Murray, the third editor of the Oxford English Dictionary).

Our tour began at the top terrace, with sweeping views across parkland (undoubtedly the school's selling point) and 120 acres of green belt. The panorama is one of immaculately kept lawns, gravelled walkways, ponds and a smorgasbord of varying architecture which marry beautifully from arts and crafts buildings to the glass exterior of the new Favell building. The previous head, we are told, wanted to 'massively transform' the school for its bicentenary. We poked our heads into the beautiful, basilica-style chapel, designed by architect Basil Champney (best known for his work at Oxford and Winchester College). For students it means a compulsory weekly chapel visit, although the school is officially a non-conformist foundation.

Very much a campus school with little access to urban reality, some distance from the gates. It's a vast space for seemingly few pupils (nearly 650 in total) and indeed the walk to the furthest boarding house is so far that we were going to suggest adding Nordic walking to the syllabus. Around a quarter board, many on a weekly basis. No longer has Saturday morning school – 'the best thing the school could have done,' a parent told us, and a major factor in her deciding to send her son there. Another parent disagreed and says it gave her son structure and all he'll do now is just 'watch TV.' Day pupils stay on site during the academic day and are members of one of seven day houses. Pupils can hang out in their houses between classes.

Boarders are allowed out after lessons to the local (limited) high street. Those who opt for full boarding are offered a Saturday morning programme of academic workshops and other activities. One boarder told us: 'I have been offered so much help with filling out my UCAS form, which is something those with parents around may take for granted.' Boarding house we saw was slightly tired looking – in need of updating.

Although a fully co-ed school since 1997, it is still very male-centric – around 70 per cent boys and 30 per cent girls. This has put some prospective parents off sending their daughters there. One parent told us: 'Any school which is not balanced worries me slightly. You wonder if it is as well geared around girls as it so clearly is for boys.' However, a girl we spoke to disagreed. 'The diversity here makes it a really unique place where everyone is accepted,' she said. Indeed the girls we met on our tour didn't appear to be the shy, retiring types who would worry about being outnumbered. Pupils generally seemed a happy and spirited bunch.

Has now merged with The Mount School.

Pastoral care and discipline: Uniform is their thing – 'extremely strict,' one parent told us, and the deputy head is often seen reprimanding students for this reason outside the school gates. The result is an extremely well turned out (and good-looking), bunch of teenagers in traditional dark blazers adorned with the school motto and a myriad of ties denoting their houses. Sixth formers wear their own suits.

Housemasters and housesmistresses are the first point of contact for students or parents with concerns. A full-time boarder told us: 'They have become like a surrogate family to me. I came over from Africa when I was 13 without anyone to look after me. My housemaster and my teachers made me feel so welcome and went step by step through everything. The pastoral care is great.' Another said: 'It can be quite a daunting school to come to and I kept getting lost, but I had an excellent mentor and settled in quickly.'

Considered to be a kind and gentle school, consistently praised by parents and officials for its outstanding pastoral care – 'very good at giving children their freedom,' one parent told us. Another parent said you can spot a Mill Hill child in a crowd. 'They always seem to be the most social and well rounded.' One pupil told us: 'It's like being part of a big family.' His only criticism was that 'you can't do an extra year.' This 'freedom' has led some parents

---

Another parent said you can spot a Mill Hill child in a crowd. 'They always seem to be the most social and well rounded.'

---

to feel that the school is fairly slack in some areas, though. One criticised the fact that pupils get the same detention for smoking behind the bikeshed as for chewing gum. She added that the head has improved the standard of the school greatly and praises him for not having double standards or being swayed by money or influence. She said: 'It seems to have been a problem with heads before, that it was one rule for one, and another if you had money.'

Formal exclusions are few and far between. Unlike some other schools, with their zero policy on drugs, this head is realistic, but not lax. 'If you are found with drugs once, it's a suspension, twice, you're out.' He says it nearly 'broke his heart' to permanently exclude a very bright and promising

student for bringing drugs onto the premises. But 'you can't start making exceptions,' he told us. 'It blurs the line.'

Pupils and parents: No typical Mill Hill pupil. Quite a lot live locally, even boarders, though in the sixth form there's a significant influx from China, Africa, Germany, France and Russia. Diverse ethnic and religious mix – Catholic, Jewish and Greek possibly the most prominent. Strong entrepreneurial element and urban professionals among the parents, together with 'the seriously rich.' The odd celebrity parent has also been known to grace the hallowed halls. Former pupils include Richard Dimbleby, Francis Crick, Simon Jenkins, Timothy Mo, Denis Thatcher, Katharine Whitehorn and Norman Hartnell.

Entrance: Total of 140 places in year 9, with about 70 or 80 going to pupils from the junior school (Belmont) and a handful of other feeder schools. No place is guaranteed, though – 'the school will politely tell you if they don't think your child is up to it.' Approx 20 places reserved for boarders. Sets its own exams in January before entrance in English, maths, French and science and uses the CE pass mark for setting. Oversubscribed, so 'we want to know what a child will bring. It's partly personality, and partly other factors like sport, music or drama.'

Entry to the sixth form requires two As and three Bs at GCSE, a requirement that applies both externally and internally. These requirements have not always been strictly adhered to, but one of the head's first acts was to enforce it, involving about 15 pupils leaving. 'We've always had a minimum grade requirement, now we're insisting it's met,' he said. One parent grumbled: 'The school is always moving the bar. It used to be automatic entrance into the sixth form.'

Exit: Most leavers to good universities. Three medics in 2014, others to study eg history of art, law, mechanical engineering and French.

Money matters: Middle to higher end of fee-paying schools in London. A selection of scholarships in academic subjects, the arts and sports. Fully-funded bursaries awarded each year and a range of other bursaries up to 90 per cent of the fees, on a carefully graded system of finance. The head's intention is that by 2020, 20 students a year will be offered full bursaries.

Remarks: Suits a busy, engaged child happy to try out a wide range of activities and use all the facilities and range of opportunities. A well-balanced school, with a head determined to put the academic underpinning firmly in place.

Palmers Green Lower School

Linked school: Palmers Green High School, 543

---

104 Hoppers Road, London, N21 3LJ

Independent • Pupils: 160 • Ages: 3–11 • Non-denom
• Fees (per term): £1,605 – £3,425

Tel: 020 8886 1135
Fax: 020 8882 9473
Email: office@palmersgreen.enfield.sch.uk
Website: www.pghs.co.uk

20

Headmistress: Since 2002, Mrs Christine Edmundson BMus MBA LRAM ARCM PGCE (Cantab) (early fifties). Originally from the Isle of Man, studied music at Royal Holloway, University of London where she was a choral scholar, as an undergraduate and postgraduate. Completed her PGCE following a bizarre twist of events that meant she was unable to continue with her doctoral research subject: 'Someone from New Zealand working at the British Museum had published his doctoral thesis on my unpublished manuscript, so I changed course.' She worked at a number of co-educational and girls' day and boarding schools before coming to this school in 2002. 'I wasn't going to stay long but it was so lovely, it's addictive.' An approachable person who still teaches some topics – ICT, RE, general studies – and stands at the gates to welcome pupils in the mornings and to see them off at the end of the day, which parents like very much. One of her strong points is the ability to spot and respond to opportunities to improve teaching at the school. She will often work with specialists that she 'may have heard at a conference or on radio'.

One of these was a specialist in early years from Homerton College in Cambridge who helped when the early years foundation stage was just being introduced. 'It was great as she was working at the forefront of what was happening, so the staff had her expertise. Where other schools were thinking, "well, how do you do that?" here teachers had a specialist to tell them how.'

Entrance: Most pupils join the school from the linked Alice Nursery, situated about a mile and a half away. Others come from nearby nursery schools such as Start Right Montessori, Leapfrog, Cedar Park, Bumble Bees Montessori and Leading Strings. Entrance to the prep department at age 4 and the junior department at age 7 is by assessment of ability and potential by one of the primary school teachers. This involves a timed test for children in years 5 and 6 but is less formal for those in year 4 and below. The school welcomes 'pupils with special educational needs, providing that our individual needs department can offer them the support they require'.

Exit: Majority go on to Palmers Green High School, others on to other independent or selective state schools in the area. Some parents would like 'a greater focus on preparing children for 11+ exams in the same way some other schools do'.

Remarks: Single form entry school with a maximum class size of 24 and a teacher pupil ratio of 1:9. Most children are working above the national average and a few are at level 6 in English, reading and maths. They are taught by mature (average age is 45) and well-qualified teachers. The small classes, say parents, are 'why we chose this school'. They also like the fact that specialist teaching in art, DT, drama, PE and music is introduced to children from as early as year 1 and in some subjects from reception. While core subjects such as English, maths, science and humanities are taught by form tutors, from year 3 girls have specialist French tuition and year 5s have taster courses in a range of languages, including Latin. Year 6 girls receive specialist DT teaching. 'DT is really fun,' remarked one year 6 girl. 'We've been doing models of playground rides and we solder too.' Her classmate showed us some prototypes but admitted that the teacher helped her with the soldering part as 'I was a bit scared' – then again, she had only joined the school in year 5 and said, 'In my old school we didn't do any DT, they didn't trust us.' Parents comment on

the 'teaching with substance'. Early introduction to subjects such as Latin and DT helps to develop the children's reasoning skills and their understanding of a wide variety of topics.

It is a very friendly school where teachers insist you come in and have a look around the classrooms and the children appear wholly interested in what they are learning and readily talk about their work. A year 4 science class shared with us what they were learning about the comparison of light and dark. Another class showed off their work on historical toys, including specimens they had brought in from home. Learning is supported by visits to places like the British Schools Museum, Hatfield House, Whipsnade Zoo and the year 5 residential trip to Flatford Mill where they develop their skills in navigation, using a compass, and trekking. The school magazine shows off impressive artwork and writing. About half of the girls learn one or more instruments at school. Specialist music teachers come in to teach instrument lessons and pupils' skills range from beginners to grade 4 and even 5.

There are no sports fields or courts on site and the main hall was, until recently when the new gymnasium was completed, being used for assemblies, indoor games, gym, dance and drama. Despite the shortage of onsite sports facilities, opportunity and enthusiasm for PE across ages is evident. Pupils travel to the nearby Walker Ground for games and to Southgate pool for swimming lessons. Gymnastics is popular, and now takes place in the new gym/dance studio. Pupils from year 2 upwards compete successfully in the week long Enfield Primary Schools Gymnastics Festival and Enfield netball tournament; there is an inter-house netball tournament for years 5 and 6, and there is a school swimming gala. Gymnastics and dance are taught on half term rotation. Drama is popular too, and year 3 to 6 girls perform at the local theatre. Year 6s take the lead roles in the annual summer play (which includes pupils from year 3 upwards) – 'we put on a play, we sing and dance and dress up in nice costumes'. Titles are adapted and new characters are introduced to popular productions to ensure everyone has the opportunity to take part. One year they 'did the 12 dancing princesses and 10 of their cousins because there were 22 of us'. Some girls played 'the jury in Goldilocks Goes to Court... she is charged with breaking in, and there are witnesses, the three ugly sisters, the bad wolf, the three bears, the bad fairy. Goldilocks won in the end. Everyone joins in and helps'.

As Christmas approaches the lower school and seniors as come together to practise songs and to make decorations for the carol service. The younger children make stars, sheep and angels whilst years 3 to 6 prepare to recite two poems. The school has close links with the local churches, although 'we have pupils of all faiths and none,' head says.

The prep and junior departments are located on the ground and middle floor of a building shared with the senior school. This supports the close knit pastoral environment where pupils in the younger pupils benefit from keen mentoring by the older pupils upstairs – 'during fire drills an older girl must grab a younger one,' said the head, 'and can get upset as there aren't enough little ones to go around'. She says the school believes in teach-

---

Children are encouraged to 'play to strengths, to support their friends and learn from them as well as the staff'.

---

ing children 'to work smart, not hard and long, but smart'. Good peer-to-peer relationships are a key part of this. Children are encouraged to 'play to strengths, to support their friends and learn from them as well as the staff'. There is 'good support for all children … with girls in higher years being a mentor to younger girls,' said a parent. 'My daughter is really happy and we are really happy.'

All junior pupils learn to be responsible by taking on roles like helping out in the prep school or library, or as head and deputy head girls. These roles – called 'duties' – alongside the range of extracurricular activities on offer, give pupils plenty to do and they both enjoy and thrive from the responsibility despite their busy schedules: 'I find it amazing that I'm a head girl,' said one pupil. 'I have prep duties two days a week; orchestra on Wednesdays, Thursdays is choir and on Friday we do library.'

'Doing library' involves acting 'as librarians, recommending books and putting them away, and learning about how the library works,' but pupils say the most exciting part is the badge they get to wear. They share the library with the senior school so there is a tight rota in place. Adjacent to the library is the main school hall – called Avondale – which is, in effect, the original school building. They relocated here in 1918, 13 years after the school was founded by a Quaker called Alice Hum. Since then a number of extensions have been added to Avondale Hall, including classrooms, a dining room and more recently the newly built Elizabeth Smith Hall and purpose-built medical room. This is expected to make things a lot easier for the girls, especially in drama and indoor PE, as previously everything took place in the main hall and its use was restricted during exam times.

Extracurricular activities range from sewing, junior orchestra, violin club and several choirs to art and maths puzzle club, speech and drama, netball and gym. The junior choir performs regularly at local events such as the N21 summer festival and Christmas festival. In the speech and drama club, 'we write our own mini plays and act them out', say pupils. 'We get certificates. They're displayed upstairs in the corridor.' There is 'something for everybody, whether you're arty, sporty, or not …' said a parent, 'we encourage our daughter to do as much as possible'.

Head says, 'We expect them to work hard and to be involved in things so that if something goes wrong (eg, a girl appears to be struggling or is behaving out of character) we pick it up.'

Parents certainly think highly of the school and most agree that their daughters are being adequately stretched academically. However, if they could wave a magic wand it would be to have more breakfast and after school clubs to support working parents.

Palmers Green High School

Linked school: Palmers Green Lower School, 541

---

104 Hoppers Road, London, N21 3LJ

Independent • Pupils: 120 • Ages: 11-16 • Non-denom • Fees (per term): £4,465

Tel: 020 8886 1135
Fax: 020 8882 9473
Email: office@palmersgreen.enfield.sch.uk
Website: www.pghs.co.uk

21

Headmistress: Since 2002, Mrs Christine Edmundson BMus MBA LRAM ARCM PGCE (Cantab) (early fifties). Came to London from the Isle of Man to study music at Royal Holloway, University of London, where she was a choral scholar undergraduate and a postgraduate, and entered teaching after a bizarre twist of events. 'Someone from New Zealand working at the British Museum had published his doctoral thesis on my unpublished manuscript, so I changed course.' This launched her teaching career at a day school for girls in Warwick, which, with its link to a local boys' school 'was great for co-educational productions'. She went on to become director of music at a co-educational day and boarding school in Ascot and then deputy head at a girls' day and boarding school in Bath.

She is a chirpy and warm character with a great sense of humour, a sort of mother figure, which fits well in a school where the atmosphere is like one big family. Parents say she is 'approachable, you can talk to her,' and that 'it's good to see her at the gates in the mornings rather than like some [heads] tucked up in the office'. Interestingly, in the head's view, her presence helps to see off 'parents who are naughty and park on the zigzag lines'. She is known for getting to the bottom of things when parents complain but is no pushover for those who try to pull the wool over her eyes and ask for things like days off to 'go to a family wedding in Scotland'.

She has been here long enough to see a whole generation of children come through, which is 'nice... just one or two left that weren't my generation'. She still teaches, not music but ICT, RE, and general studies. 'I don't get involved in music except through general studies or for Founder's Day and the carol service.' She is vocal about changes in education, and because she talks about these issues during general studies, the girls are also clued up on current debates – 'Oh good,' she says, 'general studies is working'. She says her speeches at the annual prize giving ceremony are not the norm – she uses them to remind parents of changes afoot in education, eg the debacle around GCSE exams and competition for university places.

Academic matters: Consistently high GCSE results: 73 per cent A*/A grades in 2014. Relationships between pupils and teachers are strong; class sizes are small, between 10 and 16. 'That's why we chose this school,' said a parent. 'It was pretty tough to see how overstretched the teachers were at our previous state primary school.' With a teacher pupil ratio of 1:9, 'we get the attention we need', say pupils.

The school offers iGCSE French and Spanish. French currently compulsory to iGCSE, with Spanish as an additional extra; from 2014 girls will be able to choose either or both. A few girls study additional maths; firm favourites when choosing options are history, geography and ICT. Parents will be pleased to know, however, that the school is flexible towards subject choice catering to, for example, those who study a language outside school or who have taken a GCSE/iGCSE early (frequently in a modern foreign language spoken at home), allowing them to continue to study the subject at school.

Head believes in teaching 'children to work smart and play to strengths'. She sees the school as moving more toward iGCSE because GCSE 'doesn't stretch the brightest of students'. Parents agree: 'Ms Edmundson made no bones about the school being selective,' said a parent. 'I wanted my daughter to be in that environment.'

Majority of pupils do D of E bronze level and the UK Maths Challenge. There are visiting teachers, educational trips and residential stays to enhance learning – eg year 8 geography trip to Dorset to prepare pupils for their GCSE fieldwork, trips to Poland and Berlin for GCSE history and to the Isle of Wight where pupils study the impact of the festival. 'We've just returned from a trip to Spain,' said a pupil. 'Every morning we had Spanish lessons with a native speaker; even if we asked what a word meant they would explain it in Spanish.'

Pupils say the trips aid what they learn in the classroom: 'it's so amazing to go and see everything expanded... it is all very well learning from a text book...' They particularly look forward to the annual year 9 visit to the Guardian newspaper

Whatever the school lacks in space it greatly makes up for it in friendliness: if there were a prize for the most welcoming atmosphere this school would be in the running

office as part of the English curriculum, where 'you get to see how everything is put into action, you choose the stories, you choose a name and print the papers'. They bring the papers back to school and stick the front pages up on the walls.

School introduces specialist teaching in subjects like Latin and DT much earlier than most (in the junior school) and this clearly benefits pupils in the senior school. Older students are able to access AS level course material – this is mainly in modern foreign languages and for those who have already successfully attained an A* in year 9 and year 10. 'The main purpose is to enrich and extend language skills in preparation for taking A levels.' Head says pupils often surprise others with their knowledge due to their early access to specialist teaching or advanced materials: one went for a sixth form interview 'and the interviewer said, "how did you know that? You shouldn't know that at your stage."' However, one parent said that highly able students could be better challenged: 'There have been several instances where the homework has been so basic that my daughter has become demotivated.'

Teachers generally described as friendly; head of history praised by pupils for making the subject one of the most popular. Head of maths also praised: 'In year 7 I didn't like maths and now I'm doing additional maths. They made me enjoy it and that's really good as it's so important. I know that's the case for lots of people in the class.'

No children at present who do not speak fluent English but EAL support can be provided. Around 20 to 25 girls are identified with SEN, mostly dyslexia, and a few pupils have autistic spectrum disorders (ASDs). They can have support in lessons and there is some help for the ASDs in social skills arranged by the individual needs coordinator, who can involve outside agencies if necessary. Extra classes before and after school and one-to-one tuition are also available at an extra charge.

The school helps prepare the girls for moving on to a sixth form elsewhere – 'we want to make sure they have lots of opportunities when they leave because of the opportunities they have had here,' says the head. 'It doesn't matter if they are not strong academically as they will have other strengths which may help them to get a sixth form place somewhere.'

Games, options, the arts: Although the school no longer offers PE as a short course at GCSE, the opportunity and enthusiasm for sport across the years is evident. This is commendable given the shortage of sporting facilities at the school. Until 2012, the main hall was the only space available for assemblies, gymnastics, drama and exams. The newly built Elizabeth Smith Hall now provides a multi-purpose space for all these activities and leaves the main hall free during exams.

Not much of a playground, just a small yard used by junior pupils, and there are no fields. Girls travel 10 minutes by coach to nearby Walker Grounds for outdoor games and to Southgate for swimming lessons. Year 10 and 11 travel to Southbury Leisure Centre for a range of sports. Still, nothing is lost and time is well managed so that, for example, pupils receive pre lesson instruction in transit, 'with the added advantage that they don't stand freezing listening' on the fields. Parents certainly don't view this as a problem, since 'it's not that far and they are not in the bus for half an hour'. Another said: 'My daughter isn't particularly sporty but we go and support netball matches.'

Dance and gymnastics are taught on half term rotation, and netball is popular. They have won the Barnet Netball League for four years consecutively, 'playing bigger schools', adds the head, 'who have 200-odd in each year group, where we have only 30 girls to choose from.' She puts it all down to the fact that this is a small school where the girls 'know each other incredibly well', something parents attest to.

Around half choose art and design at GCSE and the self-portraits mounted in the art corridor show there is plenty of talent here, as do pupils' willingness to talk thoughtfully about their work. Classrooms are well equipped with colour wheels for guidance and artefacts for inspiration, 'to help you make a decision about what you are trying to express through colours, shapes, textures, perspectives... which is helpful if you are not too familiar with art,' said one pupil. Another commented: 'We did 3D art and I found that is my niche'. She showed us the model of a figure drowning in money, explaining that it was to show 'how greed can take over... how too much money is never enough for some people. People always want just a little bit more.' The remedy? 'It depends on the sort of person you are,' she said.

Around a third of the girls choose drama at GCSE. It is also popular as an extracurricular activity, as is dance: pupils have performed in the Nutcracker ballet at the Bloomsbury Theatre in Euston. Not many take music at GCSE (15 per cent). At the time of our visit, there was only one girl studying music in year 11 and five in year 10. The music department offers timetabled lessons in different instruments: sax, trumpet, singing – but pupils say that if you want to learn an instrument not offered, the school will get a teacher in. Around 80 girls across the whole school take lessons inside school and many more take lessons outside school hours. Their music skills range from beginners to above grade 8. There is an open door culture in the music department where 'you can come during break if you want to practice your instrument'. There is a senior school orchestra and and two choirs, plus other instrumental groups.

Plenty on offer in terms of extracurricular clubs, though, again, some (particularly working parents) say they would like to see more after school provision. The school currently offers netball, choir, music, knitting, drama, debating, swimming and a Christian union, and tries to ensure everyone gets involved in something. As well as lunchtime and after school activities, there's a gym club at 8am and

weekend cross-country competitions, D of E expeditions and training. They also take part in eg inter-school debating competitions.

There is a 'very competitive' annual house choral competition. Pupils describe it as a 'bit like a musical but not'. The girls choose songs on some pretty powerful themes – 'about war, politics, women in power, the economy, green issues'. 'People sing, play instruments, costumes get dragged into that... but most important, you don't want your competitor to know what you're doing so it's very secretive, all covered up.' 'Green house won last year,' another butted in, 'yellow house won year before, and we won year before that. So far we're equal... but we're worried about what will happen this year [after we leave] so we will have to come back and see how they get on without us.' The audience for the house choral competition always includes some recent leavers.

Background and atmosphere: Founded in 1905 by a Christian Quaker called Alice Hum whose motto, 'By Love, Serve One Another', still guides the ethos here. The building was originally located in nearby Osborne Road and opened with 12 pupils. It had grown to 300 when it moved to its present location in Hoppers Road in 1918. The original and main building, Avondale Hall, is still the heart of the school. Classrooms and a dining room were added between the 1960s and 1990s. Over the next decade a new office block was built and more recently the new Elizabeth Smith Hall (with a couple of one bed flats above – which the school says will suit student teachers) and a medical room. The school could do with more space but as the site is on a residential street, neatly tucked between houses, expansion is difficult.

Despite its age, the school has a modern feel. The building is intimate and compact yet the rooms, hallway and stairwells are airy and bright. Most spaces, including the head's office, double up for other uses, and there are well thought out rotas for use of the hall and library resource centre to accommodate the needs of both the junior and senior pupils. The prep department shares the same building, and the linked pre-school (Alice Nursery) is about a mile and half away.

Whatever the school lacks in space it greatly makes up for it in friendliness: if there were a prize for the most welcoming atmosphere this school would be in the running. Teachers invited us into lessons, and pupils showed impeccable manners. A science class in the middle of an experiment gladly redid the combustion exercise just for our visit – or so they claimed. Pupils are keen to talk about their work displayed on classroom walls, like the 'wonder posters' they created about different countries that took part in the Olympics.

Pastoral care and discipline: As a relatively small school contained in one building, it would be hard for any child's problem or unhappiness to go unnoticed – 'it is quite common for a member of staff to take a girl aside if she seems troubled in any way'. Very good staff-parent relations as all share the ethos of: work hard and your reward will be a good career.

Pupils told us that settling into the school was easy. 'If teachers can see you are struggling they introduce you to someone'. Pupils have two induction days before they start plus a three-day team building residential trip within the first few weeks of September, 'so we made friends straight away'.

Small group sizes here mean no-one gets lost. 'We have an open door policy so we can talk to any teacher and get help if we need to,' as 'you can feel closer to one particular teacher'. In such a small school teachers 'can spot if something is wrong', and pupils develop good relationships with their form tutors – two to a form – who sometimes stay with the groups as they move up.

The house system also helps them know and support each other well across the school: during the fire drill 'one older girl must each grab a younger child and walk them to the meeting place'. Parents mentioned this 'nurturing environment' with girls 'across different year groups interacting and playing with each other' as one of the appealing characteristics of the school. Senior pupils mentor younger pupils and take up roles as head girls, house captains, form and other types of prefects. Prep prefects help out in the prep school, form prefects help year 7s to settle in and career and public relations prefects help out in their relevant areas. Sometimes they double up on roles to share duties.

This culture of active citizenship means that hhe girls are consulted on lots of important decisions. They formed a committee to help choose a new catering company for the school – the winner was not only chosen because of its great home made yoghurt (which has gone on to become a favourite), but also because it creates menus linked to the curriculum. Pupils also formed a panel to choose a new uniform to mark the school's centenary – they hated the old green one, says the head. We walked into a geography lesson where the girls were being consulted on what colour book to use for a new GCSE unit. They went for green.

Behaviour is good and incidences of bullying are rare: 'I've never had a problem... you would know about it,' said a pupil. 'I've been here since reception and never heard of anything.' Another said, 'The worst is you have an argument with your friend but that happens anywhere.' PSHE includes lessons in study and life skills and careers guidance.

Encouragement to work hard includes a star chart, embraced by even the most senior pupils, with stars awarded for high results in the weekly French and Spanish vocab tests – 'if you get 10 out of 10 you get a star, it's a good way to ensure you learn the vocabulary'. Parents praise the commendation system because it means their daughters are 'stretched in individual subjects... achievement and effort even within the subject gives more to aim for'. Notices on classroom walls include injunctions to 'turn up on time', 'help friends', 'have a good attitude', 'show respect'.

Pupils and parents: Parents are mostly professionals and come from a mixture of cultures and backgrounds. There are no parent governors: 'it avoids problems if there are financial difficulties', says the head. However, the parents' association organises events like theatre trips, quiz nights, the summer fair and other fundraising events and has raised money for benches for the grounds, an audio system for the hall and the school mini bus. It also helps new families settle in, 'especially if you have moved to London from outside,' said a parent who moved from Cardiff.

Notable past pupils include Marion Tait CBE, prima ballerina and assistant director of the Birmingham Royal Ballet.

Entrance: Girls joining at 11 sit English, maths, science and reasoning tests, with those who show promise invited for interview. However, the vast majority come up from the lower school.

Exit: 'I always say we have the largest sixth form in London. It just happens to be located in all my colleagues' schools,' says the head. Many move on to selective state sixth forms eg Latymer, Dame Alice Owen's and St Michael's. A few to Woodhouse College; others to independents eg City of London School for Girls, Haberdashers' Aske's School for

Girls, Highgate, North London Collegiate, St Albans High School for Girls and St Paul's Girls'.

Money matters: Academic scholarships, music awards and means-tested bursaries are available to cover up to 100 per cent of fees at 11+. There are also other internal awards related to progress within the school.

Remarks: A small, cosy and nurturing school which prepares girls well to move on to a wider world at 16.

Queen Elizabeth's Girls' School

High Street, Barnet, Hertfordshire EN5 5RR

State • Pupils: 1,150 • Ages: 11–18 • Non-denom

Tel: 020 8449 2984
Fax: 020 8441 2322
Email: office@qegschool.org.uk
Website: www.qegschool.org.uk

13

Headteacher: Since 2001, Mrs Kate Webster (50s) BA PGCE MA (education management). Studied geography at Sheffield University and taught at Furze Platt School in Maidenhead and Herschel Grammar school in Slough, before joining Henrietta Barnett as deputy head, followed by acting head, 'I realised I quite liked the idea of being in charge.' Also realised her heart was in comprehensive schools.

Mrs Webster's slightly school ma'am ish appearance belies a sense of humour and a refreshing modesty. Although she took this school to

outstanding status when she first started (recently downgraded by Ofsted) – she will tell you that it was already pretty good when she arrived. 'Pupils are motivated and they know how to learn. They have excellent relationships with their teachers.' She's also a realist. 'Although we aim to deliver a good education across the board, we also need to be flexible and realise that GCSEs and A levels aren't an end in themselves. The future is somewhat different.'

Her slightly disorganised office may seem endearingly scatty, but don't be fooled. Mrs Webster is most definitely on the ball. One parent told us, 'she is quick to act on any disciplinary issues.' Another said, 'She's battled endlessly to lower the skirt level of her pupils.' (A losing battle, we feel.) Her approachable and down to earth manner has made her popular with pupils and parents alike, 'She makes school assemblies very humorous', one pupil told us. Married for 35 years 'I think'. No children. Enjoys music of all sorts, walking (with a keen interest in her surroundings being a former geographer), theatre and art.

Mrs Webster's response to Ofsted's recent downgrading of the school from 'outstanding', to 'needs improvement' is robust. 'We have submitted a formal complaint.. as we believe.. that there has been a misinterpretation of the data.. I always try to see the positive side of everything and whether or not our complaint is upheld, we will be re-doubling our efforts to give each and every child the best possible opportunities.'

Academic matters: 'A love of learning is our priority' says the school, but the recent Ofsted report criticised the school for failing the students on pupil premium who are not making good progress. Contrary to this report however, the school's GCSE English results are considerably above the national average, as well as above average for girls. All the more impressive when one takes into account that nearly a quarter of the pupils come from homes where English is not a first language.

The school generally produces commendable results. In 2014, 74 per cent got 5+ A*-C at GCSE (including English and maths); 28 per cent A*/A. Nearly all girls achieve 5+ A*-C grades overall and the vast majority get at least a C in maths. At A level, 47 per cent A*/B and 21 per cent A*/A. Biology, chemistry, maths, philosophy and ethics, sociology and psychology are all popular A level choices, alongside English and geography. Vocational courses in product design and business studies are also offered.

Media arts specialism means a focus on English, drama, art and media studies, but head is quick to point out that while the arts have always been strong, the school's main priority is to deliver a broad curriculum for everybody: 'We tend not to make a big thing about our specialisation, we aim to deliver a high calibre of subjects across the board and not get labelled as one thing.'

Spanish taught in year 7 and more able pupils can study French from year 8. Languages set from year 8 but all other subjects taught in mixed ability groups. 'We tried setting for science, but the results didn't improve.' Maths has historically been one of the weaker subjects, 'but we've made lots of

None of this seemed to bother the pair of perpetually positive students, who took us on our tour. So proud they were of their school, 'one big family', that it might as well have been Versailles

progress in key stage 3 and the school now has a high performing specialist school second specialism in mathematics and computing.' This has allowed increased investment and focus on maths, producing strong results at GCSE and A level. Homework club offered every day until 4.30pm with teachers in every subject on tap to help students.

Good SEN support, mostly within the classroom. Split level site unsuitable for children with physical disabilities: 'Because we're on a hill and because of the age of the building, we can't accommodate students with significant mobility issues.' Around 10 per cent of pupils have special educational needs, including specific learning difficulties, dyslexia and dyspraxia. The gifted and talented co-ordinator identifies very able girls, who are encouraged to take on extension research projects – 'but we don't want to be exclusive, others can join in too.' Good careers advice – has Investors in Careers status, recently renewed.

Games, options, the arts: As befits school's media specialism, arts are big here. The QEGS bronze art award has been recently introduced to recognise achievement, focusing on personal progress. Annual arts festival is an opportunity for the school and its community to celebrate the events of the past year and includes drama, song, poetry and music.

Drama GCSE very popular, involving regular showcases for parents. Christmas production is written and directed by sixth formers and performed to the whole school. At Film Skool (an extracurricular activity) professional film makers and producers work with pupils who write, edit and direct their own films, culminating in a private screening in a West End cinema. SMAKS (stretch your media arts knowledge and skills), is a programme of after school workshops, designed to encourage students (as well as the wider community) to try new media skills, including theatre set design, cartoon caricature, and portrait photography. The school hosts two drama studios and media editing suites.

Music is also strong, though relatively few take it to GCSE or A Level where it is available through Barnet Music Centre. Senior and junior orchestras, a jazz band, and various ensembles depending on the strengths and numbers of the musicians. Links with the ENO.

Several (rather basic) art studios, with some eye-catching art dotted around, including a pop art display. Dance an increasingly popular subject, as is sport – including the less traditional, fencing, boxercise and roller-skating. Great indoor facilities include a mammoth sports hall, gymnasium and a pristine, Olympic size swimming pool, 'I only learned to swim once I started QE Girls', a 13-year-old student told us. Outdoor tennis courts. Girls have competed in county football and cross-country. Girls doing PE GCSE often organise dance and games tournaments for local primary schools.

'There's so much going on, you're never bored to death', one pupil told us. And she wasn't wrong. On top of all the media stuff, other extracurricular activities include karate club, music clubs and debating societies, Portuguese, cheerleading, rock challenge, archery, football, swimming, Young Enterprise etc. Blossoming hacks join the journalism club and can take part in the BBC School Report. Trips abroad include skiing in the Alps, language trip, art / drama trips to New York and history trips to the battlefields of France and Belgium.

Background and atmosphere: First opened in 1888 as a grammar school; has been comprehensive since the 1970s. Hilly site on the edge of London's green belt, and set back from busy Barnet High Street. Buildings range from Victorian to 1960s. Rather tatty round the edges and could do with a major influx of cash for refurbishment – which doesn't look imminent: 'We're often at the back of the queue because our results have been good,' the head told us. A parent commented that in her opinion, the

only weakness of the school is that 'it is very old, with small, sometimes manky classrooms.'

On the plus side, the loos were revamped at a cost of £150,000 at the request of the school council when the head first joined and have been refurbished regularly since (although many pupils

---

Beautiful grounds adorned with smart benches and a few small Japanese style feature bridges. 'It's lovely in summer for picnics,' one pupil told us

---

still cited the toilets as a downside of the school). During our tour we noticed that new windows were being installed – something the head believes only happened because of the switch to academy status. 'Apart from that, and our sporting facilities which used to be shared, becoming an academy doesn't make much of a difference in real terms.'

'None of the school set-up really makes much sense', Mrs Webster told us cheerfully at the start of our tour, and she had a point. After walking through a myriad of corridors which didn't seem to correlate to one another, over an internal bridge (which linked two buildings), we lost our bearings on several occasions. General impression is of bright, sparse spaces painted pale blue. Rather Victorian and wanting in imagination, we felt. None of this seemed to bother the pair of perpetually positive students, who took us on our tour. So proud they were of their school, 'one big family', that it might as well have been Versailles.

Large, well stocked library that was busy and buzzing (but what caught our eye was a student stuffing a sandwich in her mouth directly in front of a sign which read 'no eating in the library'). The canteen was pretty pukka too, with its mouthwatering and beautifully presented selection of hot food, generous salad bar and divine desserts. Thumb print ID system.

The outside space is a pleasant surprise – beautiful grounds adorned with smart benches and a few small Japanese style feature bridges. 'It's lovely in the summer for picnics', one pupil told us. Hard to believe we were only a stone's throw from Barnet High Street. Very much a community comprehensive, 'we have students whose grandmothers came to this school', with a relaxed atmosphere and confident, articulate girls, used to speaking up in public.

Pastoral care and discipline: Renowned for making new girls feel at home quickly – 'we want parents and girls to feel confident about their choice of secondary school,' says the school. The dedicated head of year 7 spends much time and effort visiting feeder primary schools in the summer term to meet students and staff. Sixth formers are also on tap to help out and plan team-building activities for the year 7s which encourages each form to work together – 'a crucial part of the friend making process during the first week of term.'

The head says: 'One of the hallmarks of the school is that girls find the staff very approachable'. High expectations of good behaviour and discipline do not appear to be unrealistic. Only five permanent exclusions since the head's tenure and although 'regrettable', they were left with 'no other choice'. Clear policy on drugs and bullying, 'Obviously girls are exposed to drugs outside, but inside it is not an issue. Our PHSE programme is very good and we put a lot of effort into equipping girls to make informed decisions on all aspects of life.' The form tutor or head of year is the first port of call if a girl is troubled, but, 'my daughter knows she can go to the head if she really needs to', one parent told us.

Students' progress is closely monitored with regular reports, academic reviews and parents' evenings. Great emphasis is placed on parents' inclusion – 'we are kept very well informed via texts, newsletters and emails.' However, the same parent added: 'Parents' evenings can be a bit shambolic. It often feels like speed dating without the fun. I feel it could be better organised.' 'Time for

Pupils and parents: Pupils from across the board. One parent told us: 'You get pupils who come from massive houses in Hadley Wood, and those that come from the local council estate, nature of the beast – you just have to hope they respect each other.' However, higher than average percentage of girls on free school meals. Ethnically diverse – largest share is white British 40 per cent, the remainder a variety of different ethnicities 'which reflect the population of Barnet as a whole.' Old girls: actress and singer Elaine Paige and actress Stephanie Beacham.

Entrance: Oversubscribed, but not heavily – roughly around three applicants for every place. First in line are girls with statement of social or medical needs specifying the school; then siblings, then those living closest ('we moved into the area to get our daughter into the school'), – which in practice tends to mean within two miles. Girls entering the sixth form (about 18 each year) need five grade Cs or above at GCSE, though many A level courses specify a B grade in the A level subject.

Exit: About a third leave after GCSEs for selective sixth forms, co-ed sixth form colleges or FE colleges. Most sixth form leavers go on to higher education, courses including medicine, dentistry and law. One or two to Oxford most years.

Money matters: Not a rich school – low down in the queue for government cash for refurbishment, but does its best with available funds. Loyal parent body works hard at raising money.

Remarks: A successful comprehensive with high expectations that produces self-assured girls used to discussion and debate.

'My daughter did a Ready Steady Cook afternoon with her dad. She loved it and it was great bonding.'

You' sessions have proved very popular; parents are invited to informal meetings every half term which cover topics from self esteem and friendship to e-safety. Sessions also offered just for dads and daughters. 'My daughter did a Ready Steady Cook afternoon with her dad. She loved it and it was great bonding,' one parent told us.

Lessons start immediately at 8.40am and pupils are registered electronically during the first session. The head feels that this way she gets the most out of her students in the morning before they start to flag. Plus, she says, it has a magical impact on lateness, 'Students don't like to miss teaching time – they are less worried about making it for registration.'

Various incentives and rewards schemes are offered to students who work hard and take an active part in school life.

Queen Elizabeth's School, Barnet

Queen's Road, Barnet, Hertfordshire EN5 4DQ

State • Pupils: 1,180 • Ages: 11–18 • Non-denom

Tel: 020 8441 4646
Fax: 020 8440 7500
Email: hmoffice@qebarnet.co.uk
Website: www.qebarnet.co.uk

14

Headmaster: Since 2011, Neil Enright MA (Oxon) MBA NPQH FRSA (30s). Educated at St. John's College, Oxford, and has worked at Queen Elizabeth's School, Barnet, since 2002, rising to become head of department (humanities – a geographer), head of year, deputy head. MBA in 2010 from the University of London, Institute of Education, which focused on aspects of leadership, management and systems of effective learning.

Sees himself as 'an experienced educational leader committed to safeguarding the academic, pastoral and spiritual interests of able boys, irrespective of their ethnic, religious or socio-economic background'. Aim is to preserve and build upon the reputation of Queen Elizabeth's as a school where able boys who have entered on academic merit will become well-rounded and responsible young men with unbounded opportunities to succeed at university and their chosen careers beyond.

Academic matters: Consistently top of the academic league tables, rivalling most schools, independent or state, in its exam results. Definitely not a school for slackers. You work hard here and you work consistently hard, which can be stressful for

some, particularly in the early years. Testing is very much part of the modus operandi. Baseline assessment in year 7, then setting in all subjects, with half-termly tests thereafter. 'It's quite nerve-racking at the beginning,' says one sixth former, 'but it does mean by the time we get to GCSEs we don't find exams a problem.' Certainly not. A*s the norm at GCSE (average 10 A*s). In 2014, 90 per cent

---

'Rugby serves boys so well,' says the head. 'It has a gentlemanly ethos, of which I enormously approve.'

A*/A grades. All take French and Latin from year 7 and German from year 8, continuing at least one to GCSE, with Mandarin and Spanish offered as extras. A level choices are decided by tests in years 10 and 11 designed 'to tease out' aptitude. 'GCSE grades are not a good indicator,' says the head. 'Of 180 boys here, 165 will get A*s in maths, but not all will be good enough to do maths.' Seventy per cent of boys do four A levels, most get four A*/A grades (82 per cent of grades were A*/A in 2014); 60 per cent take maths, two-thirds some science, many do a mix. No fluffy options whatsoever. 'We don't want to dilute the curriculum,' says the head.

Most departments and most teaching is very strong – 'so many departments get all A*/As'. Boys enthuse particularly about geography and history. Homework load is strenuous (one and a half hours in year 7, one hour per subject per night at A level), but few problems with hungry dogs here. 'We don't need to whine and cajole, it's a culture of achievement.' The school has recently extended its extracurricular enrichment with the Williams Society's weekly tutorials in informal logic, literary theory and analysis of concepts. 'We talk to them about the social sciences and concepts such as liberty,' no doubt helping to up the school's Oxbridge success rate.

Class sizes, 30 in year 9, 18-23 in year 10, 17 at A level. All the latest gewgaws throughout with up-to-the minute ICT and all labs refurbished in the last 10 years. 'Special needs' at this school tends to be on the gifted-and-talented end of the spectrum, but every department runs a clinic to support the struggling and challenge the most able. School says it can accommodate mild autism, Asperger's and dyslexia.

Games, options, the arts: This is a school where competing is important and a big part of the competition takes places on the sports field. All play rugby in year 7. 'Rugby serves boys so well,' says the head. 'It has a gentlemanly ethos, of which I enormously approve.' England under-16 head coach coaches the rugby squad and the school fields up to D teams on a regular basis. (Sport, however, is setted from year 7, and it can be difficult to move up the scrum, according to one pupil). Swimming, water polo, Eton Fives, tennis, cross-country and fencing also popular. Plenty of county and national representation in sport, bridge, chess. (Old Boy Tom Aggar recently won a gold medal for rowing in the Paralympics.) Eight-lane swimming pool, all-weather tennis courts, multi-gym and plenty of neatly trimmed green fields for team sports.

School has three full-time music teachers, 12 peripatetic teachers and a music suite where boys can study A level music technology with all the latest recording equipment. Big band, jazz quartet, north and south Indian collection ensemble. 'We are in the vanguard of international music development. It epitomises a strength of the world, the dialectic between different cultures. It's beautiful to listen to a group which includes the sitar, the sax and the violin.' Visual arts take place in open-plan, light-filled art rooms but plenty going on elsewhere, with a daily art club held in the lunch hour, an exhibition space for displays of work and field trips to arty destinations like St Ives and Paris

Head is against the 'industry of preparation' that leaves children trembling in the exam queue. 'It's a waste of time stressing children out.' Parents, however, wouldn't necessarily agree

for A level candidates. Growing national reputation for chess. Outside the classroom, the school has invested heavily in infrastructure. In recent years, the school has seen the launch of a dramatic, architect-designed new hall, which, as well as drama productions and debating competitions, will host recording sessions for professional orchestras. New food technology facility; DT also focuses on product design and ICT.

As one might expect, careers advice taken very seriously. From year 7, pupils have half-termly meeting on their future. 'We want them to ask early on: What do I want to do in life? After the age of 14, they won't do it for their parents or teachers; they do it because they believe it themselves.' Decision making is aided by extensive work experience from

year 10. Loyal old boys, too, come back for an organised meeting with sixth formers to chat about university and subject choice. Some act as Oxbridge buddies for the next generation. Boys also do voluntary work related to their career aspirations.

Background and atmosphere: Founded in 1573 by Robert, Earl of Leicester, with a charter from Elizabeth I, the school was rebuilt in 1931-32 by Hertfordshire County Council in a noble civic style with terrazzo flooring, parquet and panelling, all kept in spick-and-span condition. Still relatively well endowed with land held in perpetuity and its own Foundation Trustees, QE went comprehensive in the '60s, reverted to grant-maintained status in 1989 and became a grammar school once more in 1994. Difficult to imagine a more orderly and focused environment. Even in traditional chatty art, boys work with heads down, quiet as mice. Significant increases in responsibility from year 11, when own suits are allowed. Ninety prefects voted for by staff and students, monitor lunch (fresh food produced daily), playgrounds and classrooms. 'They lead the school in so many ways.' School captain and house captains appointed from on high.

Pastoral care and discipline: Boys motivated by reward and praise with loads of 'celebratory occasions'. (Homework diaries with merit stickers for every subject in the early years; hand-written notes home later on.) Certainly not a school where misbehaviour is the norm. 'I will expel a boy for violence on the premises aimed at staff, consciously creating racial disharmony or bringing drugs into school, but no boy has been expelled in over 14 years,' says the head. Occasional fixed-term exclusions, however, for persistent 'failure to carry out school protocols' or misbehaving in lessons. Registration twice a day and homework diaries are also monitored for extracurricular activities. 'If a boy is not sufficiently engaged in extracurricular activities, that's often the first warning sign.' If concern is felt, the year head will be involved, then, depending on the issues, parents, special needs or an ed psych.

Pupils and parents: Defies the traditional middle class grammar school profile in its diverse student body. Over 80 per cent of boys come from ethnic minorities, predominantly Asian. Most are first generation, most speak English as a second language. 'Our boys come from very ordinary backgrounds,' says the head. 'In our last Oxbridge intake, many boys had parents who hadn't gone to university, and in recent years one was a refugee from Rwanda.' The head feels the school 'contributes massively to social mobility and social cohesion. Here, they have to interact across the divides, whether they're scrumming down on the rugger field or playing chess.'

Entrance: More than 2,000 boys apply for 180 places. Tests now take place in September, and boys are told whether or not they have met the 'standard required' before they have to make their choice of schools, so they have nothing to lose by taking the test. NB Meeting the 'standard required' does not guarantee a place. Pupils come from around 90 primary schools, but the ability range is narrow; most are in the top 10 per cent nationally. Head is against the 'industry of preparation' that leaves children

> 'In our last Oxbridge intake, many boys had parents who hadn't gone to university, and in recent years one was a refugee from Rwanda.'

trembling in the exam queue. 'It's a waste of time stressing children out.' Parents, however, wouldn't necessarily agree. Occasional vacancies between years 7 and 10, offered to those on the waiting list. No sixth form entry for external candidates. 'This is a seven-year education and I don't want to tread on any of my colleagues' toes.' Automatic transfer to sixth form for virtually all but pupils have to be recommended for individual subjects. Further maths is particularly hard to gain access to.

Exit: Some boys leave after GCSE (13 per cent in 2014). Some prefer mixed sixth forms, are looking for subjects the school doesn't teach (law, psychology, media studies) or are not offered the subjects they want to take. Some win scholarships to independent schools. Other just prefer a more

relaxed environment. Others don't make the grade. Virtually all who stay go on to top universities. In 2014, a record 37 Oxbridge offers, and one to Williams College USA. Otherwise to eg Nottingham, Imperial, UCL and Warwick. Economics most popular degree, 20 plus to medicine and medical-related degrees. History and law also popular. The school gives excellent UCAS guidance.

Money matters: State aid is minimal and the head has to put up with the fact he gets less money than many local comps. Gaps are filled with funds from the Foundation and with carefully husbanded donations from parents, old boys and friends, which underwrite school trips and new buildings.

Most parents contribute £60 a month, though this is entirely voluntary. 'We say to them, if you want to have a sound education and provide the polish for boys to go to the best universities, you can't do it on state funding.' The head has managed to raise £10m during his time at the school.

Remarks: An extraordinary school that offers the able, the diligent and the aspiring, whatever their social or ethnic origins, an education hard to rival in the state or private sector. You do, however, have to be the right boy. Not a good option for those who would struggle with the workload, rebel against the discipline or dislike competition.

Rhodes Avenue, London, N22 7UT

State · Pupils: 565 · Ages: 3–11 · Non-denom

Tel: 020 8888 2859
Fax: 020 8881 7090
Email: admin@rhodes.haringey.sch.uk
Website: www.rhodes.haringey.sch.uk

Headteacher: Since 1996, Mrs Christine Witham (40s), definitely the driving force behind this remarkably successful primary school. In her 14 years at the helm, she has taken the school from mediocre to marvellous and to the top of every league table, both academic and sporting. Positive and upbeat, she's widely liked by parents, pupils and teachers. 'She's very approachable,' said one.

'She loves children,' said another. 'She knows all their names, sees them all as individuals and is very visible about the school.' Optimistic and determined, even the recent threat to the school rebuild did not leave her deterred. Her skill at dealing with the sometimes demanding clientele is also worthy of note. 'When one parent went into complain that their child was special and deserved special treatment, she just replied, "We feel all our children are special."' Married, with two children.

Retiring in July 2015.

Entrance: Recently moved to three-form entry with 90. Admission by means of the local authority criteria, which means that, on the whole, first come siblings and then those living as near as possible. With four applications for every place, this has meant within a quarter of a mile. The success of the school – and its neighbouring comprehensive – has undoubtedly had an impact on local property prices.

Exit: The school backs directly on to Alexandra Park, one of the borough's best secondaries, and the majority of pupils proceed there. Others to Fortismere, Channing and Dame Alice Owen's and a few to eg Henrietta Barnett, JCoSS, Latymer, North London Collegiate, Park View Academy, Queen Elizabeth School for Boys and Ashmole.

Remarks: Has for some years consistently dominated the local authority league tables and Ofsted can barely think of a word of criticism. Sats results here are truly outstanding, with the majority reaching the highest levels – results that would put a smile on the face of most prep school heads. 'There's a good mix of the thoroughly experienced and young and enthusiastic teachers,' said one mother, and the pupils agree: 'The teaching is really great,' said a boy. Though the pupils are of above average ability on entry, the school gives everyone that little bit more, particularly in the later years.

An extensive enrichment programme in art, drama and creative writing (in which teachers receive regularly training) includes workshops and specials events, such as book week. A string of well-known children's authors pitch up to entertain, but the highlight of the week is The Bedtime Story evening, when, accompanied by teddies, children are given hot chocolate and gripping fiction. Hardly surprising, then, that a recent nationwide writing competition saw nine Rhodes Avenue finalists.

Academic progress is charted minutely and parents kept well informed, with three parents' evenings and three reports a year. Strong support, too, for the struggling. 'My son has a special literacy person and she's fantastic,' said one parent. 'He gets taken out during the literacy hour and taught in a small group to ensure he'll cope at secondary school.' French taught from year 3 and 'parlez-vous' is supplemented with fun activities like a French breakfast, croissants included.

Music and sport are as high up the agenda as the three Rs. All year 4 learn cello, violin, trumpet or clarinet and specialist teachers, provided by the local authority, offer individual tuition during the school day. Sport is taken seriously – tends to

sweep the board in local competitions, whether it's athletics or tennis, football or netball. 'There's an exceptionally good PE teacher,' said one mother, adding that in-school provision is also often supplemented with private coaching. Loads of trips, clubs and workshops, with outings to the cinema, theatre and museums and a regular stream of visiting artists, actors and dancers. Plenty of activity on the pupils' parts, too, with impressive assemblies and

---

A string of well-known children's authors pitch up to entertain, but the highlight of the week is The Bedtime Story evening, when, accompanied by teddies, children are given hot chocolate and gripping fiction

regular performances and concerts. 'A lot is done around creativity,' said one parent. After-school clubs include cross-country, orchestra, cricket, recorder, choir, Bollywood dance, Spanish, French, pottery, drama, yoga, computer, netball and badminton. Lots of competitions entered and usually won, whether that's for the school's abundant and much-loved vegetable garden or for pupils' Christmas card designs. After-school play centre on site 3.30-6pm.

A local primary school and most families live within feet of the gates, giving a strong community feel, though whether increased numbers will dilute this remains to be seen. Major rebuilding programme to incorporate increased numbers now complete. Strong pupil involvement. School council, with two elections a year, debates hot topics like school uniform, sustainability and healthy eating. Peer mediators protect against playground perils. Plenty of praise is the recipe for good behaviour and the naughty are given focused 'reflection' on wrong doing. Despite the friendly upbeat mood, some feel the school places too great an emphasis on obvious winners, whether in the classroom or the sports fields. 'If you are slightly unusual and don't fit in,' said one parent, 'you can slip under the wire a bit.'

Parents, who are increasingly prosperous and professional, are heavily involved. Those with interesting jobs – like astronauts or newspaper editors – come in to share their expertise with the kids. Needless to say, the Parents' Association is buzzing, organising a hectic cycle of events including a summer and Christmas fair, school raffle, jumble sale, fireworks and Burns supper. Class reps are required to stage two cake sales a year. Oodles of extra funds raised.

St Michael's Catholic Grammar School

Nether Street, London, N12 7NJ

State • Pupils: 760 (co-ed sixth form) • Ages: 11–18 • RC

Tel: 020 8446 2256
Fax: 020 8343 9598
Email: office@st-michaels.barnet.sch.uk
Website: www.st-michaels.barnet.sch.uk

15

Headmaster: Since 2012, Julian Ward BA PGCE MBA (60s). Born in Lancashire and educated at the Pilgrim School, Bedford, and Manchester University, where he read modern history and economics. Then went on to study for an MBA at Bradford, before deciding that 'business was not my cup of tea' and training to be a teacher at Christ's College, Liverpool. ('I enjoyed every minute.') Has spent his entire professional career in London, where he started out teaching economics in 'front-line' local authority schools (Bishop Challoner in Tower Hamlets, John Paul II in Wandsworth, Sir John Cass's Foundation and Redcoat in Stepney), before moving to St Michael's in 1988.

Became sole deputy head in 1995, and his close working relationship with his predecessor, Ursula Morrisey, means he sees his current role more as evolution than revolution. Throughout his time at the school, has been a driving force in setting the highest academic targets, helping move the school from a middle-of-the road grammar to one that consistently sits at the top of the league tables. Since becoming head, has put particular emphasis on improving the percentage of A*s at A level, developing the gifted and talented programme and improving the school-parent partnership. A measured presence with a firm vision of what the school is about. 'Girls like him,' said one mother. 'They think he's strict, but fair.' 'Very dedicated,' said another. Married with three adult children, he continues to teach citizenship and RE.

Academic matters: St Michael's has won numerous awards (including Sunday Times State Secondary School of the Year 2013) for providing an outstanding education and is now one of the country's leading

Language offering particularly vibrant, with French, German, Spanish, Latin, classical Greek and Italian all on the timetable

secondary schools, always sitting within the top 20 grammar schools (often in the top 10) nationally at A level, usually in the top five at GCSE. 2014 saw 87 per cent A*-B grades at A level. At GCSE, an equally impressive 86 per cent A*/A. Teaching is undoubtedly a strength ('There are very clever teachers who provide very good teaching,' said one parent) and the school works hard to maximize both pupils' and parents' aspirations. 'We give a great deal of time to thinking about it,' says the head.

All the girls accepted here are bright, but St Michael's still offers significant added value, with a packed, fast-paced curriculum ('You need to enjoy academic work and want to find out about things,' says the head). Almost all take 11 GCSEs, including a large compulsory core, which includes English, maths, history and/or geography, RS, a science (about a third take all three) and a modern foreign language (large numbers take two). Language offering particularly vibrant, with French, German, Spanish, Latin, classical Greek and Italian all on the timetable, and Japanese and Mandarin offered outside it. Italian and Spanish particularly popular A levels (as well as psychology, RS and maths). Sixth form has its own building ('St Michael's is really two schools, with two distinct regimes,' says the head, 'a girls'-only school in years 7-11, and a co-ed sixth form college.') Only small numbers with special needs, but strugglers are provided with generous support. Homework is pushed hard. 'If you're ill you have to catch up on what you've missed,' said one mother.

Games, options, the arts: No playing fields and only a handful of courts, so team games not a forte (no

Attractive gardens, once the convent orchard, are graced by a monkey puzzle tree, large redwood and shrine to the Virgin Mary

hockey, for example), but a spacious new-ish sports hall (the largest school gym in Barnet) is used to the full to deliver high standard athletics, netball, volleyball, gymnastics, table tennis and badminton. Professional basketball and netball coaches bring out the best in nascent stars and the school is successful at local and regional level in a number of sports. The top performing school in the Borough's inter-sports competitions for girls.

Academic music is excellent, with dedicated practice rooms and a recording suite, though the head is pushing for higher standards of extracurricular involvement. 'Lots of girls participate in choir and orchestra, but I would like us to have a greater opportunity for high quality performance.' Large, well-equipped art and DT studio (offering material technology, food technology and graphics) with plenty of enthusiastic participants.

Good range of clubs (mainly in the lunch hour rather than after school as many pupils live far away) and trips (including skiing, modern languages and faith-centred activities, such as retreats and a visit to Lourdes).

Background and atmosphere: Founded by the Congregation of the Sisters of the Poor Child Jesus in 1908 as a prep school in the grounds of its convent. In 1958, a girls' grammar school was launched to share the site, and eventually the prep school was closed to allow the grammar school to expand.

Still quite a compact school housed in a motley collection of periods and styles. The Grange, which now accommodates the sixth form, was once a 19th century private house, and has the elegant proportions reflective of this history. The main school was built in the 1950s and comes with large windows and bright views. Modernisation is a constant theme (and drain on finances), but recent additions include an air-conditioned media suite and sixth form study centre. Classrooms remain a mix of old and new, but all are equipped with interactive whiteboards. Attractive gardens, once the convent orchard, are graced by a monkey puzzle tree, large redwood and shrine to the Virgin Mary.

The school, which is voluntary aided, is conducted by its governing body as part of the Catholic church and the Catholic ethos remains fundamental. Prayers are said daily and every pupil attends a weekly religious assembly, as well as mass on Feast days. But this is contemporary Catholicism. 'They go to mass, but they don't expect them to be cleaning the vestry floors,' said one parent. Attractive chapel with superior stained glass windows by Patrick Reyntiens, a master craftsman whose work also features at Liverpool and Coventry cathedrals. Girls put their faith into practice with charity work, helping in the community and giving food to homeless. Generally, the atmosphere is kind, warm and supportive. 'Academically, they push them to their limits, but they do look after them,' said one parent.'There's a very nice feeling to the school.' 'No one gets lost,' says another.'It feels very safe.'

Pastoral care and discipline: The primary aim here is the formation of responsible and committed Catholic citizens. 'We try and create a relaxed and happy atmosphere,' says the head, 'but we expect high standards of behaviour, self-discipline and responsibility.' Those from bohemian families are advised to think carefully about their choice. Even those who aren't acknowledge that the regime is firm. 'There is very strong discipline, which can irritate the girls,' says a parent. 'They will stamp on anything – possibly too hard. '

The pre-GCSE years have a slightly old-fashioned air. 'There's no talk of drugs,' said one mother. 'They do go to parties, but there's no big modern teenage culture.' Girls leap to attention if Mr Ward is spotted in the corridor and pupil pressure as much as

'We try and create a relaxed and happy atmosphere,' says the head, 'but we expect high standards of behaviour.' Those from bohemian families are advised to think carefully about their choice

teacher pressure patrols the classroom. 'My daughter said to me in astonishment, "a new girl in the school keeps answering the teacher back. Nobody will be friends with her. We like our teachers. They're on our side; we're on theirs".'

In the pre-GCSE years, uniform strictly enforced, with purple skirts at the knee or close to it, no jewellery or make-up. In the sixth form, mufti is permitted and the dress code becomes 'decency'.

Pupils remain accountable for what happens outside of the gates if in uniform. Few problems, however. 'Most people who come here are impressed by the behaviour and friendliness of the pupils.'

But this is contemporary Catholicism. 'They go to mass, but they don't expect them to be cleaning the vestry floors,' said one parent

Pupils and parents: Cradle Catholics from all over London and the world, with increasing numbers of Eastern Europeans, particularly Poles. Not as skewed to the professional middle classes as some other grammar schools, with more new immigrants (33 per cent do not speak English as their first language at home).

Entrance: Not perhaps as tricky to get into academically as some of the other North London grammar schools (390 apply for 96 places), simply because of its single-sex faith criteria. That said, the Catholic hurdle is not for slackers. Applicants at 11 plus must provide proof of First Holy Communion and at least one parent must also be a Catholic with a written reference from their parish priest stating they attend Mass on Sunday with the applicant. There is no catchment ('you can come from Sheffield if you want') but only girls who meet the religious criteria are allowed to sit the admissions tests (in verbal and non-verbal reasoning, English and maths). Sixth-form applicants are not required to be Catholic (about 20 per cent come from other faiths) but 'must subscribe to the Catholic ethos'. At this stage, there are a further 60 places (open to boys and girls with at least six GCSE passes at A* to A, with at least an A in the subjects they wish to study and no lower than a B in English and maths). Boys in this relatively large sixth form remain in the minority, with about 30 a year. 'The boys have to be quite brave,' said one parent.

Exit: About 14 or 15 girls leave post-GCSE, to nearby sixth form colleges, like Woodhouse, or larger co-ed selective schools. Most sixth formers go onto the older universities. A handful each year (eight in 2014), to Oxbridge, guided by the school's own Oxbridge specialist.

Money matters: St Michael's is a voluntary-aided school and parents are expected to contribute towards the cost of the buildings and facilities. 'The school would fall down otherwise,' says the head. An annual contribution of £275 a year is asked for and 90 per cent of parents contribute something. 'We don't go chasing the other 10 per cent.'

Remarks: A happy school, with firm discipline, high expectations and outstanding results.

St Michael's CofE Voluntary Aided Primary School

North Road, London, N6 4BG

State · Pupils: 465 · Ages: 3–11 · Non-denom

Tel: 020 8340 7441
Fax: 020 8340 9452
Email: admin@stmichaelsn6.com
Website: www.stmichaelsn6.com

30

Head Teacher: Since April 2013, Mrs Geraldine Gallagher. Trained and worked in Liverpool, then spent 16 years teaching in Islington before joining St Michael's. Three young children, all at the school.

Background and atmosphere: One of north London's most sought-after primary schools, St Michael's has high academic standards and a high proportion of pupils who reach well beyond the government's expectations at 7 and 11. This is partly due to intake – 'average children here would be above average in most other schools,' says the head – but also due to strong teaching throughout and well-organised classrooms where calm and well-behaved boys and girls sit quietly in their neat and practical navy uniform.

The curriculum is a particular strength of the school, with specialist subject teaching from year 3, Italian (courtesy of the Italian government), and a notable maths programme with an early-morning maths club for the most able run with neighbouring Highgate prep and booster lessons in curriculum time for the struggling.

Afternoon teaching unique, with specialist subject teaching in extension maths, PE, art, science, geography, history and music from year 3. 'I wanted to play to teachers' strengths,' says Mrs Smith. 'We had all these specialists in the school and only a proportion of the children were getting the benefit. It made absolute sense.'

A good range of sport – gymnastics, football, tennis, cricket, netball and basketball – taught in lesson time. Swimming too, taught in years 5 and 6, a strength – the school has won the Haringey swimming shield so often it's now on permanent display.

Founded in the mid 19th century as a school to train up young locals to go into service, by 1852 it was on its current three-and-a-half acre site. The green fields and listed Victorian buildings have since been joined by a block built in the 1970s, two large, well-equipped playgrounds and a large, new all-weather court. The immaculately maintained grounds are still the pride of the school. 'The school manager, Troy, has to be one of the best in London,' enthused one parent – and, as well as play time and games, the grounds are made full use of for the popular summer fair and Bonfire night festivities.

Excellent drama, with two or three plays annually, plus a nativity play and annual summer concert. Dynamic extra-curricular programme, with after-school cricket, drama (led by the school's celebrated drama teacher, Bob Williams, CBE), orchestra, recorder groups, French, chess, etc. Higher than average special needs, with a good SENCo, plus a gifted and talented co-ordinator.

Unusually energetic Parents' Association, which raises impressive sums each year with an endless medley of social events. 'I have never come across such a strong body of parents' reps,' says Mrs Smith. Fund raising drives have paid for a £35,000 computer suite, resurfacing and remodelling the infant playground, new cloakrooms, new stage lights and books galore.

Children mainly from comfortably off professional and media homes who are more than happy to use the state if it's as near to private as you can get. 'The parents here are wonderfully involved but you can feel excluded if you aren't in with the right set,' said one 'and parents can be quite demanding'. 'They sometimes don't seem to realise this isn't a prep school,' says the head.

Very much a community school, however, which children remain very attached to, often turning up to annual celebrations well into their secondary school years. 'It's one of unique things about the school.'

Entrance: Heavily oversubscribed at nursery and reception. Around 100 apply for 52 nursery places; 60 reception places, which are allocated on a points system. (Five points for church attendance at St Michael's Church, three for living in N6. Thereafter, local Christians, siblings, other faiths.) Christianity

---

A community school to which children remain very attached, often turning up to annual celebrations well into their secondary school years

very much part of the ethos, but the school tries to be as wide-ranging as possible in its intake. Open days every term and, if a vacancy is available, parents are welcome to look round. Places do arise, particularly in the higher years.

Exit: On the border of three boroughs – Haringey, Islington and Camden – St Michael's sends its leavers to as many as 30 secondary schools. About half to independent schools (many with scholarships)

– particularly Highgate, with which the school has a close association – and City of London, but also Channing, UCS, Westminster, North London Collegiate, Haberdashers' Aske's and South Hampstead, plus top grammars Henrietta Barnett, Latymer, St Michael's Catholic Girls and Queen Elizabeth's Boys. Two boys, too, have recently been accepted by Eton. A considerable chunk each year to Fortismere School, the popular local comprehensive in Muswell Hill. The school doesn't prepare children for entry tests but parents tend to be very clued up (with a secondary school evening run by the Parents' Association) and coach accordingly.

Remarks: One of north London's most sought-after primary schools, St Michael's has high academic standards and a high proportion of pupils who reach well beyond the government's expectations at 7 and 11. This is partly due to intake but also due to strong teaching and well-organised classrooms where calm and well-behaved boys and girls sit quietly in their neat and practical navy uniform.

The curriculum is a particular strength of the school, with specialist subject teaching from year 3, Italian (courtesy of the Italian government), and a notable maths programme with an early-morning maths club for the most able run with neighbouring Highgate prep, and booster lessons in curriculum time for the struggling.

Afternoon teaching unique, with specialist subject teaching in extension maths, PE, art, science, geography, history and music from year 3. 'I wanted to play to teachers' strengths,' said the previous head. 'We had all these specialists in the school and only a proportion of the children were getting the benefit. It made absolute sense.'

A good range of sport – gymnastics, football, tennis, cricket, netball and basketball – taught in lesson time. Swimming too, taught in years 5 and 6, a strength – the school has won the Haringey swimming shield so often it's now on permanent display.

Founded in the mid 19th century as a school to train up young locals to go into service, by 1852 it was on its current three-and-a-half acre site. The green fields and listed Victorian buildings have since been joined by a block built in the 1970s, two large, well-equipped playgrounds and a large, new all-weather court. The immaculately maintained grounds are still the pride of the school. 'The school manager, Troy, has to be one of the best in London,' enthused one parent – and, as well as play time and games, the grounds are made full use of for the popular summer fair and bonfire night festivities.

Excellent drama, with two or three plays annually, plus a nativity play and annual summer concert. Dynamic extracurricular programme, with after-school cricket, drama (led by the school's celebrated drama teacher, Bob Williams, CBE), orchestra, recorder groups, French, chess, etc. Higher than average special needs, with a good SENCo, plus a gifted and talented co-ordinator.

Unusually energetic Parents' Association, which raises impressive sums each year with an endless medley of social events. Fundraising drives have paid for a £35,000 computer suite, resurfacing and remodelling the infant playground, new cloakrooms, new stage lights and books galore.

Children mainly from comfortably-off professional and media homes who are more than happy to use the state if it's as near to private as you can get. 'The parents here are wonderfully involved but you can feel excluded if you aren't in with the right set,' said one, 'and parents can be quite demanding'.

Very much a community school, to which children remain very attached, often turning up to annual celebrations well into their secondary school years. 'It's one of unique things about the school.'

Tetherdown Primary School

Grand Avenue, London, N10 3BP

State · Pupils: 420 · Ages: 4–11 · Non-denom

Tel: 020 8883 3412
Fax: 020 8883 3414
Email: admin@tetherdownschool.org
Website: www.tetherdownschool.org

31

Headteacher: Since September 2013, Tony Woodward, previously head of Warren Mead Junior School in Surrey. Specialises in music (plays piano and clarinet), art and gymnastics (trampolining is his speciality – came second in the European Championships). Has worked in Surrey as a local leader in education, supporting the leaders of struggling local schools, and as an additional Ofsted inspector.

Entrance: The school has recently doubled in size to admit 60 pupils in reception, but there's still fierce competition to get in. In the past it was only siblings and those living feet from the gates who

reasonably stood a chance, now at least an address in the same street might reasonably be expected to do the trick. (Needless to say property prices nearby have their own exotic micro-climate.) Parents can view the school in the autumn term prior to entry, kids visit in the summer term before they start.

Exit: Not only is Tetherdown one of the country's top-performing primary schools, if you're clever enough to have got your child in here you're also pretty much guaranteed a smooth transition to one of the capital's best comprehensives. Smug parents, who've sorted it all by the age of 4, tend to assume their children will proceed to Fortismere and the vast majority go on here. The rest to north London grammar schools or leading independents ('This is Muswell Hill,' said one mother, 'parents tutor without hesitation.')

Remarks: This is a school which regularly sits near the top of the local authority league tables and, even in an average year, over 50 per cent of pupils reach level 5 in English and maths. 'Teaching is consistently good, with some that is outstanding,' says Ofsted, which demoted it from outstanding to good in the latest inspection, partly because 'A few high-attaining pupils are not always sufficiently challenged'. With meticulous monitoring, a dollop of regular homework ('there's not a lot of pressure') and dedicated parents willing to supervise nightly reading from reception to year 6 and you get some idea how these results happen. The school follows the national curriculum but adds its own flourishes.

Fun is very much part of the academic recipe, both in the classroom and outside, whether that's learning fractions in history by means of tricky Tudor recipes, studying maths with the help of a visiting Maths Clown or sharpening up those multiplication tables in Beat the Parents at Mental Maths. 'The children have a lovely education,' says one parent. Pupils are grouped, extended and supported according to ability. 'If they're struggling, it gets noticed. My son was given extra spelling and extra handwriting.' Special needs are caught early by a dedicated special needs coordinator, who works with classroom teachers and outside specialists to set appropriate targets. The recent requirement for the inclusion of modern language teaching is provided (courtesy of the Italian consulate) by weekly Italian lessons, and French is also offered as an after-school club.

Plenty of stretching and thinking in all directions, whether in an opera workshop or an after-school street dance club. Plenty of creative parents, too, who come in to share their expertise. All children learn to play the recorder and read music in year 3 and individual instrumental tuition, subsidised by the local authority, is provided during the working day. Sport is perhaps the school's weakest link, 'There isn't much and what there is isn't competitive,' said one mother of boys. In recent years, this has been partially due to a rebuild. Now the outdoor space is both more expansive and better equipped. In year 6, all children learn swimming and travel outside the school for specialist coaching. School's meals are nutritious – parents have their own tasting to ensure their experience matches their kids' – and naughty sweets, chocolates and fizzy drinks are banned from the premises. Plenty of after-school clubs – football, drama, etc – and while there's no after-school care on site, those who want it can be collected from the playground and taken to a nearby club. Regular school trips include an annual outing to the seaside for years 2 and 5, where the deputy head sets a good example by leading the troops into the bracing waves.

Virtually all parents and pupils live within a few surrounding streets and the school has always offered an exceptionally tight-knit community. Expansion has marginally diluted the atmosphere, but has brought advantages. 'It used to be very much like a village school, where everyone knew each other and older pupils looked out for the younger ones,' says one mother with children at both ends of the spectrum. 'That was comforting, but sometimes your child didn't have a particularly wide choice of friends. Now there's plenty of scope.'

Until 2009, Tetherdown was a square and solid Victorian board school, but an exciting £6.5 million redesign has provided lots of lovely light interiors and well-planned playgrounds for infants and juniors. The make-over has also brought up-to-the-minute wireless IT, with interactive whiteboards in every classroom and two computer suites.

The school has no uniform and rules are kept to a minimum. 'We have just two rules. Respect yourself, and respect others. If you respect yourself you are going to work hard to become the best you can.' Parents admire the way these principles are implemented. Those demonstrating behavioural difficulties are given the same support as those with academic problems, with intervention and

The school has no uniform and rules are kept to a minimum. 'We have just two rules. Respect yourself, and respect others.'

targets. Children are encouraged to get involved: with the school council; with each other's welfare (by becoming play leaders and buddies); and with the broader community (for example, running a soup kitchen at harvest time). They are also lavished with praise. Regular 'Achievements Assemblies' recognise work, effort and attitude.

Tetherdown is located in north London's prosperous, professional Muswell Hill and the parent body is a mirror of the locality, with plenty of engaged parents who devote the same attention to reading rotas and library duty they give to successful careers. Parents, too, provide support in a very concrete fashion and the enthusiastic Parent School Association generously underwrites school trips and playground extras. Parents know each other well in and out of school, are ambitious for their kids and for the school.

Woodhouse College

Woodhouse Road, London, N12 9EY

State · Pupils: 1300 · Ages: 16–19 · Non-denom

Tel: 020 8445 1210
Fax: 020 8445 5210
Email: enquiries@woodhouse.ac.uk
Website: www.woodhouse.ac.uk

16

Principal: Since September 2013, John Rubinstein BSc (50s). Has been a teacher for over 25 years and still teaches A level maths, 'because it keeps me in touch with students, with the experience of colleagues, but most of all, because I love it.' His wife is also a teacher and they have three children, two of whom attended Woodhouse and are now at university. Mr Rubinstein is also a part-time Ofsted inspector. Enjoys running and takes part in 10K and half marathon races, 'four or five times a year.'

Academic matters: Woodhouse is one of the country's leading sixth-form colleges, always in the top five nationally, usually in the top three. This is essentially an academic place, whose main focus is on A levels. In 2014, 31 per of grades were A*/A and two-thirds A*-B.

Undoubtedly a key part of the success is enthusiastic, experienced and focused teaching. 'I've become much better at teaching A levels here,' said one department head. 'In the comprehensive where I taught before, I was always worried about my year 9s.' Parents are very positive. 'Most of the teachers seem very, very good,' said one, whose son transferred from an independent school. 'They're excellent at monitoring and keep their finger on the pulse.' Results are certainly not achieved by hothousing or editing, and all students who pass AS level can continue to A2s.

A wide range of options on offer, with 30 subjects in almost any combination. As well as two applied A Levels, there are also two BTecs in business and ICT ('We provide some vocational courses, primarily for students coming from our partner

Values here are traditional. 'We believe in honesty, hard work, mutual respect and taking responsibility for your own learning.'

schools,' says the head.) Maths is the most popular A level choice (with 45 per cent taking it) and results are notably strong. One of London's largest providers of A level science, with many going on to science-related degrees. Four languages, including

Italian, and an abundance of 'ologies', from sociology to music technology. Critical thinking and the extended project also available, as well as GCSEs in English and maths for those who require resits.

Though the majority at Woodhouse tend to favour professional courses at university, social science and arts-based studies are strong, with thriving theatre studies, economics, English literature and geography. 'Independent learning' is high on the agenda. 'We want students to prepare for lessons, so they can understand and interpret the

---

'If there isn't a club you'd like to do,' said one student, 'the sports department are happy to try and set something up.'

---

information, using the teacher and their fellow students as a resource,' says the head. Motivated students respond well to this approach. 'Teachers assume if you're interested in your subjects, you will want to read around them,' said one. 'They don't force you to work, but they'll give you the resources and make themselves available to you,' said another.

All students have access to two learning mentors – one for humanities, the other, science and maths – to sort out any day-to-day tangles. One full-time SENCo, plus two part-time specialists, providing individual support for those with dyslexia and dyspraxia, as well as study skills aid for those who need it. The buildings are 99 per cent adapted for those with physical disabilities.

Games, options, the arts: Woodhouse prides itself on providing 'a broad and civilising education' and all are expected to participate in at least two six-week courses of 'enrichment', the majority of which take place on Wednesdays afternoons, when there are no lessons. Most relish the opportunities to develop new skills in everything from observational drawing to street dance. Duke of Edinburgh and Amnesty International also on offer.

Art and dance are strong curricular subjects here, with excellent A level results, and the college has a lovely bright dance studio and art department. Sports facilities, too, are good, with a new sports hall and floodlit all-weather pitch. Official team sports include football (girls' and boys'), netball and basketball, but individualists can also enjoy cross-country, squash, trampolining and kick boxing. 'If there isn't a club that you'd like to do,' said one student, 'the sports department are happy to try and set something up.'

Woodhouse students like to get involved and there's an active college council, which has recently helped introduce a daily loan system for netbooks. Plenty of outside speakers and activities including art trips, foreign exchanges, a ski trip and the opportunity to undertake voluntary work abroad.

Background and atmosphere: Located in a pleasant leafy suburb, Woodhouse began it educational life as Woodhouse Secondary School in 1925, but became one of the capital's rare sixth-form colleges in the 1980s. Today all pupils are aged between 16 and 18 and all are studying A levels. With 660 new pupils a year, the college is significantly larger than a traditional school sixth form, but smaller than a FE college.

The original stately Victorian façade (deriving from its former incarnation as the home of ornamental plasterer Thomas Collins) has now been joined by a motley timeline of newer buildings, leaving it today with well-equipped facilities. The state-of-the art Learning Zone is one of the most recent innovations, offering space to work in solitary silence as well as in small groups, and supervised open-access IT. 'Quite a lot of students here can't work in silence at home and don't have the facility to do the "hard hours",' says the head. 'We wanted to create learners who can work on their own.'

Values here are traditional. 'We believe in honesty, hard work, mutual respect and taking responsibility for your own learning.' The atmosphere is generally enthusiastic, as much for work as for play. 'Here it's cool to work, cool to be involved,' says one student. 'The atmosphere is incredible,' says another. 'There's a massive sense of community. There are always things happening.'

Pastoral care and discipline: Not every 16-year-old is ideally suited to the self-motivation required by an academic sixth form college, but here high expectations are supported by a well-thought-out tutorial system and plenty of individual guidance. Every student has their own tutor, 'My son sees a guy two or three times a week, whom he likes and respects,' said one mother. 'When he was having trouble at home, they really kept an eye on him.'

The college sees itself as a bridge between school and university, and new students are eased into this more adult world with an induction day in the summer before they start. The enrichment programme helps aid new friendships beyond the classroom. 'Everyone makes friends ridiculously fast because there are so many people in the same position,' said one boy. Boundaries are firm and there's zero tolerance on punctuality. 'It's an issue they have to grasp,' says the head. 'If they're not making the effort, why should other students suffer?'

In lessons, students are attentive. 'If a teacher leaves the room, people get on with their work,' says one boy, 'They want to do well.' One recent arrival, who'd left a successful local comprehensive, said, 'I came here because I felt I would be made to work. I've really grown up quickly into a different person. The change is on a biblical scale.' Few significant discipline problems. 'Issues found elsewhere are not even on the radar here,' notes the

'Everyone makes friends ridiculously fast because there are so many people in the same position,' said one boy

head gratefully. Standard formula of oral and written warnings, with a code of conduct signed by all parents and pupils, but exclusion is a rarity. 'We have pupils from quite challenged backgrounds, but I have thrown out just one student,' says the head. 'My predecessor excluded two.' Parents agree that discipline is firm but reasonable. 'They run quite a tight ship, but it makes them responsible,' said one father. 'When my son's attendance was only 90 per cent, he had to see the senior tutor every week. As his attendance improved, he went less frequently.' There's no dress code, but pupils don't push it. Relaxed but neat is the general rule.

Pupils and parents: An eclectic mix – 'some nerdy kids, some cool kids, all sorts, colours and creeds.' The core is probably typical of the reasonably prosperous 'squeezed middle' of north London, but with a far higher ethnic intake than you'd assume from the location, and a far higher proportion of those who require some type of financial support. 'Last year, we did a survey and were surprised to find that over a third of pupils were on the full EMA [now abolished],' says the principal.

Parents tend to be involved and supportive, students upbeat, mature, outgoing and energetic. They clearly enjoy the school – more than half volunteered on the annual open day held on a Saturday. 'They want to do well and they want to enjoy themselves,' says the principal. 'They're trying to get the balance right of working hard and having a good social life.' A parent agrees: 'My son is so happy. He really appreciates the fact that people are there because they want to learn, not because their parents are pushing them. Most students here are trying to better themselves and work really, really hard.' Past students include journalist Johann Hari, comedian Michael McIntyre and actress Naomie Harris.

Entrance: Priority is given to two local secondary schools, Friern Barnet and The Compton. Students from these schools make up about 20 per of the intake. After that, it's predicted grades and/or interview. Competition is ferocious (about 4,500 apply for 660 places), particularly for in-demand subjects. 'We can afford to be choosy,' says the head, 'but we're looking for a range.' Those with high predicted grades, excellent references and a clear sense of direction (about 160 students) are invited to three 'direct offer' evenings for a talk. 'They have already demonstrated that they meet the requirements we would need to ask about at an interview.' The rest with minimum predicted grade requirements (evaluated on a point system, with specific grades for individual subjects) are given a 20-30 minute interview (with optional parental accompaniment) in the February/March prior to entry. 'We're looking for maturity,' said one teacher. 'We want them to demonstrate that they are committed to A levels and really want to work, but we also want people who will get involved on a wider basis.' The interview is frequently of as much benefit to the student as to the college. 'We often spend it giving careers advice,' says the head.

Travel time is also taken into consideration. 'We generally consider an hour and a quarter by bus the maximum desirable distance.' Applications available from the time of the open day in November until the closing deadline in January. All candidates require a confidential report from their current school and must be between 16 and 18 when starting at the college. The college operates a waiting list for the re-shuffle that often takes place after results day in August.

Exit: Over 95 per cent to university with the most popular destinations being London universities, Kent, Leeds, Manchester and Sussex. Most popular subject choices are economics, law, engineering, business and psychology. Six to Oxbridge and 13 to medical school in 2014. Good advice about careers and courses, including a full time careers co-ordinator. Regular tutorials on university admissions and interview practice for those who require it.

Money matters: Parents are asked for £100 contribution for the two-year stint, enabling the college to keep up to date with books and underwrite the enrichment programme and facilities (those who can't afford it, don't pay). A £50 refundable deposit also required for text books. The college has attempted to replace some money lost through EMA cuts with bursaries.

Remarks: An upbeat environment, with strong teaching and results. A firm stepping stone between school and university.

Wren Academy

Hilton Avenue, London, N12 9HB

State • Pupils: 990 • Ages: 11–18 • C of E

Tel: 020 8492 6000
Email: firstcontact@wrenacademy.org
Website: www.wrenacademy.org

17

Principal: Since June 2007, some 15 months before the academy opened, Mr Michael Whitworth (40s). Previously head of Kelmscott School in Walthamstow. Born and brought up in Northumberland, he graduated as a historian and has recently taught history and religious studies. After working in both private and industry and the civil service, he entered teaching and has worked in schools in London, Hertfordshire and Essex. He was attracted by the 'unusual opportunity to create a brand new school from scratch', and built up the school's reputation very rapidly. 'I think the governors recognised my capacity to stick to a task and see it through.' Understated but extremely caring, say parents, very driven and with sights set very high. Married with two young children.

Academic matters: This is a comprehensive, but the nature of the students in this leafy area means it is primarily an academic one. The biggest initial challenge was achieving a truly comprehensive intake: the previous school on the site had a very poor reputation and Barnet has a variety of popular state schools, including three grammars. However, within a short space of time Ofsted stated that 'the teaching at Wren is stunning', and this is not something you read very often. 'As well as maximising achievement – because children need that currency to move on – we teach learning skills and aptitudes,' says the head. 'Children need the capacity to think for themselves. They are encouraged to seek out their own answers, to be flexible and take risks.' GCSE results in 2014 saw 76 per cent of pupils achieving five A*-C grades including English and maths with 31 per cent A*/A grades. The first cohort of sixth formers achieved nearly 40 per cent A-B grades in their AS exams.

Parents are enthusiastic. 'The teachers are very wisely chosen.' 'They're great at finding and encouraging talents.' 'They really encourage them to aim high.' Newsletters all include brainteasers for parents and pupils to solve, and articles on ways of building learning power.

English, maths and science are taught in single sex classes. 'This gives us opportunities to stretch children in gender-specific ways. For example, in English boys can look at their powers of reflectiveness and empathy, whilst in girls' maths classes we

This young school has already established a reputation for high teaching standards, courteous students and excellent enrichment activities

can encourage them to take risks and concentrate on answering quickly. It helps to broaden their skill sets, and they enjoy it.' Research suggests that girls taught in single sex groups are more likely to continue with maths and science, and a good percentage of girls is choosing single science GCSEs.

The school sets for English, maths, science and foreign languages from part of the way through year 7. 'We like to get data of our own rather than relying on Sats results.' Everyone studies a language (generally French, though some take Japanese or Spanish) and most are expected to take it to GCSE. Regular language days involve a range of linguistic activities. GCSE courses start in year 9.

The specialism of design and the built environment enhances rather than dominates the curriculum, says the head. 'It influences our culture and our ways of thinking about tasks. We have a high emphasis on creativity, and each task has a creative phase, a planning phase and an evaluation phase. But we also have the opportunity to plan projects in architecture and civil engineering.'

Those who need extra help are identified at the beginning of year 7 and follow a six week key skills programme to help bring them up to speed. There are also after-school support groups that help with spelling and comprehension. Although some get one-to-one help from teaching assistants, 'the aim is for everyone to be unsupported in lessons eventually. We do what helps them to access the curriculum in the appropriate lesson.'

Games, options, the arts: The school week includes three extended days, with compulsory enrichment activities from 3 – 4pm. These range from samba band, Latin and knitting to debating. Staff and students learn together and either can win Excellent Learner of the Week awards.

Houses – named for Wren churches – give the main opportunities for sporting rivalry, but football, netball, basketball, badminton and athletics teams also take part in borough and regional competitions with increasing success. There's a sports hall, netball courts and a football pitch. Opponents have commented on Wren teams' good sportsmanship. Pupils can take sports GCSE or BTec, and enrichment options include rugby, trampolining and table tennis.

Art, design and technology very strong and creative – as one would expect in a school with a design specialism. Projects include designing sculptures of dream ice cream sundaes, creating a piece of artwork inspired by the River Thames and designing an Olympic stadium.

Music is keen – there's an orchestra, samba band, gospel choir, Indian drumming club – and increasing in quality as musicians move up the school and hone their skills. Drama also finding its feet; eagerly awaited annual school musical – eg Bugsy Malone and Hairspray. Wren's Got Talent showcases singers, magicians and musicians.

Background and atmosphere: Named for Sir Christopher Wren, designer of St Paul's Cathedral, which reflects its C of E status and specialism in design and the built environment. Opened in 2008 on the site of a failed school next door to Woodhouse College. Partly refurbished but mostly newly built, it has an open plan feel, with roof lights and large north windows, grey carpets and aluminium cladding. Steps leading down from the entrance hall to the library, 'the heart of the school', are lined by ledges where children can sit and chat, under treble-height rooflights, giving an amphitheatre-like atmosphere. There is a feeling of space and airiness throughout. Corridor walls are decorated with graphics of the footprint of St Paul's Cathedral, and with murals quoting inspiring biblical texts eg 'Be willing and available to provide support and guidance to others'.

The school is sponsored by the London Diocesan Board for Schools, hence its Christian character, and by Berkhamsted School, which provides some of the governors. The schools work together on areas such as curriculum development, Wren stu-

> 'In English boys can look at their powers of reflectiveness and empathy, whilst in girls' maths classes we encourage them to take risks.'

dents go over to Berkhamsted for activities, including a year 7 residential retreat, and Berkhamsted sixth formers have visited Wren to give their views on appointing a new head of sixth form. 'It's a partnership, and we hope that both schools will get an equal amount from it.'

Pastoral care and discipline: 'The teachers don't tolerate any bad behaviour,' say parents. 'It is a lovely, safe environment for learning'; and indeed the school had a supremely ordered feel during our visit. Three different breaks and lunchtimes help. So does the design of the building: staff and pupils share uni-sex toilets, and there is no staff room, so everyone socialises in the restaurant. 'It's a philosophy that when staff and students share the same space there is passive supervision, and students feel secure. They're encouraged to sit in here and chat – it's part of the curriculum.' 'Focus days' concentrate on matters ranging from sexual health to university choices.

Much emphasis on good manners and courtesy. Common sanctions include litter duty and community service. There's a Reflection Room for 'those who would benefit from time on their own to reflect'. Pupils have a high degree of autonomy, with plenty of opportunities to get involved in the way the school is run, from becoming prefects to interviewing potential teachers to taking part in curriculum reviews. 'In return, they generally play their part. There's a high level of buy-in.'

The chaplain, who plays a counsellor-like role, is generally considered a good egg. The only parental criticism is that some feel the school doesn't take their views on board. 'When you start a new school you have to put in place structures that will work. We opened with a very clear idea of what we wanted. We've always listened and explained to parents, but we haven't always amended our ways as a result.'

Pupils and parents: A diverse range, about 25 per cent white British, and characteristic of this leafy outer-London suburb; mostly 'ambitious people who want to do well'. Pupils have taken GCSEs in 13 different home languages. Active PTA which organises quiz nights and festivals, organises second hand uniform sales and has raised funds for the gazebo, which offers a shady outdoor place to socialise

Entrance: Takes 180 into year 7, with 90 foundation (church) places and 90 community places. First priority for community places to looked after children, those with SEN statements or exceptional medical or social need. Points for having a sibling at the school and for attending a Barnet primary school, then by distance – generally within about half a mile. For foundation places, points for siblings and for regular church attendance, with distance as a tie-break. Has waiting lists for occasional places in other years. Internal and external sixth form applicants need at least five B grades at GCSE including maths, English, and the subjects they want to study at A level; prospective maths, further maths, science and French students need A grades in these subjects. At least 25 external sixth form places.

Exit: Some 80 per cent of those who achieve the grade requirements stay on post-GCSE. No sixth form leavers as yet.

Remarks: This young school has already established a reputation for high teaching standards, courteous students and excellent enrichment activities. Likely to go from strength to strength.

East

Barking & Dagenham
Havering
Redbridge
Tower Hamlets
Waltham Forest

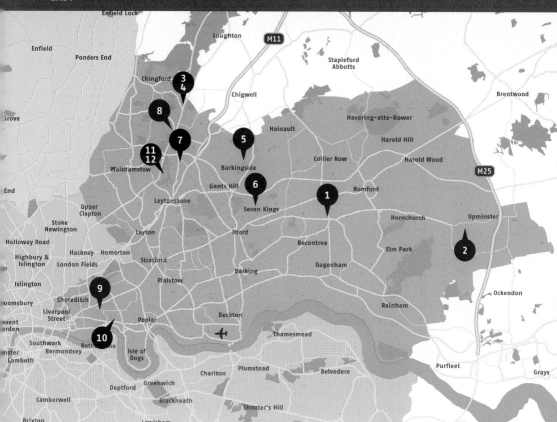

EAST

BARKING & DAGENHAM

1 Robert Clack School 594

HAVERING

2 The Cooper's Company And Coborn School 583

REDBRIDGE

3 Bancroft's Preparatory School 577

4 Bancroft's School 578

5 Ilford County High School 590

6 Seven Kings High School 597

7 Snaresbrook Preparatory School 605

8 Woodford County High School 608

TOWER HAMLETS

9 Sir John Cass Foundation And Redcoat Church Of England Secondary School 600

10 Sir William Burrough Primary School 603

WALTHAM FOREST

11 Forest Preparatory School 585

12 Forest School 586

An introduction to East London and its state schools

Barking & Dagenham

Barking and Dagenham, with the Thames as its southern boundary, stretches north to encompass the green belt area of Chadwell Heath. Once, companies such as the Ford Motor Company provided settled blue collar employment. Now, most of the employment is in low-paid service industries. A large proportion of the population lives in the vast Becontree estate. Robert Clack qv is a top secondary: this once-failing school was captained to success by Sir Paul Grant, who took the helm in the late 90s, and is now massively over-subscribed. The Sydney Russell School is rated outstanding; Barking Abbey, Jo Richardson and All Saints Catholic School are all popular.

William Ford Junior School – linked with Village Infants on the same site – was founded in 1841, when Dagenham was a village surrounded by fields. Manor Infants/Manor Longbridge are also rated outstanding, as is Warren Junior School. Most Barking and Dagenham primary schools are large, with only a couple of faith schools being one form entry, and many having four forms in a year group.

Havering

Havering is the most easterly of the London boroughs. Its main town is Romford, a major metropolitan area, but it also includes large areas of green belt land. Coopers Company and Coburn school qv in Upminster is one of the most popular secondaries and has a 'religious character': it will only consider regular worshippers from any of the major faiths. Admissions arrangements are convoluted: it gives preference to children of staff and former students; a certain percentage of places to those living in specific areas; 10 sport and nine music places. Other high performing secondary schools are both Catholic and both in Upminster: Sacred Heart of Mary girls' school and The Campion boys' school. Both give preference to practising Catholic families living in specific local parishes.

Ardleigh Green Junior and Scott's Primary, both in Hornchurch, are rated outstanding, as is Engayne primary in Upminster. Several Catholic primaries do well: St Peter's in Romford, St Joseph's in Upminster and La Salette in Rainham.

Newham

Newham – home of most of the Olympic Park – is also one of the most deprived boroughs in the country. It also has rapidly improving public transport, including Stratford Station, Docklands Light Railway and – in future – several Crossrail stations. Plashet School in East Ham is very well thought of, as are St Bonaventure RC school for boys and St Angela's Ursuline Convent school for girls (these two have a joint sixth form). The new selective sixth college, the London Academy of Excellence, is in Stratford; it was the brainchild of the heads of the local Kingsford Community School and independent Brighton College, one of its backers.

Elmhurst Primary ranks highly, as do Vicarage, Central Park, St Stephen's Primary, St Edward's Catholic Primary and Upton Cross (which is expanding to five form entry on a new site and will have some 1,200 pupils by 2016). Tollgate in Plaistow is also rated outstanding, as is St Luke's C of E in Canning Town.

Redbridge

Redbridge is one of the greenest boroughs, with plentiful parks and open spaces. Woodford County High for girls qv and Ilford County High for boys qv are the local selective grammar schools, with results to match (priority to high achievers who live within the school catchment areas). But there is a also a high proportion of non-selective schools rated as outstanding, including Seven Kings High qv, Loxford

School, Valentines High, Beal High, Oaks Park High, Chadwell Heath Academy and Trinity Catholic High. Understandably, a large proportion of pupils go on to university.

The primary schools are good too. Christchurch Primary, a secular school in spite of its name, is one of the largest in the country with five forms in each year group. St Bede's RC primary and Our Lady of Lourdes RC primary are high-achieving, as are Redbridge, Nightingale and Gearies.

Tower Hamlets

Tower Hamlets, one of the oldest parts of London (tribal, pre-Roman, silted and swampy at the time), was in more recent times home to most of London's Cockney dock workers. Wapping and the areas along that length of the river were lined with docks and warehouses for the thousands of ships and workers in London's port, characterised as well by Dickensian levels of poverty and crime. Those same docks, winding streets and riverside warehouses now contain very high end flats, served by the best butcher in east London and lively cafes and trendy restaurants (one, for example, in a converted power hydraulic station), but some areas still have high levels of poverty.

This is a vibrantly multi-ethnic borough – successive waves of immigrants, including Huguenot refugees, Irish weavers, Askanazi Jews and most recently Bangladeshis have congregated here. As well as the largest city farm in the country – the 32 acre Mudchute Park and Farm in the middle of the Isle of Dogs – it has the oldest surviving music hall in the world, Wilton's.

In the 90s it had some of the worst performing schools in the country; now it has some of the best. It reduced absences, set ambitious targets and used its extra funding as a deprived area to attract some high quality teaching staff and heads.

Sir John Cass's Foundation and Redcoat School qv is one

of the most popular secondary schools. Although a C of E school, only a small minority of places is for committed Christians, and the vast majority of pupils, mirroring the ethnic make-up of the area, are Bangladeshi. Mulberry School for Girls, with a similar demographic, is also rated as outstanding, as are Morpeth School and Swanlea School. St Paul's Way Trust, undersubscribed and rated as 'satisfactory' a few years ago, is now, in a new building with greatly improved reports, another of the most sought-after schools in the borough.

Amongst many popular primary schools are Sir William Burrough qv with its international primary curriculum, Old Palace, Bygrove, Bonner, Old Ford and Clara Grant – interesting that many of the top-performing primaries in this area are secular. A controversial free school, Canary Wharf College (a primary in spite of its name) has hit the news for having only two per cent of pupils on free school meals in an area where most schools have 50 per cent, and limiting class sizes to 20. A second College opened in September 2014, again with 50 per cent of places for Christian church goers.

Waltham Forest

Waltham Forest is a borough of contrasts: the area south of the North Circular Road is mostly built-up and urban, with the socially and ethnically mixed population characteristic of inner cities. The northern area encompasses lots of open space, including parts of Epping Forest, and several reservoirs, and has a suburban feel. Walthamstow School for Girls is a flagship secondary; Highams Park is also popular.

St Mary's Catholic Primary in Chingford in the leafy northern part is highly rated, as are Henry Maynard, Hillyfield on the Hill and Greenleaf, Handsworth and Dawlish Road.

Bancroft's Preparatory School

Linked school: Bancroft's School, 578

611–627 High Road, Woodford Green, Essex IG8 0RF

Independent · Pupils: 260 · Ages: 7–11 · C of E · Fees (per term): £4,085

Tel: 020 8506 6751
Fax: 020 8506 6752
Email: prep.office@bancrofts.org
Website: www.bancrofts.org

Headmaster: Since September 2012, Mr Joe Layburn MA, previously acting head. MA in German literature from University College London, followed by a 15-year career as investigative journalist and TV reporter, primarily for Channel 4. Retrained as a teacher and joined Bancroft's Prep in 2004. Author of a trilogy of children's books. Married with three sons, two at Bancroft's and one at a special needs school. Keen on running, cycling and West Ham United.

Entrance: At 7+ – over-subscribed by about 3:1. Testing in English – reading and writing – and maths for year 3 entry takes place on beanbags. Children seen (and offered doughnuts) in small groups with head and deputy – it's 'as informal and low key as possible'. Around 70-75 places offered – Bancroft's will be first choice for most applicants.

Exit: Vast majority to senior school; a few to local grammars, including Woodford County High, KEGS and Latymer. Others to local schools like West Hatch, Valentines. Other pupils move because families are moving out of the area (one to Putney High this year).

Remarks: Two conjoined, inviting-looking, modern red-brick buildings at the lower right hand side of the main school playing fields – two-storeyed and with big windows. From the main school they appear small and modest; the main school, viewed from the prep, looks imposing and a little awe-inspiring, but the prep children spend time in the main school, and sensible links so that 'It's a bit scary as it's so big and the students are so big, but we had a meeting with Mrs Ireland so we know much more about it now and I'm not really scared any more'. Quite! And senior pupils trot over to visit their junior siblings in break too. However the prep is its own world and, as you descend the slope to its entrance, between the playing field and the tennis court, a gentleness and palpable sense of fun envelops you.

The prep has splendid new rooms which have greatly enhanced its overall space and provision. New science, drama, music and DT rooms, a good-sized hall with flexible seating – lots of IT and new laptops. Around 23 children in a class, but the rooms are big and airy enough not to feel crowded – we did not feel the need to open windows, as one so often does. The library is well-stocked and a good mix of fact and fiction. Outside space good and super all-weather surface for littlies with monster chess set and apparatus – not surprisingly, 'Everyone loves coming out here'.

Classrooms busy, not over-orderly and relaxed – we wanted to look at the displays, all of which seemed interesting and not as predictable as they so often are. We liked the alternatives to 'said' and loved the paper collages showing variations on the Arcimboldo fruity face and the glittery, sparkly, firework ones. We also approved some of the interesting work in progress, especially the lesson on moulds – 'We had to throw them away as they were beginning to smell,' was a rueful observation. Year 6 has critical thinking lessons – 'to expand our minds, to think out of the box, to widen our imagination,' we were told, earnestly. We were impressed by the sensible 'traffic light' system whereby pupils assess their grasp of what they have learnt and where they need help. All entrants assessed for SpLD at 7 and SENCo-led help laid on where needed – mostly mild dyslexia.

Exuberant sports, music and drama and lots of inspiring extracurricular stuff. Outgoing, relaxed and confident children from a vast range of local backgrounds, as you'd expect.

A true preparatory school in that what goes on here is sound, sensible and confidence-building for what is to follow. But is not just preparatory for senior school – four happy years here are a solid foundation for life. Apply early – and cross your fingers.

Bancroft's School

Linked school: Bancroft's Preparatory School, 577

611 – 627 High Road, Woodford Green, Essex IG8 0RF

Independent• Pupils: 855 • Ages: 11–18• C of E
• Fees (per term): £5,016

Tel: 020 8505 4821
Fax: 020 8559 0032
Email: stephanie.wallis@bancrofts.org
Website: www.bancrofts.org

4

Head: Since January 2008, Mrs Mary Ireland BSc DipEd Member Soc of Biologists, chartered biologist (early 50s). Career began with Proctor and Gamble, but light dawned, she took her teaching qualification and has taught all three sciences and maths in both state and independent schools.

Prior to Bancroft's, she was deputy head of Christ's Hospital, before which she had been housemistress at Ardingly and head of science at King's Hall.

Married, with a grown-up musician son, brisk, open, energetic, easy to talk to, attractive Scots intonation. True, professional head, clear about her modernising agenda – lost no time in implementing changes – and as clear about the values upon which Bancroft's was founded and which still inform its ethos. She has clearly been won over by the school and its community. 'The buildings have a wow factor – though I tell parents that they are not what the school is about – but the thing that really appealed to me was the children. They are London children who tell it how it is, multi-racial, striving children who want to do well – they are incredibly competitive. They do everything here that we did at Christ's Hospital, only they cram it into a school day'.

A safe pair of hands – and not hands that mind getting dirty: she cleared up a lunch that slid off a pupil's plate onto the floor when we visited. She is involved, busy and available. Some of her changes not immediately understood by school community, restructuring of the school council and the popular Stars in their Eyes extravaganza being two. Introduction of new Virtual Learning Environment – internet school-home communications system – hit by predictable teething troubles and much groused about, but now a useful asset. She manages to teach some GCSE biology – we applaud. Bancroft's has continued to thrive under her eager eye and hands-on regime.

Academic matters: Notable results across the board (in 2014 nearly 84 per cent A*/A grades at GCSE) but maths is a star performer by any standards. English more of a spread, despite reports of some brilliantly inspirational teaching. Modern langs getting a boost – all year 7s learn German and Spanish; Russian is an option from year 9; Mandarin recently introduced. Greek and Latin have healthy numbers. Remarkable science results – especially in chemistry. History and geography also impressive. Few takers for art, music and DT – surprising, given the facilities – but a school which takes its academics seriously. No trendy subjects, though drama has seduced its way into the timetable and options list. A particular, enlightened feature is that subjects can be chosen not, as elsewhere, from 'blocks' but from the whole curriculum. If they can manage it at Bancroft's, why not everywhere?

A level results similarly impressive – 90 per cent A*-B, 68 per cent A*/A in 2014. Maths and chemistry popular and successful. Demand for maths and sciences has led to creation of new maths room and science lab. Economics and geography good and, at this level, English also impresses. Greek and Latin survive, though the numbers taking modern langs are, we would suggest, a cause for concern, though may reflect the immense diversity of backgrounds here.

A place where serious learning happens and in which learning is taken seriously. The library, recently revamped with a stylish new mezzanine floor beautifully integrated into the whole, is a proper scholarly resource – not something you see everywhere these days, when for 'library' you can so often read 'IT suite'. Pupils appreciate the

---

This is one of his more benign and attractive buildings, with towers, crenellations and oriel windows, a splendid central quad and admirably generous corridors

---

library and its staff – 'they are fantastic – they get in anything you need'. Sixth form has a very recent, dedicated library and quiet study area plus university-type lecture theatre – used for societies, debates and visiting speakers. IT everywhere – lots of rooms with new PCs, including a tiptop language lab, which should give the languages a deserved boost.

Learning support department screens all at 11+ (the prep also screens at 7+). Mrs Ireland appointed the school's first SENCo and has also ensured that all new staff get some training in SpLD. All on the LS register (mostly mild dyslexics) have an IEP and get some kind of individual support – the younger ones come out of different lessons each term and older ones get one-to-one. A TA in class helps those who are happy to be helped in that way. Lower sixth get help to 'develop individual learning skills'. 'They are wonderfully flexible over special needs,' says a parent.

Games, options, the arts: Sports are 'big' and well-resourced. Large playing fields on site plus vast sports hall with 25m pool. Five minutes away is school's own West Grove with pitches, courts, tracks etc. Achievement to match – triumphs in netball, rugby and cricket as well as tours in these and hockey to, eg, New Zealand, Australia, South Africa and Sri Lanka. Heart-felt pupil and parental complaints that sport is too elitist – 'if you're not in a squad, they don't give a monkey's' – seen by Mrs Ireland as a priority and B and C teams now being developed, along with soccer. 'We are encouraging more staff to help so we can run more teams. It's something we need to work on.'

CCF is huge, very popular and enthusiastically pursued by those who surprise themselves by how

A safe pair of hands – and not hands that mind getting dirty: she cleared up a lunch that slid off a pupil's plate onto the floor when we visited

much they get out of it, girls as well as boys – 'It's taught me how to get on with people I'd never mix with normally'; 'It's good that the sixth form help with it – you can have a bit of a laugh with them': not common in what is still, more or less, a London school. Thriving D of E and Sea Scout group with cubs, scouts and explorer sections.

Equally, Mrs Ireland was determined to boost time for arts across the school and has steadily increased provision. Music and drama enthusiastic and popular – annual concert in Drapers' Hall the big annual event, with bands, solo performances and musical mix the main features. Vast range of instruments studied – music maybe more pop and jazz than classical, though we are told around eight classical concerts each year. Drama had a recent fillip with conversion of old gym to good, large new studio and subject now on the curriculum at all levels. Not all musicals here, either – The Caucasian Chalk Circle and Macbeth among recent productions; year 9 and 10 performers taught to fence for their production of The Three Musketeers. Productions at Edinburgh Fringe Festival.

Art, electronics and DT departments produce lively work – we liked the clever clocks, mobiles and the remote control cars and, within the remit of the task, pupils are given their head to be creative with the actual design. Art, exceptionally well-displayed throughout school, originates in one of two brand new studios with kilns and exhibition space – light, spacious and full of quiet artists. Nice ceramics. Art could and should be bigger here – perhaps textiles and photography (on the way), as more than a club?

Tons of trips and tours – though some parental gripes about not enough places on trips for eager applicants. Extracurricular stuff is good, though some cries for more from the inexhaustible.

Background and atmosphere: Founded in 1737 by the Drapers' Company on behalf of Francis Bancroft as a school for poor boys; moved to Woodford from Mile End in 1889 into the present large and imposing red-brick Victorian Gothic revival building – clearly designed to impress, with serious scholarly credentials by architect, Sir Arthur Blomfield, also responsible for Selwyn College, Cambridge,

The RCM, much of Charterhouse, The Bank of England, Wellington, Eton Lower Chapel etc etc, as well as an astounding number of parish churches. This is one of his more benign and attractive buildings, with towers, crenellations and oriel windows, a splendid central quad and admirably generous corridors which, though originally intended for 200 boys, still feel spacious for today's quadrupled numbers.

A truly impressive school with twisty, brick staircases and leaded lights which grab eager 10 year olds immediately – 'I chose it because it was like Hogwarts': a unique selling point in Essex, to be sure. Large Great Hall – typical of date and type. Excellent Courtyard Building with colonnaded atrium and sitting area, dining room (all eat together; good food, though popular vegetarian option can run out too fast for true veggie latecomers, we're told), servery and sixth form common room and café: large and well-used. Some typically dismal 1960s add-ons but much better later additions (such as enormous multi-purpose sports hall) and adjoining buildings, eg vast head's house now used for admin and offices too, with head's garden open to everyone for quiet time and 'well-respected'. Very recent physics labs and modern language rooms.

Integral chapel one of the best bits (complete with much-loved chaplain who is 'lovely, a wonderful person for a chat, a laugh and advice – he takes Salsa club'), into which everyone comes once weekly for an ecumenical service. Brass plaques to former heads and a vast stained glass east window set the tone for the services, which are inclusive in all ways, given the mix of pupils. Chapel also used for arts events – words and music etc, a classy extra-curricular feature here.

Parental tributes to general efficiency of school and its communications. Sense of order, purposeful activity and common sense all-pervasive.

Pastoral care and discipline: When asked what was good about the school, all the parents and pupils we spoke to – lots – said, as with one voice, 'the pastoral care' – we can't recall such unanimity on any other school feature anywhere. Tributes to the teaching staff, overall friendliness, care and attention given to individuals pour from everyone and are a delight to hear: 'My teacher is amazing – he's given me extra lessons every week. He's ordered in around 30 extra books just to help me. They'll help with anyone – not just the Oxbridge candidates'; 'The teacher gave my daughter as much time as she needed when she was struggling'; 'The staff commitment is excellent; pastoral care couldn't be better'; 'My children love it – they look forward to every day.'

Pupils and parents: From as far away as Potter's Bar, Winchmore Hill and Cheshunt, though most from between 10 and 20 minutes' drive away. Transport from local tube station to encourage pupils to look out of town towards green space for schooling. Vast

---

Complete with much-loved chaplain who is 'lovely, a wonderful person for a chat, and laugh and advice – he takes Salsa club.'

---

ethnic and social intake – 'very well-handled by school,' say parents: around 30-35 per cent South Asian, 10-15 per cent Jewish, 40 per cent white. Most parents first-time buyers who 'work very hard to pay fees'.

OB notables include Dennis Quilley, Sir Frederick Warner, Sir Neil McFarlane, Hari Kunzru, Adam Foulds, Yolanda Browne, Andrew Saul, Anita Anand, Lord Pannick QC, Samantha Spiro and Mike Lynch.

Entrance: At 11, 50 come up from the school's own prep. Around 400 apply for 60 additional places. Tests in maths and English plus interviews. In practice around a third of those whose first choice is Bancroft's will get in. Umpteen feeders, though several from St Aubyn's, Loyola and Woodford Green Prep. Around a quarter from state primaries.

Candidates for the sixth form sit the school's own entrance exam in two proposed AS subjects, need six As at GCSE plus the usual references. Around 20 places at this level – very few (around 10 per cent) leave.

Exit: Ten to Oxbridge in 2014. Other popular choices were Durham, UCL, Warwick, Nottingham, Birmingham and Queen Mary University of London. In 2014 11 per cent left after GCSEs.

Money matters: Fifteen Drapers' scholarships offered annually at 11+ worth a quarter to a half of fees. No means-testing – based solely on performance at entrance exams. Also music scholarships worth half or quarter fees plus free tuition in one instrument. Several Francis Bancroft scholarship awards – means-tested but with a generous financial threshold, worth up to full fees, based on a sliding scale dependent on family income. Bancroft's Foundation set up in 2012 to mark 275th anniversary has already raised significant amounts to increase means-tested provision – enough to fund six Foundation scholars.

Remarks: A splendid school, catering for bright children and those who will seize opportunities. Deservedly over-subscribed. Brings glory to Essex well beyond its immediate catchment.

The Coopers' Company and Coborn School

St Mary's Lane, Upminster, Essex RM14 3HS

State · Pupils: 1384 · Ages: 11–18 · Christian

Tel: 01708 250500
Fax: 01708 226109
Email: info@cooperscoborn.org.uk
Website: www.cooperscoborn.org.uk

Head: Since May 2013, Dr David Parry; had been deputy of the school since 2005, including a stint as acting headteacher. Was involved in setting up the school's link with Canterbury Christ Church University and also works with the University of London as a visiting research associate.

Academic matters: You 'can expect to do well', said Ofsted in its most recent response to pupils, and so they do. Learning takes place in a culture of success led by passionate and well-qualified teachers, who clearly benefit from the school's third and most recently awarded specialist status, as a teacher training school (the other two are sport and humanities). School has therefore consistently achieved near top GCSE results nationally and the proportion of pupils achieving the highest grades is significantly above the national average – 83 per cent of candidates gained five or more A*-C passes including English and maths in 2014, and 27 per cent of grades were A*/A. They are especially strong in English lang, English lit, mathematics and art and design, but pupils do exceptionally well in RS, DT, textiles technology and music.

At sixth form pupils are offered a wide curriculum of traditional subjects but are also introduced to new courses – media studies, psychology and politics. Popular choices are the sciences, esp biology, business studies, history, maths and psychology. In 2014, 62 per cent A* – B and nearly 31 per cent A*/A grades.

Curriculum options are as standard for most schools that follow the national curriculum with years 7 and 8 studying all 10 subjects but a second MFL introduced in year 8. Work on careers is introduced for year 9s. At GCSE pupils study mainly full course GCSEs but the school also allows them to choose one or two short GCSE courses. Popular choices are history, German, geography and sport/PE but fair numbers also choose Spanish and French.

Pupils are setted only for maths, at the end of year 7. From year 7 to sixth form, homework is considered an essential part of shaping pupils' academic experience, particularly in relation to independent learning and thinking skills. School says 'regular homework would be equivalent to an extra year of education with consequent benefits', so expects parents to support their children's completion of homework and to sign their homework diaries. Parents are informed of what is expected at the beginning of each school year.

Despite high results and a NACE award for its gifted and talented programme, the school is working on improving grades. Reason for this is that teacher assessment at KS3 shows that though most pupils start well (all achieve the nationally expected levels 5 and 6 in English, maths and science, with a fair number achieving level 7 and even 8 in mathematics, which is outstanding), Ofsted notes that even better progress at key stages 3 and 4 is possible. Having recognised this, the school introduced TRIPS – a Tracking, Reporting, Intervention and Planning System to monitor progress, and 'early indications' of change look successful. Parents receive regular TRIPS reports (at least every half term) showing an academic target grade, pupils' present attainment grade and an effort grade, enabling all three parties to monitor progress and make any necessary interventions to keep grades on track. Underachieving pupils receive support from either the SEN department, LSAs or learning mentors. Just six per cent currently receive some type of extra support and less than one per cent of these have been statemented.

Games, options, the arts: Games and PSHE remain compulsory throughout the school years, even at sixth form. PE is outstanding with pupils winning many national competitions: 'There have been many times when we were behind and looked unlikely to win, but we won', observed former head, capturing pupils' exceptional achievement, resilience and aptitude for sport and learning in general.

Pupils enjoy a rich curriculum ranging from circuit gym training to trampolining, cricket and netball to indoor rowing. Coopers Cats has received natural recognition as an outstanding star programme for athletes, so lots of opportunity to be

---

Coopers Cats has received natural recognition as an outstanding star programme for athletes, so lots of opportunity to be stretched

---

stretched. Sports and athletics have been so successful at the school that several teams often represent the school at national and international events and pupils took part in the opening ceremony for the 2012 Olympics.

Well-equipped art studios, arranged as individual cubicles where pupils have their own designated area in which to work. Its 'open house' policy approach encourages independent work and, along with the clearly outstanding levels of work on display, creates a wonderful 'art school' atmosphere. Pupils consistently have work displayed in exhibitions around the country.

Music and drama are also both strong here. Pupils take part in several national ensembles and theatrical events. Connection to the Worshipful Company of Coopers means there are various concerts and events throughout the year. Around 250 pupils have instrumental lessons in school and at least another 50 have lessons outside school. Standard is high, up to grade 8, and students with exceptional achievement attend the Guildhall and Trinity Saturday College.

Huge range of extracurricular choice. Pupils are expected to get involved in music, drama and sport as well as the academic curriculum since school feels this has a great impact on the sense of culture and engagement. 'There is something for everyone,' said a year 11 pupil. Before and after and school lunch time clubs cover almost every conceivable area, from chess to fishing (under music alone there are 28 weekly activities including four wind bands, two orchestras, four jazz bands, a swing and brass band, five choirs and numerous rock bands). Several clubs have been instigated and are run by pupils.

Overseas trips are important. Language trips (year 8) and exchange trips (year 10) support Spanish, German and French but there are many others eg a rugby trip to New Zealand and a tennis trip to Florida, plus other trips to explore interesting places such as Namibia and Botswana. Year 12 and 13 pupils visited Madagascar to build a secondary school block. The school is developing links with China. Pupils praised the language exchange programme: 'They match you really well so you have lots in common and are able to make real friends, which is a good motivation for wanting to actually have a conversation'.

Background and atmosphere: A rich history dating to 1536 when it was first established as a free school for boys. Its name came in 1552 when the Coopers' Company was asked to take over the running of the school. It was then located in Stepney, Tower Hamlets. In 1891, it joined foundations with the Coborn school for boys and girls and remained at sites at Mile End and Bow until it moved to Upminster in 1971.

At its present location, situated a good distance from the main road amid 25 acres of greenery, and home to a pond visited by ducks and geese, the school very much resembles an independent school. However, because 'the school's been here since 1971 ... it needs improvement,' and modernisation and development have seen new buildings regularly erected since the 80s, the latest being a sixth form block. Other smaller but notable modern developments include a solar panel roof, i-desks (computers that pop up out of the desk) and a laser cutter, with which pupils confessed: 'we have gone to town'. The outcome of their efforts is the various metal placards signposting the DT, textile technology and design and art departments. 'The best way to protect the future is to design it,' says the laser-cut sign on the front of the main DT building, as if to help create an atmosphere of vitality and aspiration for future success.

Pastoral care and discipline: Organised by heads of year. Years 7 -11 form tutors are responsible for about 30 pupils, who remain in the same form group throughout the five years. Sixth form tutors look after about 20 students each. School tries to create a good mix with external entrants to the sixth form easily assimilated. Two forms allocated to each of three houses, a system which helps create vertical links as well as the horizontal year groupings. The school also selects school captains from year 12 pupils, who must apply for the position. These are prestigious positions and the selection process includes interviews by the head. The one boy and one girl selected hold office throughout their final year. Whole school council plays a key role in the decision-making processes – including the appointment of senior staff. Pupils are given a sense of importance and are consulted on important developments, 'because it won't work if the students don't like it'.

Peer to peer mentoring, and around 150 sixth formers work with younger pupils. Very high expectations of conduct. Parents and students report an effective response to the few incidents of bullying and racism; they are dealt with quickly by form tutors and heads of years. The school's approach to remedying problems is to get those concerned to accept responsibility and consequences for their actions. Bad behaviour is just simply 'uncool'. Instead pupils exhibit very positive attitudes to learning and life. 'We do try to look after each other, standards are high, it's tough love and there is a genuine sense of commitment.'

Pupils and parents: Mainly white middle class and clearly aspirational. A 'Christian school with an eclectic mix from all recognised world religions'. Pupils seem proud of their school and very contented. In a day when many young people seem to take what they have for granted, it was refreshing to meet a group of pupils who seemed extremely appreciative. They clearly thrive on their many opportunities for responsibility – 'you have these free periods and you soon learn that you need to

work independently, so you use it to complete essays and extra research'.

Everyone is welcoming – greeting visitors with smiles and hellos, saying thank you, holding doors open and even singing to themselves as they pass by. Many parents are supportive of the school and help out at school events. Active PTA of about 30 members, very good for a secondary state school. They arrange various fundraising events including a monthly sale of supermarket vouchers to parents and staff which enables school to raise over £10,000 per year to buy eg a minibus.

Entrance: Unusually large number of feeder schools (around 100); admissions rules complicated due to the school's historic links to east London and wish to preserve the principles of the Coopers' Company and Coborn Educational Foundation.

No doubt this helps intensify competition for places – over 800 applications for just 180 places and a fair number go to appeal. Ten sport and nine music places. All other applicants must be actively connected to one of the main world faiths. Some places for children of staff and former students; others by promixity; others to those who live in specific areas including Havering, Brentwood and Billericay.

Most stay on to the sixth form after GCSE. Around 50 places for students from outside but, again, massively popular with over 300 applications. Applicants need at least eight A*-C grades to be considered for a place, to be sympathetic to the school's Christian character and be willing to uphold its 'Love as Brethren' ethos by giving time to serve the school. Oversubscription criteria prioritise looked after children, highest predicted grades and then availability in specific sets.

Exit: Around a fifth leave after GCSE. Around three-quarters of sixth formers to university (three Oxbridge offers in 2014). School provides a range of opportunities to prepare for post school eg science pupils attend conferences, workshops, competitions and special events at Nottingham and Cambridge. Many go on to study pure science subjects and vocational courses such as medicine, veterinary science and dentistry. Other popular subjects include psychology, economics, architecture, art history, journalism, politics and theatre design.

Money matters: The school allocates £10k to assist pupils that need help and also provides music and sports grants of up to £500.

Remarks: An impressive and dynamic school that prepares pupils for success. Dazzling reputation in the local community and the word on the street blames it for increased house prices in the Upminster area. World class in true sense of the word.

Forest Preparatory School

Linked school: Forest School, 586

College Place, London E17 3PY

Independent · Pupils: 270 · Ages: 4–11 · C of E · Fees (per term): Prep £3,400 – £3,943

Tel: 020 8520 1744
Fax: 020 8520 3656
Email: prep@forest.org.uk
Website: www.forest.org.uk

Head: Since 2012, Mr Andrew Noakes MA Education, Open University (late 30s). Previously head of Northampton Junior School. Studied at Reed's, Surrey, then De Montfort, where he read European studies and French. Entered teaching later after working in education for a few years. He trained at St George's College before landing his first teaching job at Parkside and Bedford Modern Junior School. Described as 'calm and unflappable', he is married to a teacher and has two daughters.

Entrance: Main entries at 4 and 7 via play-based or literacy/numeracy assessments. Most pupils come from the local area and there is a good mix of ethnic backgrounds.

Exit: Prep pupils are automatically offered a place at either the boys' or girls' sections of Forest School and majority take up the offer.

Remarks: Tucked away from the main roads, surrounded by the ancient Epping Forest, and accessible by what resembles a narrow dirt track lane, the school stands as a closely hidden secret in its inner city surroundings. However, once we had cleared the highly secure, gated reception area to enter the school grounds, the bustle of life at the school immediately greeted us. We heard string and brass instruments sounding out from one of the many lunchtime concerts at the chapel, and saw brightly clad prep pupils at play or through their open classroom windows, merrily chanting foreign words in rote-like fashion. Pupils seem to be busy, happy and oblivious. They are taught in buildings alive with a heritage dating back to the school's foundation in 1834. Even with its Georgian buildings, this school has a distinctively bright, spacious and airy feel. Expect to see lively but small groups of pupils actively involved in learning, lots of writing and artwork displays in and outside of the classrooms, and tiny, well-behaved pupils following behind their teacher in duckling-like fashion from one part of the school to another.

In the pre-prep (4 to 7), children are taught in co-ed classes and follow the EYFS; in the prep they begin to experience single-sex teaching preparation for their later move to the boys' and girls' senior schools. Class sizes 16 in the pre-prep and 22 in the prep school. Teaching based on national curriculum with specialists brought in for art, PE, drama, foreign languages and, in particular, music.

All of the children have the opportunity to learn an instrument here for at least a year. The prep school music department is led by a teacher prized for her ability to spot the 'differences between concert and worship' voices, as well as knowing how hard to push the youngest of performers to discover their best. Each May, the school organises Composition Week, where year 5 pupils are transformed into a team of songwriters, singers and composers to produce, most recently for example, a signature melody inspirited by the retelling of Arachne. The experience is 'demanding but rewarding' for the pupils, and this spirit is one of the prized characteristics of the school: even the youngest of pupils is stretched and pushed to learn.

There is plenty else to do aside from music-making – pupils are also actively involved in dance, drama and sports. The prep school sits between the main school buildings and senior pupils behave like older siblings to the younger ones. The prep children use senior school facilities, including the sports fields, theatre and a modern leisure centre with swimming pool and gymnasium.

Many trips organised – to 'help us to learn', say the children – some local to eg Strawberry Hill Ponds and the Suntrap Centre, others further afield eg Paradise Park, the Europa Centre and the Royal Observatory in Greenwich, others even as far as Berlin.

None of the pupils here have a statement of special educational need but about 16 receive some kind of learning support. They all speak English as their main language, so no EAL needs here either; the ISI describes them as highly articulate and well above average ability. Many win academic, sport or music scholarships, to Forest senior school and elsewhere, but only a few move away.

The chapel and chaplaincy are central to learning here. The chapel is where pupils begin and end each term with events such as breakfasts for parents followed by a welcome service. Last year all of the new pupils brought in a cardboard brick to build a 'prayer wall' showing their aspirations for the term. These included learning to read, wishing to play football for the school, becoming a monitor, making lots of friends and, simply, 'I want to make my teacher and parents proud.'

Prep pupils make respectable contributions to a very lively school diary of events, such as the pre-prep nativity play, a dramatised festival service and an idiom recital day to mark the 400-year anniversary of the King James version of the Bible. They also have house competitions in eg acting, singing and rounders, and charity fundraising events. They compete in the UK chess championships and have hosted a prep-level junior science competition involving over 20 schools. They won a school prize in a wildlife foundation global art competition, with 10 year 4 and 5 pupils selected among entrants from around the world, including Hong Kong, Nigeria and Arabia. Cricket is popular but football is 'something special', and there are several teams and matches played in and outside of the borough.

Parents describe it as a school where 'teaching is good but not too pushy', teachers 'know your child well' and 'there is a very active PTA'. In fact, the majority of the parents involved in the parents' association are from the prep school. They are kept up to speed via a newsletter and the school website.

Forest School

Linked school: Forest Preparatory School, 585

College Place, Snaresbrook, London E17 3PY

Independent • Pupils: 770 • Ages: 11–18 • C of E • Fees (per term): £5,238

Tel: 020 8520 1744
Fax: 020 8520 3656
Email: info@forest.org.uk
Website: www.forest.org.uk

12

Warden: Since 2009, Mrs Sarah Kerr-Dineen MA. Read English at Cambridge followed by postgraduate study at Oxford and NPQH. Taught at Open University, Kelly College, Oxford High School (where she was an acting subject head) and St Edward's Oxford (where she was housemistress and responsible for the pastoral care of 80 girls, then director of studies). Senior leadership team of about eight. Sees herself as 'a teacher, not a CEO', and despite the school's size, treats her job as if she was 'running a small school and knowing every pupil', believing that the 'way to keep a school from becoming impersonal is to keep units of care small'. Nevertheless, as warden she is strategic in approach to building this 'happy school': you 'set a vision but then look at how to express that at every stage – there's no point saying you have a vision to be one thing and then not doing anything to live up to it'. She still teaches, including all the year 7s, has

---

It is close to the bustling City of London and yet surrounded by the quietness of ancient forest

pupils to lunch weekly and the youngest pupils are invited to come to the house where 'they learn to appreciate the significance of the school's history.' Parents say, 'It's a very well run school' and describe its leadership as 'first rate'.

Moving on in July 2015 to head Oundle School. Her successor will be Mr Antony Faccinello (late 40s), currently senior deputy head of Alleyn's School. English degree from Oxford and PGCE. Has also taught at Cheltenham College, Haberdashers' Aske's Boys' School in Elstree and RGS Guildford. Loyal supporter of Manchester City football club.

Academic matters: 'Both of my daughters are scholars,' said one very pleased parent. Single-sex teaching in this co-educational environment 'creates a study environment that boys and girls feel comfortable with and which enables them

to achieve their best', says school. Teachers are committed, about a third of them have been here more than 10 years and all of them are specialists in their subjects; also large number part time eg music, drama and dance specialists. Most pupils are of above average ability. They do well across the board, notably in English, history, geography, maths and the sciences. From year 8, some setting occurs for maths, English, MFLs and science. There is a free choice from French, German and Spanish. Latin is taught to all pupils during the first two years, then it becomes a GCSE option along with ancient Greek.

In 2014, 73 per cent A*/A at GCSE and 51 per cent at A level. Extended projects, which allow GCSE and A level students to flex their academic muscles beyond the norm, are popular. With topics and titles such as 'A legal definition of torture' and 'Love and the Adversary' (a treatise on the representation of Satan in English literature), pupils demonstrate their capacity for critical thought.

Courses in both the boys' and girls' schools run broadly in line with the national curriculum. This leads some parents to make the same complaint heard of state schools, that lessons can have 'too much focus on teaching for success in the sometimes dull GCSE syllabus rather than to wider lateral thought.. but I think this is what happens everywhere'. Hence, by and large, parents also prize the school for its 'good academic expectations but not [being] too pushy'. As one parent echoed, 'I don't consider that [my daughters] are always adequately stretched, but the humanities and arts subjects appear to be particularly well taught',

adding that they had turned down places at more academic schools in favour of Forest's 'more balanced experience'. '

The number of academic challenges, competitions, tournaments and Olympiads these pupils enter is dizzying: maths challenges, chemistry masterminds, physics Olympiads, and even the informatics Olympiad – where pupils have competed in Thailand against the best young computer scientists in the world.

Trips to eg the Battlefields, Munich (history), Devon (geography), China, Russia, Japan and the USA.

Majority of pupils stay on at sixth form where courses include classical civilisation, government and politics (with visits to key places in London, Washington DC and New York, and supported by guest speakers such as Iain Duncan Smith, John Bercow, George Galloway and Nigel Farage), philosophy (a popular university choice) and economics. The A level economics department has links with the City of London, the Economics Association and Institute of Economic Affairs.

Extra support for those who need it; school publishes an excellent guide to independent study to help struggling pupils find their own answers or at the very least to formulate thoughtful and clear questions before asking for help.

Games, options, the arts: You will find them all here: aerobics, basketball, cricket, even fencing. Extensive playing fields, netball and tennis courts, various pitches, a sports centre housing two heated swimming pools, cricket nets and a fitness suite. At sixth form, PE covers sports psychology, history and exercise physiology. Pupils can try out other sports eg karate, cross-country and golf during activities afternoons and house matches. Several record achievements gained at county, regional and national level in netball, rounders, hockey, tennis, badminton and athletics.

A large (one of the largest in London) and busy music department with over 700 instrumental and vocal lessons a week. Every pupil has the opportunity to try out an instrument free of charge and pupils are encouraged to take the lead in musical activities, often leading to specialisms. With seven orchestras, 10 bands, 14 choirs and more than 40 specialist teachers, numerous opportunities to perform. School is extensively equipped with practice, recital and technology rooms. On the day of our visit one of the bands was preparing for a lunch time concert in the chapel, the norm at this school that presents more than 80 concerts and other performances a year both in and out of the school. Tours take place in the UK, Spain, Italy, Netherlands and France and the school regularly sends pupils to major conservatoires. Regular choral and organ scholarships to Oxford and Cambridge.

Drama and art also taken seriously. The purpose-built Deaton Theatre seats 350 and has state-of-the-art lighting and sound equipment. Pupils act in large-scale productions and learn design or technical skills. As part of the house drama competition, they can select, cast and direct their own productions. A long tradition of excellence in drama with present and past pupils making successful careers in this area (the West End show Stomp was founded by former pupils) and pupils have been involved in many well known television and theatre productions, including East Enders and The Bleak Old Shop of Stuff for the BBC, and a West End production of Oliver! Art and design studios are well-resourced and pupils allowed to develop their passion outside classroom learning hours.

Co-curricular opportunities in sport, music, drama, dance and visual arts. CCF linked to the Royal Green Jackets offers field days, annual camps and weekly training. The Duke of Edinburgh Award is popular. Other opportunities include student-led societies, video production, languages, musical theatre, and journalism. Pupils also take part in raising money for charity, in public speaking competitions, and community work such as visiting the elderly and riding for the disabled.

Background and atmosphere: Old and new exist side by side here. It is close to the bustling City of London and yet surrounded by the quietness of ancient forest. The St John the Baptist chapel, where pupils regularly congregate for services and other events, is at the heart of the school and reminiscent of a history that goes back to 1834 when it began with just 22 pupils. Although Anglican in tradition, the outlook is ecumenical to cater to the broad range of backgrounds, faiths and cultures. Pupils enjoy this and say 'It is good to have the school come together and talk about different faiths.' Alongside the old, are new buildings like the Sylvestrian Leisure Centre – built with the aid of a 'buy a brick' fundraiser organised by the parents' association, used by the public at weekends and as a quiet camp for Team GB during the 2012 London Olympics – and the Martin Centre for Innovation, with digital teaching and learning facilities for the whole school.

Pastoral care and discipline: Form and house groups, headed by a housemistress or master, provide a sense of belonging and stability. Because classes are small, community atmosphere is strong; 'pupils are well known individually by the staff,' say parents. Pastoral care gives each child 'the support they need to progress socially, morally and academically'. Housemasters and mistresses stay with a child through his or her time at the school and are there to advise on any aspect of school life. This continues at sixth form. Pupils are allocated a tutor who oversees academic progress, helps with university applications, and advises on careers.

There is heavy emphasis on the code of conduct in the school prospectus: 'all observed behaviour, which indicates a lack of mutual regard, will be fully investigated', 'the school stands firmly against any form of verbal or physical bullying or any behaviour which is intended to cause distress to pupils', and the 'Warden may require the permanent exclusion of a pupil if, in her opinion, it is in the interest of the pupil of the school community'. Approach is good lines of communication. 'Children are encouraged to talk and are listened to' and to report incidents of bullying to an appropriate person, says school. 'Where bullying is detected, we acknowledge our responsibility to support both the bully and the victim'.

Parents say, 'Bullying – the school deals with this very well'. Others say 'We hear mixed things about how long it takes the school to home in and deal with these issues; but no direct experience'. Most say their children learn 'in a secure, supportive and encouraging environment'. 'The children know they are lucky but they don't see themselves as special', warden says. 'If children are not happy

they won't learn, get that right and the grades will come.'

The best thing about being at the school, said a pupil, is the 'diversity, I like the mix, staff are kind, they encourage you to do the best you can do.'

Pupils and parents: A diverse ethnic mix. They come from the surrounding east and north London and Essex areas. Most are the children of professional parents and no-one speaks English as a second language. Past pupils include actor Ian Beale and cricketer Nasser Hussain.

Entrance: Most from the prep move to the senior school at 11, joined by a large number from other state and private schools (English and maths tests). Variable numbers admitted at 13+ depending on spaces.

Exit: Virtually all to university, more than half to Russell Group universities in 2014. Most popular courses are sciences, engineering and medicine.

Money matters: Bursaries and scholarships – academic and music awards at 11+, academic, music and sports at 13, academic, art, music, drama and sports at 16.

Remarks: A happy school with committed staff, and pupils who clearly display a strong sense of independence and enjoyment of school life. While remaining true to its traditional roots, this is a forward-thinking school, humane and open-minded, with both feet on the ground. Its clear grasp of the rich inter-relationship between the curricular, the co-curricular and the pastoral ensures children do well.

Ilford County High School

Fremantle Road, Ilford, Essex IG6 2JB

State · Pupils: 955 · Ages: 11–18 · Non–denom

Tel: 020 8551 6496
Fax: 020 8503 9960
Email: enquiries@ichs.org.uk
Website: www.ichs.org.uk

5

Acting head: Mrs Rebecca Drysdale, previously deputy head, is taking the reins until September 2015 whilst a new head is appointed.

Academic matters: In 2014, 60 per cent A*/A grades at GCSE, with strongest results shown in the sciences and mathematics. French in year 7 and in year 8 pupils take up either German or Spanish as well. Everyone takes one language at GCSE, though few take two or continue languages to A level, despite European trips and work experience opportunities. The school is developing partnerships with schools and colleges in Germany, Spain, Switzerland and Denmark and has British Council International School status. It has historic links with Southern Africa and is seeking to develop links with India and China and explore alternative learning styles.

School has introduced enquiry-based learning to develop critical thinking skills.

At A level popular subjects are biology, chemistry, economics, mathematics and physics; most stick to academic rather than creative subjects. In 2014, 72 per cent A*/B and 45 per cent A*A grades. Subject-based reviews help to monitor each subject and data tracking to monitor pupil progress helps spot and tackle underperformance; not that there is much of that here, according to parents. The school was rated outstanding by Ofsted at the last full inspection. Maximum class sizes, at 30 (and 22 in the sixth form), are at the higher end. Some 560 pupils with EAL requirements plus 30 or so who need SEN support.

Games, options, the arts: Sporting trophies for cricket and swimming, and a Sportsman of the Year award, all point to an environment where sport is taken seriously and given plenty of room for expression. Pupils enjoy taking part in swimming galas and pointed out to us the 'basketball court where we play football'. They explained, 'There is space for both but the football is the most popular though cricket is what we are best at, we tend to do well at cricket.' At the entrance to the sports hall is a notice board invitation to follow the PE department on Twitter to keep up with fixtures, lessons, inter-house competitions and results. There is plenty to report on, given the substantial provision, from ultimate frisbie to indoor rowing and rugby.

The building is traditional, with beautiful oak stairwells, large wooden boards with lists of past notables – headteachers, year captains and the like – and display cabinets

On-site facilities include an artificial cricket strip, two football pitches and a 400m running track. The sports hall itself houses a heated swimming pool. There are also four badminton courts, a full size basketball court, with two small courts and provision for volleyball, five-a-side football, and tennis. Upstairs there is a fitness/weights room, an aerobics area and a viewing gallery and a 'theory room for people taking GCSE or A level' – currently about 31 at GCSE and three at A level. A few boys take PE GCSE and A level.

Drama is compulsory for year 7s as part of the English curriculum, and they all take part in an annual production, but after that it disappears from the curriculum.

Those few students who do choose art produce rich, bold and inspiring work, much of it on display in corridors throughout the school. It includes drawings, paintings, photography and sculpting. Curriculum is enriched by visits to national museums and art galleries.

Provision for music is as rich as sport, though it is not so popular as an option. Around 62 pupils have timetabled music lessons and some exceptional talent can be found here. Some lessons take place at the Redbridge Music School and specialist music teachers visit to teach. Pupils have plenty of opportunity to develop their gifts on piano, violin, cello, double bass, saxophone, drum, voice and more through orchestra, jazz ensemble, choirs and various bands. There are concerts and performances

in London and abroad. Few pupils take art or music A level.

Extracurricular provision across the school is rich, with clubs, groups and ensembles covering every interest. There are debating societies, rugby, sailing and indoor rowing clubs and, for those wishing to stick to the academic, clubs to deepen awareness of astronomy, philosophy or physics.

Background and atmosphere: The school was founded in 1901 as Park High Grade School. It was a boys' and girls' school back then and located in Balfour Road. The boys' school split in 1929 and moved to its present location in Freemantle Road in 1935. This is a built-up residential area but the school has a secluded feel. The building is traditional, with beautiful oak stairwells, large wooden boards with lists of past notables – headteachers, year captains and the like – and display cabinets. The cabinets line either side as you enter the reception area and show off a big collection of plaques and trophies, a reminder of the sort of school this is. They include awards for the Bank of England and Times Interest Rate Challenge, an Acknowledgement of Educational Excellence in Academic A Levels from Edexcel, an award from

Help the Aged for helping to unite generations, and, most impressive of all, an award for best A level results achieved by boys taking critical thinking at an English grammar school, from the Good Schools Guide.

The school layout resembles two adjacent squares, with two stories of classrooms organised around these in circular fashion. This makes it very easy for new pupils to learn their way round as where you start is usually where you will finish. Near the front is 'the hall where assemblies happen – we have them in the afternoon,' a pupil explains, 'and variety nights where students and teachers perform'.

The atmosphere is bustling and lively, especially in the music department where boys frequently practice and experiment. A new learning resource centre and library was opened by the author Chris Ryan and has remained true to the celebration of literature with regular live and video conference talks by visiting authors. Other talks also take place there, including, for example, one for students interested in medicine, organised by York University. The school is planning further expansion, including an enlarged sixth form, which will increase funding. Building work will provide more independent study space for the sixth form.

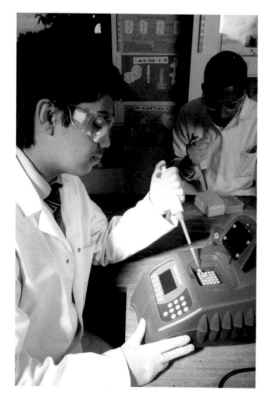

This makes it very easy for new pupils to learn their way round as where you start is usually where you will finish

Pastoral care and discipline: Parents comment on being drawn to the school by its 'ethos of competitiveness and success... it nurtures the boys and prepares them for the future'. Sometimes it is just the small things, like planners 'to ensure their homework is completed on time and all timescales are met' and the even distribution of that homework across the week. A parent said this allows his son time to complete and hand in work. This helps because 'He has music and drama lessons outside school in the evening and on weekends, which he enjoys. He also does sports two days a week.'

Noticeboards for each house, year and department keep pupils updated... 'notices on helping out, tours, linguist of the month..' Department specific news is also tweeted and there is a Facebook page for prefects.

Pastoral care arrangements at the school have moved from a horizontal year-based one to a vertical house system. There is a head of house and a team of five form tutors who work with and support pupils as they progress through the school. Form tutors are generally responsible for pupil welfare and progress. The new system provides greater opportunity for the boys to develop stronger skills in leadership, mentorship and responsibility, plus opportunities to develop relationships across year groups, right to sixth form. Pupils report that keenly-contested form sports competitions have been replaced by equally high-spirited house competitions.

Year 7s receive peer mentoring from older pupils in year 9, 10 and sixth form. 'They're a bit of a role model for the younger kids, someone to look up to...' and 'if you have any problems settling in you [can] go to see them.' For one pupil, who joined at sixth form, this was 'one of the things I liked when I came, people always willing to help'. He told us that bullying, or rather the lack of it, was another nice surprise for him, as at his previous school 'fights were a common occurrence. It was a radical change for me; since I've been here I haven't seen one'. 'The school has a strict anti-bullying policy,' said another sixth form pupil who has been at the school since year 7. 'I haven't really come across many cases of bullying in the school. I think most boys are fairly clued up on that it's wrong.'

It is this reputation for strict discipline that was given by several parents as one of the school's strong points. They said, 'The boys are well behaved', the school has 'a good approach to bullying' and 'I do not hear of any violent incidences at the school.' Evidently there is the occasional event, but 'in that one experience the head of house got in touch quickly to explain the situation; it was quickly settled. Thankfully my son has not had any further incidents and we hope it remains that way.'

Pupils and parents: Overall, pupils come across as happy and well-adjusted. They come from a wide mix of ethnic backgrounds, and from the borough of Redbridge and surrounding areas like Waltham Forest, Newham, Barking and Dagenham. They range from bubbly, stumbling and oblivious year 7s making their way between lessons, to the year 11s who showed us around and were articulate, mature and friendly. One told us about the cooking lessons the school organises for sixth formers to help them prepare for university. He said: 'I think I am fairly confident for a boy of my age.' He then added, with honesty, 'I can't fault it and I have achieved as good a grade as I can. I didn't motivate myself as well as I could have before but now I've put my foot down.'

The majority of parents believe their children are being well taught and that all round provision at the school is good, although one mentioned that it would be nice to see pupils involved in more volunteer work and fundraising and more 'events such as leadership conferences, etc' to stimulate boys' minds. There is an enormous sense of relief

---

One told us about the cooking lessons the school organises for sixth formers to help them prepare for university

---

at having got a place at the school, which is unsurprising given that it is the only boys' grammar in the borough. One parent said that the school 'has lived up to our expectations'. They appreciate the 'emphasis on all-round development and not just academics'.

There is a parents association that helps to raise money for resources at the school but, like many high schools, it dreams of getting more involved. 'The general trend here is that parents do not get involved,' said an active parent, 'they are of the feeling that once their child is in the school that is all they need to do. The school is not greatly funded and some parental support could help pay for things that are needed. It's not only about the

fundraising but the community spirit, which I am afraid is very lacking.' School understands that 'parents have busy lives' but says 'in some cases parent don't get involved enough, we still have parents you never see other than at parents' evening'.

School is more anxious about boys whose parents 'have unrealistic aspirations for them'. The main message to parents is that it is about the education, not just the grades, 'about the breadth of roundness'. It is not just pupils that need to learn to think outside of the box, parents do too. 'If a boy's real interest and passion is for humanities and not science, fine, as that it is where they will get real satisfaction and achievement.' School tries to instil into both parents and pupils that, 'If you want to do engineering at university you can't just concentrate on maths and physics, your GCSE profile needs to be high quality across all 10 subjects, you can't afford to have A*, A*, A*,.., A, C. It is the quickest route to an admissions tutor's waste paper basket.' Most parents get this and some have little sympathy for those that do not. One said, 'there are always a few parents who do not take this on board, despite the school's best efforts, and end up disappointed when their sons fail to get into their chosen university.'

Notable former pupils include Raymond Baxter, TV personality (Tomorrow's World), Sir Trevor Brooking, footballer, and David Miller, Deputy Chief Inspector of Air Accidents.

Entrance: More than 850 boys in the borough of Redbridge and nearby compete for the 120 places available each year by sitting the 11+ examination. The test is administered by the borough. School manages its own admission to the sixth form, with places offered dependent on predicted GCSE grades.

Exit: Almost all (some 85 per cent) stay on to sixth form. Leavers go on to study subjects such economics, architecture, dentistry, medicine, law, physics and engineering. Majority choose to study in London at eg King's College and UCL. Eight to Oxbridge in 2014.

Remarks: A school that delivers a high standard of education and produces young men who seem well prepared for the wider world. Somehow seems to be a victim of its own success, constantly having to grapple with the challenge of how to progress and maintain its impressive record and position among high performing secondary schools.

Robert Clack School

Gosfield Road, Dagenham, Essex RM8 1JU

State · Pupils: 1,965 · Ages: 11–18 · Non-denom

Tel: 020 8270 4200
Fax: 020 8270 4210
Email: office@robert-clack.bardaglea.org.uk
Website: www.robertclack.co.uk

Headteacher: Since 1997, Sir Paul Grant MA PGCE (60s), famously promoted from head of humanities when the school was at its lowest ebb and has since transformed it into an outstanding success story. He is the eldest of seven children from a working-class Liverpudlian family. A keen football fan, he once hoped to turn professional. He went to the Salesian Grammar School in Bootle, where an influential teacher inspired him to study history at Hull University. He completed a PGCE at Durham and an MA at London University, and taught in north Yorkshire, Australia and Newham before joining Robert Clack in 1990.

At this point the school was sliding downhill. Weak leadership meant a lack of support for those teachers who did try to keep order and behaviour was deteriorating rapidly. There was a serious gang culture, children smoked in the corridors and caused chaos in the community at lunchtime. Pupils rode bicycles inside and it was commonplace to set off fireworks indoors. In 1996, only 17 per cent of pupils gained five or more A–C grades at GCSE and the school was on the verge of special measures. The humanities department, however, was going from strength to strength. Sir Paul was

appointed headteacher with an emergency plan of action which included a tough, transparent code for bad behaviour and a new system of rewards. He suspended 300 troublemakers in his first week.

'He led by example,' says a deputy, who had then just left the school as a pupil. 'I saw him stopping a bus outside the school and talking to passengers about how the school was going to change and inviting them to phone the school if they had any problems with Robert Clack pupils.' Most teachers were delighted by the new regime but some parents were outraged. Sir Paul insisted on meeting every one and gradually won them round. Changing behaviour was a gradual process which included driving around picking up truants and talking to local shopkeepers, local councillors, council employees such as housing officers, and police.

Sir Paul was knighted for services to education, a few weeks after the school received an Evening Standard award for excellence in challenging circumstances. Larger than life in build and character and described by Ofsted as 'tireless', he is married with three daughters. The school has been his life's work, he says. 'I wanted to prove that the children in this school could be excellent and my colleagues could be excellent. I'm incredibly proud of the children, parents and staff.'

Pupils are proud too. 'He always works hard to make us succeed in life.' 'He's strict but fair. You know not to get on his wrong side but he always congratulates you when you do well.'

Academic matters: The school is one of 12 outstanding secondary schools fêted by Ofsted for excelling against the odds. Some 40 per cent of pupils are on the special needs register and 40 per cent have free school meals, but results have improved steadily from the 1996 nadir: in 2014, 65 per cent of pupils got five or more good GCSEs including maths and English. At A level, nearly 80 per cent A*/C and 20 per cent A*/A grades.

Alongside a strict disciplinary procedure, high quality teaching from a mostly young staff has helped the school achieve outstanding status. The 'Robert Clack good lesson' is a template devised by staff which involves explaining to pupils the objective, content and process of each lesson. We met one teacher who was off to Suffolk, appointed to help a school there achieve 'outstanding' status by using his experience at Robert Clack.

The school is a specialist science, maths and computing college and has recently added a modern languages specialism – a bold move in a strongly working-class school. Although everyone takes French and Spanish for the first three years, at present only 15–20 per cent continue to GCSE. However, the department plans to increase this considerably over the next few years and hopes to introduce Spanish A level alongside the new French course. Everyone takes double science, with some opting for the vocational applied science option and 100 or so taking three separate sciences. Other vocational options include health and social care, business studies, catering, beauty and ICT.

'We have got where we are because all the children feel there is a pathway for them. They're not finding themselves stranded in set 11 for everything.' The school sets right from the start for English, maths, science and languages. 'We're auditing progress all the time and a significant number have worked their way right up through the sets'. Other subjects, such as history, geography and RE, are taught in mixed ability groups from year 10 onwards. The ability range is massive, from those aiming at A*s to those who joined the school with a reading age of 5 or 6. 'Teaching a huge range is possible if the behaviour is excellent and class sizes are small, so we make sure that they are'.

Learning support and mentor rooms where children can come to catch up on literacy and numeracy, perhaps because they have had time off sick or are middle of the road and tend to be

This is one of the smartest and most ordered schools we have ever visited. Children are immaculate in blazers and ties, orderly in corridors and attentive in lessons

overlooked in class. Or they may come here because they are upset because of family problems and can't cope amongst their peers – 'if children are in the wrong place they will disrupt the lesson. We want to be proactive and avoid problems if possible'. But the 40 per cent on the SEN register – including partially sighted and deaf children – are mostly integrated into the classrooms. We saw a boy with cerebral palsy putting his views across forcefully to the class, despite speech problems. 'The children are very protective of each other'.

The sixth form is part of the North East Consortium with three other local schools, offering more than 40 courses at different levels. Over 800 sixth formers in the consortium, including some 450 at Robert Clack. No minimum entry requirements, as courses range from a certificate in motor vehicle servicing to further maths, though students

who want to take A levels must have at least five grades Cs at GCSE – 'many of these students are the first in their families to stay on at school after 16. We don't want to set the benchmark too high, despite the risk of being marked down by Ofsted, because we want to give these children a chance'. Media studies and general studies are the most popular A level courses; maths, further maths, physics and chemistry the most successful. BTecs in business, IT and sport are popular too, as is beauty therapy, taught in a state-of-the-art on-site beauty salon – 'we give everyone the opportunity to be successful here'.

Games, options, the arts: Sport is hugely important here and the school is frequently borough champion at athletics, swimming, rugby and cross-country. It has also been county champion at rugby and netball, a huge achievement against the Essex selective schools. A rugby academy attracts talented players to the sixth form. Pupils have competed nationally at sports ranging from netball to skiing and their team shirts are displayed proudly alongside photos and trophies. 'If you're good at something we'll encourage you and give you recognition,' said a deputy. 'Paul is very good at reinforcing our successes and using them to motivate pupils.'

A plush leisure centre includes a sports hall and fitness suite, open to the local community outside school hours. There are also tennis and netball courts and a large playing field which includes an all-weather pitch. Numerous sports clubs before, during and after school, and even on Saturday mornings, range from hockey to dance to girls' boxing.

The girls' and boys' choirs performed movingly in assembly during our visit – the boys' choir was recently voted best in the borough and one pupil has starred in a West End musical. Instrumental lessons are free, and there's an orchestra and a jazz group. Sixty pupils are studying for music GCSE and a few each year move on to music technology A level. The school puts on major performances of eg Oliver! and High School Musical. Plenty of high-quality art displayed around the school and DT is another popular option at GCSE. The school debating team recently won 'best delegation' at a Model UN conference.

School trips range from French exchanges to sports trips to Canada and Barbados and a conservation expedition to Egypt. Few parents could afford to pay for these trips, so the school raises funds from eg the Worshipful Company of Chartered Surveyors, and children fundraise enthusiastically too. 'We believe these trips are vitally important to our children's development, and our wonderful staff will always go the extra mile to make sure they happen.'

Background and atmosphere: This is a huge, split-site school, named after local legend Bob Clack, who was mayor from 1940 to 1942. The lower school site, which houses years 7 and 8 and most of year 9, opened in 1935, the upper school buildings, half a mile away, in 1953. The tower blocks of the Becontree Estate – one of the largest in England – bear down on the school like a fortress. It is one of the most deprived areas of the country and has been a BNP stronghold. Staff and pupils alike express delight that the BNP was routed in the last election and credit the school with considerable influence. 'The school is the centre of the community.' 'You can't be racist here.'

The buildings range from shabby prefabs put up 'temporarily' in the '40s to the bright new science block and the media block with facilities for drama, music and media studies, as well as the pristine beauty salon. There are plentiful computers and whiteboards, but the planned rebuild now seems to be receding into the far distance as government funds are cut. However, a £3 million expansion of the lower school site has seen 18 new state-of-the-art classrooms.

The school was the highest placed education establishment in a Sunday Times Best Hundred Companies to Work For list and winner in the medium-sized company section. It also came first for the quality of its leadership, for personal growth and for its employees' pride in working there.

Pastoral care and discipline: This is one of the smartest and most ordered schools we have ever visited. Children are immaculate in blazers and ties, orderly in corridors and attentive in lessons. 'People know not to mess about,' say pupils. 'But it's all fair – punishments are fair. The rules are good ones.' The school works on a combination of iron

> 'It makes you feel proud to wear our uniform, when you see pupils from other schools prancing around in polo shirts and trainers.'

discipline and plenty of praise. There are colours for sport, music and performing arts. During the assembly we attended large numbers of children lined up to receive merit awards. They approve of their uniform. 'It makes you feel proud to wear our uniform, when you see pupils from other schools prancing around in polo shirts and trainers.'

Children feel very safe here. 'If something happens here they get straight on top of it. This school really does hate bullying – they don't tolerate it.' There's a close bond between pupils and teachers. 'They're always really cheerful. They'll make a joke out of things if they can. And they treat us like grown-ups. They respect our feelings.' Staff are stationed in corridors between lessons and outside the school when pupils leave at the end of the day. No-one below sixth form is allowed out at lunchtime. Sir Paul tours classrooms daily, greeting pupils with words of praise or good-natured censure.

The pupil referral unit handles children who have disrupted lessons, breached the uniform code, started a fight or played truant. 'We get in quickly

– we're proactive – and so we've only had two permanent exclusions in the last 10 years.'

Pupils and parents: Largely from the surrounding estates, though proximity to the school puts a premium on the prices of the few houses for sale in the area. Large numbers of single parent families and those with several generations of unemployment. The school employs a parental adviser who visits families under stress and helps with housing, clothing and food allowances. Around 20 per cent Afro-Caribbean families, the rest mostly white working class: Robert Clack was the only London school on Ofsted's 'excelling against the odds' list with a preponderance of children from such typically under-achieving backgrounds

Entrance: Takes 300 children into year 7 but there are over 200 appeals every year, so the intake invariably increases. Looked-after children get priority, as do those with special educational needs, then by distance from the upper school site – generally within a mile or so. Some 2,000 applications for the 300 places. Large numbers from other schools join the sixth form.

Exit: About 70 per cent of pupils move up to the sixth form, up from around 20 per cent 10 years ago. Two students off with scholarships to study for A levels at Eton recently. Excellent careers advice and encouragement to aim high. The school has links with Oxford, Cambridge, Essex, York and east London universities, with visiting speakers, university visits and summer schools. Three off to study medicine at King's College London in 2014.

Remarks: Outstandingly successful comprehensive in one of the most deprived areas of the country. Excellent leadership by a tireless head has transformed a failing school into one that is a source of pride for staff, parents and pupils. 'This school gets you ready for the future,' said a pupil.

Seven Kings High School

Ley Street, Ilford, Essex IG2 7BT

State · Pupils: 1,400 · Ages: 11–18 · Non-denom

Tel: 020 8554 8935
Fax: 020 8518 2975
Email: enquiries@skhs.net
Website: www.skhs.net

6

Head Teacher: Since 2008, Ms Tracy Smith BA PGCE (40s). Educated at St Martin's School, Brentwood. Read history and sociology at Warwick, PGCE

at Goldsmith's College, London, then taught at Barking Abbey School for seven years. Moved to Seven Kings as head of sixth form in 1995, then deputy to former head Sir Alan Steer, and a key player in the team which transformed this east London school into one of the country's most successful comprehensives. Before taking over the headship, she led a project on Assessment for Learning carried out by King's College, Cambridge and the Institute of Education and continues to sit on a number of influential committees, including the SSAT London Headteachers' Steering Group. Energetic, level-headed and good-humoured, she's undoubtedly a safe pair of hands to keep this school top of the form. Married with two teenage children. A keen West Ham supporter, she spends down time watching football, going to the theatre, hill walking and travelling.

Academic matters: If academic matters are uppermost in your schooling choice, then you have very little to fret about at Seven Kings. Despite its 'very average' intake, Seven Kings seems to sail effortlessly to the top of the league tables. Seventy-eight per cent of GCSE candidates in 2014 achieved 5+ A*-C grades including English and maths; over 33 per cent of grades were A*/A. The hugely oversubscribed sixth form produced equally dazzling results – 60 per cent A*/B grades and nearly 33 per cent A*/A. Teaching is vibrant and committed – 'the quality of the teaching manages to challenge every student,' said one parent – and teacher-pupils relationships strong. 'Teachers know you well and know how you are feeling,' said one boy. 'You can ask them anything.'

Success is down to monitoring, tracking and a can-do approach, and certainly no one here gets lost at the back. 'You won't find a pupil we haven't

spoken to in the past three weeks about their learning,' says the head. 'They don't give us grades, they give us comments,' said one student. 'They tell you what you can do to improve and what you've already done well. They know what you need to do to get better.' Every student is also given two one-to-one interviews about academic progress. 'We track, interview and talk.' 'This isn't an exam factory,' says the head, 'but we do know the syllabus and the exam requirements.' And not only can they distinguish their Pre-Us from their A levels, they know how to prioritise a UCAS form, with a large chunk of the high-powered sixth form going on to

Success is down to monitoring, tracking and a can-do approach, and certainly no one here gets lost at the back

all the country's top universities.

Three languages on offer – French, Spanish and Mandarin – with well over half the students studying at least one language to GCSE. Science newly energised by a 'skills-based' approach, and bangs and smells part of the fabric of school life. 'Students now say science is their favourite subject,' says the head. 'There are about 50 experiments going a day.' After-school clubs include the academic as well as the just for fun, providing support with homework and coursework.

Games, options, the arts: Art, DT and PE all highly valued and popular. 'Our kids do two hours PE a week and even on days when they don't have sport, we make sure they get off their bottoms,' says the deputy. Football, cricket, netball, rugby, running and athletics all core to the curriculum. One basketball superstar recently won a scholarship to a top US university. Music and drama are popular options with plenty on offer for aspiring performers. Plenty of other extracurricular activities are available for spiritual, social and cultural nourishment such as Amnesty International, chess, model airplanes, astronomy and a film club.

Background and atmosphere: The school began life as a girls' grammar in the 1930s, and some remaining original features give a feel of the inter-war years, with an expansive spread of low rise brick buildings and a Betjemanesque assembly hall ideal for listening to the clock ticking away the exam minutes. Inside the tall-windowed classrooms, the focus is on learning, helped by full range of thoroughly modern additions, from a new lecture theatre and a spacious, glass entrance hall to a wheelchair park and interactive whiteboards. The motto is 'friendship, excellence, opportunity,' which most pupils and parents believe the school more than delivers. 'The kids know we really care about them,' says the head. Seven Kings is particularly noted for its SEN provision and has a national reputation as a centre of excellence for disabled children. As well as the specially adapted entrance and well-equipped medical centre, classrooms are accessible by wheelchair and there is well-staffed highly-skilled SEN department.

Pastoral care and discipline: Seven Kings serves a neighbourhood that is certainly on the less affluent side of the rich-poor divide, with the social problems and deprivation typical of many parts of urban London. But despite its relatively stark surrounding streets, the school itself is a haven of purposeful

'Our kids do two hours PE a week and even on the days when they don't have sport, we make sure they get off their bottoms,' said the deputy

calm. Discipline is assumed, corridors are quiet, classes orderly. That's not to say, of course, that every child's an angel. 'We have 1,500 hormonal kids,' says the head. 'Of course we have discipline problems.' But few that aren't sorted out rapidly.

An expansive spread of low rise brick buildings and a Betjmanesque assembly hall, ideal for listening to the clock ticking away the exam minutes

'We haven't excluded anyone permanently since I've been head.' Short sharp shocks for fighting or cheeking the teacher. 'Expectations are very clear, as are sanctions, but we try and apply them sensitively. This isn't a zero-tolerance environment.' Positive peer pressure is a definite help keeping potential bad boys on the straight and narrow. 'Some kids are definitely from challenging homes and we do our best to keep them going.' No-one from years 7-11 let off-site at breaks or lunchtimes. Proactive pastoral and timetabling used constructively. 'How you timetable the school day has a massive impact on behaviour,' says the deputy.

Pupils and parents: This is a neighbourhood comprehensive and more than three-quarters of the pupils come from Indian, Pakistani or Bangladeshi backgrounds. Parents here want their children to do well and give their full backing to the education on offer, with nearly all seats filled at parents' evenings. They aren't, however, a cake-baking, raffle-holding crowd and the school has no PTA. The kids themselves support their parents' aspirations, work hard and behave well. 'The kids are bright and ambitious,' says the head.

Entrance: The school is extremely popular and oversubscribed with 1,800 eager candidates queuing for the 180 year 7 places and a waiting list well into the hundreds. 'Fortunately, that's all done by the local authority,' says the head. Strict catchment rules apply, though those with statements automatically go to the top of the admissions ladder. Around 80 per cent go through to the sixth form, which attracts a massive number of outside applications every year – those successful have predicted GCSE grades that meet the entrance criteria for their chosen A level subjects.

Exit: Around half to Russell Group universities; rest to other good universities or destinations such as internships in the City.

Remarks: An inspiring place, where any parent could feel confident their child's needs will be met and where every child will reach or exceed expectations.

Sir John Cass Foundation and Redcoat Church of England Secondary School

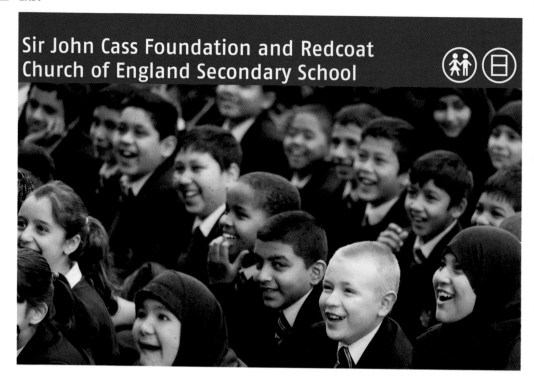

Stepney Way, London E1 0RH

State · Pupils: 1600 · Ages: 11–19 · C of E

Tel: 020 7790 6712
Fax: 020 7790 0499
Email: sirjohncass@sjcr.net
Website: www.sjcr.net

9

Headteacher: Since 1995, Mr Haydn Evans (60s), who arrived in Stepney after deputy headships in Tonbridge and, briefly, at a large rural comprehensive in Bridgend. His then school-age children failed to settle in Wales, and he returned happily to commute in from Kent to the headship of this inner-city church school. Praised as a strong, determined, strategic thinker and very successful head ('exemplary', said Ofsted), he has overseen the opening of the sixth form and the upward trajectory of the whole school, transforming it from an undersubscribed comprehensive with exam results on the minimal side to one with over 1,200 applicants for 180 places. The (now-defunct) Building Schools for the Future programme has now extended the school buildings to give it increased accommodation and capacity.

A hands-on head, he teaches chemistry to A level and is frequently out and about in the school with other senior managers, helping to police the comings and goings between lessons as 1,600 pupils move round a school built for 800. 'We act as an unobtrusive presence – we rarely have to say or do anything.'

Academic matters: Consistently near the top of the value-added tables and has three times been ranked the most improved school in the country. Most pupils come in with lower than average achievement, but in 2014, 81 per cent got at least five A*-C grades at GCSE or equivalent. This falls to about half if you include maths and English, unsurprisingly since English is a second language for around 80 per cent of the pupils. They come from a huge range of primaries and many have difficult home lives. 'Our first focus is on behaviour, on creating a climate for learning. Then we engage them with exciting teaching.'

The latest Ofsted report, which rated the school 'outstanding', praised its very high expectations of all pupils. New year 7s are tested and placed in sets for maths, English, science and RE. These are fluid and there's plenty of scope to move up as one's English improves or down should the maths start to prove tricky. There are vocational as well as academic courses at KS4, for example in science and IT. The school keeps a close eye on pupils' progress, targeting those who need extra help to ensure that everyone gets the grades they need to move on to the next stage. 'They have very high aspirations for my daughter,' said a parent. 'They push the children very hard to succeed.'

It is a specialist language college and everyone studies two languages for the first three years, from a choice of French, Spanish and Bengali, continuing at least one to GCSE. There is also a choice of 11 languages in twilight classes (for parents as well

---

The school has links with an instituto in rural Spain, and children who had rarely left the East End of London have found themselves travelling to school by horse and cart

---

as pupils), and many pupils take a GCSE in their own native language before year 11. Many go on French or Spanish exchanges. The school has links with an instituto in rural Spain, and children who had rarely left the East End of London have found themselves travelling to school by horse and cart.

It also has a business and enterprise specialism and good links with Canary Wharf and City firms, with some offering work placements, scholarships to cover university fees and jobs after graduation to talented students. Sixth form business studies students can have mentoring from business partners, visits and seminars, lectures and summer internships. One pupil recently spent the summer in America, having won a coveted place on a student leadership programme.

The large sixth form, with some 600 pupils, has its own new centre, including a library, IT suite, mixed and girls' only common rooms (the latter with pink net curtains) and a popular café. It offers a variety of vocational courses alongside A levels and GCSE retakes. Many students come in from elsewhere to join those moving up, and quite a few have relatively low qualifications. Some start with intermediate level courses then move up to higher levels en route to university. Science and maths A levels are particularly popular and successful, alongside psychology, RE and sociology; results average three B grades.

About 10 per cent of pupils have some kind of special need. 'We have an elaborate academic support team. The governors have decided to invest heavily in this and it is a very worthwhile investment.' Gifted and talented pupils are also identified for extra support. Learning mentors and assistants work through teachers and directly with pupils, helping to track their progress and

ensure they know what they need to do to improve. There are regular extension and catch-up classes. Staff recruitment is not a problem, with over 60 applicants for a recent RE vacancy. 'We have a high profile and we attract high quality applicants.'

Games, options, the arts: Sports facilities include a swimming pool (everyone learns to swim by the end of their first term) and a sports hall with space for basketball, badminton, football and cricket. Football and basketball teams play enthusiastic and successful matches against other schools. Table tennis, boxing and fencing are also on the agenda. A level sports science students coach younger pupils. Girls and boys have separate PE and sports lessons, as well as separate entrances and playgrounds – an innovation that is very popular with pupils and parents.

Actors perform at the Mile End Theatre and the steel band has played at the Albert Hall. Guitar club and a gospel choir, and many pupils have individual music lessons. Trips to operas and musicals. A school ski trip in the Easter holidays, D of E, ice skating, rock climbing and canoeing trips. Sixth formers organise societies, including Christian Union and Muslim Students' Society.

Background and atmosphere: Formed in 1964 by the governing body of Red Coat School (established

in 1714 for boys born within Mile End Old Town) and the governors of the Sir John Cass Foundation (a charity set up in 1710 by Sir John Cass for poor children in the East End of London). The school is owned by the Foundation, one of London's oldest educational charities, and Founder's Day in St Botolph-without-Aldgate church is one of the highlights of the school year. Its present site, with its pleasant redbrick buildings, dates from 1965. It is right in the middle of the East End but in a deceptively rural-seeming setting with a city farm opposite, a park next door and the school church and its tranquil graveyard beyond.

The school has been refurbished to include up-to-date science labs and learning centres stocked with computers. These are open before and after school and on Saturday mornings, with learning mentors around to help. Many pupils have no computer at home, nor quiet space in which to do homework. The great hall with stage and balcony doubles as a lecture theatre and can accommodate the entire school for assemblies. 'These are important for setting the behaviour tone for the school.' Lower school pupils wear a traditional uniform including a blazer, which becomes more informal higher up the school. Honours boards line the reception area. Although this is a C of E school, the vast majority of pupils are Muslims and they have their own prayer room.

Pastoral care and discipline: An orderly atmosphere is central to the ethos of the school. 'Security and mutual respect are very high priority. First of all we make them feel secure and safe, then we start to cultivate respect for all. A feeder primary school may be less traditional than we are but we're confident that when they come here we'll get them into our ethos by the end of the first half term.' The atmosphere is indeed calm and orderly, with some exuberance in the corridors between lessons but quiet concentration in the classrooms. There are CCTV cameras throughout, which, say staff, discourage vandalism and add to students' sense of security. Staff check on the destinations of those wandering the corridors between lessons.

By all accounts very little racial tension and very few exclusions. 'We do very occasionally have some challenging behaviour but it does not threaten the learning environment. We try hard not to exclude if we can possibly avoid it.' Two qualified counsellors on the staff. 'It's a very happy school,' said a parent, 'but the kids are expected to knuckle down and achieve.'

Pupils and parents: About two-thirds of the pupils are Bangladeshi, the rest from a variety of ethnic minorities, including many Somali refugees. Parents mostly very supportive of the school and its high expectations for their children. They join in maths workshops and twilight language classes and become involved in the numerous community projects. Pupils form strong peer groups. 'There's a very strong ethos of care for one another,' said a parent.

Entrance: Some 1,200 applicants for 180 places. Everyone is placed in one of four ability bands, assessed by the standard Tower Hamlets primary school test, with equal numbers of places offered from each band. This is a C of E school, so it does allocate a minority of places to committed Christians. Thirty-six places go to worshippers in a recognised Christian church, with looked-after children, social and medical needs, living in one of the listed parishes and then siblings in order of priority. The other 144 places have a similar priority order, but 20 are offered to first-born children. Families in the area tend to be large and siblings would otherwise monopolise the intake. Distance from the school is the tie-break.

The sixth form is also highly over-subscribed, with over 1,000 applicants for 300 outside places. Most advanced level courses require five or more A* – C grades at GCSE including English and maths, with some higher stipulations eg an A in maths for maths or further maths A level. But those with lesser qualifications can take lower level courses, and the majority of pupils from year 11 go through to the sixth form.

Exit: Those who leave after GCSEs – about 10 per cent of year 11s – mostly go on to another sixth form or straight into a job. All year 13 leavers for the past three years – and some of these may have spent several years in the sixth form improving their qualifications – have gone straight to university. For social and cultural reasons, the vast majority choose London universities, but some venture further afield. Has had several successful Oxbridge candidates. 'I am confident that once they start coming back to tell our students about it we'll have more applicants.' Some students return to the school as teachers or learning mentors.

Remarks: A beacon of excellence in a deprived area of London, which takes in students with low levels of attainment and sends the majority off to university with commendable exam results. A strong head and committed staff insist on good behaviour, provide expert teaching and inspire high aspirations. 'It's gone from strength to strength,' said a parent. 'It's a great school.'

Sir William Burrough Primary School

Salmon Lane, London E14 7PQ

State • Pupils: 375 • Ages: 3–11 years • Non–denom

Tel: 020 7987 2147
Fax: 020 7515 1858
Email: admin@sirwilliamburrough.
towerhamlets.sch.uk
Website: sirwilliamburrough.net

Headteacher: Since 1995, Mrs Avril Newman BEd (early 60s), who was educated at Hendon County Grammar School and has a first class degree in education from Goldsmith's. She has spent her entire career in east London primary schools and is a National Leader of Education and a JP. A slight and engaging lady, married with two grown-up children, she is viewed by Ofsted as 'inspirational' and an 'outstandingly good leader.'

Together with her highly experienced leadership team, she is evidently the driving force behind the school's immense success. She believes that every child must aspire to read, write and calculate to the highest possible standards and insists on formal skills-based programmes for the three Rs.

Entrance: The usual priorities: special needs, siblings, then distance, which is not very far. This is a massively oversubscribed school in a highly populated urban area.

Exit: To a variety of local state secondaries; occasionally children go off to eg City Boys or Girls, sometimes on scholarships.

Remarks: Not far off the A13 Commercial Road, overshadowed by building sites, this is an oasis of colour and calm. Inside the tall Victorian building, brightly painted walls form a background to swathes of fabric, flowers, displays of work and photos of outings, with children in red, blue, green or yellow sweatshirts.

The school has an excellent mix of cultures and ethnicities. Small majority of the pupils are of Bangladeshi heritage, others are of Somalian, Eastern European and indigenous white British background. All are expected to do well, and they do. 'We do not wish to take deprivation, culture, class or gender into account,' says the school. 'We're in the business of teaching and learning and the children do that for seven years here. We're ferocious about them learning to read, write and calculate – no-one falls through the net. Unless they have serious problems, we guarantee that they will meet or exceed government expectations.'

The school uses synthetic phonics to teach reading – 'they all learn very quickly and early.' As children become more proficient, they use an online accelerated reader system which monitors their progress, suggests books to read, sets quizzes and awards prizes. Maths is also taught by an online system: 'they always know what they need to learn next. They're not waiting for the teacher to hand

Children Skype their peers in South Korea – 'they want our creativity, we want their maths results.'

out the next bit of learning.' Children requested, and received, a system that allows them to assess themselves and take time to fill in any gaps. They can also compete against children from other countries. As a result, around 90 per cent reach the expected level 4 in year 6 SATs, and a large proportion reach level 5. A small number reach Level 6. The vast majority progress at national expectation.

However, this emphasis on the basics does not preclude an exciting, creative curriculum with a global dimension. Sir William Burrough was one of the first state primaries in the country to adopt the International Primary Curriculum (IPC). Originally developed for international schools run by petrol giant Shell, the IPC focuses on cross-curricular topics such as fashion, chocolate or treasure. There's an emphasis on hands-on learning with

Children studying treasure start with a treasure hunt round the school then go off to the Tower of London to see the crown jewels

huge numbers of trips out: children studying treasure start with a treasure hunt round the school then go off to the Tower of London to see the crown jewels. Year 6s learning about WW2 have an interactive show about an evacuee, delivered by an actor, and visit the Britain at War Experience at nearby London Bridge. Children Skype their peers in South Korea – 'they want our creativity, we want their maths results' – and some have travelled to Rome and Washington on exchange trips. The IPC and the British Council send many foreign visitors, and staff travel all over the world to see how other IPC schools operate. 'We're always scanning the horizon for better ideas.'

The children's experiences are well-documented: they make iMovies, animations and multi-media presentations as well as printing books of photos. 'Even the year 3s can edit their own presentations.' A room full of Apple Mac computers, plus plenty of laptops, are testimony to the school's profitable partnerships with several City firms, which also send in reading partners and chess mentors. The school business manager is a skilled fund-raiser, providing welcome extra funding for playground equipment, sports coaches, visiting artists, actors and storytellers.

The school's catch-phrase is 'you can do it'. 'If you can't do something you always keep trying,' say pupils. 'We're very independent and we never give up.' Pupils help to staff the reception desk and show round international visitors. The debating team has won competitions across London, and many pupils get merit or distinction in English Speaking Board assessments. When we visited, year 6 were rehearsing for a performance of Joseph and the Amazing Technicolour Dreamcoat. Assembly, which involves plenty of vigorous singing, happens at the end of the day. 'It harnesses their collective energy and sends them home feeling good about the day.'

The choreographer-in-residence organises spectacular dance displays; the 70-strong choir makes many public performances. Everyone plays the recorder. The three playgrounds include a wooded area where the children build camps and play on the jungle gym, and an all-purpose sports pitch. There are not many opportunities for inter-school matches, but plenty of sport: the cricket team has played at Lords, they swim at Mile End

Leisure Centre and skate at Canary Wharf, play handball, baseball, hockey and rounders. Year 5 has a challenging outdoor pursuits week. After-school clubs include wide variety of sports, yoga, street dance, animation, cookery, chess, sailing, Spanish and lots more.

The school has a strong relationship with the local community. 'We never stop asking the question: how can we do things better? We have regular parents' forums, and listen and act on their excellent suggestions. Parents help run the toddlers' group, and organise an opening doors programme of families meeting in each other's homes which creates strong bonds across different ethnic groups.' The children are doing this from the moment they start. 'We all get along with each other,' they say. 'We have brilliant friendships.' 'If Martin Luther King came along to our school today he would think to himself: my dream has come true.'

Snaresbrook Preparatory School

75 Woodford Road, South Woodford, London E18 2EA	Tel: 020 8989 2394
	Fax: 020 8989 4379
Independent • Pupils: 165 • Ages: 3–11 • Non-denom	Email: office@snaresbrookprep.org
• Fees (per term): £2,520 – £3,368	Website: www.snaresbrookprep.org

Head: Since 2013, Mr Christopher Curl MA BEd TEFL, studied English and drama at Exeter. Taught in a mixture of prep and senior schools, including his own, King's Canterbury. Has been boarding house-master, head of English and drama, i/c co-curricular activities. Third headship – chose this school because of its size, family atmosphere and autonomy. Active and involved governors – including some of the original founding family – give him scope to shape the school. They also give lots of practical support, from HR to decorating. 'On some other boards you see some three times a year for large lunches and no one knows who they are,' says the head.

He aims to 'make learning more interesting' while 'trying not to fiddle with everything', especially since the school already has an outstanding report. Parents think he strikes a good balance, especially in the difficult role of following 'a much-loved, very long-standing incumbent'. One said, 'He is doing a great job of listening to parents and making positive changes.' Parents describe him as a 'very visible', 'open, approachable', and a 'supremely capable steward' who 'genuinely cares about the school'.

He is hands on, helping with drama and musical productions, at the gate before and after school, and teaching. Every Monday he starts with year 6 and works his way down to the nursery, teaching the older ones current affairs and conducting story time sessions with younger pupils. He likes to avoid being 'this remote head who sits in an office'.

Years 4 and 5 are excited about the annual trip to France where they visit a chocolate factory (they like this better than the snail farm)

Head also provides weekly lunch time cover for his secretary, so he 'gets to see the front of the organisation, what she is dealing with, what's happening, who comes in, what people are saying'. He thinks that 'if as a head you stop doing the kinds of things other members of staff are asked to do, you become out of touch'.

Entrance: Most come in at nursery and go though to year 6. There is a low-key family interview with the head; sibling priority. Places higher up subject to a family interview and in-class assessment. Pupils come from various nurseries in the local area, from Canary Wharf and Stratford out to Epping, Woodford Green, Romford and Loughton, and beyond.

Exit: Many go on to win scholarships to eg City of London, Forest, Chigwell, St Edmund's Ware and Bancroft's. Others go off to grammars like Woodford County High and Ilford County High.

Remarks: Small size and family atmosphere mean pupils settle in quickly. 'You don't have to be scared to talk to a year 6 because everyone knows each other,' a pupil said. One parent said that during her son's first year at the school he has 'waved and greeted any older pupil we met in the street. And the bigger kids have invariably waved back.'

The main school is set in a 1930s Victorian house and was managed by the same family for 50 years. Its small, quaint classrooms are close together and the corridors are dainty, but it is an intimate rather than cramped feel. The nursery and reception are housed in a separate, purpose-built building overlooking a small playground, with the hall and a multi-purpose library room on the other side of the playground. Beyond that is a covered sensory garden, designed and constructed by an architect governor. The children grow plants here, and experiment with different climates and seasons. There is a huge blackboard where they chalk

to their heart's content and above it a huge, colourful mural painted by year 6s.

The governors, as mentioned, are very much involved in everyday school life, often to be seen popping in and out. They are helping to extend the hall to create more storage space, they have helped decorate the staff room and to build the new canopied decking area outside the nursery so pupils can enjoy year round outdoor play free of leaves and rain. 'They are very sensitive to the needs of the staff and children,' said the head.

Single form entry, with class sizes of roughly 24 in the infants and 18 in the juniors, and plenty of classroom assistants. 'It is mixed ability here,' says the head. 'What is exciting is seeing children who didn't come in as high fliers leave having made massive progress.' Most extra support for those with learning difficulties is provided in class, with a part-time specialist available as required.

French from nursery, optional German and Spanish, year 6 learn Latin and also embark on self-directed projects. Lots of investment in IT. We saw year 5 listening to a live commentary on an Arsenal v Southampton match and learning how to extract key information from a database to write up their news reports.

The school adventure service challenge is 'like a mini Duke of Edinburgh... we do camping, rowing, bird watching, cooking and it's lots of fun,' say

pupils. Years 4 and 5 are excited about the annual trip to France where they visit a chocolate factory in Boulogne (they like this better than the snail farm). Whilst in France they spend time with penfriends and complete a shopping task in French, although some confess they have found ways around this: 'Luckily the lady that was serving us knew English'. Year 5 has a history trip to York and year 6 an end of year trip to Shropshire.

Before and after-school clubs include the usual range of sports plus country and maypole dancing, scooter club, creative writing, art club and knitting. Popular sports are football and netball, and considering how small the school is, they do well: 'Once we played in a tournament and there were two Snaresbrook teams in the football play-off and they ended up playing each other,' a pupil said with pride. There are no fields here so pupils take a minibus to Redbridge Sports Centre and Ashton playing fields.

One parent commented: 'I feel the school works hard to optimise the use of space available.' At breaktimes a daily games timetable saves the tiny playground from being dominated by football (football still an option at lunchtime when playtimes are staggered) and the children can try out a different game each day. 'Our new games teacher came up with the idea,' said a pupil. It was inspired by Olympics sports such as handball, dodgeball and basketball. Most of the children take part and girls and boys play together. Other activities are on

---

We saw year 5 listening to a live commentary on an Arsenal v Southampton match and learning how to extract key information from a database to write up their news reports

offer, too – they can read, do art, play table tennis. The head says: 'In my last school we had acres and acres of green grass and the children didn't use it as well. Here they are much more appreciative, and the lack of space can be an advantage rather than a disadvantage.'

When we visited, years 1 and 2 were in the hall preparing for a dress rehearsal of Rise and Shine. 'All have a part to play in the production,' said their teacher. The school tries to offer a taste of a wide range of drama and music, and each class gets a chance to perform. 'Lots of parents come to see the productions whether they have children in that

---

After examining video evidence following one race, the head sent out an urgent email saying parents had in fact lost

year group or not.' Around 20 per cent of children learn to play the recorder, violin or flute.

House system gives everyone a chance to shine in different areas. 'Browns usually win on sports day, blues dominate swimming, yellows are good at choir singing and pancake races,' a pupil told us, 'so we each have our fair share of glory'. The many charitable and fundraising activities include readathons, movie nights to raise funds for Redbridge Night Shelter, sports events for the NSPCC and Great Ormond Street and harvest collections for the British Red Cross. Year 4 girls created a magazine, 'packed with quizzes, gossip and pictures. They made £61 by selling it to everyone'.

Pupils help inside school too. A year 6 pupil said of the nursery: 'We come in our free time and help the children and teachers with projects. It's also fun for us as this was our room when we were in the nursery.' It invokes a sense of service: 'This morning I was holding the door for a parent and I heard one of the year 4s say, "Dad, when I'm in year 6 I will be able to hold the door, I will say good morning to everyone".'

Support is good, say parents, with teachers always wiling to discuss and address problems. Plenty of incentives and rewards for doing well, including Good Marks assemblies and commendation awards. The merit board includes an award to teachers for 'making a good start on the return after holidays'.

A new system of online live reports, with up-to-date comments from teachers that parents can access at any time, has replaced yearly written reports. The plan is to produce a detailed picture of how each child learns and how they are progressing.

Very active parents association – '40 donations for the bake sale the other day', said a member – with an impressive participation rate considering that many, if not most, families have two working parents. Hotly-contested annual pancake race involves children, staff and parents. After examining video evidence following one race, the head sent out an urgent email saying parents had in fact lost and parents retorted: 'Mr Curl, wait till next year.'

Woodford County High School

High Road, Woodford Green, Essex IG8 9LA

State • Pupils: 880 • Ages: 11–18 • Non-denom

Tel: 020 8504 0611
Fax: 020 8506 1880
Email: head@woodford.redbridge.sch.uk
Website: www.woodford.redbridge.sch.uk

8

Headteacher: Since 2010, Ms Jo Pomeroy (40s), MA in English language and literature (St Andrews), BEd (Open), NPQH. Spent two years in a comprehensive in rural Scotland before going to work in France at a mixed grammar school for three years. It was at this high achieving international school that she became aware of 'what can be achieved', 'what is possible' and 'what bright students are capable of if they are given enough challenge,' she says. So the aim here 'is for students always to be working just beyond what they are comfortable with'. Back in the UK she spent another three years working in a comprehensive school with strong bias for European languages and at that point 'got interested in management, in getting into position where you could make a bigger change'. Sure enough, at her next appointment at a girls' grammar in Surrey, where she spent 16 years, she eventually became deputy head. 'There is enormous satisfaction in seeing incrementally what can be achieved in one place,' she says. Academic life at Woodford is very much influenced by this passion for great leadership as well as head's English teaching background. 'What excites me the most is working from what you may

be able to stimulate in your own life and career and then being able to share that with students so that they can enjoy challenges themselves.'

Academic matters: Best results in Redbridge. These are bright girls taught by committed teachers, a third of whom have been here for over 10 years. As a selective school (there are only some four students with SEN), it has maintained an outstanding record of achievement, with 75 per cent A*/A grades at GCSE in 2014. And these stats despite most students – in fact well over half of the school population – speaking English as a second language. 'The joy of being in a school like this is that it is self-propagating, when students come in and they see other students valuing learning and success, and working hard on collaborative projects, it really affects everything else they do.'

This school models leadership extremely well. It has an impressive mentoring structure in place where older pupils mentor younger ones. There are literacy mentors who provide targeted additional support for year 7s where needed, and this 'sustained focus on academic literacy across the

curriculum has been highly successful'. Head says, 'I have an interest in a great many subjects and I think the joy of English being my subject is that it takes you into everything, history, philosophy, art

---

With the great pastoral and peer support in place and strong academic atmosphere there is no reason why a pupil should not do well here

---

and music, and it is wonderful being able to investigate and enjoy literature and other languages as well.' These pupils have the opportunity to be mentored in other subjects as well, by sixth formers who relish the opportunity to 'give something back', though 'teachers still keep a close eye...'

In some classrooms desks are arranged to encourage interaction between students, not only with teachers. In the English department, year 7s are introduced to Shakespeare texts usually reserved for later years and invited to write an essay on what they have learnt. They also have lots of opportunity to visit theatres. Pupils take two languages from year 7 (French and either German or Latin). English, languages and science are all strong here and around 87 per cent of girls take triple science GCSE. Lots of information and support provided to both students and parents on choosing options.

In the sixth form, where roughly a quarter of students come from other schools, Woodford maintains good A level results with 72 per cent A*/B grades, 47 per cent A*/A, in 2014, with students off to Oxford and Cambridge and on to medical careers. Academic mentoring and university preparation at sixth form, and guidance to final transition here is second to none, or in one parent's words, 'really very strong'.

Games, options, the arts: Head's commitment to leading a school that offers plenty of opportunity to be stretched is evident across the whole curriculum. Reasonable range of games on offer – badminton, athletics, netball, rounders, gymnastics and dance – and girls can pursue their interest in multi-cultural dance options such as Bhangra, African and street dance. Games either take place outside on the field and tennis courts or indoors in the newly built Lottery funded sports hall, which looks gorgeously fresh next to the main school building, already well over 100 years old when it opened as a school in 1919. Outdoor Greek theatre recently restored. The girls do well at games; they

recently reached the UK badminton national finals, and they seem willing to try their best at everything, keen or not: 'Sport, I'm not good at, but it's a popular subject.'

Pupils speak highly of the sports leadership qualification offered in years 10 and 11: 'It gives you skills in being responsible, listening skills and classroom theory. We learn to create lesson plans.' Another said it 'opens us up to new areas; we realise there is more to our skill set and that motivates and opens us up to aim higher'. D of E also offered.

School does well at art and has had pupils featured in a Saatchi Exhibition. Major drama event each term as well as an annual musical (most recently, Oliver!) plus a summer production run by teachers and a spring production organised by students. A beautiful patchwork tapestry displayed under glass in the technology department harks back to the days when the school offered textiles. These days the girls focus their design skills in technology, where they recently emerged winners of the National Technology Design Prize.

Instrumental and vocal lessons at all levels on offer, though most who learn do so out of school. Many are involved in one of a large number of ensembles and clubs: guitar, singing, Carnatic music. There is a large junior choir and band, a folk group, a brass project, woodwind ensemble, and a staff choir too. Girls have also participated in Redbridge Choral Festival at the Royal Albert Hall.

Lots of trips to support lessons and extracurricular activities, including expeditions to eg Ghana, Morocco, Indonesia, China, Cambodia. Annual geography trip to Iceland.

Older students preside over all manner of different extracurricular opportunities, such as talks, clubs and charity events, and there is a society for everything – even to discuss current affairs. 'We have house competitions,' head says, 'and sometimes there can be more drama off stage than on stage'. But because there is no adult intervention the girls learn to work together and develop great

---

A beautiful patchwork tapestry displayed under glass harks back to the days when the school offered textiles

---

teamwork skills: 'that is a real success and selling point of the school.' It all comes good in the end, as evidenced by the year 11-led assembly held on the morning of our visit. In their well-structured presentation the girls demonstrated what they had learnt about self, learning and approaching life, showing extraordinary wisdom and the ability to work together. Head says, 'They listen to each other very well, and coming up the school younger students see this and that sets their aspirations.'

Background and atmosphere: Main building dates from 1768 when it was built as the country manor home of the Highams; school opened here in 1919, and its venerable features lend an atmosphere of tradition – from the beautiful open air Greek theatre that stands in the grounds near to the tennis courts, to the hymnals still used in assemblies – 'I'm not a Christian but I enjoy it', a pupil remarked.

With its small classrooms, narrow stairwells and corridors, the school has an intimate feel. The lack of space noted at our last visit has been remedied by using Portakabins for some lessons. Population is not that large, with just 600 in the main school, but there is a larger than average sixth form of 280 students. Still, the girls lack nothing in terms of modern resources, thanks to a very active PFTA.

Pastoral care and discipline: Pupils receive support from their form tutors and also have prefects to help school life run smoothly. 'Teachers are approachable, and there are some small classes so you get to know everyone.' When issues of bullying

> *Main building dates from 1768 when it was built as the country home of the Highams; and its venerable features lend an atmosphere of tradition – beautiful open air Greek theatre*

come up, 'once staff are aware of it the response is immediate and caring'.

Lots of careful thought has gone into ensuring peer support is strong. 'Our greatest glory is not in never failing but in rising up every time we fail' says a poster on the PSHCE board in the corridor. The board provides information about the peer support service run by older pupils. 'So important,' said a pupil; 'petty things getting out of hand is rare.' Pupils say they 'can't imagine peer support not being there. It's natural.' Also, 'Form prefects develop close relationships so you stay in contact even after leaving, like on Facebook.' House groups are active and help mobilise the girls to get involved in drama performances and fundraising events for the chosen recipient of charity week. Events like the five-penny race are popular and encourage heated competition, raising as much £2000 in one hour.

As said, career support is good. There is a university success board to inspire the girls and year 11s have a review day including one-to-one meetings with teachers. Year 12s spend two hours per week in voluntary service, often working with children or the elderly or the disabled. 'It's a steep learning curve and you find yourself going back for several months.'

Pupils and parents: Multi-ethnic population: over 40 languages spoken here and there is a significant Tamil and Indian population. One parent said, 'My daughter benefits from being with children from many different ethnic backgrounds'. Parents support the PFTA as an opportunity to solve many of the school's cash problems (£25,000 raised for digital language lab, a mini bus, external lighting).

Girls seem confident, resilient and creative. Former pupils here include Lucy Kirkwood, playwright (RSC, National Theatre), Sarah Winman, best-selling novelist (When God was a Rabbit) and Peggy Reynolds, Radio 4 broadcaster in the arts.

Entrance: Massively oversubscribed, with some 900 applying for 120 years 7 places. The verbal and non-verbal reasoning tests are written exclusively for the borough's only two grammar schools (the other being the brother school, Ilford County for Boys). It is one of just three all-girls schools in the area (the other two are independent and Catholic). Common catchment area with boys' grammar school. Head says the girls are tested on 'wit rather than what's been studied in the classroom'.

Nearly all girls stay on to the sixth form, joined by 30 or so from other schools.

Exit: A few (11 per cent in 2014) leave post-GCSE but nearly all that stay go on to university. Subject choices are academic but varied: physics, law, medicine, languages (most likely French), mathematics, geography, English or economics. A few go on to study business or architecture. Some success in applications to top universities and competitive courses with nine Oxbridge places in 2014. Other destinations include UCL, Queen Mary's, Kent, King's College London, Birmingham, Nottingham.

Remarks: With the great pastoral and peer support in place and strong academic atmosphere there is no reason why a pupil should not do well here. The message from pupils to any year 6s considering the school is: 'If you love academic study, close relationships with teachers, clubs and societies, and you want to get involved, this is the place for you.'

"If everyone is thinking alike, then no one is thinking."

Benjamin Franklin

At Frensham Heights, we are proud to think differently. Founded on values of tolerance, respect and creativity, we treat every child as an individual and ensure that everyone truly flourishes.

Our unique approach to learning begins in our vibrant nursery and extends our thriving sixth form. Situated in 120 acres of beautiful Surrey countryside and less than an hour from London, we provide unrivalled opportunities to both day and boarding students.

Visit www.frensham.org or call 01252 792561 to find out more.

Frensham Heights | Think, Create, Explore

Frensham Heights, Rowledge, Farnham, Surrey GU10 4EA . Tel. 01252 792561 Charity No. 312052

Schools to watch

The Good Schools Guide generally gives new schools plenty of time to bed down, create an ethos and generate a track record before we review them. However, there are so many new schools emerging in London that we have asked our writers to tell us about those they feel are ones to watch.

West London Free School
Cambridge Grove, Hammersmith, London W6 0LB
020 8600 8670
Website: www.westlondonfreeschool.co.uk
Email: admin@wlfs.org

Head: Hywel Jones took over in September 2014 after the abrupt departure of previous head Sam Naismith, who himself took over when the founding head went off to become an Ofsted inspector. Mr Jones was previously a history teacher at St Mary's School in Hertfordshire. We also hear that there's been some turnover of senior staff.

Entrance: Complicated to say the least, including priority to the children of the school founders, music aptitude places, distance and ballots for those living further out.

Remarks: Established in 2011, this was one of the first free schools to be set up under the present coalition government. Co-founded by journalist and writer, Toby Young (now a poster boy for the free school movement), who has since gone on to set up two further free schools in West London and has written a book about how to do it.

The school is still partly based at its temporary home in Cambridge Grove (a former special needs school building) with no immediate prospects of moving to its new premises at nearby Palingswick House (except into portakabins). At least part of the school is taking up residence in a £9.25m office block in King Street.

Maximum class size is 24. 'It's like having a private school on the doorstep,' says one parent. 'They've tried to create a grammar school feel,' explains another. However, the intake is mixed socially and 25 per cent of students are on free school meals.

Latin is compulsory until year 9. Music is particularly strong, with the head of music being described by parents as 'inspirational.' 'He manages to get these inner-city kids to sing Gregorian chants without feeling at all self conscious. He's truly amazing.' The school already has an orchestra, two choirs and an a capella group, as well as numerous bands and ensembles. Some parents wish that art provision could be better, though. 'It's a shame there's not the same emphasis on art as there is on music,' confided one.

Sports are strong, with hockey and rugby for boys and hockey and netball for girls. 'My daughter has never been that into sport before,' says one parent, 'but this Christmas all she wanted was a hockey stick!' 'Sport is a big thing there and a non-sporty, sensitive child can find that difficult,' says one parent. Others complain about the lack of football for boys and the fact that students have to travel by bus to Duke's Meadows in Chiswick for sports practice.

The school has an extended day with extracurricular clubs (funded by monthly contributions from parents) until 5pm on Mondays to Thursdays. Parents approve but 'The children are exhausted by the end of the week,' said one. Discipline and pastoral care good so far. 'They've set the bar at just the right level,' explains one parent. 'There's just the right amount of fear, but not too much.'

London Academy of Excellence

Broadway House, 322 High Street, Stratford, E15 1AJ.
020 3301 1480
Website: excellencelondon.ac.uk
Email: office@excellencelondon.ac.uk

Head: Since September 2014, John Weeks, previously deputy head of Brighton College. He took over after founding head Robert Wilne moved on after two years.

Entrance: At least five A grades at GCSE, with B or higher in maths and English, and A*/A grades in A level subjects, plus 'colossal ambition and motivation'.

Remarks: Has recently hit the headlines for getting four Oxbridge places amongst its first A2 students (and boasts 43 per cent A*/A grades in its first A2 results). A free school that opened in September 2012 in a converted 1980s council office building next to Stratford station, it was set up with the help of a group of independent school and the intention of propelling ambitious local teenagers into top universities.

The school's backers – Brighton College, Eton College, Roedean, City of London School, King's College School, Wimbledon, Highgate School, Forest School and Caterham Schools – donate not money but expertise, each looking after a different area of the curriculum. The school's six houses are named after the schools, and each student is paired with a 'buddy' from their partner establishment. It is a two-way partnership, with staff and sixth formers visiting each and sharing lessons. LAE students insist that they don't feel envious of the rolling acres and sumptuous facilities of the partner independent schools: 'We have this free.'

All 12 A levels on offer, except for religious studies, are in 'facilitating subjects' eg sciences, maths and languages. Lessons are aimed to be challenging, with discursive, 'Socratic' teaching style, and students talk of the 'passion and knowledge' of their teachers. Extracurricular clubs are definitely on the boffin side, ranging from Latin to chemistry to music appreciation. The school team made the 2014 final of the national HSBC Mandarin speaking competition, coming second in points to St Paul's Girls.

No outdoor space, but there is a weekly afternoon of sport, overseen by City of London School at various venues around Newham – options include football, netball, judo and rowing, with matches against local and partner schools. Non-sporty thespians can opt for theatre performance instead, and speaking out with confidence is one of the academy aims.

It aims to feel like a transition between school and university. The building, unprepossessing from the outside, is decorated in white and grey with lime green and bright pink upholstery – 'like a dotcom start-up,' said The Guardian; canvases with the faces of famous scientists, artists and writers decorate the walls, dotted with their words of inspiration. Students wear sober office dress. There are plentiful university visits and huge encouragement to take up opportunities. The school's aim is to equip them with social confidence and a passion for their subject as well as the results needed to aim for top universities.

The Archer Academy

3 Beaumont Close, Bishops Avenue, London N2 0GA
020 8365 4110
Website: thearcheracademy.org.uk
Email: info@thearcheracademy.org.uk

Head: Since its opening in September 2013, Mick Quigley BEd. Early 50s with an education career that spans 30 years, Mr Quigley has worked across a range of environments – from early years through to FE. A genial and likeable chap who has his feet firmly planted on the ground, and who glows with enthusiasm when talking about his school, particularly the new proposed site on Stanley Road, due to be opened in 2015.

Entrance: At 11+, 150 places split into six tutor groups of 25. Priority given in accordance with the usual standard local authority criteria of siblings etc, followed by children living within the N2, N3 and NW11 postcodes.

Remarks: The Archer Academy derives its name from the landmark of an archer firing an arrow from a bow, which sits above East Finchley tube station. It opened its doors in September 2013, following a rigorous campaign by local parents frustrated by the lack of mixed, non-selective, non-denominational secondary provision in the area. The excitement was almost tangible in East Finchley. One parent told us; 'We've waited so long for a school around here. You see, people will be moving into the area soon to get in.'

We were particularly struck when we visited by very well behaved students thoroughly engaged in the subjects they were learning, who barely gave us a cursory glance when we walked in, so engrossed were they in their books. Perhaps they were inspired by the impressive list of authors including Michael Morpurgo, who have already visited the school to give talks.

The current site is on Beaumont Close, a small turning off the extremely affluent Bishops Avenue, and occupies the building formerly home to The Institute – an adult educational college which ran into financial difficulties and was forced to sell. The building itself is attractive – bright and airy – but the interior of the school is still rather basic, with few distinguishing features (except for a giant totem pole in the foyer made by a student and his mum). It has yet to get a lived-in feel, but judging by the enthusiasm of the staff, we don't doubt it will get there.

An urban campus school with few outdoor facilities, pupils go to nearby Cherry Tree Woods for outdoor play or Saracens in Mill Hill for sports. However, all will change in 2015 when the Stanley Road site – a 10 minute walk away – opens its doors to the lower school with sports facilities to be shared with the upper school. This site, designed by leading architects Jestico and Whiles, promises to be a bright and modern space, with first class indoor and outdoor sports facilities and 'flexible zones for teaching and learning.'

Radnor House
Pope's Villa, Cross Deep, Twickenham, Middlesex TW1 4QG
020 8891 6264
Website: www.radnorhouse.org
Email: info@radnorhouse.org

Head: Since the school's opening in 2011, David Paton BComm MA PGCE (forties). Tall, omni-present, very hands on (even answered phone sometimes in early days). Was head of sixth form at nearby Harrodian and briefly deputy head of the senior school at Dulwich College. Runs popular D of E, loved by all – though is also school's owner and widely held view by parents is that he has half an eye on impressing fellow investors.

Entrance: Twenty places in year 3 by assessment (not tests); a further 20 places in year 7 by English and maths tests and interview; another 20 places in year 9 by pre-test in year 7; into new sixth form by at least five grade B passes at GCSE.

Remarks: At last a decent co-ed independent on the doorstep, think locals from Richmond and Kingston environs, who make up vast majority of intake. Currently rich pickings from state sector as population boom sees cross-borough school building programme and class sizes at maximum in Richmond primary/secondary schools. Has also become default choice for some prep parents (eg Newland House) whose children are unlikely to strike gold in high-pressure fight for places at LEH/Hampton.

Some limitations. No DT or food tech (space is the issue). Overall, though, 'so much better than any teachers I've ever had before,' says local comprehensive escapee – bar occasional teacher who can't keep order. Lots of praise from parents. 'Young, clever and energetic staff,' thought one.

Art burgeoning, music enthusiastic, sports ditto – with lots of encouragement for those struggling with discipline and commitment to team sports.

Emphatically not a hothouse (fair few come with mild SEN – three or so per class) and not desperately selective. Not, however, the default school for anyone who can't get a place elsewhere, and if it sticks to sixth form entry criteria (Bs or better is the official line), even less so in the future.

For now, though, highly praised for boosting confidence – those with dyslexia in particular, though all need to be able to cope with mainstream curriculum. Following some parental grousing about learning support provision, new and well-regarded SENCo joined in 2013, though some feel she has a rough ride, what with combining individual help with full teaching timetable on top.

Compact, historic site, originally home to Alexander Pope. Right next to river – playground under water on occasion. Adds to the charm, say parents. 'They do maths in classroom overlooking the river – idyllic,' says mother of junior pupil.

Games played on St Mary's pitches nearby. Next door public park also used. Space shortage now permanently addressed with acquisition of additional land two minutes' walk away which, once developed, will provide own place for games.

Opposite St Catherine's girls' school, accounts for slight boy heaviness (numbers, not weight) in a few year groups, now evening out – though some years have just a handful of girls.

Going great guns, though prospectus description as 'one of the leading co-educational independent day schools in London' may be a little previous. Parents take long term view. 'Will get every child to their pinnacle – but maybe not in first year,' thought one. Signs, however, augur well.

Sir William Perkin C of E High School

Oldfield Lane North, Greenford, Middlesex UB6 8PR
0208 832 8950
Website: www.williamperkin.org.uk
Email: office@williamperkin.org.uk

Head: Alice Hudson, the much respected former head of the hugely successful and oversubcribed Twyford C of E High School in Acton, is now executive head of both Twyford and William Perkin. The school is her brain-child and was founded under the umbrella of the Twyford C of E Academies Trust. The schools are run by the directors of the Trust, but William Perkin is run on a day to day basis by associate head teacher Keir Smith – previously one of Alice Hudson's long-serving deputy heads at Twyford.

Entrance: Co-ed school with 180 year 7 places (from 2018, 30 external places for sixth form too). The single most important criterion is proximity to the school (whereas at Twyford there are various hoops to jump through to prove a commitment to the Christian faith). The school also reserves 20 places for pupils of Horsenden Primary School and 20 places for those from the Edward Betham C of E primary school, both in North Greenford. Current pupils all live close to the school.

Remarks: Opened with its first year 7 intake in September 2013 (they squeezed in 183 pupils as it was so oversubscribed). The idea was to create an outstanding school with the ethos and intellectual ambition of Twyford, sharing the same Christian values but open to all-comers, in a relatively deprived area of the borough of Ealing, Greenford, with limited school provision. The specialisms, music and languages – already proved to be excellent at Twyford – also include science and chaplaincy (school says chaplaincy 'operates to make faith across the breadth of school interests a living reality'). To emphasise the importance of science, the school houses (which will be vertical through the year groups) each named after scientists – Newton, Einstein and Isambard are three of the seven.

The school was officially opened in grand style in May 2014 by Michael Gove and Professor Lord Winston, by which time the high tech premises were complete. These include excellent labs for science as well as a good sized sports hall, and performance centre. With the track record of the energetic, focused and passionate Twyford staff, and a solid foundation and backing from the diocese, this school is looking as promising as its cheerful purple uniform. Check out properties in the catchment area before prices go through the roof.

ARK Priory Primary Academy

Acton Lane, London W3 8NR
0203 110 0717
Web: arkprioryprimary.org
Email: info@arkprioryprimary.org

Head: Run by experienced and popular head Jacqueline Steele, who was the founding head of Ark Academy Primary school in Brent. Positive and energetic.

Entrance: Admission is allocated according to proximity to the school, with children of staff and siblings taking priority. For a nursery place from 3 years apply directly to the school.

Remarks: A two-form entry primary school, ARK Priory opened in its sparklingly modern new premises on the 'Chiswick side' of Acton in September 2013 with two full reception classes and one nursery class. It is a well oiled machine, born into the very successful family of ARK schools (that include secondary, as well as primary, both inside and outside London). ARK is a trust that seems to have mostly bankers of some sort on their boards, but a lot of expertise in education on the ground. Children smartly turned out in grey, blue trimmed blazers, and their shiny blue school bags. Full change for PE and for summer.

A mix of parents, with fair proportion being more well-heeled than those at a lot of inner London primaries – the school is attractive to the working parent with its long school day, and a few yummy mummies from the Chiswick environs can be spotted with a skinny latte in the playground. The school day starts at 8.30am and finishes at 4pm but your little one may not get home until after 5pm when they have finished their after-school club. This might include ballet, multi-sports and art, though some parents observe that their child is just too exhausted by then to enjoy them. A lot of enthusiasm for the head who is very good at listening to suggestions. As a result, the amount of homework has been reduced and there is more free play during the day. It's a tightly run ship, lots of awards and rewards (like being invited to sit with the head teacher at top table at lunch time), but sanctions too. Stars awarded for exciting qualities like 'courage' and 'exploration' as well as the more predictable 'excellence' and 'endeavour' – very much in keeping with school motto, a poem by Christopher Logue:

'Come to the edge. We might fall. Come to the edge. It's too high! Come to the edge! And they came, and we pushed, and they flew.'

Kew House School

6 Capital Interchange Way, London TW8 0EX
020 8742 2038
Web: www.kewhouseschool.com
Email: info@kewhouseschool.com

Head: Mark Hudson, previously senior deputy head of Thomas Telford Academy in Shropshire, is married with teenage children. Most impressive: parents talk of having been sold on the school as soon as they met him.

Entrance: Three classes – 66 places per year group. Entrance exam, but the school says it places as much, if not more, importance on the interview and school reports.

Remarks: An independent co-ed secondary school, Kew House admitted its first year 7, 8 and 9 pupils in September 2013. It is the first secondary school in the group of schools owned by Maria Gardner and her family (LPS Ltd), which include Ravenscourt Park Prep School and Kew Green Prep School. Class sizes up to 22; vertical tutor groups will have no more than 15. These give pupils the opportunity to make friendships and learn from each other across age and year groups.

An orange-brick building, situated on the busy end of Chiswick High Road just before you reach Kew Bridge, it doesn't at first appear the most attractive spot to send your precious child, but practically everyone comes out impressed and amazed by the Tardis-like quality of the premises that have been created here. Classrooms look out onto strategically planted trees around the edge of the building, and there is room for a games area (football, basketball etc) as well as for hanging out.

Kew House has adopted many of the innovative teaching strategies of Thomas Telford Academy. Four hour-and-a-half lessons a day give extra teaching time; GCSE courses start in year 9, with potential for fast-tracking some pupils. Food technology is part of the curriculum, and Spanish and German as well as French are available from year 7. Everyone takes the Individual in Society course until the end of year 11, covering a wide range of subjects from national and global politics to body language.

Eden Primary School

79 Creighton Avenue, London N10 1NR
020 8883 9527
Web: edenprimary.org.uk
Email: louise@edenprimary.org.uk

Head: Since its opening in September 2011, Jo Sassienie, BA in developmental psychology, MSc in leadership for educational change, PGCE in primary education. Late 40s and originally from North London, Jo (as she is known to all her staff and pupils) is laid back, approachable and relaxed. She spent the first 14 years of her career as a primary school teacher in London. Head-hunted to lead Eden Primary because of her work as principal of Beit Rabban Day school in Manhattan. One parent governor told us, 'Eden is all about inclusivity, and Jo had an outstanding track record in leading a pioneering, inclusive Jewish primary school in New York.'

Entrance: Single form entry. Fifty per cent of places to those practising the Jewish faith and 50 per cent open places, based on proximity. Although nominally inclusive, non-Jewish parents should be aware that Hebrew and Jewish studies make up 17 per cent of the curriculum.

Remarks: A strikingly beautiful building that stands out amongst the more traditional architecture of Creighton Avenue in Muswell Hill. The organic, timber clad, circular design reflects the ancient Coldfall Woods across the road. Every classroom has access to the outside and views of open space. A bright, airy building on three floors, with large communal areas where pupils from all classes can mingle.

The fluidity of the building and the communal 'piazzas' are based on the Reggio Emilia school of teaching – an idea developed around the villages of Reggio Emilia in Italy after World War II. A 'cutting edge' approach to early education, we are told – with a strong focus on social collaboration, working in groups, where each child is an equal participant. Parents are a vital component to the Reggio Emilia philosophy, viewed as partners, collaborators and advocates for their children, involved in every aspect of the curriculum. However, many people wonder what happens to Reggio children when they make the transition from this style of education to a non Reggio Emilia school. (We witnessed very happy and spirited students, partaking in slightly noisier activities than we are used to observing).

In the school canteen, Café Eden, pupils and staff eat together, and pupils have designated tasks. While the kibbutz-style system has pleased many, the strictly Kosher canteen has been a bone of contention for some parents.

A large classroom has been equipped and dedicated to children with varying physical disabilities, and there is a daily rota of on-call occupational and physiotherapists (more for the following year's intake, we are told).

Now in its third year, Eden has recently been rated by Ofsted as a 'good school': although the head is quick to point out that the ethos of the school is not about 'academic brilliance or a being a pressure cooker, but rather to create an environment where pupils are stimulated to learn.'

Children with special educational needs

Whether you are moving to London or already live here, the process of choosing a school is fraught with difficulties; throw into the mix a child with special needs and the challenges increase. You want your child to have an unparalleled education, but what are your options, and how do you work out what really is best?

What counts as a special need?

If your child has a difficulty that makes learning harder for them than for most children of the same age – whether the difficulty is social, emotional, intellectual, behavioural, physical, sensory or a mixture – then they may well have a special need. The most complex needs are generally diagnosed at birth or soon after, but other conditions, such as mild autistic spectrum disorders or specific learning difficulties such as dyslexia, may not be identified until well into their schooling. Indeed, you may well have to work hard to have your child's need recognised as 'special'. These needs may be transitory or permanent, but what matters is getting good help and support as soon as possible.

State schools – your choices

All state schools are in theory open to children with special needs – though for grammar schools they will need to pass the entrance exams. If your child has a Statement or, since September 2014, an Education Health and Social Care plan (EHC plan – see below) then it may be possible to add special schools to the list.

Independent schools – their choice

Independent schools choose the pupils they want to teach – if they don't want your child there is not a lot you can do about it. Some, such as Finton House in Wandsworth, keep a handful of places especially for children with special needs, others have a healthy, helpful attitude and will look at each child on merit.

London is blessed with some very good SEN specialist schools but the number and type of places available are limited. They tend to be expensive, too. Occasionally, an LA may agree to fund a place at an independent school (even if it is not in their own borough) but such places and funding are increasingly rare.

If a special or specialist school catches your eye, approach the school and ask them if they think your child might fit. They are likely to ask you to send reports, visit, even pay for an assessment. If they subsequently think they can help, they may offer assistance with the knotty process of securing LA funding, but be prepared for a long, fraught, frustrating fight with no guarantees.

SEN: a state of flux

Since September 2014 any new assessment for the two per cent or so of children with greatest needs is via an EHC plan rather than a Statement. Many of the finer details of EHC plans have yet to be worked out, but they are intended to cover both education and health needs, giving greater flexibility and greater autonomy for the child and their family. The picture is less clear for those whose needs are less severe, but most likely schools will have to provide help for them with no extra funding.

School admissions

If your child has an EHC plan or Statement you can, with the help of your LA, name the school you would like them to attend. Mainstream or special state schools, and independent special schools, must in theory admit your child unless the governing body thinks doing so would be 'unsuitable for the age, ability, aptitude or SEN of the child or young person; or the attendance of the child or young person there would be incompatible with the efficient education of others; or the efficient use of resources'. If the school says no, you can appeal to the SEND tribunal.

Evaluating schools for children with SEN

Before signing on the dotted line, check out inspection reports, school policies, school websites and any independent reviews such as those by The Good Schools Guide – do they reflect a positive approach to SEN?

Once you've done the virtual work, arrange to visit schools, request a tour and ask to meet with the head and SENCo. Do they have a flexible and positive approach to SEN? Is support an integral part of school life? How is individual progress monitored? Is there a widespread celebration of achievement? Is the school generally geared up for diverse needs?

Try to visit two or more schools so you can compare them and make the best choice possible. Keep an eye on entry requirements and deadlines; rules and timings can and do change. Finally, remember to look beyond your child's special needs to ensure their strengths, talents and interests will be well catered for too.

For more information, visit www.goodschoolsguide.co.uk/sen

Tutors and tutoring in London

Tutoring is endemic in the UK these days, and nowhere more so than in the capital, where top agencies have parents queueing to pay £70+ an hour to buy children as young as 2 an advantage. But keep your head, even if your child's already turned 2. Remember, an anxious mother and her money are soon parted, and the race has only just begun.

Two is too early

Seriously, there are folks out there offering to tutor children as young as 2, but don't be taken in. Spend the money at one of London's wonderful bookshops and read to your child instead. What pre-school-age children need is not tutoring and angst, but time and love from the grownups who care for them. If you're reading this article, you are by default an educated, thinking parent who wants the best for your child, so give her the treasures of your mind, your vocabulary, your tastes; for a pre-school child they will far out-class anything a tutor can provide.

When do you need a tutor?

Put simply, when there is a clear and specific reason for using one. Your child may need help with the 11+ or 13+ entry to an academically selective senior school. Or perhaps he's struggling with a particular GCSE/A level subject. Or she may be falling behind at school. Or he may have missed school through illness or some other crisis. Where there is a known goal to work towards, or a genuine problem to address, tutoring comes into its own.

For a shy child who's under-performing, a friendly tutor can be a godsend. Free from the distractions of the classroom and other pupils, he or she can sit quietly with your child and concentrate solely on whatever's confusing her, filling in gaps in her knowledge and building up her confidence. Grades start to improve, and the child becomes a happier learner, keener to put her hand up in class and more relaxed about going to school. For a teenager who's struggling with maths, demoralised by always coming last in his set and stressed about approaching exams, quality one-to-one teaching from someone with no preconceptions about him can make the difference between failure and success; between giving up and keeping on.

It could be that you're putting your child through the state system to begin with while you save up for the independent senior school you hope he'll attend. If this is the case, he will need help with exam preparation. You may feel confident going through maths and English 11+ preparation books and past papers with him, but if not, tutoring is pretty much essential. No matter how bright your child, he'll be up against other children who have been intensively coached. If he's to stay in the game, you'll have to do likewise.

Perhaps you feel your child needs a tutor even though he's already at a good preparatory school. Well, maybe. Be very sure, though, that the need is real. Depending on where he is, a year's tutoring in the run-up to common entrance may make sense, if only because it'll bring you peace of mind. But to have your tutored 7-year-old win a place at a high-achieving prep and then immediately start having him tutored some more just because everyone else is doing it, will only exhaust him and your bank account. Wave him off to St Brainiac's with a proud smile, and let the school do its work.

But tutoring is one of those things parents usually do in secret, either because they don't choose to tell it around that their child struggles at school, or because they've no wish to increase the opposition's chances in the race for places.

On the other hand, if you've just relocated to the UK from overseas, using a tutor is an excellent way to get your kids up to speed with the English system and help them to feel more assured and comfortable in lessons. This in turn will help them to make friends, and the whole settling-in process will be smoother. For a child in a new country, confidence is key.

If you want a tutor for your child, how do you find one? The best way should be word of mouth, of course. But tutoring is one of those things parents usually do in secret, either because they don't choose to tell it around that their child struggles at school, or because they've no wish to increase the opposition's chances in the race for places. Try asking a friend with an older child, who won't begrudge your using what they no longer need. If this doesn't bring results, don't worry. This is London, and you have plenty of options.

If a person's replies to your messages are semi-literate, don't engage them as an English tutor.

Tutor companies

We review many of the best tutor companies on the Good Schools Guide website, and using them has a number of benefits. They'll be skilled at matching your child to the right person, and will give you redress if you're not happy. This is the most expensive way of employing a tutor, however. Almost all companies charge a registration fee, anything from a few quid to a hair-raising £180, and the hourly rate for tuition is high (be prepared for at least £45), because the company takes a cut before paying the teacher. Some of the really big tutorial companies cover too wide a geographical area to interview all their tutors in person, but they will have interviewed them by phone, and checked their references and DBS record.

Tutor websites

A cheaper option is finding a tutor online. There are a number of websites on which tutors can advertise, and whose contact details you buy, usually for around £20, after you've had an exchange of messages with your selected tutor to see if they're the right fit. Tuition rates vary from £16 ph – probably an undergraduate trying to earn a bit of extra cash – to £45+ ph for an experienced and qualified teacher. The website companies run checks to ascertain whether the tutor advertising is who they claim to be, but otherwise it's down to you to judge people's suitability. Websites like these can be very useful and we regularly hear reports from satisfied parents, ourselves included. Again, use your common sense. If a person's replies to your messages are semi-literate, don't engage them as an English tutor.

Don't believe them when they say they can get from Wood Green to Putney in half an hour, they absolutely can't.

Do your homework

Self-employed individuals are unlikely to be DBS-checked, because the law prevents them from running a check on themselves, so ask to see references or to speak to previous clients. In fact, do this even if they are DBS-checked. Interview the tutor on the phone before fixing a first date, and don't feel pressured into accepting someone who doesn't sound right. Don't be afraid to sit in on the first lesson, and afterwards ask your child what she thought. If the tutor is travelling to you, check that they can get there easily. Don't believe them when they say they can get from Wood Green to Putney in half an hour, they absolutely can't. Lastly – and this wisdom comes from years of weary experience – insist on punctuality. A tutor who is routinely late will soon drive you up the wall.

With careful preparation, your child's tutoring experiences should be happy, productive and affordable. Good luck.

Child protection

If you are preparing to entrust your child to a school – whether day or boarding – you will most likely assume that your child will be safe and that all members of the school's staff will take the greatest care to ensure that this is always the case. The chances are that your expectations will be fulfilled. Unfortunately in a sad minority of cases that is not what happens.

What can you do?

Parents can warn their children – gently but seriously – of the dangers, however remote these may be, so they feel that it is easy to speak to you should they meet them. It is worth pointing out that abuse can come from anyone – including a teacher or an adult they know well.

At any school you may be considering, inquire about the steps taken to safeguard children in the same way you might ask about bullying or learning support. As always, much can be gleaned from the head's attitude when questions about child protection are asked. Openness is what you're looking for.

For those who want to probe further:

Where can I find the school's child protection policy?
Every school is required to have a child protection policy that is made available to staff, volunteers and parents on request.

How can we find out who the child protection officers are?
Ideally, a school should have more than one designated person and they should be named on a public notice board, so that everyone knows who to talk to.

What training do staff receive in child protection?
Training is mandatory every two years for designated officers, and every three years for all staff who work with children.

Is it the school's written policy to report child protection allegations to the Local Authority Designated Officer ('LADO')?
A good head will have a good working relationship with their LADO, so that both can have confidence that incidents will be well managed.

How many 'referrals' have been made to the Department of Education in the past three years and for what reasons?
A referral means a member of staff has left the school in circumstances which indicate they were unfit to work with children. Do not rule out a school because a case of abuse has been brought to light there. Tabloid coverage can be the price the school pays for handling a case of abuse or bullying openly.

HURTWOOD HOUSE

THE
BOARDING
SCHOOL
FOR THE
CREATIVE
PERFORMING
ARTS

www.hurtwoodhouse.com

City slippers – boarding for Londoners

Boarding, like sheep herding, polytunnelling and plume scrumpling, is something many Londoners assume to be an exclusively rural activity.

Not too rural, of course. These days, families are increasingly selective about just how countrified they want the boarding experience to be. Greenery, yes. Day-long hikes to sports day, on the whole, not.

It's no coincidence that boarding schools whose yield per hectare, if not quite a match for top cash crops, comes close, hit greatest density levels within easy reach of London's top postcodes – no more than a sonic boom's echo from Heathrow or Gatwick.

Most famous of the lot are Eton and Harrow. While other schools have not just rolled over in response to parental requests for part-time boarding but also offered to juggle a couple of hoops with their front paws, there are no such concessions here. When boys' only full boarding for all has worked for centuries, you can't really blame them.

It's the same story for the girls at St Mary's Ascot, which held its nerve through the dark days of the recession and has been rewarded with record demand. Parents who don't buy in to the idea of boarding the traditional way are gently – but firmly – urged to look elsewhere.

Some city slickers don't buy into boarding, full stop. Others start to wonder whether the bracing two hour trek across London to and from that excellent day school and in the dark both ways during winter really is as character-forming as they'd hoped.

For these families, boarding can seem life-enhancing, making it possible to start early and stay late with food and friends provided – and without a punitive journey at the beginning and end of the day.

INSPIRATIONAL
Box Hill School
for girls and boys aged 11–18

BELIEVE IN YOURSELF

Box Hill School, Mickleham, Dorking, Surrey RH5 6EA
Telephone: +44 (0)1372 373382
Email: enquiries@boxhillschool.com

www.boxhillschool.com

B&B

Many schools make a virtue – and success – of combining education with what can feel like a large-scale bed and breakfast operation: some pupils day only, some there pretty much full time, others opting for in-school sleepovers because of parental commitments, exam revision, late night games or early morning training.

Girls' schools offering boarding and day places within or close to M25 range from Woldingham in Surrey, Marymount in Kingston-upon-Thames and St George's Ascot to the south and south west, while the Royal Masonic School for Girls and St Margaret's fill a similar niche north of the river.

Boarding, like every other aspect of education, has its fair share of curiosities.

Boy boarders, meanwhile, can opt for Reed's School in Cobham, Surrey (girls are admitted in the sixth form) or Dulwich College, though day pupils dominate at both.

Those in search of a co-ed environment are, if not spoiled for choice close to London, far from being deprived, with Epsom College in Surrey and LVS in Ascot among those giving their accommodation eye-popping makeovers, from colour-coordinated furnishings (it's hard to spot a cushion that isn't tonally related to the curtains) to unlimited fresh fruit to snack on. Further north, there's Mill Hill School, with 80 weekly and full boarders.

Boarding, like every other aspect of education, has its fair share of curiosities. Like the ravens at the Tower of London, boarders at the City of Freemen's School in Ashtead, Surrey, specified by statute, must always be part of the community (though, unlike the ravens, wing-clipping isn't required to keep them there).

Honing skills

There are the specialists – such as the Yehudi Menuhin School (music) and Tring Park (performing arts) – where boarding helps the super talented to hone their skills in and out of hours, free from tube strike blues and similar aesthetic lows; the different (St James Senior Boys' School with just 20 weekly boarders and a distinctive, thought-provoking approach to education), and the new (flushed with the success of its first boarding house, Whitgift School, in the non-plush territory of South Croydon, is already mulling over a second).

Costs don't necessarily need to be sky high if you opt for a state boarding school such as Cranbook (selective) and Gordon's (all-comers) where parents pay for accommodation while teaching comes courtesy of the ever-generous taxpayer.

For any dyed in the wool Londoners who come over all faint at the prospect of breathing air outside the congestion zone, no longer enhanced with flavoursome carcinogens, it's hard to beat boarding, literally, on your doorstep.

Westminster School, with 170 or so boarders (including girls, admitted in the sixth form), is pretty much as close as you can get to total immersion in the beating heart of the city without squatting in Big Ben. 'You get that sense of community,' says a former Westminster parent. 'You have more time to get involved and people tend to stay late anyway.'

For some London parents, day places will always be the educational black, the only goal worth pursuing, with boarding the reserve choice when all other options have been exhausted. Others, relishing the out of hours opportunities, from extra tuition to drama, debate, music and sport, feel very differently. Costs permitting (and boarding is, undeniably, costly) it could well be worth taking a look at both.

Ilford County High School

A Specialist Boys Grammar School

Creating Future Leaders. Empowering to Excel.

Ilford County High School has established a tradition of excellence at A Level, GCSE and KS3 with a proven track record of successfully supporting students to progress to competitive universities and courses.

The school recognises that personal development, in addition to academic success is central to an excellent education. An established House system delivers outstanding pastoral care. Ilford County High School provides many opportunities for its students to further develop their skills: responsibility, leadership, and teamwork are central to the learning experience of students.

In the Sixth form, A Level examination results are testament to the success achieved in helping students build upon their GCSE achievement. Experienced teaching staff guide and support learning and nurture a real interest and depth of knowledge essential both to high level achievement and successful progression into Higher Education. Many students join the sixth form following GCSE courses studied elsewhere and comment positively upon the support they receive in making this change.

Applying to university is complicated and good advice, based on experience, is essential if young people are to make the best of the opportunities they have. The school has excellent relationships with universities, including Oxford and Cambridge and other Russell Group institutions. A personalised support package enables students to make the best university choices for them. Young people benefit from past students who return to offer advice based upon their own experience of starting university courses whether these be in Medicine, Engineering, Law, Business, Pure Science, Mathematics, the Humanities or the Arts.

Ilford County High School offers opportunities for learning that would be difficult to find elsewhere; a proven record of examination success supported by experienced and highly qualified staff and engaged students, a commitment to the personal development of the students and established relationships with universities. It is this combination of experience, knowledge and commitment that helps our students to compete successfully for the best Higher Education opportunities available.

Ilford County High School, Fremantle Road, Barkingside, Ilford, IG6 2JB. Telephone: 0208 551 6496. www.ichs.org.uk

---

ALTA PETO

Shrewsbury House Preparatory School

"This is a first class Prep School where academic rigour is balanced by an equally strong offering in arts and sports."

The Good Schools Guide

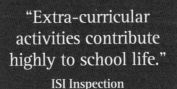

"Extra-curricular activities contribute highly to school life."

ISI Inspection

Shrewsbury House School, 107 Ditton Road, Surbiton, Surrey KT6 6RL
Tel: 020 8399 3066 Email: office@shspost.co.uk
www.shrewsburyhouse.net

You may also like to read

The Good Schools Guide 19th edition
Features independent and unbiased views of over 1,200 state and independent schools throughout Britain, written by parents for parents.

The Good Schools Guide online subscription
Read all our reviews plus exam data, catchment maps, university entrance information, and advice on choosing a school, tutors, SEN, talented children and much more.

Uni in the USA
Written by students who have been through the US system, features in-depth descriptions of 65 US universities, plus the inside track on getting in and preparing for life across the pond.

Uni in the USA and Beyond online subscription and ebook
Also includes unis in Europe and the East, from Alberta to Abu Dhabi, and advice from SATS to visas.

The Good Schools Guide International online subscription
The one-stop educational shop for ex-pats, it reviews the best state and independent schools round the globe, plus insider knowledge on life overseas.

All available via http://www.goodschoolsguide.co.uk/shop-online/all/all/all

If you're moving to London from abroad, *Living in London: a Practical Guide* might help explain the nitty-gritty. It's written by volunteers from the Junior League of London who have hundreds of years of expat experience between them. We appreciate their permission to draw on some of their descriptions of London districts.

London North districts index

District (London borough)	Region	Page

Senior school index

Junior school index

List of advertisers

Notes